ISBN 978-0-265-05821-3
PIBN 10952822

# 1 MONTH OF
# FREE
## READING

### at
### www.ForgottenBooks.com

By purchasing this book you are eligible for one month membership to ForgottenBooks.com, giving you unlimited access to our entire collection of over 1,000,000 titles via our web site and mobile apps.

To claim your free month visit:
www.forgottenbooks.com/free952822

English
Français
Deutsche
Italiano
Español
Português

# www.forgottenbooks.com

**Mythology** Photography **Fiction**
Fishing Christianity **Art** Cooking
Essays Buddhism Freemasonry
Medicine **Biology** Music **Ancient
Egypt** Evolution Carpentry Physics
Dance Geology **Mathematics** Fitness
Shakespeare **Folklore** Yoga Marketing
**Confidence** Immortality Biographies
Poetry **Psychology** Witchcraft
Electronics Chemistry History **Law**
Accounting **Philosophy** Anthropology
Alchemy Drama Quantum Mechanics
Atheism Sexual Health **Ancient History**
**Entrepreneurship** Languages Sport
Paleontology Needlework Islam
**Metaphysics** Investment Archaeology
Parenting Statistics Criminology
**Motivational**

*John F. Tobey*

# ACTS AND RESOLVES

PASSED AT THE

## MAY SESSION

(AND THE ADJOURNMENT THEREOF IN JUNE)

OF THE

# ENERAL ASSEMBLY

OF THE

### State of Rhode Island

AND PROVIDENCE PLANTATIONS.

1876.

PROVIDENCE:
PROVIDENCE PRESS COMPANY, PRINTERS TO THE CITY.
1876.

☞ The General Assembly convened at Newport, on the last Tuesday in May, 1876, (being the 30th day of the month,) in conformity with the provisions of Article 4, of the Constitution as amended by the electors on the first Tuesday of November, 1854, and adjourned on Friday, the 2d day of June following, to meet at Newport on the 13th day of June, 1876, at 10.30 o'clock A. M., and on the 14th day of June, 1876, adjourned to meet at Providence on the second Tuesday in January, (January 9th,) 1877, at 11 o'clock A. M.

# INDEX.

APPENDIX CONTAINING THE FOLLOWING DOCUMENTS:

# ACTS AND RESOLVES

PASSED AT THE

## MAY SESSION, 1876,

### AND THE ADJOURNMENT THEREOF IN JUNE, 1876.

[The Public Laws are numbered continuously from the General Statutes, Revision of 1872.]

---

## CHAPTER 565.

AN ACT TO ENABLE THE SEVERAL TOWNS AND CITIES TO CELEBRATE THE APPROACHING ANNIVERSARY OF OUR NATIONAL INDEPENDENCE.

Passed June 1, 1876.

Amended. see chap. 570.

*It is enacted by the General Assembly as follows:*

SECTION 1. The several town and city councils of this state are hereby authorized in their discretion to appropriate a sum of money, not exceeding five thousand dollars, for the proper celebration of the approaching anniversary of our national independence, and to cause to be delivered on that day a historical sketch of said town or city from its foundation, and cause one copy of said sketch, in print or manuscript, to be deposited in the clerk's office of said town or city, and one copy thereof in the office of the secretary of state, and one in the office of the librarian of congress.

Fourth of July, 1876. Town and city councils may appropriate not exceeding $5,000 for celebration of.

## CHAPTER 566.

Passed June
1. 1876.

AN ACT IN ADDITION TO CHAPTER 47 OF THE GENERAL STATUTES, "OF THE POWERS AND DUTIES OF TOWNS, AND OF THE DUTIES OF TOWN TREASURER AND TOWN CLERK."

*It is enacted by the General Assembly as follows:*

Exclusive right to lay water pipes in public highways, may be granted, how.

SECTION 1.  The town council of any town or the city council of any city may grant to any individual or corporation the exclusive right to lay water pipes in any of the public highways of such town or city for supplying the inhabitants of such town or city with water, for such term of time and upon such terms and conditions as they may deem proper, including therein the power and authority to exempt such pipes and the works connected therewith from taxation.

## CHAPTER 567.

Passed June
2, 1876.

AN ACT PROVIDING FOR THE APPOINTMENT OF A PUBLIC ADMINISTRATOR IN THE CITY OF PROVIDENCE.

*It is enacted by the General Assembly as follows :*

Public administrator, city of Providence,—how appointed.

SECTION 1.  The city council of the city of Providence may appoint some suitable person, being an inhabitant of said city, to be public administrator therein ; and the person so appointed shall hold his office during the pleasure of the city council.

Duties of.

SEC. 2.  Such administrator shall take out letters of administration and faithfully administer upon the estate of any person who dies intestate within the city of Providence or elsewhere, leaving property in the said city to be administered, such person at the time of his decease not being an inhabitant or resident of any other town in this state, and not leaving a known husband, widow or next of kin, which fact shall be established by proof satisfactory to the municipal court of the city of Providence.

Sec. 3. Administration shall not be granted to a public administrator within thirty days next after the decease of such intestate. *Administration not to be granted, when.*

Sec. 4. After granting letters of administration to a public administrator, and before the final settlement of the estate, if the husband, widow or any next of kin of the deceased, in writing claims the right of administration, or requests the appointment of some other suitable person to the trust, the municipal court in the city of Providence shall grant letters of administration accordingly. Upon the appointment of a successor, and his giving the bond required, the powers of the public administrator over the estate shall cease. *Administration to cease, when.*

Sec 5. Such public administrator shall deliver into the municipal court his letters of administration upon the estate of any person deceased, if a will of such person is thereafter allowed and proved. Upon the appointment of an executor or administrator as his successor in any case, he shall surrender his letters of administration into the municipal court with an account upon oath of his doings thereon; and upon the allowance of his account by the municipal court, shall pay over and deliver to his successor all sums of money in his hands, and all property, effects and credits of the deceased not administered. *Same subject.*

Sec. 6. Such public administrator shall give bond to the municipal court for the faithful performance of his duties, in like manner as required of other administrators, with the further condition to comply with the provisions of the preceding section. *Public administrator's bond.*

Sec. 7. Such public administrator may be licensed to sell real estate for the payment of debts, and shall administer estates and render his account, in the same manner as other administrators, except as herein otherwise provided. *License to sell real estate.*

Sec. 8. When an estate has been fully administered by such public administrator, and the debts paid according to law, he shall deposit the balance of such estate remaining in his hands with the treasurer of the city of Providence, who shall receive and hold it for the benefit of those who may have lawful claims thereon. *Balance of estate to be paid to city treasurer.*

SEC. 9. Such public administrator shall render an account of his proceedings to the municipal court of said city, at least once in each year, until the trust has been fulfilled. And when, upon a final settlement of any estate, it appears that moneys remain in the hands of such administrator, which by law should have been deposited with the city treasurer, the municipal court shall certify that fact and the statement of the amount to said treasurer, who, unless such deposit is made within thirty days after the receipt of such notice, shall cause the bond of the administrator to be prosecuted for the recovery thereof.

SEC. 10. All money or other property received by the city treasurer of the city of Providence, under the provisions of this act, shall be held for the same uses, as provided by chapter 177 of the General Statutes.

SEC. 11. Upon the death, resignation or other disqualification of a public administrator leaving an estate or estates not fully administered, it shall be the duty of the municipal court, upon application of the city treasurer, to appoint some suitable person to have the charge and care of the personal estate not administered, to hold the same until a successor to such deceased, resigned or disqualified public administrator shall be duly appointed, to whom the municipal court shall grant letters of administration *de bonis non* upon his giving the required bond.

SEC. 12. Upon the death, resignation or other disqualification of a public administrator, the city council shall fill the vacancy forthwith.

SEC. 13. When a public administrator neglects to return an inventory, settle an account, or perform any other duty incumbent upon him, (and there appears no heir entitled thereto), the city treasurer shall, in behalf of the said city of Providence, prosecute all suits and do all acts necessary and proper to ensure a prompt and faithful administration of .the estate, and the payment of the proceeds thereof into the treasury.

# CHAPTER 568.

AN ACT IN AMENDMENT OF CHAPTER 185, TITLE XXV, OF THE GENERAL STATUTES, "OF JUSTICE COURTS, THEIR ORGANIZATION AND CIVIL JURISDICTION."

Passed June 2, 1876.

*It is enacted by the General Assembly as follows:*

SECTION 1. No trial justice or clerk of a justice court shall sell any blank writs by him officially signed, to any person except an attorney at law, or to a justice of the peace authorized by the town council to issue warrants, or shall deliver to any person other than an attorney at law or to a justice of the peace so authorized, any such writ, with permission in the absence of such trial justice or clerk to fill up such writ, or to cause the same to be filled and served, under a penalty of ten dollars for each offence, and of ineligibility as a justice of the peace for the term of two years next after conviction.

Trial justices and clerks of justice courts not to sell writs, except.

SEC. 2. All acts and parts of acts inconsistent herewith are hereby repealed.

SEC. 3. This act shall take effect from and after its passage.

# CHAPTER 569.

AN ACT IN AMENDMENT OF AN ACT ENTITLED, "AN ACT IN AMENDMENT OF CHAPTER 84 OF THE GENERAL STATUTES, 'OF BIRDS,' AND OF THE SEVERAL ACTS IN AMENDMENT THEREOF AND IN ADDITION THERETO," BEING CHAPTER 554 OF THE PUBLIC LAWS.

Passed June 2, 1876.

*It is enacted by the General Assembly as follows:*

SECTION 1. Section 2 of chapter 554 of the Public Laws is hereby amended so as to read as follows:

Penalty for unlawful taking, killing, etc., of certain game birds.

"Every person who shall take or kill, sell, buy or offer for sale or have in his possession any woodcock from January 1st to July 4th, any ruffed grouse or any partridge from February 1st to September 1st, or any quail from January 1st to October 15th, any bartrams, sand-piper or grass plover from April 1st to August 1st, any dusky or black duck from March 1st to September 1st, any wood or summer duck from March 1st to September 1st, any blue or green winged teal from March 1st to September 1st, in any year, shall be fined for every such bird twenty-five dollars."

SEC. 2. This act shall take effect from and after its passage.

## CHAPTER 570.

Passed June 14, 1876.

AN ACT IN AMENDMENT OF AN ACT ENTITLED "AN ACT TO ENABLE TOWNS AND CITIES TO CELEBRATE THE APPROACHING ANNIVERSARY OF OUR NATIONAL INDE-PENDENCE," BEING CHAPTER 565 OF THE PUBLIC LAWS.

*It is enacted by the General Assembly as follows :*

Fourth of July, 1876,— act authoriz-ing appropri-ations for, to take effect immediately.

SECTION 1. The act entitled "An act to enable the several towns and cities to celebrate the approaching anniversary of our national independence," being chap-ter 565 of Public Laws, passed June 1, 1876, shall take effect immediately.

SEC. 2. This act shall take effect on its passage.

## CHAPTER 571.

Passed June 14, 1876.

AN ACT IN ADDITION TO CHAPTER 144 OF THE GENERAL STATUTES, "OF FOREIGN INSURANCE COMPANIES."

*It is enacted by the General Assembly as follows:*

Insurance commissioner to report vio-lations of law.

SECTION 1. The insurance commissioner shall report to the attorney general any violation of the provisions of chapter 144 of the General Statutes, which shall come to his knowledge, and the attorney general shall insti-tute the proper legal procedings, in the name of the state, against any person violating such provision.

SEC. 2. This act shall take effect from and after its passage.

## CHAPTER 572.

AN ACT IN AMENDMENT OF AN ACT ENTITLED "AN ACT IN REPEAL OF SECTION 7, CHAPTER 240, OF THE GENERAL STATUTES, 'OF JAILS AND THE CARE AND DISCIPLINE OF JAILS,'" AND THE ACTS IN AMENDMENT THEREOF.

*Passed June 14, 1876.*

*It is enacted by the General Assembly as follows:*

SECTION 1.    Section 2 of chapter 387 of the Public Laws, is amended so as to read as follows: "This act shall take effect on the first day of July, A. D. 1877."

*Of use of jail in Providence county, by cit y of Providence.*

SEC. 2.    All acts and parts of acts inconsistent herewith are hereby repealed.

SEC. 3.    This act shall take effect from and after its passage.

---

## CHAPTER 573.

AN ACT IN AMENDMENT OF CHAPTERS 430 AND 528 OF THE PUBLIC LAWS.

*Passed June 14, 1876.*

*It is enacted by the General Assembly as follows:*

SECTION 1.    The city council of the city of Providence may provide by ordinance that the principal and interest on any bonds of said city which may be issued under chapter 430 of the Public Laws, passed February 16th, 1875, and under chapter 528 of the Public Laws, passed April 12th, 1876, may be payable in such gold coin as said city council shall determine, and all of said bonds so made payable, shall be binding upon and paid by said city according to the terms thereof.

*Water loan, city of Providence, may be payable in gold coin.*

SEC. 2.    This act shall take effect from and after its passage.

## CHAPTER 574.

AN ACT IN AMENDMENT OF CHAPTER 596 OF THE STAT-
UTES, ENTITLED "AN ACT TO REVISE, CONSOLIDATE,
AND AMEND THE ACT ENTITLED 'AN ACT TO INCORPO-
RATE THE CITY OF PROVIDENCE.' AND THE SEVERAL
ACTS IN ADDITION THERETO, AND IN AMENDMENT
THEREOF."

Passed June
. 14, 1876.

*It is enacted by the General Assembly as follows:*

City of Provi-
dence.—
annual elec-
tion of city
council to be
on 4th Tues-
day in Novem-
ber.

SECTION 1.   Section 1 of chapter 311 of the Public
Laws, is hereby amended so as to read as follows : "The
qualified voters of each ward in the city of Providence
shall, on the fourth Tuesday of November in each year,
give in their votes in their respective wards for one
alderman and four common councilmen, to serve for
one year from the first Monday in January next ensuing, and until others are elected and qualified to fill
their places."

Annual elec-
tion of city
officers to be
on 4th Tues-
day in Novem-
ber.

SEC. 2.   Section 2 of said chapter 311 is hereby
amended so as to read as follows : "The electors of said
city of Providence, qualified to vote for general officers,
shall, on the fourth Tuesday of November in each year,
give in their votes in their respective wards, for a mayor,
a city treasurer, a harbor master, an overseer of the
poor, a superintendent of health, and also for a warden
and a ward clerk of their respective wards and voting
districts, who shall hold their respective offices for the
term of one year from the first Monday of January next
ensuing, and until others are elected and qualified to fill
their places."

SEC. 3.   This act shall take effect from and after its
passage, and all acts and parts of acts inconsistent herewith are hereby repealed.

## CHAPTER 575.

AN ACT ENABLING THE TOWN COUNCIL OF THE TOWN OF WOONSOCKET TO ELECT A JUDGE OF PROBATE FOR SAID TOWN.

*Passed June 14, 1876.*

*It is enacted by the General Assembly as follows:*

SECTION 1. The town council of the town of Woonsocket may annually, in the month of June, elect a judge of probate for said town, who shall exercise all the jurisdiction conferred by law upon the court of probate of the said town, and receive therefor the fees by law allowed to courts of probate, or such annual salary as the said council may fix and determine.

*Town of Woonsocket, election of probate judge.*

SEC. 2. This act shall take effect from and after its passage.

## CHAPTER 576.

AN ACT TO ALLOW THE TOWN COUNCIL OF WOONSOCKET TO APPROPRIATE A SUM OF MONEY TO DEFRAY A PORTION OF THE EXPENSE OF PREPARING A HISTORY OF THE OLD TOWN OF SMITHFIELD.

*Passed June 14, 1876.*

*It is enacted by the General Assembly as follows:*

SECTION 1. The town council of Woonsocket are hereby allowed, in their discretion, the right to appropriate a sum of money not exceeding three hundred dollars, for the purpose of preparing a history of the old town of Smithfield.

*Town of Woonsocket, —appropriation for history of old town of Smithfield.*

SEC. 2. This act shall take effect on and after its passage.

## CHAPTER 577.

AN ACT TO APPROVE AND PUBLISH, AND SUBMIT TO THE ELECTORS A PROPOSITION OF AMENDMENT TO THE CONSTITUTION OF THIS STATE.

*Passed June 14, 1876.*

WHEREAS, Articles of amendment to the constitution of this state were proposed by the last general assembly, by the votes of a majority of all the members elected to each house, and the same have been published and read to the electors at their annual town and ward meetings in April last, as required by the thirteenth article of the constitution of this state, and are now presented to this general assembly for their action thereon; and a majority of all the members elected to each house at said annual meeting, being present and approving of said proposed amendments:

*It is enacted by the General Assembly as follows :*

Proposed amendment to the constitution approved.

SE. TION 1.    The following proposition of amendment to the constitution of this state, proposed by the last general assembly, is hereby declared approved, and for the purpose of publication and submission to the electors, shall be designated as follows:

## ARTICLE V.

Bills to create corporations, continuance of.

Section 17, article IV, of the constitution of the state is hereby annulled and rescinded.

Amendment to voted on Nov. 7, 1876.

SEC. 2.    The said proposition of amendment shall be submitted to the electors for their approval or rejection, at meetings of the electors, to be held on the first Tuesday in November, A. D. 1876.    The voting places in the various cities and towns shall  be kept open during the hours now required by law for voting for state officers.

To be published in the newspapers;

SEC. 3.    The secretary of state shall  cause the said proposition of amendment to be published in all the papers publishing the laws of the state, for four weeks successively, next preceding the day of said meetings of said electors; and the said proposition shall be inserted

Inserted in warrants;

by the town and city clerks in the warrants or notices by them to be issued previous to said meetings of the electors, for the purpose of warning the town or ward

To be read to the electors.

meetings; and said proposition shall be read by the town, ward and district clerks to the electors in the town, ward and district meetings to be held as aforesaid.

Ballots to be printed and distributed.

SEC. 4.    The secretary of state shall cause twenty-five thousand copies of said proposition of amendment to be printed, with the word "approved" upon the same, and a like number with the word "reject" thereon, and shall cause such ballots to be distributed among the town and ward clerks in suitable proportions, previous to the day of said meetings of electors.

SEC. 5. The town, ward and district meetings to be held as aforesaid shall be warned, and the list of voters shall be canvassed and made up, and the said town, ward and district meetings shall be conducted in the same manner as now provided by law, for the town, ward and district meetings for the election of general officers. *Of warning the meetings, etc.*

SEC. 6. At the close of the polls on said day of said meetings of the electors, the moderator and town clerk, or the warden and ward clerk, or the moderator and district clerk, shall, in open town, ward or district meetings, count said ballots, and seal up the same, and shall certify that the ballots by them sealed up are the ballots given in at said meetings of the electors, the number of such ballots, and that the number of ballots on said proposition does not exceed the number of electors voting at said meetings, and shall deliver or send such ballots, so sealed up and certified, to the secretary of state before the first day of December, A. D. 1876. *Of counting the ballots at close of polls, etc.*

SEC. 7. The governor and secretary of state shall count said ballots on or before the fifteenth day of December, A. D. 1876, and the governor shall announce the result by proclamation, on or before the first day of January, A. D. 1877, and if said proposition of amendment shall have been approved by three-fifths of the electors of the state present and voting thereon in said town, ward and district meetings, the same shall be declared to be a part of the constitution of the state, and shall be numbered as an additional article in amendment thereto. *Ballots to be counted by governor and secretary of state, and proclamation made of the result.*

## CHAPTER 578.

AN ACT TO APPROVE AND PUBLISH, AND SUBMIT TO THE ELECTORS A PROPOSITION OF AMENDMENT TO THE CONSTITUTION OF THIS STATE. *Passed June 14, 1876.*

WHEREAS, Articles of amendment to the constitution of this state were proposed by the last general assembly,

by the votes of a majority of all the members elected to
each house, and the same have been published and read
to the electors at their annual town and ward meetings
in April last, as required by the thirteenth article of the
constitution of this state, and are now presented to this
general assembly for their action thereon; and a majority
of all the members elected to each house at said annual
meeting, being present and approving of said proposed
amendments:

*It is enacted by the General Assembly as follows :*

posed
1endment
the consti-
tion
proved.

SECTION 1.   The following proposition of amendment
to the constitution of this state, proposed by the last
general assembly, is hereby declared approved, and for
the purpose of publication and submission to the electors, shall be designated as follows :

## ARTICLE VI.

of reg-
7 tax and
formance
military
y as quali-
tions of
ters.

Every male native citizen of the United States, of the
age of twenty-one years, who has had his residence and
home in the state two years, and in the town or city in
which he may offer to vote, six months next preceding
the time of voting, whose name shall have been registered in the town or city where he resides, on or before
the last day of December, in the year next preceding
the time of his voting, shall have a right to vote in the
election of all civil officers, and on all questions in all
legally organized town, district or ward meetings ;
provided, that no person shall, at any time, be allowed
to vote in the election of the city council of any city, or
upon any proposition to impose a tax, or for the expenditure of money, in any town or city, unless he shall
within the year next preceding have paid a tax assessed
upon his property, valued at least at one hundred and
thirty-four dollars.   This amendment shall take, in the
constitution of the state, the place of sections 2 and 3
of article II, which sections are hereby annulled and
rescinded.

endment
be voted on
v. 7, 1876.

SEC. 2.   The said proposition of amendment shall be
submitted to the electors, for their approval or rejection,
at meetings of the electors, to be held on the first Tues-

day in November, A. D. 1876. The voting places in the various cities and towns shall be kept open during the hours now required by law for voting for state officers.

SEC. 3.   The secretary of state shall cause the said proposition of amendment to be published in all the papers publishing the laws·of the state, for four weeks successively, next preceding the day of said meetings of said electors ; and the said proposition shall be inserted by the town and city clerks in the warrants or notices by them to be issued previous to said meetings of the electors, for the purpose of warning the town or ward meetings ; and said proposition shall be read by the town, ward and district clerks to the electors in the town, ward and district meetings to be held as aforesaid. *To be published in the newspapers; Inserted in the warrants; Read to the electors.*

SEC. 4.   The secretary of state shall cause twenty-five thousand copies of said proposition of amendment to be printed, with the word "approved" upon the same, and a like number with the word "reject" thereon, and shall cause such ballots to be distributed among the town and ward clerks in suitable proportions, previous to the day of said meetings of electors. *Ballots to be printed and distributed.*

SEC. 5.   The town, ward and district meetings to be held as aforesaid shall be warned, and the list of voters shall be canvassed and made up, and the said town, ward and district meetings shall be conducted in the same manner as now provided by law, for the town, ward and district meetings for the election of general officers. *Of warning the meetings, etc.*

SEC. 6.   At the close of the polls on said day of said meetings of the electors, the moderator and town clerk, or the warden and ward clerk, or the moderator and district clerk, shall, in open town, ward or district meetings, count said ballots, and seal up the same, and shall certify that the ballots by them sealed up are the ballots given in at said meetings of the electors, the number of such ballots, and that the number of ballots on said proposition does not exceed the number of electors voting at said meetings, and shall deliver or send such ballots, so sealed up and certified, to the secretary of state before the first day of December, A. D. 1876. *Of counting the ballots at close of the polls.*

SEC. 7.   The governor and secretary of state shall count said ballots on or before the fifteenth day of

Ballots to be
counted by
governor and
secretary of
state, and
proclamation
made of the
result.

December, A. D. 1876, and the governor shall announce the result by proclamation, on or before the first day of January, A. D. 1877, and if said proposition of amendment shall have been approved by three-fifths of the electors of the state present and voting thereon in said town, ward and district meetings, the same shall be declared to be a part of the constitution of the state, and shall be numbered as an additional article in amendment thereto.

## CHAPTER 579.

Passed June
14, 1876.

AN ACT TO APPROVE AND PUBLISH, AND SUBMIT TO THE ELECTORS A PROPOSITION OF AMENDMENT TO THE CONSTITUTION OF THIS STATE.

WHEREAS, Articles of amendment to the constitution of this state were proposed by the last general assembly by the votes of a majority of all the members elected to each house, and the same have been published and read to the electors at their annual town and ward meetings in April last, as required by the thirteenth article of the constitution of this state, and are now presented to this general assembly for their action thereon; and a majority of all the members elected to each house at said annual meeting, being present and approving of said proposed amendments:

*It is enacted by the General Assembly as follows:*

Proposed
amendment
to the consti-
tution
approved.

SECTION 1. The following proposition of amendment to the constitution of this state, proposed by the last general assembly, is hereby declared approved, and for the purpose of publication and submission to the electors, shall be designated as follows:

## ARTICLE VII.

All soldiers and sailors of foreign birth, citizens of the United States, who served in the army or navy of the United States during the late war, from this state, and who were honorably discharged from such service, shall have the right to vote in the election of all civil officers, and on all questions in all legally organized town, district or ward meetings, upon the same conditions, and under and subject to the same restrictions, as native born citizens.

*Foreign born soldiers and sailors of the late war entitled to vote, without property qualification.*

SEC. 2. The said proposition of amendment shall be submitted to the electors, for their approval or rejection, at meetings of the electors, to be held on the first Tuesday in November, A. D. 1876. The voting places in the various cities and towns shall be kept open during the hours now required by law for voting for state officers.

*Amendment to be voted on Nov. 7, 1876.*

SEC. 3. The secretary of state shall cause the said proposition of amendment to be published in all the papers publishing the laws of the state, for four weeks successively, next preceding the day of said meetings of said electors; and the said proposition shall be inserted by the town and city clerks in the warrants or notices by them to be issued previous to said meetings of the electors, for the purpose of warning the town or ward meetings; and said proposition shall be read by the town, ward and district clerks to the electors in the town, ward and district meetings to be held as aforesaid.

*To be published in the newspapers;*

*Inserted in the warrants;*

*Read to the electors.*

SEC. 4. The secretary of state shall cause twenty-five thousand copies of said proposition of amendment to be printed, with the word " approved " upon the same, and a like number with the word " reject " thereon, and shall cause such ballots to be distributed among the town and ward clerks in suitable proportions, previous to the day of said meetings of electors.

*Ballots to be printed and distributed.*

SEC. 5. The town, ward and district meetings to be held as aforesaid shall be warned, and the list of voters shall be canvassed and made up, and the said town, ward and district meetings shall be conducted in the same manner as now provided by law, for the town, ward and district meetings for the election of general officers.

*Of warning the meetings, etc.*

SEC. 6. At the close of the polls on said day of said meetings of the electors, the moderator and town clerk, or the warden and ward clerk, or the moderator and

*Of counting the ballots at close of the polls.*

district clerk, shall, in open town, ward or district meetings, count said ballots, and seal up the same, and shall
certify that the ballots by them sealed up are the ballots
given in at said meetings of the electors, the number of
such ballots, and that the number of ballots on said
proposition does not exceed the number of electors
voting at said meetings, and shall deliver or send such
ballots, so sealed up and certified, to the secretary of
state before the first day of December, A. D. 1876.

Ballots to be counted by governor and secretary of state, and proclamation made of the result.

SEC. 7.   The governor and secretary of state shall
count said ballots on or before the fifteenth day of December, A. D. 1876, and the governor shall announce
the result by proclamation, on or before the first day of
January, A. D. 1877, and if said proposition of amendment shall have been approved by three-fifths of the
electors of the state present and voting thereon in said
town, ward and district meetings, the same shall be
declared to be a part of the constitution of the state,
and shall be numbered as an additional article in
amendment thereto.

# ACTS

OF A

# 𝕷𝖔𝖈𝖆𝖑 𝖆𝖓𝖉 𝕻𝖗𝖎𝖛𝖆𝖙𝖊 𝕹𝖆𝖙𝖚𝖗𝖊,

INCLUDING

## ACTS OF INCORPORATION.

---

### AN ACT TO INCORPORATE THE KINGSTON RAILROAD COMPANY.

*It is enacted by the General Assembly as follows:*

Passed June 1, 1876.

SECTION 1. Thomas P. Wells, Thomas M. Potter, J. Hagadorn Wells, Nathaniel C. Peckham, John H. Tefft, Thomas A. Gardner, John R. Eldred, their associates, successors and assigns, are hereby created a corporation by the name of the Kingston Railroad Company.

SEC. 2. Said corporation are hereby authorized to locate, lay out, construct, finally complete and operate a railroad, commencing at a point on the New York, Providence and Boston Railroad at or near Kingston Station in the town of South Kingstown, thence running, in the most practicable direction, to or near Kingston Village, in said town, and thence southerly or easterly or southerly and easterly to tide water in said town, and for that purpose the said corporation are authorized to lay out their said road not exceeding six rods wide through its entire length ; and for the purpose of cutting embankments, and obtaining stone and gravel, may take as

2

much more land as may be necessary for the proper construction of said road: *Provided*, that all damage that may be occasioned to any person, company or corporation, by taking of such land or materials for the purposes aforesaid, shall be paid for by said corporation in the manner hereinafter provided.

SEC. 3. The capital stock of said corporation shall not exceed one hundred thousand dollars, to be divided into shares of fifty dollars each; and the immediate government and direction of the affairs thereof shall be vested in not less than three nor more than five directors, who shall be chosen by the stockholders of the corporation, and shall hold their offices for one year and until others are elected and qualified to take their places. And a majority of them shall form a quorum for business and may fill vacancies in their number. The directors shall elect one of their number president of the board, who shall also be president of the company, and said directors may choose a clerk and treasurer, who shall give bonds to the corporation, with sureties, to the satisfaction of the board of directors for the faithful discharge of his trust, and may choose such other officers as may be deemed necessary for the proper transaction of the business of the corporation.

SEC. 4. Said board of directors may from time to time make assessments upon the shares of the company, as they may deem expedient and necessary in the progress and execution of the work, and direct the same to be paid to the treasurer, and the treasurer shall give notice to the stockholders of all such assessments, and in case any stockholder shall neglect to pay his assessment for the space of thirty days after notice by the treasurer, the directors may order the treasurer to sell the share or shares of such delinquent stockholder at public auction (after giving not less than twenty days notice of such sale in one newspaper at least printed in this state), to the highest bidder, and the treasurer shall thereupon transfer such stock so sold to the purchaser, and such delinquent stockholder shall be entitled to the surplus, if his share or shares shall sell for more than the assessment due, with the interest and expenses of sale, *provided, however*, that no assessment shall be made upon any share in said corporation of a greater amount in the whole than the par value of such share.

SEC. 5. Said corporation may establish rates of fare and of freight and change the same from time to time.

SEC. 6. The annual meeting of said corporation shall be held at such time and place within this state as the corporation shall by by-law direct.

SEC. 7. Whenever said corporation shall have located said road or any part thereof, they shall make report thereof, and file the same with the clerk of the court of common pleas, within and for the county of Washington, in which report they shall particularly describe the bearings of the route so located, and the names of the owners of the land through or over which the same may pass, so far as they can be ascertained; whereupon the same proceedings shall be had as prescribed by general law, and said court shall appoint three disinterested persons from said county (vacancies, if any happen, to be filled by the court,) commissioners to estimate all damages which any person or persons whose lands are described or mentioned in said report shall sustain, *provided*, such railroad or any appendage or appurtenance thereof be constructed thereon, and said commissioners before they proceed to execute their duties shall be sworn to a faithful and impartial discharge thereof, and they shall give reasonable notice in such manner as said court shall direct, to all persons interested to file their claims, if any they have, which have not been released to said corporation, with some one of said commissioners, or with the clerk of said court, within thirty days from the date of such notice. At the end of the term allowed for filing such claims for damages, the commissioners, or a majority of them, having previously given notice to all parties interested as far as they can be ascertained, of the time and extent of the route to be examined, by publishing in a newspaper printed in the county of Washington, an advertisment for three successive weeks at least, shall meet on the premises so intended to be used by said corporation, and after hearing the parties interested, shall estimate all such damages as they shall think any person shall sustain by the construction of said railroad through his

land, which the said commissioners shall judge may
accrue to such person from the construction of said
railroad through said lands, and said commissioners, or a
majority of them, shall make report of their doings, as
soon as may be to said court of common pleas, and the
said court shall thereupon order the said report, or the
substance thereof, to be published forthwith in a newspaper printed in the county of Washington, three weeks
successively, at the expense of the corporation. Said
corporation or any other person interested who may be
dissatisfied, may apply to said court at its term for said
county next after the expiration of said notice, for a
jury to examine and determine the amount of damages
as aforesaid to be paid by said corporation, and a trial
shall be had thereon, under direction of said court; and
if the party applying for such jury fail to obtain an
alteration of the estimate or assessment in favor of such
party applying, such party shall pay all costs accruing
after the entry of such application, and the court shall
render judgment and issue an execution or executions
to carry out said judgment; and if within sixty days
after said corporation shall have entered on the land of
any person and begun to construct their road thereon,
and no application is made for a jury, they shall not
pay the damages assessed as aforesaid, such person
may have an action of debt against said corporation to
recover the same. And the report of said commissioners if not appealed from or the verdict of a jury
and judgment thereon when paid, settled and discharged,
shall forever be a bar to any other action against said
corporation for any injury for which said damages were
awarded, and said commissioners in all cases shall be
allowed and paid three dollars each per day for their
services, and shall at the request of any one whose
lands or materials are to be taken by said corporation
require said corporation to give security to the satisfaction of said commissioners, to such person for the payment of all damages which may be awarded by said
commissioners or by a jury and for costs and expenses,
and thereupon said corporation shall not enter such
person's land for any other purpose than surveying until
such security is given.

Sec. 8. When the land or property of any infant or person *non compos mentis*, shall be necessary for the construction of said road, the guardian of such person may release all damages done as aforesaid, *provided*, the same be done under the advice and direction of the court of probate of the town in which the land lies.

Sec. 9. Said corporation may alter and vary the location of their road, or make a new location in whole or in part, in which case like proceedings shall be had as are hereinbefore directed; but the time herein allowed for completing the road shall not be extended thereby.

Sec. 10. In case of any new location, said corporation shall report what portion of the former location is abandoned; and if the land or materials of any person included in the former location have not been taken or used, all proceedings for estimating such damages shall cease, but the company shall pay to such person his costs and reasonable expenses incurred in the prosecution of his claims up to that time, to be taxed and allowed by the court. And if such land or materials have been taken or used, in whole or in part, said corporation may give such abandonment in evidence in diminution of damages, said corporation in such case paying all costs and expenses of estimate and litigation.

Sec. 11. If the stock be not subscribed, the corporation organized and said location be not filed as aforesaid on or before the first day of February, A. D. 1880, or if said corporation fail to complete said road by the first day of February, A. D. 1885, then this act shall so far as it relates to that part of said road then not completed be void and of no effect.

Sec. 12. Said corporation shall have an office or place of business in the town of South Kingstown, and shall be entitled to all the powers and privileges and be subject to all the duties and liabilities set forth in chapters 139 and 145 of the General Statutes, and of all acts in amendment thereof or in addition thereto.

Sec. 13. Said corporation shall be subject to all the provisions and liabilities as to fires, fences and passways and gates at passways to which the New York, Providence and Boston Railroad company are made liable by the act amending their charter, passed at the

June session of this general assembly, A. D. 1836, and persons aggrieved shall be entitled to all the remedies provided by the said act in the same manner and to the same extent as if said provisions had been incorporated into this act at length.

SEC. 14.    This act shall take effect immediately.

---

Passed June
1. 1876.
AN ACT TO INCORPORATE THE PAWTUCKET LUMBER AND BUILDERS' SUPPLIES COMPANY.

*It is enacted by the General Assembly as follows:*

SECTION 1.    James T. Bliss, James Davis, James M. Bishop, Alfred W. Carr, John L. Perrin, Daniel A. Jillson and Thomas Horton, their associates, successors and assigns, are hereby constituted and created a body corporate and politic, under the name of the Pawtucket Lumber and Builders' Supplies Company, for the purpose of manufacturing lumber, sash, blinds, doors, packing boxes for goods of all kinds, and all sorts of builders' supplies, and for transacting other business connected therewith; with all the powers and privileges, and subject to all the duties and liabilities set forth in chapters 139 and 142 of the General Statutes, and all acts in amendment thereof and in addition thereto.

SEC. 2.    The capital stock of said company shall be not more than one hundred thousand dollars, to be divided into shares of one hundred dollars each; the amount to be fixed by vote of the stockholders.

SEC. 3.    Said company shall have an office in Pawtucket; and there shall be an annual meeting of the stockholders in Pawtucket, at such places and times as may be designated by the by-laws of the company, for the election of officers and such other business as may properly come before said meetings.

AN ACT TO INCORPORATE THE NEW ENGLAND RAILROAD AUTOMATIC GATE COMPANY.

Passed June 1, 1876.

*It is enacted by the General Assembly as follows:*

SECTION 1.   Charles Moies, Stephen A. Jenks, Henry A. Stearns, John R. Fales, Alvin F. Jenks, William D. Hilton and Lysander Flagg, their associates, successors and assigns are hereby made a corporation by the name of the New England Railroad Automatic Gate Company, for the purpose of making, selling and using railroad automatic and other gates, with all the powers and privileges, and subject to all the duties and liabilities set forth in chapters 139 and 142 of the General Statutes, and in any acts in amendment thereof or in addition thereto.

SEC. 2.   The capital stock of said corporation shall be not exceeding one hundred thousand dollars, to be divided into shares of one hundred dollars each.

SEC. 3.   No stockholder shall transfer his stock, or any portion thereof, without first giving said corporation the refusal of the same at the lowest price for which he is willing to sell such stock.

SEC. 4.   The stock or shares of every stockholder shall be pledged and liable to said corporation for all debts and demands owing from such stockholder to said company, and whether over due or due at a day future, and whether arising from assessments or instalments, or in any other manner; and said stock or shares may be sold for the payment of such debts and demands in such manner as the by-laws of said company may prescribe.

SEC. 5.   Said corporation shall have a counting-room or place of business in Pawtucket, at which the annual meetings thereof shall be held.

AN ACT TO INCORPORATE THE CHATTAN OIL AND PAINT WORKS.

Passed June 1, 1876.

*It is enacted by the General Assembly as follows:*

SECTION 1.   Charles E. Boon, Donald D. Cattanach, Henry Barton,  James A. Leckie and Oscar Lapham, their associates, successors and assigns, are hereby constituted and created a body corporate and politic by the name of the "Chattan Oil and Paint Works," for the purpose of refining and treating oils, and the manufacture of paints and varnishes, and all purposes connected therewith, with all the powers and privileges, and subject to the duties and liabilities set forth in chapters 139 and 142 of the General Statutes, and all acts in amendment thereof or in addition thereto.

Sec. 2. The capital stock of said corporation shall not exceed one hundred thousand dollars, to be fixed in amount by vote of the company, and to be divided into shares of one hundred dollars each.

Sec. 3. At all meetings of the corporation a majority of the shares shall be required to constitute a quorum, but a less number may adjourn the meeting from time to time, as they shall see fit, and a majority of the votes present shall be required to decide any matter, allowing each stockholder in person, or by proxy, one vote for every share by him owned, but no stockholder shall vote on more than one-fourth part of the whole capital stock.

Sec. 4. The stock and shares of each and every stockholder shall be pledged and liable to said company for all debts and demands due from such stockholders to said company, or to become due at a day future, whether from assessments, instalments, or any other cause, and such stock, or so much thereof as said company may deem expedient, may be sold by said company at public auction, for the payment of such debts and demands and the incidental expenses, and said company may likewise have their action against such debtors at any time before the whole of said indebtedness shall be paid.

Sec. 5. C. E. Boon or Donald D. Cattanach is hereby authorized to call the first meeting of the stockholders for the purpose of organization, and any other business of said company which said stockholders may think proper, at such time and place, and upon such notice as he may deem reasonable and proper.

Sec. 6. Said company shall have an office in the city of Providence.

Sec. 7.   This act shall take effect on and after its passage.

---

AN ACT TO INCORPORATE THE LADD WATCH CASE COMPANY.

Passed June 1, 1876.

*It is enacted by the General Assembly as follows:*

Section 1.   John A. Brown, George W. Ladd, and their associates, successors and assigns are hereby constituted a corporation by the name of the Ladd Watch Case Company, for manufacturing watch cases and jewelry, and for the transaction of other business connected therewith, with all the powers and privileges, and subject to all the duties and liabilities set forth in chapters 139 and 142 of the General Statutes, and in the Statutes in amendment thereof, and in addition thereto.

Sec. 2.   The capital stock of said corporation shall be the sum of one hundred thousand dollars, divided into one thousand shares of one hundred dollars each, and at every meeting of the corporation the stockholders therein shall be entitled to one vote for each share of stock held by them.   The stock or shares of each stockholder shall be pledged and liable to the corporation for all debts and demands due and owing from such stockholder to the corporation, whether over due or due at a future day, and whether arising from assessments or in any other manner, and said shares may be sold for the payment of such debts and demands, in such manner as the corporation may by by-law prescribe, and in case the proceeds of such sale shall be insufficient to satisfy such debt or demand, with incidental expenses of sale, the corporation may have their action against the debtor for the balance due.

Sec. 3.   Said corporation shall have a counting-room and place of business in the city of Providence.

Passed June
2, 1876.

AN ACT IN AMENDMENT OF AND IN ADDITION TO THE
CHARTER OF THE OLD COLONY RAILROAD COMPANY.

*It is enacted by the General Assembly as follows:*

SECTION 1.  The Old Colony Rail Road Company is
hereby authorized to purchase, take, hold and enjoy the
Rail Road, of the Fall River, Warren and Providence
Rail Road Company, with the franchise and property
of the last named corporation, and to operate and use
the said Rail Road, property, and franchise, when purchased, as a part of the Rail Road property of the said
Old Colony Rail Road Company.

Passed June
2, 1876.

AN ACT TO INCORPORATE THE JOHNSTON MINING
COMPANY.

*It is enacted by the General Assembly as follows:*

SECTION 1.  Benjamin Hunt, Jr., Amasa S. Westcott,
Lycurgus Sayles, their associates, successors and assigns, are hereby constituted and created a body politic
and corporate, with perpetual succession, by the name
of the Johnston Mining Company, for the purpose of
acquiring, holding, working and mining gold, silver,
copper and other minerals in the state of Rhode Island
or elsewhere in the United States, in any lands which
they may at any time own in fee simple, or possess by
lease, or which they may acquire the right to use for
mining purposes, and for the transaction of all other
business connected therewith or incidental thereto ; with
all the powers and privileges, and subject to all the
duties and liabilities set forth in chapters 139 and 142
of the General Statutes of this state, and of any acts in
amendment thereof or in addition thereto.

SEC. 2.  The capital stock of said corporation shall
consist of one hundred thousand dollars, to be divided
into four thousand shares of the par value of twenty-five
dollars each.  Said shares shall be deemed personal
estate and the ownership thereof be evidenced by certificates, and said certificates shall be issued and said
shares shall be transferred in such manner as the by-

laws of said corporation shall provide. The stock and shares of each and every shareholder shall be pledged and held liable for all debts and demands due and owing from him to said corporation, whether the same be over due or due at a day future, and whether the same shall arise from instalments or assesments, or from any other contract made with said corporation; and said stock or shares may be sold for the payment of such debts, demands, instalments or assessments, in such manner as the by-laws of the corporation may prescribe; and in case the proceeds of such sale be insufficient to pay and discharge said debts and demands, with the incidental expenses of sale, the corporation may have their action against such debtor for the balance due.

SEC. 3.    There shall be an annual meeting of the stockholders in the city of Providence to be holden on the second Monday in June, in each year, or at such time as the by-laws shall prescribe, for the election of not less than five nor more than nine directors (a majority of whom shall be residents of the state of Rhode Island) who shall be stockholders in said company, all of whom shall hold their offices for one year and until others are elected and qualified in their places, who shall choose all necessary officers of the corporation.

SEC. 4.    Special meetings of said corporation may be called and held in such manner as may be provided by the by-laws of the corporation.

---

AN ACT TO INCORPORATE THE NATIONAL SPOOL COMPANY.

Passed June 1, 1876.

*It is enacted by the General Assembly as follows:*

SECTION 1.    Thomas V. Stillman, Otis P. Chapman, Thomas Vincent, their associates and successors are hereby created a body corporate by the name of the National Spool Company, for the purpose of manufacturing spools and bobbins, and for the transaction of other business incidentally connected therewith, with all the powers and subject to all the duties and liabilities set forth in chapters 139 and 142 of the General Statutes, and of all acts in amendment thereof or in addition thereto.

Sec. 2.  The capital stock of said corporation shall not exceed one hundred thousand dollars, to be fixed in amount by the stockholders of said company, to be divided into shares of one hundred dollars, the same to be transferred in such manner as the by-laws of the corporation shall prescribe; but no stockholder shall transfer his stock or any portion thereof, without first giving the corporation the refusal of the same, at the price for which he is willing to sell.

Sec. 3.  The stock or shares of every stockholder shall be pledged and liable to the corporation for all debts and demands due and owing from such stockholder to the corporation, and whether over due or due at a day future, and whether arising from instalments or assessments, or in any other manner, and said stock or shares may be sold for the payment of such debts and demands, in such manner as the by-laws of said corporation may prescribe; and in case the proceeds of such sale shall be insufficient to discharge said debts or demands, with the incidental expenses of sale, the corporation may have their action against the debtor for the balance due.

Sec. 4.  There shall be an annual meeting of said corporation in the village of Westerly, at such day in each year, and for the choice of such officers as the by-laws may prescribe.

Sec. 5.  Said corporation shall have a counting room and place of business in the village of Westerly.

---

Passed June 1, 1876.   AN ACT TO INCORPORATE THE PROVIDENCE AND PASCOAG
                    TELEGRAPH COMPANY.

*It is enacted by the General Assembly as follows:*

Section 1.  Charles E. Paine, Amos N. Beckwith, John T. Fiske, James O. Inman, H. A. Kimball, H. R. Sayles, Albert L. Sayles, their associates, successors and assigns are hereby incorporated and made a body politic and corporate, by the name and style of "The Providence and Pascoag Telegraph Company," for the purpose of constructing and maintaining lines of telegraph from the city of Providence to the village of Pascoag in

the town of Burrillville, and thence. to the boundary
lines of the states of Massachusetts and Connecticut,
with power to connect the same with other lines of
telegraph in this state and other states, and to and from
any other points in this state as they may deem expedient for commercial purposes and the transmission of
intelligence, and shall have by such name all the powers
and privileges, and be subject to all the duties, liabilities and restrictions, applicable to such corporations set
forth in chapter one hundred and thirty-nine of the
General Statutes, and the several acts in amendment
thereof.

Sec. 2.   The capital stock· of said corporation shall
not exceed fifty thousand dollars, and may be fixed from
time to time by vote of the corporation, and shall be
divided into shares of fifty dollars each.

Sec. 3.   There shall be an annual meeting of said
corporation holden in the city of Providence on such
day in each year as the by-laws of said corporation shall
prescribe, for the election of officers and the transaction
of such business as may properly come before the corporation.

Sec. 4.   Said corporation shall have a place of business in the city of Providence.

---

AN ACT TO INCORPORATE "THE PROVIDENCE HEATING
GAS COMPANY."

Passed June
1, 1876.

*It is enacted by the General Assembly as follows:*

SECTION 1.   William Harkness, John T. Mauran,
Sullivan Moulton, Walter M. Jackson, their associates,
successors and assigns, are hereby created a body corporate and politic, by the name of The Providence
Heating Gas Company, for the purpose of making,
selling and distributing heating gas, to heat the buildings, public and private, in the city of Providence and
its adjoining territory, and to be used for such purposes
as fuel is generally employed, and for the transaction of
any business connected therewith, or incidental thereto,
with all the powers and privileges, and subject to all
the duties and liabilities set forth in chapters 139 and

142 of the General Statutes, and of all acts in amendment thereof or in addition thereto.

Sec. 2.   The capital stock of said corporation shall
be one hundred thousand dollars, to be divided into
shares of one hundred dollars each.   Said capital stock
may be increased by a vote of said corporation to any
amount not exceeding the sum of five hundred thousand
dollars.

Sec. 3.   The stock or shares of every stockholder
shall be pledged and liable to the corporation for all
debts and demands due and owing from such stockholder to the corporation, and whether over due or due at
a day future, and whether arising from instalments or
in any other manner; and said stock or shares may be
sold for the payment of such debts and demands, in
such manner as the by-laws of the corporation may prescribe; and in case the proceeds of such sale shall be
insufficient to discharge such debts and demands, the
corporation may have their action against the debtor for
the balance due.

Sec. 4.   Said corporation shall have power and
authority to open the ground in any highway, street,
lane, alley, park or other public places within the
limits aforesaid, with the approval of the city or town
council as the case may be, and lay and repair therein
their pipes for conducting gas; said corporation restor-
ing the same to as good condition as before, within a
reasonable time thereafter; said corporation being required in so doing not to injure any gas or water pipe
or connection or sewer laid therein, and to be subject
to such reasonable regulations as the municipal authorities of the said city of Providence or the town councils
of the adjoining towns, within the limits of which said
corporation shall lay pipes, shall prescribe for their respective limits.

Sec. 5.   If any person shall wilfully or maliciously
do or cause to be done any act whatever whereby the
works of said corporation, or any part thereof, or any
pipe, conduit, plug, cock, reservoir, or any engine,
machine, meter, or structure, or any matter or thing
appertaining to the same shall be injured, destroyed,
stopped, obstructed, impaired, weakened or interfered
with, the person so offending shall forfeit and pay to

said corporation double the amount of damages sustained by means of such offence or injury, to be recovered in an action of debt, to be brought in the name of said corporation in any court of competent jurisdiction, together with costs of suit.

SEC. 6. Any person or persons who shall without right wilfully or fraudulently injure or suffer to be injured any pipes, fittings or meter belonging to the corporation, or prevent any meter from duly registering the quantity of gas supplied through the same, or shall alter the index of any such meter, or in any way hinder or interfere with its proper action or just registration, or shall fraudulently burn the gas of this corporation or waste the same, shall, for every such offence, forfeit and pay to this corporation the sum of twenty-five dollars, and in addition thereto shall pay to said corporation the amount of damage by them sustained by reason of such injury, prevention, waste, consumption or hindrance.

SEC. 7. Any person duly authorized in writing by this corporation, over the signature of the president or treasurer, at all proper hours of the day, may, on presenting such written authority, enter any dwelling, store, room, place or building supplied with heating apparatus by this corporation, for the purpose of inspecting and examining the meters, pipes, fittings and works for supplying and regulating the quantity of gas consumed or supplied ; and in case of non-payment of any sum due for gas previously supplied according to his or their contract with this corporation, to prevent and stop the gas from entering the premises of such person or persons, and take and carry away any such meter, pipe, fittings or other works from the mains or pipes of this corporation.

SEC. 8. There shall be an annual meeting of the stockholders in the city of Providence, at such time as the by-laws of said corporation shall prescribe, for the choice of officers and for such other business as shall come before them.

SEC. 9. Said corporation shall have a counting-room and place of business in the city of Providence.

SEC. 10. This act shall take effect from and after its passage.

Passed June
1, 1876.   AN ACT TO INCORPORATE THE TURKEY RED DYEING
                         COMPANY.

*It is enacted by the General Assembly as follows:*

SECTION 1.   James Sutcliffe, John Tattersall, James
Butterworth, Henry Ashworth, Robert Reoch, Thomas
Rawlinson, Henry P. Clough, their associates, successors and assigns are hereby made a corporation by the
name of the Turkey Red Dyeing Company, for the purpose of manufacturing, bleaching, dyeing, printing and
finishing cotton yarns and other textile goods, and for
the transaction of other business connected therewith or
incidental thereto, with all the powers and privileges,
and subject to all the duties and liabilities set forth in
chapters 139 and 142 of the General Statutes, and in
any acts in amendment thereof or in addition thereto.

.SEC. 2.   The capital stock of said corporation shall
be not exceeding one hundred thousand dollars, to be
divided into shares of one hundred dollars each.

SEC. 3.   No stockholder shall transfer his stock, or
any portion thereof, without first giving said corporation
the refusal of the same at the lowest price for which he
is willing to sell such stock.

SEC. 4.   The stock or shares of every stockholder
shall be pledged and liable to said corporation for all
debts and demands owing from such stockholder to said
company, and whether overdue or due at a day future,
and whether arising from assessments or instalments or
in any other manner, and said stock or shares may be
sold for the payment of such debts and demands in such
manner as the by-laws of said company may prescribe;
and in case the proceeds of such sale be insufficient to discharge said debts or demands, with incidental expenses of sale, the corporation may have their
action against the debtor for the balance due.

SEC. 5.   There shall be an annual meeting of the
stockholders at such time as the by-laws shall prescribe
for the choice of officers, and for such other business as
may come before them.

SEC. 6.   Said corporation shall have a counting room
or place of business in the city of Providence or town
of Cranston.

Sec. 7. This act shall take effect from and after its passage.

---

AN ACT TO INCORPORATE "THE BULLOCK LAND COMPANY."

Passed June 2, 1876.

*It is enacted by the General Assembly as follows:*

Section 1. Edward Pearce, Harriet Pearce, Julia Bullock, William T. Bullock, Jerauld Bullock, Thomas Harris and their associates, successors and assigns, are hereby constituted a corporation by the name of "The Bullock Land Company," with the right to purchase real estate, and to hold and improve the same, and for other purposes connected therewith or incidental thereto, with all the powers and privileges, and subject to all the duties and liabilities set forth in chapter 139 of the General Statutes, and in all acts in amendment thereof or in addition thereto.

Sec. 2. The capital stock of said company shall not exceed one thousand shares of one hundred dollars each, and said shares shall be transferable and certificates shall be issued in such manner as said corporation shall prescribe.

Sec. 3. There shall be held an annual meeting of the stockholders of said corporation at such time as the by-laws shall prescribe.

Sec. 4. The stock or shares of every stockholder shall be pledged and liable to the corporation for all debts and demands due and owing from such stock holder, whether over due or due at a future day, and whether arising from assessments, or in any other manner, and such shares may be sold for the payment of such debts and demands in such manner as the corporation by the by-laws prescribes, and in case the proceeds of such sale shall be insufficient to satisfy such debts or demands, with incidental expenses of sale, the corporation may have their action against the debtor for the balance due.

Sec. 5. Said corporation shall have a counting room and place of business in the city of Providence.

3

Passed June
2, 1876.

AN ACT TO INCORPORATE THE BRISTOL COUNTY SAVINGS
BANK IN THE TOWN OF BRISTOL.

*It is enacted by the General Assembly as follows:*

Section 1. Theodore P. Bogert, John B. Munro,
Henry Goff, Augustus O. Bourn, Charles H. R. Do-
ringh, Stephen T. Church, John G. Watson, Lemuel
A. Bishop, Otis Munro, Andrew R. Trotter, George H.
Farrington, John B. Pearce, John W. Monro, Nathan
C. Bedell, James A. Miller, William H. Spooner, J.
Howard Manchester, Thomas G. Holmes, Jonathan D.
Waldron, Josephus Gooding, S. Pomroy Colt, John
Turner, Isaac F. Williams, Elisha M. Wardwell, Par-
menas Skinner, Jr., with such other persons as may be
associated with them, in manner hereinafter provided,
are hereby created and made a body corporate by the
name of the "Bristol County Savings Bank" in the
town of Bristol.

Sec. 2. Said corporation shall meet in the town of
Bristol, on the first Wednesday in June, annually, and
as much oftener as they may deem expedient; any
seven members of said corporation shall be a quorum,
of which two at least shall be directors; and at said
annual meeting said corporation shall have power to
elect a president, three vice presidents, secretary, and
not more than ten directors, who, together, shall constitute a board of trustees, together with such other officers as shall appear necessary, which officers shall in
all cases be chosen by ballot, and shall continue in
office one year, and until others are chosen in their
places.

Sec. 3. Said corporation shall be capable of receiving from any person or persons, any deposit or deposits
of money, and to use and improve the same for the purposes and according to the directions herein provided:
*provided, however*, that the amount of the whole sum
received by said corporation and remaining under its
management shall never exceed, at any time, the sum
of five hundred thousand dollars.

Sec. 4. All deposits of money received by said corporation shall be used and improved to the best advan-

tage, and the income or profits thereof shall be by them
applied and divided among the persons making the said
deposits, their legal representatives or assigns, in just
proportion, with such reasonable deductions as the
management of the affairs of said corporation may require; and the principal of such deposits may be withdrawn at such times and in such manner as said corporation shall direct, the interval to be limited.

Sec. 5.   Said corporation shall have power and
authority at any legal meeting, to elect by ballot any
other person or persons members of said corporation.

Sec. 6.   The following shall be the regulations for
the government of said corporation as part of this act,
viz.:

1st.   *Object of this Corporation.*—To enable all persons to invest such part of their earnings or property as
they may choose, in a manner which will afford them
security and profit.

2d.   *Management.*—The affairs of said corporation
shall be managed by a president, three vice presidents,
a treasurer, and not more than ten directors, who shall,
together, constitute the board of trustees as aforesaid.
They shall have power to elect such officers, not provided for in the second section of this act, as they may
deem expedient, and to fill all vacancies in their board
which may happen during the year.   They shall meet
at least twice in every year, in the months of June and
December, and as much oftener as they may deem necessary, and whenever meetings shall be called by the
president or any two directors; and it shall be the duty
of the treasurer to notify such meetings either by
personal notice or by advertisement in one of the newspapers printed in Bristol or Providence, and at all
meetings of the board of trustees five members shall
make a quorum.   The members of the board, excepting
the treasurer, shall not receive any emolument for their
services, nor shall any money be loaned to or for any
member of the board, or other officer of the corporation,
and any member of the board who shall be present
when any such loan shall be made, and shall not at that
time cause a protest to be entered in writing on the
records of the proceedings of the board against the
same, shall be considered and held liable for the amount

of such loan, in his individual person and property. And the said members of the board, (except as aforesaid), shall not be responsible for any losses which may happen from whatever cause, except their willful corrupt misconduct, in which case those only who were present and guilty of such misconduct shall be responsible for the same. And the board of trustees at any meeting of which seven at least of them shall be present, and after due notice of such intention at a previous meeting, may make such further rules, regulations, and by-laws, or alterations of those already by them made, as they may deem necessary; *provided, however,* that the same may be disallowed by said corporation at their next annual meeting.

3d. *The Treasurer.*—The treasurer, before he enters on the duties of his office, shall give bonds with sufficient surety or sureties, to the corporation, to be determined by the board of trustees, for the faithful execution of the duties of his office; he may receive such reasonable compensation for his services as may be allowed by the board of trustees; he shall receive all the deposits, enter the same in the books of the corporation, pay out all dividends which shall be declared, and render an account of the property and funds of the corporation to the board of trustees, or the corporation when requested thereto by a vote.

4th. *Deposits.*—All deposits shall be made at the office of the treasurer, in the town of Bristol. The smallest deposit shall be five cents, and the lowest sum which shall be put upon interest shall be one dollar. An account shall be given in a book to each depositor, by the treasurer, of the sum deposited, which shall be the evidence of the depositor's property in said corporation, who shall, on making the first deposit, subscribe and thereby signify his assent to the rules, regulations and by-laws of the corporation. Any depositor, at the time of making his deposit, may designate the period for which he is desirous the same should remain, and the person for whose benefit the same is made, which shall be binding on him and his legal representatives; *provided, however,* that said deposit and its accruing dividends may be paid off according to the provisions hereinafter mentioned. Every person making a deposit personally, may withdraw the money deposited, and the dividends that may have accrued thereon, notwithstanding the person at the time of withdrawing the same may be a married woman or a minor, and the receipt of such married woman or minor, unless under guardianship, shall be a sufficient discharge of said corporation for the sum so withdrawn.

5th.    *Dividends.*—At such times as the board of trustees may determine there shall be declared and paid on all sums of and above one dollar, which shall have been deposited, a dividend of such per centum per annum as the board shall determine, and a proportionate rate of interest shall be paid on any such sum which shall have been deposited for the space of three months preceding.   No interest shall be paid on any sums withdrawn for the period which may have elapsed since the last dividend, unless otherwise determined by the board of trustees ; *provided*, that at the time of making any dividend, or within one month thereafter, the board of trustees may, at their pleasure, pay off the whole of any deposit due to any depositor; *provided, however*, that in such case interest shall be paid on such deposit up to the time of such payment.

6th.    *Mode of Receiving Dividends, and of Withdrawdrawing Deposits.*—Dividends may be received either personally or by the order in writing of the depositor, or by letter of attorney.   Deposits shall only be withdrawn by the depositor, or some person legally authorized ; but no person shall receive any part of his principal or dividends without producing the original book, that such payment may be entered thereon; *provided, however*, that in case of loss of the original book, the board of trustees may determine upon what terms a new book may be granted.   The board of trustees may require that sixty days' notice of the intention of withdrawing any money shall be given to the treasurer in writing.   All dividends not called for, after they shall have been declared, shall be added to the principal.

7th.    *Institution, how Dissolved.*—The board of trustees, by a vote of three-fourths of the whole number, may at any time divide the whole property among the depositors, in proportion to their respective interests therein, upon giving six months notice thereof, and shall also have power to refuse any deposits at their pleasure.

SEC. 7.   Notice of the annual meetings shall be published for three weeks previously to holding the same, in one of the newspapers in the town of Bristol, or the city of Providence.

SEC. 8.   Said corporation shall be entitled to all the powers and privileges, and subject to all the duties and liabilities set forth in chapters 139, 140 and 141 of the General Statutes, and of all acts in amendment thereof, or in addition thereto.

SEC. 9.   This act shall take effect on and after its passage.

---

Passed June
13, 1876.

### AN ACT IN AMENDMENT OF AN ACT ENTITLED "AN ACT TO INCORPORATE THE BRISTOL COUNTY SAVINGS BANK IN THE TOWN OF BRISTOL."

*It is enacted by the General Assembly us follows:*

SECTION 1.   Section 8 of the act entitled "An act to · incorporate the Bristol County Savings Bank in the town of Bristol," passed at the present session of the general assembly, is hereby amended by adding the following, viz.:

Parmenas Skinner, Jr., is hereby authorized to call the first meeting of said corporation at such time and place as he may deem proper, but notice of such meeting shall, seven days at least before the meeting, be delivered to each member or published in some newspaper of Bristol county.

SEC. 2.   This act shall take effect immediately.

---

Passed June
2, 1876.

### AN ACT TO INCORPORATE THE NEW AMERICAN FILE COMPANY.

*It is enacted by the General Assembly as follows:*

SECTION 1.   William F. Sayles, Stephen A. Jenks, Earl P. Mason, Frederick C. Sayles and Charles A. Nichols, their associates, successors and assigns, are hereby constituted and created a body corporate and

politic, by the name of the " New American File Company," for manufacturing files and other articles of
hardware, and by that name shall have perpetual succession. may have and use a common seal, the same to
alter, break and renew at pleasure, and generally may
do and execute all acts, matters and things which may
be necessary to carry into effect the powers and privileges herein granted.

SEC. 2.    The capital stock shall not exceed the sum
of two hundred thousand dollars, to be fixed in amount
by a vote of the company, and to be divided into shares
of one hundred dollars each.    The shares in said
capital stock are hereby declared to be personal estate,
and shall be transferred by bill of sale, and recorded in
the office of the treasurer or agent of said corporation
in a book provided for that purpose.

SEC. 3.    There shall be an annual meeting of said
stockholders, holden at the office of the corporation on
the third Wednesday of July in each year, for the choice
of such officers as they may deem expedient, who shall
respectively hold their offices during one year, and until
others are chosen in their stead, unless removed by
death, incapacity, or by a vote of the corporation, and
at any legal meeting said corporation may elect such
officers as may be deemed necessary, and may declare
any offices vacant, and may fill any vacancy that may
happen in any office created by said corporation, and if
said corporation should fail, from any cause or circumstances, to hold their annual meeting on the day aforesaid, it shall not work a forfeiture of this charter, but
the business of such meeting may.be transacted at any
legal meeting called for that purpose. Special meetings
may be called in such manner as shall be prescribed by the by-laws of the corporation, and at all
meetings of the corporation, not less than a majority of
the shares shall constitute a quorum for doing business,
and all matters shall be decided by a majority of the
votes present, allowing each person, in person or by
proxy, one vote for each share by him owned.

SEC. 4. The stock or shares of each and every stockholder shall be pledged and liable for all debts and
demands due and owing from such stockholders to said
corporation, whether overdue or due at a day future,

and whether the same shall arise from assessments or instalments, or from any other contract originally made with said corporation; and in case the proprietor of any share or shares shall neglect or refuse to pay such debt or demand to the treasurer or agent thereof, within twenty days after the same becomes due and payable, the treasurer or agent of said corporation is hereby authorized to sell at public auction the share or shares of such delinquent proprietor, sufficient to discharge such demand, and all incidental expenses, first giving notice in one of the newspapers printed in the city of Providence, of the time and place of sale, for two weeks successively, once in each week next before the sale, and also giving written notice two weeks next before the sale to such delinquent proprietor, in case he shall not reside in this state, and his residence shall be known to said corporation, and the treasurer or agent is authorized to transfer said stock to the purchaser at such sale in the form and manner by which stock is transferrable by the regulations of said corporation, and such sale and transfer shall vest in such purchaser, the legal title to such stock or shares, and the balance of the money arising from the sale of such stock or shares, after discharging the debt or demand for which the same was pledged, with the expenses, shall be paid to the delinquent proprietor; and provided, that if the proceeds of such sale shall not be sufficient to discharge said debt, or demand, the corporation may have their action against the debtor for the balance due.

SEC. 5. William F. Sayles, Stephen A. Jenks and Charles A. Nichols or either of them, are hereby authorized to call the first meeting of stockholders for organization and any other business of the corporation hereby formed at such time and place, and giving such notice of such meeting as they may deem reasonable and proper.

SEC. 6. The liabilities of members of this company for debts of the corporation, its members and officers, shall be fixed and limited by, and the corporation, its members and officers shall, in all respects be subject to the provisions of chapters 139 and 142 of the General Statutes, and all acts and parts of acts in amendment thereof or in addition thereto.

SEC. 7. This act shall take effect from and after its passage.

AN ACT IN AMENDMENT OF AN "ACT TO INCORPORATE THE PROVIDENCE LAND AND WHARF COMPANY," PASSED AT THE MAY SESSION, A. D. 1865.

Passed June 1, 1876.

*It is enacted by the General Assembly as follows:*

SECTION 1.  Section second of "An Act to incorporate the Providence Land and Wharf Company," passed at the May session, A. D. 1865, is hereby amended, by striking out in line second the word "five," and inserting in lieu thereof the word "six."

AN ACT IN AMENDMENT OF AN ACT ENTITLED "AN ACT TO INCORPORATE THE CHRISTIAN CHAPEL SOCIETY IN WESTERLY."

Passed June 1, 1876.

*It is enacted by the General Assembly as follows:*

SECTION 1.  The name of said "Christian Chapel Society in Westerly," is hereby changed to the "Broad Street Christian Church in Westerly," and said society shall hereafter be known by said last mentioned name.

SEC. 2.  Said corporation may take, hold, transmit and convey real and personal estate to an amount not exceeding twenty thousand dollars.

SEC. 3.  So much of the act of which this act is in amendment as is inconsistent herewith is hereby repealed, and this act shall take effect from and after its passage.

AN ACT IN AMENDMENT OF AN ACT TO INCORPORATE KING SOLOMON'S LODGE, NUMBER 4, PASSED JANUARY SESSION, A. D. 1873.

Passed June 3, 1876.

*It is enacted by the General Assembly as follows:*

SECTION 1.  Section one of an act entitled "An act to incorporate King Solomon's Lodge, No. 4, F. and A. M., of Providence," is hereby amended by striking out "4," in the fifth line and inserting in its stead the figure "5."

SEC. 2. This act shall take effect from and after its passage.

---

AN ACT TO INCORPORATE THE BROWN CHAPTER OF PHI KAPPA ALPHA.

Passed June
2, 1876.

*It is enacted by the General Assembly as follows:*

SECTION 1. Alfred G. Langley, Thomas E. Bartlett, W. Whitman, Charles S. Scott, S. O. Edwards, D. W. Hersey, F. W. Bliss, Herbert L. Pierce, Francis H. Viets, J. C. Lamb and H. S. Babcock, their associates and successors, are hereby made a corporation by the name of Brown Chapter of Phi Kappa Alpha, for the purpose of educational and mutual improvement, with all the powers and privileges, and subject to all the duties and liabilities set forth in chapter 139 of the General Statutes, and in any acts in amendment thereof or in addition thereto.

SEC. 2. Said corporation may take, hold, transmit and convey real and personal estate to an amount not exceeding ten thousand dollars.

---

AN ACT TO INCORPORATE THE ST. MARY'S TOTAL ABSTINENCE AND BENEVOLENT SOCIETY AND MUSIC BAND IN THE CITY OF PROVIDENCE.

Passed June
14, 1876.

*It is enacted by the General Assembly as follows:*

SECTION 1. James Donnelly, John Donnelly, Thomas Haggerty, Charles Burrows, Patrick Magner, Luke Padien, James Monahan, their associates and successors are hereby made a corporation by the name of St. Mary's Total Abstinence and Benevolent Society and Music Band in the City of Providence, for the purpose of promoting temperance, for mutual benefit and charitable purposes, and for practising the art of music, with all the powers and privileges, and subject to all the duties and liabilities set forth in chapter 139 of the General Statutes, and in any acts in amendment thereof or in addition thereto.

SEC. 2. Said corporation may take, hold, transmit and convey real and personal estate to an amount not exceeding three thousand dollars.

AN ACT IN AMENDMENT OF AN ACT ENTITLED "AN ACT TO INCORPORATE THE 'SOCKANOSSETT HORSE RAILROAD COMPANY.'"

Passed June 14, 1876.

*It is enacted by the General Assembly as follows:*

SECTION 1. Section one of an act entitled "An act to incorporate the 'Sockanossett Horse Railroad Company'" is hereby amended by striking out all after the word "to" in the fourteenth line of said act down to and including the word "Cranston" in the 25th line, and inserting in place thereof the words "the intersection of the Knightsville road (so called) with said Reservoir avenue."

# RESOLUTIONS

# PUBLIC AND PRIVATE NATURE.

---

No. 1.    RESOLUTION adopting joint rules and orders.

*Resolved*, That the joint rules and orders of the senate
and house of representatives, adopted at the May session of the general assembly, 1875, be and the same are
hereby adopted as the joint rules and orders of the
present senate and house of representatives.

---

No. 2.    RESOLUTION authorizing the joint committee on Engrossed Bills to employ a clerk.

*Resolved*, (The house of representatives concurring
herein,) that the joint committee on engrossed bills be
and hereby are authorized to employ a clerk.

---

No. 3.    RESOLUTION for distribution of the General Statutes to
members of the General Assembly.

*Resolved*, That the secretary of state be hereby
authorized to distribute to each member of the present
general assembly, who has not already received the
same, a copy of the General Statutes, and of the
amendments thereto.

RESOLUTION to suspend Joint Rules six, seven, eight and nine. No. 4.

*Resolved*, (The honorable senate concurring herein.) that so much of joint rules, numbered six, seven, eight and nine, as requires the engrossing of acts of incorporation, and amendments thereof, be suspended for the remainder of the present session, at Newport.

---

RESOLUTION instructing the Secretary of State to prepare a Legislative Manual. No. 5.

*Resolved*, That the secretary of state be instructed to prepare, for the use of the general assembly, a legislative manual, containing the rules and orders of the general assembly, and such other information as he may deem expedient, and that he cause five hundred copies thereof to be printed. Also one hundred and fifty copies in pocket size, containing the roll of members, the committees, and the rules and orders of the two houses, with such other matters as he may see fit.

---

RESOLUTION of enquiry respecting the Public Schools. No. 6.

*Resolved*, (The senate concurring,) that the commissioner of public schools be instructed to report to the general assembly at the next January session, whether any, and what means are used in the public schools " to implant and cultivate in the minds of all children " therein " the principles of morality and virtue," as provided in section 6 of chapter 54 of the General Statutes.

---

RESOLUTION in relation to the Annual Reports of the State Auditor and other officers. No. 7

*Resolved*, (the senate concurring with the house in the passage hereof,) that the state auditor, general treasurer, and commissioners ou shell fisheries be and hereby are directed to present their next annual

reports to 'the general assembly on the second day o
the next January session thereof.

---

No. 8.

RESOLUTION to procure plans and estimates for furnish
ing Providence County Court House.

*Resolved*, That Messrs. Amasa S. Westcott, Edwir
Darling, and Thomas P. Shepard be and hereby are
appointed commissioners to procure plans and estimate:
for furnishing the new court house for the county of
Providence, and to report to this general assembly at it:
January session.

---

No. 9.

RESOLUTION for the payment into the state treasury of
moneys received by the Board of State Charities and
Corrections.

*Resolved*, (The honorable senate concurring,) that the
board of state charities and corrections shall cause to be
paid into the state treasury, as provided in section 14,
chapter 25, of the General Statutes, all moneys received
by them for board of inmates, labor and materials, and
from all other sources ; which sums so paid into the
treasury shall be added to the appropriations already
made for the use of said board for the fiscal year ending
April 30th, 1877.

---

No. 10.

RESOLUTION to appoint a committee to transfer seals,
books and papers and other property of the Supreme
Court and Court of. Common Pleas of the county of
Kent.

*Resolved*, (The senate concurring herein,) that Thomas
A. Pierce, Jr., of East Greenwich, be, and he is hereby
appointed a committee to transfer the seals, books and
papers and other property of the supreme court and
court of common pleas, of the county of Kent, from
Albert R. Greene, former clerk of said courts, to
Thomas M. Holden, newly elected clerk of said courts,
he taking and giving receipts therefor.

RESOLUTION transferring Records, &c., Court of Com-  No. 11.
mon Pleas, Washington county.

*Resolved,* That John G. Perry, Esq., of South Kingstown, be, and hereby is appointed a committee to receive the books, files, papers, seal and other property
in the clerk's office of the court of common pleas, in
the county of Washington, from the former clerk of said
court, and transfer the same to clerk elect, J. Henry
Wells, he giving and taking receipt therefor.

---

RESOLUTION appointing a joint special committee in  No. 12.
regard to verbatim reports of general assembly proceedings.

*Resolved,* (The honorable senate concurring.) that
Messrs. Alfred H. Littlefield, of Lincoln, William H.
Spooner, of Bristol, and Isaac M. Potter, of Providence,
on the part of the house, and Messrs. Samuel H. Cross,
of Westerly, and Charles H. Handy, of Warren, on the
part of the senate, be a committee to ascertain what
arrangements can be made to have a verbatim report of
the proceedings of the general assembly published each
day and furnished to the members of the respective
houses ; said committee to report as soon as possible,
and said reports to commence with the January session.

---

RESOLUTION authorizing the loan of a state flag to the  No. 13.
First Light Infantry Regiment of Providence.

*Resolved,* That his excellency the governor be and
he hereby is authorized to loan to the first light infantry
regiment the revolutionary flag, with which is associated
the name of General Greene, for use in the centennial
parade at Philadelphia, July 4th ; said regiment having
been selected to represent this state in the centennial
legion, which is to be composed of one militia organization from each of the original thirteen states.

No. 14.

RESOLUTION making appropriation for the state law library.

*Resolved*, (The house of representatives concurring herein,) that the sum of eight hundred dollars be, and the same is hereby appropriated out of the general treasury for the purpose of supplying deficiencies in the state law library, to be expended under the direction of the justices of the supreme court, and the books when purchased to be suitably labelled as the property of the state.

No. 15.

RESOLUTION making an appropriation for the repair of the state house and jail in the city of Newport.

*Resolved*, That a sum not exceeding fourteen hundred dollars is hereby appropriated for the repair of the state house and jail in the city of Newport, to be expended under the direction of Mr. Frederick A. Pratt, of Newport, and the state auditor is hereby directed to draw his order for said sum or so much thereof as may be needed, upon the state treasurer, to be paid out of any money not otherwise appropriated.

No. 16.

RESOLUTION making appropriation for fence around the soldiers' cemetery on Dutch Island.

*Resolved*, That the sum of two hundred and fifty dollars, or so much thereof as may be necessary, is hereby appropriated for the construction of a suitable fence around the soldiers cemetery on Dutch Island, and for necessary repairs on said cemetery; to be expended under the direction of the committee of inquiry appointed by resolution No. 14, January session, 1876, and the state auditor is hereby directed to draw his order on the general treasurer for said sum or so much thereof as may be necessary, payable to the order of said committee.

RESOLUTION granting use of grand jury room, Kent No. 17. county, to Greenwich Lodge and others.

*Resolved*, (the house concurring herein,) That the use of the grand jury room in the court house in Kent county be, and the same is hereby allowed to Greenwich Lodge, No. 62, I. O. of G. T., and also to Douglass Lodge, No. 45, I. O. of G. T., for the purpose of lodge and other meetings, when not required for the use of the courts.

---

RESOLUTION upon the petition of Edward Everett Hare, No. 18. for change of name to that of Edward Everett Lee.

*Resolved*, That the prayer of said petition be and the same hereby is granted, and the name of said petitioner be and hereby is changed to that of Edward Everett Lee, and all contracts and grants heretofore made by or to him in the name of Edward Everett Lee are hereby made valid to the same extent and of the same effect as if made by or to him in the name of Edward Everett Hare, and that by the name of Edward Everett Lee he is and shall be entitled to all the rights and privileges, and be subject to all the duties and liabilities he would have been subject and entitled to, had the same always been his true and legitimate name.

---

RESOLUTION upon the petition of Levi B. Brown, praying No. 19. for a pardon and release from imprisonment in the Providence county jail.

*Voted and Resolved*, That the senate do hereby advise and consent to the granting of the prayer of the petition of the said Levi B. Brown, as recommended by his excellency the governor, and that the warden of the state prison and the keeper of the Providence county jail be directed to release the said Levi B. Brown from his said imprisonment.

4

No. 20.　　RESOLUTION upon the petition of Thomas B. Davis, of
Newport, praying for a pardon and release from imprisonment in the Newport county jail.

*Voted and Resolved,* That the senate do hereby advise
and consent to the granting of the prayer of the petition
for the pardon of Thomas B. Davis, as recommended
by his excellency the governor, and that the keeper of
the county jail in and for the county of Newport be
directed to release said Thomas B. Davis from his said
imprisonment.

---

No. 21.　　RESOLUTION upon the petition of E. C. Arnold and others,
praying for a pardon and release from imprisonment
in the State Prison, of George Arnold, of Woonsocket.

*Resolved,* That the senate do hereby advise and consent to the granting of the prayer of the petition for the
pardon of the said George Arnold, as recommended by
his excellency the governor, and that the warden of the
state prison be directed to release said George Arnold
from his said imprisonment forthwith.

---

RESOLUTIONS authorizing disabled Rhode Island soldiers
and citizens to peddle without cost for license.

*Resolved,* That the general treasurer be and he is
hereby directed to issue to the following disabled
soldiers:

No 22.　　Henry T. Ayers,
No. 23.　　Richard A. Brown,
No. 24.　　Thomas Byron,
No. 25.　　Frank P. Chase,
No. 26.　　James Farrell,
No. 27.　　John Fauls,
No. 28.　　Eugene A. Fish,
No. 29.　　Nelson Gardner,
No. 30.　　Joseph Grant,

James Kerr, — No. 31.
James McCann, — No. 32.
John McGinn, — No. 33.

licenses to peddle any merchandise, except watches, jewelry, gold, silver, and German silver ware, for the term of one year, without cost to the said persons, and that said licenses be not transferable.

RESOLUTION to appropriate $400 for the purpose of aid-  No. 34.
ing in the distribution of the history of the 2d R. I.
Volunteers, throughout the state.

*Resolved,* That the secretary of state be and hereby is instructed to purchase a sufficient number of copies of "Woodbury's History of the Second R. I. Volunteers," to furnish each and every public library in the state with one copy; also to distribute other copies as directed in section 5, chapter 19, of the General Statutes; and he is hereby authorized to draw upon the state treasurer for an amount not to exceed $400, out of any money not otherwise appropriated.

RESOLUTION for extra allowance for rent of armory of  No. 35.
Battery B, 1st Battalion Light Artillery.

*Resolved,* That the quartermaster general be and he is hereby directed to allow the sum of two hundred dollars to Battery B, (formerly known as the "Tower Light Battery,") instead of one hundred dollars, as provided by section 3 of chapter 251 of the General Statutes, as contained in chapter 476, of the Public Laws.

RESOLUTION concerning the unexpended balance of ap-  No. 36.
propriations for the erection of a new State Prison,
&c.

*Resolved,* (the honorable senate concurring,) That the unexpended balance of the appropriations for the erection of a new state prison, made at the January sessions

of the years 1875 and 1876, be and the same is hereby
carried to the credit of the state prison commission;
and the state auditor is hereby directed to draw his orders for such portions thereof, as may be required from
time to time, upon the receipt of properly authenticated
vouchers.

No. 37.     RESOLUTION making an appropriation for carpeting office
of the clerk of Supreme Court and Court of Common
Pleas for Newport County.

*Resolved*, That a sum not exceeding forty dollars be
and the same is hereby appropriated for the carpeting
of the office of the clerk of the supreme court and the
court of common pleas for Newport county; and the
auditor is hereby directed to draw his order on the
general treasurer for the same, to be paid to said clerk,
upon the presentation of satisfactory vouchers, out of
any money in the treasury not otherwise appropriated.

No. 38.     RESOLUTION to appropriate moneys for repairs upon the
State's Jail in Kent County.

*Resolved*, (the senate concurring herein,) That the
sum of three hundred dollars be and the same is hereby
appropriated, to be expended in repairs upon and about
the state's jail in Kent county, under the care and direction of the sheriff of said county; the same to be paid
out of any moneys not otherwise appropriated.

No. 39.     RESOLUTION making an appropriation for the support
and maintenance of Evening Schools.

*Resolved*, That the sum of twenty-five hundred dollars
be and the same is hereby appropriated for the support
of evening schools, to be expended under the direction
of the state board of education, and the governor is
hereby authorized to draw his order on the general
treasurer of the state, in favor of the board of education, for the said sum of twenty-five hundred dollars.

RESOLUTIONS for the payment of sundry accounts against the state.

*Resolved*, That the following accounts against the state be and the same are hereby allowed and ordered to be paid; and the state auditor is directed to draw his order on the general treasurer for the said several amounts out of any money unappropriated in the treasury:

| | | |
|---|---:|---|
| Nicholas Van Slyck, Grand Master of Masons, for expenses contracted in laying corner stone of Providence county court house. .......... .... ..... ....... | $238 42 | No. 40. |
| Tillinghast and Mason News Co., for stationery for senate........... ........... | 40 82 | No. 41. |
| Tillinghast and Mason News Co., for stationery for house of representatives.... | 95 95 | No. 42. |
| Davis and Pitman, for printing for the senate...................... ......... | 8 00 | No. 43. |
| Davis and Pitman, for printing for the house, | 24 00 | No. 44. |
| Newport Light Infantry, for services of band at inaugural of state officers...... | 100 00 | No. 45. |
| Newport Brass Band, for services on May 29th and 30th, 1876 ......... ...... | 260 00 | No. 46. |
| Davis & Pitman, for advertising election programme............... .......... | 16 25 | No. 47. |
| John P. Sanborn, for publishing election programme........ . ........... | 15 00 | No. 48. |
| Anthony Stewart, for drawing guns for the Newport Artillery................... | 10 00 | No. 49. |

RESOLUTION to pay officers and attendants of the general assembly at the May session, A. D. 1876.                    No. 50.

*Resolved*, That the following sums be paid to the following persons, officers and attendants of the general assembly at the May session, A. D. 1876:

| | |
|---|---|
| Nathaniel P. S. Thomas .............. .... | $75 00 |
| Charles F. Ballou..................... | 75 00 |
| Henry T. Braman........ ............ | 75 00 |
| Nathan F. Dixon, Jr............... ... | 75 00 |
| George Manchester .................... | 30 00 |
| Henry N. Ward...................... | 20 00 |
| Thomas W. Wood, Jr. .............. .... | 20 00 |
| John R. Ward ............. ..... ........ | 20 00 |
| B. E. Remington Ward ............... | 20 00 |
| Clarence A. Hammett... ............. | 20 00 |
| Benjamin C. Weaver..... ............ | 20 00 |
| James Coggeshall........ .. ......... | 20 00 |
| Edward S. Hammond............... . | 20 00 |

No. 51.  RESOLUTION of adjournment.

*Resolved*, (the house of representatives concurring,) That when the general assembly adjourns on Friday, June 2d, 1876, it adjourn at 12 o'clock M., to meet at the state house, Newport, on Tuesday the 13th day of June, 1876, at 10.30 A. M.

No. 52.  RESOLUTION suspending Joint Rule No. Nine.
(Passed June 14, 1876.)

*Resolved*, That joint rule No. 9 be suspended so far that all Public Laws passed at the present session of the general assembly, shall be engrossed after the passage thereof, and the secretary of state is hereby authorized to certify the same and place them on file in his office.

No. 63.  RESOLUTION of adjournment to the 2d Tuesday in January, 1877.

*Resolved*, (the senate concurring,) That this general assembly adjourn June 14th, at 2 o'clock P. M., to meet in Providence on the second Tuesday in January, 1877, at 11 o'clock A. M.

SECRETARY OF STATE'S OFFICE,
Providence, Rhode Island.

I certify the acts, resolutions, record of officers elected, and reports contained in this volume to be true copies of the originals on file in this office.

IN TESTIMONY WHEREOF, I have hereto set my hand and affixed the seal of the State, this                    day of            A. D.

# APPENDIX.

At the General Assembly of the State of Rhode Island and Providence Plantations, begun and holden at Newport on the last Tuesday of May, (being the 30th day of the month,) in the year of our Lord one thousand eight hundred and seventy-six, and of Independence the one hundredth.

### PRESENT :

His Excellency HENRY LIPPITT, Governor, and *ex-officio* President of the Senate.

His Honor HENRY T. SISSON, Lieut. Governor, and *ex-officio* senator.

## SENATORS FROM THE SEVERAL TOWNS.

| | |
|---|---|
| Newport, | JAMES M. DRAKE. |
| Providence, | BENJAMIN N. LAPHAM. |
| Portsmouth, | ALFRED SISSON. |
| Warwick, | JONATHAN BRAYTON. |
| Westerly, | SAMUEL H. CROSS. |
| New Shoreham, | RAY S. LITTLEFIELD. |
| North Kingstown, | JOHN REMINGTON. |
| South Kingstown, | WILLIAM G. CASWELL. |
| East Greenwich, | HENRY A. THOMAS. |
| Jamestown, | THOMAS CARR WATSON. |
| Smithfield, | SAMUEL W. FARNUM. |

# APPENDIX.

| | |
|---|---|
| Scituate, - - | JEREMIAH H. FIELD. |
| Glocester, - - | ZIBA O. SLOCUM. |
| Charlestown, - | GEORGE C. JAMES. |
| West Greenwich, - | JOHN T. LEWIS. |
| Coventry, - - | JOHN WARNER. |
| Exeter, - - | DANIEL L. MONEY. |
| Middletown, - | ROBERT S. CHASE. |
| Bristol, - - | AUGUSTUS O. BOURN. |
| Tiverton, - - | GIDEON H. DURFEE. |
| Little Compton, - | NATHANIEL CHURCH. |
| Warren, - - | CHARLES H. HANDY. |
| Cumberland, - - | HENRY B. METCALF. |
| Richmond, - | DANIEL C. KENYON. |
| Cranston, - - | WILLIAM ELSBREE. |
| Hopkinton, - | OLIVER LANGWORTHY. |
| Johnston, - - | SAMUEL A. IRONS. |
| North Providence, | WILLIAM H. ANGELL. |
| Barrington, - - | HARRISON H. RICHARDSON. |
| Foster, - - | JOSHUA PAINE. |
| Burrillville, - - | WILLIAM H. CLARK. |
| East Providence, | OLIVER CHAFFEE. |
| Pawtucket, - - | WILLIAM F. SAYLES. |
| Woonsocket, - | NATHAN T. VERRY. |
| North Smithfield, - | WILLIAM H. SEAGRAVE. |
| Lincoln, - - | JONATHAN CHACE. |

## JOSHUA M. ADDEMAN,

Secretary of State, and *ex-officio* Secretary.

NATHANIEL P. S. THOMAS, Clerk.

---

## REPRESENTATIVES OF THE SEVERAL TOWNS.

| *Newport.* | *Providence.* |
|---|---|
| William P. Sheffield, | Allen Greene, |
| Henry H. Fay, | Henry W. Gardner, |
| Augustus P. Sherman, | Henry J. Spooner, |
| William C. Townsend, | James W. Blackwood, |
| Frederick A. Pratt. | Isaac M. Potter, |

Henry H. Ormsbee,
Gorham P. Pomroy,
Nelson W. Aldrich,
Harvey E. Wellman,
Edmund S. Hopkins,
George H. Pettis,
Joseph F. Brown.
*Portsmouth.*
Jonathan A. Sisson.
*Warwick.*
Christopher R. Greene,
Stephen W. Thornton,
John H. Collingwood,
J. Torrey Smith.
*Westerly.*
Nathan F. Dixon,
J. Alonzo Babcock.
*New Shoreham.*
Joshua T. Dodge.
*North Kingstown.*
Thomas C. Peirce.
*South Kingstown.*
John G. Clarke.
*East Greenwich.*
Thomas A. Pierce, Jr.
*Jamestown.*
Isaac B. Briggs.
*Smithfield.*
Andrew B. Whipple.
*Scituate.*
Benjamin Wilbur.
*Glocester.*
Raymond Colwell.
*Charlestown.*
Charles Cross.
*West Greenwich.*
John Tillinghast.
*Coventry.*
Thomas C. Peckham,
Dexter B. Potter.
*Exeter.*
Nathan B. Lewis.

*Middletown.*
Nathaniel Peckham.
*Bristol.*
William H. Spooner,
Samuel P. Colt.
*Tiverton.*
Holder N. Wilcox.
*Little Compton.*
Jedediah Shaw.
*Warren.*
George Lewis Cooke.
*Cumberland.*
Dexter Clark,
James C. Dexter.
*Richmond.*
Reynolds C. Phillips.
*Cranston.*
Henry Whitman,
John Beattie.
*Hopkinton:*
Thomas H. Greene.
*Johnston.*
Alfred A. Williams,
George W. White.
*North Providence.*
Benjamin Sweet.
*Barrington.*
Earl C. Potter.
*Foster.*
Thomas E. Phillips.
*Burrillville.*
John A. Wood,
David Mathewson.
*East Providence.*
Alvord O. Miles.
*Pawtucket.*
Claudius B. Farnsworth,
William E. Gilmore,
Almon K. Goodwin,
Pardon E. Tillinghast,
Joseph E. Dispeau,
Oren S. Horton.

*Woonsocket.*
William E. Hubbard,
Nathaniel Elliott,
John A. Bennett,    .
Amos Sherman.
*North Smithfield.*
Arlon Mowry.

*Lincoln.*
Thomas Moies,
Alfred H. Littlefield,
Elisha S. Aldrich,
Edward L. Freeman.    `

NELSON W. ALDRICH, Speaker.

CHARLES F BALLOU, ⎫
HENRY T. BRAMAN, ⎭ Clerks.

## PROCEEDINGS IN GRAND COMMITTEE.

NEWPORT, TUESDAY, May 30th, 1876.

The two houses of the general assembly met in grand committee for the purpose of receiving, counting and declaring the votes for general officers, given at the annual election held on the first Wednesday in April, 1876.

His Excellency Henry Lippitt, governor, in the chair.

The ballots were delivered in by the secretary of state.

On motion the following select committee were appointed to assort and count the votes and declare the result of said election, viz.:

### COMMITTEE TO COUNT VOTES.

*Newport County.*—James M. Drake, Jedediah Shaw, Holder N. Wilcox.

*Providence County.*—Samuel W. Farnum, James W. Blackwood, Alfred H. Littlefield, Amos Sherman, Oren S. Horton.

*Washington County.*—Charles Cross, John G. Clarke, J. Alonzo Babcock.

*Bristol County.*—Charles H. Handy, Samuel P. Colt, Earl C. Potter.

*Kent County.*—John Warner, John Tillinghast, John H. Collingwood.

The secretary and clerks were added.

The grand committee took a recess till 3 o'clock
P. M., and on re-assembling the following report was
presented, viz. :

The committee appointed to count the votes for
general officers, beg leave to submit the following

### REPORT.

That the whole number of electors voting for governor is 19,037, and that 9,519 votes are necessary for
a choice.

That 8,689 electors voted for Henry Lippitt, of Providence.

That 6,733 electors voted for Albert C. Howard, of
East Providence.

That 3,599 electors voted for William B. Beach, of
Providence.

That 16 electors voted scattering.

They further report that there is no election of governor.

That the whole number of electors voting for lieutenant-governor is 18,986, and that 9,494 votes are
necessary for a choice.

That 8,677 electors voted for Henry T. Sisson, of
Little Compton.

That 6,588 electors voted for Alfred B. Chadsey, of
North Kingstown.

That 3,704 electors voted for Ziba O. Slocum, of
Glocester.

That 17 electors voted scattering.

They further report that there is no election of lieutenant-governor.

That the whole number of electors voting for secretary of state is 19,081, and that 9,541 votes are necessary for a choice.

That 15,395 electors voted for Joshua M. Addeman,
of Providence.

That 3,684 electors voted for John B. Peirce, of
North Kingstown.

That 2 electors voted scattering.

They further report that Joshua M. Addeman, of Providence, is elected secretary of state by a majority of 11,709 votes over all others.

That the whole number of electors voting for attorney general is 18,902, and that 9,452 votes are necessary for a choice.
That 9,232 electors voted for Willard Sayles, of Providence.
That 6,056 electors voted for Warren R. Perce, of Providence.
That 3,609 electors voted for . Oscar Lapham, of Providence.
That 5 electors voted scattering:
They further report that there is no election of attorney general.

That the whole number of electors voting for general treasurer is 18,879, and that 9,440 votes are necessary for a choice.
That 9,275 electors voted for Samuel Clark, of Lincoln.
That 6,059 electors voted for Alonzo D. Vose, of Woonsocket.
That 3,542 electors voted for William P. Congdon, of Newport.
That 3 electors voted scattering.
They further report that there is no election of general treasurer.

The committee in conformity with their report recommend the passage of the following resolutions:
*Resolved*, That the following named person be, and is hereby declared elected to the following office for the ensuing year:
Joshua M. Addeman, of Providence, secretary of state.
*Resolved*, That there is no election of governor, lieutenant-governor, attorney general and general treasurer.
For the committee,
JOHN G. CLARKE, *Chairman.*

The foregoing report was read, received and the accompanying resolutions adopted.

On motion, the grand committee proceeded to elect by ballot a governor, with the following result, viz.:

Whole number of ballots cast............ ... 103
Necessary for a choice... ......... ....... ... 52
   Of which Henry Lippitt received........ 74
   Albert C. Howard received.. .......... 29

and HENRY LIPPITT, of Providence, was declared elected governor.

The grand committee proceeded to elect by ballot a lieutenant-governor, with the following result, viz.:

Whole number of ballots cast..... ......... ... 98
Necessary for a choice........····· ............. 50
   Of which Henry T. Sisson received.... 70
   Alfred B. Chadsey received........... 28 .

and HENRY T. SISSON, of Little Compton, was declared elected lieutenant-governor.

The grand committee proceeded to elect by ballot an attorney general, with the following result, viz.:

Whole number of ballots cast. ... ........ .. 103
Necessary for a choice... , .............. 52
   Of which Willard Sayles received...... 96
   Warren R. Perce received ...... . .... 7

and WILLARD SAYLES, of Providence, was declared elected attorney general.

The grand committee proceeded to elect by ballot a general treasurer, with the following result, viz.:

Whole number of ballots cast........ .... 103
Necessary for a choice........... .... ........... 52
   Of which Samuel Clark received........ 97
   Alonzo D. Vose received........ .. .. 6

and SAMUEL CLARK, of Lincoln, was declared elected general treasurer.

The oath of office was administered to the governor and lieutenant-governor by the secretary of state, and the governor next administered the oath of office to the secretary of state.

Proclamation was then made by the sergeant-at-arms of the several officers elected, in accordance with ancient usage.

---

IN SENATE, May 31, 1876.

The governor announced the following executive appointments:

*Commissioner of the Narragansett Indians.*—John A. Wilcox, of Charlestown.

*Commissioner of the Indian School.*—William F. Tucker, of Charlestown.

*Commissioners of Pilots.*—Capt. Silvanus D. Willis, of New Shoreham, for two years, for the unexpired term of Thomas Hull, deceased.

Capt. Jeptha Nickerson, of Providence, for three years.

*Inspectors of the State Prison.*—Rev. Augustus Woodbury, Rev. Alexis Caswell, D. D., Stephen R. Weeden, Lewis Fairbrother, William Binney, Jesse Metcalf, Benoni Carpenter, M. D.

*Board of State Charities and Corrections.*—Thomas Coggeshall, of Newport, for six years; James M. Pendleton, of Westerly, for two years, for the unexpired term of Horace Babcock, resigned.

*Inspector of the Hartford, Providence and Fishkill Railroad.*—George A. Spink, of Warwick.

*Sealer of Weights, Measures and Balances.*—John H. Appleton, of Providence.

*State Assayer of Liquors.*—Henry W. Vaughan, of Providence.

*Aids to the Commander-in-Chief.* — Charles Warren Lippitt, of Providence; Edward C. Ames, of Providence; Henry J. Spooner, of Providence; Theodore M. Cook, of Woonsocket; Samuel Pomeroy Colt, of Bristol; James Fludder, of Newport.

*Commissioner for Pawtucket River.*—John D. Earle, of Pawtucket.

IN GRAND COMMITTEE, May 31, 1876.

His Excellency governor Lippitt in the chair.
The following officers were elected :

*State Auditor.*—Joel M. Spencer, of Coventry.
*Inspector of Beef and Pork.*—Henry M. Kimball, of Providence.
*Inspector of Scythe Stones.*—Thomas H. Hughes, of Johnston.
*Inspector of Lime.*—Stephen W. Wright, of Lincoln
*Inspector of Cables.*—George H. Pettis, of Providence

#### CLERKS OF THE SUPREME COURT.

*Newport County.*—Thomas W. Wood, of Newport.
*Providence County.*—Charles Blake, of Providence.
*Washington County.* — John G. Clarke, of South Kingstown.
*Bristol County.*—Charles A. Waldron, of Bristol.
*Kent County.*—Thomas M. Holden, of Warwick.

#### CLERKS OF THE COURT OF COMMON PLEAS.

*Newport County.*—Thomas W. Wood, of Newport.
*Providence County.*—George E. Webster, of Providence.
*Washington County.* — J. Henry Wells, of South Kingstown.
*Bristol County.*—Charles A. Waldron, of Bristol.
*Kent County.*—Thomas M. Holden, of Warwick.

#### SHERIFFS.

*Newport County.*—George Manchester, of Portsmouth
*Providence County.*—Christopher Holden, of Providence.
*Washington County.*—Henry Whipple, of Westerly
*Bristol County.*—Charles A Greene, of Bristol.
*Kent County.*—Thomas J. Tilley, of East Greenwich

*State Board of Education.*— Samuel H. Cross, o Westerly, and Thomas H. Clarke, of Newport, each for three years.

*Justice Court of the City of Newport.*—James G. Topham, trial justice ; Henry N. Ward, clerk.
*Justice Court of the City of Providence.*—James W. Blackwood, trial justice ; Ervin T. Case, clerk.
*Justice Court of the Town of Woonsocket.*—George A. Wilbur, trial justice ; William H. Jenckes, clerk.

Willard Sayles, attorney general elect, and Samuel Clark, general treasurer elect, being present, were engaged by the governor.

(NOTE.—For notaries public and justices of the peace elected this day see pages 67–78.)

### IN GRAND COMMITTEE, JUNE 1, 1876.

His excellency the governor in the chair.
James W. Blackwood, of Providence, was elected trial justice of the justice court of the city of Providence.
The following candidates for state scholarships in Brown University were nominated:
Richard B. Comstock, Providence.
Augustus A. Greene, Providence.

### IN GRAND COMMITTEE, JUNE 14, 1876.

The following candidates for state scholarships in Brown University were nominated:
John J. Greene, Hopkinton.
Friend P. Thompson, Providence.

### IN SENATE, JUNE 14, 1876.

The governor announced the following executive appointments :

*Ladies' Board of Visitors to the Penal and Correctional Institutions of the State* :
Mrs. Elizabeth B. Chace, of Lincoln.
Mrs. Eliza C. Weeden, of Westerly.

5

Mrs. Abby D. Weaver, of Newport.

Mrs. Harriet A. Cook, of Burrillville.

Mrs. Abby W. Chace, Mrs. Emily A. Hall, and Mrs. Sarah E. H. Doyle, all of Providence.

*Harbor Commissioners.*—(Pursuant to chapter 556 of the Public Laws.)

J. Herbert Shedd, of Providence, for three years.

Nathaniel F. Potter, of Providence, for two years.

Jedediah Williams, of Providence, for one year.

## PROCEEDINGS IN JOINT ASSEMBLY,

NEWPORT, JUNE 14, 1876.

The two houses convened in joint assembly to complete the election of a senator in congress from this state.

His Excellency Governor LIPPITT in the chair.

The rolls of the two houses were called, and a quorum of each declared to be present.

The journal of the proceedings of the senate of yesterday, and the journal of the proceedings of the house of representatives of yesterday were severally read; and it appearing therefrom that HENRY B. ANTHONY, of Providence, received a majority of the votes in each house, the said HENRY B. ANTHONY was by the governor declared duly elected senator to represent this state in the congress of the United States for the term of six years from the fourth day of March, A. D 1877.

The following notaries public for the state, and justices of the peace for the several towns and cities named, were elected during the session:

Charles P. Adams,
J. M. Addeman,
John Aigan,
Clarence A. Aldrich,
Edwin Aldrich,
William D. Aldrich,
C. Henry Alexander,
Alfred Allen,
Frank G. Allen,
Henry W. Allen,
Herbert Almy,
Edward C. Ames,
Samuel Ames,
Albert L. Andrews,
Louis L. Angell,
Pardon Angell,
Rufus J. Angell,
Charles F. Anthony,
Charles C. Armstrong,
Frank S. Arnold,
Lyman Arnold,
Stephen C. Arnold,
William G. Arnold,
Edward C. Ashley,
George A. Atwood,
Ira C. W. Aylsworth,
Harmon S. Babcock,
William M. Bailey, Jr.,
Charles E. Ballou,
Charles F. Ballou,
Daniel R. Ballou,
Henry G. Ballou,
Henry L. Ballou,
G. Walter Barnefield,
Thomas P. Barnefield,
Charles Barrows,
Edwin Barrows,

George B. Barrows,
Charles H. Bartlett,
James H. Barry,
Edward D. Bassett,
William B. Beach,
George F. Beane,
Stephen Gano Benedict,
E. Sylvester Binford,
William Binney,
James W. Blackwood,
Charles Blake,
Ellis L. Blake,
George N. Bliss,
William H Bliss,
Benjamin J. Bliven,
Samuel C. Blodget,
W. W. Blodgett,
John H. Bongartz,
Charles E. Boon,
Bailey E. Borden,
Charles Bradley,
Charles R. Brayton,
William W. Brayton.
John M. Brennan,
Frederick A. Brigham,
Benjamin F. Brown,
Charles Henry Brown,
George H. Browne,
George T. Brown,
James W. Brown,
John A. Brown,
George W. Brownell,
Edwin C. Budlong,
James W. Bullock,
Thomas Burgess,
George H. Burnham,
Edgar D. Burrill,

Duncan Campbell,
Roger F. Capwell,
Albert P. Carpenter,
Ansel Carpenter,
Edgar A. Carpenter.
George M. Carpenter, Jr.,
William A. Carpenter,
Irving Champlin,
William C. Chase,
Joseph A. Chedel,
Nelson E. Church,
Edwin Clapp,
William H. Clapp,
Horace Clarke,
Langford P. Clarke,
William Coggeshall,
James C. Collins,
Francis Colwell,
Welcome G. Comstock,
Edmund L. Cook,
Edward Cooke,
Emory Cook,
James E. Cook,
Lorin M. Cook;
Samuel P. Cook,
Stephen A. Cooke, Jr.,
Daniel J. Cordery,
William H. Corey,
James M. Cosgrove,
Walter H. Crowninshield,
Andrew J. Currier,
Adoniram J. Cushing,
David L. Daboll,
Francis A. Daniels,
Edwin Darling,
Oliver P. Davis,
Arthur W. Dennis,
A. B. Dike,
James R Dorrance,
Samuel T. Douglas,
William W. Douglas,
William C. Downs,
Thomas A. Doyle,

Henry J. Dubois,
William Duffy,
William W. Eddy,
John W. Elsey,
Joseph C. Ely,
George A. Emerson,
Carl W. Ernst,
Stephen Essex,
Samuel W. Farnum,
Claudius B. Farnsworth,
Preston M. Farrington,
O. E. Fitzgerald,
John B. Fitzpatrick,
George Fuller,
Osmond T. Fuller,
John A. Gardner,
Fred. W. Gilmore,
Fred. N. Goff,
Isaac L. Goff,
John E. Goldsworthy,
Osmond C. Goodell,
James B. Gooding,
William H. Gooding,
Charles E. Gorman,
Arnold Green,
Paul Greene,
Welcome A. Greene, Jr.,
William H. Greene,
John P. Gregory,
James H. Haberlin,
John F. Haberlin,
Christopher A Hall,
George W. Hall,
William H. Hall,
William B. W. Hallett,
B. B. Hammond,
H. A. Harrington,
Earl C. Harris,
William J. Harris,
Samuel A. Haswell,
Charles C. Havens,
William D. S. Havens,
Philip O. Hawkins,

Wingate Hayes,
Samuel Hedly,
Thomas W. Hedly,
William H. Herrick,
James C. Hidden,
William Hill,
Henry Hirons,
William H. Hodges,
Edwin R. Holden,
Henry A. Horton,
Horace F. Horton,
Sylvanus D. Horton,
James I. Hotchkiss,
Lester Howard,
Albert Hubbard,
James E. Hudson,
Daniel A. Hunt,
Edwin L. Hunt,
Oliver A. Inman,
Frank A. Irons,
Samuel A. Irons,
Elias M. Jenckes,
Alonzo L. Jenks,
Ethan A. Jenks,
Frank Jenks,
Edwin Jerauld,
Francello G. Jillson,
Allen T. Johnson,
Joseph G. Johnson,
Ralph Jolley,
Henry V. A. Joslin,
Joseph H. Kendrick,
George A. Kent,
George A. Kenyon,
Peter Kiernan,
Andrew A. Kimball,
Jerome B. Kimball,
Walter C. King,
Bradford F. Knapp,
Walter P. Knickerbocker,
Charles L. Knight,
B. N. Lapham,
Cyrus E. Lapham.

Oscar Lapham,
Simon S. Lapham,
Samuel D Larned,
Joseph A. Latham,
George Lawless,
Royal Lee,
Frank Leonard,
J. Erastus Lester,
Joseph W. Lewis,
Eugene H. Lincoln,
Freeman P. Little,
Eben N. Littlefield,
John F. Lonsdale,
John S. Lynch,
Michael Maloney,
James G. Markland,
Henry Marsh, Jr.,
George E. Martin,
Henry Martin,
Horace Martin,
Charles B. Mason,
Thomas W. D. Mason,
John G. Massie,
Arnold P. Mathewson,
Rollin Mathewson,
George H. McCann,
John McCann,
Bernard McGuinness,
Walker A. Medbury,
Josephus R. Merriam,
Edwin Metcalf,
George Metcalf, Jr.,
Augustus S. Miller,
Thomas A. Millett,
Francis W. Miner,
Charles P. Moies,
David Moore, Jr.,
Revilo F. Morton,
William P. Morton,
Elisha C. Mowry,
Marquis D. L. Mowry,
Spencer Mowry,
Wilson P. Moulton,

George A. Mumford,
Abel C. Munroe,
George B. Nichols,
William W. Nichols,
James P. Nickerson,
Sparrow H. Nickerson,
Samuel A. Nightingale,
John L. Noyes,
Joseph O'Connor,
Francis L. O'Reilly,
Josiah H. Ormsbee,
Franklin P. Owen,
Charles H. Page,
Simon S. Page,
George T. Paine,
Joseph H. Paine,
John Palmer,
Charles H. Parkhurst,
Robert C. Parker,
James H Parsons,
Alonzo Passmore,
Andrew J. Patt,
Andrew B. Patton,
Arthur D. Payne,
Allen M. Peck,
Samuel W. Peckham,
John C. Pegram,
Warren R. Perce,
Joseph H. Perkins,
Marsden J. Perry,
George W. Phillips,
William A. Phillips,
Horace M. Pierce,
Hiram C. Pierce,
Isaac W. D. Pike,
Andrew J. Pitcher,
John T. Pitman,
Joseph S. Pitman,
Raymon G. Place,
Cornelius C. Plummer,
Charles H. Plummer,
Ebenezer Plummer,
D. B. Potter,

Walter L. Potter,
William K. Potter,
Zuriel Potter,
Charles T. Pratt,
John C. Purkis,
John R. Randolph,
Edmund W. Raynsford,
Charles M. Read,
F. P. Read,
George S. Read,
Samuel B. M. Read,
Albert J. Reeve,
Christopher Rhodes,
Elisha H. Rhodes,
Lawrence Rhoades,
Addison B. Rice,
William W. Rickard,
John E. Risley, Jr.,
Gilbert F. Robbins,
Augustus W. Robinson,
Charles P. Robinson,
Henry H. Robinson,
Thomas Robinson,
Thomas W. Robinson,
Arthur O. Rockwell,
Lucius O. Rockwood,
William G. Roelker,
Horatio Rogers,
Squier H. Rogers,
Charles M. Salisbury,
Levi Salisbury,
William H. Sandford,
Isaac Saunders,
Herbert L. Sayles,
Simon A. Sayles,
W. R. Sayles,
Willard Sayles,
Charles E. Scott,
James M. Scott,
Philip C. Scott,
William H. Scott,
Ira O. Seamans,
Charles Selden,

# APPENDIX.

Clinton D. Sellew,
Charles H. Sheldon, Jr.,
Robert Sherman,
Isaac Shove,
Samuel Shove,
Waldo F. Slocum,
Z. O. Slocum,
Charles H. Smith,
George H. Smith,
James F. Smith,
John W. Smith,
Richard B. Smith,
Simon T. Smith,
Joseph E. Spink,
Henry J. Spooner,
Charles Staples,
Frank N. Stearns,
Charles L. Steere,
P. B. Stiness, Jr.,
Walter R. Stiness,
Raymond Stone,
George Stuart,
William T. Stuart,
H. O. Sturges,
Cornelius S. Sweetland,
Edward A. Taft,
Oscar A. Tanner,
Charles H. Thurber,
Frank A. Thurber,
Alfred O. Tilden,
James Tillinghast,
John J. Tillinghast,
Jos. W. Tillinghast,
Pardon E. Tillinghast,
Oscar A Tobey,
William C. Townsend,
Nathan H. Truman,

Edward A. Turner,
Cæsar A. Updike,
Nicholas Van Slyck,
Nathan T. Verry,
Walter B. Vincent,
Augustus F. Wade,
Samuel H Wales,
John P. Walker,
Kenrick Walker,
David A. Waldron,
Walter A. Walling,
Charles A. Warland,
Richard Waterman,
Frank B. Webster,
Amasa S Westcott,
George Wheaton, 2d,
Jonathan M. Wheeler,
Amos A. White,
Addison H. White,
Cornelius A. White,
Willson T. White,
Samuel Whitney,
George S. Whitman,
Henry B. Whitman,
David R. Whittemore,
Gilbert E. Whittemore,
George A. Wilbur,
Charles A. Wilson,
James Wilson,
William P. Winslow,
Ira Winsor,
Alanson P. Wood,
Brown S. Wood,
Charles F. Wood,
Daniel G. Wood,
Herbert B. Wood,
J. C. B. Woods.

## NEWPORT COUNTY.

Samuel Allen,
A. Prescott Baker,
Darius Baker,

Francis Brinley,
Daniel P. Bull,
Henry Bull, Jr.,

Albert L. Chase,
Philip B. Chase,
Lucius D. Davis,
Joshua T. Dodge,
George N. Durfee,
John Fadden,
William Gilpin,
Nathan H. Gould,
Charles D. Hammett,
Edward H. Hayes,
Samuel R. Honey,
William Hunt,
William D. Lake,
William P. Lewis,
George P. Leonard,
Philip F. Little,
Alamanza Littlefield,
George Manchester,
Benjamin Marsh, 2d,

Charles B. Marsh,
Francis B. Peckham, Jr.,
Nathaniel Peckham,
Theophilus T. Pitman,
Frank B. Porter,
James T. Powell,
Ambrose N. Rose,
William P. Sheffield,
Anthony S. Sherman,
Alfred Smith,
Howard Smith,
William G. Stevens,
Charles N. Tilley,
John Henry Tilley,
Wm. Lovie Tilley,
Chas. C. Van Zandt,
John E. Watson,
Henry N. Ward,
Thomas W. Wood.

## BRISTOL COUNTY.

Ozro C. Barrows,
Albert C. Bennett,
Benjamin M. Bosworth, Jr.,
Lyman B. Bosworth,
Orrin L. Bosworth,
Frederick A. Burgess,
Joseph B. Burgess,
Luther Cole,
Samuel P. Colt,
LeBaron B. Colt,
George Lewis Cooke, Jr.,
George T. French,
George T. Gardner,
Peter Gladding,
Nathan Goff, Jr.,

Charles A. Greene,
Nathaniel S. Greene,
Henry H. Luther,
Charles B. Mason,
Bennett J. Munro,
John B. Pearce,
Nathaniel T. Sanders,
Parmenas Skinner, Jr.,
William R. Taylor,
John Turner,
Thomas F. Usher,
Charles A. Waldron,
J. Henry Weed,
Robert Wilson,
Mark H. Wood.

## KENT COUNTY.

Joseph F. Arnold,
Vernum A. Bailey,
John A. Bates,

E. C. Capwell,
William Carder,
Hugh J. Carroll, Jr.,

Wm. A. Champlain,
Sam W. Clarke,
John C. Colvin,
J. W. Congdon,
Albert R. Greene,
Thomas C. Greene,
Stephen W. Griffin,
Thomas M. Holden,
Henry A. Holmes,
Pardon Hopkins,
Benjamin H. Horton,
John J. Kilton,
George T. Lanphear,
Wm. G. Luther,
Enos Lapham,
Charles H. Martin,

S. R. Nicholas,
Arnold Phillips,
Thomas A. Pierce, Jr.,
Elisha R. Potter,
Thomas A. Reynolds,
J. Clarence Reeve,
George F. Sheldon,
Charles W. Smith,
Edward Stanhope,
Wm. C. Tibbitts,
Henry S. Vaughn,
Eugene F. Warner,
John Warner,
Silas Weaver,
Israel Whaley.

## WASHINGTON COUNTY.

Edwin R. Allen,
J. Alonzo Babcock,
David S. Baker, Jr.,
Henry T. Braman,
John A. Brown,
Henry T. Chadsey,
Charles H. Chapman,
Elisha C. Clarke,
Halsey P. Clarke,
John G. Clarke,
Wm. E. Cozzens,
William P. Coy,
Albert B. Crafts,
Elisha W. Cross,
Samuel H. Cross,
E. G. Cundall,
Nathan F. Dixon,
Nathan F. Dixon, Jr.,
James P. Dockray,
Elisha Dyer, Jr.,
Joseph Eaton, Jr.,
Thomas A. Gardner,
Anson Greene,

William Hoxsey,
Alfred W. Kenyon,
John L. Kenyon,
John D. Langworthy,
Nathan B. Lewis,
Franklin Metcalf,
George H. Olney,
Thomas H. Peabody,
John B. Peirce,
Eugene B. Pendleton,
Nathan L. Richmond,
William F. Segar,
Benjamin B. Sheldon,
Charles Sisson,
Herbert W. Stillman,
Abel Tanner,
N. P. S. Thomas,
Robert Thompson,
Enoch W. Vars,
Henry Whipple,
Thomas S. Wightman,
Charles W. Wilcox.

## JUSTICES OF THE PEACE.

### PROVIDENCE COUNTY.

*City of Providence.*
Henry W. Allen,
Herbert Almy,
Samuel Ames,
Louis L. Angell,
Frank S. Arnold,
Nathan T. Arnold,
John W. Atwood,
William H. Ayer,
Charles F. Baldwin,
George E. Barnard, Jr.,
Charles Barrows,
George B. Barrows,
Charles H. Bartlett,
James W. Blackwood,
Albert D. Bean,
John H. Bongartz,
Charles Bradley,
George H. Brayton,
Arthur L. Brown,
Charles Henry Brown,
James W. Brown,
Samuel W. Brown,
Walter F. Brown,
George H. Bucklin,
George H. Burnham,
Roger F. Capwell,
George M. Carpenter, Jr.,
Ervin T. Case,
John Chorlton,
Samuel Clough,
J. S. G. Cobb,
John H. Cokely,
Welcome G. Comstock,
Lorin M. Cook,
Erastus H. Cook,
Francis A. Daniels,

Henry R. Davis,
James R. Dorrance,
Samuel T. Douglas,
William W. Douglas,
William C. Downs,
Louis J. Doyle,
Thomas A. Doyle,
Henry J. Dubois,
Charles L. Ellis,
Carl W. Ernst,
Stephen Essex,
George T. French,
Edward K. Glezen,
A. W. Godding,
James C. Goff,
Charles E. Gorman,
George Lewis Gower,
Arnold Green.
William H. Greene,
William B. W. Hallett,
Edward I. Ham,
B. B. Hammond,
Benjamin Harrington,
Chas. N. Harrington, Jr.,
Charles Hart,
Thomas W. Hayward,
Thomas W. Hedly,
William H. Herrick,
James C. Hidden,
Edmund S. Hopkins,
William L. Hopkins,
Seth L. Horton,
Edwin L. Hunt,
Elias M. Jenckes,
Joseph G. Johnson,
J. A. D. Joslin,
George W. Kennedy,

Henry C. Knight,
John M. Knowles,
William Knowles,
John F. P. Lawton,
James C. Lester,
D. F. Longstreet,
Wm. F. Macomber,
James G. Markland,
Henry Martin,
John G. Massie,
H. A. McKenney,
Edwin Metcalf,
Ezra J. Morris,
William P. Morton,
Elisha C. Mowry,
William W. Nichols,
Simon S. Page,
Charles H. Parkhurst,
James H. Parsons,
Alonzo Passmore,
Arthur D. Payne,
Warren R. Perce,
George H. Pettis,
Edwin C. Pierce,
John C. Purkis,
John H. Purkis,
John R. Randolph,
Frederick A. Ray,
Edmund W. Raynsford,
Samuel B. M. Read,
Christopher Rhodes,
Addison B. Rice,
Alfred Rickard,
J. M. Ripley,
Lycurgus Sayles,
Charles H. Scott,
Philip C. Scott,
Charles Selden,
Milton H. Shattuck,
F. J. Sheldon,
A. B. Slater,
Richard B. Smith,
Edwin H. Snow,

Henry J. Spooner,
Lucien M. Stayner,
Charles Staples,
Charles M. Stone,
M. H. Sullivan,
Theodore B. Talbot,
A. Marshall Terence,
Charles H. Thurber,
John D. Thurston,
James Tillinghast,
Nicholas Van Slyck,
Nelson Viall,
Walter B. Vincent,
Amos M. Warner,
George E. Webster,
Joseph D. Whitaker,
Cornelius A. White,
Gilbert E. Whittemore,
George W. Wightman,
G. A. Williamson,
J. C. B. Woods,
William H. Wood.

*North Providence.*

John Angell,
George Eddy.

*Pawtucket.*

T. P. Barnefield,
Stephen Gano Benedict,
Edwin Clapp,
William H. Clapp,
John J. Dempsey,
Wm. W. Eddy,
John F. Haberlin,
Royal Lee,
Lewis Pearce,
Thomas Robinson,
Thomas W. Robinson,
Isaac Shove,
Alden W. Sibley,
Oscar A. Tanner,
Alfred O. Tilden,
Pardon E. Tillinghast.

*Cumberland.*
Davis Cook,
George L. Dana,
Horace A. Follett.
*North Smithfield.*
Wellington Aldrich,
Ansel Holman,
Arlon Mowry,
William H. Seagrave,
George W. Smith, Jr.
*Lincoln.*
William D. Aldrich,
Bailey E. Borden,
Geo. F. Crowninshield,
Andrew J. Currier,
Samuel Fessenden,
Frederick N. Goff,
J. E. Goldsworthy,
Wm. H. Gooding,
Welcome A. Greene,
John P. Gregory,
Samuel D. Larned,
George A. Kent,
Josephus R. Merriam,
Daniel Pearce,
Simon A. Sayles,
Frank A. Thurber,
Joseph W. Tillinghast.
*Cranston.*
William H. Hall,
William Hill,
Francis W. Miner,
Jonathan M. Wheeler.
*Burrillville.*
Henry M. Chase,
Oliver A. Inman,
Samuel W. Millard,
Lafayette Reynolds,
John M. Smith,
Charles L. Steere,

Francis M. Wood.
*Johnston.*
Horace Clarke,
William A. Phillips,
Isaac W. D. Pike,
Andrew B. Patton.
*Glocester.*
Alexander Eddy,
Henry A. Randall,
Ziba O. Slocum.
*Woonsocket.*
Alfred Allen,
Edwin Aldrich,
Darius D. Farnum,
Albert E. Greene,
William E. Hubbard,
William H. Jenckes,
Francello G. Jillson,
Francis L. O'Reilly,
Nathan T. Verry,
George A. Wilbur.
*Foster.*
Daniel N. Paine,
George S. Tillinghast.
*Scituate.*
Auldis Barden,
Caleb W. Johnson,
David Howland,
Charles H. Page,
Sylvester Patterson,
Daniel H. Remington.
*East Providence.*
Francis Armington,
George N. Bliss,
John A. Flagg,
Alonzo Freeman.
*Smithfield.*
Michael Maloney,
Martin Mann,
Wilson S. Mowry.

## NEWPORT COUNTY.

*City of Newport.*
Darius Baker,
Francis Brinley,
William Gilpin,
Edward S. Hammond,
Benjamin Marsh, 2d,
Francis B. Peckham, Jr.,
James G. Topham,
Henry N. Ward,
Thomas W. Wood.
*Little Compton.*
Ephraim W. Brownell,

Frederick R. Brownell,
Philip F. Little,
Henry M. Tompkins.
*Middletown.*
Eugene Sturtevant.
*Tiverton.*
Benjamin C. Borden,
Thomas H. Borden,
Joshua T. Durfee.
*Portsmouth.*
Asa B. Anthony,
Philip B. Chase.

## BRISTOL COUNTY.

*Bristol.*
John Turner,

John P. Reynolds.

## KENT COUNTY,

*Warwick.*
John F. Brown,
Thomas W. D. Clarke,
Albert R. Greene,
Thomas M. Holden,
Oliver P. Sarle,
Ira O. Seamans,
Thomas Spencer,
William V. Slocum,
Charles W. Smith,
John C. Sweet,
Norman G. Tefft,
Daniel Warner,
John F. Woodmancy.

*West Greenwich.*
John A. Bates,
George T. Brown,
John A. Hall,
John T. Lewis.
*East Greenwich.*
Lowell Pitcher,
Elisha R. Potter,
Christopher A. Shippee,
Thomas J. Tilley,
Samuel L. Tillinghast,
Sidney S. Tillinghast.
*Coventry.*
Resolved Harvey,
John J. Kilton,
Oliver Lewis.

## WASHINGTON COUNTY.

*South Kingstown.*
Charles H. Aldrich,

John Babcock,
Henry T. Braman,

John L. Brown,
Benjamin W. Case,
Elisha C. Clarke,
Joseph C. Clarke,
Robert Thompson,
J. Henry Wells.
*North Kingstown.*
David S. Baker, Jr.,
Wm. E. Cozzens,
Harrison G. O. Gardner,
Edwin R. Johnson,
Allen Reynolds,
Thomas S. Wightman.
*Charlestown.*
Charles Cross.
*Exeter.*
Nathan B. Lewis,

George P. Rose,
John C. Tillinghast.
*Hopkinton.*
George H. Olney,
Nathan L. Richmond.
*Richmond.*
James C. Baker,
Halsey P. Clarke,
Isaac Collins,
Nelson K. Church,
Clarke B. Lillibridge.
*Westerly.*
Samuel H. Cross,
Nathan F. Dixon, Jr.,
William Hoxsey,
Thomas H. Peabody,
Thomas Vincent.

---

## JUSTICES OF THE PEACE ELECTED BY TOWNS.

### PROVIDENCE COUNTY.

*City of Providence.*
Emory Cook,
Royal Chapin,
Stephen S. Salisbury,
Edward Field,
Edward D. Bassett,
William S. Hayward,
Arthur W. Dennis,
Augustus M. Wheeler,
George H. Pettis,
Philip B. Stiness, Jr.
*East Providence.*
Thomas B. Wall,
David S. Anthony,
Miles B Lawson,
Cyrus E. Goff,

Alvord O. Miles,
Nathaniel Cole.
*Pawtucket.*
Alden Sibley,
Walter Wheeler,
Arthur R. Sweet.
*Scituate.*
John C. Colvin,
Thomas S. Olney,
William H. Chandler,
Daniel H. Remington,
Joseph W. Potter,
David B. Knight,
George W. Leach.
*Foster.*
Daniel N. Paine,

# APPENDIX.

George S. Tillinghast.

### Cranston.
John Beattie,
Eben C. Thaxter,
Frank L. Sheldon,
F. Wayland Potter,
John Treen,
John Cornell,
Walter L. Potter,
Arad Wood,
James M. Cornell,
Frederick Smith.

### Glocester.
Reuben J. Brown,
Henry A. Randall,
Clovis W. Steere,
Charles W. Farnum.

### Cumberland.
Horace A. Follett,
Stephen I. Dexter,
William H. Tobey,
Wilson T. White,
Davis Cook.

### North Providence.
Albert L. Andrews,
John Angell,
Barber A. Wilcox,
James V. Corey,
Philip A. Sweet, 2d.
George Eddy.

### Woonsocket.
Henry L. Ballou,
Spencer Mowry,
Jefferson Aldrich,
Joshua E. Blood,
Darius D. Farnum,

Samuel P. Cook,
Bradbury C. Hill.

### Johnston.
George W. White,
Andrew H. Remington,
Horace Clarke,
Henry C. Arnold,
Theodore S. Hughes.

### North Smithfield.
William H. Seagrave,
Ansel Holman,
Charles A. Smith,
George W. Smith, Jr.,
Augustus M. Aldrich.

### Burrillville.
Oliver A. Inman,
Francis Carpenter,
Nelson Armstrong,
Simon T. Smith,
Smith Mowry,
Francis M. Wood,
Henry M. Chase.

### Smithfield.
Wilson S. Mowry,
John A. Brown,
Walker A. Medbury,
George A. Cornell,
Orin Barnes.

### Lincoln.
Daniel Pearce,
George F. Crowningshield,
Simon A. Sayles,
William D. Aldrich,
Samuel Fessenden,
Joseph Olney,
John Aigan.

## NEWPORT COUNTY.

### Portsmouth.
Asa B. Anthony,
Charles H. Potter,
George Manchester.

### Middletown.
Nathaniel Peckham,
John Gould,
George A. Brown.

*Tiverton.*
Thomas H. Borden,

Isaac D. Manchester,
William Hunt.

## BRISTOL COUNTY.

*Warren.*
Benjamin M. Bosworth, Jr.,
George L. Cooke, Jr.,
Nathaniel T. Sanders,
John A. Umfreeville,
Joseph M. Smith.
*Barrington.*
Mark H. Wood,

Isaac F. Cady,
Hiram F. Perry.
*Bristol.*
Bennett J. Munro,
James Lawless,
George H. Reynolds,
Silas H. Munro.

## KENT COUNTY.

*West Greenwich.*
Ambrose Brown,
Isaac C. Andrews,
John A. Hall.
*Warwick.*
Pardon Spencer,
Cyrus Holden,
William Carder,
Caleb R. Hill,
Henry A. Holmes,
David G. Ross,
Joseph Lawton,
Sam W. Clarke,
William V. Slocum,

John C. Sweet,
Alpheus F. Angell,
Caleb Westcott,
Thomas Spencer,
Thomas W. D. Clark,
John F. Brown,
Dwight R. Adams.
*East Greenwich.*
Walter Spencer,
James M. Cook,
Charles A. Vaughn,
Christopher V. Spencer,
Arnold Nichols.

## WASHINGTON COUNTY.

*South Kingstown.*
Henry W. Babcock.
*North Kingstown.*
Allen Reynolds,
Charles Allen,
John Westcott, Jr.,
William E. Cozzens,
Daniel G. Allen.
*Richmond.*
Abel Tanner,
James C. Baker,
George S. Gould,

George H. Clarke,
Daniel C. Kenyon,
John C. Ennis.
*Exeter.*
Stephen B. Weeden,
Moses D. Lewis.
*Charlestown.*
Oliver D. Clarke.
*Hopkinton.*
Nathan L Richmond,
John J. Babcock.

# Report of the General Treasurer,

## MAY SESSION, A. D. 1876.

GENERAL TREASURER'S OFFICE,
PROVIDENCE, May 30th, 1876. }

*To the Honorable the General Assembly of the State of Rhode Island :*

In compliance with the requirements of law I have the honor to submit herewith the following report of the Receipts and Expenditures of Public Money, commencing with the fiscal year May 1st, A. D. 1875, and ending April 30th, A. D. 1876.

Balance in Treasury April 30th, 1875.................... $475,850 23

Receipts from May 1st, 1875, to April 30th, 1876....... $1,026,612 26

    Amounting to.............................. $1,502,462 49

Payments from May 1, 1875, to April 30, 1876.......... $1,106,276 96

Balance in the Treasury............................... $396,185 53

Funded Debt of the State....... .................... $2,558,500 00

## RECEIPTS.

| | |
|---|---:|
| Balance in Treasury April 30, 1875 .................... | $475,850 23 |
| State Tax......................................... | 492,586 10 |
| Institutions for Savings.......................... | 115,356 10 |
| State Insurance Companies......................... | 18,224 09 |
| Foreign Insurance Agents.......................... | 30,913 94 |
| Supreme Court.................................... | 5,259 37 |
| Court of Common Pleas............................ | 8,963 84 |
| Justice Court, Providence. ....................... | 3,500 00 |
| Justice Court, Newport............................ | 369 81 |
| Justice Court, Pawtucket.......................... | 958 20 |
| Justice Court, Woonsocket......................... | 485 60 |
| Trial Justices.................................... | 843 18 |
| Auctioneers...................................... | 1,754 51 |
| Town Councils................................... | 73,594 24 |
| Peddlers' Licenses................................ | 5,800 00 |
| Dividends on School Fund.......................... | 20,033 50 |
| Civil Commissions. ............................... | 1,730 00 |
| Charters......................................... | 4,050 00 |
| Jailers........................................... | 2,458 16 |
| Interest on Deposits of Revenue.................... | 17,746 77 |
| General Statutes.................................. | 110 50 |
| Rhode Island Reports............................. | 30 00 |
| Envelopes........................................ | 9 00 |
| Schedules........................................ | 31 30 |
| State Constables ................................. | 868 40 |
| Cove Lands....................................... | 200,000 00 |
| National Bank of North America, award of referees...... | 15,196 53 |
| Oyster Lots...................................... | 5,300 00 |
| Miscellaneous.................................... | 439 12 |
| | $1,502,462 49 |

## PAYMENTS.

| | |
|---|---:|
| Salaries.......................................... | $71,065 24 |
| Expenses of the General Assembly.................. | 19,936 99 |
| Supreme Court.................................... | 19,639 82 |
| Court of Common Pleas............................ | 26,213 43 |
| Justice Court, Providence......................... | 3,811 10 |
| Justice Court, Newport ........................... | 364 55 |

| | |
|---|---:|
| Justice Court, Pawtucket........................... | $413 05 |
| Justice Courts...................................... | 1,117 44 |
| Orders of the Governor............................. | 671 80 |
| Public Printing.................................... | 10,621 52 |
| Secretary of Board of Charities and Corrections......... | 97,000 00 |
| Commissioners of Sinking Funds..................... | 181,000 00 |
| Public Schools..................................... | 90,000 00 |
| Special Appropriations.............................. | 8,713 48 |
| Insane and other Dependents......................... | 9,607 02 |
| Jailers............................................. | 1,829 59 |
| Reform School...................................... | 20,636 58 |
| Military............................................ | 15,797 31 |
| Court Houses and Jails.............................. | 3,092 17 |
| Fuel and Gas....................................... | 2,639 17 |
| Care of State House, Providence...................... | 1,260 00 |
| Care of State House, Newport........................ | 300 00 |
| Care of Elizabeth Building.......................... | 335 73 |
| Care of College Street Court Room.................... | 396 00 |
| Narragansett Indians................................ | 300 00 |
| Normal School...................................... | 10,000 00 |
| Rents.............................................. | 3,800 00 |
| Law Library........................................ | 1,874 75 |
| Trial Justices...................................... | 855 54 |
| Officers............................................ | 2,587 80 |
| Accounts allowed by General Assembly................ | 6,169 45 |
| Interest on State Debt.............................. | 153,960 00 |
| Registration of Births, Marriages and Deaths........... | 350 00 |
| Inland Fisheries.................................... | 1,137 23 |
| Mileage State Normal School......................... | 1,340 20 |
| Teachers' Institutes................................ | 305 00 |
| Soldiers' and Sailors' Testimonials................... | 25 00 |
| Evening Schools.................................... | 1,968 00 |
| New State Prison................................... | 128,214 97 |
| Lectures and Addresses, Public Schools............... | 112 87 |
| Providence County Court House...................... | 40,000 00 |
| Decennial Census A. D. 1875........................ | 14,219 81 |
| State Library....................................... | 52 00 |
| National Centennial Exhibition....................... | 324 35 |
| Town House Lot.................................... | 146,468 15 |
| Miscellaneous...................................... | 5,749 85 |
| | $1,106,276 96 |

## RECEIPTS.

### *State Tax.*

| | | |
|---|---:|---:|
| Warren | $7,042 72 | |
| Discount | 81 00 | |
| | | $6,961 72 |
| Newport | $44,210 33 | |
| Discount | 248 69 | |
| | | $43,961 64 |
| East Providence | $5,685 80 | |
| Discount | 19 89 | |
| | | 5,665 91 |
| New Shoreham | | 673 62 |
| Scituate | | 4,065 48 |
| Smithfield | | 3,504 88 |
| Tive·ton | | 2,675 32 |
| Charlestown | | 995 94 |
| Exeter | | 916 14 |
| East Greenwich | | 2,804 78 |
| Barrington | | 2,596 69 |
| Portsmouth | | 3,925 15 |
| Hopkinton | | 2,718 39 |
| Coventry | | 6,187 43 |
| Bristol | | 7,940 97 |
| Woonsocket | | 17,246 34 |
| Middletown | | 4,167 23 |
| North Providence | | 1,544 77 |
| Johnston | | 6,350 09 |
| Glocester | | 1,788 41 |
| Richmond | | 1,933 23 |
| North Kingstown | | 4,328 30 |
| Providence | | 252,821 59 |
| South Kingstown | | 8,154 05 |
| Little Compton | | 1,914 13 |
| Burrillville | | 4,142 20 |
| Cumberland | | 8,990 57 |
| Cranston | | 12,393 72 |
| Foster | | 993 98 |
| North Smithfield | | 4,021 67 |
| Westerly | | 8,161 08 |

| | | |
|---|---:|---:|
| Lincoln.......................................... | | $12,879 03 |
| West Greenwich................................. | | 822 18 |
| Jamestown...................................... | | 1,001 35 |
| Warwick........................................ | | 16,504 44 |
| Pawtucket.............................$26,758 82 | | |
| Interest........................... 124 86 | | 26,883 68 |
| | | |
| | | $492,586 10 |

*Institutions for Savings.*

| | |
|---|---:|
| Ashaway Savings Bank......................... | $163 40 |
| Bristol Institution for Savings................. | 755 75 |
| Citizens Savings Bank, Providence ............. | 590 08 |
| Citizens Savings Bank, Woonsocket............. | 905 24 |
| City Savings Bank, Providence................. | 5.546 80 |
| Coddington Savings Bank, Newport............. | 1,326 28 |
| Coventry Savings Bank, Anthony............... | 557 90 |
| East Greenwich Institution for Savings......... | 446 87 |
| Franklin Savings Bank, Pawtucket............. | 3,677 23 |
| Hopkinton Savings Bank....................... | 561 92 |
| Island Savings Bank, Newport................. | 228 89 |
| Jackson Institution for Savings, Providence..... | 797 25 |
| Kingston Savings Bank, Kingston.............. | 648 49 |
| Mechanics Savings Bank, Providence........... | 14,625 69 |
| Mechanics Savings Bank, Westerly............. | 597 73 |
| Merchants Savings Bank, Providence........... | 597 00 |
| Niantic Savings Bank......................... | 961 06 |
| Pascoag Savings Bank, Pascoag,............... | 1,494 34 |
| Pawtucket Institution for Savings............. | 5,633 65 |
| Peoples Savings Bank, Providence............. | 10,067 33 |
| Peoples Savings Bank, Woonsocket............. | 1,300 13 |
| Phenix Savings Bank, Warwick................. | 860 23 |
| Producers Savings Bank, Woonsocket........... | 666 72 |
| Providence Institution for Savings............. | 19,542 94 |
| Providence County Savings Bank, Pawtucket..... | 9,597 48 |
| Rhode Island Institution for Savings........... | 1,912 71 |
| Savings Bank, Newport....................... | 9,597 34 |
| Smithfield Savings Bank, Smithfield.......... | 461 31 |
| Union Savings Bank, Providence............... | 3,398 21 |
| Wakefield Institution for Savings............. | 835 06 |

| | | |
|---|---:|---:|
| Warwick Institution for Savings...................... | $3.409 | 37 |
| Westerly Savings Bank................................ | 2,446 | 95 |
| Wickford Savings Bank, Wickford.................... | 1,241 | 46 |
| Woonsocket Institution for Savings.................. | 8,344 | 40 |
| Warren Institution for Savings...................... | 1,563 | 89 |
| | $115,356 | 10 |

### *State Insurance Companies.*

| | | |
|---|---:|---:|
| Atlantic Insurance Co............................... | 450 | 07 |
| City Insurance Co................................... | 991 | 57 |
| Equitable Insurance Co.............................. | 855 | 66 |
| Merchants Insurance Co............................. | 1,187 | 56 |
| Providence Washington Insurance Co................. | 716 | 70 |
| Roger Williams Insurance Co........................ | 1,073 | 42 |
| Newport Insurance Co............................... | 685 | 80 |
| Blackstone Mutual Insurance Co..................... | 633 | 18 |
| Butler Mutual Insurance Co......................... | 324 | 07 |
| Firemens Mutual Insurance Co....................... | 1,706 | 27 |
| Franklin Mutual Insurance Co....................... | 567 | 79 |
| Manufacturers Mutual Insurance Co.................. | 1,453 | 45 |
| Pawtcket Mutual Insurance Co....................... | 987 | 76 |
| Providence Mutual Insurance Co..................... | 1,769 | 04 |
| Rhode Island Mutual Insurance Co.................. | 1,625 | 55 |
| State Mutual Insurance Co.......................... | 1,675 | 01 |
| Tiverton and Little Compton Insurance Co........... | 51 | 93 |
| Union Mutual Insurance Co.......................... | 562 | 91 |
| Mcchanics Mutual Insurance Co..................... | 608 | 49 |
| American Mutual Insurance Co...................... | 66 | 45 |
| Enterprise Mutual Insurance Co..................... | 39 | 25 |
| Merchants Mutual Insurance Co..................... | 96 | 12 |
| What Cheer Mutual Insurance Co.................... | 97 | 04 |
| | $18,224 | 09 |

### *Foreign Insurance Agents.*

| | | |
|---|---:|---:|
| William Kellen...................................... | 102.04 | |
| C. G. McKnight..................................... | 44 | 28 |
| C. E. Tillinghast................................... | 952 | 02 |
| G. H. Ware......................................... | 382 | 99 |
| James H. DeWolf................................... | 68 | 44 |

| | |
|---|---:|
| R. B. Averill.......................................... | $9 23 |
| G. R. Drown......................................... | 20 50 |
| E. P. Church......................................... | 19 17 |
| C. Banning.......................................... | 147 20 |
| Angell & Bicknell................................... | 154 82 |
| A. H. White......................................... | 1,526 70 |
| William DeWolf...................................... | 17 88 |
| William J. Potter.................................... | 329 45 |
| Asa Lyman.......................................... | 52 06 |
| R. B. Averill........................................ | 71 68 |
| Joel M. Spencer, Insurance Commissioner.............. | 1,100 21 |
| Farnum & Harris..................................... | 7 74 |
| Collins & Greene..................................... | 28 82 |
| John R. Dorrance.................................... | 302 36 |
| Charles A. Warland.................................. | 81 04 |
| Wm. R. Taylor....................................... | 5 59 |
| James G. Topham.................................... | 19 72 |
| J. M. Pendleton..................................... | 223 65 |
| J. M. Pendleton & Co.....:........................... | 105 99 |
| Pendleton & Co...................................... | 40 69 |
| Commercial Assurance Co., London.................... | 16 00 |
| Addison H. White ................................... | 1,389 29 |
| Collins & Greene..................................... | 434 47 |
| J. S. Parish......................................... | 147 27 |
| Searle & Williams.................................... | 33 86 |
| George C. Foster..................................... | 86 |
| J. E. Ellis.......................................... | 96 |
| Thomas J. Tilley.................................... | 14 07 |
| M. N. Davidson...................................... | 110 68 |
| Samuel Shove........................................ | 1,741 44 |
| Henry C. Ormsbee................................... | 348 66 |
| Thomas M. Holden................................... | 21 59 |
| Bull & Powell....................................... | 420 64 |
| Isaac Shove......................................... | 154 18 |
| M. E. Torrey........................................ | 179 18 |
| Charles H. Beach.................................... | 119 07 |
| C. S. Durfee........................................ | 418 87 |
| O. H. Aldrich....................................... | 8 25 |
| Langley & Engs...................................... | 186 76 |
| B. B. Hammond...................................... | 92 16 |
| Fred. W. Arnold..................................... | 278 56 |

| | |
|---|---:|
| H. H. Richardson | $5 41 |
| E. P. Patterson | 165 55 |
| Asa Lyman | 301 18 |
| J. L. Smith | 123 98 |
| George T. Paine | 540 54 |
| George H. Bunce | 180 10 |
| Thomas Ely | 230 48 |
| P. Skinner, Jr | 80 31 |
| George F. Bunce | 541 12 |
| C. A. Hopkins | 4,705 99 |
| A. Lapham | 24 31 |
| Immanuel Searle | 943 36 |
| D. A. Keyes | 19 37 |
| A. S. Sherman | 100 31 |
| Rhodes B. Chapman | 341 66 |
| Robert B. Chapman | 338 69 |
| E. P. Patterson | 100 86 |
| Wm. Kellen | 18 27 |
| George M. Carpenter | 322 19 |
| Wm. Kellen | 69 35 |
| Sparrow H. Nickerson | 92 43 |
| D. A. Keyes | 882 72 |
| C. Banning | 62 72 |
| John R. Dorrance | 276 03 |
| L. L. Barnard | 2,205 52 |
| W. L. Watson | 10 64 |
| Sidney Williams | 20 72 |
| Caleb Farnum | 81 82 |
| Snow & Barker | 400 19 |
| George S. Shepley | 95 48 |
| Daniel Murphy | 1,003 58 |
| George S Shepley | 59 50 |
| Wm. Y. Potter | 39 49 |
| Farnum & Harris | 540 55 |
| C. Farnum for Wm. G. Arnold | 7 09 |
| D. R. Whittemore | 143 68 |
| R. J. Angell | 213 13 |
| R. P. Smith | 505 84 |
| J. H. D'Wolf | 54 36 |
| J. M. Spencer, Insurance Commissioner | 1,091 97 |
| A. G. Godding | 1,129 02 |

| | |
|---|---:|
| Amos Sherman................................... | $200 43 |
| George H. Ware................................. | 751 06 |
| E. P. Church.................................. | 17 85 |
| | $30,913 94 |

### Supreme Court.

| | | |
|---|---:|---:|
| Entries.................................. | $937 75 | |
| Jury Fees.................................. | 36 85 | |
| Fines.................................... | 95 00 | |
| Jurors................................... | 1,223 60 | |
| Miscellaneous, Writs, &c................. | 294 14 | |
| Costs.................................... | 1,491 63 | |
| Officers................................. | 252 40 | |
| Witnesses................................ | 150 70 | |
| Clerks................................... | 777 30 | |
| | | $5,259 37 |

### Court of Common Pleas.

| | | |
|---|---:|---:|
| Entries.................................. | $11 00 | |
| Jury Fees................................ | 69 55 | |
| Fines.................................... | 631 00 | |
| Jurors................................... | 1,441 30 | |
| Miscellaneous............................ | 98 05 | |
| Costs.................................... | 3,970 44 | |
| Officers................................. | 247 35 | |
| Witnesses................................ | 2,053 00 | |
| Clerks................................... | 76 00 | |
| Recognizances............................ | 366 15 | |
| | | $8,963 84 |

### Justice Court, Providence.

| | |
|---|---:|
| Fines................................... | $1,438 00 |
| Costs................................... | 2,062 00 |
| | $3,500 00 |

### Justice Court, Newport.

| | |
|---|---:|
| Entries................................. | $110 00 |
| Fines................................... | 71 06 |
| Costs................................... | 174 80 |
| Writs................................... | 13 95 |
| | $369 81 |

### Justice Court, Pawtucket.

| | |
|---|---:|
| Entries............................................ | $300 00 |
| Fines............................................. | 160 50 |
| Costs............................................. | 460 90 |
| Writs............................................. | 36 80 |
| | **$958 20** |

### Justice Court, Woonsocket.

| | |
|---|---:|
| Entries............................................ | $94 60 |
| Fines............................................. | 320 00 |
| Costs............................................. | 52 70 |
| Writs............................................. | 18 30 |
| | **$485 60** |

### Trial Justices.

| | |
|---|---:|
| George F. Tillinghast, Foster...................... | $10 00 |
| Wm. Hill, Cranston................................ | 49 00 |
| Geo. N. Bliss, East Providence..................... | 44 00 |
| Horace Clark, Johnston............................ | 32 00 |
| Geo. F. Crowningshield, Lincoln.................... | 17 00 |
| Mark H. Wood, Barrington.......................... | 15 00 |
| F. M. Wood, Burrillville........................... | 79 50 |
| Thos. S. Wightman, North Kingstown................ | 25 00 |
| Emor H. Mowry, Smithfield......................... | 21 00 |
| Benj. W. Case, South Kingstown.................... | 15 00 |
| Alexander Eddy, Glocester......................... | 2 00 |
| F. M. Wood, Burrillville........................... | 59 08 |
| Geo. L. Cooke, Warren............................. | 47 00 |
| Bennett J. Munro, Bristol.......................... | 18 00 |
| Horace A. Follett, Cumberland..................... | 24 00 |
| Thomas H. Borden, Tiverton........................ | 5 00 |
| Nathan B. Lewis, Exeter........................... | 2 00 |
| John E. Watson, Warden, Jamestown................ | 2 00 |
| F. M. Wood, Burrillville........................... | 176 10 |
| T. A. Gardner, Clerk Justice Court, South Kingstown... | 15 00 |
| Wilson S. Mowry, Smithfield....................... | 5 00 |
| M. F. Perry, South Kingstown...................... | 4 00 |
| Bennett J. Munro, Bristol.......................... | 58 00 |

| | | |
|---|---|---|
| Horace A. Follett, Cumberland........................ | $15 | 00 |
| Geo. N. Bliss, East Providence....................... | 98 | 00 |
| Nelson K. Church, Richmond......................... | 5 | 50 |
| | **$843** | **18** |

## *Auctioneer's.*

| | | |
|---|---|---|
| S. A. Driscol, Warren............................... | $6 | 47 |
| William Hill, Cranston.............................. | 18 | 26 |
| Geo. F. Barber, Exeter.............................. | | 47 |
| Auldis Barden, Scituate.∴........................... | 1 | 86 |
| Abel C. Monrow, Woonsocket........................ | 1 | 45 |
| Wm. N. Sherman, East Greenwich.................... | | 67 |
| Holder N. Wilcox, Tiverton.......................... | 1 | 07 |
| Ansen S. Barr, Scituate............................. | 1 | 89 |
| Nathaniel Peckham, Middletown...................... | 1 | 27 |
| Job W. Hazard, Jamestown.......................... | | 81 |
| F. W. Simmons & N. Church, Little Compton......... | 12 | 69 |
| Ira Winsor, Foster................................. | 2 | 56 |
| Thomas Burlingame, Newport....................... | 38 | 50 |
| H. F. Ferrin & Jas. F. Davidson, Providence.......... | 11 | 84 |
| O. A. Inman, Burrillville............................ | 1 | 98 |
| Jos. O. Osborn, Tiverton............................ | 18 | 85 |
| F. N. Goff, (Lincoln)............................... | 20 | 00 |
| John C. Ellis, East Greenwich....................... | | 15 |
| S. B. Hoxie, Charlestown........................... | | 21 |
| Chas. Wilcox, South Kingstown...................... | 1 | 16 |
| David R. Kenyon, Hopkinton........................ | | 18 |
| Martin Mann, Smithfield............................ | 1 | 02 |
| Olney M. Cook, Cumberland........................ | 8 | 29 |
| John A. Brown, Smithfield.......................... | 1 | 12 |
| W. A. Phillips, Johnston............................ | 15 | 88 |
| Sheldon & Draper, Providence....................... | 78 | 44 |
| Ichabod Allen, Smithfield........................... | 4 | 55 |
| Wm. H. Crandall, Newport.......................... | | 21 |
| Chas. S. Sweetland, Providence...................... | 20 | 40 |
| Nathan T. Verry, Woonsocket........................ | 7 | 27 |
| S. Gano Benedict, Pawtucket........................ | 5 | 64 |
| Robert Sherman, Pawtucket.......................... | 82 | 85 |
| Stedman Kenyon, Richmond......................... | | 94 |
| P. M. Farrington, Providence........................ | 8 | 58 |

| | |
|---|---|
| H. C. Budlong, Warwick............................... | $5 66 |
| Edward S. Babcock, South Kingstown................. | 15 20 |
| Albert S. Wilbur, Providence........................ | 18 00 |
| Charles A. Warland, Pawtucket..................:... | 9 32 |
| Gideon T. Collins, Westerly......................... | 5 28 |
| Wm. P. Lewis, New Shoreham....................... | 1 18 |
| Geo. H. Burnham, Providence........................ | 303 01 |
| John M. Eddy, Glocester............................ | 2 62 |
| Stephen P. Brown, Scituate......................... | 1 50 |
| William Hill, Cranston.............................. | 21 04 |
| Francis Armington, East Providence......·.......... | 6 13 |
| S. A. Driscol, Warren.............................. | 77 |
| B. F. Smith, Hopkinton............................. | 82 |
| George R. Kinnecut, Barrington..................... | 16 10 |
| Alanson M. Barr, Scituate.......................... | 05 |
| Charles P. Adams, Pawtucket........................ | 8 42 |
| John C. Ellis, East Greenwich....................... | 28 |
| Henry Staples, Providence.......................... | 23 38 |
| John A. Brown, Smithfield.......................... | 67 |
| F. N Goff, Lincoln................................. | 53 85 |
| C. S. Sweetland, Providence........................ | 9 33 |
| Charles W. Wilcox, South Kingstown................. | 1 90 |
| Olney M. Cook Cumberland.......................... | 7 42 |
| John G. Moore, Providence.......................... | 4 31 |
| Walter A. Medbury, Smithfield...................... | 07 |
| Emory Cook, Providence............................ | 1 03 |
| Sheldon & Draper, Providence ...................... | 45 72 |
| Charles A. Warland, Pawtucket................ ...... | 8 00 |
| Albert G. Wilbur, Providence....................... | 21 42 |
| Stedman Kenyon, Pichmond......................... | 13 32 |
| W. A. Phillips, Johnston........................... | 8 10 |
| A. G. Barton, Providence .......................... | 20 75 |
| Gideon T. Collins................................. | 2 25 |
| Herbert E. Dodge, Providence....................... | 8 02 |
| H. F. Ferrin & James F. Davidson................... | 13 37 |
| George H. Burnham, Providence..................... | 270 40 |
| Chris. A. Hall, Providence.......................... | 6 08 |
| N. T. Verry, Woonsocket........................... | 2 34 |
| David S. Moore, Providence......................... | 2 35 |
| Ichabod Allen, Woonsocket.......................... | 1 03 |
| Charles L. Ellis, Providence........................ | 1 46 |

A. G. Sanford, Warren.............................. $24 11
P. M. Farrington, Providence....................... 6 13
Henry C. Budlong, Warwick......................... 5 74
Oliver Chaffee, Providence......................... 14 02
George H. Burnham, Providence..................... 205 47
George Stewart, East Providence.................... 28 87
Georgh H. Reynolds, Bristol........................ 12 03
Henry Staples, Barrington.......................... 2 67
Abel C. Monrow, Woonsocket....................... 7 61
Holder N. Wilcox, Tiverton......................... 2 56
Henry C. Card, Charlestown........................ 92
Wm. P. Lewis, New Shoreham...................... 16

$1,754 51

## Town Councils.

| | | | |
|---|---|---|---:|
| Town Treasurer, | | South Kingstown..................... | $60 00 |
| " | " | Burrillville........................... | 25 00 |
| " | " | East Greenwich...................... | 3 00 |
| " | " | East Providence..................... | 40 00 |
| " | " | South Kingstown.................... | 12 50 |
| City | " | Providence.......................... | 633 00 |
| Town | " | Warren.............................. | 37 50 |
| " | " | Warren............................. | 40 00 |
| " | " | Charlestown......................... | 75 00 |
| " | " | Woonsocket ........................ | 4,973 00 |
| " | " | North Providence.................... | 250 00 |
| " | " | East Providence.................... | 20 00 |
| " | " | Johnston........................... | 1,400 00 |
| " | " | Richmond........................... | 300 00 |
| " | " | N. Kingstown....................... | 20 50 |
| City | " | Providence......................... | 54,413 74 |
| " | " | Newport........................... | 6,475 00 |
| Town | " | Westerly........................... | 15 00 |
| " | " | West Greenwich..................... | 300 00 |
| " | " | Cranston........................... | 1,050 00 |
| " | " | Warwick............................ | 3,000 00 |
| " | " | East Greenwich..................... | 450 00 |
| " | " | Tiverton........................... | 1 00 |

$73,594 24

## Peddlers' Licenses.

| | |
|---|---|
| Cornelius Quinn, Providence County.................... | $50 00 |
| Benjamin H. Rugg, State ........................... | 100 00 |
| George A. Taylor, Providence County................. | 50 00 |
| George S. Winn, Providence County.................. | 50 00 |
| Charles Bourigard, Providence County................ | 50 00 |
| L. E. Remington, Providence County................. | 50 00 |
| Edward J. Corey, Providence County................. | 50 00 |
| W. F. Olin, Washington County..................... | 25 00 |
| John B. Jette, Providence County................... | 50 00 |
| Leonard Mountney, Providence County............... | 50 00 |
| Oliver H. Magoon, Providence County............... | 50 00 |
| Welcome A. Ballou. Providence County.............. | 50 00 |
| Francis Hackett, Providence County................. | 50 00 |
| Henry Hammond, Kent County...................... | 25 00 |
| Patrick McKenna, Providence County................ | 50 00 |
| Jacob Besman, Providence County................... | 50 00 |
| Alvin Miller, Providence County.................... | 50 00 |
| James Gaddes, Providence County................... | 50 00 |
| Israel Versofski, Providence County................. | 50 00 |
| Z. Evarski, Newport County....................... | 25 00 |
| Asa T. Davol, Newport County..................... | 25 00 |
| Abraham Burnstine, Providence County.............. | 50 00 |
| Jacob Verstufski, Providence Co................... | 50 00 |
| R. Marcus, Providence County..................... | 50 00 |
| Charles W. Farrington, Providence County........... | 50 00 |
| Nelson James Arnold, Providence County............ | 50 00 |
| Thomas Sawyer, Providence County................. | 50 00 |
| George Allen Loomis, Providence County............ | 50 00 |
| Patrick Drew, Providence County................... | *50 00 |
| Wm. B. Davis, Providence County.................. | 50 00 |
| John Joseph Scattergood, Providence County......... | 50 00 |
| Heskey Shove, Providence County.................. | 50 00 |
| George J. Collins, Providence County.............. | 50 00 |
| Lewis Young, Providence County................... | 50 00 |
| Owen G Gardiner, Kent County.................... | 25 00 |
| Isaac Abraham, Providence County............ ...... | 50 00 |
| James Lewis, Providence County................... | 50 00 |
| Josiah Besse, Bristol County...................... | 25 00 |
| D. J. O'Connor, Providence County................. | 50 00 |

| | | |
|---|---:|---:|
| James McGlinchy, Providence County | $50 | 00 |
| D. C. O'Connor, Providence County | 50 | 00 |
| Wm. Pritchard, Providence County | 50 | 00 |
| Bernard McCaughey, Providence County | 50 | 00 |
| Wm. Carroll, Providence County | 50 | 00 |
| Bernard Harris, Providence County | 50 | 00 |
| Frederick Taylor, Providence County | 50 | 00 |
| John Cowley, Providence County | 50 | 00 |
| Henry Clarkson, Providence County | 50 | 00 |
| Frank Salmon, Providence County | 50 | 00 |
| Joseph Boisclair, Providence County | 50 | 00 |
| Patrick C. Landry, Providence County | 50 | 00 |
| Wm. Salmon, Providence County | 50 | 00 |
| Isaiah C. Haswell, Providence County | 50 | 00 |
| Z. Evarski, Providence County | 50 | 00 |
| Aaron Lewis, Providence County | 50 | 00 |
| Bernard Harris, Kent County | 25 | 00 |
| M. Eisenstadt, Newport County | 25 | 00 |
| Henry Passinski, Newport County | 25 | 00 |
| Lewis Guinsburg, Newport County | 25 | 00 |
| Wm. Greeley, Providence County | 50 | 00 |
| John Lamoine, Kent County | 25 | 00 |
| Charles H. Clifford, Bristol County | 25 | 00 |
| Henry D. Smith, State | 100 | 00 |
| Warren Smart, State | 100 | 00 |
| Charles Furrell, Providence County | 50 | 00 |
| Joseph Patenand, Providence County | 50 | 00 |
| Samuel O. Gardiner, State | 100 | 00 |
| T. Jefferson White, Patented Article, State | 50 | 00 |
| Lascom E. Rice, Kent County | 25 | 00 |
| Anthony Morse, Washington County | 25 | 00 |
| James A. Makepeace, Bristol County | 25 | 00 |
| William Hardman, Providence County | 50 | 00 |
| Sylvester W. Marden, Newport County | 25 | 00 |
| J. H. Lee, Washington County | 25 | 00 |
| F. S. Brault, Providence County | 50 | 00 |
| Charles P. Card, Providence County | 50 | 00 |
| Ian Fischer. Newport County | 25 | 00 |
| Peleg A. Fletcher, Providence County | 50 | 00 |
| Edward Beaudrv, Providence County | 50 | 00 |
| Thomas P. Locke, Washington County | 25 | 00 |

| | |
|---|---|
| George F. Bixby, Newport County...................... | $25 00 |
| Terrence Coughlin, Providence County................ | 50 00 |
| Lucian Learned, State................................. | 100 00 |
| B. Hoye, Providence County............... ........... | 50 00 |
| Wm. F. Jennison, Providence County................. | 50 00 |
| Charles Barrows, Providence County.......... ..... | 50 00 |
| James Gough, Kent County.......................... | 25 00 |
| Wm. L. Darling, Kent County....................... | 25 00 |
| Wm. L. Darling, Washington County.................. | 25 00 |
| S. P. Dana, State .................................. | 100 00 |
| A. R. Battey, Kent County........................... | 25 00 |
| Frank Early, Providence County...................... | 50 00 |
| Peter Moran, Providence County..................... | 50 00 |
| Ennis Mathewson, Providence County................ | 50 00 |
| Samuel Robinson, Providence County................. | 50 00 |
| John S. Kenyon, Providence County................. | 50 00 |
| John E. Boyce, Providence County................... | 50 00 |
| Herbert F. Lasell, State............................. | 100 00 |
| Charles E. Lazell, Providence County................ | 50 00 |
| Charles H. Briggs, Kent County..................... | 25 00 |
| Beriah Potter, Kent County.......................... | 25 00 |
| Ennis Mathewson, Bristol County.................... | 25 00 |
| Edward Beaudry, Providence County................. | 50 00 |
| James Connors, Providence County.................. | 50 00 |
| Joel T. Sherman, Washington County................ | 25 00 |
| Robert A. Mills, Providence County................. | 50 00 |
| Fayette Barrows, Washington County................ | 25 00 |
| John Friedland, State............................... | 100 00 |
| John D. Waite, Providence County ................. | 50 00 |
| T. W. Priest, Providence County..................... | 50 00 |
| C. P. Gardiner, Washington County.................. | 25 00 |
| Moses Biermount, Providence County................ | 50 00 |
| Joseph Bedard, Providence County.................. | 50 00 |
| A. F. Scattergood, Providence County............... | 50 00 |
| John Riley, Providence County...................... | 50 00 |
| Oliver D. Hall, Washington County.................. | 25 00 |
| George L. Vibbert, Providence County............... | 50 00 |
| Christopher Vaughan, Kent County and Washington Co.. | 50 00 |
| Erastus Brown, Newport County.................... | 25 00 |
| Charles W. Wilcox, Kent County and Washington Co... | 50 00 |
| Thomas Heap, Providence County................... | 50 00 |

| | |
|---|---:|
| Max Faldman, Kent County.......................... | $25 00 |
| William McMahan, Providence County................ | 50 00 |
| Patrick Price, Providence County.................... | 50 00 |
| Samuel C. Davis, Washington County................ | 25 00 |
| | $5,800 00 |

### *Dividends on School Fund.*

| | |
|---|---:|
| Globe National Bank................................ | $4,000 00 |
| National Bank of North America.................... | 2,915 00 |
| Rhode Island National Bank........................ | 45 00 |
| American National Bank............................ | 1,092 00 |
| Mechanics National Bank........................... | 830 00 |
| National Bank of Commerce......................... | 1,626 00 |
| American National Bank............................ | 1,092 00 |
| Globe National Bank............................... | 3,000 00 |
| National Bank of North America.................... | 2,915 00 |
| National Bank of Commerce......................... | 1,626 00 |
| Mechanics National Bank........................... | 830 00 |
| Rhode Island National Bank........................ | 45 00 |
| National Exchange Bank, Newport................... | 17 50 |
| | $20,033 50 |

### *Civil Commissions.*

| | |
|---|---:|
| John B. Pearce.................................... | $26 00 |
| Charles A. Greene................................. | 52 00 |
| George Manchester................................. | 104 00 |
| J. M. Addeman.................................... | 526 00 |
| Christopher Holden................................ | 500 00 |
| Thomas J. Tilley.................................. | 120 00 |
| Christopher Holden................................ | 152 00 |
| George W. Burlingame.............................. | 112 00 |
| Henry Whipple.................................... | 138 00 |
| | $1,730 00 |

### *Charters.*

| | |
|---|---:|
| Peoples' Horse Railroad Co......................... | $200 00 |
| American Diamond Rock Boring Co.................. | 150 00 |
| Ocean Highlands Co............................... | 100 00 |
| Providence Land Co............................... | 100 00 |
| Lyman Spool Co.................................. | 100 00 |
| McWilliams Manufacturing Co...................... | 100 00 |

2

| | | |
|---|---:|---:|
| Providence Gas Burner Co | $100 | 00 |
| Capital Nail Co | 100 | 00 |
| Rhode Island Cotton Gin Co | 100 | 00 |
| Relief Washing Machine Co | 100 | 00 |
| City Gas Co | 1,000 | 00 |
| Pontiac Branch Railroad | 100 | 00 |
| Ballou Manufacturing Co | 500 | 00 |
| The Cliff Avenue Association | 100 | 00 |
| Infantry Building Association | 200 | 00 |
| Conant Thread Co., increase | 1,000 | 00 |
| | $4,050 | 00 |

### Jailers.

| | | |
|---|---:|---:|
| S. B. Springer, Bristol County | $3 | 10 |
| Edward D. Jones, Newport County | 58 | 65 |
| Nelson Viall, Providence County | 1,283 | 85 |
| Joatham S. Smith, Kent County | 5 | 20 |
| Edward D. Jones, Newport County | 80 | 98 |
| C. W. Wilcox, Washington County | 17 | 33 |
| Edward D. Jones, Newport County | 42 | 25 |
| Nelson Viall, Providence County | 938 | 10 |
| Charles W. Wilcox, Washington County | 28 | 70 |
| | $2,458 | 16 |

### Interest on Deposits of Revenue.

| | | |
|---|---:|---:|
| Rhode Island Hospital Trust Co | $9,464 | 38 |
| Rhode Island Hospital Trust Co | 8,282 | 39 |
| | $17,746 | 77 |

### General Statutes.

| | | |
|---|---:|---:|
| J. M. Addeman, Secretary of State | $110 | 50 |

### Rhode Island Reports.

| | | |
|---|---:|---:|
| J. M. Addeman, Secretary of State | $30 | 00 |

### Envelopes.

| | | |
|---|---:|---:|
| J. M. Addeman, Secretary of State | $9 | 00 |

### Schedules.

J. M. Addeman, Secretary of State.... ................     $31 80

### State Constables.

| | |
|---|---:|
| James Wilson........................................ | $281 60 |
| Nathaniel S. Greene............................... | 54 40 |
| John P. Case....................................... | 152 70 |
| Samuel B. M. Read................................. | 45 00 |
| Charles N. Gifford................................. | 82 60 |
| George W. Burlingame............................. | 252 10 |

$868 40

### Cove Lands.

City of Providence, redemption of bond...... ........   $200,000 00

### National Bank of North America.

Award of Referees in case of State of Rhode Island vs. National Bank of North America................   $15,196 53

### Miscellaneous.

| | |
|---|---:|
| City of Newport, for costs in cases not sustained........ | $20 90 |
| Money repaid, a matter for the town of Johnston to settle | 17 53 |
| Philip H. Clark, for enlistment bounty, refunded.... .... | 75 00 |
| William W. Chapin, Sec'ry of Charities and Corrections.. | 135 40 |
| Joshua M. Addeman, Sec'ry of State, (old carpet)...... | 35 38 |
| J. M. Addeman, Sec'ry of State, repayment of freight... | 9 82 |
| Christopher Holden, Sheriff, for old carpet and matting .. | 35 57 |
| William W. Chapin, Sec'ry of Charities and Corrections, (State Work House).......................... | 10 00 |
| Newport Artillery Co., gun house.................... | 41 70 |
| George Lewis Cooke, sum overpaid for services as member of General Assembly........................ | 21 00 |
| Thomas B. Stockwell, Commissioner of Public Schools, on account of Teachers' Institute.............. | 37 32 |

$439 12 :

## PAYMENTS.

### *Salaries.*

| | |
|---|---:|
| Henry Lippitt............................ ................... | $932 07 |
| Henry T. Sisson................................... | 466 04 |
| Henry Howard.............................. ............ | 69 64 |
| Charles C. Van Zandt ............................. | 34 82 |
| Joshua M. Addeman................................ | 2,500 00 |
| Willard Sayles.................................... | 2,500 00 |
| Samuel Clark................ ..................... | 2,000 00 |
| Joel M. Spencer................................... | 2,500 00 |
| George A. Brayton..................... ............... | 3,500 00 |
| Thomas Durfee.................................... | 4,425 00 |
| Walter S. Burges................................. | 4,000 00 |
| Elisha R. Potter................................. | 4,000 00 |
| John H. Stiness.................................. | 4,000 00 |
| Charles Mattison................................... | 3,934 78 |
| John R. Randolph................................ | 2,000 00 |
| Ervin T. Case.................................... | 3,000 00 |
| Thomas B. Stockwell................... .......... | 2,500 00 |
| George A. Wilbur................................. | 1,000 00 |
| William H. Jenckes.............................. | 800 00 |
| James G. Topham................................ | 700 00 |
| Henry N. Ward.................................. | 790 76 |
| James C. Collins.................................. | 400 00 |
| George N. Bliss................................. | 400 00 |
| Thomas Arnold.................................. | 400 00 |
| George Manchester.............................. | 400 00 |
| Charles A. Waldron............................. | 400 00 |
| Christopher Rhodes............................. | 1,000 00 |
| Augustus L. Miller.............................. | 1,200 00 |
| Thomas W. Wood................................ | 1,199 72 |
| Arnold Greene................................... | 625 00 |
| Charles Blake................................... | 4,571 63 |
| Daniel R. Ballou................................ | 210 60 |
| Charles T. Northup............................. | 304 36 |
| Charles R. Dennis.............................. | 400 00 |
| Daniel W. Fink................................. | 300 00 |
| William W. Eddy................................ | 1,238 23 |

| | |
|---|---:|
| Samuel B. M. Read.................................... | $228 26 |
| Henry Staples...................................... | 500 00 |
| Ira O. Seamans..................................... | 1,500 00 |
| Isaac N. Shove..................................... | 1,510 86 |
| George E. Webster.................................. | 2,390 49 |
| Jeremiah Peabody................................... | 228 26 |
| James Wilson....................................... | 228 26 |
| Charles N. Gifford................................. | 228 26 |
| Nathaniel S. Greene................................ | 228 26 |
| Heber LeFavour..................................... | 600 00 |
| James W. Monroe.................................... | 600 00 |
| Jabez C. Knight.................................... | 200 00 |
| Benjamin W. Case................................... | 303 26 |
| John G. Clark...................................... | 303 26 |
| Charles A. Greene.................................. | 411 24 |
| Albert R. Greene................................... | 606 52 |
| Franklin P. Owen................................... | 1,098 92 |
| Thomas S. Tilley................................... | 340 22 |
| Henry Whipple...................................... | 400 00 |
| John P. Case....................................... | 228 26 |
| George W. Burlingame............................... | 228 26 |
| | $71,065 24 |

### B.—*Expenses of the General Assembly.*

| | |
|---|---:|
| Pay of members of the General Assembly.............. | $14,116 66 |

### C.

| | |
|---|---:|
| Pay of officers, clerks, pages, stationery, &c........... | 5,820 33 |

### D.—*Supreme Court.*

| | | |
|---|---:|---:|
| Jurors..................................... | $13,320 40 | |
| Witnesses.................................. | 1,615 95 | |
| Clerks.... ................................ | 201 80 | |
| Officers................................... | 3,442 35 | |
| Incidentals................................ | 1,059 32 | |
| | | 19,639 82 |

### Court of Common Pleas.

| | | |
|---|---:|---:|
| Jurors.................................................. | $14,050 40 | |
| Witnesses............................................. | 7,715 45 | |
| Clerks................................................. | 185 45 | |
| Officers............................................... | 3,568 48 | |
| Incidentals........................................... | 693 65 | |
| | | 26,213 43 |

### Justice Court, Providence.

| | |
|---|---:|
| Officers.................................................. | 3,811 10 |

### Justice Court, Newport.

| | | |
|---|---:|---:|
| Officers................................................. | $233 90 | |
| Witnesses.............................................. | 130 65 | |
| | | 364 55 |

### Justice Court, Pawtucket.

| | | |
|---|---:|---:|
| Officers................................................. | $232 40 | |
| Witnesses.............................................. | 180 65 | |
| | | 413 05 |

### Justice Courts.

| | | |
|---|---:|---:|
| Officers................................................. | $709 26 | |
| Witnesses.............................................. | 408 18 | |
| | | 1,117 44 |

### E.

| | |
|---|---:|
| Orders of the Governor................................ | 671 80 |

### F.

| | |
|---|---:|
| Public Printing......................................... | 10,621 52 |

### H.

| | |
|---|---:|
| Charities and Corrections............................. | 97,000 00 |

## Commissioners of Sinking Funds.

| | |
|---|---|
| For bonds due 1882....................$119,000 00 | |
| "      "      "    1883.................... 20,000 00 | |
| "      "      "    1893.................... 20,250 00 | |
| Å      "      "    1894.................... 21,750 00 | |
| | 181,000 00 |

### Public Schools.

| | |
|---|---|
| Barrington........................................ | $485 65 |
| Bristol.......................................... | 1,863 55 |
| Burrillville...................................... | 2,513 57 |
| Charlestown...................................... | 832 75 |
| Coventry......................................... | 2,365 70 |
| Cranston......................................... | 2,034 86 |
| Cumberland....................................... | 1,979 85 |
| East Greenwich................................... | 1,013 56 |
| East Providence.................................. | 1,318 22 |
| Exeter........................................... | 1,183 72 |
| Foster........................................... | 1,559 49 |
| Glocester........................................ | 1,611 48 |
| Hopkinton........................................ | 1,573 46 |
| Jamestown........................................ | 218 16 |
| Johnston......................................... | 2,254 62 |
| Lincoln.......................................... | 3,383 32 |
| Little Compton................................... | 899 28 |
| Middletown....................................... | 584 30 |
| Newport.......................................... | 5,070 04 |
| New Shoreham..................................... | 723 64 |
| North Kingstown.................................. | 1,900 20 |
| North Providence................................. | 510 68 |
| North Smithfield................................. | 1,491 09 |
| Pawtucket........................................ | 4,757 16 |
| Portsmouth....................................... | 1,102 14 |
| Providence....................................... | 24,556 83 |
| Richmond......................................... | 1,528 10 |
| Scituate......................................... | 2,213 38 |
| Smithfield....................................... | 1,864 85 |
| South Kingstown.................................. | 2,868 81 |
| Tiverton......................................... | 1,330 04 |

| | |
|---|---:|
| Warwick | $4,212 81 |
| Warren | 1,274 40 |
| Westerly | 2,871 33 |
| West Greenwich | 1,014 34 |
| Woonsocket | 4,034 98 |
| | $90,000 00 |

## Special Appropriations.

| | |
|---|---:|
| George L. Cooke, Commissioner on Exemption from Taxation | $62 00 |
| Thomas G. Hazard, Commissioner on Exemption from Taxation | 6 00 |
| James W. Pollock, Washington County Court House | 123 61 |
| C. Maxon & Co., Washington County Court House | 2,871 39 |
| Justice Court Room, Woonsocket | 150 00 |
| State House and Jail, Newport | 600 03 |
| Aquidneck Agricultural Society | 500 00 |
| Rhode Island Horticultural Society | 300 00 |
| Rhode Island Society for the Encouragement of Domestic Industry | 1,000 00 |
| Washington County Agricultural Society | 500 00 |
| Woonsocket Agricultural and Horticultural and Industrial Society | 500 00 |
| Isaac Shove, Justice Court Room, Pawtucket | 500 00 |
| A. R. Greene, Kent County Records | 350 00 |
| Newport Light Infantry | 125 00 |
| C. Maxon & Co., Washington County Court House | 802 46 |
| S. Northup & Co., Washington County Court House | 117 99 |
| J. M. Addeman, Index to | 200 00 |
| | $8,713 48 |

## Miscellaneous Accounts.

| | |
|---|---:|
| Insane and other dependents | $9,607 02 |
| Jailers | 1,829 59 |
| Reform School | 20,636 58 |
| Military | 15,797 31 |
| Court Houses and Jails | 3,092 17 |
| Fuel and Gas | 2,639 17 |
| Care of State House, Providence | 1,260 00 |
| Care of State House, Newport | 300 00 |

| | | |
|---|---:|---:|
| Care of Elizabeth Building............................ | $335 | 73 |
| Care of College Street Court Room.................... | 396 | 00 |
| Narragansett Indians................................ | 300 | 00 |
| Normal School...................................... | 10,000 | 00 |
| Rents.............................................. | 3,800 | 00 |
| Law Library........................................ | 1,874 | 75 |
| Trial Justices...................................... | 855 | 54 |
| Officers............................................ | 2,587 | 80 |
| Accounts allowed by General Assembly........ ....... | 6,169 | 45 |
| Interest on State debt............................... | 153,960 | 00 |
| Registration of Births, Marriages and Deaths.... ...... | 350 | 00 |
| Inland Fisheries.................................... | 1,137 | 23 |
| Mileage, State Normal School........................ | 1,340 | 20 |
| Teachers' Institutes................................. | 305 | 00 |
| Soldiers and Sailors' Testimonials.................... | 25 | 00 |
| Evening Schools.................................... | 1,968 | 00 |
| New State Prison................................... | 128,214 | 97 |
| Lectures and Addresses, Public Schools............... | 112 | 87 |
| Providence County Court House........... ........... | 40,000 | 00 |
| Decennial Census, A. D. 1875........................ | 14,219 | 81 |
| State Library....................................... | 52 | 00 |
| National Centennial Exhibition....................... | 324 | 35 |
| Town House Lot.................................... | 146,468 | 15 |
| Miscellaneous...................................... | 5,749 | 85 |

The following investments constitute the Stock of the Permanent School Fund :

| | | | | |
|---|---|---|---:|---:|
| 2,000 shares | Globe National Bank, Providence.......... | | $101,008 | 19 |
| 546 " | American National Bank, Providence...... | | 28,659 | 12 |
| 1,166 " | National Bank of North America, Providence | | 50,289 | 57 |
| 813 " | National Bank of Commerce, Providence.... | | 42,935 | 24 |
| 332 " | Mechanics National Bank, Providence...... | | 15,600 | 00 |
| 45 " | Rhode Island National Bank, Providence. .. | | 1,534 | 25 |
| 7 " | Newport National Bank, Newport......... | | 350 | 00 |

|  | | |
|---|---:|---:|
| | $240,376 | 37 |

*Statement of School Fund subject to investment.*

| | | |
|---|---:|---:|
| Amount reported May, 1875........................ | $14,766 | 14 |
| Auctioneers' duties to April 30, 1876................ | 1,754 | 51 |
| | $16,520 | 65 |

### Touro Fund in account with Agent.

| | | |
|---|---|---|
| To paid Agent............................................ | $42 | 00 |
| Deposited in Savings Bank, Newport..................... | 10,822 | 48 |
| Deposited in Newport National Exchange Bank......... | 2,782 | 15 |
| | $13,646 | 63 |

### Credit.

| | | |
|---|---|---|
| Balance from old account............................. | $11,434 | 10 |
| Dividends, Lime Rock National Bank, Providence....... | 63 | 00 |
| "         Blackstone Canal National Bank, Providence.. | 350 | 00 |
| "         Weybosset National Bank, Providence....... | 120 | 00 |
| "         Roger Williams National Bank, Providence... | 90 | 00 |
| "         Manufacturers National Bank, Providence.... | 360 | 00 |
| "         Savings Bank, Newport.................... | 719 | 53 |
| "         Commercial National Bank, Providence...... | .90 | 00 |
| "         Merchants National Bank, Providence....... | 192 | 00 |
| "         Rhode Island National Bank, Providence..... | 102 | 00 |
| "         Newport National Bank, Newport........... | 126 | 00 |
| | $13,646 | 63 |

The following Stocks constitute the

### Touro Jewish Synagogue Fund.

| | | |
|---|---|---|
| 30 shares Manufacturers National Bank, Providence..... | $3,277 | 25 |
| 32   "   Merchants National Bank, Providence......... | 1,788 | 27 |
| 20   "   Weybosset National Bank, Providence........ | 1,095 | 14 |
| 10   "   Roger Williams National Bank, Providence... | 841 | 50 |
| 24   "   Commercial National Bank, Providence...... | 1,301 | 00 |
| 200  "   Blackstone Canal National Bank, Providence.. | 5,106 | 90 |
| 18   "   Lime Rock National Bank, Providence....... | 926 | 40 |
| 51   "   Rhode Island National Bank, Providence..... | 1,806 | 53 |
| 21   "   Newport National Bank, Newport........... | 1,291 | 85 |
| | $17,434 | 84 |

### Funded Debt of the State.

| | | | | | | |
|---|---|---|---|---|---|---|
| Bonds issued October 1st, A. D. 1861, payable 1881..... | | | | | $500 | 00 |
| "      "   September 1st, " 1862, " 1882..... | | | | | 989,000 | 00 |
| "      "   April 1st,     " 1863, " 1883..... | | | | | 200,000 | 00 |
| "      "   July 1st,      " 1863, " 1893..... | | | | | 631,000 | 00 |
| "      "   August 1st,    " 1864, " 1894..... | | | | | 738,000 | 00 |
| | | | | | $2,558,500 | 00 |

*Sinking Funds, in account with Commissioners of Sinking Funds.*

| | | |
|---|---:|---:|
| To note of City of Providence, date June 16th, A. D. 1875, payable one year from date, at 5 per cent. per annum, interest payable semi-annually........ | $175,000 | 00 |
| To certificate of indebtedness State of Rhode Island, No. 120, par value. $5,000, purchased December 23, A. D. 1875, with interest from September 1, 1875.. | 5,400 | 00 |
| Deposited with Rhode Island Hospital Trust Co......... | 5,284 | 83 |
| | $185,684 | 83 |

*Credit.*

| | | |
|---|---:|---:|
| By General Treasurer's Checks........................ | $181,000 | 00 |
| By interest on deposits to October 31, 1875............ | 309 | 83 |
| By six months interest on City of Providence note...... | 4,375 | 00 |
| | $185,684 | 83 |

Respectfully submitted,

SAMUEL CLARK,

*General Treasurer.*

# REPORT

OF THE

# STATE AUDITOR,

MADE TO THE

# GENERAL ASSEMBLY,

AT ITS

## MAY SESSION, A. D. 1876.

PROVIDENCE:
PROVIDENCE PRESS COMPANY, PRINTERS TO THE STATE.
1876.

# REPORT.

State Auditor's Office,
Providence, R. I., May 28, 1876.

*To the Honorable General Assembly of the State of Rhode Island:*

In accordance with the requirements of our laws, I respectfully present the following report of the condition of the finances of the State on the 30th day of April, 1876, including receipts and expenditures for the fiscal year ending on that date, with a summary of the same and a transcript of all orders given upon the General Treasurer, naming the date, amount, to whom made payable, and appropriation to which the same was charged. I have found the proper vouchers for all payments made by the Treasurer, and find upon examination of the books and accounts of that office, the following results, viz.: Moneys in the treasury May 1st, 1875, $475,850.23; receipts from all sources during the year, $1,026,612.26; making the total resources, $1,502,462.49. The expenditures were $1,106,276.96, including $181,000.00 paid Commissioners of Sinking Funds, and $153,960.00 paid for interest upon the bonded debt, leaving a balance in the treasury April 30, 1876, of $396,185.53. The receipts from Institutions for Savings show an increase from previous year of $2,432.93; from State Insurance Companies, a small increase from previous year, while the sum realized from companies of other States, and foreign countries for taxes, licenses, fees, etc., is considerably less than received the previous year, owing mainly to a repeal of laws in the States of Pennsylvania and New York exacting licenses, fees, etc., for filing statements, and agencies, annual tax from companies of other States doing business therein, our receipts during two or three years past being augmented by collections under our retaliatory laws, having reference to the collection of the same charges that companies of our own State are required to meet for the privilege of transacting business in said States.

The receipts from all the courts during the past year, which includes fines, penalties, fees of clerks of the higher courts, and all other costs, show a decrease from the previous year of nearly fifteen thousand dollars, accounted for in part by the operation of the law repealing that portion of the fee table exacting certain fees in civil cases previously paid to clerks of the higher courts. I again respectfully recommend the re-enactment of said law in reference to the collection of said fees, believing it in consonance with real equity and justice towards the tax payers of our State.

The receipts from town councils during the past year, being mostly for liquor licenses, exceed those of the previous year in the sum of $70,524.51. The receipts for peddler's licenses, show an increase of $2,100.00. The aggregate of receipts from the regular sources from which our annual income is derived was $811,415.73; for the previous year, $763,276.07.

The sum total of payments for the actual expenses of the State government for the year ending April 30, 1876, excluding moneys expended for Providence County Court House, and land upon which it is located, New State Prison, sinking funds and interest on bonded debt was $456,633.84; for the previous year, $411,201.92, the increase arising from the sum paid for salaries to clerks of the higher courts and sheriffs of the several counties (excepting the county of Providence) being about $9,000. and an increase of $32,000. allowed to the Board of Charities and Corrections for support of the State Farm and other expenses. The funded debt of the State May 1st, 1876, was $2,563,500, less the sum of $181,000 paid to the Commissioners of Sinking Funds, June 1st, 1875, to be applied towards the extinguishing of this liability, incurred that our nation might live. The investments constituting the stock of the permanent school fund, are stocks in various National Banks of the State, costing $250,376.37, as shown by the following tables. A summary of receipts and expenditures for the past eight years is given, with payments on account of bonded debt and transcript of coupon and registered bonds outstanding, a bond of $5,000, issued Sept. 1, 1862, and payable in 1882 having been purchased by the Commissioners of Sinking Funds, Dec. 23, 1875, the account of Commisioners being appended to this report, The investment of Touro Jewish Synagogue Fund, with account of agent, is also given.

All of which is respectfully submitted,

JOEL M. SPENCER,
*State Auditor.*

---

### Summary of Receipts and Expenditures.

|  | RECEIPTS. | EXPENDITURES. |
|---|---|---|
| For year ending April 30, 1869 ....... | $714,434 66 | $634,165 13 |
| " " " 1870........ | 631,886 98 | 584,880 12 |
| " " " 1871........ | 703,215 65 | 742,618 84 |
| " " " 1872........ | 710,476 84 | 670,177 59 |
| " " " 1873........ | 700,132 59 | 709,500 55 |
| " " " 1874........ | 821,194 67 | 688,648 53 |
| " " " 1875........ | 763,276 07 | 581,731 92 |
| " " " 1876........ | 1,026,612 26 | 1,106,276 96 |
|  | $6,071,229 72 | $5,717,999 14 |

Add amount in Treasury, May 1, 1868.. 42,954 95.

$6,114,184 67
Deduct Expenditures................ 5,717,999 14

Balance in Treasury, April 30, 1876....$396,185 53

*Summary of Payments on account of Bonded Debt.*

| | AMOUNT REDEEMED. | INTEREST. |
|---|---|---|
| For year ending April 30, 1869........ | $132,000 00 | $182,384 27 |
| "          "      " 1870........ | 25,000 00 | 173,209 43 |
| "          "      " 1871........ | 127,000 00 | 183,170 54 |
| "          "      " 1872........ | 73,000 00 | 164,618 77 |
| "          "      " 1873........ | 75,000 00 | 159,249 16 |
| "          "      " 1874........ | 75,000 00 | 149,949 47 |
| "          "      " 1875........ | ......... | 160,530 00 |
| "          "      " 1876........ | 5,000 00 | 153,960 00 |
| Total........................... | $512,000 00 | $1,327,071 64 |

Coupon Bonds and Registered Certificates of Indebtedness are payable as follows:

| | |
|---|---|
| Bonds of October 1, 1861, payable 1881........... | $500 00 |
| "    Sept.   1, 1862,    "    1882............ | 989,000 00 |
| "    April   1, 1863,    "    1883............ | 200,000 00 |
| "    July    1, 1863,    "    1893............ | 631,000 00 |
| "    Aug.    1, 1864,    "    1894............ | 738,000 00 |
| | $2,558,500 00 |

The following investments constitute the Stock of the Permanent School Fund:

| | | |
|---|---|---|
| 2,000 | shares Globe National Bank, Providence.......... | $101,008 19 |
| 546 | "    American National Bank, Providence....... | 28,659 12 |
| 1,166 | "    National Bank of North America, Providence | 50,289 57 |
| 813 | "    National Bank of Commerce, Providence.... | 42,935 24 |
| 332 | "    Mechanics National Bank, Providence...... | 15,600 00 |
| 45 | "    Rhode Island National Bank, Providence.... | 1,534 25 |
| 7 | "    Newport National Bank, Newport.......... | 350 00 |
| | | $240,376 37 |

*Statement of School Fund subject to investment.*

| | | |
|---|---:|---:|
| Amount reported May 1875............................ | $14,766 | 14 |
| Auctioneers' duties to April 30, 1876................. | 1,754 | 51 |
| | $16,520 | 65 |

*Touro Fund in account with Agent.*

| | | |
|---|---:|---:|
| To paid Agent...................................... | $42 | 00 |
| Deposited in Savings Bank, Newport.................. | 10,822 | 48 |
| Deposited in Newport National Exchange Bank......... | 2,782 | 15 |
| | $13,646 | 63 |

*Credit.*

| | | |
|---|---:|---:|
| Balance from old account........................... | $11,434 | 10 |
| Dividends, Lime Rock National Bank, Providence....... | 63 | 00 |
| " Blackstone Canal National Bank, Providence.. | 350 | 00 |
| " Weybosset National Bank, Providence,....... | 120 | 00 |
| " Roger Williams National Bank, Providence.... | 90 | 00 |
| " Manufacturers National Bank, Providence..... | 360 | 00 |
| " Savings Bank, Newport.................·......... | 719 | 53 |
| " Commercial National Bank, Providence........ | 90 | 00 |
| " Merchants National Bank, Providence........ | 192 | 00 |
| " Rhode Island National Bank, Providence...... | 102 | 00 |
| " Newport National Bank, Newport............ | 126 | 00 |
| | $13,646 | 63 |

The following Stocks constitute the

*Touro Jewish Synagogue Fund.*

| | | | |
|---|---|---|---:|
| 30 shares | Manufacturers National Bank, Providence.... | $3,277 | 25 |
| 32 " | Merchants National Bank, Providence........ | 1,788 | 27 |
| 20 " | Weybosset National Bank, Providence....... | 1,095 | 14 |
| 10 " | Roger Williams National Bank, Providence.... | 841 | 50 |
| 24 " | Commercial National Bank, Providence....... | 1,301 | 00 |
| 200 " | Blackstone Canal National Bank, Providence.. | 5,106 | 90 |
| 18 " | Lime Rock National Bank, Providence....... | 926 | 40 |
| 51 " | Rhode Island National Bank, Providence...... | $1,806 | 53 |
| 21 " | Newport National Bank, Newport......... ... | 1,291 | 85 |
| | | $17,434 | 84 |

*Sinking Funds, in account with Commissioners of Sinking Funds.*

To note of City of Providence, date June 16th, A. D.
 1875, payable one year from date, at 5 per cent.
 per annum, interest payable semi-annually....... $175,000 00
To certificate of indebtedness State of Rhode Island, No.
 120, par value, $5,000, purchased December 23,
 A. D. 1875, with interest from September 1, 1875..   5,400 00
Deposited with Rhode Island Hospital Trust Co.........   5,284 83

                                                 $185,684 83

### Credit.

By General Treasurer's Checks....................... $181,000 00
By interest on deposits to October 31, 1875............     309 83
By six months interest on City of Providence note......   4,375 00

                                                 $185,684 83

### RECEIPTS.

| | |
|---|---:|
| State Tax............................................. | $492,586 10 |
| Institutions for Savings............................... | 115,356 10 |
| State Insurance Companies............................. | 18,224 09 |
| Foreign Insurance Companies.......................... | 30,913 94 |
| Supreme Court....................................... | 5,259 37 |
| Court of Common Pleas............................... | 8,963 84 |
| Justice Court, Providence............................. | 3,500 00 |
|        "      Newport............................... | 369 81 |
|        "      Pawtucket............................. | 958 20 |
|        "      Woonsocket............................ | 485 60 |
| Trial Justices......................................... | 843 18 |
| Auctioneers.......................................... | 1,754 51 |
| Town Councils,....................................... | 73,594 24 |
| Peddlers' Licenses.................................... | 5,800 00 |
| Dividend on School Fund.............................. | 20,033 50 |
| Civil Commisions .................................... | 1,730 00 |

| | |
|---|---|
| Charters | $4,050 00 |
| Jailers | 2,458 16 |
| Interest on Deposits of Revenue | 17,746 77 |
| General Statutes | 110 50 |
| Rhode Island Reports | 30 00 |
| Envelopes | 9 00 |
| Schedules | 31 80 |
| State Constables | 868 40 |
| Cove Lands | 200,000 00 |
| National Bank of North America | $15,196 53 |
| Oyster Lots | 5,800 00 |
| Miscellaneous | 439 12 |
| | $1,026,612 26 |
| Balance in Treasury, May 1, 1875 | $475,850 23 |
| Aggregate | $1,502,462 49 |

## PAYMENTS.

| | |
|---|---|
| Salaries | $71,065 24 |
| Expenses of the General Assembly | 19,936 99 |
| Supreme Court | 19,639 82 |
| Courts of Common Pleas | 26,213 43 |
| Trial Justices | 855 54 |
| Officers of Justice Courts | 4,986 66 |
| Witnesses of Justice Courts | 719 48 |
| Officers in Criminal Cases | 2,587 80 |
| Public Schools | 90,000 00 |
| State Normal School | 10,000 00 |
| "    "    "    (Mileage) | 1,340 20 |
| Teachers' Institutes | 805 00 |
| Reform School | 20,636 58 |
| Public Printing | 10,621 52 |
| Insane and other Dependent Persons | 9,607 02 |
| Militia and Military Affairs | 15,797 31 |
| Court Houses and Jails | 8,092 17 |
| Jails and Jailers | 1,829 59 |
| Fuel and Gas | 2,689 17 |
| Rents | 3,800 00 |

| | | |
|---|---:|---:|
| Law Library........................................ | 1,874 | 75 |
| State Library...................................... | 52 | 00 |
| Orders of the Governor............................. | 671 | 80 |
| Registration of Births, Marriages and Deaths........... | 350 | 00 |
| Narragansett Indians............................... | 300 | 00 |
| Care of State House, Providence...................... | 1,260 | 00 |
| "      "      "      Newport...................... | 300 | 00 |
| "      College Street Court Rooms ................... | $396 | 00 |
| "      Elizabeth Building, Providence................ | 335 | 73 |
| Interest on State Bonds............................. | 153,960 | 00 |
| Miscellaneous Expenses............................. | 5,749 | 85 |
| Accounts allowed by the General Assembly.............. | 6,169 | 45 |
| Inland Fisheries................................... | 1,137 | 23 |
| Charities and Corrections........................... | 97,000 | 00 |
| Evening Schools................................... | 1,968 | 00 |
| New State Prison................................... | 128,214 | 97 |
| Soldiers and Sailors' Testimonials.................... | 25 | 00 |
| Washington County Court House...................... | 3,920 | 45 |
| Providence County Court House................ ....... | 40,000 | 00 |
| State House and Jail, Newport........... ..... ......... | 600 | 08 |
| Aquidneck Agricultural Society....................... | 500 | 00 |
| Washington County "      "  ................... | 500 | 00 |
| R. I. Horticultural      "  ................... | 300 | 00 |
| Woonsocket Agricultural  "  ................... | 500 | 00 |
| R. I. Society for Encouragement of Domestic Industry.... | 1,000 | 00 |
| Justice Court Room, Woonsocket...................... | 150 | 00 |
| "      "      "      Pawtucket...................... | 500 | 00 |
| Decennial Census.................................. | 14,219 | 81 |
| Lectures and Addresses, Public Schools................ | 112 | 87 |
| Commissioners of Sinking Funds...................... | 181,000 | 00 |
| Town House Lot.................................... | 146,468 | 15 |
| Kent County Records............................... | 350 | 00 |
| National Centennial Exhibition....................... | 324 | 35 |
| Index to Charters and Resolutions.................... | 200 | 00 |
| Committee on exemption from Taxation................ | 68 | 00 |
| Newport Light Infantry..........................:..... | 125 | 00 |
| | $1,106,276 | 96 |
| Balance in Treasury, April 30, 1876.................. | 396,185 | 53 |
| | $1,502,462 | 49 |

A transcript of orders upon the General Treasurer, issued by the State Auditor, from May 1, 1875, to April 30, 1876, inclusive, with the amount, to whom made payable, and appropriation to which the same was charged.

## SALARIES.

### *Governor.*

1875.

| | | | |
|---|---|---|---|
| July 22. | Henry Howard | $69 | 64 |
| Sept. 17. | Henry Lippitt | 182 | 07 |
| Nov. 1. | Henry Lippitt | 250–00 | |

1876.

| | | | |
|---|---|---|---|
| Feb. 1. | Henry Lippitt | 250 | 00 |
| Apr. 29. | Henry Lippitt | 250 | 00 |

### *Lieutenant-Governor.*

1875.

| | | | |
|---|---|---|---|
| June 11. | Charles C. Van Zandt | $34 | 82 |
| Sept. 17. | Henry T. Sisson | 91 | 04 |
| Nov. 1. | Henry T. Sisson | 125 | 00 |

1876.

| | | | |
|---|---|---|---|
| Feb. 1. | Henry T. Sisson | 125 | 00 |
| Apr. 29. | Henry T. Sisson | 125 | 00 |

### *Secretary of State.*

1875.

| | | | |
|---|---|---|---|
| July 31. | Joshua M. Addeman | $625 | 00 |
| Nov. 1. | Joshua M. Addeman | 625 | 00 |

1876.

| | | | |
|---|---|---|---|
| Feb. 1. | Joshua M. Addeman | 625 | 00 |
| Apr. 29. | Joshua M. Addeman | 625 | 00 |

### *Attorney General.*

1875.

| | | | |
|---|---|---|---|
| July 31. | Willard Sayles | $625 | 00 |
| Nov. 1. | Willard Sayles | 625 | 00 |

1876.

| | | | |
|---|---|---|---|
| Feb. 1. | Willard Sayles | 625 | 00 |
| Apr. 29. | Willard Sayles | 625 | 00 |

### *General Treasurer.*

1875.

| | | | |
|---|---|---|---|
| Aug. 2. | Samuel Clark | $500 | 00 |
| Nov. 1. | Samuel Clark | 500 | 00 |

1876.
Feb.    1.    Samuel Clark................................$500 00
Apr.   29.    Samuel Clark................................ 500 00

### Chief Justice of Supreme Court.
1875.
Aug.    2.    Thomas Durfee...........................$1,050 00
Nov.    1.    Thomas Durfee........................... 1,125 00
1876.
Feb.    1.    Thomas Durfee........................... 1,125 00
Apr.   29.    Thomas Durfee........................... 1,125 00

### Associate Justices of Supreme Court.
1875.
July   31.    E. R. Potter................................ 1,000 00
Aug.    2.    Walter S. Burges........................... 1,000 00
        2.    Charles Matteson........................... 1,000 00
        2.    John H. Stiness............................. 1,000 00
Nov.    1.    E. R. Potter................................ 1,000 00
        1.    Walter S. Burges........................... 1,000 00
        1.    John H. Stiness............................. 1,000 00
        3.    Charles Matteson........................... 934 78
1876.
Feb.    1.    E. R. Potter................................$1,000 00
        1.    Walter S. Burges........................... 1,000 00
        1.    John H. Stiness............................. 1,000 00
        1.    Charles Matteson........................... 1,000 00
Apr.   29.    E. R. Potter................................ 1,000 00
    29.    Walter S. Burges........................... 1,000 00
    29.    John H. Stiness............................. 1,000 00
    29.    Charles Matteson........................... 1,000 00

### Retired Chief Justice, Supreme Court.
1875.
Aug.    2.    George A. Brayton..........................$875 00
Nov.    1.    George A. Brayton......................... 875 00
1876.
Feb.    1.    George A. Brayton ......................... 875 00
Apr.   29.    George A. Brayton......................... 875 00

### State Auditor.
1875.
Aug.    2.    Joel M. Spencer............................. 875 00
Nov.    1.    Joel M. Spencer............................. 875 00

1876.
Feb. 1. Joel M. Spencer.............................. 375 00
Apr. 29. Joel M. Spencer.............................. 375 00

### Commissioner Public Schools.

1875.
July 31. Thomas B. Stockwell.........................$625 00
Nov. 1. Thomas B. Stockwell......................... 625 00
1876.
Feb. 1. Thomas B. Stockwell......................... 625 00
Apr. 29. Thomas B. Stockwell......................... 625 00

### Insurance Commissioner.

1875.
Aug. 2. Joel M. Spencer..............................$250 00
Nov. 1. Joel M. Spencer.............................. 250 00
1876.
Feb. 1. Joel M. Spencer.............................. 250 00
Apr. 29. Joel M. Spencer.............................. 250 00

### Reporter of Decisions of Supreme Court.

1875.
May 15. Arnold Greene...............................$125 00
Nov. 3. Arnold Greene.............................. 250 00
1876.
Feb. 1. Arnold Greene............................... 125 00
Apr. 29. Arnold Greene.............................. 125 00

### Commissioners of Shell Fisheries.

1875.
July 31. James C. Collins............................$100 00
Aug. 2. George N. Bliss ............................. 100 00
      2. Thomas Arnold .............................. 100 00
Nov. 1. James C. Collins............................ 100 00
      1. George N. Bliss ............................. 100 00
      1. Thomas Arnold......................... ...... 100 00
1876.
Feb. 1. James C. Collins............................ 100 00
      1. George N. Bliss ............................. 100 00
      1. Thomas Arnold............................. 100 00
Apr. 29. James C. Collins............................ 100 00

1876.
Apr. 29.    George N. Bliss ............................$100 00
     29.    Thomas Arnold................................ 100 00

### Sheriff of Newport County.

1875.
Aug. 2.    George Manchester............................$100 00
Nov. 1.    George Manchester............................ 100 00
1876.
Feb. 1.    George Manchester............................ 100 00
Apr. 29.    George Manchester............................ 100 00

### Sheriff of Bristol County.

1875.
May 8.    Charles A. Greene............................ $11 24
Aug. 2.    Charles A. Greene............................ 100 00
Nov. 1.    Charles A. Greene. ........................... 100 00
1876.
Feb. 1.    Charles A. Greene............................. 100 00
Apr. 29.    Charles A. Greene............................ 100 00

### Sheriff of Washington County.

1875.
Aug. 14.    Henry Whipple................................$100 00
Nov. 1.    Henry Whipple................................ 100 00
1876.
Feb. 1.    Henry Whipple................................ 100 00
Apr. 29.    Henry Whipple ................................ 100 00

### Sheriff of Kent County.

1875.
Nov. 1.    Thomas J. Tilley.............................$140 22
1876.
Feb. 1.    Thomas J. Tilley.............................. 100 00
Apr. 29.    Thomas J. Tilley.............................. 100 00

### Clerk of Secretary of State.

1875.
Aug. 2.    Christopher Rhodes............................$250 00
Nov. 1.    Christopher Rhodes............................ 250 00

1876.

Feb. 1.  Christopher Rhodes.............................. 250 00
Apr. 29.  Christopher Rhodes.............................. 250 00

### Assistant Attorney General.

1875.

Aug. 2.  Ira O. Seamans..............................$375 00
Nov. 1.  Ira O. Seamans.............................. 375 00
1876.
Feb. 1.  Ira O. Seamans.............................. 375 00
Apr. 29.  Ira O. Seamans.............................. 375 00

### Railroad Commissioner.

1875.

Aug. 2.  Henry Staples..............................$125 00
Nov. 1.  Henry Staples.............................. 125 00
1876.
Feb. 1.  Henry Staples.............................. 125 00
Apr. 29.  Henry Staples.............................. 125 00

### Clerk of Supreme Court, Providence.

1875.

May 28.  Charles Blake..............................$2,071 63
Aug. 13.  Charles Blake.............................. 625 00
Nov. 1.  Charles Blake.............................. 625 00
1876.
Feb. 1.  Charles Blake.............................. 625 00
Apr. 29.  Charles Blake.............................. 625 00

### Assistant Clerk of Supreme Court, Providence.

1875.

July 31.  Augustus S. Miller ..........................$300 00
Nov. 3.  Augustus S. Miller.......................... 300 00
1876.
Feb. 1.  Augustus S. Miller.......................... 300 00
Apr. 29.  Augustus S. Miller.......................... 300 00

### Clerk of Court of Common Pleas, Providence.

1875.

June 8.  Daniel R. Ballou.............................. 210 60
Aug. 2.  George E. Webster.............................. 414 41
Nov. 1.  George E. Webster.............................. 625 00

1876.
Feb.  1.  George E. Webster................................. 625 00
Apr. 29.  George E. Webster................................. 625 00

*Assistant Clerk of Court of Common Pleas, Providence.*

1875.
July 31.  Franklin P. Owen.................................$198 92
Aug.  2.  'George E. Webster .............................. 101 08
Nov.  3.  Franklin P. Owen................................ 300 00
1876.
Feb.  1.  Franklin P. Owen................................ 300 00
Apr. 29.  Franklin P. Owen................................ 300 00

*Clerk of Supreme Court and Court of Common Pleas, Newport.*

1875.
Aug.  6.  Thomas W. Wood................................. 224 72
Nov.  3.  Thomas W. Wood................................. 325 00
1876.
Feb.  1.  Thomas W. Wood................................. 325 00
Apr. 29.  Thomas W. Wood........ ..................... 325 00

*Clerk of Supreme Court and Court of Common Pleas, Bristol County.*

1875.
Aug.  2.  Charles A. Waldron............................. 100 00
Nov.  1.  Charles A. Waldron. ........................... 100 00
1876.
Feb.  1.  Charles A. Waldron............................. 100 00
Apr. 29.  Charles A. Waldron............................. 100 00

*Clerk of Supreme Court, Washington County.*

1872.
Aug.  6.  John G. Clarke...................................$78 26
Nov.  1.  John G. Clarke................................. 75 00
1876.
Feb.  1.  John G. Clarke................................. 75 00
Apr. 29.  John G. Clarke................................. 75 00

*Clerk of Court of Common Pleas, Washington County.*

1875.
June 10.  Benjamin W. Case.............................. $11 67
Dec. 17.  Benjamin W. Case.............................. 141 59

1876.

| | | | |
|---|---|---|---|
| Feb. | 1. | Benjamin W. Case............................ | $75 00 |
| Apr. | 29. | Benjamin W. Case............................ | 75 00 |

### Clerk of Supreme Court and Court of Common Pleas, Kent County.

1875.

| | | | |
|---|---|---|---|
| Aug. | 3. | A. R. Greene................................. | $156 52 |
| Nov. | 1. | A. R. Greene................................. | 150 00 |

1876.

| | | | |
|---|---|---|---|
| Feb. | 1. | A. R. Greene................................. | 150 00 |
| Apr. | 29. | A. R. Greene................................. | 150 00 |

### Crier of Courts, Providence County.

1875.

| | | | |
|---|---|---|---|
| July | 31. | James W. Munroe............................ | $150 00 |
| Nov. | 1. | James W. Munroe............................ | 150 00 |

1876.

| | | | |
|---|---|---|---|
| Feb. | 1. | James W. Munroe............................ | 150 00 |
| Apr. | 29. | James W. Munroe............................ | 150 00 |

### Librarian of Law Library.

1875.

| | | | |
|---|---|---|---|
| July | 31. | Daniel W. Fink ............................. | $75 00 |
| Nov. | 1. | Daniel W. Fink............................. | 75 00 |

1876.

| | | | |
|---|---|---|---|
| Feb. | 1. | Daniel W. Fink............................. | 75 00 |
| Apr. | 29. | Daniel W. Fink............................. | 75 00 |

### Adjutant General.

1875.

| | | | |
|---|---|---|---|
| Aug. | 2. | Heber Le Favour............................ | $150 00 |
| Nov. | 1. | Heber Le Favour............................ | 150 00 |

1876.

| | | | |
|---|---|---|---|
| Feb. | 1. | Heber Le Favour............................ | 150 00 |
| Apr. | 29. | Heber Le Favour ........................... | 150 00 |

### Quartermaster General.

1875.

| | | | |
|---|---|---|---|
| Aug. | 2. | Charles R. Dennis........................... | $100 00 |
| Nov. | 1. | Charles R. Dennis........................... | 100 00 |

2

1872.

Feb.  1.   Charles R. Dennis...............................$100 00
Apr. 29.   Charles R. Dennis.................. ............ 100 00

### Paymaster General.

1875.

Aug.  2.   Jabez C. Knight.................................$50 00
Nov.  1.   Jabez C. Knight............................... 50 00
1876.
Feb.  1.   Jabez C. Knight............................... 50 00
Apr. 29.   Jabez C. Knight............................... 50 00

### Justice Court, Providence.

1875.

Aug.  2.   John R. Randolph.............................$500 00
Nov.  1.   John R. Randolph............................. 500 00
1876.
Feb.  1.   John R. Randolph............................. 500 00
Apr. 29.   John R. Randolph............................. 500 00

### Clerk of Justice Court, Providence.

1875.

June 25.   Ervin T. Case..........,..................$1,500 00
1876.     -
Apr. 29.   Ervin T. Case...............,............. 1,500 00

### Justice Court, Newport.

1875.

Aug.  2.   James G. Topham, Trial Justice.................$175 00
      2.   Henry N. Ward, Clerk.......................... 175 00
      6.   Henry N. Ward, Clerk  ....,................... 15 76
Nov.  1.   James G. Topham, Trial Justice................ 175 00
      1.   Henry N. Ward, Clerk.......................... 200 00
1876.
Feb.  1.   James G. Topham, Trial Justice................ 175 00
      1.   Henry N. Ward, Clerk.......................... 200 00
Apr. 29.   James G. Topham, Trial Justice................ 175 00
     29.   Henry N. Ward, Clerk.......................... 200 00

### Justice Court, Woonsocket.

1875.

| | | | | |
|---|---|---|---|---|
| Aug. | 2. | George A. Wilbur, Trial Justice | $250 | 00 |
| | 2. | William H. Jenckes, Clerk | 200 | 00 |
| Nov. | 1. | George A. Wilbur, Trial Justice | 250 | 00 |
| | 1. | William H. Jenckes, Clerk | 200 | 00 |

1876.

| | | | | |
|---|---|---|---|---|
| Feb. | 1. | George A. Wilbur, Trial Justice | 250 | 00 |
| Apr. | 17. | William H. Jenckes, Clerk | 200 | 00 |
| | 29. | George A. Wilbur, Trial Justice | 250 | 00 |
| | 29. | William H. Jenckes, Clerk | 200 | 00 |

### Justice Court, Pawtucket.

1875.

| | | | | |
|---|---|---|---|---|
| May | 17. | Isaac Shove, Trial Justice | $510 | 86 |
| June | 30. | W. W. Eddy, Clerk | 438 | 23 |
| Nov. | 22. | Isaac Shove, Trial Justice | 400 | 00 |

1876.

| | | | | |
|---|---|---|---|---|
| Apr. | 29. | Isaac Shove, Trial Justice | 600 | 00 |
| | 29. | W. W. Eddy, Clerk | 800 | 00 |

### State Constable.

1875.

| | | | | |
|---|---|---|---|---|
| July | 8. | Charles T. Northup | $304 | 86 |

### Deputy State Constables.

1875.

| | | | | |
|---|---|---|---|---|
| June | 30. | Elisha C. Clarke, order of John P. Case | $228 | 26 |
| July | 6. | Samuel B. M. Read | 228 | 26 |
| | 7. | Charles N. Gifford | 228 | 26 |
| | 7. | James Wilson | 228 | 26 |
| | 13. | Nathaniel S. Greene | 228 | 26 |
| Aug. | 6. | Jeremiah Peabody | 228 | 26 |

1876.

| | | | | |
|---|---|---|---|---|
| Feb. | 20. | George W. Burlingame | 228 | 26 |

Aggregate of Salaries...........................$71,065 24

## GENERAL ASSEMBLY.

### *Pay and Mileage.*

1875.

| | | | | |
|---|---|---|---|---|
| June 28. | John A. Adams, | May Session | .................... | $35 80 |
| " | Peleg Arnold, | " | .................... | 43 00 |
| " | Thomas G. Carr, | " | .................... | 52 50 |
| " | William G. Caswell, | " | .................... | 62 20 |
| " | Robert S. Chase, | " | .................... | 49 24 |
| " | Nathaniel Church, | " | .................... | 50 20 |
| " | William L. Clarke, | " | .................... | 71 80 |
| " | Francis Colwell, | " | .................... | 32 44 |
| " | James S. Cook, | " | .................... | 50 20 |
| " | Samuel H. Cross, | " | .................... | 68 60 |
| " | William Elsbree, | " | .................... | 38 20 |
| " | Samuel Farnum, | " | .................... | 39 00 |
| " | John Hoxie, | " | .................... | 58 20 |
| " | Samuel A. Irons, | " | .................... | 34 20 |
| " | George C. James, | " | .................... | 60 60 |
| " | Alfred W. Kenyon, | " | .................... | 57 40 |
| " | Job Kenyon, | " | .................... | 40 60 |
| " | Timothy A. Leonard, | " | .................... | 35 00 |
| " | A. B. Lewis, | " | .................... | 43 80 |
| " | John T. Lewis, | " | .................... | 49 40 |
| " | Ray S. Littlefield, | " | .................... | 70 20 |
| " | Henry H. Luther, | " | .................... | 41 40 |
| " | Daniel W. Lyman, | " | .................... | 35 00 |
| " | Henry B. Metcalf, | " | .................... | 39 80 |
| " | Joseph Osborn, | " | .................... | 45 24 |
| " | Charles H. Page, | " | .................... | 41 40 |
| " | Joshua Paine, | " | .................... | 47 80 |
| " | Samuel Powel, | " | .................... | 40 36 |
| " | John Remington, | " | .................... | 49 40 |
| " | Harrison H. Richardson, | " | .................... | 39 80 |
| " | W. F. Sayles, | " | .................... | 35 00 |
| " | W. H. Seagrave, | " | .................... | 51 32 |
| " | Alfred Sisson, | " | .................... | 55 80 |
| " | Ziba O. Slocum, | " | .................... | 50 20 |
| " | John Turner, | " | .................... | 43 80 |

1875.

| | | | | |
|---|---|---|---|---|
| June 28, | N. T. Verry, | May Session | ................. | $45 40 |
| " | E. L. Freeman, | " | ................. | 35 80 |
| " | Elisha S. Aldrich, | " | ................. | 88 20 |
| " | N. W. Aldrich, | .. | ................. | 32 44 |
| " | William H. Ashurst, | " | ................. | 46 36 |
| " | Warren J. Ballou, | " | ................. | 42 20 |
| " | J. B. Barnaby, | .. | ................. | 82 44 |
| " | John A Bennett, | " | ................. | 45 40 |
| " | Grenville R. Brown, | " | ................. | 35 80 |
| " | Richmond Brownell, | " | ................. | 56 60 |
| " | George L. Clarke, | " | ................. | 32 44 |
| " | John G. Clarke, | .. | ................. | 55 80 |
| " | George Lewis Cooke, | " | ................. | 39 80 |
| " | James M. Cook, | .. | ................. | 45 40 |
| " | Charles Cross, | .. | ................. | 67 80 |
| " | Edwin Darling | .. | ................. | 35 80 |
| " | Thomas Davis, | .. | ................. | 33 08 |
| " | James C. Dexter, | " | ................. | 36 60 |
| " | Joseph Dispeau, | .. | ................. | 35 80 |
| " | Nathan F. Dixon, | " | ................. | 63. 80 |
| " | Joshua T. Dodge, | " | ................. | 70 20 |
| " | Joseph Eaton, Jr., | " | ................. | 60 60 |
| " | Nathaniel Elliott, | " | ................. | 45 40 |
| " | Henry S. Fairbanks, | " | ................. | 35 80 |
| " | George S. Fales, | .. | ................. | 35 80 |
| " | C. B. Farnsworth, | " | ................. | 35 80 |
| " | Henry H. Fay, | .. | ................. | 46 36 |
| " | Thomas N. Fry, | .. | ................. | 41 24 |
| " | William E. Gilmore, | " | ................. | 35 80 |
| " | Almon K. Goodwin, | " | ................. | 35 80 |
| " | Allen Greene, | " | ................. | 32 44 |
| " | Edward N. Hammond, | " | ................. | 52 60 |
| " | Cyrus Harris, | " | ................. | 41 40 |
| " | Albert F. Hill, | .. | ................. | 39 80 |
| " | William Hill, | .. | ................. | 35 80 |
| " | Edmund S. Hopkins, | " | ................. | 32 44 |
| " | William E. Hazard, | " | ................. | 45 40 |
| " | Benjamin Kenyon, | " | ................. | 67 00 |
| " | Nathan H. Langworthy, | " | ................. | 63 80 |
| " | Andrew H. Manchester, | " | ................. | 48 12 |

1875.

| | | | | |
|---|---|---|---|---:|
| June 28. | David Mathewson, May Session | .................. | | $50 20 |
| " | Alvord O. Miles, | " | .................. | 84 20 |
| " | Robert I. Moore, | " | .................. | 55 80 |
| " | Jacob Morse, | -- | .................. | 46 20 |
| " | Nathaniel Peckham, | " | .................. | 50 20 |
| " | Thomas C. Peckham, | " | .................. | 46 20 |
| " | George H. Pettis, | " | .................. | 82 44 |
| " | Thomas E. Phillips, | " | .................. | 48 60 |
| " | Thomas C. Peirce, | " | .................. | 48 60 |
| " | Andrew Potter, | -- | .................. | 43 00 |
| " | Isaac M. Potter, | " | .................. | 82 44 |
| " | William H. Reynolds, | " | .................. | 82 44 |
| " | Horatio Rogers, | " | .................. | 82 44 |
| " | W. P. Sheffield, | -- | .................. | 86 20 |
| " | Jeremiah Sheldon, | " | .................. | 47 80 |
| " | Augustus P. Sherman, | " | .................. | 46 36 |
| " | Jonathan A. Sisson, | " | .................. | 53 40 |
| " | Henry Smith, | -- | .................. | 89 48 |
| " | Martin S. Smith, | -- | .................. | 37 40 |
| " | Henry J. Spooner, | " | .................. | 82 44 |
| " | George A. Spink, | " | .................. | 89 00 |
| " | Benjamin Sweet, | -- | .................. | 85 80 |
| " | John Tillinghast, | " | .................. | 47 80 |
| " | William B. Tillinghast, | " | .................. | 67 80 |
| " | William C. Townsend, | " | .................. | 46 36 |
| " | N. Van Slyck, | " | .................. | 82 44 |
| " | William T. C. Wardwell, | " | .................. | 43 80 |
| " | Andrew B. Whipple, | " | .................. | 89 80 |
| " | George W. White, | " | .................. | 86 60 |
| " | Henry Whitman, | -- | .................. | 85 80 |
| " | Alfred A. Williams, | " | .................. | 86 60 |
| " | Isaac F. Williams, | " | .................. | 43 80 |
| " | John A. Wood, | -- | .................. | 48 60 |

1876.

| | | | | |
|---|---|---|---|---:|
| April 20. | John A. Adams, | January Session, | .............. | 79 20 |
| " | Peleg Arnold, | " | .............. | 84 96 |
| " | Thomas G. Carr, | " | .............. | 100 82 |
| " | W. G. Caswell, | | .............. | 100 82 |
| " | Robert S. Chase, | | .............. | 97 76 |

1876.

| | | | |
|---|---|---|---|
| April 20 | Nathaniel Church, | January Session............$104 80 |
| " | W. L. Clark, | " | ............ 108 00 |
| " | Francis Colwell, | " | ............ 76 64 |
| " | James S. Cook, | -- | ............ 90 72 |
| " | Samuel H. Cross, | •• | ........ ..... 106 08 |
| " | William Elsbree, | -- | ............ 81 12 |
| " | Samuel Farnum, | •• | ............ 81 76 |
| " | John Hoxie, | .. | ............ 97 12 |
| " | Samuel A. Irons, | •• | ............ 77 92 |
| " | George C. James, | .. | ............ 99 04 |
| " | Alfred W. Kenyon, | | ............ 96 48 |
| " | Job Kenyon, | -- | ............ 83 04 |
| " | Timothy A. Leonard, | -- | ............ 78 56 |
| " | A. B. Lewis, | •• | ............ 85 60 |
| " | John T. Lewis, | -- | ............ 90 08 |
| " | Ray S. Littlefield, | -- | ............ 114 40 |
| " | Henry H. Luther, | -- | ............ 83 04 |
| " | Daniel W. Lyman, | -- | ............ 78 56 |
| " | Henry B. Metcalf, | -- | ............ 82 40 |
| " | Joseph Osborn, | •• | ............ 92 00 |
| " | Charles H. Page, | | ............ 83 68 |
| " | Joshua Paine, | •• | ............ 88 80 |
| " | Samuel Powel, | -- | ............ 61 20 |
| " | John Remington, | | ............ 90 08 |
| " | Harrison H. Richardson, | " | ............ 82 40 |
| " | W. H. Seagrave, | .. | ............ 92 00 |
| " | Alfred Sisson, | .. | ............ 98 40 |
| " | Ziba O. Slocum, | -- | ............ 90 72 |
| " | John Turner, | -- | ............ 85 60 |
| " | N. T. Verry, | -- | ............ 86 88 |
| " | Edward L. Freeman, | | ............ 79 20 |
| " | Elisha S. Aldrich, | | ............ 81 12 |
| " | Nelson W. Aldrich, | | ............ 76 64 |
| " | Warren J. Ballou, | | ............ 72 04 |
| " | J. B. Barnaby, | | ............ 76 64 |
| " | John A. Bennett, | -- | ............ 86 88 |
| " | Grenville R. Brown, | -- | ............ 79 84 |
| " | Richmond Brownell, | | ............ 101 60 |
| " | George L. Clarke, | -- | ............ 76 64 |
| " | John G. Clarke, | .. | ............ 95 20 |

1876.

| | | | | |
|---|---|---|---|---|
| April 20. | George Lewis Cooke, January Session | | ............ | $80 40 |
| " | James M. Cook, | " | ............ | 86 88 |
| " | Charles Cross, | " | ............ | 104 80 |
| " | Edwin Darling, | -- | ............ | 79 20 |
| " | Thomas Davis, | -- . | ............ | 76 64 |
| " | James C. Dexter, | -- | ............ | 79 20 |
| " | J. E. Dispeau, | -- | ............ | 79 20 |
| " | Nathan F. Dixon, | -- | ............ | 101 60 |
| " | Joshua T. Dodge, | -- | ............ | 114 40 |
| " | Joseph Eaton, Jr., | -- | ............ | 100 96 |
| " | Nathaniel Elliott, | -- | ............ | 86 24 |
| " | Henry S. Fairbanks, | -- | ............ | 79 20 |
| " | George S. Fales, | -- | ............ | 79 20 |
| " | C. B. Farnsworth, | -- | ............ | 79 20 |
| " | Henry H. Fay, | -- | ............ | 96 48 |
| " | Thomas N. Fry, | -- | ............ | 89 44 |
| " | W. E. Gilmore, | -- | ............ | 79 20 |
| " | Almond K. Goodwin, | -- | ............ | 79 20 |
| " | Allen Greene, | -- | ............ | 76 64 |
| " | Edward N. Hammond, | " | ............ | 100 96 |
| " | Cyrus Harris, | | ............ | 83 68 |
| " | Albert F. Hill, | | ............ | 84 32 |
| " | William Hill, | -- | ............ | 79 84 |
| " | Edmund S. Hopkins, | | ............ | 76 64 |
| " | W. E. Hubbard, | -- | ............ | 86 88 |
| " | Benjamin Kenyon, | | ............ | 104 16 |
| " | N. H. Langworthy, | -- | ............ | 104 80 |
| " | Andrew H. Manchester, | " | ............ | 94 56 |
| " | David Mathewson, | -- | ............ | 90 08 |
| " | Alvord O. Miles, | -- | ............ | 78 56 |
| " | Robert I. Moore, | | ............ | 95 20 |
| " | Jacob Morse, | | ............ | 87 52 |
| " | Nathaniel Peckham, | -- | ............ | 98 40 |
| " | Thomas C. Peckham, | -- | ............ | 87 52 |
| " | George H. Pettis, | -- | ............ | 76 64 |
| " | Thomas E. Phillips, | -- | ............ | 89 44 |
| " | Thomas C. Peirce, | -- | ............ | 95 20 |
| " | Andrew Potter, | -- | ............ | 84 96 |
| " | Isaac M. Potter, | -- | ............ | 76 64 |

1876.

| | | | |
|---|---|---|---|
| April 20. | Fred. A. Pratt, | January Session | $96 48 |
| " | William H. Reynolds, | " | 88 64 |
| " | Horatio Rogers, | " | 46 32 |
| " | W. P. Shetfield, | | 94 48 |
| " | Jeremiah Sheldon, | | 90 72 |
| " | Augustus P. Sherman, | " | 96 48 |
| " | Jonathan A. Sisson, | | 101 60 |
| " | Henry Smith, | | 82 40 |
| " | Martin S Smith, | | 85 60 |
| " | Henry J. Spooner, | | 76 64 |
| " | George A. Spink, | | 81 76 |
| " | Benjamin Sweet, | | 79 20 |
| " | John Tillinghast, | | 88 80 |
| " | William B. Tillinghast, | " | 105 44 |
| " | William C. Towrsend, | " | 96 48 |
| " | Nicholas Van Slyck, | | 76 64 |
| " | W. T. C. Wardwell, | | 85 60 |
| " | Andrew B. Whipple, | | 81 76 |
| " | George W. White, | | 79 84 |
| " | Henry Whitman, | | 79 20 |
| " | Alfred A. Williams, | | 79 84 |
| " | I. F. Williams, | | 85 60 |
| " | John A. Wood, | | 90 08 |

Total............................................$14,116 66

*Clerks, (General Assembly.)*

1875.

| | | | |
|---|---|---|---|
| June 28. | Walter B. Vincent, | May Session | $15 00 |
| " | Nathaniel P. S. Thomas, | " | 155 00 |
| " | Charles F. Ballou, | " | 155 00 |
| " | Henry T. Braman, | | 155 00 |
| " | Nathan F. Dixon, Jr., | " | 155 00 |

1876.

| | | | |
|---|---|---|---|
| April 22. | Nathaniel P. S. Thomas, January Session | | 380 00 |
| " | Charles F. Ballou, | " | 380 00 |
| " | Henry T. Braman, | " | 380 00 |
| " | Nathan F. Dixon, Jr., | | 380 00 |

Total......................................$2155 00

#### Officers, (*General Assembly.*)

1875.

| | | | |
|---|---|---|---:|
| June 28. | Christopher Holden, May Session | ................ | $63 00 |
| " | Lyman Upham, | " ................ | 42 00 |
| " | Phineas Fairbrother, | " ................ | 42 00 |
| " | J. Aborn Gardiner, | " ................ | 42 00 |
| " | Fred. N. Goff, | -- ................ | 42 00 |
| " | George Manchester, | " ................ | 18 00 |
| " | Henry N. Ward, | -- ................ | 12 00 |
| " | Edward S. Hammond, | " ................ | 12 00 |

1876.

| | | | |
|---|---|---|---:|
| April 22. | Phineas Fairbrother, January Session | .............. | 152 00 |
| " | Lyman Upham, | " ............. | 152 00 |
| " | J. Aborn Gardiner, | " ............. | 152 00 |
| " | Fred. N. Goff, | -- ............. | 152 00 |
| " | Christopher Holden, | -- ............. | 228 00 |

Total........................................$1,109 00

#### Pages, (*General Assembly.*)

1875.

| | | | |
|---|---|---|---:|
| June 27. | Salmon W. Davis, May Session | ................. | $42 00 |
| " | Richard S. Devlin, | " ................. | 42 00 |
| " | Edward J. Holden, | " ................. | 42 00 |
| " | H. A. Olney, | -- ................. | 42 00 |
| " | Clarence Kingsbury, | " ................. | 42 00 |
| " | Sullivan Ballou, | -- ................. | 42 00 |
| June 28. | C. T. Griffiths, | -- ................. | 12 00 |
| " | Herbert Bliss, | -- ................. | 12 00 |
| " | Benjamin C. Weaver, | " ................. | 12 00 |
| " | B. E. Remington Ward, | " ................. | 12 00 |
| " | John R. Ward, | " ................. | 12 00 |
| " | Thomas W. Wood, Jr., | " ................. | 12 00 |

1876.

| | | | |
|---|---|---|---:|
| April 22. | Edwin J. Holden, January Session | .............. | 152 00 |
| " | S. Arnold Aplin, Jr., | " ............. | 152 00 |
| " | Hendricks A. Olney, | " ............. | 152 00 |
| " | Clarence Kingsbury | -- ............. | 152 00 |

1876.
April 22.  Sullivan Ballou,      January Session............$152 00
    "     Salmon W. Davis,      "          ............ 152 00

      Total.......................................$1,236 00

*Stationery and Newspapers, (General Assembly.)*

1875.
July 9.  Tillinghast & Mason News Co., May Session....... $161 34
1876.
April 28.  Tillinghast & Mason News Co., January Session...1,158 99

      Total .......................................$1,320 33

      Total Expenses of General Assembly.............$19,936 99

## JUDICIAL EXPENSES.

### *Clerks.*

1875.
May 31.  A. R. Greene, S. C., Kent........................$135 20
June 4.  Thomas W. Wood, C. C. P., Newport............. 46 15
  " 22.  A. R. Greene,       "     Kent................ 139 30
July 2.  John G. Clarke, S. C., Washington ............... 66 60

      Total.......................................$387 25

### *Jurors.*

1875.
May 4.  Benjamin W. Case, C. C. P., Washington......... $500 00
  " 12.  Thomas W. Wood,      "     Newport............ 300 00
  " 31.  Charles Blake,  S. C., Providence................ 3.000 00
  " 31.  A. R. Greene,     "    Kent.  .................... 155 20
June 10.  George E. Webster, C. C. P., Providence......... 2,000 00
  " 22.  Charles Blake, S. C., Providence ................ 45 70
July 24.  Nathaniel D. Thurber, C. C. P., Providence....... 12 70
Aug. 12.  John G. Clarke, S. C., Washington.............. 500 00
  " 23.  A. R. Greene,      "    Kent.................... 600 00
Sept. 10.  George F. Webster, C. C. P., Providence.......... 1,800 00
  " 11.  C. A. Waldron,  S. C., Bristol.................... 400 00
  " 16.  Thomas W. Wood,  "    Newport............... 800 00
Oct. 11.  A. R. Greene, C. C. P., Kent.................... 250 00

1875.

| | | | |
|---|---|---|---:|
| Oct. 15. | Thomas W. Wood, S. C., Newport.............. | | $28 60 |
| " 22. | C A. Waldron, C. C. P., Bristol................. | | 200 00 |
| " 29. | B. W. Case,       "       Washington............ | | 500 00 |
| Nov. 10. | Thomas W. Wood, "       Newport............... | | 375 00 |
| " 16. | Charles Blake, S. C., Providence................ | | 2,500 00 |
| Dec. 1. | Benjamin W. Case, C. C. P., Washington......... | | 562 70 |
| " 9. | John G. Clarke, S. C., Washington.............. | | 400 00 |
| " 15. | George E. Webster, C. C. P., Providence.......... | | 2,000 00 |

1876.

| | | | |
|---|---|---|---:|
| Jan. 3. | Charles Blake, S. C., Providence................ | | 2,500 00 |
| Feb. 14. | George E. Webster, C. C. P., Providence......... | | 3,000 00 |
| " 18. | John G. Clarke, S. C., Washington.............. | | 500 00 |
| Mar. 1. | John G. Clarke,    "    Washington............... | | 87 30 |
| " 3. | C. A. Waldron,     "    Bristol................... | | 400 00 |
| " 11. | A. R. Greene,      "    Kent..................... | | 600 00 |
| " 13. | George E. Webster, C. C. P., Providence.......... | | 1,500 00 |
| " 15. | Thomas W. Wood, S. C., Newport............... | | 500 00 |
| " 30. | D. R. Kenyon,      "    Washington............. | | 1 80 |
| " 30. | H. A. Philips,      "    Washington............. | | 1 80 |
| Apr. 7. | A. R. Greene, C. C. P., Kent.................... | | 300 00 |
| " 7. | Charles Blake, S. C., Providence................ | | 300 00 |
| " 28. | C. A. Waldron, C. C. P., Bristol............... | | 250 00 |

Total........................................$27,370 80

*Officers of Supreme Court and Court of Common Pleas.*

1875.

| | | | | |
|---|---|---|---|---:|
| May 3. | Christopher Holden, S. C., | Providence.......... | | $99 00 |
| " | Lyman Upham, | " | " | 22 00 |
| " | Roger W. Potter, | " | " | 66 00 |
| " | P. Fairbrother, | " | " | 22 00 |
| May 14. | W. D. Lake, | C. C. P., | Newport, estimate..... | 50 00 |
| " | Henry Whipple, | " | Washington, " ..... | 50 00 |
| June 1. | Michael Maloney, | " | Providence........ | 45 70 |
| June 2. | Christopher Holden, S. C., Providence............ | | | 66 00 |
| " | Roger W. Potter, | " | " | 44 00 |
| " | J. A. Gardiner, | " | " | 44 00 |
| " | Lyman Upham, | -- | | 44 00 |
| " | P. Fairbrother, | -- | | 44 00 |

1875.

| | | | | |
|---|---|---|---|---|
| June 2. | Edward S. Hammond, C. C. P., Newport.......... | | | $6 00 |
| June 4. | C. H. Martin, C. C. P., Kent.................... | | | 9 90 |
| " | Patrick Eagan, " Providence.............. | | | 2 00 |
| June 7. | Joseph Arnold, S. C., Kent................ ......... | | | 20 00 |
| " | Lowell Pitcher, " " .................... | | | 20 00 |
| " | Joatham S. Smith, " " .................... | | | 30 50 |
| " | C. A. Greene, C. C. P., Bristol................. | | | 17 70 |
| " | H. B. Macomber, " " ............... | | | 4 00 |
| " | John N. Miller, " " ............... | | | 4 00 |
| " | William Bradford, " -- ............... | | | 4 00 |
| " | J. Hoard, Jr., -- ............... | | | 7 60 |
| " | L. B. Bosworth, " " ............... | | | 14 70 |
| June 16. | George Manchester, " Newport................. | | | 15 40 |
| " | James G. Topham, " " ............... | | | 6 00 |
| " | Henry N. Ward, " " ............... | | | 8 00 |
| " | I. R. Romes, -- -- ............... | | | 6 00 |
| " | W. L. Riley, -- -- ............... | | | 6 00 |
| " | Frank G. Harris, " " ............... | | | 2 00 |
| " | John Flynn, -- -- ............... | | | 3 25 |
| " | David Case, -- -- ............... | | | 50 |
| " | Alexander Steele, " " ............... | | | 10 00 |
| " | Stephen G. Chace, " " ............... | | | 3 55 |
| " | Benjamin Holland, " " ............... | | | 50 |
| " | I. B. Briggs, -- " ............... | | | 16 50 |
| " | A. W. Colvin, -- " ............... | | | 30 00 |
| June 19. | J. Aborn Gardiner, " Providence, estimate.... | | | 200 00 |
| June 24. | Joseph Arnold, " Kent................. | | | 6 00 |
| June 25, | George W. Burlingame, S. C. and C. C. P., Kent... | | | 39 00 |
| July 2. | Christopher Holden, C. C. P., Providence......... | | | 60 00 |
| " | J. Aborn Gardiner, " " ........... | | | 22 00 |
| " | O. C. Goodell, -- " ........... | | | 40 00 |
| " | S. G. Benedict, " -- ........... | | | 32 00 |
| " | M. H. Shattuck, " -- ........... | | | 38 00 |
| July 6. | Christopher Holden, S. C., " ........... | | | 72 00 |
| " | Roger W. Potter, " -- ........... | | | 44 00 |
| " | P. Fairbrother, " -- ........... | | | 8 00 |
| " | J. Aborn Gardiner, " -- ........... | | | 2 00 |
| " | Lyman Upham, -- -- ........... | | | 10 00 |
| " | O. C. Goodell, -- ........... | | | 6 00 |
| " | M. H. Shattuck, " -- ........... | | | 6 00 |

1875.

| | | | |
|---|---|---|---:|
| July 7. | John A. Ward, C. C. P., Providence | | $10 00 |
| July 9. | Oliver O. Colvin, S. C., Kent | | 6 70 |
| " | Lowell Pitcher, S. C., and C. C. P., Kent | | 14 80 |
| " | J. S. Smith, C. C. P., Kent | | 10 00 |
| July 10. | A. W. Colvin, S. C., and C. C. P., Kent | | 18 00 |
| " | David R. Kenyon, S. C., Washington | | 72 90 |
| " | J. Aborn Gardiner, S. C., Providence | | 4 10 |
| July 12. | C. A. Greene, S. C., Bristol | | 15 00 |
| July 14. | Henry Whipple, " Washington | | 39 70 |
| " | C. W. Wilcox, " " | | 43 30 |
| " | B. F. Smith, " " | | 12 00 |
| " | Henry C. Pollard, C. C. P., Providence | | 14 40 |
| " | David Douglass, S. C., Washington | | 24 00 |
| " | Stephen Gardiner, " | | 24 00 |
| " | Geo. W. Greenman, " | | 20 00 |
| " | J. C. Church, " | | 14 60 |
| " | David R. Kenyon, " | | 6 90 |
| " | William Bliven, | | 14 50 |
| " | S. S. Barber, | | 1 00 |
| July 14. | P. P. Palmer, | | 2 50 |
| " | George H. Austin, " | | 1 00 |
| " | John Palmer, | | 2 00 |
| " | W. N. Collins, | | 1 50 |
| " | Charles W. Austin, " | | 1 50 |
| " | John V. Coon, | | 1 50 |
| " | Amos J. Dawley, " | | 3 00 |
| July 15. | L. B. Bosworth, S. C., Bristol | | 20 50 |
| July 21. | John B. Pearce, " " | | 2 10 |
| " | Henry Whipple, C. C. P., Washington | | 28 85 |
| " | C. W. Wilcox, " | | 22 60 |
| " | B. F. Smith, | | 2 00 |
| " | David Douglas, | | 16 00 |
| " | Stephen Gardiner, " | | 16 00 |
| July 24. | Hail Turner, S. C., Bristol | | 14 50 |
| " | H. B. Macomber, " | | 4 00 |
| " | John N. Miller, -- | | 12 00 |
| " | W. Brad'ord, -- | | 10 00 |
| " | Robert N. Turner, " | | 2 00 |
| " | James Hoard, Jr., " | | 9 00 |
| Aug. 5. | C. Holden, S. C, Providence | | 45 00 |

1875.

| | | |
|---|---|---:|
| Aug. 5. | P. Fairbrother, S. C., Providence | $28 00 |
| " | Lyman Upham, " | 80 00 |
| " | Roger W. Potter, " | 80 00 |
| Aug. 12. | C. Holden. C. C. P., Providence | 83 00 |
| " | M. H. Shattuck, " | 24 00 |
| " | S. G. Benedict, " | 22 00 |
| " | J. Aborn Gardiner, " | 22 00 |
| " | O. C. Goodell, " | 24 00 |
| Sept. 14. | Henry Whipple, S. C., Washington | 25 00 |
| Sept. 12. | W. R. Johnson, C. C. P., Washington | 2 40 |
| Sept. 15. | C. A. Waldron, S. C., Bristol | 15 00 |
| Sept 16. | J. Aborn Gardiner, C. C. P., Providence, estimate.. | 200 00 |
| " | Henry C. Pollard, " " | 4 80 |
| Sept. 17. | W. D. Lake, S. C., Newport | 100 00 |
| Sept. 21. | John M. Knowles, C. C. P., Providence | 8 60 |
| Oct. 2. | C. Holden, " " | 66 00 |
| " | J. S. Smith, S. C., Kent | 22 00 |
| " | J. Aborn Gardiner, C. C. P., Providence | 42 00 |
| " | M. H. Shattuck, " | 42 00 |
| " | O. C. Goodell, " | 42 00 |
| " | A. C. Johnson, " | 42 00 |
| " | F. N. Goff. " | 2 00 |
| Oct. 15. | Thomas J. Tilley, S. C., Kent | 83 00 |
| " | Henry N. Ward, S. C., Newport | 22 00 |
| " | Geo. Manchester, " | 88 95 |
| " | W. D. Lake, " | 24 55 |
| " | I. R. Romes, " | 16 00 |
| " | W. L. Riley, " | 22 00 |
| " | Edward S. Hammond, " | 16 00 |
| " | John Hambly, ' | 13 90 |
| " | Greene Tripp, " | 1 00 |
| Oct. 16. | Lowell Pitcher, S. C., Kent | 22 00 |
| " | W. P. Andrew, " | 20 00 |
| " | W. F. Miller, " | 20 00 |
| Oct. 18. | George Manchester, S. C., Newport | 1 95 |
| Oct. 22. | C. A. Greene, C. C. P., Bristol | 15 00 |
| Nov. 1. | T. J. Tilley, " Kent | 2 00 |
| Nov. 3. | C. Holden, S. C., Providence | 72 00 |
| " | P. Fairbrother, " | 46 25 |

1875.

| | | | |
|---|---|---|---|
| Nov. 3. | Lyman Upham, S. C., Providence................ | $48 | 00 |
| " | J. Aborn Gardiner,      "       ................ | 42 | 00 |
| " | Roger W. Potter,        "       ................ | 48 | 00 |
| " | W. H. Pullen,           "       ................ | 8 | 00 |
| Nov. 6. | C. A. Greene, C. C. P., Bristol................ | 13 | 00 |
| Nov. 9. | H. B. Macomber,         "       ................ | 2 | 00 |
| " | W. Bradford,            "       ................ | 2 | 00 |
| " | John N. Miller,         --      ................ | 2 | 00 |
| " | James Hoard, Jr.,       "       ................ | 2 | 00 |
| " | D. T. Potter,           "       ................ | 2 | 95 |
| " | Thomas J. Tilley, C. C. P., Kent.............. | 9 | 00 |
| " | J. S. Smith,            "       ................ | 10 | 00 |
| " | Lowell Pitcher,         "       ................ | 6 | 00 |
| " | W. F. Miller,           --      ................ | 6 | 00 |
| " | W. P. Andrew,           "       ................ | 4 | 00 |
| " | B. L. Gammon, C. C. P., Providence........... | 9 | 60 |
| Nov 12. | W. D. Lake,        "      Newport, estimate...... | 50 | 00 |
| Nov. 24. | J. Aborn Gardiner, S. C., and C. C. P., Providence. | 75 | 50 |
| Nov. 29. | Edward S. Hammond, C. C. P., Newport........ | 28 | 00 |
| Dec. 1. | C. Holden,      S. C.,  Providence............... | 75 | 00 |
| " | P. Fairbrother,         "       ................ | 50 | 00 |
| " | Lyman Upham,            "       ................ | 50 | 00 |
| " | J. Aborn Gardiner,      "       ................ | 48 | 00 |
| " | Roger W. Potter,        "       ................ | 50 | 00 |
| Dec. 10. | George Manchester, C. C. P., Newport.......... | 13 | 70 |
| " | W. D. Lake,             "       ............ | 8 | 00 |
| " | Henry N. Ward,          --      ............ | 8 | 00 |
| " | W. L. Riley,                    ............ | 6 | 00 |
| " | I. W. Romes,                    ............ | 4 | 00 |
| " | Alexander Steele,               ............ | 5 | 80 |
| " | F. B. Garnett,          "       ............ | 4 | 50 |
| Dec. 13. | J. Aborn Gardiner, C. C. P., Providence, estimate... | 200 | 00 |
| Dec. 16. | Henry Whipple, C. C. P., Washington........... | 8 | 40 |
| Dec. 20, | Henry Whipple,          "       ............. | 57 | 00 |
| " | C. W. Wilcox,           "       ............. | 38 | 00 |
| " | C. H. Chapman,          --      ............. | 6 | 00 |
| " | Benjamin F. Smith,      "       ............. | 2 | 00 |
| " | David Douglas,                  ............. | 38 | 00 |
| " | Stephen Gardiner,       "       ............. | 44 | 00 |
| " | George W. Greenman, "           ............. | 44 | 00 |

1875.

Dec. 21. George Manchester, C. C. P., Newport............ $3 00

1876.

Jan. 3. Roger W. Potter, S. C., Providence............... 52 00
  "   Christopher Holden, S. C., and C. C. P., Providence. 144 00
  "   P. Fairbrother, S. C., Providence................ 52 00
  "   Lyman Upham,     "     ................ 52 00
  "   J. Aborn Gardiner, C. C. P., Providence............ 40 00
  "   O. C. Goodell,     "     ............... 42 00
  "   M. H. Shattuck,     "     ............... 40 00
  "   A. C. Johnson,      ............... 40 00
  "   Fred. N. Goff,     "     .............. 2 00

Jan. 31. C. A. Greene, S. C., Bristol...................... 24 00

Feb. 1. Christopher Holden, S. C., and C. C. P., Providence. 138 00
  "   P. Fairbrother, S. C., Providence................. 32 00
  "   Lyman Upham,     "     ................. 32 00
  "   Roger W. Potter,     "     ................. 40 00
  "   I. W. D. Pike,     "     ................. 8 00

Feb. 1. J. Aborn Gardiner, C. C. P., Providence........... 40 00
  "   O. C. Goodell,     "     ............. 52 00
  "   M. H. Shattuck,     "     ............. 50 00
  "   A. C. Johnson,     "     ............. 52 00

Feb. 5. L. B. Bosworth, S. C., Bristol................ 16 30
  "   H. B. Macomber,     "     ................. 14 00
  "   William Bradford,     "     ................. 16 00
  "   John N. Miller,     --     ................. 16 00
  "   James Hoard, Jr.,     ".     ................. 20 70
  "   J. Hazard,     "     ................. 1 00

Feb. 11. A. H. Gates, C. C. P., Providence................. 2 00
  "   R. R. Baker,     "     ................. 2 00
  "   George H. Dary,     "     ................. 2 00
  "   J. A. Brown,     ................. 2 00
  "   R. S. Howland,     --     ................. 2 00
  "   F. Morton,     ................. 2 00
  "   N. Lawton,     ................. 2 00
  "   C. Hendrick,     ................. 2 00
  "   O. W. Baker,     ................. 2 00
  "   J. R. Ross,     ................. 2 00
  "   L. L. Allen     ................. 2 00
  "   Q. S. Hooper,     "     ................. 2 00

Feb. 14. C. W. Wilcox, S. C., Washington................ 80 00

3

1876.

| | | | | |
|---|---|---|---|---|
| Feb. 19. | Henry Whipple, S. C , Washington | | | $64 00 |
| Feb. 25. | David Douglas, | " | | 26 00 |
| " | Stephen Gardiner, | " | | 32 00 |
| " | George W. Greenman | " | | 28 00 |
| " | B. F. Smith, | " | | 2 00 |
| " | John Slocum, | | | 8 30 |
| " | Jason W. Gorton, | " | | 2 60 |
| " | Sheffield Palmer, | " | | 2 00 |
| " | John I. Gardiner, | " | | 2 00 |
| Mar. 1. | J. Aborn Gardiner, C. C. P., Providence | | | 137 80 |
| Mar. 3. | C. A. Greene, S. C., Bristol | | | 30 00 |
| Mar. 6. | A. C. Johnson, C. C. P., Providence | | | 50 00 |
| " | M. H. Shattuck, | " | | 50 00 |
| " | O. C. Goodell, | " | | 50 00 |
| " | Christopher Holden, | " | | 75 00 |
| Mar. 7. | Henry Whipple, S. C., Washington | | | 1 25 |
| Mar. 10. | J. Aborn Gardiner, C. C. P., Providence | | | 200 00 |
| " | T. J. Tilley, S. C., Kent | | | 75 00 |
| Mar 13. | C. W. Wilcox, S. C., Washington | | | 18 75 |
| " | Geo. W. Greenman, " | | | 4 00 |
| " | David Douglass, " | | | 4 00 |
| Mar. 17. | W. D. Lake, S. C., Newport | | | 150 00 |
| Mar. 25. | C. Holden, S. C., Providence | | | 75 00 |
| " | Roger W. Potter, " | | | 50 00 |
| " | I. W. D. Pike, " | | | 50 00 |
| Apr. 6. | Henry C. Pollard, C. C. P., Providence | | | 72 60 |
| Apr. 7. | P. Fairbrother, S. C., Providence, | | | 5 30 |
| Apr. 8. | W. H. Pullen, C. C. P., Providence | | | 31 98 |
| " | Edward S. Hammond, | " | | 9 40 |
| " | C. Holden, | " | | 72 00 |
| " | M. H Shattuck, | | | 44 00 |
| " | O. C. Goodell, | | | 46 00 |
| " | A. C. Johnson, | | | 44 00 |
| " | Fred. N. Goff, | | | 2 00 |
| " | I. W. D. Pike, | | | 4 00 |
| " | Frank Jenks, | | | 1 00 |
| Apr. 10. | P. Cavanagh. | | | 4 00 |
| Apr. 11. | B. L. Gammon, | " | | 1 00 |
| Apr. 18. | W. F. Miller, S. C., Kent | | | 12 00 |

1876.

| | | | |
|---|---|---|---:|
| Apr. 21. | Thomas J. Tilley, S. C., Kent | | $21 70 |
| " | Lowell Pitcher, | " | 10 85 |
| Apr. 20. | Warren P. Andrew, | " | 7 15 |
| " | J. S. Smith, | " | 12 00 |
| Apr. 27. | T. J. Tilley, C. C. P., Kent | | 4 10 |

Total ........................................$7,010 88

*Witnesses Supreme Courts and Courts of Common Pleas.*

1875.

| | | | |
|---|---|---|---:|
| May 3. | Barney McLaughlin, C. C. P., Providence | | $3 60 |
| May 7. | John McLaughlin, | " | 3 20 |
| May 12. | Walter L. Clarke, | " | 6 80 |
| May 14. | W. D. Lake, C. C. P., Newport | | 100 00 |
| " | Henry Whipple, " Washington | | 100 00 |
| May 17. | Asa Cushman, " Providence, | | 1 60 |
| May 31. | Charles Baird, O. C. P., Providence | | 3 20 |
| June 1. | Michael Maloney, | " | 2 20 |
| June 2. | W. S. Kent, | " | 5 70 |
| June 4. | Alba Watson, C. C. P., Kent | | 1 50 |
| " | J. H. Bradford, | " | 1 50 |
| " | J. S. Essex, | " | 1 60 |
| " | Lewis Arnold, | .. | 1 60 |
| " | A. Harrington, | .. | 1 60 |
| " | Mason Walker, | .. | 1 60 |
| " | C. A. Jordan, | .. | 1 60 |
| " | A. Sherman, | .. | 1 80 |
| " | Job Card, | .. | 1 80 |
| " | A. B. Card, | .. | 1 60 |
| " | J. Capwell, | " | 1 60 |
| " | Patrick Eagan, C. C. P., Providence | | 1 70 |
| June 8. | W. H. Bullock, | " | 1 70 |
| June 9. | L. B. Bosworth, C. C. P., Bristol | | 55 |
| " | S. H. Downing, | " | 55 |
| " | John F. Munroe, | " | 55 |
| " | Susan Canfield, | .. | 55 |
| " | John Canfield, | " | 55 |
| June 12. | Michael Maloney, C. C. P., Providence | | 1 55 |

1875.

| | | | | |
|---|---|---|---|---|
| June 16. | Alexander Steele, C. C. P., Newport | | | $1 65 |
| " | Stephen G. Chase, | " | | 55 |
| " | J. B. Briggs, | " | | 55 |
| " | Benjamin Holland, | -- | | 55 |
| " | J. M. Davis, | | | 55 |
| " | I. Gould, | | | 55 |
| " | Eben Dow, | | | 55 |
| " | W. Brightman, | | | 1 65 |
| " | Martin Tifft, | | | 1 65 |
| " | Martha Rhine, | | | 55 |
| " | John Mahoney, | | | 1 65 |
| " | W. Edgar, | | | 55 |
| " | John Armstrong, | | | 55 |
| " | George W. Carr, | | | 55 |
| " | W. Taylor, | " | | 65 |
| June 17. | A. W. Colvin,   C. C. P., Kent | | | 38 40 |
| " | A. W. Colvin,   S. C., | " | | 82 50 |
| June 19. | J. Aborn Gardiner, C. C. P., and S. C., Providence. | | | 1,200 00 |
| June 25. | Geo. W. Burlingame, C. C. P., and S. C., Kent | | | 82 90 |
| July 9. | William Whitford, S. C., Kent | | | 95 |
| " | Jesse Carr, | " | | 90 |
| " | Henry Shippee, | " | | 95 |
| " | John Whitford, | -- | | 95 |
| " | Burrell Hopkins, | -- | | 85 |
| " | Layton Hopkins, | -- | | 85 |
| " | Caleb Whitford, | -- | | 95 |
| " | Byron Shippee, | -- | | 95 |
| " | Enos O. Sweet, | -- | | 90 |
| " | George P. Howard, | " | | 65 |
| " | Ephraim Howard, | -- | | 65 |
| " | Searles Capwell, | -- | | 65 |
| " | David Howard, | -- | | 65 |
| " | A. H. Bentley, | -- | | 75 |
| " | Darius Hart, | -- | | 55 |
| " | Peleg Card, | -- | | 55 |
| " | Charles Spencer, | -- | | 55 |
| " | Edward Stanhope, | -- | | 55 |
| " | Erank Burlingame, | " | | 55 |
| " | S. A. Edwards, | -- | | 1 10 |

1875.

| | | | | |
|---|---|---|---|---|
| July 9. | George N. Howland, S.C., Kent.................. | | | $0 55 |
| July 10. | D. R. Kenyon, S. C., Washington................ | | | 1 65 |
| " | J. Aborn Gardiner, S. C., Providence............. | | | 29 20 |
| July 14. | David R. Kenyon, S. C., Washington............. | | | 55 |
| " | Peter P. Palmer, | " | ............... | 65 |
| " | W. N. Collins, | | ............... | 65 |
| July 20. | Thomas J. Champlin, | " | ............... | 1 00 |
| " | John B. Eldred, | | ............... | 1 00 |
| " | Henry H. Whalley, | " | ............... | 1 00 |
| " | Stanton F. Barber, | " | ............... | 60 |
| " | Robert D. Brown, | " | ............... | 1 00 |
| " | Jesse Potter, | | ............... | 1 65 |
| " | Henry Barnes, | | ............... | 2 25 |
| " | John Spicer, | | ............... | 2 25 |
| " | Margaret Taylor, | | ............... | 2 85 |
| " | Peter Taylor, | | ............... | 2 85 |
| " | Benjamin Briggs, | | ............... | 1 40 |
| " | Lydia A. Saunders, | " | ............... | 5 00 |
| " | Franklin Burton, | | .......A...... | 2 10 |
| " | C. H. Joslyn, | | ............... | 1 10 |
| " | Erastus D. Miner, | " | ............... | 2 85 |
| " | Harriet E. Collins, | " | ............... | 65 |
| " | Henry Pendleton, | " | ............... | 55 |
| " | Annie E. Palmer, | " | ............... | 65 |
| " | C. P. W. Wheeler, | " | ............... | 65 |
| " | Everett Palmer, | | ............... | 65 |
| " | George Edwards, | " | ............... | 65 |
| " | I. B. Potter, | | ............... | 55 |
| " | James Briggs | | ............... | 60 |
| " | Thomas B. Briggs, | " | ............... | 60 |
| July 21. | E. T. Case, order of Austin Williams, S. C., Bristol. | | | 28 70 |
| " | John B. Pearce, S. C., Bristol.................... | | | 2 15 |
| July 24. | James Hoard, Jr., | " | .................... | 3 85 |
| " | Norman N. Mason, | " | .................... | 6 50 |
| " | Peter Gladding, | " | .................... | 2 75 |
| " | Spencer Rounds, | " | .................... | 1 10 |
| " | Susan Canfield, | " | .................... | 2 20 |
| " | Ellen M. Howard, | " | .................... | 55 |
| " | Job. W. Osgood, | " | .................... | 5 00 |

1875.

| | | | | | |
|---|---|---|---|---|---|
| July 24. | Florence Fitzgerald, S. C., Bristol | | | $1 | 10 |
| " | Minnie Belts, | " | | 1 | 10 |
| " | Charles Evans, | " | | 1 | 10 |
| " | Charles Bullock, | " | | 1 | 10 |
| " | Barney Keene, | " | | 1 | 05 |
| " | Charles Evans, Jr., | " | | | 55 |
| " | John S. Newman, | " | | | 55 |
| " | W. H. Church, | " | | 37 | 80 |
| " | John A. Ingraham, | " | | | 55 |
| " | W. H. Spooner, | " | | 1 | 05 |
| " | Samuel Lindsey, | " | | | 55 |
| " | Samuel D. Wardwell, | " | | 1 | 05 |
| " | James A. Miller, | " | | 1 | 05 |
| " | James E. White, | " | | 1 | 20 |
| " | E. C. Horton, | " | | 1 | 95 |
| " | Silas H. Munroe, | " | | | 55 |
| " | Nathan C. Bedell, | " | | | 55 |
| " | Gildersleeve Bedell, | " | | | 55 |
| Aug. 9. | C. H. Tourtellott, | " | | 28 | 60 |
| Aug. 14. | W. A. Carroll, C. C. P., Providence | | | 6 | 60 |
| " | Henry Whipple, S. C., Washington | | | 75 | 00 |
| Aug. 25. | W. H. Ayer, C. C. P., Providence | | | 2 | 20 |
| Sept. 15. | C. A. Greene, S. C., Bristol | | | 85 | 00 |
| Sept. 17. | J. Aborn Gardiner, C. C. P., Providence | | 1,500 | 00 |
| " | Henry C. Pollard, | " | | 2 | 30 |
| Sept. 17. | W. D. Lake, S. C., Newport | | | 300 | 00 |
| Oct. 16. | Herbert Clement, | " | | | 95 |
| " | Fred. Clement | " | | | 95 |
| " | John Clement, | " | | | 95 |
| Oct 20. | A. J. Kennedy, C. C. P., Providence | | | 8 | 10 |
| Oct. 22. | C. A. Greene, | " | Bristol | 85 | 00 |
| Oct. 26. | W. H. Scott, C. C. P., Providence | | | 2 | 00 |
| " | F. H. Mason, | " | | 2 | 00 |
| Oct. 28. | Catherine Riley, | " | | 9 | 60 |
| " | Margaret Richards, | " | | 8 | 20 |
| Oct. 30. | Ann McLear, | | | 8 | 20 |
| Oct. 31. | Thomas McCormick, | " | | 16 | 80 |
| " | Patrick Smith, | ' | | 9 | 20 |
| " | Richard Mathews, | " | | 9 | 60 |

1875.

| | | | | | |
|---|---|---|---|---|---|
| Oct. 31. | Sarah Mathews, C. C. P., Providence | | | | $9 60 |
| Nov. 1. | Thomas J. Tilley, " | Kent | | | 8 40 |
| " | C. A. Greene, " | Bristol | | | 6 00 |
| Nov. 3. | A. H. Gates, C. C. P., Providence | | | | 1 60 |
| " | W. H. Pullen, " | | | | 85 |
| Nov. 6. | R. McDonald, " | | | | 3 20 |
| " | John Phillips, - | | | | 1 60 |
| " | Rufus P. Swinburne, " | | | | 3 20 |
| Nov. 9. | David T. Potter, C. C. P., Bristol | | | | 60 |
| " | David H. Potter, " | | | | 60 |
| " | Samuel R. Andrew, " | | | | 60 |
| " | J. T. Burnham, " | | | | 60 |
| " | B. L. Gammon, C. C. P., Providence | | | | 85 |
| " | James McCabe, " | | | | 3 20 |
| Nov. 12. | W. D. Lake, C. C. P., Newport | | | | 150 00 |
| Nov. 24. | J. Aborn Gardiner, S. C., Providence | | | | 198 60 |
| Dec. 7. | James Mason, C. C. P., Providence | | | | 1 60 |
| Dec. 10. | Alexander Steele, C. C. P., Newport | | | | 1 10 |
| " | F. B. Garnett, " | | | | 2 20 |
| Dec. 11. | James Harrigan, " | | | | 55 |
| " | J. B. Hawley, | | | | 55 |
| " | Richard Robertson, | | | | 55 |
| " | John Dillon, | | | | 1 10 |
| " | Margaret Lawton, | | | | 1 10 |
| " | Mary W. Lawton, | | | | 1 10 |
| " | George Stevens, | | | | 1 10 |
| " | James Dowling, | | | | 55 |
| " | A. Russell Manchester, " | | | | 1 10 |
| " | Stephen S. Ward, | | | | 1 10 |
| " | Frank Sylvia, | | | | 55 |
| " | Charles Dowling, | | | | 1 10 |
| " | O. P. Peckham, | | | | 1 70 |
| " | B. W. Brigham, | | | | 50 |
| " | George Dunn, | | | | 55 |
| " | James Boyle, | | | | 55 |
| " | Henry Rooney " | | | | 55 |
| Dec. 13. | J. Aborn Gardiner, C. C. P, Prov., est. Dec. Term | | | | 1,000 00 |
| Dec. 16. | Michael W. Ryan, " Providence | | | | 2 00 |
| " | Henry Whipple, " Washington | | | | 43 30 |
| Dec. 21. | Edward N. Baker, " Providence | | | | 3 20 |

1875.

| | | | |
|---|---|---|---:|
| Dec. 21. | A. Chanley, C. C. P., Providence | | $3 20 |

1876.

| | | | |
|---|---|---|---:|
| Jan. 1. | J. Aborn Gardiner, C. C. P., Providence | | 1,000 00 |
| Jan. 4. | Michael Keefe, | " | 8 20 |
| Feb. 5. | James Hoard, Jr., S. C., Bristol | | 55 |
| " | S. S. Drury, | " | 55 |
| " | Gardiner W. Sisson, | " | 55 |
| " | Elnora Mahew, | " | 55 |
| " | Joanna Bowers, | | 55 |
| " | Henry Doty, | " | 55 |
| " | Sophia A. Mott, | | 55 |
| " | Phebe R. Mott, | " | 55 |
| Feb. 19. | Henry Whipple, S. C , Washington | | 150 00 |
| " | W. W. Packard, C. C. P., Providence | | 1 60 |
| Feb. 21. | Henry L. Bowers, | " | 1 60 |
| Feb. 25. | Jason W. Gorton, S. C., Washington | | 95 |
| " | Charles Perkins, | " | 1 00 |
| " | Sally Hawkins, | " | 95 |
| " | N. B. L. Palmer, | | 1 00 |
| " | J. W. Richmond, | | 95 |
| " | Amasa Pratt, | · | 95 |
| " | Jeremiah W. Congdon, | " | 1 00 |
| " | Eliza A. Chappell, | " | 95 |
| Mar. 1. | J. Aborn Gardiner, C. C. P., Providence | | 724 60 |
| Mar. 3. | C. A. Greene, S. C., Bristol | | 70 00 |
| Mar. 10. | J. Aborn Gardiner, C. C. P., Providence | | 1,500 00 |
| " | T. J. Tilley, S. C., Kent | | 125 00 |
| Mar. 17. | W. D. Lake, " Newport | | 300 00 |
| Apr. 6. | C. Chapman, C. C. P., Providence | | 1 60 |
| " | H. C. Pollard, | " | 5 00 |
| Apr. 7. | E. C. Brown, | " | 2 70 |
| Apr. 8. | W. H. Pullen, | | 7 35 |
| " | Frank Jenks, | | 4 60 |
| Apr. 11. | A. G. Whidden, | " | 2 55 |
| " | B. L. Gammon, | " | 7 35 |
| " | W. W. Packard, | " | 2 55 |
| " | Edward W. Baker, | " | 1 60 |
| Apr. 14. | C. H. Thurber, | " | 7 35 |
| Apr. 15. | Addie A. Whitney, | " | 1 60 |

1876.

| | | | |
|---|---|---|---|
| Apr. 20. | W. H. Kenyon, C. C. P., Providence............. | $2 55 |
| Apr. 20. | Q. A. Hooper, C. C. P., Providence............. | 2 55 |
| Apr. 22. | B. S. Howland, " ............. | 2 55 |
| Apr. 24. | John V. Symonds, " ............. | 2 55 |
| Apr. 27. | Thomas J. Tilley, C. C. P., Kent................ | 22 90 |
| Apr. 29. | C. F. Church, " Providence........... | 2 55 |

Total............. .........................$9,331 40

*Incidental Expenses Supreme Courts and Courts of Common Pleas.*

1875.

| | | |
|---|---|---|
| May 14. | Christopher Holden, S. C., and C. C. P., Prov....... | 14 45 |
| May 17. | C. A Waldron, C. C. P., Bristol ................ | 10 88 |
| May 28. | Charles Blake, S. C., Providence.................. | 60 20 |
| June 1. | A. R. Greene, S. C., Kent...................... | 2 50 |
| June 7. | Thomas W. Wood, C. C. P., Newport............. | 6 40 |
| June 9. | A. Crawford Greene, S. C., Kent................. | 19 50 |
| " | S. S. Rider, " ................. | 10 60 |
| June 10. | D. Gillies, C. C. P., Washington.................. ........ | 28 00 |
| " | T. A. Gardiner, " ................. | 4 76 |
| " | B. W. Case, " ................. | 70 |
| June 16. | Davis & Pitman, C. C. P., Newport............. | 7 50 |
| " | Charles E. Hammett, Jr., " ............. | 40 |
| June 19. | J. Aborn Gardiner, C. C. P., Providence........... | 7 65 |
| June 22. | A. R. Greene. " Kent................ | 1 10 |
| July 2. | John G. Clarke, S. C., Washington............... | 35 21 |
| July 3. | A. Crawford Greene, C. C. P., Kent.............. | 12 00 |
| July 9. | S. S. Rider, " ............. | 16 87 |
| July 12. | C. A Greene, S. C., Bristol..................... | 14 50 |
| " | C. A. Waldron, " ..................... | 6 60 |
| July 24. | Ackerman & Co., " ..................... | 16 00 |
| July 26. | C. Holden, S. C., Providence.................... | 9 20 |
| July 30. | W. H. Fenner & Co., C. C. P., Providence......... | 15 00 |
| " | Valpey, Angell & Co., C. C. P., " ........... | 63 41 |
| Sept. 15. | C. A. Greene, S. C., Bristol..................... | 14 25 |
| Oct. 11. | J. Aborn Gardiner, C. C. P., Providence........... | 2 10 |
| " | Bugbee & Hall, S. C., Providence................ | 2 50 |
| " | M. H. Shattuck, C. C. P., Providence........... .. | 1 55 |
| " | O. C. Goodell, " ............. | 5 50 |

| | | |
|---|---|---:|
| **1875.** | | |
| Oct. 11. | S. S. Rider, C. C. P., Providence................. | $4 75 |
| " | Charles Blake, S. C., Providence................ | 46 01 |
| " | Valpey, Angell, & Co., " ................... | 82 13 |
| " | Ackerman & Co., " ................... | 33 57 |
| " | Angell, Burlingame & Co., S. C., Providence....... | 85 29 |
| " | A. R. Greene, S. C., Kent.... ................... | 3 30 |
| Oct. 15. | Thomas W. Wood, S. C., Newport................ | 7 87 |
| Oct. 16. | Charles E. Hammett, Jr., " ................ | 2 50 |
| " | John P. Sanborn, " .... ............ | 20 00 |
| " | Davis & Pitman, ................. | 2 75 |
| " | James Atkinson, .. ................. | 6 00 |
| " | R. H. Tilley, ................. | 8 00 |
| " | S. B. Brewster, " ................. | 56 00 |
| " | A. Crawford Greene, S. C., Kent................. | 21 00 |
| " | Henry N. Ward, S. C., Newport.................. | 2 05 |
| Oct. 23. | Valpey, Angell & Co , C. C. P., Providence........ | 34 68 |
| " | Christopher Holden, " ......... | 1 70 |
| Oct. 25. | George E. Webster, " ......... | 29 05 |
| Oct. 28. | Ackerman & Co., ......... | 87 37 |
| " | O. C. Goodell, ......... | 1 20 |
| Nov. 3. | J. Aborn Gardiner, ......... | 1 20 |
| Nov. 6. | Manton H. Luther, " ......... | 30 00 |
| Nov. 9. | Charles A. Waldron, C. C. P., Bristol............. | 8 17 |
| " | Sidney S. Rider, " Kent.............. | 8 00 |
| " | A. Crawford Greene, C. C. P., Kent.............. | 6 50 |
| " | A. R. Greene, " ............... | 2 30 |
| Nov. 17. | M. V. Newton, S. C., Bristol.................... | 12 00 |
| " | C. A. Waldron, " .................... | 19 52 |
| Nov. 24. | J. Aborn Gardiner, S. C., Providence............ | 7 20 |
| Nov. 29. | Thomas W. Wood, C. C. P., Newport............. | 1 30 |
| Dec. 10. | C. E. Hammett, Jr., " ............. | 2 75 |
| Dec. 11. | Davis & Pitman, " .............. | 2 75 |
| Dec. 16. | Tillinghast & Mason News Co.,C. C. P., Washington | 7 95 |
| " | T. A. Gardiner, C. C. P., Washington............. | 7 44 |
| " | D. Gillies, " ............. | 13 50 |
| Dec. 20. | Henry Whipple, " . ........•.... | 14 88 |
| **1876.** | | |
| Jan. 31. | C. A. Greene, S. C., Bristol..................... | 14 50 |
| Feb. 8. | John G. Clarke, " Washington................. | 23 62 |
| Feb. 19. | Henry Whipple, " " ................ | 19 83 |

1876.

| | | | |
|---|---|---|---|
| Mar. 1. | John G. Clarke, S. C., Washington............... | $6 | 00 |
| Mar. 7. | Geo. E. Webster, C. C. P., Providence............. | 8 | 70 |
| " | C. Holden, " ............. | 8 | 40 |
| " | J. Aborn Gardiner, " ............. | 4 | 25 |
| " | O. C. Goodell, ............. | 2 | 55 |
| " | Milton H. Shattuck, " ............. | 11 | 05 |
| " | Providence Press Co., " ............. | 148 | 80 |
| " | Valpey Angell & Co., C. C. P., and S.C., Providence. | 208 | 11 |
| " | C. Blake, S. C., Providence................. | 25 | 81 |
| " | Akerman & Co., " ................. | 81 | 00 |
| " | Angell, Burlingame & Co., S. C. Providence....... | 96 | 96 |
| " | Bugbee & Hall, " ........ | 1 | 75 |
| " | Sidney S. Rider, " ........ | 4 | 00 |
| Apr. 11. | C. A. Greene, S. C., Bristol.................. | 14 | 25 |
| " | W. H. Buffington, " " .................. | 14 | 92 |
| Apr. 20. | A. Crawford Greene, S. C., Kent................. | 19 | 00 |
| " | S. S. Rider, " ................. | 23 | 71 |
| Apr. 25. | Albert R. Greene, " ................. | 1 | 25 |

Total.........................................$1,752 97

## Trial Justices and Justices of the Peace.

1875.

| | | | |
|---|---|---|---|
| May 10. | C. W. Smith................................. | $14 | 05 |
| May 11. | George N. Bliss.............................. | 77 | 70 |
| " 12. | Walter L. Clarke, order of Horace Clarke.......... | 85 | 75 |
| " 13. | Resolved Harvey ............................. | 96 | 10 |
| " 20. | George F. Crowningshield...................... | 70 | 85 |
| June 1. | Emor H. Mowry ............................. | 86 | 85 |
| " 3. | Mark H. Wood............................... | 7 | 20 |
| " 4. | C. W. Smith................................. | 4 | 80 |
| " 9. | B. J. Munroe................................ | 7 | 80 |
| " 10. | John L. Brown............................... | 1 | 80 |
| June 10. | F. M. Wood................................. | 48 | 95 |
| " | Thomas S. Wightman ......................... | 17 | 64 |
| June 16. | John E. Watson.............................. | 8 | 65 |
| " 25. | C. W. Smith.... ........................... | 2 | 85 |
| July 9. | Resolved Harvey............................. | 2 | 05 |
| " | John T. Lewis............................... | 8 | 20 |

1875.

| | | | |
|---|---|---|---|
| July | 9. | S. L. Tillinghast ...................... .......... | $4 65 |
| July | 14. | Bennett J. Munro.............................. | 42 65 |
| " | | M. S. Greene .................................. | 5 60 |
| " | | Nelson K. Church ............................. | 6 20 |
| " | | N. L. Richmond............................... | 7 80 |
| " | | Alexander Eddy............................... | 15 15 |
| July | 24. | Albert L. Andrew ............................ | 7 70 |
| Sept. | 15. | S. L. Tillinghast .............................. | 7 20 |
| Oct. | 16. | Thomas H. Borden......'..................... | 2 05 |
| " | 19. | John T. Lewis................................. | 7 40 |
| " | 21. | F. M. Wood.......................... ........ | 26 20 |
| " | 26. | George L. Cooke, Jr........................... | 29 65 |
| Nov. | 5. | Bennett J. Munro............................. | 28 05 |
| " | 9. | M. H. Wood.................................. | 2 05 |
| " | 9. | Horace A. Follet............................. | 23 00 |
| " | 17. | George N. Durfee............................. | 2 35 |
| " | 22. | Thomas H. Borden ........................... | 1 80 |
| " | 23. | Nathan B. Lewis.............................. | 1 80 |
| Dec. | 11. | H. M. Tompkins.............................. | 2 85 |
| 1876. | | | |
| Jan. | 26. | George L. Cooke, Jr........................... | 1 80 |
| " | 31. | Charles Cross................................. | 4 90 |
| Feb. | 5. | Bennett J. Munro............................. | 3 85 |
| " | 25. | N. B. Lewis .................................. | 8 45 |
| Mar. | 1. | Charles Cross................................. | 35 |
| " | 8. | F. M. Wood.................................. | 31 75 |
| Apr. | 11. | T. A. Gardiner............................... | 2 30 |
| " | 20. | W. S. Mowry.... ............................. | 1 50 |
| " | 25. | John L. Brown................................ | 3 85 |
| " | 27. | Bennett J. Munro............................. | 24 05 |
| ' | | George N. Bliss............................... | 124 35 |
| | | Total......................................... | $855 54 |

### Officers of Justice Courts.

1875.

| | | | |
|---|---|---|---|
| May | 8. | Henry N. Ward................................ | $28 65 |
| " | 10. | C. W. Smith.................................. | 20 70 |
| " | 11. | George N. Bliss............................... | 78 15 |

1875.

| | | |
|---|---|---:|
| May 12. | Walter L. Clarke, order of Horace Clarke.......... | $48 40 |
| " 20. | George F. Crowningshield....................... | 49 40 |
| " 21. | Charles Gifford, order of Ed. S. Hammond........ | 10 80 |
| " 24. | Hiram Mann...... ............................. | 8 60 |
| " 31. | W. F. Miller..... ............................. | 5 70 |
| June 1. | Michael Maloney.............................. | 36 40 |
| " 3. | W. H. Pullen.................................. | 24 00 |
| " 3. | Mark H. Wood................................ | 8 20 |
| " 10. | Thomas S. Wightman.......................... | 15 40 |
| " 29. | W. H. Pullen................................. | 16 00 |
| " 30. | W. W. Eddy.................................. | 232 40 |
| July 2. | O. A. Inman ................................. | 36 50 |
| " 15. | Lyman B. Bosworth ........................... | 4 70 |
| " 23. | B. F. Newhall................................ | 7 10 |
| July 23. | Benjamin F. Payne............................ | 1 10 |
| " | Walter Buckley............................... | 2 80 |
| " | J. B. Curtis.. ................................ | 5 60 |
| " | Timothy McDonough........................... | 1 10 |
| " | J. O. Swan................................... | 6 00 |
| " | P. E. Worsley................................ | 1 10 |
| " | M. L. Geary.................................. | 1 10 |
| " | E. F. O'Connor............................... | 8 85 |
| " | P. J. Magill.................................. | 11 70 |
| " | W. T. Robinson .............................. | 1 10 |
| " | Benjamin H. Childs............................ | 5 25 |
| " | W. J. Nickerson.. ............................ | 10 85 |
| " | George H. Rounds............................. | 1 10 |
| " | Benjamin T. White............................ | 9 60 |
| " | James P. Scott................................ | 2 60 |
| " | John A. Murray............................... | 5 65 |
| " | Medbury M. Heath........................... . | 1 60 |
| " | I. Fairbrother................................ | 1 10 |
| July 27. | James H. Hoard, Jr........................... | 4 10 |
| " | J. S. Ingraham............................... | 1 00 |
| " | H. B. Macomber.............................. | 2 20 |
| Aug. 2. | W. H. Pullen................................. | 18 00 |
| " 3. | John M. Knowles.............................. | 33 50 |
| " 7. | Henry N. Ward............................... | 56 90 |
| Sept. 2. | W. H. Pullen................................. | 18 00 |

1875.

| | | |
|---|---|---:|
| Sept. 21. | John M. Knowles................................$3,478 80 | |
| Oct.   1. | W. H. Pullen................................... | 18 00 |
| "  16. | W. F. Miller................................... | 2 80 |
| Oct. 19. | George G. Bullock............................. | 1 30 |
| " | J. S. Smith...................................... | 1 00 |
| " | Lowell Pitcher................................. | 1 80 |
| " | A. B. Steere................................... | 1 00 |
| " | Charles A. Slocum ............................. | 6 00 |
| " | E. W. Garfield.................................. | 5 40 |
| " | Wilmarth Gross................................ | 1 00 |
| , " | John A. Staples................................ | 4 00 |
| " | Hiram Mann................................... | 9 60 |
| " | E. McDonald................................... | 1 00 |
| Oct. 21. | F. M. Wood.................................... | 52 90 |
| " | C. W. Smith................................... | 1 00 |
| Oct. 22. | Oliver O. Colvin................................ | 3 10 |
| " | Joseph F. Arnold.............................. | 1 70 |
| Oct. 26. | George L. Cooke, Jr............................ | 18 70 |
| Nov.  1. | W. H. Pullen.................................. | 16 00 |
| "  5. | Bennett J. Munro.............................. | 25 10 |
| "  6. | Henry N. Ward................................. | 64 95 |
| Nov. 17. | Dewitt C. Smith............................... | 1 90 |
| " | John Hambly................................... | 2 80 |
| " | James W. Millard.............................. | 3 10 |
| Nov. 22. | Thomas H. Borden............................. | 3 70 |
| " | John C. Lewis................................. | 3 50 |
| Dec.  1. | W. H. Pullen.................................. | 18 00 |
| 1876. | | |
| Jan.  1. | W. H. Pullen.................................. | 18 00 |
| "  26. | George L. Cooke, Jr............................ | 3 00 |
| "  27. | J. E. Taylor................................... | 5 10 |
| Feb.  1. | W. H. Pullen.................................. | 18 00 |
| "  7. | Henry N. Ward................................. | 59 85 |
| Mar.  1. | W. H. Pullen.................................. | 16 00 |
| "  1. | Charles Cross.................................. | 5 30 |
| "  8. | F. M. Wood.................................... | 58 50 |
| " 15. | John A. Staples................................ | 14 50 |
| " 20. | C. W. Wilcox................................... | 4 80 |
| Apr.  1. | W. H. Pullen.................................. | 18 00 |
| "  8. | W. H. Pullen.................................. | 10 56 |

1876.

| | | | |
|---|---|---:|---:|
| Apr. 11. | T. A. Gardiner | $4 | 70 |
| " 20. | W. S. Mowry | 4 | 30 |
| Apr. 25. | F. B. Garnett | 8 | 05 |
| " | Ed. S. Hammond | | 50 |
| " | W. P. Denman | 4 | 70 |
| Apr. 27. | Bennett J. Munro | 19 | 00 |
| " 29. | George N. Bliss | 111 | 20 |
| " 29. | W. H. Pullen | 16 | 00 |

Total ................................................$4,986 66

*Witnesses of Justice Courts.*

1875.

| | | | |
|---|---|---:|---:|
| May 8. | Henry N. Ward | $7 | 70 |
| " 10. | C. W. Smith | 6 | 65 |
| " 11. | George N. Bliss | 28 | 90 |
| " 12. | Walter L. Clarke, order of Horace Clarke | 32 | 25 |
| " 14. | W. H. Clarke | 2 | 35 |
| " 14. | John A. Wood | 2 | 30 |
| " 14. | Clovis E. Keach | 2 | 35 |
| " 19. | George S. Tillinghast | 6 | 50 |
| " 20. | George F. Crowningshield | 8 | 95 |
| " 24. | George Angell | 1 | 50 |
| June 1. | Emor H. Mowry | 9 | 80 |
| " 2. | Norman N. Mason | 34 | 70 |
| " 3. | Mark H. Wood | 2 | 80 |
| " 10. | F. M. Wood | 27 | 25 |
| " 10. | Thomas S. Wightman | 35 | 00 |
| " 10. | W. H. Stone | 1 | 50 |
| " 10. | Jeremiah Gilmore | 1 | 50 |
| " 16. | John E. Watson | 2 | 78 |
| " 23. | F. M. Wood | 2 | 35 |
| " 30. | W. W. Eddy | 180 | 65 |
| July 7. | George F. Crowningshield | 9 | 35 |
| " 26. | T. J. Usher | 1 | 10 |
| July 27. | James H. Hoard, Jr | 2 | 20 |
| " | Peter Gladding | 6 | 60 |
| " | W. H. Church | 8 | 20 |
| " | Charles H. Burke, | 1 | 50 |

1875.

| | | | |
|---|---|---|---|
| July 27. | Chris. M. Baker.............................. | $0 | 55 |
| " | David A. Fiske............................... | | 60 |
| " | W. J. Whitford.............................. | | 55 |
| " | Albert C. Greene............................ | | 65 |
| " | Charles H. Thurber......................... | 1 | 25 |
| " | Silas Holmes................................ | | 55 |
| " | William Tourgee............................ | | 55 |
| " | Champlin Brown............................ | | 55 |
| " | Robert Dunbar.............................. | | 55 |
| " | Abbie Hazard............................... | | 55 |
| " | Ida Hazard.................................. | | 55 |
| " | Michael Christie............................ | | 55 |
| " | Samuel White............................... | | 60 |
| Aug. 7. | Henry N. Ward.............................. | 26 | 40 |
| Oct. 19. | Dyer S. Essex............................... | | 55 |
| " | John Edwards............................... | | 60 |
| " | Eben Johnson............................... | | 55 |
| " | Francis Greene ............................. | | 55 |
| " | Jesse Carr.................................. | | 55 |
| " | C. Burton .................................. | | 65 |
| " | Nicholas Wood ............................. | | 65 |
| " | Pardon Hopkins............................. | 1 | 10 |
| Oct. 19. | Lowell Pitcher.............................. | 1 | 10 |
| " | Lyman Himes............................... | | 55 |
| " | Eleanor B. Kenyon.......................... | | 55 |
| " | George W. Howland......................... | 1 | 10 |
| " | W. H. Hunt................................. | | 55 |
| " | W. H. Jacoy................................ | | 70 |
| " | W. W. Hawkins............................. | | 55 |
| " | D. S. Durfee................................ | | 70 |
| " | Enoch Steere............................... | | 70 |
| " | James B. Wood............................. | | 55 |
| " | Benedict Aldrich............................ | | 55 |
| " | Mrs. Joseph S. Olney........................ | | 55 |
| " | Eugene T. Eddy............................. | | 55 |
| " | Silas Steere................................. | | 70 |
| " | Olive Steere ................................ | | 70 |
| " | W. H. Knight............................... | | 85 |
| " | Walter Knight.............................. | | 85 |

1875.

| | | | |
|---|---|---|---|
| Oct. 19. | Susan Knight | $0 | 85 |
| " | Lousia Knight | | 85 |
| " | George W. Knight | | 85 |
| " | E. W. Garfield | | 55 |
| " | Wilmarth Gross | | 55 |
| " | Hiram Mann | | 85 |
| " | F. M. Wood | 10 | 00 |
| Oct. 21. | C. W. Smith | 2 | 00 |
| " 26. | George L. Cooke, Jr | 12 | 10 |
| Nov. 5. | Bennett J. Munro | 9 | 90 |
| " 5. | Henry N. Ward | 41 | 55 |
| Nov. 17. | Job Almy | | 80 |
| " | James L. Gray | | 80 |
| " | Fred. Wilcox | | 80 |
| " | Carmi Potter | | 80 |
| " | Peleg Wilcox | | 80 |
| " | C. F. Wilcox | | 80 |
| " | W. A. Gray | | 65 |
| " | Edward J. Cory | | 80 |
| " | I. G. White | | 80 |
| " | James W. Millard | 2 | 40 |
| " | John Tanner | 1 | 25 |
| " | Hazard W. Burdick | 1 | 25 |
| " | Halsey D. Larkin | 1 | 25 |
| " | Benjamin G. Palmer | | 80 |
| " | Benjamin W. Pendleton | 1 | 30 |
| " | Daniel W. Coon | 1 | 30 |
| " | Asher M. Palmer | 1 | 30 |
| Nov. 22. | Charles Rose | | 55 |
| " | Ephraim Lake | | 70 |
| " | Clark Estes | | 55 |
| " | Nathan B. Lewis | 4 | 40 |
| 1876. | | | |
| Jan. 26. | George L. Cooke, Jr | 2 | 20 |
| " 27. | J. E. Taylor | 1 | 05 |
| Feb. 7. | Henry N. Ward | 27 | 50 |
| " 10. | Benjamin Waldron | 1 | 10 |
| Mar. 1. | Charles Cross | 11 | 55 |
| " 8. | F. M. Wood | 19 | 45 |

4

1876.

| | | | |
|---|---|---:|---:|
| Mar. 14. | David Coggin | $1 | 10 |
| " | Jacob Weaver | 2 | 75 |
| " | Mary Leddy | 1 | 10 |
| " | Dennis Mahan | 2 | 20 |
| " | Jeremiah Shea | | 55 |
| " | William Hollihan | | 55 |
| " | Bridget Haggerty | | 55 |
| " | Kate McMahon | | 55 |
| " | Bridget Bohanna. | | 55 |
| " | Betsy Heath | | 55 |
| " | Thos. B. Garnett | 2 | 20 |
| " | Thomas Gharty | | 55 |
| " | Daniel Hurley | | 55 |
| " | Joseph Taylor | 1 | 65 |
| " | George Braham | 1 | 65 |
| " | Thomas Lennor | 1 | 65 |
| " | George Kernan | 1 | 65 |
| " | Michael Hallisy | | 55 |
| " | Michael O'Donnell | | 55 |
| " | Flory Sullivan | | 55 |
| " | Henry Bryer | | 55 |
| " | W. Slavin | | 55 |
| " | Peter Christian | | 55 |
| " | Daniel Graham | 1 | 10 |
| " | George C. Kaull, Jr | 1 | 10 |
| " | William C. Tennant, Jr | | 55 |
| Apr. 8. | E. C. Brown | | 90 |
| " | W. H. Pullen | | 85 |
| " | Frank Jenks | | 65 |
| Apr. 11. | A. G. Whidden | | 85 |
| " | B. L. Gammon | | 85 |
| " | W. W. Packard | | 85 |
| " | T. A. Gardiner | 4 | 55 |
| Apr. 14. | C. H. Thurber | | 85 |
| Apr. 20. | W. H. Kenyon | | 85 |
| " | Q. A. Hooper | | 85 |
| " | W. S. Mowry | 4 | 50 |
| Apr. 24. | B. S. Howland | | 85 |
| " | John V. Symonds | | 85 |

1876.

| | | |
|---|---|---|
| Apr. 27. | Bennett J. Munroe.............................. | $3 30 |
| Apr. 29. | C. F. Church......................... | 85 |
| " | George N. Bliss............................. | 26 45 |

Total........................................$719 48

*Officers in Criminal Cases.*

1875.

| | | |
|---|---|---|
| May 3. | C. W. Wilcox................................. | $20 35 |
| May 8. | H. B. Macomber............................. | 2 90 |
| May 13. | Patrick Conway.............................. | 8 90 |
| " | George W. White............................ | 2 30 |
| " | F. I. Clarke.... | 2 30 |
| May 14. | John Kenyon................................ | 1 70 |
| " 17. | O. A. Inman................................. | 6 10 |
| " 19. | C. Holden..... | 13 05 |
| " 19. | O. A. Inman................................. | 4 70 |
| " 20. | Barton A. Cook............................. | 23 80 |
| " 21. | Charles Gifford, order of E. S. Hammond.......... | 7 00 |
| " 24. | Andrew J. Patt.............................. | 1 90 |
| June 1. | Alonzo Healy................................ | 1 30 |
| " 1. | O. C. Goodell................................ | 2 70 |
| June 2. | C. A. White................................ | 90 |
| " | Edward S. Hammond......................... | 7 10 |
| " | James H. Collins............................ | 8 10 |
| " | W. C. Dring................................ | 8 10 |
| June 3. | C. H. Hunt................................. | 92 40 |
| " | O. A. Inman................................ | 10 80 |
| June 4. | John B. Pearce,............................. | 23 85 |
| " 12. | O. C. Goodell............................... | 5 80 |
| " 14. | P. Cavanagh................................ | 8 10 |
| " 15. | Lyman B. Bosworth.......................... | 5 10 |
| " 17. | A. W. Colvin................................ | 2 70 |
| " 18. | D. R. Kenyon............................... | 9 70 |
| " 23. | Barton A. Cook............................. | 17 20 |
| " 23. | John Kenyon................................ | 5 10 |
| " 28. | Alonzo Healy................................ | 85 |
| July 1. | Alexander Steele............................. | 16 20 |
| July 3. | S. S. Beaumont.............................. | 16 20 |
| July 6. | O. A. Inman................................ | 6 10 |
| July 7. | C. H. Hunt................................. | 94 50 |

1873.

| | | | |
|---|---|---|---:|
| July | 7. | Edward S. Hammond | $15 20 |
| " | 9. | George W. Whipple | 55 80 |
| " | 13. | George A. Atwood | 2 70 |
| " | 14. | O. C. Goodell | 2 70 |
| " | | J. Beaumont | 16 20 |
| July | 15. | L. B. Bosworth | 5 10 |
| " | 20. | Peter Taylor | 1 70 |
| " | 20. | Alexander Steele | 8 10 |
| " | 21. | Patrick Cawley | 3 10 |
| " | 23. | S. S. Beaumont | 8 10 |
| July | 26. | Barton A. Cook | 23 90 |
| " | | F. B. Garnett | 8 10 |
| " | | John Kenyon | 1 70 |
| " | | Christopher Holden | 19 80 |
| July | 31. | George O. Fairfield | 9 40 |
| " | | C. H. Hunt | 98 70 |
| Aug. | 2. | O. C. Goodell | 5 40 |
| " | | W. H. Pullen | 9 75 |
| Aug. | 3. | Thomas J. Tilley | 9 90 |
| Aug. | 10. | P. K. Potter | 4 50 |
| " | | Alexander Steele | 8 10 |
| " | | F. B. Garnett | 8 10 |
| Aug. | 13. | C. E. Sisson | 10 70 |
| Aug. | 14. | L. B. Bosworth | 10 20 |
| " | | P. K. Potter | 4 50 |
| Aug. | 26. | C. E. Sisson | 10 70 |
| Aug. | 30. | J. Beaumont | 8 10 |
| " | | S. H. Rogers | 11 00 |
| Sept. | 2. | O. A. Inman | 15 70 |
| Sept. | 4. | John Kenyon | 1 70 |
| " | | J. Beaumont | 8 10 |
| Sept. | 7. | C. H. Hunt | 111 30 |
| Sept. | 13. | Charles Dickerman | 1 10 |
| " | | Stephen G. Chase | 8 10 |
| Sept. | 16. | Henry C. Pollard | 1 90 |
| Sept. | 17. | O. A. Inman | 6 10 |
| " | | L. B. Bosworth | 14 10 |
| " | | H. B. Macomber | 7 20 |
| Sept. | 20. | Alonzo Healy | 2 90 |

1875.

| | | | |
|---|---|---|---:|
| Sept. 21. | John M. Knowles | $241 | 40 |
| " | O. A. Inman | 6 | 10 |
| Oct. 1. | C. H. Hunt | 107 | 10 |
| Oct 2. | George Manchester | 14 | 20 |
| " | John P. McGaughan | 15 | 50 |
| Oct. 6. | Frank A. Thurber | 7 | 00 |
| Oct. 11. | O A. Inman | 14 | 10 |
| " | J. Beaumont | 21 | 80 |
| Oct. 13. | Robert Negus | 2 | 90 |
| " | H. B. Macomber | 4 | 30 |
| " | Christoher Holden | 23 | 70 |
| " | Fred. N. Goff | 1 | 90 |
| " | Alonzo Healy | 5 | 80 |
| Oct. 16. | W. F. Miller | 2 | 50 |
| " 18. | Fdward S. Hammond | 8 | 10 |
| " 20. | Lewis Haynes | 38 | 50 |
| Oct. 21. | W. R. Page | 7 | 80 |
| " | A. J. Kennedy | 2 | 10 |
| Oct. 23. | John Kenyon | 1 | 70 |
| " | Christopher Holden | 34 | 20 |
| Oct. 26. | L. B. Bosworth | 9 | 00 |
| " 28. | O. C. Goodell | 10 | 80 |
| " 30. | F. B. Garnett | 7 | 10 |
| " 30. | S. S. Beaumont | 8 | 10 |
| Nov. 2. | Randall H. Rice | 13 | 80 |
| " 3. | A. J. Patt | 7 | 00 |
| " 3. | J. H. Collamore | 5 | 80 |
| " 4. | C. H. Hunt | 69 | 30 |
| " 5. | S. H. Rogers | 4 | 10 |
| " 5. | John Kenyon | 2 | 95 |
| " 6. | O. C. Goodell | 10 | 80 |
| " 8. | Barton A. Cook | 8 | 10 |
| " 13. | C. W. Wilcox | 5 | 50 |
| " 16. | E. C. Gardner | 7 | 00 |
| " 19. | James V. Corey | 2 | 90 |
| Nov. 22. | George Manchester | 7 | 10 |
| " | John Kenyon | 1 | 70 |
| " | John C. Tillinghast | 4 | 30 |
| Nov. 24. | G. H. Clough | 2 | 10 |
| " | Alexander Steele | 7 | 10 |

1875.

| | | | |
|---|---|---|---:|
| Nov. | 24. | W. P. Denman | $7 10 |
| Nov. | 26. | O. C. Goodell | 10 80 |
| " | 29. | Edward S. Hammond | 16 20 |
| Dec. | 8. | J. P. McGaughan | 3 70 |
| " | 9. | John Hambly | 6 70 |
| " | 9. | F. J. Clarke | 6 90 |
| " | 10. | S. S. Beaumont | 8 10 |
| " | 13. | Edward S. Hammond | 8 10 |
| " | 15. | S. S. Beaumont | 7 10 |
| " | 16. | John Kenyon | 1 70 |
| " | 16. | Henry Whipple | 4 00 |
| " | 20. | W. R. Page | 8 70 |
| " | 23. | A. C. Johnson | 90 |
| " | 30. | John Kinnecom | 2 70 |
| " | 31. | George W. Whipple | 81 00 |

1876.

| | | | |
|---|---|---|---:|
| Jan. | 4. | O. C. Goodell | 5 40 |
| " | 5. | O. T. Fuller | 5 50 |
| " | 7. | C. W. Wilcox | 10 70 |
| " | 7. | W. R. Page | 3 70 |
| " | 11. | Charles H. Hunt | 90 30 |
| " | 18. | O. T. Fuller | 5 50 |
| " | 18. | Edward S. Hammond | 8 10 |
| " | 21. | L. B. Bosworth | 5 10 |
| " | 22. | O. A. Inman | 9 40 |
| " | 22. | Frank A. Thurber | 8 50 |
| " | 24. | O. A. Inman | 10 80 |
| " | 25 | Frank A. Thurber | 8 50 |
| " | 25. | O. A. Inman | 9 40 |
| " | 26. | George O. Fairfield | 9 40 |
| " | 26. | O. T. Fuller | 11 00 |
| " | 26. | C. W. Wilcox | 16 50 |
| " | 27. | Stephen G. Chace | 8 10 |
| " | 31. | W. C. Dring | 7 10 |
| " | 31. | S. S. Beaumont | 8 10 |
| Feb. | 3. | J. P. McGaughan | 9 30 |
| " | 5. | A. J. Patt | 7 00 |
| " | 7. | C. W. Wilcox | 5 50 |
| " | 10. | Edward S. Hammond | 21 30 |

1876.

| | | | |
|---|---|---|---:|
| Feb. | 10. | E. C. Reynolds | $2 30 |
| " | 11. | S. E. Paterson | 1 45 |
| " | 14. | C. W. Wilcox | 11 00 |
| " | 17. | John A. Ross | 3 10 |
| " | 19. | C. H. Chapman | 9 90 |
| " | 19. | Andrew J. Patt | 3 50 |
| " | 19. | George Kidder | 1 90 |
| " | 21. | J. P. McGaughan | 3 10 |
| " | 23. | C. W. Wilcox | 14 60 |
| " | 23. | W. R. Page | 5 90 |
| " | 26. | Henry Whipple | 13 40 |
| Mar. | 1. | Alonzo Healy | 1 80 |
| " | 8. | W. F. Miller | 3 90 |
| " | 16. | F. A. Allen | 1 70 |
| " | 18. | C. H. Hunt | 121 80 |
| " | 20. | C. W. Wilcox | 5 50 |
| " | 20. | Edward S. Hammond | 24 30 |
| " | 23. | O. T. Fuller | 4 10 |
| " | 27. | O. A. Inman | 6 10 |
| " | 27. | W. A. Medbury | 3 70 |
| " | 28. | L. B. Bosworth | 3 70 |
| Apr. | 4. | Thomas J. Tilley | 11 10 |
| " | 7. | Barton A. Cook | 8 20 |
| " | 7. | A. J. Patt | 3 50 |
| " | 8. | Christopher Holden | 82 70 |
| " | 10. | O. C. Goodell | 2 90 |
| " | 20. | C. W. Wilcox | 5 50 |
| " | 21. | L. B. Bosworth | 5 10 |
| " | 22. | Andrew J. Patt | 3 50 |
| " | 24. | E. C. Reynolds | 2 10 |
| " | 24. | Barton A Cook | 8 20 |
| " | 25. | F. B. Garnett | 8 10 |
| " | 25. | Edward S. Hammond | 8 10 |
| " | 25. | Lowell Pitcher | 1 90 |
| " | 27. | J. P. McGaughan | 3 10 |
| " | 27. | O. A. Inman | 12 20 |
| " | 28. | T. W. Hayward | 20 45 |
| " | 29. | George W. Whipple | 9 30 |
| " | 29. | C. E. Sisson | 10 70 |

Total ......................................$2,587 80

### Public Schools.

**1875.**

| | | | | | |
|---|---|---|---|---|---|
| July 15. | Town Treasurer, East Providence | | | $502 | 33 |
| " | " | " | Barrington | 251 | 16 |
| " | " | " | Burrillville | 941 | 86 |
| " | " | " | Charlestown | 502 | 33 |
| " | " | " | Coventry | 1,130 | 23 |
| " | " | " | Cranston | 627 | 91 |
| " | " | " | East Greenwich | 313 | 95 |
| " | " | " | Exeter | 753 | 49 |
| " | " | " | Foster | 1,130 | 23 |
| " | " | " | Glocester | 941 | 86 |
| " | " | " | Hopkinton | 753 | 49 |
| " | " | " | Jamestown | 125 | 58 |
| " | " | " | Johnston | 1,004 | 65 |
| " | City | " | Newport | 1,444 | 17 |
| " | Town | " | North Providence | 188 | 37 |
| " | " | " | North Smithfield | 690 | 70 |
| " | " | " | Pawtucket | 502 | 33 |
| " | " | " | Portsmouth | 502 | 33 |
| " | " | " | Richmond | 941 | 86 |
| " | " | " | Scituate | 1,193 | 08 |
| " | " | " | Smithfield | 627 | 91 |
| " | " | " | Tiverton | 753 | 49 |
| " | " | " | Warren | 376 | 74 |
| " | " | " | Westerly | 879 | 07 |
| " | " | " | West Greenwich | 630 | 70 |
| July 29. | " | " | Little Compton | 627 | 91 |
| " | " | " | Lincoln | 753 | 49 |
| July 31. | " | " | Bristol | 439 | 53 |
| " | " | " | North Kingstown | 941 | 86 |
| July 3. | City | " | Providence | 1,820 | 93 |
| July 10. | Town | " | Cumberland | 879 | 07 |
| July 16. | " | " | Middletown | 313 | 95 |
| July 23. | " | " | South Kingstown | 1,381 | 40 |
| " | " | " | Woonsocket | 627 | 91 |
| July 26. | " | " | New Shoreham | 376 | 74 |
| Oct. 22. | " | " | Warwick | 1,067 | 44 |
| Dec. 31. | " | " | North Smithfield | 800 | 39 |

1875.

| | | | | | |
|---|---|---|---|---|---|
| Dec. 31. | Town Treasurer, | Barrington | $234 | 49 |
| " | " | " | Bristol | 1,424 | 02 |
| " | " | " | Burrillville | 1,571 | 71 |
| " | " | " | Charlestown | 330 | 42 |
| " | " | " | Coventry | 1,235 | 47 |
| " | " | " | Cranston | 1,406 | 95 |
| " | " | " | Cumberland | 1,100 | 78 |
| " | " | " | East Greenwich | 699 | 61 |
| " | " | " | East Providence | 815 | 89 |
| " | " | " | Exeter | 430 | 23 |
| " | " | " | Foster | 429 | 26 |
| " | " | " | Glocester | 669 | 57 |
| " | " | " | Hopkinton | 819 | 77 |
| " | " | " | Jamestown | 93 | 02 |
| " | " | " | Johnston | 1,249 | 97 |
| " | " | " | Lincoln | 2,629 | 83 |
| " | " | " | Middletown | 270 | 85 |
| " | " | " | Little Compton | 271 | 32 |
| " | City | " | Newport | 3,625 | 87 |
| " | Town | " | New Shoreham | 346 | 90 |
| " | " | " | North Kingstown | 958 | 84 |
| " | " | " | North Providence | 322 | 31 |
| " | " | " | Pawtucket | 4,254 | 83 |
| " | " | " | Portsmouth | 599 | 81 |
| " | City | " | Providence | 22,735 | 90 |
| " | Town | " | Richmond | 586 | 24 |
| " | " | " | Scituate | 1,020 | 35 |
| " | " | " | Smithfield | 736 | 44 |
| " | " | " | South Kingstown | 1,487 | 41 |
| " | " | " | Tiverton | 576 | 55 |
| " | " | " | Warwick | 3,145 | 87 |
| " | " | " | Warren | 897 | 66 |
| " | " | " | Westerly | 1,492 | 26 |
| " | " | " | West Greenwich | 323 | 64 |
| " | " | " | Woonsocket | 8,407 | 07 |

Total.....................................$90,000 00

### *State Normal School.*

1875.
June 23.   George L. Locke, treasurer....................$2,500 00
June 12.   George L. Locke, treasurer.................... 2,500 00
  1876.
Jan. 21.   George L. Locke, treasurer.................... 2,500 00
Apr. 10.   George L. Locke, treasurer.................... 2,500 00

      Total.......................................$10,000 00

### *Mileage State Normal School.*

1875.
June 23.   George L. Locke, treasurer....................$750 00
  1876.
Jan. 21.   George L. Locke, treasurer.................... 590 20

      Total........................................$1,340 20

### *Reform School.*

1875.
June  2.   Providence Reform School ....................$5,245 43
Sept.  2.   Providence Reform School..................... 5.341 43
Dec.  2.   Providence Reform School..................... 5,198 29
  1876.
Mar.  3.   Providence Reform School..................... 4,851 43

      Total............................ .........$20,636. 58

### *Teachers' Institutes.*

1875.
June. 24.   Thomas B. Stockwell......................... $55 00
Oct.  25.   Sarah I. Carpenter........................... 75 00
Dec.  8.   Sarah I. Carpenter........................... 75 00
  1876.
Jan. 22.   B. V. Gallup................................. 100 00

      Total........................................$305 00

*Insane and other Dependent Persons.*

1875.

| | | | |
|---|---|---|---|
| May | 12. | City of Boston............................ | $54 00 |
| July | 12. | Perkins Inst. and Mass. Asylum for the Blind.... | 3,725 00 |
| July | 12. | Mass. School for I. and F. M. Youth............ | 800 00 |
| July | 21. | Butler Hospital............................ | 806 13 |
| Oct. | 4. | American Asylum for Deaf and Dumb........... | 883 93 |
| Oct. | 13. | Butler Hospital............................ | 931 26 |

1876.

| | | | |
|---|---|---|---|
| Jan. | 15. | Butler Hospital............................ | 1,165 95 |
| Apr. | 18. | Butler Hospital............................ | 1,128 25 |
| Apr. | 29. | American Asylum for Deaf and Dumb........... | 612 50 |

Total.......................................$9,607 02

*Militia and Military Affairs.*

1875.

| | | | |
|---|---|---|---|
| May | 10. | Armstrong & Burlingame, rent of rooms, Hay Building, from Jan. 1, to April 1, 1875....... | $50 00 |
| June | 2. | C. R. Dennis, Freight, Carriage Hire, &c., Q. M. General's Department.................... | 17 85 |
| July | 21. | Armstrong & Burlingame, rent of rooms, Hay Building, to July 1, 1875................. | 50 00 |
| Oct. | 19. | Armstrong & Burlingame, rent of rooms, Hay Building, to Oct. 1, 1875................. | 50 00 |
| " | 26. | Geo. Greene, labor of men, 1st Brigade Muster.. | 20 00 |
| " | 30. | Board of Aldermen, Newport, rent of Armory, Redwood Band, year ending Dec. 30, 1874... | 100 00 |
| Nov. | 3. | N. Y., P. & B. R. R. Co., transportation of Westerly Rifles and Kentish Guards to Providence and return........................ | 277 54 |
| " | 24. | G. W. Easterbrooks, repairs Tower Lt. Battery. | 151 54 |
| " | 26. | Prov. & Worcester R. R. Co., transportation of Military to Providence and return.......... | 69 00 |
| " | 29. | American Steamboat Co., transportation of Military to Providence and return............. | 64 75 |
| " | 29. | Prov., Warren & Bristol R. R. Co., transportation of Military to Providence and return.... | 80 00 |

1875.

| | | | |
|---|---|---|---|
| Dec. | 3. | Thomas Phelan, services as Armorer, Co. F, R. I. Guards .............................. | $37 80 |
| " | 3. | Army and Navy Journal, 100 copies Wingate's Manual Rifle Practice, Adj't. Gen. Dept...... | 100 00 |

1876.

| | | | |
|---|---|---|---|
| Jan. | 3. | D. W. Reeves, services of American Band, 1875. | 150 00 |
| " | 6. | L. A. Tillinghast, Rations 1st and 2d Brigades, Muster Day.............................. | 320 75 |
| " | 7. | Lyman Himes, services Co. C, 3d Battalion, 1st Brigade, and Armorer, 1875............... | 235 00 |
| " | 11. | P. A. Cosgrove, services Co. C, 5th Battalion 2d Brigade, and Armorer, 1875.............. | 259 00 |
| " | 11. | B. M. Bosworth, Jr., services Co. A, 2d Battalion, 2d Brigade, and Armorer, 1875......... | 290 50 |
| " | 11. | E. L. Freeman, services of Armorer, Lincoln Union Guards to disbandment.............. | 89 43 |
| " | 11. | Chickering & Miller, teaming and drawing guns, Q. M. Gen. Dept......................... | 20 00 |
| " | 11. | Thomas Chambers, services of Co. B, 2d Battalion, 1st Brigade, and Armorer, 1875......... | 220 00 |
| " | 11. | Patrick McHugh, services of Co. A, 5th Battalion, 2d Brigade, and Armorer, 1875........... | 328 00 |
| " | 11. | W. McPherson, services of Co. F, 5th Battalion, 2d Brigade, and Armorer, 1875............. | 263 50 |
| " | 11. | Thomas W. Chace, services of Self and Staff, 1st Brigade, 1875.......................... | 46 50 |
| " | 11. | A. N. Crandall, services of Field and Staff, 3d Battery, 1st Brigade, 1875.................. | 26 50 |
| " | 11. | W. B. W. Hallet, services of Co. B, 4th Battalion, 2d Brigade, and Armorer, 1875......... | 355 00 |
| " | 11. | Edward Thayer, services of Co. B. 1st Battalion of Lt. Artillery, and Armorer, 1875......... | 757 50 |
| " | 11. | John Cullen, services of Co. B, 5th Battalion, 2d Brigade, and Armorer.................... | 256 00 |
| " | 11. | Joseph M. Kendrick, services of Co. A, 1st Battalion, 2d Brigade, and Armorer, 1875...... | 356 50 |
| " | 11. | E. Frank Annable, services of Co. B, 1st Battalion, 2d Brigade, and Armorer, 1875......... | 350 50 |

1876.

Jan. 11. W. Frankland, services of Co. C, 1st Battalion,
2d Brigade, and Armorer, 1875.............. $313 00

" 11. Edwin Draper, services of Co. D, 1st Battalion,
2d Brigade, and Armorer,1875.............. 329 50

" 11. R. H. I. Goddard, services of Field and Staff, 1st
Battalion, 2d Brigade, 1875................ 85 50

" 11. Daniel Champlin, services of Co. A, 3d Battalion, 1st Brigade, and Armorer, 1875......... 337 00

" 11. J. Albert Brown, services of Co. B, 3d Battalion, 1st Brigade, ard Armorer, 1875........ 280 00

" 12. Fred. Miller, services of Self and Staff, 2d Brigade, 1875.............................. 42 00

" 14. George A. Emerson, services of Field and Staff 1st Battalion Light Artillery, 1875.......... 64 50

" 14. J Lippitt Snow, services of Co's. A and B, Self and Staff, 1st Battalion of Cavalry 1875.... 906 50

" 14. James E. Curran, services of Co. D, 5th Battalion, 2d Brigade, and Armorer, 1875........ 284 50

" 17. Jeremiah Costine, services of Field and Staff, 5th Battalion, 2d Brigade, 1875.............. 43 00

" 18. Armstrong & Burlingame, rent of room, Hay Building, to Q. M. General................ 50 00

" 22. Thomas Brinn, services of Co. B, 5th Battalion, 1st Brigade, and Armorer, 1875............ 265 00

" 22. Lewis Kenegee, services of Co. C, 5th Battalion, 1st Brigade, and Armorer, 1875............ 301 00

" 22. Amos Sherman, services of Field and Staff, 1st Battalion of Infantry, 1875................ 53 50

" 22. Alexander Strauss, services of Co. C, 1st Battalion of Cavalry, and Armorer, 1875.......... 436 00

" 24. A. Marshall Terrence, services of Co. A, 6th Battalion, 1st Brigade, and Armorer, 1875 ...... 263 50

" 24. John H. Munroe, services of Field and Staff, 1st Brigade, 1875........................... 48 50

" 24. Thomas Cahill, services of Co. C, 2d Battalion, 1st Brigade, and Armorer, 1875............ 313 00

" 27. Joseph A. Sheffield, services of 1st Brigade Band, 1875....... ... ................... 68 00

" 27. James W. Johnson, services of Co. D, 6th, Battalion, and Armorer, 1875................. 265 00

1876.

| | | | | |
|---|---|---|---|---|
| Jan. | 31. | C. R. Dennis, allowance for Annual Inspection.. | $200 | 00 |
| Feb. | 1. | Town Council of Lincoln, rent of Armories..... | 188 | 85 |
| " | 1. | Board of Aldermen, Newport, rent of Armories. | 200 | 00 |
| " | 1. | Town Council of Westerly, rent of Armories.... | 200 | 00 |
| " | 1. | Town Council of Pawtucket, rent of Armories.. | 300 | 00 |
| " | 1. | Town Council, Bristol, rent of Armory........ | 100 | 00 |
| " | 1. | Fred. Miller, use of tents, Camp Henry Lippitt, 2d Brigade............................ | 23 | 00 |
| " | 1. | Sidney Williams, use of field for Muster, 2d Brigade.............................. | 10 | 00 |
| " | 1. | George C. Jenks, carting tents, &c., General Muster................................ | 8 | 95 |
| " | 1. | Frank McKenzie & Co., posts &c., Camp Henry Lippitt................................ | 14 | 27 |
| " | 1. | A. A. White, tents, 5th Battalion of Infantry, Muster Day............................ | 5 | 00 |
| " | 1. | L. F. Pease, tents, 1st Battalion of Light Artillery, Muster Day........................ | 8 | 50 |
| " | 1. | C. E. Chickering, oats for Battery B, 1st Battalion of Lt. Artillery, Muster Day........... | 12 | 00 |
| " | 3. | W. R. Walker, services of Self and Staff, 1875.. | 46 | 50 |
| " | 3. | I. A. Sherman, carting guns, equipments, &c., to Store House, Elizabeth Building.......... | 32 | 90 |
| " | 3. | Charles H. George & Co.,....:.............. | 12 | 76 |
| " | 4. | C. F. Pope & Co., ammunition............... | 515 | 76 |
| " | 4. | J. Harry Welch, use of tents, 1st and 2d Brigades, Muster Day....................... | 126 | 00 |
| " | 5. | James M. Jaques, services of Co. B, 2d Battalion, 1st Brigade, 1875....................... | 78 | 00 |
| " | 5. | C. R. Dennis, postage, freight and other expenses, Q. M. Gen. Dept.................. | 64 | 94 |
| " | 8. | Fourth Battalion of Infantry, tents and putting up of same, Muster Day.................. | 5 | 00 |
| " | 8. | Board of Aldermen, Prov., rent of Armories.... | 1,800 | 00 |
| " | 10. | Day, Sprague & Co., oats, 1st Battalion of Cavalry, Muster Day...................... | 10 | 75 |
| " | 11. | First Battalion of Infantry, Tents and putting up of same, Muster Day.................... | 10 | 00 |
| " | 14. | Philip Whaland, services of Co. E, 5th Battalion, 2d Brigade, and Armorer, 1875......... | 275 | 50 |

1876.

Feb. 15. Albert E. Greene, services of Co. A, 4th Battalion, 2d Brigade, and Armorer, 1875......... $191 50

" 29. Benjamin B. Martin, services of Field and Staff, 2d Battalion of Infantry, 1875.............. 29 00

Mar. 6. Frank G. Allen, services of Co. A, 1st Battalion, Light Artillery, and Armorer, 1875......... 1,404 00

Mar. 14. Co. C, 1st Battalion of Cavalry, rations for men and forage for horses, May 29, 1875......... 26 30

Apr. 8. Rufus Waterman, Trustee, rent of room No. 16, Elizabeth Building, Q. M. General...»...... 41 67

" 14. Samuel Clark, order of C. A. Greene, services of Bristol Artillery, and Armorer, to Apr. 17, 1875.................................... 139 50

" 24. George G. Stillman, camp equipage, Muster 3d Brigade, 1875........................... 28 00

" 25. J. Harry Welch, American flags, 1st Brigade... 101 50

Total......................................$15,797 31

*Public Printing.*

1875.

May 7. Knowles, Anthony & Danielson, advertising for Committee of Gen. Assembly and for Insurance Commissioner.......................... $394 54

May 8. C. A. Greene, advertising Amendment to Constitution................................ 1 50

May 8. A. Crawford Greene, advertising Amendment to Constitution, and publishing Laws of State, one year..........................'.... 99 20

May 13. Providence Press Co., printing for Commissioner of Public Schools....................... 67 95

May 14. Mercury Office, advertising General Order, No. 3, New Militia Law...................... 9 00

May 20. Davis & Pitman, advertising General Order No. 3, New Militia Law, &c.................. 17 50

May 21. Providence Press Co., printing blanks &c., for Attorney General....................... 46 35

1875.

| | | |
|---|---|---|
| May 31. | Providence Press Co., printing Schedule Public Laws, &c., for Sec. of State............... | $748 47 |
| June 10. | Providence Press Co., printing for Sec. of State, Adjutant Gen. and Clerk of House.......... | 151 65 |
| June 16. | Davis & Pitman, printing Roll of Senate and House of Representatives, May Session...... | 53 50 |
| June 28. | W. N. Sherman,............................ | 8 50 |
| June 29. | Providence Press Co., printing Sec. of State..... | 58 05 |
| June 29. | W. N. Sherman, publishing Laws............. | 47 00 |
| July 1. | G. B. & J. H. Utter, publishing Laws, &c., in Narragansett Weekly,..................... | 58 50 |
| July 6. | Providence Press Co., printing Orders on Treasurer, for State Auditor................... | 31 50 |
| July 13. | Brownell & Barrows, binding for Sec. of State, Commissioner of Public Schools, and Adjutant General............................... | 364 52 |
| July 15. | Providence Press Co., printing blanks, &c., for Sec. of State and Justice Court, Woonsocket. | 83 75 |
| July 22. | Providence Press Co., printing for Clerk of Senate, May Session...................... | 64 80 |
| July 31. | Providence Press Co., printing for Clerk of House of Representatives, May Session........... | 31 50 |
| Aug. 10. | Providence Press Co., printing Schedules for Sec. of State............................. | 295 45 |
| Aug. 18. | Brownell & Barrows, binding for sundry offices.. | 72 46 |
| Aug. 23. | D. Gillies, advertising Public Laws for Sec. of State................................. | 58 00 |
| Aug. 25. | Providence Press Co., printing Report of Ins. Commissioner........................... | 908 65 |
| Sept. 7. | Brownell & Barrows, binding for sundry offices. | 74 15 |
| Sept. 7. | Providence Press Co., printing for Sec. of State and Justice Court Providence............. | 96 09 |
| Sept. 10. | Providence Press Co., printing for Justice Court, Newport................... ............. | 18 00 |
| Sept. 21. | Providence Press Co., printing for Joint Com. of Legislature.............................. | 30 00 |
| Sept. 21. | J. W. Barton, advertising Public Laws in Warren Gazette, 1874–5..................... | 47 00 |
| Sept. 21. | Providence Press Co., printing for Gen. Treas. and Adjutant Gen........................ | 82 08 |

1875.

| | |
|---|---|
| Sept. 28. Providence Press Co., printing, Commissioner of Public Schools........................... | $27 75 |
| Oct. 11. Brownell & Barrows, binding Ins. Reports...... | 28 50 |
| Oct. 11. Providence Press Co. printing, blanks, Jus. Court, Providence............................... | 114 80 |
| Oct. 13. Providence Press Co., printing Auditor's Report................................. | 120 51 |
| Oct. 23. H. M. Coombs & Co., binding, sundry offices... | 40 48 |
| Nov. 17. Providence Press Co., printing blanks, &c., Adjt. General................................. | 17 55 |
| Dec. 7. Providence Press Co., printing Taxation of Cost Blank, State Auditor and for Jus. Court, Prov. | 208 35 |
| Dec. 9. H. M. Coombs, binding, sundry offices ........ | 10 50 |
| Dec. 17. Providence Press Co., printing Registration of Births, Marriages and Deaths Report, and other work for Secretary of State............... | 524 27 |
| Dec. 21. Providence Press Co., printing, Justice Court, Pawtucket....................... | 17 10 |
| Dec. 21. Prov. Press Co., printing Rhode Island Manual, | 343 52 |

1876.

| | |
|---|---|
| Jan. 3. E. L. Freeman & Co., publishing Laws in Visitor from Oct. 1, 1874 to Oct. 1, 1875........... | 60 00 |
| Jan. 4. Spectator Co., printing Blanks for Ins. Commissioner.................................. | 126 89 |
| Jan. 11. Samuel H. Row, printing Blanks for Ins. Commissioner.............................. | 54 08 |
| Jan. 11. H. M. Coombs & Co., binding, &c., Sec. of State | 134 06 |
| Jan. 13. Providence Press Co., printing, Sec. of State... | 515 66 |
| Jan. 15. C. A. Greene, adv. Laws and Thanksgiving Proclamation.............................. | 59 00 |
| Jan. 18. Knowles, A. & Dainelson, adv. for sundry offices.. | 93 17 |
| Jan. 21. Providence Press Co., adv. and printing Blanks for sundry offices......................... | 59 99 |
| Jan. 25. S. B. Keach, publishing Laws in Town and Country, 1875........................... | 40 00 |
| Jan. 31. H. M. Coombs & Co., binding for Sec. of State, Ins. Commissioner, and House of Rep....... | 100 04 |
| Feb. 1. Mercury Office, publishing Laws, &c. in Mercury and printing for Sheriff of Newport......... | 57 00 |

5

1876.

| | | | |
|---|---|---|---|
| Feb. | 3. | Providence Press Co., printing Gov's Message and Report of R. R. Commissioner.......... | $172 21 |
| Feb. | 4. | S. S. Foss, publishing Laws, &c. in Woonsocket Patriot................................. | 61 00 |
| " | 10. | LeRoy B. Pease, publishing Laws, &c. in Woon. Daily Reporter......................... | 60 00 |
| " | " | S. S. Foss, adv. Amendments to Constitution... | 2 00 |
| " | 14. | Nickerson & Sibley, publishing Laws, &c., and adv. meeting of Joint Committee, General Assembly. ............................... | 69 00 |
| " | 17. | Providence Press Co., publishing Laws in Evening Press and Morning Star, from May 5, 1873 to June. 1875............................. | 325 00 |
| " | 21. | Providence Press Co., printing Report of Com. of Public Schools......................... | 895 93 |
| " | 24. | Providence Press Co., printing Second Annual Report of New State Prison Committee, &c... | 34 77 |
| Mar. | 1. | Providence Press Co., printing for Senate. House of Representatives and Sec. of State, and adv. Legislative Hearing....................... | 171 90 |
| " | 3. | Providence Press Co., printing, Justice Court, Newport and Sec. of State................. | 39 22 |
| " | 4. | Providence Press Co., printing for General Treasurer and House of Representatives.......... | . 40 26 |
| " | 6. | Providence Press Co., printing Adjutant General's Report, and Blanks for Jus. Court, Woonsocket | 118 76 |
| " | " | H. M. Coombs & Co., binding, sundry offices... | 54 12 |
| " | 8. | Davis & Pitman, publishing Laws, &c., in Newport Daily News and Journal............... | 66 00 |
| " | 9. | E. L. Freeman & Co., publishing Bills, &c., Sec. of State and House of Representatives....... | 16 00 |
| " | 10. | H. M. Coombs & Co., binding, wrapping and mailing Reports of School Commissioner..... | 180 13 |
| " | 16. | Providence Press Co., printing for Senate, House of Representatives, Sec. of State and Ins. Commissioner............. .............. | 149 43 |
| " | 18. | Davis & Pitman, publishing Laws in Newport Journal and adv. Legislative Hearing........ | ˙67 50 |
| " | 18. | Mercury Office, advertising Legislative Hearing, | 2 00 |
| " | 20. | Providence Press Co., printing, State Auditor and Commissioner of Public Schools............ | 245 98 |

1876.

Mar. 23. Providence Press Co., printing Inspectors of State Prison Report, &c.................... $86 04

" 27. H. M. Coombs & Co., binding, sundry offices... 44 00

" 31. Providence Press Co., printing for Senate, House of Representatives and Secretary of State... 188 95

April 4. Providence Press Co., printing Report of Board of Charities and Corrections .............. 134 19

" 6. Providence Press Co., printing Quartermaster General's Report......................... 112 10

" 20, Providence Press Co., printing, Gen. Assembly.. 69 98

" 21. Providence Press Co., printing Report of Joint Committee on State Farm, &c............. 82 41

" 24. H. M. Coombs & Co., binding, sundry offices.. 20 01

" 25. A. Crawford Greene, adv. Amendments to Constitution in Advertiser and Gazette.......... 18 00

" 29. Knowles, Anthony & Danielson, publishing Laws 1875, and adv. Legislative Hearings......... 314 45

"  " Knowles, Anthony & Danielson, adv. examination of State Farm by Com. of G. A........ 3 30

"  " Davis & Pitman, advertising Reward in News and Journal........................... 5 00

Total.........................................$10,621 52.

*Court Houses and Jails.*

1875.

May 3. C. W. Wilcox, sundry articles, Washington County Jail............................ $10 93

" 4. James Tucker, Jr., cuspadors, tumblers, &c., State House, Providence................. 11 00

" 8. C. A. Greene, sundry articles, Bristol County Jail and Court House...... 9 80

" 12. Eveline G. Smith, making mattresses, &c., and putting on paper, Kent County Jail......... 7 40

" 17. Thomas Halstead, carting 17 loads of ashes from State House, Providence................... 12 75

" 20. Edward D. Jones, whitewashing and sundry articles, Newport County Jail............. 25 50

"  " W. C. Cozzens & Co., paper and border, Newport County Jail...................... 7 5L

1875.

| | | | |
|---|---|---|---|
| May | 20. | Benjamin B. Cornell, hanging paper, Newport County Jail............................... | $7 00 |
| " | " | Barker, Whitaker & Co., 1 lawn mower, State House, Providence......................... | 20 00 |
| " | " | Cattanach & Cliff, painting, setting glass, &c., Court House, Providence................... | 34 33 |
| " | 31. | George Manchester, work on flag and staff, State House, Newport..................... | 2 50 |
| " | " | Mary Lyons, cleaning offices in State House, Providence, and Elizabeth building.......... | 40 50 |
| " | " | George L. Slocum, repairs on locks, State House, Newport................................ | 2 25 |
| " | " | Providence S. C. Cleaning Establishment, cleaning carpets for Public offices ............... | 22 70 |
| June | 2. | S. G. Snow, re-covering and finishing desks, S. House Newport.......................... | 23 75 |
| " | 3. | Isabel F. Spinning, sundry articles, Bristol County Jail.............................. | 53 00 |
| " | 11. | Newport Gas Lt. Co., repairing fixtures, State House and Jail, Newport .................. | 2 22 |
| " | 16. | George Nason, chairs, mirror, &c., Sheriffs Office, Newport ........................... | 15 90 |
| " | 29. | Providence Concrete Co., concrete and labor on premises of Kent County Court House ...... | 67 00 |
| " | " | Cleveland Brothers......................... | 2 00 |
| July | 1. | Mary Lyons, cleaning water closets, State House, Providence, from April 15 to July 1, 1875.... | 12 00 |
| " | 1. | D. Brainard Blake, repairing clocks, Auditor and Adjutant General........................ | 2 00 |
| " | 1. | George Manchester, directory, &c., State House, Newport................................ | 3 25 |
| " | 2. | W. S. Fifield, sundry articles for Court House and Col. Street, C. R., Providence .......... | 46 03 |
| " | 3. | James L. Congdon, lime and nails for Kent Co. Jail.................................. | 2 53 |
| " | 2. | James Tucker, Jr., sundry articles for Elizabeth building and State House, Providence........ | 25 75 |
| " | 8. | Freeman & Kelly, moving and setting up stoves, State House, Providence ................. | 2 95 |
| " | 9. | Providence S. C. Cleaning Establishment, cleaning carpets, State House, Providence........ | 5 40 |

1875.

| | | | |
|---|---|---|---|
| July | 9. | John H. Eddy, two feather dusters............ | $5 62 |
| " | " | John R. Macomber, chandelier, labor, &c., Col. Street Court Room........:............... | 21 35 |
| " | 16. | W. C. Cozzens & Co., towels, matting, &c., State House, Newport.................... | 78 49 |
| " | 20. | James Clark, repairs of Jail, Bristol.......... | 10 50 |
| " | " | Henry C. Gray, repairs of Jail, Bristol........ | 5 25 |
| " | " | William H. Pitman, " " " ........ | 27 89 |
| " | " | W. H. Bell, " " " ........ | 23 03 |
| " | " | Charles Stone, " " " ........ | 4 00 |
| " | " | E. P. Brownell, " " " ........ | 9 80 |
| " | " | B. M. Lincoln, " " " ........ | 20 27 |
| " | " | James Hoar, " " " ........ | 4 50 |
| " | " | John H. Munro, " " " ........ | 3 18 |
| " | " | James F. Munro, " " " ........ | 37 00 |
| " | " | James Hoar, " " " ........ | 10 08 |
| " | " | J. B. F. Smith, paint, labor, &c., State House and Jail, Newport...................... | 26 60 |
| " | 22. | Tillinghast & Sherman, oil cloth, &c., Secretary of State................................ | 33 00 |
| " | 24. | John Dugan, re-glazing glass, State House, Newport....... ........................... | 11 25 |
| " | 30. | Belcher Brothers, nails, Kent County Court House.... ............................ | 1 70 |
| " | " | W. H Hunt & Son, paint and lead, Kent Co. C. H. | 4 35 |
| " | 31. | John McIver, labor and sundry articles, Court House, Providence...................... | 419 94 |
| Aug. | 3. | W. Barstow & Co., carpeting, oil cloths, matting, sundry offices.......................... | 330 23 |
| " | 9. | Providence Wire Works.................... | 5 00 |
| " | 10. | Edward D. Jones, sundry articles, Newport County Jail........................... | 23 00 |
| " | 13. | Borgon & Ohlson, new cushions, Kent County Court House........................... | 20 00 |
| " | 23. | D. G. Wilbur, sundry articles, Kent County Jail.................................. | 6 83 |
| " | " | J. S. Smith, labor, Kent County Jail..:....... | 29 00 |
| " | 24. | W. C. Cozzens & Co., oil cloth, State House, Newport............................... | 5 00 |
| " | " | David Cady & Co., carpets and matting, &c., Kent County Court House................ | 204 30 |

1875.

| | | |
|---|---|---|
| Sept. 13. | John A. Howland, iron pipe and labor, Court House, Providence........................ | $47 30 |
| " ' 16. | Newport Ice Co., ice, S. House, Newport, 1875. | 8 40 |
| Oct. 1. | David Cady, carpet, Kent County Court House . | 2 50 |
| " " | Mary Lyons, cleaning water closets, July 1, to Oct. 1, 1875........................... | 12 00 |
| " 1. | John Sherson, cutting grass, &c., season of 1875, State House, Providence............. | 30 00 |
| " 2. | Browning & Fitts, sundry articles, Kent County Jail.............................. | 11 69 |
| " 4. | Mary Lyons, cleaning paint, &c., State House Providence............................ | 18 00 |
| " ' 11. | W. Barstow & Co., 50 yards lining, Adjutant General's Office....................... | 7 50 |
| Oct. 11. | Chambers, Calder & Co., sundry articles, Court House, Providence...................... | 22 50 |
| " 11. | J. A. Brown, weather vane Washington County Court House........................... | 70 00 |
| " 20. | D. Brainard Blake, repairing clock, State House Providence,........................ | 5 00 |
| " 27. | Providence S. C. C. Establishment, cleaning carpets, sheriff Providence County........... | 8 00 |
| Nov. 6. | Samuel Cliff, paint, glass, labor, etc., Court House, Elizabeth Building and College street Court Room, Providence...................... | 89 89 |
| " 8. | Thos. Stevens, watering street in front of Jail and State House, Newport.................... | 28 00 |
| " 13. | Edward D. Jones, washing, whitewashing, etc., Newport County Jail................... | 19 55 |
| " 13. | C. W. Wilcox, sundry articles, Washington County Jail.......................... | 17 84 |
| " 16. | F. J. Sheldon safe for Sheriff's Office, Providence, | 33 10 |
| " 27. | Thos. Halstead, carting ashes from State House and College street Court Room. Providence... | 9 00 |
| Dec. 6. | H. A. Freeman, labor, etc., Court House and College Street Court Room, Providence...... | 40 80 |
| " 10. | John B. Munro, crockery, Bristol County Court House................................ | 2 25 |
| " 16. | Newport Gas Light Co., repairing fixtures, Newport County Jail.....,................. | 4 23 |

1875.

| | | |
|---|---|---:|
| Dec. 22. | N. A. Woodward & Co., repairing furnace, Washington County Jail...................... | $14 90 |
| " 23. | N. Gladding, repairs Bristol County Jail...... | 60 |
| 1876. | | |
| Jan. 3. | Mary Lyons, cleaning water closets, State House, Providence, Oct. 1, 1875, to Jan. 1, 1876..... | 12 00 |
| " 3. | W. S. Fifield, sundry articles, College street Court Room and Court House, Providence... | 22 43 |
| " 3. | E. W. Lovell & Co., sundry articles, Court House and Jail, Kent County.... ................. | 17 35 |
| " 3. | Henry Miller, watering street in front of State House, Providence, April 2 to Nov. 1....... | 29 00 |
| " 6. | J. A. Howland, chimney cap, State House, Prov. | 9 00 |
| " 7. | Newport Ice Co., ice, State House and Jail, Newport.............................. | 9 90 |
| " 11. | Browning & Fitts, articles, Kent County Jail... | 26 20 |
| " 15. | P. O'Conner, plumbing, State House, Providence, | 10 10 |
| " 18. | C. B. Sawyer, labor on water closets, State House, Providence....................... | 5 70 |
| " 21. | W. H. Fenner & Co., articles and labor, Kent County Jail............................. | 23 42 |
| " 22. | Earl Carpenter & Son, ice, public offices, 1875. | 119 89 |
| " 22. | T. T. Allen & Co., blankets, Bristol County Jail, | 5 79 |
| " 26. | H. N. Foster, making new fastenings, Kent County Jail............................ | 10 00 |
| " 26. | Cleveland Brothers, repairing lounge, etc., State House, Providence........................ | 8 50 |
| " 26. | Thos. J. Tilley, sundry articles, Kent County Jail and Court House.................... | 26 43 |
| " 28. | Ann Devine, cleaning paint, State House, Prov.. | 10 50 |
| " 31. | Providence Water Works, city water, State House, Providence....................... | 13 17 |
| Feb. 1. | Mary Lyons, cleaning paint, State House, Prov. | 10 50 |
| " 1. | D. F. Thorpe, soap, State House, Providence... | 1 00 |
| " 3. | Edward W. Lawton, six pair blankets, Newport County Jail.............................. | 24 60 |
| " 3. | A. C. Titus & Co., sundry articles, Newport County Jail and State House.............. | 133 80 |
| " 3. | C. L. Holden, two dozen towels, State House, Providence.............................. | 5 50 |

1876.
Feb. 7.   C. W. Wilcox, sundry articles, Washington
          County Jail.............................. $15 82
 "   7.   W. S. Roberts, clothing, Kent County Jail..... 4 75
 "   8.   Geo. W. Sheldon & Co., pipe, shovel, poker, etc.,
          Washington County Court House........... 30 90
 "  11.   Edward D. Jones, sundry articles, Newport Jail, 21 50
 "  11.   Finch, Engs & Co., cement, Newport Jail...... 1 25
 "  11.   Joseph Higgins, repairing pump, Newport Jail.. 1 50
 "  11.   Sheffield Arnold, repairing clock, Kent County
          Court House.......  ..................... 2 00
 "  12.   Thos. Halstead, carting ashes from State House
          and Court Room, Providence........  ...... 12 75
 "  24.   Owen & Bennett, sundry articles, Kent County
          Jail................................  .... 10 99
Mar. 6.   W. S. Fifield, sundry articles, State House and
          Court of Common Pleas, Providence........ 69 91
 "   8.   H. M. Coombs & Co., one criminal record, Kent
          County Jail.......................  ...... 8 00
 "   8.   Newport Gas Light Co., putting fixtures in cel-
          lar, State House, Newport................. 2 37
 "  20.   H, A. Freeman, pipes, labor, etc., State House,
          Providence............................... 6 79
Apr. 3.   Mary Lyons, cleaning water closets to April 1,
          1876........................................ 12 00
 "   3.   C. F. Southwick, re-bottoming chairs and stool,
          Adjutant General's Office.................. 4 75
                                                  _____
          Total........................................$3,092 17

## *Fuel and Gas.*

1875.
May  3.   C. W. Wilcox, charcoal, Washington County
          Jail..................................... $6 30
June 3.   Isabel F. Spinning, coal and wood, Bristol
          County Jail............................. 22 00
 "  11.   Newport Gas Light Co., gas, Court House and
          Jail, Newport........................... 87 20
 "   "    Rufus Waterman, heating Elizabeth building,
          December 15, 1874, to May 15, 1875........ 262 50

1875.

| | | | |
|---|---|---|---|
| June 16. | Cushman, Wilcox & Co., wood and kindlings, Justice Court Room, Pawtucket............ | $8 85 |
| " 22. | Joseph Bradford & Co., coal, Court House and Jail, Newport............................ | 79 35 |
| July 3. | Providence Gas Co., gas, Public Offices, Prov... | 39 76 |
| " 10. | Joseph Bradford, & Co., coal, Newport Jail and Court House........................... | 23 55 |
| " " | Bristol Gas Light Co., gas, Court House and Jail, Bristol............................ | 32 00 |
| " 26. | A. T. & T. J. Usher, wood.................... | 2 26 |
| " " | Tucker, Swan & Co., coal, State House and Col. street Court Room........................ | 297 23 |
| Aug. 23. | Joseph Bradford & Co., coal and wood, Newport Jail and Court House.................... | 141 60 |
| Sept. 28. | N. N. Cole, wood and coal, Bristol County Jail. | 84 38 |
| Oct. 11. | Providence Gas Co., gas, Public Offices, Prov... | 23 52 |
| " 22. | Thomas G. Allen, charcoal, Kent County Jail... | 24 70 |
| Nov. 5. | Bristol Gas Light Co., gas, Court House and Jail, Bristol................................. | 30 00 |
| " " | Edwin A. King, charcoal, Court House, Prov... | 17 85 |
| " 13. | Watson & Wells, coal, Court House and Jail, Washington County.................. ....... | 117 57 |
| " " | C. W. Wilcox, wood, Washington County Jail.. | 12 50 |
| " 23. | Edwin A. King, charcoal, Court House, Prov... | 12 95 |
| Dec. 16. | Newport Gas Light Co., gas, Court House and Jail, Newport........................... | 46 55 |
| " 17. | E. A. King, charcoal, Court House, Providence. | 10 50 |
| " 28. | R. H. Champlin, coal, Court House and Jail, Kent County............................ | 84 85 |
| " 30. | Newport Coal Co., wood and coal, State House, Newport............................ ......... | 50 25 |

1876.

| | | | |
|---|---|---|---|
| Jan. 7. | Joseph Bradford & Co., charcoal, Newport Jail. | 2 00 |
| " " | Providence Gas Co., gas, Public Offices, Prov... | 71 50 |
| " " | Tucker, Swan & Co., coal, State House and Col. street Court Room........................ | 298 40 |
| " 15. | Watson & Wells, coal, &c., Court House and Jail, Washington County.................. | 39 58 |
| " " | Bristol Gas Light Co., gas, Court House and Jail, Bristol................................. | 60 00 |

1876.

| | | | |
|---|---|---|---|
| Feb. | 7. | C. W. Wilcox, wood, Washington County Jail.. | $34 42 |
| Mar. | 18. | Newport Gas Light Co., gas, Court House and Jail, Newport............................ | 36 05 |
| " | 25. | R. H. Champlin, coal, Kent County Jail........ | 41 75 |
| " | 30. | W. H. Knight, charcoal, Court House, Prov.... | 7 00 |
| April | 6. | Watson & Wells, coal, Court House and Jail, Washington County........................ | 41 77 |
| " | 15. | Bristol Gas Light Co., gas, Court House and Jail, Bristol.............................. | 62 05 |
| " | 27. | Providence Gas Co., gas, Public Offices, Prov... | 72 75 |
| " | 28. | Tucker, Swan & Co., coal, Court House and College street Court Room................ | 335 80 |

Total.........................................$2,639 17

### *Jails and Jailers.*

1875.

| | | | | |
|---|---|---|---|---|
| May | 3. | C. W. Wilcox, Washington County........... | | $157 22 |
| " | 7. | George S. Burton, Kent " ........... | | 10 00 |
| " | 20. | Edward D. Jones, Newport, " ........... | | 86 66 |
| June | 3. | Isabel F. Spinning, Bristol " ........... | | 91 49 |
| Aug. | 10. | Edward D. Jones, Newport " ........... | | 173 20 |
| Oct. | 11. | J. S. Smith, Kent .. ........... | | 79 96 |
| Nov. | 13. | Edward D. Jones, Newport " ........... | | 213 80 |
| " | " | C. W. Wilcox, Washington " ........... | | 134 47 |
| " | 30. | Henry E. Turner, Newport " ........... | | 12 00 |
| Dec. | 23. | George A. Pike, M. D., Bristol " ........... | | 25 00 |

1876.

| | | | | |
|---|---|---|---|---|
| Jan. | 3. | J. S. Smith, Kent ... ........... | | 107 57 |
| " | 31. | L. B. Bosworth, Bristol .. ........... | | 85 47 |
| Feb. | 7. | C. W. Wilcox, Washington " ........... | | 321 58 |
| " | 11. | Edward D. Jones, Newport " ........... | | 153 08 |
| " | " | W. S. A. Allan, Newport " ........... | | 4 65 |
| " | 16. | Eunice Hyde, Bristol .. ........... | | 21 00 |
| " | " | Eliza Reed, Bristol .. ........... | | 7 50 |
| April | 4. | J. S. Smith, Kent .. ........... | | 144 94 |

Total.................................... $1,829 59

*Rents.*

1875.

| | | |
|---|---|---|
| June 19. | S. S. Foss.............................. | $50 00 |
| July 2. | Rufus Waterman...... .................. | 675 00 |
| " 10. | W. H. Low, Agent........................ | 250 00 |
| Oct. 2. | W. H. Low, Agent......... ............ ...... | 250 00 |
| " 4. | Rufus Waterman......................... | 675 00 |
| Dec. 21. | S. S. Foss.............................. | 50 00 |
| 1876. | | |
| Jan. 5. | Rufus Waterman......................... | 675 00 |
| " " | W. H. Low, Agent........................ | 250 00 |
| April 6. | W. H. Low, Agent........................ | 250 00 |
| " 8. | Rufus Waterman......................... | 675 00 |
| | Total... ........................... | $3,800 00 |

*Narragansett Indians.*

1875.

| | | |
|---|---|---|
| June 14. | Gordon H. Hoxie......................... | $75 00 |
| July 30. | W. D. Cross............................. | 25 00 |
| Sept. 21. | Town Treasurer, Charlestown.............. | 200 00 |
| | Total............................... | $300 00 |

*Registration of Births, Marriages and Deaths.*

1875.

| | | |
|---|---|---|
| Oct. 13. | Edward T. Caswell....................... | $350 00 |

*Law Library.*

1875.

| | | |
|---|---|---|
| May 10. | Baker, Voorhis & Co...................... | $138 25 |
| " 20. | Sidney S. Rider.............. ............. | 39 48 |
| " 21. | Baker, Voorhis & Co...................... | 65 25 |
| " 24. | Benjamin Ashworth....................... | 17 00 |
| June 22. | Baker, Voorhis & Co...................... | 12 00 |
| " 22. | John Campbell & Co...................... | 15 88 |
| " 22. | George B. Adams......................... | 199 73 |
| " 23. | S. S. Rider............................. | 32 50 |

1875.

| | | | |
|---|---|---|---:|
| July | 6. | George B. Adams | $34 25 |
| " | 13. | Baker, Voorhis & Co. | 34 00 |
| " | 31. | Baker, Voorhis & Co. | 17 00 |
| Sept. | 10. | Baker, Voorhis & Co. | 57 25 |
| Oct. | 2. | S. S. Rider. | 30 35 |
| " | 2. | S. S. Rider. | 60 00 |
| " | 19. | Baker, Voorhis & Co. | 110 50 |
| " | 19. | George B. Adams | 31 09 |
| " | 22. | George B. Adams | 35 75 |
| Nov. | 4. | S. S. Rider. | 148 75 |
| Dec. | 16. | Baker, Voorhis & Co. | 26 50 |
| " | 24. | J. Sabin & Sons. | 92 15 |
| 1876. | | | |
| Jan. | 7. | Wilbour, Jackson & Co. | 325 38 |
| " | 13. | S. S. Rider. | 135 19 |
| " | 18. | Baker, Voorhis & Co. | 206 50 |

Total..................................................$1,874 75

### Orders of the Governor.

1875.

| | | | |
|---|---|---|---:|
| Sept. | 28. | G. M. Hopkins & Co. | $12 00 |
| 1876. | | | |
| Feb. | 4. | J. M. Addeman. | 6 00 |
| Mar. | 29. | John A. Sweeney | 47 80 |
| " | 29. | Manton H. Luther. | 29 00 |
| " | 31. | Providence Press Co. | 27 00 |
| April | 28. | Henry Lippitt. | 500 00 |
| " | 29. | Cleveland Brothers. | 50 00 |

Total..................................................$671 80

### Care of State House, Providence.

1875.

| | | | |
|---|---|---|---:|
| June | 1. | J. O'Connor. | $60 00 |
| " | 1. | John Sherson. | 45 00 |
| July | 1. | J. O'Connor. | 60 00 |
| " | 1. | John Sherson. | 45 00 |
| " | 31. | John Sherson. | 45 00 |
| " | 31. | J. O'Connor. | 60 00 |

1875.

| | | | |
|---|---|---|---:|
| Sept. | 2. | J. O'Connor | $60 00 |
| " | 2. | John Sherson | 45 00 |
| Oct. | 1. | J. O'Connor | 60 00 |
| " | 1. | John Sherson | 45 00 |
| Nov. | 1. | J. O'Connor | 60 00 |
| " | 1. | John Sherson | 45 00 |
| Dec. | 1. | J. O'Connor | 60 00 |
| " | 1. | John Sherson | 45 00 |

1876.

| | | | |
|---|---|---|---:|
| Jan. | 3. | J. O'Connor | 60 00 |
| " | 3. | John Sherson | 45 00 |
| Feb. | 1. | J. O'Connor | 60 00 |
| " | 1. | John Sherson | 45 00 |
| Mar. | 1. | Joseph O'Connor | 60 00 |
| " | 1. | John Sherson | 45 00 |
| April | 3. | J. O'Connor | 60 00 |
| " | 3. | John Sherson | 45 00 |
| " | 29. | J. O'Connor | 60 00 |
| " | 29. | John Sherson | 45 00 |

Total......$1,260 00

### Care of State House, Newport.

1875.

| | | | |
|---|---|---|---:|
| Aug. | 3. | I. W. Romes | $75 00 |
| Nov. | 3. | I. W. Romes | 75 00 |

1876.

| | | | |
|---|---|---|---:|
| Feb. | 1. | I. W. Romes | 75 00 |
| April | 29. | I. W. Romes | 75 00 |

Total......$300 00

### Care of Elizabeth Building, Providence.

1875.

| | | | | |
|---|---|---|---|---:|
| June | 1. | John Crook | | $26 00 |
| July | 1. | " | " | 26 00 |
| " | 31. | " | " | 27 00 |
| Sept. | 2. | " | " | 26 00 |
| Oct. | 2. | " | " | 26 00 |
| Nov. | 1. | " | " | 29 25 |
| Dec. | 1. | " | " | 29 25 |

1876.
Jan.   3.   John Crook ....................................$30 37
Feb.   1.    "      "     .................................... 29 25
Mar.   1.    "      "     .................................... 28 12
April  3.    "      "     .................................... 30 37
  "    29.   "      "     .................................... 28 12
                                                            _____
       Total.............................................$335 73

### Care of College Street Court Rooms.

1875.
June   2.   Mary Lyons...................................$36 00
July   1.    "      "     .................................... 36 00
Aug.   2.    "      "     .................................... 18 00
Sept.  2.    "      "     .................................... 18 00
Oct.   1.    "      "     .................................... 36 00
Nov.   1.    "      "     .................................... 36 00
Dec.   1.    "      "     .................................... 36 00
 · 1876.
Jan.   3.    "      "     .................................... 36 00
Feb.   1.    "      "     .................................... 36 00
Mar.   1.    "      "     .................................... 36 00
Apr.   3.    "      "     .................................... 36 00
  "    29.   "      "     .................................... 36 00
                                                            _____
       Total.............................................$396 00

### Interest on State Bonds.

1875.
May    3.   R. I. H. Trust Co., Coupons...................   $330 00
June   2.    "      "    "      "    $810...Reg..$300..  1,110 00
  "    30.   "      "    "      "     360... " ... 30..    390 00
July   12.  Brown, Riley & Co.,      "     ..................    30 00
  "    30.   R. I. H. Trust Co.,    `"    11,190.Reg...8,280 19,470 00
Sept.  2.    "      "    "      "   10,260. " ..10.350 20,610 00
  "    6.    "      "    "      "   20,040. " ...3,750 23,790 00
  "    30.   "      "    "      "    2,400. " ...1.470  3,870 00
Oct.   1.    "      "    "      "    4 50. "  ........    450 00
  "    26.   "      "    "      "    5,970. " ...1,560  7,530 00
Dec.   1.    "      "    "      "     630. "  .....120    750 00

1875.

Dec. 31. R. I. H. Trust Co., Coupons..$180. " ....$150    $330 00

1876.

| | | | | | | |
|---|---|---|---|---|---|---|
| Jan. 25. | ' | " | " | " | 11,220.Reg...7,440 | 18,660 00 |
| Feb. 1. | " | " | " | " | ....90. " ........ | 90 00 |
| " 1. | " | " | " | " | ....30. " ....... | 30 00 |
| " 21. | " | " | " | " | 10,620. " ...9,660 | 20,280 00 |
| Mar. 1. | " | " | " | " | ...800. " .....750 | 1,050 00 |
| " 1. | Stone & Downer | | " | ...240. " ........ | 240 00 |
| " 7. | R. I. H. Trust Co., | | " | 19,830. " ...4,350 | 24,180 00 |
| Apr. 3. | " | " | " | " | 2,400. " ...1,260 | 3,660 00 |
| " 26. | " | " | " | " | 6,000. " ...1,110 | 7,110 00 |

Total......................................................$153,960 00

*Accounts allowed by the General Assembly.*

1875.

| | | |
|---|---|---|
| May 21. | E. R. Potter, given in place of check 14,192, supposed to be lost...................... | $28 50 |
| June 9. | Geo. H. Vaughn, election expenses........... | 265 00 |
| " " | Davis & Pitman, advertising Election programme in Newport News........................ | 16 25 |
| " " | John P. Sanborn, advertising Eelction programme in Newport Mercury............... | 15 00 |
| " " | Fred A. Pratt, services rendered making repairs to State House and Jail, Newport.......... | 50 00 |
| " 10. | Edwin C. Pierce, legal services rendered·State Constabulary............................. | 110 00 |
| " " | B. M. Bosworth, Jr., legal services rendered State Constabulary...................... | 15 00 |
| " 12. | American Steamboat Co., transportation 1st Brigade to Brigade Muster, Newport, 1874.. | 350 00 |
| " 16. | Stephen Essex, legal services rendered State Constabulary......... ................... | 15 00 |
| " 19. | C. D. Eaton, reimbursement for defaulted recognizance............................. | 300 00 |
| " 25. | E. T. Case, allowed for clerk hire in 1875..... | 500 00 |
| July 25. | E. T. Case, legal services rendered State Constabulary................................ | 30 00 |
| 1876. | | |
| Mar. 23. | B. R. Vaughn, rent of room, State Constable, June 1 to Aug. 1, 1875.................... | 41 67 |

1876.

Mar. 80. Samuel Currey, legal services case of State vs.
National Bank of North America before
referees appointed .......................... $500 00

"    1.   Benjamin Tallman, services rendered in case of
Robert L. Casey, who was formally convicted
of murder...............................     65 50

"   31.   W. H. King, examination of 27 disabled soldiers
for admission to Soldier's Home............     81 00

"   "    S. S. Foss, printing 200 Citations.............      2 00

"   "    George Manchester, services and personal
expenses as Sheriff in arresting Robert L.
Casey, who was formally convicted of murder,   81 00

"   "    Asa B. Anthony...........................     17 00

"   "    John McIver, putting in windows and frames,
Senate Chamber..........................    154 49

April 8.  Charles Blake, fees of referees and opening of
report in case of State vs. National Bank of
North America...........................    750 00

"   "    John McIver, shingling and repairing roof of
State House, Providence....................    150 52

"   7.   S. R. Burlingame, remittance of Jury fine and
costs...................................     23 25

"   "    Nathaniel S. Greene, sundry expenses of carting
liquors under constabulary law.............     24 00

"  15.   Jeremiah Peabody, sundry bills on account of
State Constabulary........................    166 64

"  18.   Manton H. Luther, phonographic report of
hearings before Joint Committee on State
Farm...................................    217 00

"   "    Lyman Upham, fees summoning witnesses before
Joint Committee on State Farm............      8 20

"   "    James H. Collins, witness fees, before Joint
Committee on State Farm .................      4 60

"   "    Ira B. Wilson, witness fees before Joint Committee on State Farm.....................      2 20

"   "    Harriet Marshall, witness fees before Joint
Committee on State Farm.................      2 20

"   "    Josiah W. Keene, witness fees before Joint Committee on State Farm.....................      4 50

"   "    Julia Ann Keene, witness fees before Joint Committee on State Farm.....................      4 50

1876.

Apr. 18. W. L. Roberts, witness fees before Joint Committee on State Farm...................... $1 60

" " H. B. Brockway, witness fees before Joint Committee on State Farm...................... 2 20

" 20: C. W. Wilcox, wood and oil, Washington County Jail from Aug. 1, 1871, to Oct. 31, 1875..... 243 54

" " S. B. Cushing, services and expenses of Commissioners on Reservoirs.................. 640 00

" 21. Providence Press Co., diagram of Senate and House of Representatives, January Session... 80 00

" " John W. Angell, fines paid by mistake into treasury belonging to Rhode Island Society for Prevention of Cruelty to Animals by clerk of C. C. P., Providence...................... 23 00

" " Samuel Currey, commission of 2½ per cent. of money collected in case of State vs. National Bank of North America.................. 361 15

" 22. J. Aborn Gardiner, fees on writs of scire facias, C. C. P., Providence.................. 361 40

" 24. H. B. Hunt, carting liquors, State Constabulary, 3 50

" 27. George H. Pettis, services, Joint Committee on printing, 1875 and 1876.................. 5 00

" " H. H. Richardson, services, Joint Committee on printing, 1875 and 1876.................. 5 00

" " Daniel W. Lyman, services, Joint Committee on printing, 1875 and 1876.................. 5 00

" " Albert B. Lewis, services, Joint Committee on printing, 1875 and 1876.................. 5 00

" " W. E. Gilmore, services, Joint Committee on printing, 1875 and 1876.................. 5 00

" " Alvord O. Miles, services, Joint Committee on printing, 1875 and 1876.................. 5 00

" " Henry Whipple, attending special Court in Westerly...................... 27 54

" " Warren Artillery, rent of Armory, 1873 and '74, 200 00

" " Brown & Ives, rent of rooms in Wayland building for S. Court...................... 190 00

" " George A. Brown, fees for services as Trial Justice case of Robert L. Casey........... 8 00

" " C. H. Fisher, traveling expenses as member State Board of Education, 1875........:.... 14 00

6

1876.

Apr. 27.   E. K. Parker, traveling expenses as member
           State Board of Education, 1875............     $9 10
   "    "   Thomas H. Clarke, traveling expenses as mem-
           ber State Board of Education, 1875.........     11 25
   "    "   George L. Locke, traveling expenses as member
           State Board of Education, 1875............      7 50
   "    "   Samuel H. Cross, traveling expenses as member
           State Board of Education, 1875............     15 65
                                                        ─────────
      Total.........................................    $6,169 45

### *Miscellaneous Expenses.*

1875.

May   1.   Henry Whipple, sundry services as Sheriff......    $64 73
  "   7.   Knowles, Anthony & Danielson, Providence
           Journal, one year for Secretary of State.....       9 33
  "   8.   Samuel B. M. Read, expenses as Deputy Con-
           stable....................................          22 60
  "  10.   Valpey, Angell & Co., stationery, Adjutant
           General...................................           6 25
  "  11.   James Wilson, expenses as Deputy Constable...      155 50
  "  12.   Ralph Jolly, care of Justice Court Room, Paw-
           tucket, to date...........................         21 84
  "   "    Eliza C. Weeden, expenses visiting Penal and
           Correctional Institutions..................        45 00
  "  13.   Valpey, Angell & Co., stationery, State Auditor
           and Commissioner of Public Schools........        10 82
  "  14.   Chris. Holden, distributing Civil Commissions,
           1874 and 1875...........................           75 00
  "  14.   W. D. Lake, paying witnesses and officers' fees,
           year ending March 31.....................         25 00
  "  17.   C. N. Gifford, traveling expenses as Deputy
           State Constable.........................          54 80
  "  20.   George W. Wightman, expense of Coronor's In-
           quest on body of C. H. Mowry, inmate of
           State Prison.............................          22 60
  "  22.   Jeremiah Peabody, traveling expenses as Deputy
           State Constable.........................          25 30

1875.

| | | | |
|---|---|---|---:|
| May | 31. | George Manchester, distributing Commissions, &c................................. | $12 00 |
| June | 2. | A. B. Burdick, expenses as Deputy State Constable............................... | 56 89 |
| " | 3. | Nathaniel S. Greene, expenses as Deputy State Constable.......................... | 88 40 |
| " | 10. | S. S. Rider, stationery, &c., Justice Court, Pawtucket.............................. | 47 58 |
| " | 11. | E. L. Freeman & Co., teachers' certificates, envelopes, &c., Commissioner of Public Schools, | 151 50 |
| " | " | S. S. Rider, stationery, &c., Justice Court, Prov. | 35 62 |
| " | 18. | C. R. Brayton, P. M., postage stamps, sundry offices................................ | 75 00 |
| " | 19. | J. Aboin Gardiner, paying officers and witnesses' fees, year ending, March 29, 1875........... | 200 00 |
| " | 22. | Barker, Whitaker & Co...................... | 7 20 |
| " | 80. | E. C. Clarke, order of J. P. Case, expenses as Deputy State Constable.................... | 102 10 |
| July | 8. | S. S. Rider, stationery, &c., Commissioner of Public Schools........................... | 8 60 |
| " | 9. | C. R. Brayton, P. M., rent of Post Office Boxes, Public Offices, to September 30, 1875........ | 15 13 |
| " | " | Tibbitts & Randall, stationery, &c., State Auditor.................................. | 5 00 |
| " | 10. | E. M. Snow, services and expenses as New State Prison Commissioner................ | 63 00 |
| " | " | W. B. Lawton, services and expenses as New State Prison Commissioner................. | 243 00 |
| " | " | W. D. Brayton, services and expenses as New State Prison Commissioner................. | 54 00 |
| " | " | George I. Chace, services and expenses as New State Prison Commissioner................ | 60 00 |
| " | " | Augustus Woodbury, services and expenses as New State Prison Commissioner........... | 57 00 |
| " | 20. | Tibbits & Randall, stationery, Attorney General, | 10 44 |
| " | 24. | Thomas B. Stockwell, sundry expenses, office Commissioner of Public Schools............ | 5 90 |
| | 81. | George W. Wightman, expenses, Coronor's Inquest on body of Henry Tilghman, inmate of State Prison............ ............... | 23 75 |

1875.

| | | | |
|---|---|---|---:|
| Aug. | 2, | S. S. Rider, stationery, General Treasurer...... | $26 00 |
| " | 8. | Earl & Prew's Express, delivering packages, Sec. of State................................. | 5 85 |
| " | " | C. W. Jencks & Brother, lawyers' cases, Sec. of State................................. | 19 79 |
| " | 9. | George W. Wightman, expenses of Coroner's Inquest on body John Powers, inmate of State Prison.................................. | 23 45 |
| " | 10. | B. P. Swarts, coffin for Henry Tilghman, inmate of State Prison....,................. | 12 00 |
| " | 14. | Henry Whipple, attending Indian Meeting, Charlestowr., 1875...................... | 6 00 |
| " | " | Charles H. Chapman, attending Indian Meeting, Charlestown, 1875...................... | 6 00 |
| " | 16. | L. T. Haskell, tin boxes, Justice Court, Pawtucket.................................. | 9 50 |
| " | 25. | Knowles, Anthony & Danielson, Journal, one year to Aug. 1, 1875, for Treasurer......... | 8 00 |
| Sep. | 7. | C. R. Brayton, P. M., Post Office Stamps for Public Offices.......................... | 50 00 |
| " | 10. | Valpey, Angell & Co., stationery, Adjutant General................................ | 14 77 |
| " | 15. | C. J. Whipple, allowance to Manville Library and Reading Room Association............ | 50 00 |
| " | " | George L. Cooke, Jr., allowance to Warren Library and Reading Room Association.......... | 125 00 |
| " | " | Joseph R. Williams, painting Fence around Monument, Exchange Place.............. | 70 00 |
| " | 21. | Merchant's National Bank, order Board of Education for East Greenwich Free Library Association.......................... | 125 00 |
| " | 29. | Town Treasurer, Glocester, acceptance of a Public Highway, Rhode Island and Connecticut Turnpike.......................... | 500 00 |
| Oct. | 2. | B. F. Smith, attendance, Indian Meeting, Charlestown.................................. | 6 00 |
| " | 7. | C. R. Brayton, P. M., rent of Post Office Boxes, Public Offices.......................... | 15 12 |
| " | 11. | Bugbee & Hall, arm rest for Auditor......... | 1 00 |

1875.

Oct. 11  Tibbitts & Randall, stationery, Commissioner of
Public Schools and Auditor................. $15 25
"   "  S. S. Rider, stationery, Commissioner of Public
Schools.................................. 64 68
"  22.  Samuel Clark, check stamps.................. 2 00
"  14.  Abby D. Weaver, traveling expenses, member
Board of Female Visitors to Penal Institutions,
1874–1875.............................. 12 50
"  30.  E. L. Freeman & Co., printing and numbering
checks for Treasurer..................... 54 50
Nov. 3.  J. M. Addeman, sundry expenses, Office Sec. of
State................................. 39 07
"   "  Arnold Greene........................... 171 98
"  4.  Ralph Jolly, care of Justice Court, Pawtucket,
to November 1, 1875.................... 24 04
"  6.  C. R. Brayton, P. M., stamps, Public Offices.... 24 00
"  9.  Tillinghast & Mason News Co., stationery, Sec.
of State............................... 27 07
"  10.  J. W. Vernon, cash, order of Board of Education for Narragansett Library Association.... 100 00
"   "  Tillinghast & Mason News Co., stationery, Sec.
of State............................... 62 10
Dec. 8.  Burdick Brothers, 25 tin boxes, Justice Court,
Providence.............................. 9 37
"  17.  Estate of William B. Lawton, services as Commissioner, New State Prison........ ...... 68 00
"  28.  D. M. Chace, allowance Middletown Library
Association.............................. 50 00
"  28.  Thomas G. Carr, allowance Jamestown Library
Association.............................. 50 00

1876.

Jan. 3.  E. L. Freeman & Co., envelopes, Sec. of State.. 51 00
"  4.  C. R. Brayton, P. M., stamps, Public Offices.... 75 00
"  5.  H. Jacobs, pens for Secretary of State......... 15 00
"  7.  C. W. Wilcox, attending Indian Meeting....... 6 00
"   "  Valpey, Angell & Co., stationery, General Treasurer................................. 4 72
"   "  Bugbee & Hall, stationery, &c., Auditor....... 24 00
"   "  S. S. Rider, stationery, &c., Auditor and Sec. of
State.................................. 20 52

1876.

| | | | | |
|---|---|---|---|---|
| Jan. | 3. | Joel M. Spencer, sundry expenses, Auditor's Office............................................ | $12 | 20 |
| " | 11. | C. R. Brayton, P. M., rent of Post Office Boxes to March 31.................................... | 15 | 44 |
| " | 12. | S. S. Rider, stationery, Justice Court, Prov..... | 35 | 25 |
| " | 15. | Valpey, Angell & Co., stationery, &c., sundry offices......................................... | 11 | 11 |
| " | " | S. S. Rider, stationery, &c., Commissioner of Pub. Schools.................................... | 4 | 30 |
| " | 25. | Edwin M. Snow, expenses and services, member State Prison Commission.................... | 63 | 90 |
| " | 26. | Fairbanks, Brown & Co., goods furnished J. H. Appleton, State Sealer....................... | 268 | 55 |
| " | 26. | W. D. Brayton, services as member S. Prison Commission............................... | 57 | 00 |
| " | 26. | O. A. Ballou, services as member S. Prison Commission................................... | 24 | 00 |
| " | 26. | George I. Chace, services as member S. Prison Commission................................. | 33 | 00 |
| " | 26. | Aug. Woodbury, services as member S. Prison Commission............................... | 138 | 00 |
| Feb. | 1. | Zachariah Allen, expenses preparing a plan for a geological survey of State of R. I........... | 58 | 31 |
| " | 3. | Tibbitts & Randall, stationery, School Com. and Auditor................................. | 6 | 20 |
| " | 3. | Fred. W. Arnold, premium on policies of insurance upon State Arsenal................... | 90 | 00 |
| " | 7. | C. R. Brayton, P. M., stamps, Pub. Offices..... | 100 | 00 |
| " | 10. | A J. Ward, stationery, Jus. Court, Newport.... | 5 | 47 |
| " | 10. | N. Van Slyck, clerk's fees, Supreme Court, Prov., for one copy of Trial Decree vs. Old Town House lot, so called....................... | 2 | 10 |
| " | 18. | Valpey, Angell & Co., stationery Gen. Treas... | 13 | 72 |
| Mar. | 9. | Harriet A. Cook, traveling expenses as member of Board of Visitors to Penal and Correctional Institution ................................ | 55 | 97 |
| " | 20. | C. E. Jackson, cashier order of Board of Education benefit of Harris Institute............. | 125 | 00 |
| " | 24. | S. M. Greene, order of Board of Education, benefit of old Warwick Library Association.. | 50 | 00 |

1876.

| | | |
|---|---|---:|
| Mar. 25. | Eliza C. Weeden, expenses visiting Penal and Correctional Institutions................... | $30 00 |
| " 28. | C. R. Brayton, P. M., stamps, Pub. Offices...... | 80 00 |
| " 30. | Abby D. Weaver, expenses visiting Penal and Correctional Institutions................... | 15 00 |
| " 30. | G. A. Wallace, Rubber Stamp, Sec. of State.... | 3 00 |
| Apr. 8. | W. D. Lake, Paying officers and witnesses to March 31, Newport Co.................... | 25 00 |
| " 10. | Bugbee & Hall, Stationery, Auditor and Com. of Pub. Schools........................... | 7 24 |
| " 10. | C. R. Brayton, P. M., rent of P. O. Boxes to June 30, 1876.......................... | 15 54 |
| " 11. | Sidney S. Rider, Stationery, Jus. Court. Prov... | 59 25 |
| " 17. | S. S. Rider, wrapping paper, &c., Com. of Pub. Schools. ............................. | 8 80 |
| " 17. | W. II. Jenks, making criminal record Jus. Court, Woonsocket............................ | 25 00 |
| " 28. | Tillinghast & Mason News Co., stationery Sec. of State.............................. | 13 49 |
| " 29. | C. A. Greene, sundry services as Sheriff, Bristol County............................... | 31 00 |
| " 29. | Thomas J. Tilley, sundry services as Sheriff, Kent County............................ | 35 00 |
| " 29. | Henry Whipple, sundry services as Sheriff, Washington County........................... | 40 00 |
| " 29. | Christopher Holden, sundry services as Sheriff, Providence County...................... | 75 00 |
| " 29. | George Manchester, sundry services as Sheriff, Newport County......................... | 12 00 |

Total.............................................$5,749 85

## SPECIAL APPROPRIATIONS.

*Charities and Corrections.*

1875.

| | | | | | |
|---|---|---|---|---|---:|
| May 12. | W. W. Chapin, Secretary...................$10,000 00 |
| June 9. | " | " | " | ................... | 10,000 00 |
| Aug. 9. | " | " | " | ................... | 10,000 00 |

1875.

| | | | |
|---|---|---|---|
| Aug. | 25. | W. W. Chapin, Secretary.................... | $10,000 00 |
| Sept. | 28. | "    "    " ...... ............... | 10,000 00 |
| Oct. | 14. | "    "    " .................... | 10,000 00 |
| " | 28. | "    "    " .................... | 5,000 00 |
| Nov. | 10. | "    "    " .................... | 10,000 00 |
| Dec. | 1. | "    "    " .................... | 10,000 00 |
| " | 30. | "    "    " .................... | 7,000 00 |
| 1876. | | | |
| Feb. | 7. | "    "    " .................... | 5,000 00 |

Total................................$97,000 00

### State Library.

1876.

| | | | |
|---|---|---|---|
| Jan. | 21. | G. M. Hopkins & Co............................ | $24 00 |
| Mar. | 9. | G. Sabin & Sons............................... | 28 00 |

Total.......................................$52 00

### Evening Schools.

1875.

| | | | |
|---|---|---|---|
| May | 8. | C. J. White.................................. | $300 00 |
| July | 8. | Sarah I. Carpenter.......................... | 118 00 |
| Dec. | 21. | R. S. Andrew................................ | 200 00 |
| 1876. | | | |
| Jan. | 3. | Sarah I. Carpenter.......................... | 131 25 |
| " | 3. | R. H. Paine................................. | 125 00 |
| " | 3. | Jared Morris................................ | 10 75 |
| " | 26. | James S. Cook............................... | 200 00 |
| " | 26. | H. W. Keech................................. | 50 00 |
| Feb. | 8. | S. W. Farnum................................ | 33 00 |
| " | 9. | George Lewis Cooke.......................... | 200 00 |
| Mar. | 7. | S. A. Irons................................. | 175 00 |
| " | 11. | J. A. Keech................................. | 75 00 |
| Apr. | 12. | D. M. Coggeshall............................ | 350 00 |

Total.......................................$1,968 00

### Kent County Court Records.

1876.

| | | | |
|---|---|---|---|
| Apr. | 7. | A. R. Greene................................ | $350 00 |

### New State Prison.

1875.

| | | | |
|---|---|---|---|
| May | 4. | Edwin M. Snow, Chairman | $15,000 00 |
| June | 30. | Edwin M. Snow, " | 25,000 00 |
| July | 10. | Edwin M. Snow | 1 37 |
| " | 10. | W. B. Lawton | 64 80 |
| " | 30. | Edwin M. Snow | 25,000 00 |
| Sept. | 3. | Edwin M. Snow | 25,000 00 |
| " | 16. | Tuttle & Hobbs | 105 00 |
| Oct. | 1. | Edwin M. Snow | 35,000 00 |
| " | 5. | Tuttle & Hobbs | 27 00 |
| Dec. | 17. | Edwin M. Snow | 3,000 00 |
| " | 17. | Estate of W. B. Lawton | 16 |

Total.................................$128,214 97

### Providence County Court House.

1875.

| | | | |
|---|---|---|---|
| Aug. | 2. | Amasa S. Westcott Chairman | $10,000 00 |
| Oct. | 16. | Amasa S. Westcott " | 5,000 00 |
| " | 26. | Amasa S. Westcott " | 5,000 00 |
| Dec. | 20. | Amasa S. Westcott " | 10,000 00 |
| 1876. | | | |
| Apr. | 12. | Amasa S. Westcott " | 10,000 00 |

Total...................................$40,000 00

### Soldiers' and Sailors' Testimonial.

1875.

May 12. American Bank Note Co.......................$25 00

### Committee on Exemption from Taxation.

1875.

| | | | |
|---|---|---|---|
| May | 13. | George Lewis Cooke.... | $62 00 |
| " | 17. | Thomas G. Hazard | 6 00 |

Total................................... $68 00

### Washington County Court House.

1875.

| | | | |
|---|---|---|---|
| May | 14. | James W. Pollock | $128 61 |
| Nov. | 8. | C. Maxson & Co. | 2,871 39 |

7

1876.
Apr.  27.  C. Maxson & Co............................  $802 46
"     27.  S. Northup................................  117 99

     Total..............................................$3,920 45

### Newport Light Infantry.

1876.
June   2.  Thomas Chambers..........................  $125 00

### Town House Lot.

1875.
Dec.   2.  City of Providence.........................$146,044 40
"      2.  N. Van Slyck........................... .....   423 75

     Total........................................$146,468 15

### State House and Jail, Newport.

1875.
June  9.   Brown, Goddard & Barlow...................   $23 37
"     9.   H. August Kaull...........................   110 50
"     9.   Joseph M. Lyon............................   315 00
"     9.   Fred. A. Pratt............................    21 35
"     9.   Timothy C. Sullivan.......................    37 97
"     9.   John C. Stoddard..........................    19 10
"     9.   William Peabody...........................    64 26
"     9.   Newport Gas Light Co......................     8 48

     Total.............................................  $600 03

### Inland Fisheries.

1875.
June  22.  George H. Downer........ ................   $413 46
Dec.  23.  George H. Downer.........................   322 53
     1876.
Feb.   5.  George H. Downer.... ....................   401 24

     Total.........................................  $1,137 23

### Lectures and Addresses, Public Schools.

1875.
June  24.  Thomas B. Stockwell......................   $26 61
Sept. 13.  Thomas B. Stockwell......................    3 00

1875.

| | | | | |
|---|---|---|---|---|
| Oct. | 27. | Thomas B. Stockwell ....................... | $47 | 26 |
| Dec. | 31. | Sarah I. Carpenter.......................... | 86 | 00 |

| | | |
|---|---|---|
| Total........................................ | $112 | 87 |

*Justice Court Room, Woonsocket.*

1875.

| | | | | |
|---|---|---|---|---|
| June 25. | | W. E. Hubbard............................ | $150 | 00 |
| Oct. | 9. | Aqidneck Agricultural Society............... | 500 | 00 |
| " | " | Rhode Island Horticultural Society........... | 300 | 00 |
| " | 18. | Rhode Island Society for Encouragement of Domestic Industry...................... | 1,000 | 00 |
| Nov. 15. | | Washington County Agricultural Society....... | 500 | 00 |
| Dec. 14. | | Woonsocket Agricultural, Horticultural and Industrial Society........................ | 500 | 00 |

*Commissioners of Sinking Fund.*

1875.

| | | | | |
|---|---|---|---|---|
| June | 1. | Bonds of 1882............................. | $119,000 | 00 |
| " | " | Bonds of 1883............................. | 20,000 | 00 |
| " | " | Bonds of 1893............................. | 20,250 | 00 |
| " | " | Bonds of 1894............................. | 21,750 | 00 |

| | | |
|---|---|---|
| Total........................................ | $181,000 | 00 |

*Justice Court Room, Pawtucket.*

1875.

| | | | |
|---|---|---|---|
| Dec. 28. | I. Shove................................... | $500 | 00 |

*National Centennial Exhibition.*

1876.

| | | | | |
|---|---|---|---|---|
| April 25. | | John R. Bartlett........................... | $40 | 75 |
| " | 26. | M. L. Chapin.............................. | 100 | 00 |
| " | 28. | Thomas Phillips & Co....................... | 84 | 63 |
| " | " | Providence Franklin Society................. | 128 | 97 |
| " | " | J. Harry Welch............................ | 20 | 00 |

| | | |
|---|---|---|
| Total........................................ | $324 | 35 |

*Index to Charters and Resolutions.*

1876.

April 27.  J. M. Addeman............................  $200 00

*Decennial Census.*

1875.

| | | | | |
|---|---|---|---|---|
| June | 18. | Cleveland & Brothers......................... | $37 | 00 |
| " | " | D. Gillies................................ | 1 | 50 |
| " | " | J. W. Barton.............................. | 1 | 25 |
| " | " | John H. Eddy.............................. | 4 | 05 |
| " | " | LeRoy B. Pease............................ | 1 | 25 |
| " | " | Mercury Office............................ | 2 | 50 |
| " | " | L. A. Austin.............................. | 4 | 80 |
| " | " | R. I. Pendulum............................ | 2 | 25 |
| " | " | Davis & Pitman........................... | 4 | 00 |
| " | " | S. S. Foss................................ | 3 | 00 |
| " | " | G. B. & J. H. Utter....................... | 1 | 50 |
| " | " | Providence Press Co....................... | 335 | 13 |
| " | " | Valpey, Angell & Co....................... | 35 | 00 |
| " | 19. | J. L. Richardson.......................... | 20 | 15 |
| " | " | Charles H. Plummer ....................... | 23 | 86 |
| " | " | Fred. L. Slade............................ | 47 | 25 |
| " | " | C. H. Slade............................... | 45 | 63 |
| " | " | George H. Metcalf......................... | 21 | 22 |
| " | " | Edwin S. Metcalf.......................... | 41 | 07 |
| " | " | E. M. Snow, order of S. A. Winsor.......... | 21 | 48 |
| " | " | A. J. Reeves.............................. | 12 | 61 |
| " | 22. | Cornelius Mahoney......................... | 32 | 64 |
| " | " | P. H. Conlen.............................. | 37 | 47 |
| " | " | Nicholas H. Bradford...................... | 12 | 96 |
| " | " | James D. Underwood........................ | 16 | 98 |
| " | " | Lewis W. Jones............................ | 23 | 52 |
| " | " | James L. Ripley........................... | 17 | 97 |
| " | " | Frank Johnson............................ | 25 | 80 |
| " | " | Daniel R. Clapp........................... | 7 | 41 |
| " | " | W. R. Chapman............................ | 28 | 52 |
| " | " | H. G. Adams.............................. | 21 | 57 |
| " | " | Linn S. Billings.......................... | 4 | 82 |
| " | " | Willard Smith, Jr......................... | 8 | 76 |
| " | " | John B. Livsey............................ | 20 | 22 |

1875.

| | | | | |
|---|---|---|---|---|
| June | 22. | William Pendrill | $23 | 13 |
| " | " | Nickerson & Sibley | 2 | 75 |
| " | " | George T. Thurber | 33 | 80 |
| " | " | John Randolph | 22 | 93 |
| " | " | W. R. Dix | 14 | 52 |
| " | " | John F. Hamer | 46 | 28 |
| " | " | E. T. Case, order of John Devereux | 45 | 12 |
| " | " | George W. Chase | 8 | 87 |
| " | " | Samuel Clark, order of John Angell | 39 | 63 |
| " | " | Isaac Peck | 185 | 92 |
| " | " | Frank Merry | 18 | 89 |
| " | 23. | Henry D. Miller | 16 | 98 |
| " | " | R. A. Canfield | 39 | 78 |
| " | " | John F. Doyle | 52 | 89 |
| " | " | Benjamin M. Greene, Jr | 18 | 12 |
| " | " | S. S. Tompkins | 19 | 81 |
| " | " | Samuel Gladding | 19 | 77 |
| " | 24. | Thomas F. Murphy | 44 | 68 |
| " | " | Daniel B. Ingraham | 33 | 84 |
| " | " | Frank Jenks | 61 | 19 |
| " | " | W. F. Prenfort, Jr | 21 | 16 |
| " | 25. | James Greene | 30 | 00 |
| " | " | A. Manchester Hussey | 25 | 26 |
| " | " | Joseph R. Shepard | 22 | 17 |
| " | " | J. B. Hathaway | 26 | 06 |
| " | " | Michael Ryan | 35 | 29 |
| " | " | Edwin M. Snow, order of C. R. Gibbs | 20 | 95 |
| " | " | Edwin W. Kelly | 18 | 65 |
| " | " | Jos. A. Duckworth | 30 | 56 |
| " | 27. | John D. Ghody | 24 | 60 |
| " | 28. | James M. Crawford | 45 | 99 |
| " | " | W. T. Robinson | 18 | 17 |
| " | " | W. E. Whiting | 17 | 90 |
| " | " | Edmund F. Prentiss | 47 | 85 |
| " | " | John C. Robinson | 22 | 05 |
| " | " | Robert T. Hathaway | 18 | 56 |
| " | " | J. L. Sherman | 16 | 11 |
| " | " | Sheldon Knight | 15 | 95 |
| " | " | George H. Johnson | 30 | 73 |
| " | " | W. P. Winslow | 17 | 16 |

1875.

| | | | |
|---|---|---|---|
| June | 28. | George A. Manchester...................... | $15 95 |
| " | 29. | Thomas M. Holden........................ | 51 60 |
| " | " | Byron H. Arnold.......................... | 46 84 |
| " | " | A. H. Cheetham.......................... | 23 95 |
| " | " | W. H. Polsey............................. | 15 12 |
| " | 30. | John A. Munsey.......................... | 33 51 |
| July | 1. | John A. Stone............................ | 32 72 |
| " | " | W. H. Gurney............................ | 51 02 |
| " | " | R. N. Church............................. | 42 28 |
| " | " | W. F. Eaton............................. | 50 00 |
| " | " | John Goodro............................. | 16 87 |
| " | " | George Sherman.......................... | 50 50 |
| " | " | Fred. H. Merris.......................... | 55 20 |
| " | " | Medbury M. Heath....................... | 11 25 |
| " | 2. | A. B. Brown............................. | 30 79 |
| " | " | Charles W. Smith........................ | 15 57 |
| " | " | Sidney S. Rider......................... | 11 79 |
| " | " | O. A. Inman............................. | 59 90 |
| " | 3. | John J. Watson.......................... | 23 55 |
| " | " | James H. Rickard........................ | 40 12 |
| " | " | Mechanics National Bank................. | 105 00 |
| " | " | Ira Winsor.............................. | 84 03 |
| " | " | A. P. Collins........................... | 36 50 |
| " | " | John Roberts............................ | 51 98 |
| " | " | Edward F. Dyer......................... | 42 10 |
| " | " | Frank A. Kenell......................... | 35 53 |
| " | " | Horton D. Kenny........................ | 16 53 |
| " | 6. | Daniel Warner.......................... | 54 47 |
| " | " | A. J. Patt.............................. | 42 31 |
| " | " | Arnold Lapham.......................... | 46 38 |
| " | " | W. P. Lewis............................. | 62 38 |
| " | 7. | Anna C. Sheldon........................ | 30 00 |
| " | " | M. J. Peckham.......................... | 40 00 |
| " | " | Martha G. Addeman..................... | 34 28 |
| " | " | Stephen W. Thornton.................... | 34 20 |
| " | " | Ednah F. Beane........................ | 15 71 |
| " | " | Henry C. Budlong....................... | 26 01 |
| " | " | Charles E. Andrews..................... | 42 44 |
| " | 8. | A. W. Kenyon........................... | 63 66 |
| " | " | Charles Peckham, 2d.................... | 49 10 |

1875.

| | | | | |
|---|---|---|---|---|
| July | 9. | John A. Brown | $38 | 62 |
| " | " | A. C. Munro | 30 | 63 |
| " | " | A. W. Harris | 69 | 29 |
| " | 10. | Frank B. Scribner | 49 | 23 |
| " | " | J. F. Smith | 22 | 40 |
| " | " | Walter I. Jenks | 30 | 50 |
| " | " | Isaac Peck | 84 | 62 |
| " | " | Charles W. Earle | 26 | 10 |
| " | " | S. A. Austin | 6 | 09 |
| " | " | Harvey L. Spencer | 32 | 45 |
| " | 12. | William A. Phillips | 84 | 84 |
| " | " | Fred J. Clarke | 62 | 33 |
| " | " | Peleg G. Kenyon | 40 | 48 |
| " | " | P. O. Hawkins | 45 | 35 |
| " | 13. | W. L. Darling | 23 | 12 |
| " | " | Charles Browning | 23 | 58 |
| " | " | Augustus French | 58 | 17 |
| " | " | Francis Stanhope | 39 | 32 |
| " | " | Adolphus Page | 34 | 01 |
| " | " | W. J. Holden | 6 | 39 |
| " | " | Thomas W. Gardner | 35 | 25 |
| " | " | Stephen C. Irons | 44 | 55 |
| " | " | Jos. L. Browning | 46 | 70 |
| " | " | Brownell & Barrows | 44 | 47 |
| " | 14. | B. J. Munro | 59 | 56 |
| " | " | Charles P. Nye | 65 | 34 |
| " | 15. | C. R. Brayton | 55 | 00 |
| " | 16. | A. Manuel, Jr. | 50 | 85 |
| " | " | Pardon Hopkins | 68 | 10 |
| " | " | Thomas P. Braman | 87 | 33 |
| " | 17. | John Babcock | 35 | 40 |
| " | " | Mark H. Wood | 56 | 38 |
| " | " | William A. Jack | 33 | 80 |
| " | " | Henry C. Gifford | 30 | 99 |
| " | " | William Hill | 84 | 22 |
| " | " | W. G. Smith | 73 | 00 |
| " | " | Silas B. Havens | 58 | 50 |
| " | 22. | John S. Appleby | 44 | 73 |
| " | 24. | William Hoxsie | 66 | 89 |
| " | " | Francis Armington | 65 | 38 |

1875.

| | | | | |
|---|---|---|---|---:|
| July | 24. | George E. Cranston........................ | $63 | 28 |
| " | 26. | Henry T. Braman........................ | 77 | 43 |
| " | " | George H. Johnson...................... ..... | 34 | 70 |
| " | 30. | Gustavus Snow......................... | 22 | 86 |
| " | 31. | Frank Merry........................... | 25 | 50 |
| " | " | Thomas F. Murphy...................... | 24 | 00 |
| " | " | W. Pendrill........................... | 28 | 20 |
| " | " | M. J. Peckham......................... | 40 | 00 |
| " | " | Anna C. Sheldon....................... | 40 | 00 |
| " | " | Martha G. Addeman.................... | 40 | 00 |
| " | " | Ednah F. Beane........................ | 36 | 67 |
| " | " | John P. Olney......................... | 18 | 81 |
| Aug. | 2. | John G. Wall.......................... | 63 | 50 |
| " | " | Millard F. Perry...................... | 30 | 86 |
| " | 4. | Clifford Thomas....................... | 28 | 68 |
| " | " | Sidney S. Tillinghast.................. | 40 | 67 |
| " | " | Emily E. Potter....................... | 20 | 00 |
| " | 5. | George Barton......................... | 37 | 66 |
| " | 9. | James E. France....................... | 23 | 33 |
| " | " | N. L. Richmond....................... | 49 | 78 |
| " | 14. | W. H. Bowen.......................... | 51 | 10 |
| " | " | Ansel Holman......................... | 52 | 25 |
| " | 18. | Thomas N. Stillman.................... | 34 | 97 |
| " | " | Isaac Peck............................ | 109 | 28 |
| " | " | Adolphus Page........................ | 13 | 00 |
| Sept. | 3. | Mary E. Engley........................ | 10 | 00 |
| " | " | M. J. Peckham........ ........... | 40 | 00 |
| " | " | Anna C. Sheldon....................... | 40 | 00 |
| " | " | Martha G. Addeman.................... | 30 | 72 |
| " | " | Marion B. Tillinghast.................. | 28 | 33 |
| " | " | N. F. Potter.......................... | 70 | 50 |
| " | " | Ellis L. Blake......................... | 70 | 14 |
| " | 6. | Stephen A. Aplin...................... | 73 | 85 |
| " | " | Ednah F. Beane....................... | 30 | 96 |
| " | " | William Pendrill...................... | 72 | 90 |
| " | " | Isaac Peck............................ | 104 | 00 |
| " | " | W. J. Holden......................... | 50 | 00 |
| " | 8. | Ansel Holman......................... | 10 | 00 |
| " | " | Thomas P. Braman.................... | 20 | 00 |
| " | " | Frank Jenks.......................... | 42 | 45 |

1875.

| | | | |
|---|---|---|---|
| Sept. 10. | Reuben J. Brown | $49 | 79 |
| " " | Providence Press Co | 125 | 90 |
| " 13. | O. A. Inman | 44 | 00 |
| " " | George C. Manchester | 13 | 50 |
| " " | John A. Brown | 35 | 00 |
| " " | William Hoxsie | 29 | 76 |
| " 15. | M. Herbert Pierce | 24 | 00 |
| " 16. | W. P. Lewis | 18 | 00 |
| " " | H. W. Keach | 13 | 00 |
| " 17. | Edwin S. Metcalf | 67 | 50 |
| " 20. | Ira Winsor | 22 | 00 |
| " 21. | Willard S. Walker | 20 | 00 |
| " " | George C. Cross | 20 | 60 |
| " " | John Roberts | 15 | 00 |
| " " | Nathan L. Richmond | 32 | 39 |
| " 23. | George H. Johnson | 33 | 02 |
| " " | Alfred W. Kenyon | 10 | 00 |
| " 29. | George C. Manchester | 87 | 32 |
| " " | W. J. Holden | 26 | 00 |
| " " | William H. Gurney | 26 | 25 |
| Oct. 1. | Nathaniel F. Patten | 78 | 00 |
| " " | Jared Morris | 9 | 75 |
| " 5. | Walter I. Jenks | 57 | 00 |
| " " | Millard F. Perry | 61 | 45 |
| " " | Fred. H. Merris | 49 | 50 |
| " " | Marion B. Tillinghast | 50 | 00 |
| " " | Mary E. Engley | 50 | 00 |
| " " | Martha G. Addeman | 45 | 00 |
| Oct. 1. | Ednah F. Beane | 20 | 00 |
| " " | Anna C. Sheldon | 40 | 00 |
| " " | M. J. Peckham | 35 | 00 |
| " " | S. S. Rider | 13 | 72 |
| " 6. | Edwin S. Metcalf | 90 | 00 |
| " " | Mechanics National Bank | 105 | 00 |
| " 7. | Isaac Peck | 104 | 00 |
| " " | W. Pendrill | 82 | 50 |
| " " | Stephen A. Aplin | 84 | 00 |
| " 11. | John G. Wall | 19 | 50 |
| " 13. | George Barton | 6 | 00 |
| " 14. | Edwin M. Snow | 28 | 72 |

6

1875.

| | | | | |
|---|---|---|---|---|
| Oct. | 18. | Martha G. Addeman | $21 | 67 |
| " | " | Thomas J. Thurston | 25 | 02 |
| " | 23. | Thomas M. Holden | 24 | 00 |
| Nov. | 1. | Levi L. Borden | 75 | 00 |
| " | 2. | Isaac Peck | 125 | 47 |
| " | " | Ednah F. Beane | 40 | 00 |
| " | " | Mary E. Engley | 40 | 00 |
| " | " | M. Josephine Peckham | 20 | 00 |
| " | " | Anna C. Sheldon | 40 | 00 |
| " | " | Marion B. Tillinghast | 40 | 00 |
| " | " | Nathaniel F. Patten | 135 | 00 |
| " | 6. | C. R. Brayton, P. M. | 6 | 00 |
| " | 8. | Benjamin W. Bentley | 26 | 88 |
| " | " | Bennett J. Munroe | 30 | 25 |
| " | 9. | Levi L. Borden | . 75 | 00 |
| " | 17. | Stephen A. Aplin | 75 | 00 |
| " | 18. | I. B. Cowen | 63 | 95 |
| " | " | George B. Carpenter | 36 | 02 |
| " | 22. | Henry Pollock | 250 | 00 |
| " | " | John Angell | 9 | 50 |
| Dec. | 1. | Nathaniel F. Patten | 96 | 00 |
| " | 8. | Ednah F. Beane | 40 | 00 |
| " | " | J. T. Snow | 8 | 10 |
| " | " | Anna C. Sheldon | 40 | 00 |
| " | " | M. Josephine Peckham | 17 | 00 |
| " | " | Mary E. Engley | 40 | 00 |
| " | " | Marion B. Tillinghast | 40 | 00 |
| " | " | Levi L. Borden | 39 | 20 |
| " | " | John J. Watson | 6 | 75 |
| " | 3. | Pardon Hopkins | 31 | 50 |
| " | " | Isaac Peck | 103 | 16 |
| " | 7. | A. W. Harris | 26 | 00 |
| " | " | Mary E. Engley | 20 | 00 |
| " | 15. | Francis Stanhope | 66 | 00 |
| " | 16. | Francis Armington | 36 | 00 |
| " | 18. | Walter I. Jenks | 30 | 00 |
| " | 21. | Henry C. Whipple | 30 | 00 |
| " | " | Providence Press Co | 17 | 10 |
| " | 28. | Henry Pollock | 83 | 10 |
| " | 31. | N. F. Patten | 105 | 00 |

1876.

| | | | | |
|---|---|---|---|---:|
| Jan. | 3. | Asa Sisson | | $146 49 |
| " | 4. | Mechanics National Bank | | 108 00 |
| " | " | Bessie G. Tillinghast | | 23 33 |
| " | " | Marion B. Tillinghast | | 50 00 |
| " | " | Ednah F. Beane | | 50 00 |
| " | " | S. Lolie Elliott | | 25 00 |
| " | " | Anna C. Sheldon | | 50 00 |
| " | " | M. J. Peckham | | 25 00 |
| " | 22. | Earle Carpenter & Sons | | 11 76 |
| " | 31. | H. M. Coombs & Co | | 3 75 |
| Feb. | 1. | Nathaniel F. Patten | | 105 60 |
| " | " | M. Josephine Peckham | | 32 00 |
| " | " | S. Lolie Elliott | | 40 00 |
| " | " | Anna C. Sheldon | | 40 00 |
| " | " | Mary E. Engley | | 84 30 |
| " | " | Mary A. Jones | | 85 50 |
| " | " | Ednah F. Beane | | 38 33 |
| " | " | Bessie G. Tillinghast | | 40 00 |
| " | " | Marion B. Tillinghast | | 40 00 |
| " | " | Edwin M. Snow | | 18 82 |
| " | 3. | Edwin M. Snow | | 500 00 |
| " | 8. | Henry T. Chadsey | | 55 92 |
| " | 23. | John Argell | | 58 00 |
| Mar. | 1. | Asa Sisson | | 218 05 |
| " | " | M. J. Peckham | | 36 00 |
| " | " | Anna C. Sheldon | | 40 00 |
| " | " | Mary E. McGary | | 45 90 |
| " | " | Mary A. Jones | | 45 60 |
| " | " | Ednah F. Beane | | 28 33 |
| " | " | Marion B. Tillinghast | | 40 00 |
| " | " | Bessie G. Tillinghast | | 40 00 |
| " | " | S. Lolie Elliott | | 40 00 |
| " | 2. | Nathaniel F. Patten | | 89 10 |
| " | " | Estate of I. Peck | | 130 00 |
| " | 6. | William Hill | | 18 00 |
| " | 9. | E. L. Freeman & Co | | 2 50 |
| " | 22. | Bennett J. Munro | | 5 00 |
| Apr. | 3. | Jared Morris | | 9 00 |
| " | " | Mary E. McGary | | 70 05 |
| " | " | Mary A. Jones | | 68 70 |

1876.

| | | | | |
|---|---|---|---|---:|
| Apr. | 3. | Anna C. Sheldon | | $51 45 |
| " | " | Ednah F. Beane | | 24 27 |
| " | 4. | S. Lolie Elliott | | 58 75 |
| " | " | Marion B. Tillinghast | | 53 57 |
| " | " | Bessie G. Tillinghast | | 53 10 |
| " | " | M. Josephine Peckham | | 40 00 |
| " | " | Mary E. Engley | | 52 20 |
| " | 7. | Mechanics National Bank | | 105 00 |
| " | 15. | N. F. Patten | | 6 46 |
| | | Total | | $14,219 81 |

# Report of the Railroad Commissioner.

## MAY SESSION, A. D. 1876.

*To the Honorable General Assembly of the State of Rhode Island, at its May Session, A. D. 1876:*

The Railroad Commissioner respectfully presents the following report of accidents :

January 11, 1876. E. M. HUNT, injured in yard of Providence & Worcester Railroad Company at Providence. Mr. Hunt is in the employ of the Providence & Worcester Railroad Company, and his business is to team the coal from the vessels to the bins of the Company, and owns and operates a hoisting engine stationed near the bins. He ordered the steam let off from his engine, and then started to go inside the sheds, to ascertain the quantity of coal in the bins. The shed was so completely filled with the steam from his own engine, that he could neither see nor be seen, and when in there, was hit by the tender of a locomotive backing in, and was somewhat injured. In his own testimony he states : " I am not obliged to go into these bins ; there was a ladder on the outside, but I preferred to go this way." This accident was the sole result of his own carelessness or thoughtlessness.

January 21. RICHARD IRVING, injured while attempting to cross the track of the Providence & Worcester Railroad Company, near Valley Falls. He stated to me that a train of dump cars was standing on the track ; that he, wishing to be on the opposite track, got over the fence of the Railroad Company, and on to the cars, and when there, he was thrown off, and injured in his ankle. I did not deem any further investigation necessary.

February 21. DANIEL BASSETT, injured while attempting to drive across the crossing at Hamlet, on the Providence & Worcester Railroad. I wrote the surgeon attending him at Woonsocket, and received a reply, stating that " Mr. Bassett said no one was to blame but himself; he thought he could cross before the cars would reach him." No further investigation.

March 15. CALVIN WHITE was found dead, laying near the track of the Providence & Worcester Railroad Company, between Ashton and Albion. There were some slight bruises on his head, but no marks of being run over. I could not find any employee of any train, or hear of any other person that could give me any information relating to the case.

March 16. JOHN HAMILTON, injured on Providence, Warren & Bristol Railroad, near Cedar Grove. It was the noon train, on time, and within a minute after leaving the station. The man, when first seen by the engineer, was only two or three lengths of the train off, standing still, some eight feet outside of the rail. As the train moved along, very slow, he attempted to cross in front of it, and fell. The power brake was immediately applied, and the engine was reversed, but the engine and the forward wheels of one of the passenger cars ran over one of his feet. He was promptly and carefully cared for, and was sent to the R. I. Hospital, where he now remains. Liquor was the undoubted cause of the accident.

March 17. An unknown man was slightly injured by jumping from a moving train of the Providence & Worcester Railroad Company, between Providence and Pawtucket. He had refused to pay his fare, and to avoid being arrested, jumped from the train. The train was promptly stopped, and backed to the spot. A small quantity of blood was found, and the man was seen rapidly running away, and has not since been heard from.

April 24. SAMUEL CREIGHTON was found injured laying near Smith Street bridge, Providence. As I could not find any one of the employees of any train that knew any thing about the accident, I decided that the man probably fell from the bridge wall. The Providence & Worcester Railroad Company sent him to the R. I. Hospital.

There have been one or two other slight accidents, but upon making inquiries in regard to them, did not deem a formal investigation called for.

All of which is respectfully submitted,

HENRY STAPLES,

*Railroad Commissioner.*

PROVIDENCE, May 1, 1876.

# ACTS AND RESOLVES

PASSED BY THE

# GENERAL ASSEMBLY

OF THE

## State of Rhode Island and Providence Plantations,

AT THE

## SPECIAL SESSION, DECEMBER 1, 1876,

AND AT THE

## JANUARY SESSION, 1877.

STATE OF RHODE ISLAND, ETC.,
OFFICE OF THE SECRETARY OF STATE, MAY, 1877.

---

PROVIDENCE :
ANGELL, BURLINGAME & CO., PRINTERS TO THE STATE.
1877.

☞ The General Assembly convened at Providence, on the first day of December, 1876, pursuant to a proclamation of the Governor, and on the same day adjourned to meet in Providence on the 9th day of January, 1877. On the 30th day of March following, it adjourned to meet in Newport, on the last Tuesday in May, 1877.

# INDEX.

2

---

## APPENDIX CONTAINING THE FOLLOWING DOCUMENTS.

No.

1. –Governor's Message.
2. –Semi- annual report of the Railroad Commissioner.
3. –Annual report of the Inspectors of the State Prison.
4. –Annual report of the Quartermaster General.
5. –Third Annual report of the Commission to build a new State Prison.
6. –Annual report of the Adjutant General.
7. –Eighth Annual report of the Board of State Charities and Corrections.
8. –Second report of the License Commissioners in and for the City of Providence.
9 –Statement of the condition of the State Banks and Institutions for Savings.
10. –First Annual report of the Harbor Commissioners.
11. –Annual report of the Women's Board of Visitors to the Penal and Correctiona
     Institutions of the State.
12. –Report on the Industrial Arts in the Public Schools, made by Committee on Edu
     cation to the House of Representatives.
13. –Report of State Auditor on License money paid by the several towns.
14. –Report of special Committee on Woman Suffrage.
15. –Report of Committee on Education on proposition to reduce number of Schoo
     Committee in City of Providence, and to change mode of election.
16. –Report of special Committee on State Industrial School.
17. –Seventh Annual report of State Board of Pharmacy.
18. –Seventh Annual report of Commissioners of Inland Fisheries.
19. –Annual report of the Inspector of the Hartford, Providence, and Fishkill Railroa
     Company.

# PROCEEDINGS OF THE SPECIAL SESSION

---

At the General Assembly of the State of Rhode Island and Providence Plantations, begun and holden at Providence on Friday, the first day of December, in the year of our Lord one thousand eight hundred and seventy-six, and of Independence the one hundred and first, pursuant to the following proclamation of the governor :

## PROCLAMATION.

By his EXCELLENCY, HENRY LIPPITT, GOVERNOR OF THE STATE OF RHODE ISLAND AND PROVIDENCE PLANTATIONS.

Whereas, at the election of electors of president and vice-president of the United States, held on the seventh day of November, A. D. 1876, there was not in my judgment an election of the number of electors to which the state is entitled.—

Now Therefore, I, HENRY LIPPITT, Governor of the State of Rhode Island and Providence Plantations, pursuant to the provisions of section 5, chapter 11, of the General Statutes, do issue this my proclamation convening the general assembly of this state, to meet at the state house in Providence, on *Friday, December 1, 1876, at 11 o'clock A. M.*, for the choice of electors to fill such vacancy in the manner provided by law.

And I do hereby call upon the members of both houses thereof, to assemble in their respective houses at the time and place aforesaid.

{ L. S. }   In testimony whereof, I have hereunto set my hand and caused the seal of the state to be affixed at Providence, this twenty-eighth day of November A. D. 1876.

HENRY LIPPITT.

By the Governor,
    JOSHUA M. ADDEMAN,
        *Secretary of State.*

### PRESENT:

His Excellency HENRY LIPPITT, Governor, and *ex-officio* President of the Senate.

His Honor HENRY T. SISSON, Lieut. Governor, and *ex-officio* senator.

### SENATORS FROM THE SEVERAL TOWNS.

|  |  |
|---|---|
| Newport, | JAMES M. DRAKE. |
| Providence, | BENJAMIN N LAPHAM. |
| Portsmouth, | ALFRED SISSON. |
| Warwick, | JONATHAN BRAYTON. |
| Westerly, | SAMUEL H. CROSS. |
| New Shoreham, North Kingstown, | JOHN REMINGTON. |
| South Kingstown, | WILLIAM G. CASWELL. |
| East Greenwich, | HENRY A. THOMAS. |
| Jamestown, | THOMAS CARR WATSON. |
| Smithfield, | SAMUEL W. FARNUM. |
| Scituate, | JEREMIAH H. FIELD. |
| Glocester, | ZIBA O. SLOCUM. |
| Charlestown, | GEORGE C. JAMES. |
| West Greenwich, | JOHN T. LEWIS. |
| Coventry, | JOHN WARNER. |
| Exeter, | DANIEL L. MONEY. |

| Middletown, | - | ROBERT S. CHASE. |
| Bristol, | - - | AUGUSTUS O. BOURN. |
| Tiverton, - | - | GIDEON H. DURFEE. |
| Little Compton, | - | NATHANIEL CHURCH. |
| Warren, - | - | CHARLES H. HANDY. |
| Cumberland, | | |
| Richmond, | - | DANIEL C. KENYON. |
| Cranston, | - - | WILLIAM ELSBREE. |
| Hopkinton, | - | OLIVER LANGWORTHY. |
| Johnston, | - - | SAMUEL A. IRONS. |
| North Providence, | | WILLIAM H. ANGELL. |
| Barrington, - | - | HARRISON H. RICHARDSON. |
| Foster, | - - | JOSHUA PAINE. |
| Burrillville, - | - | WILLIAM H. CLARK. |
| East Providence, | | OLIVER CHAFFEE. |
| Pawtucket, - | - | WILLIAM F. SAYLES. |
| Woonsocket, | - | NATHAN T. VERRY. |
| North Smithfield, | - | WILLIAM H. SEAGRAVE. |
| Lincoln, | - | JONATHAN CHACE. |

## JOSHUA M. ADDEMAN,

Secretary of State, and *ex-officio* Secretary.

NATHANIEL P. S. THOMAS, Clerk.

---

## REPRESENTATIVES OF THE SEVERAL TOWNS.

*Newport.*
William P. Sheffield,

Augustus P. Sherman,
William C. Townsend,
Frederick A. Pratt.
*Providence.*
Allen Greene,

Henry J. Spooner,
James W. Blackwood,
Isaac M. Potter,
Henry H. Ormsbee,

Gorham P. Pomroy,
Nelson W. Aldrich,
Harvey E. Wellman,
Edmund S. Hopkins,
George H. Pettis,
Joseph F. Brown
*Portsmouth.*
Jonathan A. Sisson.
*Warwick.*
Christopher R. Greene,
Stephen W. Thornton,
John H. Collingwood.

*Westerly.*
Nathan F. Dixon,
J. Alonzo Babcock.
*New Shoreham.*

*North Kingstown.*
Thomas C. Peirce.
*South Kingstown.*
John G. Clarke.
*East Greenwich.*
Thomas A. Pierce, Jr.
*Jamestown.*
Isaac B. Briggs.
*Smithfield.*
Andrew B. Whipple.
*Scituate.*
Benjamin Wilbur.
*Glocester.*
Raymond P. Colwell.
*Charlestown.*
Charles Cross.
*West Greenwich.*
John Tillinghast.
*Coventry.*
Thomas C. Peckham,
Dexter B. Potter.
*Exeter.*
Nathan B. Lewis.
*Middletown.*
Nathaniel Peckham.
*Bristol.*
William H. Spooner,
Samuel P. Colt.
*Tiverton.*
Holder N. Wilcox.
*Little Compton.*
Jediah Shaw.
*Warren.*
George Lewis Cooke.
*Cumberland.*
Dexter Clark.

*Richmond.*
Reynolds C. Phillips.
*Cranston.*
Henry Whitman,
John Beattie.
*Hopkinton.*
Thomas H. Greene.
*Johnston.*
Alfred A. Williams,
George W. White.
*North Providence.*
Benjamin Sweet.
*Barrington.*
Earl C. Potter.
*Foster.*
Thomas E. Phillips.
*Burrillville.*
John A. Wood,
David Mathewson.
*East Providence.*

*Pawtucket.*
Claudius B. Farnsworth,
William E. Gilmore,
Almon K. Goodwin,
Pardon E. Tillinghast,
Joseph E. Dispeau,
Oren S. Horton.
*Woonsocket.*
William E. Hubbard,
Nathaniel Elliott,
John A. Bennett,
Amos Sherman.
*North Smithfield.*
Arlon Mowry.
*Lincoln.*
Thomas Moies,
Alfred H. Littlefield,
Elisha S. Aldrich,
Edward L. Freeman.

NELSON W. ALDRICH, Speaker.

CHARLES F. BALLOU,   }
HENRY T. BRAMAN,    } Clerks.

The Governor presented the following Message:

*To the Honorable the General Assembly :—*

Grave doubts having arisen as to the eligibility of the Hon. George H. Corliss, one of the candidates for electors of president and vice president of the United States voted for by the people of this state on the 7th of November last, and who, if qualified, received a plu-rality of the legal votes given in at that election, I deemed it my duty to obtain from the supreme court an authori-tative opinion, which would settle this important ques-tion. Accordingly, on the 23d of November last, I submitted to the honorable justices of that court certain questions, prepared by the attorney general, copies of which are herewith presented.

On the 28th ult., I received from a majority of the court an opinion, also herewith presented, to the effect that Mr. Corliss, holding the office of United States centennial commissioner, did hold " an office of trust " under the United States, and therefore under the pro-visions of section 1, of article II, of the Constitution of the United States, was ineligible.

It seemed to me a clear case under the provisions of section 5, chapter 11, of the General Statutes, and following the direction of the statute, I have therefore convened you at this time to fill the vacancy in the manner provided by law.

Since issuing the warrants for convening the gen-eral assembly I have received from one of the justices of the supreme court an opinion in which he dissents from the opinion of the majority of the court upon the question of the eligibility of Mr. Corliss as an elector, but concurs with them in their views upon the other points submitted. This opinion I also present here-with for your consideration.

HENRY LIPPITT, Governor.

Providence, December 1, 1876.

(Copy of questions submitted by the Governor to the Supreme Court.)

### STATE OF RHODE ISLAND, &c.

EXECUTIVE DEPARTMENT,
Providence, November 23d, 1876.

*To the Honorable the Judges of the Supreme Court of the State of Rhode Island, &c.:*

The undersigned, Henry Lippitt, governor of said state, respectfully asks for a written opinion upon the following questions of law:

FIRST:—Is the office of commissioner of the United States Centennial Commission such an office of " trust or profit under the United States," as to disqualify him for the office of elector of president and vice president of the United States ?

SECOND:—If so, does such a candidate for the office of elector who receives a plurality of the legal votes given and declines said office, create thereby such a vacancy as is provided for in section 7, chapter 11, of the General Statutes?

THIRD:—If no, is the disqualification removed by the resignation of said office of " trust or profit " ?

FOURTH:—If not, does the disqualification result in the election of the candidate next in vote, or in a failure to elect?

FIFTH:—If by reason of the disqualification of the candidate who received a plurality of the votes given there was no election, can the general assembly in grand committee elect an elector ?

Please favor me with a reply to the above questions at the earliest possible moment.

(Signed)          HENRY LIPPITT, Governor.

OPINION OF CHIEF JUSTICE DURFEE AND ASSOCIATE
JUSTICES BURGES, POTTER AND MATTESON—ON THE
FOREGOING QUESTIONS:

*To his Excellency, Henry Lippitt, Governor of the
State of Rhode Island and Providence Plantations.*

We have received from your Excellency a communication requesting our opinion upon the following
questions, to wit:

"First—Is the office of commissioner of the United
States Centennial Commission such an office of 'trust
or profit under the United States' as to disqualify him
for the office of elector of president and vice president of the United States?

"Second—If so, does such a candidate for the office of
elector who receives a plurality of the legal votes given
and declines said office, create thereby such a vacancy
as is provided for in section 7, chapter 11, of the
General Statutes?

"Third—If no, is the disqualification removed by the
resignation of said office of 'trust or profit?'

"Fourth—If not, does the disqualification result in
the election of the candidate next in vote, or in a failure to elect?

"Fifth—If by reason of the disqualification of the
candidate who received a plurality of the votes given
there was no election, can the general assembly in
grand committee elect an elector?"

We will give our opinion upon the foregoing questions in the order in which they are propounded.

1. We think a commissioner of the United States
Centennial Commission holds an office of trust under
the United States, and that he is therefore disqualified
for the office of elector of president and vice president
of the United States.

The Commission was created under a statute of the
United States, approved March 3, 1871. That statute
provides for the holding of an exhibition of American
and foreign arts, products and manufactures, "under
the auspices of the government of the United States,"
and for the constitution of a commission to consist of

not more than one delegate from each state and from each territory of the United States, "whose functions shall continue until the close of the exhibition," and "whose duty it shall be to prepare and superintend the execution of a plan for holding the exhibition." Under the statute the commissioners are appointed by the president of the United States on the nomination of the governors of the states and territories respectively. Various duties were imposed upon the Commission, and under the statute provision was to be made for it to have exclusive control of the exhibition before the president should announce, by proclamation, the time and place of opening and holding the exhibition. By an act approved June 1st, 1872, the duties and functions of the Commission were further increased and defined. That act creates a corporation, called "The Centennial Board of Finance," to co-operate with the Commission and to raise and disburse the funds. It was to be organized under the direction of the Commission. The 7th section of the act provides "that the grounds for the exhibition shall be prepared and the buildings erected by the said corporation in accordance with plans which shall have been previously adopted by the United States Centennial Commission and the rules and regulations of said corporation, governing rates for entrance and admission fees, or otherwise affecting the rights, privileges or interests of the exhibitors, or of the public, shall be fixed and established by the United States Centennial Commission; and no grant conferring rights or privileges of any description connected with said grounds or buildings, or relating to said exhibition or celebration, shall be made without the consent of the United States Centennial Commission, and said Commission shall have power to control, change or revoke all such grants and shall appoint all judges and examiners, and award all premiums." The 10th section of the act provides that "it shall be the duty of the United States Centennial Commission to supervise the closing up of the affairs of said corporation, to audit its accounts, and submit in a report to the president of the United States, the financial results of the centennial exhibition."

It is apparent from this statement, which is but partial, that the duties and functions of the Commission were various, delicate and important; that they could be successfully performed only by men of large experience and knowledge of affairs; and that they were not merely subordinate and provisional, but in the highest degree authoritative, discretionary and final in their character. We think that persons, performing such duties and exercising such functions in pursuance of statutory direction and authority, are not to be regarded as mere employes, agents or committee men, but that they are, properly speaking, officers, and that the places which they hold are offices. It appears, moreover, that they were originally regarded as officers by congress; for the act under which they were appointed declares (sec. 7) that "no compensation for services shall be paid to the commissioners or *other officers* provided by this act from the treasury of the United States." The only other officers provided for were the "alternates" appointed to serve as commissioners when the commissioners were unable to attend.

We think, too, the office is an office "under the United States." It was created by act of congress, and all its powers and duties were conferred and imposed by congress. It was created not for the service of any particular state or section, but in the interest of all the states united. The commissioner were appointed under the act by the president, and were commissioned like other United States officers. There seems to be no room for doubt upon this point.

Is it an "office of *trust or profit* under the United States?" It is not an office of profit under the United States, for the commissioners are not entitled to any pay from the United States, nor to any perquisite or emolument under any law of the United States. But we think it is an office of trust. It is true that originally the United States had no pecuniary interest in the exhibition. The commissioners, however, were to be entrusted with a large supervisory and regulative control of the property sent for exhibition, and from the time the government gave its sanction to the exhibi-

tion, and especially after the president issued his proclamation, the honor and reputation of the United States
were pledged for its proper management to its own
citizens and to foreign nations.  From that time the
honor and reputation of the United States were largely
in the keeping of the commissioners; and in this view
there was a very delicate and important trust reposed
inf them.  It would be a narrow and we think an improper interpretation, to hold that an office is an office
of, trust only when the officer has the handling of public money or property, or the care and oversight of
some pecuniary interest of the government.  But, even
if it were so, there came a time when the United
States did become pecun.arily interested in the exhibition by the appropriation of a million and a half of
dollars for it, to be repaid out of the profits if any
should accrue; and when, also, valuable property belonging to the United States was exhibited on the exhibition grounds.  We repeat that the office is, in our
opinion an office of trust.

There is another point deserving mention before we
pass to the next question.  By the act approved June
1, 1872, the Commission was incorporated under the
name of " The United States Centennial Commission."
Did this in any manner terminate or alter its official
character.  We think not.  The change was merely
formal, and made, we suppose, to facilitate the transaction of business.  Indeed, in the papers annexed to
the report of the Commission to congress, it appears
that the Commission had assumed the name of the
United States Centennial Commission before its incorporation, and that the act of June 1, 1872, was
passed on its recommendation.  We do not see, therefore, why the commissioners were not as much United
States officers after as before their incorporation.

2. We think a centennial commissioner, who was a
candidate for the office of elector, and received a plurality of the votes, does not, by declining the office,
create such a vacancy as is provided for in the General Statutes, R. I., chapter 11, section 7.  Section 7,
is as follows:

" If any electors, chosen as aforesaid, shall, after

their said election, decline the said office, or be prevented by any cause from serving therein, the other electors when met in Bristol, in pursuance of this chapter, shall fill such vacancies, and shall file a certificate in the secretary's office of the person or persons by them appointed."

Before any person can decline under this section, he must first be elected, and no person can be elected who is ineligible, or, in other words, incapable of being elected. "Resignation," said Lord Cockburn, C. J., in *The Queen vs. Blizard*, L. R. 2, Q. B. 55, "implies that the person resigning has been elected into the office which he resigns. A man cannot resign that which he is not entitled to, and which he has no right to occupy."

3. We think the disqualification is not removed by the resignation of the office of trust, unless the office is resigned before the election. The language of the constitution is that no person "holding an office of trust or profit under the United States shall be *appointed* an elector." Under our law, Gen. Stat. R. I., chap. 11, §§1 and 2, the election by the people constitutes the appointment. The duty of the governor is to "examine and count the votes, and give notice to the electors of their election." He merely ascertains, he does not complete, the appointment. A resignation, therefore, after the election, is too late to be effectual.

4. We think the disqualification does not result in the election of the candidate next in vote, but in a failure to elect.

In England it has been held that where electors vote for an ineligible candidate, knowing his disqualification, their votes are not to be counted any more than if they were thrown for a dead man or the man in the moon ; and that in such a case the opposing candidate, being qualified, will be elected, though he has but a minority of the votes. *King vs. Hawkins*, 10 East, 211, affirmed in 2 Dow 124, *Reg. vs. Coaks*, 3 El. and B. 249. But even in England, if the disqualification is unknown, the minority candidate is not entitled to the office, the election being a failure. *Queen vs. Hiorns*, 7 Ad. and E., 960. *Rex. vs. Bridge*, 1 M. and S. 76. And it has been held that to entitle the minority candidate to the office, it is not enough that the electors know of the facts which amount to a disqualification, unless they likewise know that they amount to it in point of law. *The Queen vs. The Mayor, &c., of Tewkesbury*, L. R. 8 Q. R. 629. In this country the law is certainly not more favorable to the minority candidate. *State vs. Giles*, 1 Chand. (Wis.) 112; *State vs. Smith*, 14. Wisc. 497; *Saunders vs. Haynes*, 13 Cal. 145; *People vs. Clute*, 50 N. Y., 451; *Commonwealth vs. Cluley*, 56 Pa., St. 270. The question submitted to us does not allege or imply that the electors, knowing the disqualification, voted for the ineligible candidate in wilful defiance of the law; and certainly, in the absence of proof, it is not to be presumed that they so voted. The only effect of the disqualification, in our opinion, is to render void the election of the candidate who is disqualified, and to leave one place in the electoral college unfilled.

5. Our statute (Gen. Stat. R. I., ch. 11, s. 5,) provides that "If by reason of the votes being equally divided, *or otherwise*, there shall not be an election of the number of electors to which the state may be entitled, the governor shall forthwith convene the general assembly at Providence for the choice of electors to fill such vacancy, by an election in grand committee." We think this provision covers the contingency, which has happened, and that, therefore, the general assembly in grand committee can elect an elector to fill up the number to which the state is entitled. The law of the United States provides that "whenever any state has held an election for the purpose of choosing electors, and has failed to make choice on the day prescribed by law, the electors may be appointed on a subsequent day in such a manner as the legislature of such state may direct." U. S. Gen. Stat., p. 21, sec. 134.

THOMAS DURFEE,
W. S. BURGES,
E. R. POTTER,
CHARLES MATTESON.

OPINION OF JUDGE STINESS.

PROVIDENCE, R. I., Nov. 28, 1876.

Sir,—Upon the first question submitted by you, viz.: "Is the office of commissioner of the United States Centennial Commission an office of trust or profit under the United States, within the meaning of the constitution, so as to render a person ineligible as an elector?" etc., I find myself compelled to dissent from the opinion of the majority of the justices of the supreme court.

While the fact that the learned justices composing the majority hold an opinion different from mine might well lead me to doubt the correctness of my own conclusion, it nevertheless renders it proper that I should give some of the reasons that lead me to that conclusion.

By act of congress approved March 3d, 1871, the commission was constituted. The preamble recites that it is desirable that there should be an exhibition of the resources, arts, &c., of the country, in comparison with those of older nations, at Philadelphia, which "should have the sanction of the congress of the United States;" and the first section provides that such an exhibition shall be held under the "auspices of the government."

The act further provides that commissioners, one from each state, &c., shall be appointed, by the president, on the nomination of the governors of the respective states, "to prepare and superintend the execution of a plan for holding the exhibition," and to report such plan, with its incidents, to congress.

Did the commissioners appointed under this act hold "an office of trust under the United States," within the meaning of that term as used in the constitution?

I think not. True they are appointed by the president and hold his commission; hence, if they are officers it must be under the United States, rather than under their respective states, even though they are nominated by the governors. Nevertheless, this mode of appointment would go far to remove them from the operation of the spirit of the constitution and from that class of executive favorites against which it was the evident

intention to guard. Still the mere fact that they hold
such a commission, cannot bring them within the class
precluded by the constitution. It is difficult, if not
impossible, to conceive a case where a person, so commissioned, would not be, in some sense an officer; and
every office implies in some degree trust and confidence.
Hence it might be claimed that every such appointment imports an office of trust. But this cannot be
the meaning of the constitution, for the language is
"holding an office of trust or profit under the United
States." The words "trust or profit" are words of
limitation and restrict the operation of the remainder
of the phrase. If every officer was to be interdicted,
the prohibition would have applied to persons holding
*any* office under the United States. The words of limitation therefore clearly point to considerations other
than the mere holding an office.

While with reference to the question you have submitted, it might be conceded that the commissioners were
officers, to my mind, they would, in view of the duties
imposed upon them by the act referred to, more nearly
resemble a committee chosen outside the appointing
body, to whom was referred a subject which they were
to examine and report upon. I can hardly think that
congress intended by that act to create a new body of
public officers, or supposed that it had done so. For
example, the constitution provides "that no person holding any office under the United States shall be a member of either house during his continuance in office."
Yet it is a notable fact that the president of this very
commission was for a long time a representative in
congress.

But if it is admitted that they are officers, it does not
necessarily follow that they hold an "office of trust
or profit." They were to receive no salary, and nowhere
in the act does anything appear which indicates a
"trust" beyond that implied in every appointment,
except in the words "superintend the execution of a
plan for holding the exhibition," in the provision, that
"the functions" of the commission "shall continue
until the close of the exhibition;" and in section 8,
"That whenever the president shall be informed by
the governor of the state of Pennsylvania that provis-

ion has been made for the erection of suitable buildings for the purpose, and for the exclusive control by the commission, herein provided for, of the proposed exhibition," the president shall make proclamation, &c., and send copies to foreign nations.

But even in these words, what "trust" do the commissioners receive? What power is conferred upon them? What discretion are they to exercise on behalf of the United States? They can make no contracts; they are not by this act even authorized to carry out any plan they may devise, nor can they in any way cause or compel it to be carried out. What then are they "to superintend?" Of course, they may do what they please as individuals, and on their personal responsibility, but nothing as "officers" beyond what is specified in the act; and all that the act provides for, so far as the government is concerned, is a report to congress. That having been made their duties ceased, as to all matters over which congress then had control.

The provision for the exhibition and the erection of suitable buildings was not to be made by the United States. Indeed, the chance for any liability on the part of the government is carefully excluded by the act. If the commissioners were trustees at all, they were the trustees of such private parties as might undertake the work, and they were to act only under the "sanction" and "auspices" of the United States. The purpose of the act seems to have been simply to assure exhibitors at home and abroad that the managers of the exhibition would be selected in such a manner as to secure men worthy of their confidence, and that their rare and costly articles would not be in the hands of irresponsible adventurers, but of those who, acting under the "sanction of the United States," might be understood to be men of intelligence, integrity and responsibility.

There appears to me to be nothing in this denoting a "trust" within the meaning of the constitution.

June 1st, 1872, another act was approved which created two corporations, one by section 1, styled "The Centennial Board of Finance," naming the corporators, and the other by section 11, as follows:

" That the commission created by the act referred to in the preamble of this act is hereby made and constituted a body politic and corporate in law, with power to do such acts and to enter into such obligations as may be promotive of the purposes for which such commission was established. Its title shall be the United States Centennial Commission. It shall have a common and a corporate seal and possess all the rights incident to corporate existence."

The board of finance was to provide the means necessary to carry the plans of the United States Centennial Commission into effect, erect suitable buildings, &c., subject, however, to such rules and regulations as said commission should see fit to make. The commission was to audit their accounts, &c., report to congress, and was clothed with full power to carry forward the exhibition. In the duties allotted to the commission in this act, we see something more nearly resembling a trust; not, indeed, over anything belonging to the government, for the act provides that "nothing in this act shall be so construed as to create any liability of the United States, direct or indirect, for any debt or obligation incurred, nor for any claim by the Centennial International Exhibition, or the corporation hereby created, for aid or pecuniary assistance, from Congress or the treasury of the United States in support or liqui. dation of any debts or obligations created by the corporation herein authorized."

But suppose we assume, in view of the subsequent appropriation made by congress, that a trust is hereby conferred, it will be observed that duties are imposed not upon the commissioners as such, but upon the United States Centennial Commission, the *corporation* for this purpose and by this act created, which in the act is uniformly referred to by its corporate name. If anything remained for the commissioners to do under the act of March 3d, 1871, it was by the act of June 1st, 1872, transferred to the corporation in the same way that the general assembly, if it should pass an act to create a commission to audit all accounts of the state and to do all things theretofore done by the state auditor, would thereby take from him all his powers and duties and transfer them to the new commission.

It may be said that this corporation was merely for the convenience of the commissioners in the transaction of their duties, and that they remained officers as much as before. But when I find that before this act nothing remained for the commissioners to do as officers on behalf of the government, and that in this act every reference is to the corporation, upon which new duties are imposed, different from those originally stated, I cannot think that such was the purpose. Under the first act nothing was required of the commissioners which involved pecuniary liability. Under the second there might be; and therefore the intention was to take from them the personal relations they had hitherto held to this enterprise and merge them in a corporate body.

By the act of June 1, 1872, each commissioner became a member of the corporation. As commissioner he was *functus officio*, and the only operative effect of the commission was to designate him, or a new member in case of a vacancy, as a corporator of the new body corporate. The corporation, therefore, was the trustee and not the members as individuals.

The question, then, resolves itself into this: Is a member of a corporation which acts as the agent of the government in a matter of trust or profit to be regarded as "holding an office of trust or profit under the United States?" Clearly not. To hold such a doctrine would extend the operation of this clause of the constitution far beyond the original intention, and the limit of the mischiefs which it was designed to forestall.

I conclude, therefore, that under the original act no "office of trust under the United States" was created; that by the second act, in which duties are confided to the Commission in the nature of a trust, the corporation is the trustee, and not the members as such; that at the date of the election of electors a member of that commission did not hold such an office as rendered him ineligible as an elector.

As to the replies to the remaining questions, I concur with the other justices.

I have the honor to be,

Very respectfully your obedient servant,

JOHN H. STINESS.

To His Excellency Henry Lippitt, Governor of the
State of Rhode Island, &c.

---

RESOLUTION inviting his excellency the governor and
the honorable senate to join the house in grand
committee.

*Resolved.*—That his excellency the governor and the
honorable senate be invited to join the house in grand
committee this day at one o'clock P. M., for the purpose
of choosing an elector of president and vice-president
of the United States, and for the purpose of electing
justices of the peace and notaries public.

Pursuant to the foregoing invitation the two houses
joined in grand committee.

---

### PROCEEDINGS IN GRAND COMMITTEE.

The governor in the chair.

The rolls of the two houses were called and a quorum
declared to be present.

William S. Slater, of North Smithfield, and Charles
R. Cutler of Warren, were nominated as candidates
for elector of president and vice-president of the United
States.

A ballot was taken with the following result, viz:—

| | |
|---|---|
| Whole number of votes cast, | 100 |
| Necessary for a choice, | 51 |
| of which William S. Slater, received | 81 |
| and Charles R. Cutler received | 19 |

and WILLIAM S. SLATER of North Smithfield was declared elected.

The following named persons were elected justices

f the peace for the several cities and towns named, viz:—

*Providence.*—Pitts S. Bliven.

*Bristol.*—LeBaron B. Colt, Samuel P. Colt, George T. French.

*Tiverton.*—Charles F. Seabury.

The following named persons were elected notaries public for the state, viz:—

*Providence County.*—John F. Tobey.

*Washington County.*—Benjamin Baker.

The grand committee rose and the two houses separated.

---

RESOLUTION to dispense with printing the proceedings of the present session.

*Resolved,* That the secretary of state is hereby authorized and directed to print the proceedings of the present special session of the general assembly with the proceedings of the next January session, and not separately as provided by section 4, chapter 19 of the General Statutes.

---

RESOLUTION relative to pay of officers and attendants.

*Resolved,* That the pay of the members of the general assembly, and that of the officers, and others entitled to pay for this session be postponed to the January session.

---

JOINT RESOLUTION of adjournment.

*Resolved,* The senate concurring, that when the general assembly adjourns this day (December 1st, 1876), it adjourns to meet in Providence on Tuesday, the 9th of January, A. D. 1877, at eleven o'clock, A. M.

SECRETARY OF STATE'S OFFICE,
Providence, Rhode Island.

I certify the foregoing to be true copies of the originals on file in this office.

IN TESTIMONY WHEREOF, I have hereto
set my hand and affixed the seal of
the State, this                    day
of                A. D.

# ACTS AND RESOLVES,

PASSED AT THE

## JANUARY SESSION, 1877.

.

The Chapters of the Public Laws are numbered continuously from
the General Statutes, Revision of 1872.

## CHAPTER 580.

ACT IN AMENDMENT OF SECTION 1, CHAPTER 81, OF THE
GENERAL STATUTES, "OF BOWLING ALLEYS, BILLIARD
TABLES AND SHOOTING GALLERIES." — Passed January 25, 1877.

*It is enacted by the General Assembly as follows:*

SECTION 1. The board of aldermen of the city of
Newport may license pistol galleries, and rifle galleries
within the limits of the said city, to be located at such

*City of Newport; of licensing pistol and rifle galleries.*

places and to be carried on subject to such regu ations as the said board may prescribe.

SEC. 2. This act shall take effect from and after its passage.

## CHAPTER 581.

Passed Feb. 2, 1877.

Amended. See Chap. 595.

AN ACT IN ADDITION TO CHAPTER 33 OF THE GENERAL STATUTES, "OF THE QUORUM, GOVERNMENT, AND CONDUCT OF THE QUORUM, AND OF ORGANIZATION AND GOVERNMENT OF WARD MEETINGS."

*It is enacted by the General Assembly as follows:*

In town meetings, what questions shall be taken by ballot.

SECTION 1. Whenever any question shall be pending in any town meeting involving an expenditure of money, or the incurring of liability by the town, or the disposition of town property, the same shall be taken by ballot, if a ballot be called for, and the call is seconded by at least five electors qualified to vote upon the pending question.

## CHAPTER 582.

Passed Feb. 8, 1877.

AN ACT FOR SUPPLYING THE CITY OF NEWPORT WITH PURE WATER.

*It is enacted by the General Assembly as follows:*

Grants to Geo. H. Norman, for supplying Newport with pure water.

SECTION 1. George H. Norman, of the city of Newport, his heirs and assigns, are hereby authorized, for the purpose of supplying said city and the inhabitants thereof with pure water, as hereinafter provided, to take and convey into and throughout the city of Newport the waters of those two certain streams or brooks which unite at Lawton's Valley, in the town of Portsmouth, and to acquire, as hereinafter indicated, and to hold the said waters, the water rights therewith connected so far as may be necessary for the purposes hereof, and any real estate, hereinafter designated, requisite for the location, establishment, erection, building and maintaining of dams and reservoirs to collect, retain and store said waters, and of water works for pumping and transporting the same; and are further authorized to enter upon and excavate the highway in Portsmouth and Middletown, known as the Main Road, from said valley and streams to the north line of the city of Newport, for the purpose of laying water pipes beneath the surface of said road, and for the purpose of repairing such pipes thereafter; but said highway shall always be restored immediately after such excavating to as good order as it was in just before the excavating was commenced, and during the laying down of said pipes, said highway shall be kept passable at all times for the public.

SEC. 2.  If any owner of lands, water, or water rights required to carry out the objects of this act shall refuse to sell the same to said Norman, his heirs and assigns, or if any such owners shall not agree with said Norman, his heirs or assigns, upon the price to be paid for such property, or privileges, then said Norman, his heirs and assigns, are authorized to take and condemn so much land, water, and water rights as may be necessary for the purposes of this act, under the provisions hereof, and to proceed with the use and improvement thereof in the premises, and with the construction of dams, reservoirs and other works therein as aforesaid; but the lands so condemmed shall not exceed the quantity and limits hereinafter specified, to wit: of lands adjoining and adjacent to said streams, and lying next to and south of said Main Road, between said road and Union Street, so called,—about twenty-three acres belonging to Susan B. Thurston, Peleg L. Thurston, Lewis Thurston, Roland Thurston and Parker H. Thurston, about twelve and a half acres belonging to John Croucher, about thirteen and three-quarters acres belonging to Jacob Chase, and about sixteen and a half acres belonging to Peleg A. Coggeshall: and of lands lying near and south of said Union Street, about four acres belonging to Edward Almy, and about twenty-two acres belonging to Edward Sisson.  And upon taking any property or privilege, as aforesaid, said Norman, his heirs or assigns, shall tender to the owner or owners thereof, if in this state, a sum of money as

*Of condemning lands, water and water rights.*

*What lands may be condemned.*

*Of tender of payment.*

and for the damages sustained, or to be sustained, by
such owner or owners, by the said taking and condemnation, and if said tender shall be refused or lawfully

Bond to be given
on refusal of
tender. omitted, shall on demand give bond to such owner or
owners for the prompt payment of all damages and
costs adjudged under this act, in a form and a sum,
and with sureties satisfactory to any justice of the
supreme court.

Of application
to the supreme
court for dama-
ges. Sec. 3.    Any owner of lands, waters or water rights
so taken as aforesaid, may at any time within, but not
after one year from the time of such taking (unless the
owner be a minor or out of the state, in which case
such owner shall make his claim hereunder within one
year after his majority or after his return to the state)
apply by petition for damages to the supreme court,
holden within and for the county of Newport, at any
regular term of said court, and, upon such petition being filed, at least twenty days notice thereof shall be giv-
en said Norman,his heirs or assigns by serving him, them
or any of them with a copy of such petition; and said
court shall, after such notice, proceed to the hearing of the
petition, and shall appoint three disinterested persons,
being freeholders and residents of the state, appraisers
to determine, after reasonable notice to the parties,
what damages, if any, the petitioner has sustained; and
the award of such appraisers, or of the major part of
them, shall be returned to the court as soon as may be;
and upon acceptance thereof by the court, unless a jury
trial be applied for as hereinafter provided, judgment
shall be thereupon rendered by said court, for the party
prevailing, with costs, and execution may issue accordingly; and provided further that if either party shall be
dissatisfied with such award, such party may, immediately upon the return thereof to the court,    apply
for a trial by jury, which shall determine all questions
of fact relating to such damages and the amount thereof; and such trial shall thereupon be ordered by the
said court and had as soon as conveniently may be, and
judgment shall be entered upon the verdict of said jury,
and costs shall be allowed to the party prevailing, and
execution may be issued therefor; but no petition or
complaint shall be made, as aforesaid, for the taking of
any land, water, or water rights, until the same shall

have been actually taken by virtue of the terms of this act.

SEC. 4. Said Norman, his heirs and assigns, shall have the exclusive right of the waters aforesaid, taken, dammed, collected and stored, as aforesaid, for the purposes aforesaid, and may maintain an action against any person using the same without his or their consent. And if any person shall maliciously or wantonly divert the water of either of said streams and sources from which water shall be taken and conveyed to the city of Newport, as aforesaid, or shall corrupt or render impure the same or any water connected therewith, or shall destroy or injure any pipe, dam, reservoir, machinery or other property used in or relating to the premises, such person or persons, and his or their aiders or abettors shall forfeit to said Norman, his heirs or assigns, to be recovered in an action of trespass on the case or trespass, treble the amount of damage sustained thereby, and shall also be liable to indictment therefor, and upon conviction shall be fined not exceeding three thousand dollars, or be imprisoned not exceeding two years.

George H. Norman to have exclusive right to waters, etc.

Penalties.

SEC. 5. The lands, waters and rights taken and acquired for the purposes of this act, and all the property and improvements of every kind used in connection therewith for supplying said city of Newport with water, and all the rights and powers granted by this act may be at any time sold and transferred to and vested in said city of Newport by said Norman, or his heirs or by any person or corporation to whom he may sell the same, and thereupon shall be thenceforth fully and absolutely held, used, possessed and enjoyed by said city forever, and shall be conducted, operated, managed and maintained by said city in manner and form as the city council of said city shall by ordinance from time to time provide; and said city is hereby empowered to purchase the same and pay for the same, and for the subsequent maintenance and support thereof, as hereinafter further authorized, by the bonds, script or finances of said city, as said city council may deem best, provided such purchase shall be first voted on and approved by a majority of the electors of said city qualified to vote on any proposition to impose a

Lands, waters, etc., hereby taken may be sold to city of Newport.

City of Newport authorized to purchase the same.

tax or for the expenditure of money, voting in ward meetings, legally called for the purpose. After such purchase, said city may distribute said water throughout said city, and by ordinance regulate the use thereof

Powers of the city in the premises. and the price to be paid therefor by the inhabitants of said city and other persons using the same, and all the terms upon which the same may be used within or without the limits of said city, and may enlarge, repair, replace or strengthen dams, reservoirs, works, pipes and other structures and improvements in the premises and generally may do whatever shall be necessary, desirable or appropriate for the purposes of this act.

SEC. 6. This act shall take effect on its passage, but no property or privilege shall be condemned hereunder after three years from the passage hereof.

## CHAPTER 583.

AN ACT IN AMENDMENT OF AND IN ADDITION TO CHAPTER 27, OF THE PUBLIC LAWS, ENTITLED "AN ACT IN AMENDMENT OF CHAPTER 186, TITLE XXV., OF THE GENERAL STATUTES, 'OF THE CRIMINAL JURISDICTION OF, AND OF CERTAIN CRIMINAL PROCEEDINGS BEFORE JUSTICE COURTS.'"

*It is enacted by the General Assembly as follows:*

Fees of justices of the peace for issuing warrants etc. SECTION 1. Justices of the peace appointed by the town council to issue warrants and take recognizances, shall be allowed the following fees in full for the same:

For warrant against every person accused of a
    crime,           .        .        .        .75
For taking recognizance,        .   . .35

Said fees to be deducted from the fees allowed justice courts in criminal cases by section 4, chapter 246, of the General Statutes.

SEC. 2. All acts and parts of acts inconsistent herewith are hereby repealed.

SEC. 3. This act shall take effect from and after its passage.

## CHAPTER 584.

AN ACT IN AMENDMENT OF CHAPTER 491 OF THE PUBLIC LAWS, ENTITLED "AN ACT FOR SUPPLYING THE TOWN OF PAW-TUCKET WITH PURE WATER."

Passed Feb. 14, 1877.

*It is enacted by the General Assembly as follows:*

SECTION 1.   Section 1, of chapter 491, of the Public Laws is hereby amended by inserting after the word "of," in the third line, the words "Abbott's run in Cumberland," so that the section as amended will read as follows:

Town of Paw-tucket may take water from Abbott's Run, in addition to other sources of supply.

"SECTION 1.   The town of Pawtucket is authorized in the manner hereinafter provided to convey into and through said town the waters of Abbott's run in Cumberland, the Blackstone river, Grant's brook in Cumberland, or of Carpenter's pond, or to receive water from the city of Providence upon such terms as may be agreed upon by the city council of said city and the town council of said town, for the purpose of furnishing a supply of pure water for said town; and the town council of said town shall determine from which source to bring said water, after the electors of said town, qualified to vote upon any proposition to impose a tax, shall have decided to introduce the same into said town."

SEC. 2.   Section 2 of said act is hereby amended by inserting after the word "said" and before the word "Blackstone" in the third line the words "Abbott's run in Cumberland," so that the section as amended will read as follows:

"SECTION 2.   The said town of Pawtucket is hereby authorized to acquire by purchase, and to hold, so much of the waters of said Abbott's run in Cumberland, Blackstone river, Grant's brook in Cumberland, or of said Carpenter's pond, and any water rights connected therewith as may be necessary for the purpose aforesaid, and may also purchase, take and hold any real estate necessary for laying aqueducts and forming reservoirs, and for any of the purposes of this act; and may build one or more permanent aqueducts from said water sources selected and determined upon as

May purchase and hold waters of Abbott's Run, etc.

aforesaid, into and through said town, and secure and
maintain the same by any proper works; may erect
and maintain dams to raise and retain the waters
therein; and make and maintain reservoirs within and
without the said town; and in general may do any
other act necessary or convenient for the purpose of
this act; and may distribute the water throughout the
town, regulate its use, and the price to be paid therefor,
within and without the town; and said town, for the
purposes aforesaid, may carry any works by them to
be constructed over or under any highway, turnpike,
railroad or street, in such manner as not to permanently
obstruct or impede travel thereon; and may enter
upon and dig up any highway, turnpike, road or street,
for the purpose of laying down pipes or building
aqueducts upon or beneath the surface thereof, or for
the purpose of repairing the same."

SEC. 3.　This act shall take effect on its passage.

## CHAPTER 585.

Passed Feb. 27, 1877. AN ACT IN AMENDMENT OF AN ACT ENTITLED "AN ACT IN
ADDITION TO CHAPTER 33 OF THE GENERAL STATUTES 'OF
THE QUORUM, GOVERNMENT AND CONDUCT OF TOWN MEET-
INGS, AND OF ORGANIZATION AND GOVERNMENT OF WARD
MEETINGS,'" BEING CHAPTER 581 OF THE PUBLIC LAWS.

*It is enacted by the General Assembly as follows :*

Chapter 581 to
take effect im-
mediately.
　　　SECTION 1.　The act entitled "An act in addition to
chapter 33 of the General Statutes, 'Of the quorum,
government and conduct of town meetings. and of organization and government of ward meetings,'" being,
chapter 581 of the Public Laws, passed February 2,
1877, shall take effect immediately.

SEC. 2.　This act shall take effect from and after its
passage.

## CHAPTER 586.

Passed Feb. 28, 1877. AN ACT IN ADDITION TO CHAPTER 208 OF THE GENERAL STAT-
UTES. "OF APPEALS FROM JUSTICE COURTS IN CRIMINAL
CASES."

*It is enacted by the General Assembly as follows :*

SECTION 1.　The word "jail," as used in chapter
208 of the General Statutes, shall be construed to in-

clude the state workhouse and house of correction
and the Providence reform school.

Of claiming appeals at the State Workhouse and Providence Reform School.

Sec. 2.   This act shall take effect from and after its
passage.

---

## CHAPTER 587.

AN ACT REPEALING CHAPTER 398 OF THE PUBLIC LAWS, AND
RE-ENACTING AND REVIVING ALL PARTS OF CHAPTER 34 OF
THE GENERAL STATUTES WHICH WERE REPEALED BY
CHAPTER 398 OF THE PUBLIC LAWS.

Passed Feb. 28, 1877.

*It is enacted by the General Assembly as follows:*

Section 1.   Chapter 398 of the Public Laws, entitled "An act in amendment of chapter 34, title VII,
of the General Statutes," passed at the May session,
1874, is hereby repealed.

Town clerks to be elected annually.

Sec. 2.   All parts of chapter 34 of the General
Statutes, repealed by chapter 398 of the Public Laws,
are hereby re-enacted and revived.
Sec. 3.   The repeal of said chapter 398 shall not be
construed to remove any town clerk from office until
the expiration of the term of office for which such
town clerk was elected.
Sec. 4. This act shall take effect from and after its
passage.

---

## CHAPTER 588.

AN ACT IN AMENDMENT OF AND IN ADDITION TO CHAPTER 34
OF THE GENERAL STATUTES, "OF THE ELECTION AND QUALIFICATION OF TOWN OFFICERS."

Passed March 6, 1877.

*It is enacted by the General Assembly as follows:*

Section 1.   The mayor of every city, and the president of the town council of every town shall, as
soon as may be after the election of city clerk or town
clerk of such city or town, send to the secretary of
state a certificate of the election of such city or town
clerk, which certificate shall be kept on file in the
office of the secretary of state.

City and town clerks:—election of, to be certified to the secretary of state.

## CHAPTER 589.

Passed March 13, 1877.

AN ACT IN RELATION TO THE ADJOURNMENT OF THE SU-
PREME COURT AND COURT OF COMMON PLEAS.

*It is enacted by the General Assembly as follows:*

Of adjournment of supreme court, etc., by the clerk.

SECTION 1.  Whenever at any time appointed for the sitting of the supreme court or court of common pleas, no justice of the supreme court shall be in attendance, the clerks of said courts respectively may adjourn the same to such day not later than that fixed by law for the next regular term of such court, as he shall have been directed by a justice of the supreme court.

Sec. 5, Chap. 291 repealed.

SEC. 2.  Section 5, of chapter 291 of the Public Laws, entitled "An act in relation to the supreme court," is hereby repealed.

SEC. 3.  This act shall take effect upon its passage.

## CHAPTER 590.

Passed March 15, 1877.

AN ACT IN AMENDMENT OF SECTION 8, OF CHAPTER 195 OF THE GENERAL STATUTES, "OF WRITS, THE FORMS THEREOF, AND WHEN ISSUABLE."

*It is enacted by the General Assembly as follows:*

Of writs of arrest in actions of *scire facias* against bail in criminal cases, in addition to cases heretofore authorized.

SECTION 1.  Section 8, of chapter 195 of the General Statutes, "Of writs, the forms thereof, and when issuable," is hereby amended, in the second clause thereof, by striking out the word "and" after the word "ejectment" and before the word "trespass," and adding thereto the words, "and *scire facias* against bail in criminal cases," so that said clause shall read as follows: "In any action on penal statutes, or in any action of trover, detinue, trespass, trespass on the case, trespass and ejectment, trespass *quare clausum fregit,* and *scire facias* against bail in criminal cases."

SEC. 2.  All acts and parts of acts inconsistent herewith are hereby repealed.

SEC. 3.  This act shall take effect from and after its passage.

## CHAPTER 591.

AN ACT IN AMENDMENT OF SECTION 14, CHAPTER 211 OF THE    Passed March
GENERAL STATUTES, "OF EXECUTIONS."                       15, 1877.

*It is enacted by the General Assembly as follows:*

SECTION 1.   Section 14 of chapter 211 of the General Statutes, "Of executions," is hereby amended by inserting in the fifth line thereof, after the word "dispute" and before the word "or," the words "*scire facias* against bail in criminal cases," so that said section shall read as follows: "An execution, original, alias or pluries, may issue against the body of a defendant not exempt from arrest in an action whenever the same shall have been brought upon a penal statute, or in trover, detinue, trespass, trespass on the case, trespass *quare clausum fregit*, in which the title to the close was not in dispute, *scire facias* against bail in criminal cases, or whenever, the action being for the recovery of a debt or a state or town tax, the cause thereof accrued before the 31st day of day of March, 1870, or whenever such defendant shall have been arrested and held to bail upon an original writ or writ of mesne process therein, or whenever it shall be made to appear to the court which rendered the judgment in such action, or to any justice thereof, that such defendant is about to depart the state without leaving therein sufficient real or personal estate to satisfy such judgment, or that such defendant has been guilty of fraud in contracting the debt, for the recovery of which such judgment was rendered, or in the concealment, detention or disposition of his property."

Executions may issue against the body in actions on *sci're facias* against bail in criminal cases, in addition to the cases heretofore authorized.

SEC. 2   All acts and parts of acts inconsistent herewith are hereby repealed.

SEC. 3.   This act shall take effect from and after its passage.

## CHAPTER 592.

Passed March
15, 1877. AN ACT IN AMENDMENT OF SECTION 2, OF CHAPTER 509 OF THE PUBLIC LAWS ENTITLED, "AN ACT IN AMENDMENT OF CHAPTER 195 OF THE GENERAL STATUTES 'OF WRITS, THE FORMS THEREOF, AND WHEN ISSUABLE,' AND OF CHAPTER 196, 'OF THE SERVICE OF WRITS.'"

*It is enacted by the General Assembly as follows:*

Of service of writs in different counties.

SECTION 1. Section 2 of chapter 509 of the Public Laws, entitled "An act in amendment of chapter 195 of the General Statutes, 'Of writs, the forms thereof, and when issuable,' and of chapter 196, 'Of the service of writs,'" is hereby amended by adding the words, " provided that the officer making the attachment shall not be required to send a copy of the writ by mail, to the address of the defendant, in case the summons shall be served as by law provided," so that said section shall read as follows: "If the property attached shall be in one county, and the defendant be, or have his usual place of abode in another county, the attachment may be made by any proper officer of the county where the property was situate, and the defendant may be summoned by any such officer of any other county where the defendant may be found, or may have his usual place of abode: *Provided*, that the officer making the attachment shall not be required to send a copy of the writ by mail, to the address of the defendant, in case the summons shall be served as by law provided."

## CHAPTER 593.

Passed March
15, 1877. AN ACT IN AMENDMENT OF AND IN ADDITION TO CHAPTER 181 OF THE GENERAL STATUTES, "OF THE SUPREME COURT."

*It is enacted by the General Assembly as follows:*

Assignee of debtor to render inventory to the supreme court.

SECTION 1. The assignee or assignees named in any deed of assignment hereafter made by a debtor for the benefit of creditors, shall, within two months after the time of accepting the trusts created by said deed, render on oath to the supreme court, an inventory of all the effects, estates and credits conveyed by said deed, and a schedule of the liabilities and creditors of said debtor so far as the same can be ascertained, and file said inventory and schedule, together with a copy of such deed in the office of the clerk of said court, in the county where said debtor resides, or has his principal place of business.

SEC. 2. The supreme court in term time, and either of the justices thereof in vacation, may, upon the petition of any creditor interested in such deed of assignment, upon due notice by summary order, require the assignee or assignees named in such deed to give bond, with sufficient surety or sureties to the satisfaction of said court or justice, for the faithful performance of the trusts of said deed. *Assignee may be required to give bond.*

SEC. 3. The bond to be given under the provisions of the preceding section shall be in a penal sum to be determined by the supreme court or a justice thereof, and shall be to the clerk of said court for the county where the assignor resided at the time of making the assignment, and to the successor in office of such clerk, and shall enure to the benefit of the creditors interested in the said assignment, and an action upon any breach thereof may be brought in the name of the clerk of the court in office at the time of the commencement of said action, and the creditor for whose benefit the action shall be brought, shall endorse his name on the back of the writ, and he shall thereby be made liable for the defendant's costs in the event of not prevailing in said action. *Bond to be to the clerk of court and his successor in office.* *Action on bond, how to be brought.*

SEC. 4. The supreme court in term time, or a justice thereof in vacation, shall, upon the petition of any creditor interested in any deed of assignment made by a debtor for the benefit of creditors, upon due notice, remove any assignee named in such deed of assignment, who shall neglect to render an inventory and schedule as required in section one of this act, or shall neglect to give a bond as required by said court or justice. And upon such removal, the said court or justice shall proceed to appoint a successor, or successors, in said trust, in the same manner and with the same effect *Of removal of assignee, and appointment of successor.*

5

as provided in sections fourteen, fifteen, sixteen, seventeen, eighteen, nineteen and twenty of chapter 181 of the General Statutes.

Rights, etc., of creditors not hereby affected.

SEC. 5. This act shall not be construed to affect any of the rights or remedies secured to creditors by any of the provisions of chapter 181 of the General Statutes.

## CHAPTER 594.

Passed March 16, 1877.

AN ACT IN AMENDMENT OF AND IN ADDITION TO CHAPTER .34, OF THE GENERAL STATUTES, "OF THE ELECTION AND QUALIFICATION OF TOWN OFFICERS."

*It is enacted by the General Assembly as follows :*

Of bond of collector of taxes when he is town treasurer.

SECTION 1. Whenever any town shall elect its town treasurer collector of taxes for such town, the warrant for the collection of the taxes assessed therein shall be issued to the town treasurer as collector of taxes, by the town clerk of the town, and in such cases the bond to be given by such collector, under the provisions of section 20, of the chapter of the General Statutes to which this act is in amendment, shall be given to the town, and shall be delivered to the town council for safe keeping, and upon the happening of any breach of the condition of the said bond, an action thereon may be commenced in the name of the town to which it was given.

## CHAPTER 595.

Passed March 21, 1877.

AN ACT IN AMENDMENT OF CHAPTER 494, OF THE PUBLIC LAWS, ENTITLED "AN ACT IN AMENDMENT OF TITLE XII, CHAPTER 68, OF THE GENERAL STATUTES, 'OF THE RESTRAINT AND CURE OF THE INSANE '"

*It is enacted by the General Assembly as follows :*

Of examination of prisoners alleged to be insane.

SECTION 1. Section 1 of chapter 494 of the Public Laws is amended so as to read as follows :
 " On the petition of the agent of state charities

and corrections, or of the clerk of the supreme court or court of common pleas in any county of the state other than the county of Providence, setting forth that any person awaiting trial and imprisoned is insane, any judge of the supreme court shall have power to make such an examination of said person as in his discretion he shall deem proper."

Sec. 2. This act shall take effect on the fifth day of June, 1877.

## CHAPTER 596.

AN ACT TO VALIDATE THE ACTS OF EDGAR D. BURRILL, A NOTARY PUBLIC, DULY COMMISIONED BUT NOT SWORN.

*Passed March 2?, 1877.*

*It is enacted by the General Assembly as follows :*

Section 1. All acts, matters and things done or performed by Edgar D. Burrill as a notary public, in the State of Rhode Island, elected at the May session of the General Assembly in the year 1876, and duly commissioned, but not sworn, are hereby declared to be as valid and effectual in all respects as if said Edgar D. Burrill had taken the oath prescribed by the General Statutes, before entering upon the duties of said office.

*Edgar D. Burrill; acts of, as notary public, validated.*

Sec. 2. This act shall take effect from and after the passage thereof.

## CHAPTER 597.

AN ACT IN REGARD TO THE FRAUDULENT PUBLICATION OF BIRTHS, MARRIAGES AND DEATHS.

*Passed March 22, 1877.*

*It is enacted by the General Assembly as follows :*

Section 1. Any person who shall wilfully send to the publishers of any newspaper for the purpose of publication, a fraudulent notice of the birth of a child, or of the marriage of any parties, or of the death of any person, shall upon conviction thereof, be punished by a fine not exceeding one hundred dollars.

*Penalty for fraudulent publication of births, marriages and deaths.*

SEC. 2. This act shall take effect from and after its passage.

## CHAPTER 598.

Passed March 22. 1877.

AN ACT IN AMENDMENT OF CHAPTER 282 OF THE PUBLIC LAWS, ENTITLED " AN ACT IN AMENDMENT OF AND IN ADDITION TO CHAPTER 137, TITLE XVIII, OF THE GENERAL STATUTES, ' OF INLAND FISHERIES.' "

*It is enacted by the General Assembly as follows :*

Of fishing in Sneach Pond, Cumberland.

SECTION 1. Sneach Pond, in the town of Cumberland, is hereby exempted from the operation of chapter 539, " Of inland fisheries."

SEC. 2. This act shall take effect from and after its passage.

## CHAPTER 599.

Passed March 22, 1877.

AN ACT IN AMENDMENT OF CHAPTER 30 OF THE GENERAL STATUTES, " OF THE STATE AUDITOR, AND OF RETURNS TO HIM."

*It is enacted by the General Assembly as follows :*

Trial justices and clerks of justice courts to account for fines, &c., quarterly.

SECTION 1. Section 27 of chapter 30 is hereby amended by striking out in the second and third lines, the words " annually, and on or before the thirtieth day of April in each year," and inserting in lieu thereof the words, " four times in each year, and on or before the fifteenth day of May, August, November and February respectively," and also by striking out the word " year " in the fifth line and inserting in lieu thereof, the word " quarter," and also by striking out the words, " more than one year before said day," in the eleventh and twelfth lines, and inserting in lieu thereof, the words " since the preceding return," so that the section as amended shall read : " Every trial justice of a justice court having no clerk, otherwise every clerk of a justice court, shall four times in each year and on or before the fifteenth day of May, August, November and February respectively, make return in writing to the auditor of all fines collected by him due the state, during the preceding quarter, and the amount and circumstances of such fines, if any, by him collected ; and shall therewith return an abstract of his docket or record, showing the amount of fines by him imposed, and copies of the bills of costs on all complaints and warrants made, brought or tried before him ; and shall also make return, as aforesaid, of of any penalties or costs in any civil or criminal suit or process due the state, which have been in his hands since the preceeding return, and the amount and circumstances of such penalties and costs."

Sec. 2. This act shall take effect upon and after its passage.

## CHAPTER 600.

AN ACT DEFINING AND LIMITING THE MODE OF ENFORCING THE LIABILITY OF STOCKHOLDERS FOR THE DEBTS OF CORPORATIONS.

Passed March 27, 1877.

*is enacted by the General Assembly as follows :*

Section 1. No person shall hereafter be imprisoned, be continued in prison, nor shall the property of y such person be attached, upon an execution issued n a judgment obtained against a corporation of which such person is or was a stockholder.

Person and property of stockholders exempt, when.

Sec. 2. All proceedings to enforce the liability of a stockholder for the debts of a corporation shall be ther by suit in equity, conducted according to the tice and course of equity, or by an action of debt on the judgment obtained against such corporation ; d in any such suit or action such stockholder may ntest the validity of the claim upon which the judgnt against such corporation was obtained upon any und upon which such corporation could have contested the same in the action in which such judgment was recovered.

Proceedings to enforce liability of stockholder.

Defence of stockholder.

Sec. 3. All acts and parts of acts inconsistent herewith are hereby repealed.

Sec. 4. This act shall take effect from and after the date of the passage thereof.

## CHAPTER 601.

Passed Mar. 27.
1877.

AN ACT IN RELATION TO "PAWNBROKERS."

*It is enacted by the General Assembly as follows :*

Of granting li-
censes to pawn-
brokers.

SECTION 1. The town council of any town may grant licenses to suitable persons, residents of this state, under such conditions and regulations as they may think proper, to carry on the business of pawn-brokers within their respective towns for the term of one year ; and every person taking such license, shall pay to the to 'n treasurer of the town granting such license, a sum to be fixed by the town council granting such license, of not less than fifty dollars.

Penalty for not
taking out
license.

SEC. 2. Any person carrying on the business of pawnbroker without a license, shall be fined two hundred dollars for the first offence, and five hundred dollars for the second and every subsequent offence.

Pawnbroker to
keep a record.

SEC. 3. Every pawnbroker shall keep a book in which he shall enter the date, duration and amount of any loan made by him ; an accurate description of the property or thing pawned, and the name and residence of the pawnor, and at the same time deliver to said pawnor a written memorandum signed by him, containing the substance of the above entry, and at all reasonable times submit said book to the inspection of the mayor, city marshal or chief of police, or the deputy chief of police of any city, or to the chief of police or the town sergeant of any town, and for any violation of this section shall be fined one hundred dollars.

Property
pledged not to
be sold until,
etc.

SEC. 4. No pawnbroker shall sell or dispose of any property pledged with him by any person, until after three months from the time of the expiration of the loan, and for every violation of this section, such pawnbroker shall be fined a sum equal to double the value of the property so sold by him, and his license shall thereupon become void.

Penalty for
dealing with
lunatics, minors,
etc.

SEC. 5. If any pawnbroker shall, after being notified by any officer mentioned in the third section of this act, that any person is either of unsound mind or is

a minor, or neglects all lawful business, or that he habit-
ually misspends his time by frequenting houses of ill-
fame, gaming-houses or tippling-houses, or that from
drinking, gaming, idleness, or debauchery of any
kind, he is squandering his earnings or wasting his
estate, or that he is likely to bring himself or family to
want, or to render himself or family a public charge,
or that he is a known thief, receive from any such
person in pledge or mortgage, or by way of sale,
either absolute or with an agreement to sell back, any
s, notes, bills, checks, or other property, or assign-
nts of, or order for money or other property, such
wnbroker shall be fined a sum equal to double the
ue of the property so received by him, and his
nse shall thereupon become void.

SEC 6. Whenever complaint shall be made, by any
n, on oath to any trial justice or the clerk of any
e court authorized to issue warrants in criminal
that any property belonging to him has been
hout his consent lodged or pledged with any pawn-
ker, and that the complainant believes the same
be in some house or place within the county where
ch complaint is made, such justice or clerk shall, if
tisfied of the reasonableness of such belief, issue
a warrant directed to the sheriff, his deputy, or to
er of the town sergeants, or constables, in said
ty, commanding them to search for the property
lleged to have been lodged or pledged, and to
and bring the same before such justice court,
h warrant shall be issued and served as search
nts are now by law required to be issued and
ed.

*Of issuing search warrants.*

SEC. 7. Upon any property seized under the pro-
ons of the preceding section being brought before
h justice court, such court shall cause such property
be delivered to the person so claiming to be the
e owner thereof, on whose application the warrant
as issued, on his executing a bond as hereinafter directed, and if such bond be not executed within twenty-
four hours, exclusive of Sunday, said justice court
shall cause the said property to be delivered to the
person from whose possession it was taken.

*Of delivering property seized to the true owner.*

Of bond for restoration.

SEC. 8. The bond required to be given under the preceding section shall be in double the value of the property claimed, with such surety as such justice court shall approve, and shall be given to the person from whose possession the property was taken, with a condition that the person so claiming the same will, in case any suit shall be brought against him within ten days from the date of such bond by the pawnbroker from whose possession the said property was taken, pay all costs and damages that may be recovered against him.

Business of pawnbrokers not to be transacted on Sunday.

SEC. 9. No license granted under the provisions of this act shall authorize any business to be transacted by pawnbrokers on the first day of the week.

## CHAPTER 602.

Passed Mar. 27, 1877.

AN ACT IN AMENDMENT OF CHAPTER 240 OF THE GENERAL STATUTES, " OF JAILS AND THE CARE AND DISCIPLINE OF JAILS."

*It is enacted by the General Assembly as follows :*

Jail in county of Providence; what to constitute.

SECTION 1. Section 1, of chapter 240, of the General Statutes, is amended so as to read as follows: " The jail in the county of Providence shall be the building adjoining the state prison in the city of Providence, built for the keeper's house, and such portions of the state prison and buildings on the prison lot as are now used for 'the purpose of a jail together with such portions of the building on the state farm in Cranston, erected by the commissioners appointed for the building a new prison for the state,' under a resolution of the general assembly, passed at the May session, 1874, as shall be designated for the purposes of a jail by the board of state charities and corrections, and the several towns in Providence county, including the city of Providence, may continue the use of the Providence county jail upon the same terms and conditions, and to the extent, as they are now authorized by law to use the same."

SEC. 2. Section 9 is amended so as to read as follows :

"The board of state charities and corrections shall appoint one of their number to inspect the jail in each county except the county of Providence, at least twice in each year, and to. inquire into the state thereof as respects security, treatment and condition of the prisoners therein, and said member shall have power to direct the sheriff to take such precautions as the board shall deem necessary, against escape, and infection, and the board shall make report annually to the general assembly of the condition of the several jails, in the same manner as they are required by law to make report of the condition of the jail in Providence county." *Of inspection of jails in the several counties.*

SEC. 3. No law of this state shall be so construed as to give any town a claim upon the state for the labor or services of any person committed to jail under authority thereof. *Towns not to have claim for labor of convicts.*

SEC. 4. This act shall take effect on the fifth day of June, 1877.

## CHAPTER 603.

AN ACT PROVIDING FOR THE GOVERNMENT AND CONTROL OF THE STATE INSTITUTIONS IN THE TOWN OF CRANSTON. *Passed March 27, 1877.*

*is enacted by the General Assembly as follows :*

SECTION 1. The board of state charities and corrections shall consist of nine persons, three from county of Providence, one from each of the other counties, and one from the state at large, together with such person as may be appointed secretary of the *Board of state charities, etc; number of.*

SEC. 2. The members of the present board shall respectively hold their offices for the terms for which they were appointed unless sooner removed. *Term of present members.*

SEC. 3. The governor, with the advice and consent of the senate, shall appoint one person from the county of Providence and one person from the state at large to be members of said board, who shall hold their offices respectively, one for the term of three years, and *Appointment of new members.*

6

one for the term of six years from the fifth day of June,
A. D. 1877.

Of future appointments. SEC. 4. He shall in like manner annually at the
May session of the general assembly, upon the expiration of the term of office of any one of the said board,
appoint a person to such office, and every such person
hereafter so appointed shall hold his office for six years
unless sooner removed. Every appointment to fill a vacancy shall be for the remainder of the term.

Secretary of the board: appointment, bond and duties of. SEC. 5. Such board may appoint a secretary, who
shall, by virtue of his office, be a member thereof; he
shall hold his office during the pleasure of said board;
he shall give bond to the state in such sum as the
board may require for the faithful performance of his
duties; he shall keep a record of all the doings of the
board, and perform such other duties as may be by
them required.

Powers and duties of the board. SEC. 6. The oversight, management and control of
the state farm in Cranston, of the state workhouse
and house of correction, state asylum for the incurable
insane and state almshouse thereon, together with the
state prison and Providence county jail, shall be vested
in the board of state charities and corrections, and they
shall have, in addition, all the powers and duties heretofore vested by law in the board of inspectors of the
state prison.

No compensation allowed the board, except, &c. SEC. 7. No member of the board except the secretary shall receive any compensation for his services as
such, but every member shall be paid out of the state
treasury his necessary traveling expenses, and shall
be exempted from military and jury duty.

Agent of state charities and corrections; appointment and duties of. SEC. 8. The board shall appoint an agent of state
charities and corrections, who shall hold his office
during their pleasure. He shall, under their direction,
have the general charge of the examination of paupers
and lunatics for the purpose of ascertaining their
place of settlement and means of support, and who
may be responsible therefor; and also attend to their
removal to their homes or places of settlement, or to
the state almshouse or to the asylum for the incurable insane, and shall have like power and authority
in respect thereto as is conferred upon the overseers

of the poor. and shall perform such other duties as may
be required of him by the board.

SEC. 9. The board shall appoint a superintendent Superintendent of state institutions in Cranston; appointment and duties of.
of the state institutions in Cranston, who shall hold
office during their pleasure. Such officer shall, under
their direction, have the control and management of
state farm and of the state workhouse and house
f correction, state asylum for the incurable insane and
late almshouse thereon, and he shall have the general
versight of the state prison and Providence county
l, and report to the board from time to time upon
sir condition and management. The said board
l, upon the nomination of the superintendent of the
institutions, appoint a deputy superintendent of Of deputy superintendents;
tate workhouse and house of corrrection, a deputy
ntendent of the state asylum for the incurable in-
nd a deputy superintendent of the state alms-
who shall hold their respective offices during the
of the board. Said superintendent shall ap-
t all the assistants to the deputy superintendents, Of assistants;
such other persons employed upon said state farm
he board shall deem necessary, and shall discharge
same at his pleasure. The board shall fix the com-
sation of their secretary and of the superintendent Compensation of officers, etc.
he state institutions, the agent of state charities and
ons, the deputy superintendents and their assis-
, the warden and deputy warden of the state's
n and their assistants, and all other persons em-
ed in any manner upon said state farm, and the
tutions thereon, adopt all needful rules and regu-
ns for the government of the institutions upon
farm, and make contracts for the labor of the in-
thereof.

SEC. 10. The board may bind out any pauper child Of binding out pauper children, and discharging inmates.
o is an inmate of the state almshouse in like man-
and with like effect as overseers of the poor may
out children under their charge, and may at any
discharge any of the inmates of the state work-
and house of correction, state asylum for the incurable insane and state almshouse.

SEC. 11. Such board may cause any inmate of the Of removal to state workhouse of inmates of reform school;
Providence reform school, who shall be deemed incor-
rigible or an unfit person to remain therein by the

trustees thereof, upon their application, to be removed, with the mittimus committing him thereto, to the state workhouse, there to remain until the expiration of the term of the sentence stated in the mittimus. Said board may cause any person sentenced to the jail in the county of Providence, whenever in their opinion it shall be for the interest of the state and of such sentenced person, to be removed, with the mittimus committing him thereto, to the state workhouse, there to remain until the expiration of the term of the sentence stated in the mittimus. And every person sentenced to such workhouse, or removed thereto in the manner above provided, who shall escape or attempt to escape therefrom, may be returned thereto, and shall on conviction of such escape or attempt to escape, be imprisoned in such workhouse not less than six months nor more than twelve months, in addition to the previous sentence. The board may cause any inmate of the state workhouse and house of correction, who shall be by them deemed to be a dangerous or unfit person to remain therein, to be removed, with the mittimus committing him thereto, to the jail in the county of Providence, there to remain until the expiration of the term of the commitment stated in the mittimus.

SEC. 12. The board shall direct as they may think proper, all purchases for use on the state farm, and in any of the public institutions thereon, and also in the state prison and jail in Providence; they shall in their discretion, sell the products of said farm and institutions; they shall make such contracts respecting the labor of the inmates of the several institutions as they may think proper, and they shall cause full accounts thereof to be kept.

SEC. 13. The members of the board of state charities and corrections shall, before entering upon their duties, be sworn to the faithful performance thereof and said board shall make a full report of their doings including a statement of the names and salaries of all persons appointed or employed by them, annually to the general assembly, on or before the second week of the January session in Providence.

SEC. 14. The oversight, management and control of the state prison, shall be vested in the board of state charities and corrections and all the duties and powers heretofore vested in the inspectors of the state prison are hereby vested in the said board, excepting only as hereinafter in this act provided; and the words "inspectors of the state prison," wherever they occur or are referred to in the General Statutes and public laws, shall be construed to mean board of state charities and corrections. *State prison; oversight, &c., vested in the board.*

SEC. 15. Said board shall appoint and may remove at pleasure the warden, physician and religious instructor, and shall, upon the nomination of the warden, appoint a deputy warden. The warden shall appoint the other officers and assistants of the prison, who shall be removable at his pleasure; and said warden, officers and assistants, shall, before entering upon their duties be sworn to the faithful performance thereof, and to the observance of the rules of the prison. The religious instructor shall conduct the religious services on Sunday, at the prison and other institutions on the state farm, and perform such other duties in connection therewith as the board may prescribe, and act as agent for procuring employment for prisoners after their discharge. Said religious instructor shall reside at or near the state farm and shall receive such compensation for his services as the board may designate. *Officers of the prison. Religious instructor.*

SEC. 16. Upon the death, resignation or removal of the warden, they shall immediately give notice thereof to the sheriff of the county of Providence, and proceed as early as possible to the election of another warden. *Of vacancy in office of warden.*

SEC. 17. They shall make all lawful and necessary rules and regulations for the internal police of the prison, for the mode of employing the convicts imprisoned therein, and the place of such employment within the limits of the prison yard, or within any of the buildings on the prison lot or on any portion of the state farm, and shall determine the uniform to be worn by the prisoners. Such rules and regulations shall be entered in a book kept for that purpose, and a copy thereof given to the warden and other officers of the prison. One or more members of said board *Of rules and regulations for government of the prison.*

shall at least twice a month visit the prison, examine into the condition of the prisoners, hear any complaints that they may make, and see that the rules and regulations of the prison are strictly observed ; and the person or persons so visiting shall keep a particular record of such visits and the complaints made to them by prisoners, whether well or ill-founded, in a book kept for that purpose, open to the inspection of the whole board and to be filed with the records of said board.

SEC. 18. They shall have full power and authority over all convicts who now are or hereafter may be committed to the prison ; may enlarge their confinement and regulate their labor and exercise within the limits of the prison yard or of any building on the prison lot or any part of the state farm ; may confine, in their discretion, females sentenced to imprisonment in the state prison, in the Providence county jail ; may admit such communication to and from prisoners and their friends and between prisoners themselves, and such books and other articles to be given to them as they may deem expedient, the same being consistent with the safe keeping of the prisoners.

SEC. 19. Each member of said board may administer oaths as to all matters connected with the prison.

SEC. 20. The warden of the state prison shall before entering upon his office, give bond to the state in the sum of ten thousand dollars, with sureties to the satisfaction of the board, for the faithful performance of the duties of his office.

SEC. 21. He shall reside at the prison, and shall not absent himself therefrom for a night without the written permission of two of the board.

SEC. 22. He shall see that the rules of the prison are strictly obeyed, that the convicts regularly receive their allowance of food and clothes ; that they are cleanly in their dress and cells, and actively engaged in the work prescribed them ; and he shall enforce obedience to the prison rules, by such punish- ments as are prescribed therein ; but whipping shall no be permitted under any circumstances, nor shall an other corporal punishment be inflicted except under the direction of at least two of the board.

SEC. 23. The warden of the state prison shall receive and safe keep therein all prisoners committed thereto under the authority of any court of the United States held within this state, until such prisoner shall be discharged by the course of law of the United States, under the like penalties and liabilities as in case of prisoners committed by the authority of this state.

Warden to receive prisoners sentenced by U. S. courts.

SEC. 24. He shall report in writing once a month, at such time as the board may determine, and oftener if they require, every case of punishment inflicted in the prison, and the mode and degree of the same, together with the cause thereof.

To report every case of punishment.

SEC. 25. He may in his discretion, and without a permit from one of the board admit visitors to the state prison, under such restrictions and on payment of such fees, as the board may from time to time prescribe, to be applied as the board may direct.

May admit visitors.

SEC. 26. He shall not receive from any one confined in the state prison, nor from any one in behalf of any such prisoner, any gift or reward, or the promise of any, for any services, or supplies or as a gratuity, under the penalty of five hundred dollars.

Not to receive gifts from prisoners.

SEC. 27. He shall keep a journal, in which he shall regularly enter the reception, discharge, death, pardon, or escape of every convict, all punishments by him inflicted for breach of prison discipline, and the visits of members of the board, and physicians.

To keep a journal of prisoners.

SEC. 28. He shall keep correct accounts of all receipts and expenditures, and as far as may be, separate accounts of all expenses incurred by him for the prison and the jail; taking vouchers for all payments that he may make, specifying the articles furnished, and the labor performed for each; and as often as required by them make report and present his account to the board. He shall also, as often as required by them, present to said board a written report which shall contain the number of persons in confinement in such prison and jail, the sex, age, place of nativity, time of commitment, crime, and term of imprisonment of each; noting also what convicts have left the prison or jail during the preceding year, and under what circumstances.

To keep accounts and make reports.

In case of va-
cancy, sheriff to
be ex-officio
warden.

SEC. 29. In case of vacancy in the office of warden, by death, resignation or removal, and until the
bond of the new warden is given as by law required,
the sheriff of the county of Providence shall be, ex-
officio, warden of the state prison, and shall be entitled to receive such compensation as belongs to said
office.

SEC. 30. The warden of the state prison shall keep
a record of the conduct of each convict, and for each
month that a convict (except convicts under sentence
to imprisonment for life) appears by such record to
have faithfully observed all the rules and requirements of the prison, and not to have been subjected
to punishment, there shall, with the consent of the
governor, upon the recommendation to him of a majority of the board be deducted from the term or terms
of sentence of such convict, the same number of days
that there are years in the said term of his sentence:
provided, that when the sentence is for a longer term
than five years, only five days shall be deducted for
one month's good behavior: and provided further,
that for every day a convict shall be shut up, or

otherwise punished, for bad conduct, there shall be
deducted one day from the time he shall have gained
for good conduct.

SEC. 31. One under-keeper or assistant shall every
day inspect the cell of each prisoner, shall see that
his meals are regularly furnished, that his cell and all
its contents are in good order, and shall report in
writing to the warden, and to the board when required,
all deficiencies in these respects.

Under keepers
etc., not to be
absent without
leave; nor re-
ceive gifts from
convicts, etc.

SEC. 32. No under-keeper or assistant shall absent
himself from the prison without the leave of the
warden: nor receive from any convict confined in the
state prison, nor from any one in his behalf, any reward
or gift, or promise of any, either for services or supplies, or as a gratuity, under the penalty of imprisonment for thirty days. He shall also be immediately
dismissed, and shall not afterward be employed in
the prison.

SEC. 33. The under keepers and assistants shall
have no conversation with the convicts, other than is

necessary for understanding and supplying their wants, and enforcing industry and obedience to the rules of the prison.

SEC. 34. The buildings erected and built, and to be built, for the purpose of a state prison, on a portion of the state farm, in the town of Cranston, by the commissioners appointed under a resolution of the general assembly, passed at the May session, 1874, "for the purpose of building a new prison for the state," are hereby declared to be and are a portion of the state prison of the state of Rhode Island. *State prison, to include what.*

SEC. 35. Every convict shall, immediately on his commitment to the state prison, be examined by the warden and other officers, and his name, height, apparent and alleged age, place of nativity, complexion, color of hair and eyes, length of foot, and trade or occupation, as near as may be, ascertained and entered in a book provided for that purpose, together with such natural and accidental marks as may serve as a means of identifying his person. *Of examination and registry of convicts on commitment.*

SEC. 36. All the effects on the person of the convict, as well as his clothes, shall be taken from him; an inventory of which shall be entered under the description of his person, in his presence; after which he shall be thoroughly cleansed, conducted to the cell assigned him, clothed in the uniform of the prison, informed of the rules of the prison, and set to labor as soon as conveniently may be. The effects and clothes of each convict shall be carefully kept by the warden, and restored to him on his discharge, unless the warden shall in his discretion deem it advisable to sell them, in which case the convict shall receive the proceeds thereof on his discharge. *Of inventory of convict's effects, etc.*

SEC. 37. A change of under clothing shall be furnished to each prisoner at least once a week. *Change of underclothing.*

SEC. 38. No convict shall receive anything but the prison allowance, unless by order of the physicians. *Allowance of food.*

SEC. 39. No person shall deliver to, or receive from any convict, any letter or message whatever, not authorized by the rules and regulations adopted by the board, or supply any convict with any article of any kind, under the penalty of one hundred dollars. *Penalty for delivering letter or message to.*

Sick prisoner
not to be dis-
charged.
SEC. 40.  No prisoner shall be dismissed from the state prison while laboring under dangerous or contagious disease, although entitled to his discharge.

On his dis
charge, convict
to be clothed
and paid a por-
tion of his earn-
ings.
SEC. 41.  When a convict shall be discharged he shall be decently clothed, and the board may in their discretion pay to him a sum of money not exceeding one-tenth of his actual earnings while confined in said prison : provided however that in case of sickness of any convict by which he shall have been incapacitated for labor, he shall  in the discretion  of  the board be paid  a  sum not exceeding one-tenth of  the average compensation of convict labor in said  prison  during the  time of his sickness ; provided, moreover, that the board  shall  have  the privilege of paying said Of payment of
earnings to fam-
ily of convict. amount at any  time during the imprisonment of the convicts to the families or near  relatives of such convicts, who may  be  in  circumstances of indigence or want, instead of  paying it to the convicts themselves, at their discharge, and further provided that in no case shall the sum paid such convict at his discharge be less than five dollars.

Of allowing vis-
its to the prison.
SEC. 42.  No person not an official visitor shall be allowed to  visit the prison without the permission of the warden as aforesaid, or a written  permit from one of the board ; nor  shall any  person  other  than an official visitor have any conversation or communication with any convict except as provided for in the general rules established  for the prison.  This rule may be dispensed with in favor of any  person  visiting the prison from without the state, for the purposes of general information, by  a  written permit from two of the board.

Official visitors
ex-officio.
SEC. 43.  The governor and lieutenant-governor of the state,  the speaker of the house of  representatives, the secretary of  state, the attorney general, and justices of the supreme court, shall *ex-officio* be official visitors of the prison.

Superintendent
of state chari-
ties, etc., con-
strued to mean
agent of state
charities, etc.
SEC. 44.  The words  "superintendent of  state charities and corrections,"  wherever they occur, or are  referred  to in the General Statutes and  Public Laws,  shall  be  construed to  mean  agent of state charities and corrections.

SEC. 45. The governor may with the consent of the senate for mal-feasance or non-feasance during the sitting of the general assembly remove from office any member of the board of state charities and corrections, and when the general assembly is not in session, may suspend such member. Of removal of members of the board.

SEC. 46. Chapters 242 and 243 of the General Statutes, and chapters 304, 327, 350 and 440 of the Public Laws and all acts and parts of acts inconsistent herewith are hereby repealed. Acts repealed.

SEC. 47. This act shall take effect on the fifth day of June, 1877.

## CHAPTER 604.

AN ACT IN AMENDMENT OF CHAPTER 54 OF THE GENERAL STATUTES, "OF TEACHERS." Passed March 28, 1877.

*It is enacted by the General Assembly as follows:*

SECTION 1. Section 2 of chapter 54, of the General Statutes, is hereby amended so as to read as follows, to wit : "Such certificate, unless annulled, if signed by the school committee, shall be valid within the town for one year, or for such portion thereof as shall be specified in said certificate." Of certificates of qualification of teachers.

SEC. 2. This act shall take effect on and after its passage.

## CHAPTER 605.

AN ACT TO AMEND CHAPTER 203 OF THE GENERAL STATUTES, "OF VIEWS, WITNESSES, DEPOSITIONS AND EVIDENCE." Passed March 28, 1877.

*It is enacted by the General Assembly as follows:*

SECTION 1. Section 32 of chapter 203, of the General Statutes, is hereby amended, and shall read as follows : "No person shall be disqualified from testifying in any action at law, suit in equity, or other When parties may become witnesses.

proceeding at law or in equity, by reason of his being interested therein, or being a party thereto : *Provided,* that when an original party to the contract or cause of action is dead, or is shown to the court to be insane, or when an executor or administrator is a party to the suit, the other party may be called as a witness by his opponent, but shall not be admitted to testify upon his own offer, or upon the call of his co-plaintiff or co-defendant, otherwise than now by law allowed, unless a nominal party merely, or unless the contract in issue was originally made with a person who is living and competent to testify, except as to such acts and contracts as have been done or made since the decease of the executor's testate, or administrator's intestate."

SEC. 2. This act shall not apply to or affect any pending suit, in which either of the parties to the original contract or cause of action is now dead.

SEC. 3. All acts and parts of acts inconsistent herewith are hereby repealed.

SEC. 4. This act shall take effect from and after its passage.

## CHAPTER 606.

AN ACT IN RELATION TO THE PUTTING UP AND SALE OF COMMERCIAL FERTILIZERS.

*It is enacted by the General Assembly as follows :*

SECTION 1. Every package or parcel of a commercial, fertilizer sold, offered or exposed for sale in this state, shall show the name and place of business of the manufacturer and seller, and shall be accompanied by an analysis, (except as is hereinafter proivded,) showing its composition, &c., viz.:

1st. "The percentage of nitrogen as it exists in raw bone or refuse meat, blood and guano."

2d. "The percentage of actual ammonia."

3d. "The percentage of potential ammonia."

4th. "The percentage of anhydrous phosphoric acid, soluble in cold water."

5th. "The percentage of anhydrous reverted phosphoric acid."

6th. "The percentage of anhydrous insoluble phosphoric acid."

7th. "The source of phosphoric acid, whether from bone or mineral phosphate."

8th. "The percentage of potash."

9th. "The percentage of pure potash in the salts of potash."

10th. "The percentage of water."

11th. "The percentage of the other remaining constituents."

*Provided*, however, that no analysis shall be required for crude fish pomace or other fertilizer which is sold for a less price than fifteen dollars per ton, or which does not contain either nitrogen, phosphoric acid or potash.

SEC. 2. Any person selling, offering or exposing for sale any commercial fertilizer without an analysis, except as is provided in the first section of this act, or with an analysis representing said fertilizer to contain a larger percentage of nitrogen, phosphoric acid or potash than really exists, or of representing these elements to exist in a more available condition for "plant food" than shall be shown by analysis, shall be fined not less than one hundred nor more than five hundred for the first offence, and not less than five hundred nor more than five thousand dollars for each subsequent offence. <sup></sup>

*Penalties.*

SEC. 3. This act shall take effect from and after July 1st, A. D. 1877.

## CHAPTER 607.

AN ACT AUTHORIZING THE TOWN OF BARRINGTON TO BUILD A BRIDGE ACROSS BARRINGTON RIVER.

*Passed March 28, 1877.*

*It is enacted by the General Assembly as follows:*

SECTION 1. The town of Barrington is authorized to build across Barrington river in the northerly part of said town, a suitable bridge; provided that the

*Bridge across Barrington river.*

same be constructed at such a location, of such materials and width, and in such manner as the board of harbor commissioners shall approve.

Sec. 2. This act shall take effect from and after its passage.

---

## CHAPTER 608.

Passed March 29, 1877. AN ACT IN AMENDMENT OF AND IN ADDITION TO TITLE XXV, CHAPTER 183, OF THE GENERAL STATUTES, "OF THE TERMS OF THE SUPREME COURT AND COURT OF COMMON PLEAS, AND OF THE ADJOURNMENT THEREOF."

*It is enacted by the General Assembly as follows :*

Of holding courts at Westerly.

SECTION 1. At any term of the supreme court hereafter to be holden, within and for the county of Washington, said supreme court or any one of the justices thereof, holding or attending to hold the same may adjourn said court to Westerly in said county, and there hold the same for the trial of causes pending in said court ; and any one of said justices holding or attending to hold the court of common pleas at any term thereof hereafter to be holden, within and for said county of Washington, may adjourn said court of common pleas to Westerly, in said county, and there hold the same for the trial of causes pending in said court of common pleas, at his or their discretion, provided that the state shall be at no additional expense thereby, and further provided that all the parties, in causes pending in said courts, requested to be removed, shall consent for said causes to be heard and tried at Westerly.

Sec. 2. All acts and parts of acts inconsistent herewith are hereby repealed, and this act shall take effect from and after its passage.

## CHAPTER 609.

AN ACT IN ADDITION TO CHAPTER 152 OF THE GENERAL STATUTES, "OF THE PROPERTY OF MARRIED WOMEN AND OF THE DISPOSITION OF THE SAME."

Passed March 29, 1877.

*It is enacted by the General Assembly as follows :*

SECTION 1. Whenever a husband shall have deserted his wife, who is not a minor, without justifiable cause, for the period of six months, or who shall have neglected to provide for her a suitable support for that riod, he being of sufficient ability to make such provision, and such desertion or neglect to provide shall have been made to appear to the satisfaction of the court of probate of the town where such married woman shall reside, after notice given in pursuance of section 4 of chapter 169, of the General Statutes, such married woman may sell and convey her real and personal estate in the same way, and may have the earnings of her minor children, in her custody, and in her own name sue and be sued, as if she was sole and arried.

*Right of wife to sell property, and to earnings of minor children, in case of desertion, etc., by husband.*

SEC. 2. Whenever a husband shall be of unsound mind, his wife may apply to the court of probate the town where she may reside, setting forth that husband is of unsound mind and has been in that condition for a period of twelve months, or upwards, and if the court of probate, after notice given in accordance with the provisions of section 3 of chapter 169, of the General Statutes, shall find the facts alleged to be true, the court of probate may, in its discretion, allow such married woman to transact business as a trader and allow her to sell her real and personal estate and to have the earnings of her minor children, upon such terms, and subject to such restrictions as such court may prescribe, and she may sue for any right herein conferred upon her or be sued for any obligation which she may assume hereunder as if she was sole and unmarried.

*Wife of insane husband may be authorized to transact business as a trader, etc.*

## CHAPTER 610.

Passed March
29, 1877.

AN ACT IN AMENDMENT OF CHAPTER 463 OF THE PUBLIC LAWS
ENTITLED "AN ACT TO ESTABLISH A BOARD OF COMMISSION-
ERS OF SINKING FUNDS."

*It is enacted by the General Assembly as follows :*

Time changed
for payments to
sinking funds.

SECTION 1.  Section 7 of chapter 463 of the Publi
Laws, is hereby amended by striking out the wor
"first day of June," and substituting therefor th
words, "fifteenth of January."

## CHAPTER 611.

Passed March
30, 1877.

AN ACT IN AMENDMENT OF CHAPTER 556 OF THE PUBLIC LA
ENTITLED "AN ACT TO ESTABLISH A BOARD OF HARBOR CO
MISSIONERS."

*It is enacted by the General Assembly as follows :*

Harbor commis-
sioners to have
supervision of
harbors and tide
waters, etc.

SECTION 1.  The board of harbor commissioner
shall have the general care and supervision of all th
public harbors and tide waters within this state, wit
authority to prosecute for, and to cause to be remove
all unauthorized obstructions, and encroachment
therein, and may cause such harbors and public wate
to be surveyed and platted ; and may make such ex
aminations and observations as they may deem nece
sary to protect and develop the rights and interests o
the state in such harbors and public waters ; and ma
employ such engineers and other services as may b
necessary to this end.  They shall have an office i

To have an of-
fice in Provi-
dence.

Providence, where the maps, charts, and plans co
nected with the harbors and public waters, records o
all their doings and all documents relating to thei
business shall be kept.

To regulate de-
positing of mud,
etc., in public
tide waters.

SEC. 2.  Said board shall regulate the depositing
of mud, dirt or other substances in the public tide
waters of the state, and shall prescribe the places
where the same may be deposited ; and any person
who shall place or deposit mud, dirt or other substance

in said waters without obtaining proper authority therefor, shall be fined for each offence not exceeding five hundred dollars, to enure, one-half thereof to the use of the state and the other half to the use of the complainant.

SEC. 3.  All persons building into or over public tide waters by authority of said board of commission- or by authority of the general assembly, any wharf, pier, bridge or other structure, or who shall drive any piles into the land under public tide water or fill any flats, shall, before beginning such work, give written notice to the harbor commissioners of the work they intend to do, and submit plans of any pro- posed wharf or other structure, and of the flats to be filled, and of the mode in which the work is to be performed, and no such work shall be commenced until the plan and mode of performing the same shall be approved in writing by a majority of the said harbor commissioners.  And the said commissioners shall have power to alter the said plans at their discretion, and to prescribe the direction, limits and mode of building the wharves or other structures; provided that nothing herein contained shall be construed to impair the rights of any riparian proprietors to erect wharves authorized to be erected under any of the several laws establishing harbor lines within this state, or otherwise, by the general assembly. *Of building wharves, piers, bridges, etc.*

SEC. 4.  The harbor commissioners are authorized and empowered, whenever they deem it necessary, to apply to congress for appropriations for protecting or improving any harbor in the state. *Of application to congress for appropriations.*

SEC. 5.  All erections made into, or encroachments upon the public tide waters of the state, not author- ized by the general assembly, or by the harbor com- mission, shall be deemed to be a public nuisance, and may be prosecuted as such by the attorney general. *What is to be deemed a public nuisance.*

SEC. 6.  The members of the board of harbor com- missioners shall be allowed three dollars per day for each day's actual service; and shall keep a particular account of their services and expenses, which, when approved by the governor, shall be paid upon the order of the state auditor, from the general treasury. *Compensation of commission- ers.*

SEC. 7.  The board of harbor commissioners shall make an annual report to the general assembly, at its January session, of their doings during the preceding year, and shall recommend such further legislation as they may deem proper, for the preservation and improvement of the harbors and public tide waters and the promotion of the interests of the state connected therewith.

SEC. 8.  The waters immediately bordering upon the towns in the counties of Newport and Washington, extending to ship channel, and the harbors of said counties, are hereby exempted from the provisions of this act.

SEC. 9.  All acts and parts of acts inconsistent herewith are hereby repealed.

SEC. 10.  This act shall take effect from and after its passage.

*Marginal note: Commissioners to report annually.*

*Marginal note: Newport and Washington counties exempt.*

---

## CHAPTER 612.

AN ACT IN AMENDMENT OF AND IN ADDITION TO CHAPTER 185 OF THE GENERAL STATUTES, "OF JUSTICE COURTS, THEIR ORGANIZATION AND JURISDICTION."

*Marginal note: Passed March 30, 1877.*

*It is enacted by the General Assembly as follows :*

SECTION 1.  No trial justice or clerk of any justice court shall fill or procure to be filled, any civil writ returnable to the court of which he is trial justice or clerk, nor appear for or act as attorney for any party in any civil or criminal case originally brought before said justice court, or on appeal thereof in any court.

SEC. 2.  Any trial justice or clerk of any justice court violating any provision of the preceding section shall thereupon be disqualified to serve as such officer.

SEC. 3.  Section 2 of chapter 545 of the Public Laws, and all acts and parts of acts inconsistent herewith are hereby repealed.

SEC. 4.  This act shall take effect from and after its passage.

*Marginal note: Trial justices and clerks forbidden to fill writs, or act as attorney in certain cases.*

*Marginal note: Penalty.*

*Marginal note: Act repealed.*

## CHAPTER 613.

AN ACT IN AMENDMENT OF CHAPTER 80 OF THE GENERAL
STATUTES, " OF SHOWS AND EXHIBITIONS."

Passed March
30, 1877.

*It is enacted by the General Assembly as follows :*

SECTION 1.   No license granted by any town council, under the provisions of chapter 80 of the General Statutes, shall authorize any theatrical performance, or rope or wire dancing, or other show or performance, or any wrestling, boxing or sparring match or exhibition, to be given on the first day of the week. Shows, etc., on Sunday, forbidden.

SEC. 2.   The word "forfeit" wherever it occurs in section 4, chapter 80, of the General Statutes, is hereby stricken out, and the words " be fined" inserted in place thereof. Penalty.

SEC. 3.   This act shall take effect from and after its passage.

## CHAPTER 614.

AN ACT TO PROVIDE SECURITY AGAINST EXTRAORDINARY CON-
FLAGRATIONS, AND FOR THE CREATION OF SAFETY FUNDS
BY INSURANCE COMPANIES.

Passed March
30, 1877.

*It is enacted by the General Assembly as follows :*

SECTION 1.   Hereafter it shall be lawful for any fire insurance company organized under the laws of this state to create the funds herein provided for, to be known and designated as the " guaranty surplus fund" and the " special reserve fund," and to avail itself of the provisions of this act, upon complying with the requirements thereof. Fire insurance companies may create guaranty and reserve funds.

SEC. 2.   Any fire insurance company desiring to create such funds, is authorized to do so, upon the adoption of a resolution by its board of directors at a regular meeting thereof, to that effect, and filing with the insurance commissioner of the state a copy thereof, declaring the intention of such company to create such funds, and to do business under the pro- Funds how created.

Of examination by insurance commissioner; visions of this act; and as soon after the filing of such copy of the resolution as convenient, the insurance commissioner shall make or cause to be made, an examination of such company, and he shall make a certificate of the result thereof, which shall particularly set forth the amount of surplus funds held by such company at the date of such examination, which, under the provisions of this act, are to and may be and certificate by him. equally divided between and set apart to constitute guaranty surplus and special reserve funds, which certificate shall be recorded in the insurance department; and from and after the date of the recording of said certificate, all the policies and renewals of policies issued Policies of company to refer to this act. by said company shall have printed thereon by said company a notice that the same are issued under and in pursuance of this act, referring to the same by its chapter and title, and such policies and renewals shall be deemed to have been issued and received subject to the provisions of this act.

Dividends, how restricted. SEC. 3. After the date mentioned in any such resolution so passed and filed, such company shall not make or declare or pay in any form, any dividend upon its capital stock exceeding ten per cent. per annum thereupon, and seven per cent. upon the surplus funds to be formed hereunder, until after its guaranty surplus fund and its special reserve fund shall have together accumulated to an amount equal to its capi- Surplus profits, to be set apart to said funds. tal stock; and the entire surplus profits of such company above such annual dividend shall be equally divided between and set apart to constitute the said guaranty surplus fund, and the said special reserve fund, which funds shall be held and used as hereinafter provided, and not otherwise, and any company doing business under this act, which shall declare or pay any dividend contrary to the pro- Penalty for paying dividend contrary hereto. visions herein contained, shall forfeit its charter and be liable to be proceeded against by the attorney general for its dissolution. Whenever such company shall notify the insurance commissioner that it has fulfilled the requirements already expressed in this section, and that its guaranty surplus fund and its special reserve fund, taken together, equal its capital stock, the commissioner shall make an examination of such company and make a certificate of the result thereof, and file the same in his office, and if the commissioner shall find that said combined funds shall equal the capital stock of such company, thereafter such company may continue, out of any subsequent profits of its business, to add to such funds; provided, that when any addition is made to the special reserve fund, an equal sum shall be carried to the guaranty surplus fund. Examination by insurance commissioner.

SEC. 4. Said guaranty surplus fund shall be held and be invested by such company in the same [manner] as its capital stock and surplus accumulation may be held and be invested, and shall be liable and applicable in the same manner as the capital stock to the payment generally of the losses of such company. Of investment of guaranty surplus fund.

SEC. 5. Said special reserve fund shall be invested according to existing laws relating to investments of capital by fire insurance companies, and shall be deposited from time to time as the same shall accumulate and be invested, with the insurance commissioner of the state, who shall permit the company depositing the same to change such deposits by substituting for those withdrawn others of equal amount and value, and to collect and receive the interest or dividends upon such securities as the same may accrue; and such special reserve fund shall be deemed a fund contributed by the stockholders to protect such company and its policy holders other than claimants for losses already existing, or then incurred, in case of such extraordinary conflagration or conflagrations as is hereinafter mentioned; and said fund shall not be regarded as any part of the assets in possession of said company, so as to be or render the same liable for any claim or claims for loss by fire or otherwise, except as herein provided. Of investment of special reserve fund.

Effect of such fund.

SEC. 6. In estimating the profit of any such company for the purpose of making a division thereof between said guaranty surplus fund and such special reserve fund, until such funds shall together amount to a sum equal to the capital stock of such company, there shall be deducted from the gross assets of the Profits to be added to funds, how to be ascertained.

company, including for this purpose the amount of the special reserve fund, the sum of the following items:

*First*—The amount of all outstanding claims.

*Second*—An amount sufficient to meet the liability of such company for the unearned premiums upon its unexpired policies, which amount shall be at least equal to one-half of the premiums received on policies having less than one year to run from the date of policy, and a pro rata proportion of the premiums received on the policies having more than one year to run from the date of policy, and shall be known as the re-insurance liability.

*Third*—The amount of its guaranty surplus fund and of its special reserve fund.

*Fourth*—The amount of the capital of the company; and

*Fifth*—Interest at the rate of ten per cent. per annum upon the amount of the capital and seven per cent. per annum upon the amount of the said funds for whatever time shall have elapsed since the last preceding cash dividend. And the balance shall constitute the net surplus of the company, subject to an equal division between the said funds as is herein provided.

Restriction of dividends to continue how, long.

The said restriction of dividends upon the capital stock of such company shall continue until the said funds shall together equal the amount of such capital, but any addition to such funds, beyond an amount equal to such capital stock, may be made out of any profits of the subsequent business of such company, whether such addition shall constitute the whole of such subsequent profits or only a part thereof.

Proceedings in event of extensive conflagration.

SEC. 7.   In the event of an extensive conflagration, whereby the claims upon such company shall exceed the amount of its capital stock, and of the guaranty surplus fund provided for by this act, the said company shall notify the said insurance commissioner of the fact, who shall then make or cause to be made, an examination of said company, and shall issue his certificate of the result, showing the amounts of capital, of guaranty surplus fund, of special reserve fund, of re-insurance liability, and of other assets, and upon his issuing such certificate in duplicate, one copy to be given to the company, and one to be recorded in the insurance department, the said special reserve fund shall be immediately held to protect all policy holders of said company, other than such as are claimants upon it at the time, or such as become such claimants in consequence of such conflagration or conflagrations; and the amount of said special reserve fund and an amount equal to the unearned premiums of such company, to be ascertained as hereinbefore provided, shall constitute the capital and assets of such company for the protection of policy holders other than such claimants, and for the further conduct of its business; and such official certificate of the insurance commissioner shall be binding and conclusive upon all parties interested in such company, whether as stockholders, creditors, or policy holders, and upon the payment to the claimants, for losses or otherwise, existing at the time of or caused by such general conflagration, of the amount to which they are respectively entitled in proportion to their several claims, of the full sum of the capital of such company, and of its guaranty surplus fund, and of its assets, excepting only such special reserve fund and an amount of its assets equal to the liability of the company for unearned premiums, as so certified by such insurance commissioner, such company shall be forever discharged from any and all further liability to such claimants, and to each of them; and the said insurance commissioner shall, after issuing his said certificate, upon the demand of such company, transfer to it all such securities as shall have been deposited with him by such company as such special reserve fund; and if the amount of such special reserve fund be less than fifty per cent. of the full amount of the capital of the company, a requisition shall be issued by the said insurance commissioner upon the stockholders, to make up such capital to that proportion of its full amount, in the manner now provided by law in the case of companies with impaired capital. And provided, further, that any capital so impaired shall be made up to at least the sum of $200,000; and in case said company, after such requisition, shall fail to make up its capital to at least said amount of $200,000, as

*Special reserve fund, to be held to protect whom.*

*Capital and assets, to be what.*

*Of discharge of company from claims.*

*Of making up capital.*

therein directed, said special reserve fund shall still be
held as security, and liable for any and all l
occurring upon policies of such company after su
conflagration.    Such    company    shall,    in    its    annu

statement to the insurance commissioner of this sta
set forth the amount of such special reserve fund, an
of its guaranty surplus fund. The policy registers, insu
ance maps, books of record, and other books in use b
such company in its business, are not to be conside

as assets, but shall be held by the company for its u
in the protection of its policy-holders, not claiman
for losses at the time of such general conflagration
provided, however, that if any amount greater than
sum equal to one-half of its capital stock shall by suc
company, under the provisions of this act, have been
deposited with such commissioner, he shall retain of such

securities an amount equal to one-half of what amount
he shall so hold thereof in excess of a sum equal to
such one-half of such capital stock, and he shall transfer the balance thereof to such company as herein provided ; and the amount so transferred to such company
shall, from the time of such transfer, provided the
amount thereof shall not be less than two hundred.

thousand dollars, constitute the capital stock of such
company for the further conduct of its business a
hereinbefore provided, and the securities so retained
shall be regarded as the special reserve fund of such
company, to which additions may be made, as herein
provided, and shall be held in the same manner, and
for the same purpose, and under the same conditions
as the original special reserve fund of such company
was held.

SEC. 8.   If at any time after said special reserve

fund shall have been accumulated by any company, it
shall appear upon examination by the said insurance
commissioner that the capital of such company has
in the absence of any such extensive conflagration, become impaired so as to cause him to order a call upon
the stockholders to make up such impairment, the
board of directors of such company may either comply with such order and require the necessary payment
by the stockholders, or, at their option, they may apply,

for that purpose, so much of said special reserve fund as will make such impairment good. No company doing business under this act shall insure any larger amount upon any single risk than is permitted by law a company possessing the same amount of capital, pective of the fund hereby provided for. So ch of existing laws as are inconsistent with this are hereby made and declared to be inapplicable insurance companies doing business under and in nformity with this act.

SEC. 9. This act shall take effect from and after its ge.

## CHAPTER 615.

ACT IN ADDITION TO CHAPTER 121 OF THE GENERAL STATUTES, "OF PARTNERS AND JOINT DEBTORS." — Passed March 30, 1877.

*is enacted by the General Assembly as follows :*

SECTION 1. In case of the death of any person who at the time of his decease a member of any copart- ip, either general or limited, the surviving partner , upon the demand in writing, and within ten thereafter, of the administrator or executor, of deceased copartner, make out and deliver to said nistrator or executor, a detailed statement of the and liabilities of said copartners as they existed he time of the decease of said copartner. Said ement shall be verified by the oath or affirmation id surviving copartner. *In case of death of partner, surviving partner to return statement of assets, etc, to legal representative of deceased co-partner.*

SEC. 2. Said executor or administrator may enter u the premises and examine the books and affairs id copartnership and take an inventory of the nal property in which his testate or intestate may e had an interest at the time of his decease. *Rights of such legal representative.*

SEC. 3. This act shall take effect upon its passage, all acts or parts of acts inconsistent herewith are by repealed.

9

## CHAPTER 616.

Passed March
30, 1877.

AN ACT IN AMENDMENT OF AND IN ADDITION TO CHAPTER 580
OF THE STATUTES, PASSED JANUARY, 1865, ENTITLED, " AN
ACT IN AMENDMENT OF AND IN ADDITION TO CHAPTER 74 OF
THE REVISED STATUTES, ' OF REGULATIONS FOR THE PRE-
VENTION OF INFECTIOUS AND CONTAGIOUS DISEASES.' "

*It is enacted by the General Assembly as follows :*

City of Provi-
dence; of regu-
lations relative
to removal of
swill.

SECTION 1.   Section 1 of said chapter 580 is hereby
amended by adding thereto the following words:
" And also to make all such rules and regulations as
they shall deem necessary with reference to the collection and removal of swill and house offal in the city of
Providence, and to the person or persons who shall
collect and remove the same, being empowered and
authorized under such rules and regulations to designate and appoint such person or persons to collect and
remove the same as they shall see fit."

SEC. 2.   All acts and parts of acts inconsistent herewith are hereby repealed.

SEC. 3.   This act shall take effect from and after its
passage.

## CHAPTER 617.

Passed March
30, 1877.

AN ACT IN AMENDMENT OF AN ACT ENTITLED, " AN ACT CON-
CERNING THE ERECTION OF BUILDINGS IN THE CITY OF
PROVIDENCE."

*It is enacted by the General Assembly as follows :*

City of Provi-
dence; of erect-
ing and operat-
steam boilers in.

SECTION 1.   Section 7 of said act is hereby amended so as to read as follows : " No steam boiler shall
hereafter be erected and put in operation in said city,
unless by permission of the board of aldermen of said
city, and no steam boiler shall be operated in said city,
without such permission; and any authority or permission heretofore given, or which may hereafter be
given, to any person to operate any steam boiler in

said city, may be revoked by said board of aldermen for non-compliance with any requirement said board of aldermen may make for the protection or safety of life, health and property ; and thereupon such person shall cease to operate the same."

SEC. 2.   All acts and parts of acts inconsistent herewith are hereby repealed.

SEC. 3.   This act shall take effect from and after its passage.

---

## CHAPTER 618.

AN ACT RELATIVE TO TRUST COMPANIES.

Passed March 30, 1877.

*It is enacted by the General Assembly as follows :*

SECTION 1.   Every trust company incorporated by this state shall make return to the state auditor of its situation at the same time and in the same manner as is required by law to be made by institutions of savings, and in the case of the Rhode Island Hospital Trust Company such return shall be in lieu of the return now required by its charter. <small>Trust companies to make return of situation to state auditor.</small>

SEC. 2.   Every such trust company shall annually pay to the general treasurer twenty-five cents on each and every hundred dollars deposited therewith, on participation, or in the same manner as in savings banks.   Said sums to be ascertained from the returns required by law to be made to the state auditor, and to be paid on or before the first Monday in August. <small>Tax on deposits.</small>

*Provided*, That the Rhode Island Hospital Trust Company are hereby authorized to deduct from the amount payable to the state from said company under the provisions of this section in any year, such sum as shall have actually been paid by such company, for profits accruing during said year, under the terms of their charter, to the Rhode Island Hospital. <small>Deduction authorized in case of R. I. Hospital Trust Co.</small>

## CHAPTER 619.

Passed March
30, 1877. AN ACT IN ADDITION TO CHAPTER 59 OF THE GENERAL STAT-
UTES, "OF LAYING OUT AND MAKING HIGHWAYS AND
DRIFTWAYS."

*It is enacted by the General Assembly as follows :*

Of laying out, etc., highways in towns.

SECTION 1. Whenever the town council of any town hereinafter named shall adjudge it to be necessary to lay out, enlarge, straighten, improve or alter any street or highway, or any part thereof, in said town, it shall be lawful for said council to cause the same to be done in the manner following:—Whenever any lands shall be required for the purpose aforesaid, and the town council shall be of opinion that any estates will be specially benefited thereby, said council shall after notice to all persons interested, which notice shall specify the time and place of the meeting of the council and the nature and extent of the intended improvement, and after hearing all of said persons who desire to be heard in the matter, appoint not less than three, nor more than five discreet and disinterested persons as commissioners of estimate and assessment, who may be residents and taxpayers in said town ; and said council may at the same time determine that such portion of the damage occasioned by taking any real estate for said purpose, not exceeding three-fourths thereof, shall be assessed upon the owners of such estates as said commissioners shall find will be specially benefited, by making the proposed improvement, whether any part of such estates are taken for the improvement or not ; provided, that such owners shall not be assessed in any case beyond the amount that said commissioners shall consider their estates to be specially benefited thereby. Said commissioners, before entering upon the duties of their office, shall be severally sworn to the faithful discharge of the trust and duties required of them.

Appointment of commissioners of estimate and assessment.

Of laying out etc., highways in any city.

SEC. 2. Whenever the city council of any city shall adjudge it to be necessary to lay out, enlarge, straighten, improve or alter any street or highway, or any part thereof, in said city, and any lands shall be required for the purpose aforesaid, and the said city council shall be of opinion that any estates will be specially benefited thereby, and the said city council shall determine what portion of the damage occasioned by taking any real estate for said purpose, not exceeding three-fourths thereof, shall be assessed upon the owners of such estates as the commissioners appointed under this act shall find to be specially benefited, by making the proposed improvement, whether any part of such estates are taken for the improvement or not; provided, that such owners shall not be assessed in any case beyond the amount that said commissioners shall consider their estates to be specially benefited thereby; the board of aldermen of said city shall thereupon proceed in the same manner and with the same powers and authority as is given in section 1 of this act to town councils.

SEC. 3. The commissioners shall cause a survey and plat of the proposed alteration to be made; and shall cause notice to be given to all persons interested in the lands to be taken, or in the improvement to be made, and to all persons who are owners of lands which, in the opinion of the commissioners, will be benefited by such proposed alterations, of the time and place of making an estimate of the value of the property so required to be taken, and of the special benefits to be conferred by making such alterations; and at the time and place appointed in said notice, the commissioners shall proceed to make a just estimate of the amount of the damage occasioned to the respective owners, lessees, parties or persons entitled to or interested in the lands taken for such alteration; and also a just estimate of the value of the special benefits, if any, caused thereby, to the several owners of lands not required for the proposed improvements, but which will, in the opinion of the said commissioners, be benefited thereby. And said commissioners shall report thereon to the town council or board of aldermen without unnecessary delay. The commissioners shall set forth in said report, the name of the owners of, and persons in any way interested in any of the land taken for the proposed im-

Duties of commissioners of estimate and assessment.

provement, so far as the same can be ascertained, and a description or designation of the several parcels thereof, with the damage and benefit to each respectively. And the said commissioners shall further apportion and assess such portion of the damage and cost of improvements as the town or city council may have directed, ascertained as aforesaid, upon the owners of the estates so specially benefited, in proportion to the special benefits conferred: *provided*, that the amount of such assessment shall not exceed the amount of the special benefits, ascertained as aforesaid.

Of notice to parties interested, etc.. after filing of commissioners' report.

SEC. 4. The town council or board of aldermen shall, within fourteen days after the making of said report, cause personal notice to be served upon all persons named in said report, residing in this state, and shall also cause a copy of said notice to be published, as hereinafter provided, to the effect that such report has been filed in the clerk's office, and that any person aggrieved by said report must file with the clerk of the supreme court, for the county where such town or city is situated, a notice in writing of his intention to claim a jury trial as provided in the next succeeding section of this act; and they shall also cause a copy of said report to be filed with the clerk of the said supreme court.

Of claim for jury trial.

SEC. 5. Any person aggrieved by the report of the commissioners shall, within sixty days after the first publication of the notice of the filing of said report, named in section four of this act, file with the clerk of the supreme court a notice in writing of his intention to claim a jury trial; and in case such aggrieved person fails to file such notice, he shall not be entitled to a jury trial. Any person filing a notice, as aforesaid, may have a trial by jury before said court, to determine the amount of damage and benefit to him to be apportioned, upon issue or issues, to be for that purpose framed under the direction of said court, and if the person applying for a jury trial shall fail to obtain an increase of damages or a diminution of the amount of benefit assessed by the commissioners, such person shall pay all costs arising after such application for a jury; and the court shall enter judgment and issue execution therefor; and in other cases the costs shall be paid by said town or city as aforesaid.

SEC. 6. The town or city council shall, within one hundred and twenty days after the first publication of notice required by the fifth section of this act, elect whether they will make said improvements or not; and the town or city council may, at any time before said election, discontinue all further proceedings relative thereto, but said town or city upon said discontinuance, shall be liable for all costs, fees and expenses which shall have accrued; and the court may enter judgment and issue execution therefor as to costs accrued on said appeals. *Council to elect to make improvement, etc., when.*

SEC. 7. The said town or city, after electing by the town or city council to make said improvements as aforesaid, shall become seized of all the land in said report mentioned that shall be required for making said improvements, in trust for use as a public highway. And said town or city may, by such person, and at such time as the town council or board of aldermen shall order, take possession of the same, or any part thereof, without any process of law, and remove all buildings and other impediments as said town council shall order and direct; provided, that the owner of such land shall have the right within thirty days after the town or city council shall have elected make such improvements, or within such further time as the town council or board of aldermen may grant, to remove all crops, trees, buildings, or other improvements thereon, for his own use and benefit. *Of title to land taken, removal of buildings, etc.*

SEC. 8. The town council or board of aldermen, after the election to make said improvements, as aforesaid, shall confirm the report of the commissioners as to all persons who have not given notice of their intention to claim a jury trial as aforesaid, and shall finally confirm the said report as to those persons who shall have claimed a trial by jury, in accordance with the verdicts rendered, or in accordance with such other disposition as shall have been made of the claims for a jury trial, and such report, so confirmed, shall be final and conclusive upon the parties. *Of confirming commissioners' report.*

SEC. 9. Whenever the whole of any lot or parcel of land, or any building under lease or other contract, shall be taken as aforesaid, for any of the purposes aforesaid, upon the election of the town or city council, as provided in this act, to make said improvements, said lease or contract shall immediately cease and determine, and be absolutely discharged. And in case part only of any parcel of real estate so under lease, or other contract, shall be taken, all contracts and engagements respecting the same shall, from the time of the election aforesaid, cease and determine, and be absolutely discharged as to the part so taken, but shall remain valid as to the residue, and the rents, considerations, and payments, reserved or payable, and to be paid for or in respect to the same, shall be apportioned so that the just proportional part thereof shall be demanded or paid, or recoverable for or in respect of the same.

SEC. 10. The town or city shall, within four months after the confirmation of the report of the commissioners, pay to the person entitled thereto, the amount of damage finally awarded upon said report. And in default of such payment, the person entitled to the same, after application to the town or city council for payment thereof, may sue the town or city for and recover the same, with lawful interest, in which suit it shall be sufficient to declare generally for so much money due the plaintiff by virtue of this act, for premises taken for the purpose herein mentioned, and the plaintiff may give any special matter in evidence under such general declaration, with proof of the right of the plaintiff to the sum demanded.

SEC. 11. The amount of benefit apportioned and assessed to the owners of real estate, by the commissioners in their report, confirmed as aforesaid, and required by such report to be paid by the respective owners, shall be added to the taxes assessed against said real estate, and the owners thereof, by the assessors of taxes, at the next or any subsequent annual assessment of taxes, after the confirmation of said report, and shall be and remain a lien upon such real estates, from and after such confirmation until it is paid; and shall be collected at the same time and in the same manner as the other taxes assessed against said real estate, and the owners thereof, except in cases where the estates are owned by non-residents in the state, or minors, in which case one year in addition shall be allowed.

SEC. 12. The notice required by the first, second, third and fourth sections of this act, in addition to the personal notice, shall be given by publishing the same once each week for two succeeding weeks in at least two newspapers such as the town council may order; and they shall also cause three or more copies of such notice to be posted in conspicuous public places in or near the place where the proposed improvements are to be made; provided, however, that the first publication of the notice required by section four, shall be made within fourteen days after the filing of said report.  *Of publication of notice.*

SEC. 13. Said commissioners shall be entitled to receive for their services a reasonable compensation, to be allowed by the town council or board of aldermen, and all sums reasonably expended for maps, plats and clerk hire, and other necessary expenses shall be paid by said town.  *Compensation of commissioners, etc.*

SEC. 14. Whenever all buildings and impediments have been removed by order of the town council or board of aldermen as aforesaid, from the street, or portion thereof, taken as aforesaid, and the same shall be open for public use, the town council or board of aldermen shall declare the same, and it shall be a public highway.  *Of declaring street as public highway.*

SEC. 15. The town council of any town may, notwithstanding this act, whenever they shall deem it expedient, proceed to lay out or alter any highway within said town, as heretofore, under the general laws of this state.  *Highways may be laid out under general laws.*

SEC. 16. This act shall apply only to the towns of Pawtucket, Lincoln, Woonsocket, Cranston, Johnston, Warren, Bristol, Middletown, East Greenwich and East Providence.  *Towns to which this act applies.*

SEC. 17. Chapter 872 of the Pubic Laws, and all acts inconsistent herewith, except so far as such apply  *Laws repealed.*

10

to the city of Providence, are hereby repealed.

Sec. 18. This act shall take effect from and after its passage.

## CHAPTER 620.

Passed March 30, 1877.

### AN ACT TO PREVENT INCENDIARISM.

*It is enacted by the General Assembly as follows:*

*Of summoning special jury to inquire into origin of incendiary fires.*

SECTION 1. Whenever any building or other property in this state shall be destroyed or damaged by fire, and a complaint within ten days thereafter shall be subscribed and sworn to before any justice of the peace in and for the town or city where such fire shall happen, alleging that reasonable grounds exist for believing that said fire was not accidental in its origin, but was caused by design, it shall be the duty of such justice forthwith to issue his warrant to the town sergeant or to some constable of the town or city where such property was destroyed or damaged, requiring him to summon immediately six good and lawful men of the county to appear before said justice, at the time and place expressed in the warrant, to enquire when, how, and by what means said fire originated. And in case of the non-appearance of any person so summoned, the town sergeant or constable shall, by order of said justice, return some other person or persons to complete said number.

*Oath to be administered to jurors.*

SEC. 2. When the persons thus summoned appear, or the number be made complete, the justice shall call over their names, and then, in view of the place on which said property was destroyed or damaged, he shall administer the following oath to said jurors: You solemnly swear that you will diligently enquire, and true presentment make on behalf of this state, when, how, and by what means the fire which has here occurred, was caused, and you shall return a true inquest according to your knowledge and such evidence as shall be laid before you.

*Of summoning witnesses.*

SEC. 3. The justice may issue summons for, and compel the attendance of witnesses before the said jury, in the same way as if they had been summoned upon the part of the state, to attend court in criminal cases.

SEC. 4. The testimony of all witnesses, examined before any inquest, shall be reduced to writing by said justice, or some other person by his direction, and be subscribed by the witnesses.

*Testimony to reduced to writing.*

SEC. 5. In case of the absence or inability of the justice issuing said warrant, to serve at the time and place expressed in said warrant any other justice of the peace in and for said town or city may discharge the duties otherwise to be performed by the justice so issuing the warrant.

*What justices of the peace may hold the examination.*

SEC. 6. The jury, after hearing the testimony of the witnesses and making such other inquiry as they may deem necessary, shall draw up and deliver to the justice officiating at said inquest their inquisition, under their hands, in which they shall find and certify, when, how, and by what means such fire was caused; and said inquisition and testimony thus subscribed shall, within one week thereafter, be filed by said justice in the office of the clerk of the court of common pleas then next to be holden in the county in which such inquisition shall have been made.

*Jury to return inquisition.*

*To be filed in clerk's office o court of com². mon pleas.*

SEC. 7. The expenses of any inquest called under the provisions of this act shall be paid by the person at whose request such inquest shall be called, provided, however, that if such complaint shall be made by any officer of any town or city charged with the duty of making complaints in such cases by ordinance or other authority of such town or city, then the town or city shall pay the expenses of any inquest.

*Expenses, how paid.*

SEC. 8. The justice in any such inquest shall be allowed the fees provided for the coroner in coroner's inquests, and the jurors and officer summoning the jury serving in any proceeding under this act shall be allowed the fees provided respectively for jurors and such officer in coroner's inquests.

*Fees allowed.*

SEC. 9. This act shall take effect immediately upon its passage.

## CHAPTER 621.

Passed March
30, 1877. AN ACT TO PROVIDE FOR THE SERVICES OF A CLERK IN THE
OFFICE OF THE STATE AUDITOR.

*It is enacted by the General Assembly as follows:*

State auditor
authorized to
employ a clerk.   SECTION 1.   The state auditor is hereby authorized
to employ a clerk to assist in his duties as auditor
and insurance commissioner, at a compensation, annually, not to exceed the sum of eight hundred dollars.

SEC. 2.   This act shall take effect from the commencement of the present fiscal year, May 1st, 1876.

## CHAPTER 622.

Passed March
30, 1877. AN ACT REPEALING CHAPTER 363 OF THE PUBLIC LAWS, EN-
TITLED " AN ACT IN AMENDMENT OF CHAPTER 55, TITLE IX,
OF THE GENERAL STATUTES, 'OF LEGAL PROCEEDINGS
RELATIVE TO PUBLIC SCHOOLS,'" AND REVIVING SECTION 2,
OF CHAPTER 55 OF THE GENERAL STATUTES.

*It is enacted by the General Assembly as follows:*

Of hearing ap-
peals by one
justice of the
supreme court.   SECTION 1.   Chapter 363 of the Public Laws, entitled "An act in amendment of chapter 55, title IX,
of the General Statutes, ' Of legal proceedings relative to public schools,' " is hereby repealed.

SEC. 2.   Section 2, of chapter 55, of the General
Statutes, "Of legal proceedings relating to public
schools," repealed by said chapter 363, of the Public
Laws, is hereby revived.

## CHAPTER 623.

Passed March
30, 1877. AN ACT TO PREVENT THE DUMPING OF MUD AND OTHER MA-
TERIALS INTO A PORTION OF THE WATERS OF NARRAGAN-
SETT BAY.

*It is enacted by the General Assembly as follows:*

Dumping of
mud, etc., into
Providence
river, Warren
river, and por-
tions of Narra-
gansett bay,
forbidden.   SECTION 1.   No person shall hereafter throw or deposit any mud, earth, sand, gravel, ashes, cinders, or
other materials into the main channel of Providence
river leading to the city of Providence, or into any

part of the said river, or of Warren river, and of Narragansett bay, lying east of the said main channel, and north of a line drawn east and west across the said channel, and from the easterly line thereof to the eastern shore of the said bay, in the range of the lower buoy off Rumstick Point; but this act shall not be construed to prevent the planting of oysters within the said lines, or the properly fitting said grounds for planting oysters thereon, or the construction of any wharf from the shores of the said bay, which may have been authorized by this general assembly.

SEC. 2. Any person violating any of the provisions of this act shall be fined not exceeding one hundred dollars. *Penalty.*

---

## CHAPTER 624.

AN ACT IN AMENDMENT OF CHAPTER 508 OF THE PUBLIC LAWS, ENTITLED "AN ACT TO REGULATE AND RESTRAIN THE SALE OF INTOXICATING LIQUORS." *Passed March 30, 1877.*

*is enacted by the General Assembly as follows :*

SECTION 1. No town shall make any deduction for uses or otherwise from the one-half part received said town for licenses granted, accruing to the state, der the provisions of section 1 of said chapter 508 the Public Laws. *No deduction to be made from portion of license money due state.*

---

## CHAPTER 625.

ACT IN AMENDMENT OF CHAPTER 209 OF THE GENERAL STATUTES, " OF TAKING QUESTIONS OF LAW, IN CASES CIVIL AND CRIMINAL, TO THE SUPREME COURT." *Passed March 30, 1877.*

*is enacted by the General Assembly us follows :*

SECTION 1. Every person against whom a verdict shall have been rendered in any criminal proceeding in the court of common pleas, who shall desire to take *Of taking questions of law in criminal cases to the supreme court.*

to the supreme court any question of law, by the decision or ruling upon which in the court of common pleas he has been aggrieved, shall enter into recognizance, with sufficient surety, to proceed in and enter the record of said cause in the clerk's office of the supreme court in the same county, within ten days as the case may be, from such verdict or from the allowance of exceptions, or decision of motion to quash, motion in arrest of judgment, or other similar proceeding.

Of entry, hearing and decision of the same.    SEC. 2. Upon the entry of such record as aforesaid, the clerk of the supreme court shall forthwith enter the same if in term time, upon the docket of said court, and if in vacation, then upon the docket for the next term of the supreme court in the same county, and the supreme court shall give as speedy a hearing and decision in such a cause as shall be consistent with the ends of justice therein.

SEC. 3. All acts and parts of acts inconsistent herewith are hereby repealed.

## CHAPTER 626.

Passed March 30, 1877.

AN ACT IN ADDITION TO CHAPTER 185 OF THE GENERAL STATUTES, "OF JUSTICE COURTS, THEIR ORGANIZATION AND CIVIL JURISDICTION," AND CHAPTER 186 OF THE GENERAL STATUTES, "OF THE CRIMINAL JURISDICTION OF, AND OF CERTAIN CRIMINAL PROCEEDINGS BEFORE, JUSTICE COURTS."

*It is enacted by the General Assembly as follows:*

Of election of assistant trial justices.    SECTION 1. The town council of any town wherein a justice court, having no clerk, may be established, may select and elect from the qualified justices of the peace in such town, an assistant trial justice, who, accepting such office, shall, within twenty days after his election, file a written notice of his acceptance, with the town clerk of the town, together with proof of his engagement upon his commission; and shall hold his office for the term of one year, unless sooner removed by the election of some other person to fill his place.

SEC. 2. In case of the absence or inability to serve *Duties of.* of the trial justice, such assistant trial justice shall constitute the justice court of the town, and shall exercise and perform the same duties, with the same power and authority, imposed and conferred by law upon such trial justice.

SEC. 3. All acts and parts of acts inconsistent herewith are hereby repealed.

## CHAPTER 627.

AN ACT IN AMENDMENT OF SECTIONS 18 AND 22 OF CHAPTER 9 OF THE GENERAL STATUTES, " OF THE MANNER OF CONDUCTING ELECTIONS."

*Passed March 30, 1877.*

*It is enacted by the General Assembly as follows :*

SECTION 1. There shall be inserted in the third line of the eighteenth section of chapter 9 of the General Statutes, after the words " senator and representatives," the words " and of members of the town council," so that said line shall read, " respectively for the election of senator and representatives and of members of the town council or of any," etc.

*Of adjournment of meetings for election of members of town council.*

SEC. 2. There shall be inserted in the second line of the twenty-second section of said chapter, after the words "general assembly," the words " and of members of the town council," so that the first two lines of said section shall read as follows : " Section 22. If no election shall have been made of senator and representatives to the general assembly, and of members of the town council or of any one or more of them," etc.

*Of new election for members of town council.*

## CHAPTER 628.

AN ACT IN RELATION TO THE STATE FLAG.

*Passed March 30, 1877.*

*It is enacted by the General Assembly as follows :*

SECTION 1. The flag of the state shall be a foul anchor with the motto " HOPE," the whole to be sur-

*State flag established and described.*

rounded by a scroll, around which in a circle, shall be as many stars as there are states in the Union. The color of the anchor, motto and stars shall be blue, the scroll red in the centre of a white field.

SEC. 2. This act shall take effect from and after its passage.

## CHAPTER 629.

Passed March 30, 1877.

AN ACT FOR THE FURTHER PROTECTION OF THE MEETINGS OF RELIGIOUS SOCIETIES.

*It is enacted by the General Assembly as follows:*

Sale of liquors, merchandise, etc., prohibited within one mile of out-door religious meetings.

SECTION 1. Whenever any religious society shall hold any camp, tent, grove, or other out-door meeting for any purpose connected with the object for which such religious society was organized, no person, without the consent of such religious society or of its proper officers, shall keep in any shop, tent, booth, wagon or carriage, or other place for sale, or expose for sale any spirituous or intoxicating liquors, or other drinks, or food, or merchandise of any kind, or hawk or peddle any such liquors or merchandise within one mile of the place of such meeting, nor shall any person engage in gaming, horse-racing, or exhibit or offer to exhibit any show or play within the like distance of one mile of such meeting, and any person violating any provision of this act shall be fined not exceeding twenty dollars or less than five dollars, or be imprisoned not exceeding thirty days. *Provided, however,* that nothing herein contained shall be construed to prevent innkeepers, grocers, or other persons from pursuing their ordinary business at their usual place of doing business, nor to prevent any person from selling victuals in his usual place of abode.

Exception.

## CHAPTER 630.

AN ACT REGULATING THE ATTENDANCE UPON THE GENERAL ASSEMBLY, AND PAY FOR SAME.

*Passed March 30, 1877.*

*It is enacted by the General Assembly as follows:*

SECTION 1. The number of sheriffs or their deputies, who shall attend upon the senate and house of representatives, at any session thereof, shall not exceed three in both chambers, unless by special order of the general assembly, provided that only actual attendance shall be paid for.

*Number of officers authorized to attend general assembly*

The number of pages shall not exceed the following, viz.: for the senate, two; for the house of representatives, four.

*Pages.*

The following sums shall be paid for each day's attendance, viz.: To the clerks of either chamber, five dollars per day.

*Pay of same.*

To the sheriffs, three dollars per day; to the deputy sheriffs, two dollars per day; and to the pages, one dollar and a half per day.

## CHAPTER 631.

AN ACT IN AMENDMENT OF SECTION 23 OF CHAPTER 145 OF THE GENERAL STATUTES.

*Passed March 30, 1877.*

*It is enacted by the General Assembly as follows:*

SECTION 1. Section 23 of chapter 145 of the General Statutes is hereby amended by striking out the words "as often as twice." The section as amended will then read:

"SECTION 23. The railroad commissioner shall every year, and oftener if he deem it necessary, report to the general assembly the state, the condition and proceedings of the several railroad corporations, so far as the public interest may require the same."

*Railroad commissioner to report annually.*

SEC. 2. This act shall take effect on and after its passage.

11

# CHAPTER 632.

AN ACT MAKING APPROPRIATIONS FOR THE SUPPORT OF THE GOVERNMENT OF THE STATE, FOR THE YEAR ENDING ON THE THIRTIETH DAY OF APRIL, 1878.

*It is enacted by the General Assembly as follows:*

Appropriations of 1877-78.

SECTION 1. The following sums, or so much thereof as may be authorized by law, are hereby appropriated to the objects hereinafter expressed, for the fiscal year ending on the thirtieth day of April, A. D. 1878, to be paid out of the several appropriations herein mentioned; and the state auditor is hereby authorized to draw his orders for such portion thereof as may be required from time to time, upon the receipt by him of properly authenticated vouchers.

## FOR SALARIES.

To the governor, one thousand dollars.

To the lieutenant–governor, five hundred dollars.

To the secretary of state, twenty-five hundred dollars.

To the attorney general, twenty-five hundred dollars.

To the assistant attorney general, fifteen hundred dollars.

To the general treasurer, two thousand dollars.

To the chief justice of the supreme court, forty-five hundred dollars, and to each of the associate justices thereof, four thousand dollars each.

To the state auditor, fifteen hundred dollars.

To the insurance commissioner, one thousand dollars.

To the commissioner of public schools, twenty-five hundred dollars.

To the reporter of the decisions of the supreme court, five hundred dollars.

To the commissioners of shell fisheries, (four hundred dollars each), twelve hundred dollars.

To the clerk of the secretary of state, one thousand dollars.

Appropriations for 1877-78, (continued)

To the sheriffs of the counties of Newport, Bristol, Kent and Washington, four hundred dollars each.

To the crier of the courts in Providence county, six hundred dollars.

To the clerk of the supreme court, county of Providence, twenty-five hundred dollars.

To the clerk of the court of common pleas, county of Providence, twenty-five hundred dollars.

To the assistant clerk of the supreme court, county of Providence, twelve hundred dollars.

To the clerk of the state auditor, eight hundred dollars.

To the assistant clerk of the court of common pleas, county of Providence, twelve hundred dollars.

To the clerk of the supreme court, county of Bristol, two hundred dollars.

To the clerk of the court of common pleas, county of Bristol, two hundred dollars.

To the clerk of the supreme court, county of Newport, seven hundred and fifty dollars.

To the clerk of the court of common pleas, county of Newport, five hundred and fifty dollars.

To the clerk of the supreme court, county of Kent, three hundred dollars.

To the clerk of the court of common pleas, county of Kent, three hundred dollars.

To the clerk of the supreme court, county of Washington, three hundred dollars.

To the clerk of the court of common pleas, county of Washington, three hundred dollars.

To the trial justice of the justice court of the city of Providence, two thousand dollars.

To the clerk of the justice court of the city of Providence, fifteen hundred dollars.

To the trial justice of the justice court of the city of Newport, seven hundred dollars.

To the clerk of the justice court of the city of Newport, eight hundred dollars.

To the trial justice of the justice court of the town of Pawtucket, one thousand dollars.

To the clerk of the justice court of the town of Pawtucket, eight hundred dollars.

To the trial justice of the justice court of the town of Woonsocket, one thousand dollars.

To the clerk of the justice court of the town of Woonsocket, eight hundred dollars.

To the retired chief justice of the supreme court, thirty-five hundred dollars.

To the librarian of the law library, three hundred dollars.

To the adjutant general, six hundred dollars.

To the quartermaster general, four hundred dollars.

To the paymaster general, two hundred dollars.

### FOR THE GENERAL ASSEMBLY.

For the payment and mileage of the members of the general assembly, twelve thousand dollars.

For the pay of two clerks of the house of representatives and one clerk of the senate, fifteen hundred dollars.

For the pay of four pages for the house of representatives and two pages for the senate, nine hundred dollars.

For the pay of the sheriffs and deputies for attendance upon the general assembly, one thousand dollars.

For stationery and stamps for the general assembly, to be expended under the direction of the secretary of state, four hundred dollars.

For other expenses of the general assembly, two hundred dollars.

### FOR JUDICIAL EXPENSES.

For the payment of juror fees, thirty thousand dollars.

For the payment of trial justices, except those of the cities of Providence and Newport and towns of Woonsocket and Pawtucket, fifteen hundred dollars.

For the payment of officers' fees in the supreme courts and courts of common pleas, twelve thousand dollars, provided that only actual attendance be paid for.

For the payment of officers' fees in justice courts, four thousand dollars.

For the payment of officers' fees in criminal cases, three thousand dollars.

For the payment of witnesses' fees in the supreme courts and courts of common pleas, twelve thousand dollars.

For the payment of witnesses' fees in justice courts, three thousand dollars.

For incidental expenses of supreme courts and courts of common pleas, three thousand dollars.

Appropriations for 1877–78, (continued.)

### FOR EDUCATION.

For public schools, ninety thousand dollars, to be paid as heretofore, twenty-seven thousand dollars on and after July 15th, 1877, and the residue on and after December 31st, 1877.

For the support of Rhode Island State Normal School, ten thousand dollars, provided that no portion of this sum shall be used for the payment of clerk hire to any school officer.

For travelling expenses for the pupils of the Rhode Island State Normal School, fifteen hundred dollars.

For teachers' institutes, for defraying the expenses of procuring teachers and lecturers, to be holden under the direction of the commissioner of public schools, five hundred dollars.

### REFORM SCHOOL.

For the support of juvenile offenders sentenced to the Providence Reform School, twenty-two thousand dollars.

### FOR INSANE AND OTHER DEPENDENT PERSONS.

For the support of the insane poor at the Butler Hospital, and for the support and education of deaf, dumb, idiotic and blind persons, as authorized by existing laws, twelve thousand dollars.

### PUBLIC PRINTING.

For publishing the laws, printing the schedules, the annual report of the commissioner of public schools, annual report of the insurance commissioner, of the

Appropriations
for 1877–78.
(continued.) registration of births, marriages and deaths, all printing ordered by the general assembly, and such other
printing as may be required in the office of the secretary of state and other public offices, ten thousand
dollars.

#### FOR MILITARY AFFAIRS.

For militia and military affairs, sixteen thousand
dollars.

#### FOR COURT HOUSES AND JAILS.

For repairs of court houses and jails, and for furniture and fixtures for the same, and for offices in Elizabeth building, twenty-five hundred dollars.

#### FOR JAILS AND JAILERS.

For jailers' fees and for board of persons confined
in jail, except in Providence county, two thousand
dollars.

#### FOR FUEL AND GAS.

For fuel and gas for the several court houses and
the public offices, to be certified by the sheriffs of the
several counties, twenty-two hundred dollars.

#### FOR RENTS.

To pay rents of various offices and rooms of justice
courts, and for the accommodation of supreme court
and court of common pleas in Providence county,
three thousand dollars.

#### NARRAGANSETT INDIANS.

For support of school, two hundred dollars.
For school commissioner, twenty-five dollars.
For Indian commissioner, seventy-five dollars.

#### FOR LAW LIBRARY.

Five hundred dollars.

### ORDERS OF THE GOVERNOR.

For payment of orders of the governor, one thous- **nd** dollars.

Appropriations for 1877-78, (continued.)

### FOR REGISTRATION OF BIRTHS, MARRIAGES AND DEATHS.

Three hundred and fifty dollars.

### CARE OF STATE HOUSES AND PUBLIC OFFICES.

For two persons to take charge of the state house Providence, and the offices therein, twelve hundred sixty dollars.

For care of Newport state house, three hundred llars.

For a person to take charge of the College street -rooms, four hundred and fifty dollars.

For a person to take charge and care of the offices Elizabeth building, four hundred and fifty dollars.

For the support of the state prison, ten thousand lars.

For deficiency in appropriation for militia and mili- affairs for fiscal year ending April 30, 1877, rty-three hundred dollars.

'or deficiency in appropriation for insane and er dependent persons for fiscal year ending April 1877, fifteen hundred dollars.

?or deficiency in appropriation for court houses and for fiscal year ending April 30, 1877, eight hun- dollars.

For deficiency in appropriation for jails and jailers fiscal year ending April 30, 1877, seven hundred llars.

For deficiency in appropriation for fuel and gas for year ending April 30, 1877, eight hundred dol-

or deficiency in appropriation for officers of justice ts for fiscal year ending April 30, 1877, twenty- five hundred dollars.

For deficiency in appropriation for reform school fiscal year ending April 30, 1877, eight hundred dollars.

Appropriation s
for 1877-78.
(continued.)
For miscellaneous expenses, payment of all accounts allowed by the general assembly and other expenses not provided for by this act, ten thousand dollars.

Sec. 2. All acts and parts of acts inconsistent herewith are hereby repealed.

## CHAPTER 633.

Passed March
30, 1877.
AN ACT IN AMENDMENT OF CHAPTERS 6 AND 7 OF THE GEN-
ERAL STATUTES, "OF THE REGISTERING, LISTING AND RE-
TURNING LISTS OF VOTERS, AND OF PROOF OF THEIR
QUALIFICATION TO VOTE," AND "OF CANVASSING THE
RIGHTS, AND CORRECTING THE LISTS, OF VOTERS."

*It is enacted by the General Assembly as follows :*

The registry book: what to contain.
SECTION 1. The secretary of state shall prepare and furnish to the town clerks of the several towns a book to be entitled "The Registry Book," which book shall be ruled under suitable headings to indicate the time when, and the place where, any person desiring to be registered was born ; if the person was born or had resided without the town, when he last came to reside within the state, and if he was born or had resided without the town, when he last came to reside within the town, and if the town contains more than one thousand voters, the place in the town at which the person resided at the time of registering.

Registry voters to register themselves an-nually in certain towns.
SEC. 2. Every person who is, or within a year may be qualified to vote upon being registered and the payment of a registry tax, shall go to the town clerk of the town in which he resides, and shall annually, if the town contains more than one thousand voters, on or before the last day of December, register his name and thereby certify to the truth of the facts stated in the appropriate heads of such registry, and the like mode of registration of persons qualified to be placed on the registry shall be made in the towns containing

In other towns, triennially.
less than one thousand voters, but in such town, the registration need only be made triennially. Any person who shall knowingly make any false certificate

in registering his name in any such registry book, shall be fined not exceeding fifty dollars, or be imprisoned not exceeding thirty days.

Penalty for false registry.

SEC. 3. For the purposes of this act, the town clerk and the town treasurer of the town shall be a board of assessors of the town, and they shall annually, on or before the first Monday in January, assess a tax of one dollar, or of such sum as with the other taxes assessed against such person, shall amount to one dollar, which shall be the assessment of the registry tax required to be assessed by the constitution and laws of this state, to entitle the person registered to vote for the succeeding year.

Board of assessors under this act to assess registry tax.

SEC. 4. Every registry tax assessed to qualify a person to vote shall be paid to the town clerk of the town in which such person resides, on or before the second Saturday in January, and all taxes paid to any town clerk shall be paid over by the clerk receiving the same, to the town treasurer, on or before the 20th day of said month, and be applied to the support of public schools.

Registry tax to be paid when.

And how applied.

SEC. 5. Town clerks receiving registry taxes under the provisions of this act, shall make out and certify a list of the persons paying such taxes, and the amount of each tax paid, the time when, and the name of the person who paid the tax, and shall return the said certified list to the board of canvassers for such town, at the meeting of the board of canvassers next to be holden in such town or ward after the second Saturday in January in each year. In the city of Providence such lists shall be certified to the board of canvassers of the several wards for the said city.

Town clerks to return certified lists of persons paying registry taxes, etc.

SEC. 6. Any clerk making any false entry or certificate of any fact required to be entered or certified under the provisions hereof, shall be fined not exceeding five hundred dollars, or be imprisoned not exceeding six months.

Penalty for false entry, etc.

SEC. 7. The city clerk of the city of Providence shall annually, on or before the first day of November, certify and deliver to the several ward clerks of said city, a printed copy of the tax assessment of the said city.

City clerk of Providence to furnish copies of tax assessment.

12

Voting lists, how to be canvassed, posted up and corrected. SEC. 8. The several boards of canvassers of the several towns, and of the wards of the city of Providence, shall meet annually on the last Monday in January, for the purpose of canvassing and making up the voting lists for their respective town or ward, which list shall as soon as may be thereafter, by the town or ward clerk, be posted up in at least three public places in such town or ward, and in the city of Providence, shall post up a like list in the office of the city clerk, and the board of canvassers shall hold their last meeting within four days next preceding the first Wednesday in April in each year, to further correct, and add to the voting list for such town or ward, and shall also meet within four days of any other general or special election to further correct and add to such voting list.

Returns of military service. SEC. 9. The returns required to be made by the commanding officer of a military company by the provisions of section 35 of chapter 6 of the General Statutes, for the city of Providence, shall be made to the ward clerks of the said city, in which the members of such company respectively reside, and such returns shall be made within the city of Providence and in the several towns on the first Saturday in January in each year.

Duties of clerks of voting districts in Providence. SEC. 10. Whenever any ward of the city of Providence shall be divided into voting districts, the duties herein imposed on ward clerks shall be performed by the clerks of such districts, and for the purposes of this act the term " ward clerk " shall be construed to mean and include said district clerks.

Town clerks to attend for registration of voters. SEC. 11. The several town clerks are required to be in their respective offices for the purpose of attending to the registration of voters for the three secular days next preceding and including the last secular day of December in each year, and there to remain from nine o'clock in the forenoon until one o'clock in the afternoon, and from two o'clock to nine o'clock in the afternoon ; and shall attend to such registration at such other times as persons may apply to be registered. And such clerks shall be and remain at their respective offices during the same hours of the three days next preceding and including the second Saturday in January, for the purpose of receiving the payment of registry taxes, and shall receive such taxes at such other times before the said second Saturday in January, from persons against whom such taxes are assessed or are liable to be assessed.

And receiving payment of registry taxes.

SEC. 12. The several town and ward clerks shall annually place upon the registry list the names of the several persons who have previously been upon the voting list, according to the provisions of this act, against whom a property tax, to the amount of one dollar or upwards, shall have been assessed; and such persons need not register their names annually as is required of persons paying a registry tax.

Names of property tax payers to be put on voting lists;

And annual registry not required.

SEC. 13. Any officer required to perform any duty under the provisions of this act who shall refuse or wilfully neglect to perform such duty as required hereunder, shall be fined not exceeding five hundred dollars or be imprisoned not exceeding three months, unless a punishment for such offence is herein otherwise provided.

Penalties.

SEC. 14. So much of chapter 6 of the General Statutes, as requires the collector of taxes to receive registry taxes, and so much of chapter 7 of said Statutes as requires the several boards of canvassers to meet at times other than as herein prescribed, and so much of the said General Statutes as requires the assessors of taxes to assess registry taxes, and all acts and parts of acts inconsistent herewith, or which imposes upon other officers the duties herein imposed, are hereby repealed.

Acts repealed.

SEC. 15. So much of this act as refers to the registration of voters, and to the payment of registry taxes assessed hereunder, and as to the return of tax lists by the city clerk of Providence to the several ward clerks of said city, shall go into effect on the first day of July, A. D., 1877, and the residue hereof shall take effect on the first day of January, A. D., 1878.

This act to go into effect, when.

# ACTS

### OF A

# Local and Private Nature,

### INCLUDING

# ACTS OF INCORPORATION.

Passed January 22, 1877. AN ACT IN AMENDMENT OF AN ACT ENTITLED " AN ACT TO INCORPORATE THE NEW ENGLAND RAILROAD AUTOMATIC GATE COMPANY," PASSED AT THE MAY SESSION, 1876.

*It is enacted by the General Assembly as follows :*

SECTION 1. Section 1 of an act entitled " An Act to incorporate the New England Railroad Automatic Gate Co.," passed at the May session, A. D. 1876, is hereby amended by striking out the words " New England Railroad Automatic Gate Co.," and inserting in place thereof the words " Railway Safety Gate Co."

SEC. 2. All acts and parts of acts inconsistent herewith are hereby repealed, and this act shall take effect upon its passage.

Passed Feb. 6, 1877. AN ACT IN AMENDMENT OF AN ACT ENTITLED " AN ACT TO INCORPORATE THE ATLANTIC TUBING COMPANY," PASSED AT THE MAY SESSION, 1865.

*It is enacted by the General Assembly as follows :*

SECTION 1. Section 1 of an act entitled " An Act to incorporate the Atlantic Tubing Company," passed

the May session, A. D. 1865, is hereby amended
striking out the words, " Atlantic Tubing Com-
y," and inserting in place thereof the words
tlantic Manufacturing Company," and by inserting
the word " purposes " the words " and electrical
)lies."

sc. 2. All acts and parts of acts inconsistent.
with are hereby repealed, and this act shall take
upon its passage.

ACT IN AMENDMENT OF AN ACT TO INCORPORATE THE
DIAMOND HILL GRANITE COMPANY.

Passed Feb.
14, 1877.

*is enacted by the General Assembly as follows :*

SECTION 1. The capital stock of The Diamond
Granite Company shall not exceed two hundred
nd dollars.

2. So much of said act of which this is in
ndment, as is inconsistent herewith, is hereby reed.

SEC. 3. This act shall take effect from and after
passage.

ACT IN AMENDMENT OF AN ACT ENTITLED " AN ACT TO IN-
RPORATE THE HERRESHOFF OIL AND GUANO COMPANY."

Passed March
6, 1877.

*is enacted by the General Assembly as follows :*

SECTION 1. The place of the holding of the annual
ing of the Herreshoff Oil and Guano Company
hereafter be at Tiverton instead of at Bristol as
fore.

2. This act shall take effect from and after its

Passed March : 
28, 1877.

AN ACT IN AMENDMENT OF AN ACT INCORPORATING THE AMERICAN SHIP WINDLASS COMPANY.

*It is enacted by the General Assembly as follows:*

SECTION. 1.　Section 2 of an Act incorporating the American Ship Windlass Company, is hereby amended by striking out all of said section after the words " in a book kept for that purpose."

SEC. 2.　Section 5 of said act is hereby repealed.

Passed March
14, 1877.

AN ACT IN AMENDMENT OF AND IN ADDITION TO " AN ACT TO INCORPORATE THE KINGSTON SAVINGS BANK," PASSED JUNE 14, 1853.

*It is enacted by the General Assembly as follows:*

SECTION 1.　Section 2 of an act to incorporate the Kingston Savings Bank is hereby amended so as to read as follows :

"Section 2.　Said corporation shall meet annually at Kingston on the first Monday of July.　They shall annually elect a president and not less than four nor more than six directors who shall manage the affairs of said bank and who may elect a secretary and treasurer and such other officers as they may deem necessary, remove them at their discretion, determine their salaries, fill all vacancies in their own board until the next annual election, and make all necessary by-laws not contrary to law.　All officers of the corporation shall continue in office until others are legally appointed in their places."

SEC 2.　This act shall take effect from and after its passage.

Passed March
80, 1877.

AN ACT IN AMENDMENT OF AN ACT ENTITLED "AN ACT TO INCORPORATE THE MACHINIST TOOL COMPANY."

*It is enacted by the General Assembly as follows:*

SECTION 1.　The name of the corporation created by an act to incorporate the " Machinist Tool Company," is hereby changed to the " American Street Sweeping Machine Company."

ᴇᴄ. 2. Section 2 of the act to incorporate the
ᴀᴄhinist Tool Company" is hereby amended so
o read as follows: "Section 2. The capital stock
ᴀid corporation ᴃhall be thirty-five thousand dol-
with liberty to increase the same to fifty thousand
ᴀrs, to be divided into shares of one hundred dol-
each; the shares in said capital stock are hereby
ᴀred to be personal estate, and shall be transferred
bill of sale, and recorded in the office of the treas-
of said corporation in a book provided for that
"

ᴊ. All acts and parts of acts inconsistent
ɪ are hereby repealed.

---

T IN AMENDMENT OF AN ACT ENTITLED "AN ACT TO
ᴇᴘORATE THE FRANKLIN FOUNDRY AND MACHINE COM-
ɪ FOR PROSECUTING FURNACE AND MACHINE BUSI-
." Passed March 30, 1877.

ᴍacted by the General Assembly as follows:

ᴏɴ 1. The third section of an act entitled
Act to incorporate the Franklin Foundry and
ine Company for prosecuting furnace and ma-
business," is hereby so amended that the capital
of said corporation may be increased by vote of
corporation to an amount not exceeding three
dred thousand dollars, to be divided into shares
ᴏne hundred dollars each. Said shares shall be
ed personal estate and shall be transferable in
manner as shall be prescribed by the by-laws of
corporation.

. 2. All acts and parts of acts inconsistent here-
ᴀre hereby repealed.

. 3. This act shall take effect from and after its
e.

---

ᴀᴄᴛ TO INCORPORATE REUNION LODGE NO. 61, INDEPEN-
DENT ORDER OF GOOD TEMPLARS OF WOONSOCKET. Passed January 25, 1877.

ᴜ enacted by the General Assembly as follows:

Sᴇᴄᴛɪᴏɴ 1. John Worrall, Francis Brady, A. D.
ᴿts, Francis White, Edward H. Burt, Caleb E.
ᴀᴿd, Gilbert Roberts and such others as now are or

may hereafter become members of said lodge are hereby created a body politic and corporate by the name of Reunion Lodge No. 61, Independent Order of Good Templars in Woonsocket, for the purpose of promoting the cause of temperance and by that name shall be able and capable in law to take, hold and dispose of property and effects, real and personal or mixed, to an amount not to exceed ten thousand dollars, and shall have all the power of perpetual succession, with all the powers and privileges and subject to all the duties and liabilities set forth in chapter 139 of the General Statutes, and of the statutes in amendment of and in addition to the same.

SEC. 2. Said corporation may elect at such times and in such manner and for such period as said lodge has heretofore been accustomed to elect, a worthy chief templar, worthy vice-templar, secretary, financial secretary, treasurer, chaplain, marshal, deputy marshal and the right and left supporters, and such other officers as may be deemed necessary for transaction of their business and to continue in said office for such length of time as has heretofore been the custom of said lodge, as shall be provided for in the constitution and by-laws of said lodge.

SEC. 3. This act shall take effect from and after its passage.

sed Feb. 1877.

AN ACT IN AMENDMENT OF AN ACT ENTITLED "AN ACT TO INCORPORATE THE HOME FOR FRIENDLESS CHILDREN IN NEWPORT."

*It is enacted by the General Assembly as follows:*

SECTION 1. The amount of property the Home for Friendless Children, in Newport, may hold for the charitable object of the corporation, shall not exceed the sum of two hundred thousand dollars.

SEC. 2. The control and management of the invested property of the said corporation shall be committed to a board of three male trustees who shall be denominated the financial trustees—if the terms of any donation to the society do not otherwise provide—who, or a majority of whom, shall invest the said funds and property, and re-invest the same, from time to time, in their best discretion, for the benefit of the said corporation, and shall receive the income, dividends and profits of such investments as they may become due and receivable, and shall pay the said income, dividends and profits to the treasurer of the said corporation as the said trustees may receive the same.

SEC. 3.   Richard Cornell, Oliver Read and J. Truman Burdick shall constitute the first Board of Financial Trustees to discharge the duties imposed by the next preceding section, and whenever any vacancy shall arise in the said Board, from any cause, or either of the said trustees shall become disqualified from discharging the duties of the said office, the Board of Trustees appointed by the said corporation shall, with the approval of the remaining financial trustees, fill such vacancy, or appoint another man to act in the place of the trustee who may be disqualified.

SEC. 4.   No person shall be admitted a member of the corporation except upon a vote by ballot of the trustees appointed by the corporation, nor until the next meeting after such person shall have been proposed for admission.

SEC. 5.   All children who shall be placed in the custody of the Children's Home, who shall have no lawful guardian, shall be subject to the rules and regulations of the corporation in reference to remaining therein, or being discharged therefrom; all children who may be placed in the custody of the said Home by the overseer of the poor of any town, shall also be subject to the rules and regulations of the corporation in reference to remaining therein and being discharged therefrom; all children who shall be placed at the said Home on board during the pleasure of the parent or guardian, shall, when the board shall remain unpaid for the period of three months, be subject in like manner to the rules and regulations of the said corporation in reference to remaining therein or being discharged therefrom.

12

Passed Feb.
27, 1877.

AN ACT TO INCORPORATE "DIVISION NO. 11, ANCIENT ORDER
OF HIBERNIANS" OF PROVIDENCE.

*It is enacted by the General Assembly as follows:*

SECTION 1.  John Bannan, Peter Gaffeny, Patrick
Lynch, John Lyons, John Fitzgerald, John Powers,
John Gillan, Michael Reid, Michael Devern, their associates and successors, are hereby made a corporation
by the name of "Division No. 11, Ancient Order of
Hibernians" of Providence, for charitable and benevolent purposes, with all the powers and privileges, and
subject to all the duties and liabilities set forth in
chapter 139 of the General Statutes, and in any acts
in amendment thereof or in addition thereto.

SEC. 2.  Said corporation may take, hold, transmit
and convey real and personal estate to an amount not
exceeding ten thousand dollars.

Passed March
1, 1877.

AN ACT TO INCORPORATE "DIVISION NO. 12, ANCIENT ORDER
OF HIBERNIANS, IN THE CITY OF PROVIDENCE."

*It is enacted by the General Assembly as follows:*

SECTION 1.  James Murphy, James Kelly, John
Hanley, Edmund Knowles, their associates and successors, are hereby made a corporation by the name of
"Division No. 12, Ancient Order of Hibernians of the
city of Providence," for benevolent and charitable purposes, with all the powers and privileges, and subject
to all the duties and liabilities set forth in chapter 139
of the General Statutes, and in any acts in amendment
thereof or in addition thereto.

SEC. 2.  Said corporation may take, hold, transmit
and convey real and personal estate to an amount not
exceeding one thousand dollars.

AN ACT TO INCORPORATE THE ANCIENT ORDER OF HIBERNI- Passed March
ANS, BENEVOLENT, SICK AND BURIAL SOCIETY OF WOON- 30, 1877.
SOCKET.

*It is enacted by the General Assembly as follows :*

SECTION 1.   Edward Byrnes, Edward Prendergast,
Frank Green, Bartholomew Murray, Patrick Murphy,
Peter Mulligan, Lawrence McNally, Thomas Cannon,
John Roddy, Edward Clifford, John F. Muloy, John
Murphy, William Walsh, John Gilfillen, William
McCanna, Charles Flynn, their associates and succes-
sors, are hereby made a corporation by the name of the
Ancient Order of Hibernians, Benevolent, Sick and
Burial Society, for benevolent and charitable purposes,
with all the powers and privileges, and subject to all
the duties and liabilities set forth in chapter 139 of the
General Statutes, and in any acts in amendment there-
of or in addition thereto.

SEC. 2.   Said corporation may take, hold, transmit
and convey real and personal estate to an amount not
exceeding ten thousand dollars.

AN ACT TO INCORPORATE THE PROVIDENCE YACHT CLUB. Passed Feb.
28, 1877.

*It is enacted by the General Assembly as follows :*

SECTION 1.   Addison H. White, Henry J. Steere,
Wm. L. Beckwith, Harvey J. Flint and such other
persons as are now associated as a yacht club in the
city of Providence, or may hereafter become associated
with them, are hereby constituted a body corporate by
the name of the Providence Yacht Club, to be located
in the city of Providence for the purpose of encouraging yacht building and improvement in seamanship
and the cultivation of naval science.

SEC. 2.   The said corporation shall have power to
make and  adopt a constitution, by-laws, rules and
regulations for the admission and government of its
members, as well as for their suspension and expul-
sion; for the election of its officers and defining their
duties, and for the safe keeping, management and dis-

position of its funds. It may also from time to time alter or repeal such constitution, by-laws, rules and regulations.

Sec. 3. The trustees of said corporation shall consist of three members of the club who are or who shall be for the time being, owners of yachts duly enrolled on the records of the club. The said trustees shall be elected annually.

Sec. 4. The said corporation may purchase and hold or lease any real or personal estate, but the value of the real estate so held by it shall not exceed twenty thousand dollars.

Sec. 5. The said corporation shall also possess the powers and be subject to the restrictions and liabilities contained in the one hundred and thirty-ninth chapter, nineteenth title of the General Statutes of Rhode Island.

Sec. 6. This act shall take effect on its passage.

---

Passed Feb.
28, 1877.

AN ACT TO INCORPORATE THE PROVIDENCE CHARITABLE
FUEL SOCIETY.

*It is enacted by the General Assembly as follows :*

Section 1. William W. Hoppin, Augustus Woodbury, Robert B. Chambers, Gorham P. Pomroy, Benjamin Potter, Samuel Chace, Samuel Salsbury, Oliver W. Hopkins, Henry G. Luther, Stillman Perkins, Charles H. Tilley, Alfred A. Harrington, Charles C. James, their associates and successors, are hereby made a corporation by the name of The Providence Charitable Fuel Society, for the purpose of distributing fuel to the worthy and deserving poor of the city of Providence, with all the powers and privileges, and subject to all the duties and liabilities set forth in chapter 139 of the General Statutes, and in any acts in amendment thereof or in addition thereto.

Sec. 2. Said corporation may take, hold, transmit and convey real and personal estate to an amount not exceeding ten thousand dollars.

AN ACT TO INCORPORATE COVENANT LODGE NO. 40, I. O. O. F. IN THE TOWN OF SCITUATE, R. I. Passed Feb. 16, 1877.

*It is enacted by the General Assembly as follows :*

SECTION 1. Ferdinand H. Allen, William A. Baker, Robert H. Walker, Daniel H. Remington, Harden Steere, George A. Henrys, John Ramsdell, their associates and successors, are hereby made a corporation by the name of Covenant Lodge No. 40, I. O. O. F., r mutual benefit and charitable purposes, with all e powers and privileges, and subject to all the duties d liabilities set forth in chapter 139 of the General tutes, and in any acts in amendment thereof or in dition thereto.

SEC. 2. Said corporation may take, hold, transmit d convey real and personal estate to an amount not ceeding twenty thousand dollars.

SEC. 3. This act shall take effect at the time of its al passage and the first meeting of said lodge thereer shall be the first meeting of the corporation with· t notice, and the then existing officers of said lodge all be the officers of the corporation until others are cted and installed in accordance with the constitu-n and by-laws of said lodge.

---

AN ACT IN AMENDMENT OF AN ACT INCORPORATING GOOD SAMARITAN LODGE NO. 8, INDEPENDENT ORDER OF ODD FELLOWS. Passed Feb. 28, 1877.

*It is enacted by the General Assembly as follows :*

SECTION 1. The words " Village of Pawtucket " in 'd act of incorporation, section 1, shall be changed to as to read " Town of Pawtucket."

SEC. 2. The words " twenty thousand dollars " in section 1, of said act of incorporation shall be changed to as to read " fifty thousand dollars."

SEC. 3. This act shall take effect immediately after its passage.

Passed March
30, 1877. AN ACT TO INCORPORATE ELECTRA LODGE NO. 41, I. O. O. F.,
LITTLE COMPTON, R. I.

*It is enacted by the General Assembly as follows :*

SECTION 1. Abram Gifford, Charles H. Field, Alvah D. Macomber, David G. Hart, Caleb M. Macomber and Sylvester C. Manley, their associates and successors, are hereby made a corporation by the name of Electra Lodge, No. 41, I. O. O. F., Little Compton, R. I., for mutual benefit and charitable purposes, with all the powers and privileges, and subject to all the duties and liabilities set forth in chapter 139 of the General Statutes, and in any acts in amendment thereof or in addition thereto.

SEC. 2. Said corporation may take, hold, transmit and convey real and personal estate to an amount not exceeding thirty thousand dollars.

SEC. 3. This act shall take effect at the time of its final passage and the first meeting of said lodge thereafter shall be the first meeting of the corporation without notice and the then existing officers of said lodge shall be the officers of the corporation until others are elected and installed in accordance with the constitution and by-laws of said lodge.

Passed March
13, 1877. AN ACT TO INCORPORATE THE NEWPORT BAND IN NEWPORT.

*It is enacted by the General Assembly as follows :*

SECTION 1. Joseph Graham, William Mather, Henry C. Sherman, Thomas Simpson, and their associates and successors, are hereby made a corporation by the name of the Newport Band, for the purpose of improving themselves and practising in instrumental music, with all the powers and privileges, and subject to all the duties and liabilities set forth in chapter 139, of the General Statutes, and in any acts in amendment thereof or in addition thereto.

SEC. 2. Said corporation may take, hold, transmit and convey real and personal estate to an amount not exceeding five thousand dollars.

AN ACT IN AMENDMENT OF AN ACT ENTITLED " AN ACT TO IN-  Passed March 16, 1877.
CORPORATE 'HERRICKS BRIGADE BAND,' OF PROVIDENCE,
R. I."

*It is enacted by the General Assembly as follows:*

SECTION 1.   An Act entitled " An Act to incorporate 'Herrick's Brigade Band' of Providence, R. I.,"
passed at the January Session 1876, is hereby amended by striking out the words " Herrick's Brigade
Band" wherever the same occur and inserting in lieu
thereof the words " Herrick and Tonge's Military
Band."

SEC. 2.   This act shall take effect from and after its
passage.

---

AN ACT TO INCORPORATE THE " ADVENT CHRISTIAN CHURCH  Passed March 6, 1877.
OF NATICK," IN THE TOWN OF WARWICK.

*It is enacted by the General Assembly as follows :*

SECTION 1.   Elisha B. Card, John D. Kittle, Spencer H. Shippee, and Nehemiah Nicholas, and their associates and successors, are hereby created a body corporate, by the name of the " Advent Christian Church
of Natick," in Warwick, for the purpose of establishing and supporting the public worship of God, in the
village of Natick, town of Warwick, in any house or
place of worship which is now or hereafter may be
owned or occupied by said corporation, and by this
name shall have power to take by purchase or otherwise, and to receive and hold, grant, sell and dispose
of any real and personal estate, not exceeding in value
five thousand dollars, and to make such by-laws, rules
and regulations not contrary to the laws of this state,
as said corporation may deem expedient, and shall
have all the rights and privileges and be subject to
all the duties and liabilities set forth in chapter 139
of the General Statutes and of all acts in amendment
thereof or in addition thereto.

Passed March 20, 1877.

AN ACT IN AMENDMENT OF AN ACT ENTITLED "AN ACT TO IN-CORPORATE CERTAIN PERSONS BY THE NAME OF THE UNITARIAN CONGREGATIONAL CHURCH IN NEWPORT."

*It is enacted by the General Assembly as follows :*

SECTION 1. The Unitarian Congregational Church in Newport is hereby continued a body politic and corporate, for the purpose of maintaining Christian worship, with all the powers and privileges, and subject to all the duties and liabilities set forth in chapter 139 of the General Statutes, and in any acts in amendment thereof, or in addition thereto.

SEC. 2. The church, and lot whereon it stands, formerly held by William Ellery, Samuel St. John, Jr., Borden Wood, James Hammond, Alexander M. MacGregor, and Michael Freeborn, as trustees, and which, by an act passed at the January session of the general assembly, A. D. 1836, whereof this act is an amendment, was vested in the Unitarian Congregational Church in Newport, is hereby confirmed as the property of the said corporation, together with all property therein in law or equity belonging, and said corporation is hereby authorized to sell or exchange the same, or any part or parts thereof, provided the said sale or exchange shall be approved by a majority of the persons whose names shall appear on the records of the secretary of said corporation as pew-owners in said church, at the time of such proposed sale or exchange. Provided further, however, that the owners of pews who may be in arrears for assessments or taxes which may have been levied thereon, for a period of two years or more, shall not be entitled to vote thereon.

SEC. 3. The duly elected trustees of said corporation shall have authority to appoint three discreet and disinterested persons, not trustees of the corporation, who shall be authorized to make a special appraisement of all pews upon which the annual assessments or taxes have remained unpaid for two years or more and whenever the amount due for said unpaid assessments or taxes shall equal the valuation so appraised then the said trustees shall be authorized to take possession of said pews, for and on behalf of the said corporation, which shall thereupon become seized of the title to said pews, as fully as in the original ownership thereof. Provided, however, that before such proceedings are taken, public notice of the intention to take the same, shall be given by advertisement, at least once a week, for three weeks, in a newspaper published in the city of Newport, and that a similar notice shall be placed conspicuously in or on the church building during the same period. An affidavit that the said notices were given in the manner required, shall be recorded in the book of record of the corporation, by the secretary thereof, and the said affidavit shall constitute legal evidence that the said notices were duly given.

SEC. 4. The aforesaid corporation and their successors, are hereby empowered to take and hold, by purchase or otherwise, lands, tenements, and hereditaments, necessary and proper for a place of public worship, for the religious instruction of the young, d for the residence of a pastor ; and to receive uests, legacies, donations, sell pews in said place public worship, and otherwise to raise funds for e aforesaid purposes.

SEC. 5. The corporation aforesaid, shall consist of ch persons as are proprietors of pews in the afore-'d place of worship, together with such others as y be admitted as members of the corporation, der the limitations and restrictions which the cortion may from time to time authorize. And each on so admitted shall be entitled to vote in all ings of the corporation, and to be a member reof in all other respects, subject to the conditions reinafter named.

SEC. 6. There shall be an annual meeting of the ration on the second Monday in October, to elect president, secretary, treasurer, and ten trustees ; ree of which trustees shall be the president, secreta- and treasurer ; and all the persons so elected shall hold their offices respectively for one year there-from, or, until other persons shall be duly elected in their stead.

14

SEC. 7. At all meetings of the corporation for the transaction of business, nine members shall be necessary to constitute a quorum.

SEC. 8. If the corporation in any year shall have failed from any cause to elect on the day specified for their annual meeting, members to fill said offices of president, secretary, treasurer, and trustees, or either of them, or if from any other cause said offices or either of them, become vacant, they may be filled as the case may require ; or any other corporate business may be transacted at a special meeting of the corporation, which shall have been called at the request of five members thereof ; and of which notice shall have been given from the pulpit, at least two successive Sundays before the time appointed for such special meeting.

SEC. 9. The secretary of the corporation shall keep in a book provided for the purpose, a record of the persons owning pews, and of such transfers thereof as may from time to time occur, which records shall be considered the general evidence by which the proprietors of pews are to be ascertained.

SEC. 10. The aforesaid corporation shall be authorized to fix a valuation upon the pews in its place of worship, and from time to time to alter the same as circumstances may require, to assess and levy taxes upon the said pews at a fixed rate of percentage upon such valuation, for the purpose of defraying its current expenses of whatever nature, other than the purchase of real estate, the erection of buildings, or for improvements exceeding in cost the sum of five hundred dollars; provided, that in each case its action shall be approved by a vote of two-thirds of the members of the corporation who may be present at the time it is taken, and that the said action shall be at the same time, or subsequently approved by a majority of the pew-holders.

SEC. 11. This act shall take effect from and after its passage.

AN ACT TO INCORPORATE THE STEWART STREET BAPTIST Passed March 30, 1877.
CHURCH IN THE CITY OF PROVIDENCE.

*It is enacted by the General Assembly as follows :*

SECTION 1.    Aaron   B.   McCrillis,   Jeremiah   S.
Adams, Silas A. Sweet, members of the Stewart Street
Baptist Church and their associates, together with such
others as may hereafter become members of said church,
are hereby created a body corporate and politic with per.
petual succession by the  name of Stewart Street Bap.
tist Church, for the purpose of establishing and maintaining the  public  worship of Almighty God  in the
city of Providence, and for the purpose of supporting
 d promulgating the christian  religion  according  to
the rites and  usages  of the  churches constituting  the
Warren Baptist Association, with  all  the  rights 'and
privileges, and subject to all the duties and liabilities
set forth in chapter 139 of the  General Statutes, and
 chapters in amendment thereof or in addition there-

SEC.  2.    Said  society  may  receive,  hold,  trans-
t and convey real and personal property to an amount
ot exceeding one hundred thousand dollars.
SEC. 3.    In all financial matters or transactions in-
olving the appropriations of  money, or the  transfer
 property, except for benevolent purposes, the right
 vote shall be restricted to the adult pew  holders in
 d church, and each hirer of a  seat or sitting in any
    shall be  considered a pew  holder, provided that
 member shall be entitled to more than one vote.
SEC. 4.    At any meeting of the corporation five  of
 adult members shall constitute a quorum.
SEC. 5.    This act shall take effect immediately upon
passage.
SEC. 6.    All acts and parts of acts inconsistent here-
th are hereby repealed.

AN ACT IN AMENDMENT OF AN ACT TO INCORPORATE CER- Passed March 30, 1877.
TAIN PERSONS AS A CHURCH BY THE NAME OF THE SHAW-
OMET BAPTIST CHURCH, IN OLD WARWICK, R. I.

*It is enacted by the General Assembly as follows:*

SECTION 1.    That the act to incorporate the Shaw-
omet Baptist Church, of the  January  session 1851, is

amended as follows: From the name of the church in the title of said act and in the first section thereof strike out the word "Old" and the initials "R. I." Also from section 3 strike out the word "seven" and insert in its place the word "five."

SEC. 2. This act shall take effect from and after its passage.

Passed March 80, 1877.

**AN ACT IN AMENDMENT OF AN ACT TO INCORPORATE THE PROPRIETORS OF THE OLD WARWICK BAPTIST MEETING HOUSE.**

*It is enacted by the General Assembly as follows:*

SECTION 1. That the act to incorporate the proprietors of the Old Warwick Baptist meeting house, passed by the general assembly at the January session 1858, is amended as follows: From article 6 of the constitution contained in section 2 strike out the words "apportion and assess taxes for the necessary repairs of the meeting house, on the pews, according to the valuation made previous to their distribution, and when such apportionment and," and in place of the words so stricken out insert the words "assess and levy on the pews in said meeting house, in a ratable proportion to the valuation made previous to their distribution, and to collect from the owner or owners thereof all sums of money they may vote to be necessary and requisite for all repairs and improvements of said house and the lot on which it stands, and for insurance of said house; and when said." Also from article 9 of said constitution strike out the word "seven" and insert in its place the word "five."

SEC. 2. This act shall take effect from and after its passage.

Passed March 30, 1877.

**AN ACT TO INCORPORATE THE SECOND AFRICAN METHODIST EPISCOPAL CHURCH IN PROVIDENCE.**

*It is enacted by the General Assembly as follows:*

SECTION 1. John A. Cravatt, George W. Jones, Frederick Piper, Peter Simmes, Robert Minton, Joseph Rhodes, William A. B. Mathews, all of Providence, R. I., and their associates and successors are hereby reated a body corporate and politic with perpetual succession by the name of the Second African Methodist Episcopal Church, for the purpose of establishing and maintaining the public worship of Almighty God in the city of Providence, in the state of Rhode Island, and of propagating the christian religion according to the forms, customs, usages and discipline of the Allen Methodist Episcopal Church, and by that name shall be able and capable in law to sue and be sued, to plead and be impleaded, to defend and be defended against, in all courts and places, and before all proper and lawful judges and magistrates whomsoever, to take, receive and hold all money and other property raised by voluntary subscription, contribution, donation or otherwise accruing to said corporation within the provisions of this act. Also all legacies and devises of real and personal estate, and to have, hold, possess and acquire lands, tenements and hereditaments, goods and chattels and property of every description to an amount not exceeding fifteen thousand dollars; and all and singular the estate and property aforesaid to lease, grant, convey and dispose of in such manner as they may judge expedient for purposes of this act at their will and pleasure; to have and to use a common seal and the same to break, alter or renew at pleasure, and at any of their meetings to enact and pass such rules, regulations and by-laws for the government of said corporation or its officers and for the management of its affairs as they may deem proper and necessary; provided the same be not repugnant to the constitution and laws of this state and of the United States, and to the usages and discipline of said church.

Sec. 2. Said corporation shall have all the rights, powers and privileges, and be subject to all the duties and liabilities provided by chapter one hundred and thirty-nine of the General Statutes, of the State of Rhode Island, and the several acts in amendment thereof and in addition thereto, except as herein provided; and any three of the persons above named may call the meeting for organization at such time and place, and giving such notice of such meeting as they may deem seasonable and proper.

SEC. 3.  This act shall take effect from and after its passage.

---

Passed March 30, 1877.

AN ACT TO INCORPORATE THE PRAIRIE AVENUE CHRISTIAN SOCIETY, IN THE CITY OF PROVIDENCE.

*It is enacted by the General Assembly as follows :*

SECTION 1.  John F. Pitts, Benjamin Harrington, Welcome A. Collins, H. M. Eaton, and their associates and successors are hereby made a corporation by the name of Prairie Avenue Christian Society for establishing and maintaining christian worship in the city of Providence with all the powers and privileges, and subject to all the duties and liabilities set forth in chapter 139, of the General Statutes, and in any acts in amendment thereof or in addition thereto.

SEC. 2.  Said corporation may take, hold, transmit and convey real and personal estate to an amount not exceeding fifty thousand dollars.

---

Passed March 22, 1877.

AN ACT TO INCORPORATE THE RHODE ISLAND SCHOOL OF DESIGN.

*It is enacted by the General Assembly as follows:*

SECTION 1.  C. A. L. Richards, William B. Weeden, Francis W. Goddard, Charles D. Owen, Helen A. Metcalf, Sarah E. Doyle, Mary H. Drake, Clifton A. Hall, Claudius B. Farnsworth, and their associates and successors are hereby made a corporation by the name of the Rhode Island School of Design for the purpose of aiding in the cultivation of the arts of design, with all the powers and privileges, and subject to all the duties and liabilities set forth in chapter 139 of the General Statutes, and in any acts in amendment thereof or in addition thereto.

SEC. 2.  Said corporation may take, hold, and transmit personal and real estate to an amount not exceeding fifty thousand dollars.

AN ACT TO INCORPORATE THE " AMATEUR DRAMATIC CLUB" IN THE CITY OF PROVIDENCE. Passed March 27, 1877.

*It is enacted by the General Assembly as follows :*

SECTION 1. Wm. B. Weeden, Royal C. Taft, Samuel W. Peckham, J. C. B. Woods, their associates and successors are hereby made a corporation by the name of "Amateur Dramatic Club," for the purposes of musical, dramatic, social and literary culture, with all powers and privileges, and subject to all the duties and bilities set forth in Chapter 139 of the General utes, and in any acts in amendment thereof or in ition thereto.

SEC. 2. Said corporation may take, hold, transmit d convey real and personal estate to an amount not ceeding ten thousand dollars.

ACT TO INCORPORATE THE ST. EDWARDS ROMAN CATHOLIC TOTAL ABSTINENCE AND BENEVOLENT SOCIETY OF PROVIDENCE, R. I. Passed March 27, 1877.

*is enacted by the General Assembly as follows :*

SECTION 1. Edward McKearnan, C. A. Murphy, atrick Martin, Thomas Flynn, Harry W. Henry, Mich- Carlin, their associates and successors are hereby e a corporation by the name of the " St. Edwards an Catholic, Total Abstinence and Benevolent ety," of Providence, R. I., for the purpose of pro- ng temperance and benevolent purposes, with all powers and privileges, and subject to all the duties liabilities set forth in chapter 139 of the General tes, and in any acts in amendment thereof or in tion thereto.

SEC. 2. Said corporation may take, hold, transmit nd convey real and personal estate to an amount not ceeding two thousand dollars.

Passed March 30, 1877.

AN ACT TO INCORPORATE PROVIDENCE LODGE NUMBER 182 KNIGHTS OF HONOR.

*It is enacted by the General Assembly as follows :*

SECTION 1. Henry King, Francis B. Hayden, Ira A. Foster, William E. Boutelle, A. O. Rockwell, M. F. Morse, Henry Cram, F. W. Huntoon, Thomas Patterson and James Hiscox, their associates and successors are hereby made a corporation by the name of " Providence Lodge No. 182, Knights of Honor," for scientific, charitable and benevolent purposes, with all the powers and privileges, and subject to all the duties and liabilities set forth in chapter 139 of the General Statutes, and in any acts in amendment thereof or in addition thereto.

SEC. 2. Said corporation may take, hold, transmit and convey real and personal estate to an amount not exceeding ten thousand dollars.

SEC. 3. The persons now holding office in the association heretofore known as ·· Providence Lodge No. 182 Knights of Honor," shall continue to hold their respective offices for such length of time as heretofore has been the custom of said lodge.

SEC. 4. The said corporation shall have power to create, hold and disburse the funds of said corporation for promoting benevolence and relieving the sick and distressed ; but no funds of said corporation shall be paid out or disbursed on any account whatsoever, except under such regulations and by-laws as may from time to time be regularly established by said corporation.

SEC. 5. Any three of the persons named in the first section of this act, are hereby authorized to call the meeting of said corporation for organization, giving such notice of the same as they may deem reasonable and proper.

SEC. 6. This act shall take effect from and after its passage.

AN ACT IN AMENDMENT OF "AN ACT TO INCORPORATE THE WOMEN'S CHRISTIAN ASSOCIATION."

Passed March 30, 1877.

*It is enacted by the General Assembly as follows :*

SECTION 1. The property of the "Women's Christian Association" shall be and remain exempt from taxation, so long as it shall be used for the purposes mentioned in the charter of said association and no longer.

ACT TO CHANGE THE NAME OF THE WARREN PUBLIC READING ROOM ASSOCIATION.

Passed March 30. 1877.

*It is enacted by the General Assembly as follows :*

SECTION 1. "The Warren Public Reading Room iation" shall hereafter be known as the "War- Public Library."
SEC. 2. All acts and parts of acts inconsistent here- th are hereby repealed.
SEC. 3. This act shall take effect on and after its

ACT TO INCORPORATE BRIGADE NO. 3, OF THE ORDER OF ALFREDIANS OF RHODE ISLAND.

Passed March 30, 1877.

*is enacted by the General Assembly as follows :*

SECTION 1. John Thomas, Thomas Sainsbury, n Sainsbury, James Slater, Samuel Martin, Ed- Alexander, Caleb Merrett, William Besser, s Gibson, James Palmer, George Buckley, Wash- n Broadhead, James Broadhead, Charles Fisher, associates and successors are hereby made a cor- tion by the name of "Order of Alfredians Brigade 3, of R. I.," for the purposes of promoting the are of all concerned and for charitable and benevo- purposes, with all the powers and privileges, and subject to all the duties and liabilities set forth in chapter 139 of the General Statutes, and in any acts amendment thereof or in addition thereto.

15

SEC. 2. Said corporation may take, hold, transmit and convey real and personal estate to an amount not exceeding ten thousand dollars.

SEC. 3. Said corporation shall have its location or place of business in the city of Providence.

Passed March 30, 1877. AN ACT TO INCORPORATE THE "PROVIDENCE ASSISTING AS-SOCIATION," OF PROVIDENCE, RHODE ISLAND.

*It is enacted by the General Assembly as follows :*

SECTION 1. Barnard Holmes, Marcus Cohn, Nathan Werld, Thomas Williams, Thomas Weisman, Jacob Simon, Isidor Cohn, Moritz Hirsch, and Seelig Lepsky, of said Providence, their associates and and successors are hereby made a corporation by the name of the " Providence Assisting Association," for the purpose of mutual assistance and for charitable purposes, with all the powers and privileges, and subject to all the duties and liabilities set forth in chapter 139 of the General Statutes, and in any acts in amendment there-of or in addition thereto.

SEC. 2. Said corporation may take, hold, transmit and convey real and personal estate to an amount not exceeding five thousand dollars.

SEC. 3. This act shall take effect on and after its passage.

# RESOLUTIONS

OF A

# PUBLIC AND PRIVATE NATURE.

LUTION to print the Governor's Message.   No. 1.

*Resolved,* That one thousand copies of the govern.
s message in addition to the number for the sched-
es be printed for the use of the general assembly.

[Note. For governor's message, see Appendix, document No. 1.]


LUTION appointing a Joint Special Committee rel-   No. 2.
ative to the government and direction of the new
State Prison.

*Resolved,* The senate concurring herewith, That
essrs. Allen Greene, of Providence, Claudius B.
arnsworth, of Pawtucket, George Lewis Cooke, of
arren, John G. Clarke of South Kingstown, and
ed H. Littlefield, of Lincoln, of the house of repre-
tatives, and Messrs. Jonathan Brayton, of Warwick,
illiam Elsbree, of Cranston, and James M. Drake,
of Newport, of the senate, be a committee to take
into consideration title XXXII, of the General Statutes, to ascertain what legislation, if any, is required,
for the government and direction of the new state
prison, when it shall have been completed, and for the

transfer of the prisoners now in the state prison and
Providence county jail thereto ; to make the necessary
provisions for the transfer of the female prisoners now
in the state prison and Providence county jail, to the
state farm ; to ascertain what other changes in said
title may be advisable ; and to report by bill or
otherwise at the present session of the general assembly.

---

No. 3.

RESOLUTION authorizing the Joint Special Committee
on the new State Prison to print bills.

*Resolved,* The honorable senate concurring, that the
joint special committee on the new state prison be
authorized to print such bills as they may think fit to
report.

[Note. For bills reported, see Chapter 603, and Resolutions Nos. 4 and 5.]

---

No. 4.

RESOLUTION Continuing the Commission for building a
new State Prison.

*Resolved,* That Edwin M. Snow, William D. Brayton, George I. Chace, Augustus Woodbury, and Allen
Greene, who are now the commissioners under the resolution of the general assembly, passed at their May
session, 1874, for the purpose of building a new prison
for the state, which shall also include a jail for the
county of Providence, upon the grounds of the state
farm, are hereby appointed to and continued in their
said offices respectively until said new prison and jail
are completed and furnished.

*Resolved,* That whenever, in the opinion of said
commissioners, said new prison and jail are completed,
furnished, and ready for occupancy, they shall deliver
up the same into the possession and control of the
board of state charities and corrections.

*Resolved,* That in case of a vacancy occurring in said
commission, by reason of death, resignation, removal

LUTION empowering the Warden of the State Prison and Keeper of the Jail in the County of Providence to remove convicts and prisoners.

*Resolved*, That whenever the board of state chari- and corrections shall notify the warden of the e prison and keeper of the jail, in the county of vidence, that the new buildings on the state farm, for the purposes of a state prison and jail, and ared by act of the general assembly, to be a por- of the state prison and jail for the county of vidence, are ready and suitable for occupancy, the l warden is hereby authorized and empowered to ove the inmates of the state prison from that por- n of said prison in the city of Providence, to that rtion of the state prison situated on the state farm; d as the keeper of the said jail he is hereby author- and empowered to remove the inmates of the said from that portion thereof situated in the city of vidence, to that portion thereof situated on the farm.

---

LUTION to procure furniture for the new Prison.

*Resolved*, That the state prison commissioners be, hereby are, authorized to procure furniture for the r prison.

SOLUTIONS of thanks to the Board of Inspectors of the Rhode Island State Prison.

WHEREAS, By an act passed at this session of the eneral assembly, the present board of inspectors of t Rhode Island state prison, consisting of Augustus

Woodbury, chairman; Jesse Metcalf, secretary; William Binney, Benoni Carpenter, Lewis Fairbrother, Joseph C. Hartshorn and Stephen R. Weeden, inspectors; has been merged with the board of state charities and corrections, and will after the fifth of June next cease to have a separate existence, and—

WHEREAS, The said board of inspectors having by their wise and gratuitous labors extending through a series of years in the administration of the affairs of the Rhode Island state prison, placed the people of this state, whose interests they have served, under a deep and lasting obligation to them, therefore,

*Resolved,* That the thanks of the general assembly are hereby tendered to the above named gentlemen individually and collectively, for the able, long continued, and gratuitous services which they have rendered the state as a board of state prison inspectors

*Resolved,* That the thanks of the general assembly are in an especial manner due to the Reverend Augustus Woodbury, for the very interesting and valuable historical sketch of the old state prison embodied in the annual report of the board of inspectors for the year 1876, presented to the general assembly at its present session.

---

No. 8.

RESOLUTION for printing an additional number of copies of the report of the Inspectors of the State Prison for 1876.

*Resolved,* That in addition to the number of copies of the report of the inspectors of the state prison for 1876, authorized to be printed by the joint committee on printing, 350 copies of the same be printed for the use of the inspectors and the general assembly.

[NOTE. For report, see Appendix document, No. 3.]

Resolution in relation to an Industrial School—recom-  No. 9.
mended in the Governor's Message.

Resolved, That Messrs. Nathan T. Verry, of Woonsocket, Samuel H. Cross, of Westerly, and Jonathan
Brayton, of Warwick, of the senate, and Messrs. Henry
H. Fay, of Newport, Allen Greene, of Providence,
xter Clark, of Cumberland, Pardon E. Tillinghast,
Pawtucket, and Christopher R. Greene, of Warwick,
the house of representatives, be a committee to ex-
ine into and report by bill or otherwise, in relation
the establishment of an industrial school.

[Nota. For report, see Appendix, document No. 16.]

lution granting the use of Court House in Wash-  No. 10.
ington County to the Washington County Agricultural Society.

Resolved, That the use of the court house in the
unty of Washington, be and hereby is granted to the
ashington County Agricultural Society for the hold-
g of their annual meeting on the 8th day of March,
877.

lution granting the use of Court House in Wash-  No. 11.
ington County to Kingston Library and Reading
Room Association.

Resolved, That the use of the court house in the
unty of Washington, be and hereby is granted to the
Kingston Library and Reading Room Association for
the holding of a course of lectures upon literary and
scientific subjects, at some time to be fixed hereafter
by a committee of said association,

No. 12.

RESOLUTION granting the use of the Court House a Kingston, to the ladies of Kingston.

*Resolved,*—The senate concurring therein ; that th sheriff of the county of Washington, be, and he hereb is authorized and requested, to give to the ladies ( Kingston the use of the court house, for the pu of holding a fair or fairs, and giving entertainmen consisting of refreshments, tableaux, readings, charad &c., for the benefit of the Library and Reading Roo organized by them.

---

No. 13.

RESOLUTION of inquiry as to the payment to the Sta by towns of monies due for liquor licenses.

*Resolved,* That the state auditor report to this ge eral assembly what towns have paid over to the sta the amount due for, or on account of, liquor licen and what towns, if any, have not so paid.

[NOTE. For report, see Appendix, document No. 13.]

No. 14.

RESOLUTION relating to certain liquors seized by Sta officers.

*Resolved,* That the sheriff of the county of Provi dence be directed to demand and receive certain liq uors seized by the state constable in February, 1875 at 50 and 52 Orange street, in Providence, and to sel the same on such terms as he thinks proper, and to pa to the general treasurer the proceeds of such sal over and above the expenses thereof, and make re- port of his doings to the general assembly.

LUTION relative to the disposition of the Rhode No. 15.
Island Building at the Centennial Grounds.

*Resolved,* That the governor and the United States
tennial commissioners from this state be, and they
hereby authorized to make such disposition of the
ode Island building at the centennial exhibition
uuds, as they may deem most expedient and advis-
ble.

---

ESOLUTION for the appointment of a Committee on No. 16.
the boundary lines of the new Court House Lot in
the City of Providence.

WHEREAS, the boundary lines, on the south and west
the lot on which the new court house for the
ty of Providence is built, are irregular and not
pted for the convenience of the state or the ad-
ing proprietors, and a proper adjustment of said
s will render it necessary for the state to give and
ive title to real estate by deed, and—
WHEREAS, a question has arisen as to the power of
state to give a perfect title to real estate which
been condemned for public uses ; it is
*Resolved,* That Messrs. Nelson W. Aldrich, of Prov-
ence, and Thomas Moies, of Lincoln, on the part of
e house, and Messrs. Benjamin N. Lapham, of Prov-
ence, and Ziba O. Slocum, of Glocester, on the part
the senate, be and hereby are appointed a commit-
to procure from the city of Providence a quitclaim
of said lot, and to negotiate with the owners
ljoining land, and in their discretion to make sale
ich portions of said lot as in their opinion are not
ed for the purposes of the state, and purchase
portions of the adjoining lands as they may
nk are needed for the purposes of the state, provided the whole amount of money agreed by them to be
paid by the state shall not exceed the sum of five hundred dollars, and provided further that all deeds given
by the state or received by the state shall be examin-
16

ed by the attorney general and by him certified to
be correct.

The general treasurer is hereby authorized to execute on the part of the state the deeds of such portions
of said lot as are sold by said committee, and to receive the consideration money therefor, and to pay out
of the treasury all sums of money agreed by said committee to be paid for land purchased, provided the
excess of the money paid out over the amount of money
received shall not exceed the sum of five hundred dollars.

---

17.

RESOLUTION authorizing the Joint Special Committee
on the division of the town of Warwick to send for
persons and papers.

*Resolved,* That the joint special committee on the
division of the town of Warwick be authorized to send
for persons and papers in their discretion; provided
the same be no expense to the state.

---

18.

RESOLUTION submitting the question of the division of
the town of Warwick to the qualified electors of
said town.

*Resolved,* That the following question be submitted
to the qualified electors of the town of Warwick, at
special meetings called for that purpose by the town
council of said town, on the last Saturday of April
1877, as hereinafter provided, viz:

"Shall the town of Warwick be divided into two
towns by a line drawn from a bend in the Pawtuxet
river, about half a mile northwest of Hill's Grove, in a
southerly direction to the highway on the east side of
Gorton's Pond, and thence along said highway to the
Apponaug depot, and thence along the line of the
Stonington railroad to Apponaug creek?"

The meetings above authorized shall be held on

said last Saturday of April, 1877, as follows: The meeting of the electors of said town who reside on the easterly side of said line, shall be held at the Pawtuxet depot, on the Warwick railroad, and the meeting of the electors of said town residing on the westerly side of said line, shall be held at the town house in Apponaug.

The town council of said town is hereby authoriz- to appoint a moderator, clerk, and sergeant and her necessary officers, for the proper conduct the meeting of said electors residing on the easterly de of said line, hereinbefore authorized to be held said Pawtuxet depot, and shall fix the hours for opening and close of said meeting.

t shall be the duty of the town clerk of said town certify to the general assembly at its next May ion, the number of votes cast for and against said sion of said town, at each of said special meetings tively.

t shall be the duty of the secretary of state to ise a sufficient number of ballots to be printed and ivered to the town clerk of said town, for use in d special meetings, on one side of which ballots shall printed the above question, and on the other side all be printed on one half of said ballots the word Yes," and on the remaining half, the word " No."

LUTION appointing a joint special committee to No. 19. examine and report what repairs are necessary for the State House in the city of Providence.

*Resolved*, the house of representatives concurring erein, that a joint special committee, consisting of Nathan T. Verry, of Woonsocket, and Augus- O. Bourn, of Bristol, on the part of the senate, Messrs. Henry W. Gardner, of Providence, Henry Fay, of Newport, and Earl C. Potter, of Barrington, on the part of the house of representatives, be appointed to examine into the condition of the state house in the city of Providence, and recommend what repairs are

necessary to put said state house in a proper condition
of safety ; and also to examine and report, what alterations are necessaiy to enlarge the senate chamber and
prepare proper committee rooms in said building and
report their doings at the next May session of the
general assembly.

---

No. 20.     RESOLUTION to appoint a Joint Special Committee relative to the establishment of a new county or judicial district in the northern part of the State.

*Resolved,* The house of representatives concurring,
a joint special committee be appointed, consisting of
Messrs. Nathan T. Verry, of Woonsocket, Benjamin N.
Lapham, of Providence, and Jonathan Chace, of Lincoln, of the senate, and Messrs. William E. Hubbard,
of Woonsocket, Frederick A. Pratt, of Newport, Arlon
Mowry, of North Smithfield, Earl C. Potter, ot Barrington, and Nathan B. Lewis, of Exeter, of the house
of representatives, to consider and report on the expediency and necessity of such legislation as shall establish a new county or judicial district in the northern part of the state, making Woonsocket the shire
town.

---

No. 21.     RESOLUTION to continue Special Committee appointed
to inquire relative to establishing a county or judicial district in the northern part of the State.

*Resolved,* That the special committee relative to a
new county or judicial district in the northern part of
the state, appointed at the present session, are hereby
continued and authorized to report to the next May
session of the general assembly.

RESOLUTION to appoint a Committee to transfer seals, No. 22.
books and papers and other property of the Court
of Common Pleas, of the County of Washington.

*Resolved,* (The house of representatives concurring
herein,) That J. Alonzo Babcock, of Westerly, be and
he is hereby appointed a committee to transfer the
seals, books and papers and other property of the
court of common pleas of the county of Washington,
from J. Henry Wells, former clerk of said court, to
Benjamin W. Case, newly elected clerk of said court,
said Babcock taking and giving receipts therefor.

---

RESOLUTION continuing use of State's Armory, in East No. 23.
Greenwich, to Kent Cornet Band.

*Resolved,* That the use of the state's armory, in
East Greenwich, for two evenings in each week, be
and hereby is continued to the Kent Cornet Band,
the same to be so used as not to interfere with the
proper use of the armory by the Kentish Guards for
military purposes, till the first day of June, 1877, and
no longer.

---

RESOLUTION granting the use of the Grand Jury room No. 24.
in the Court House at East Greenwich, to the Kent
Cornet Band.

*Resolved,* The senate concurring herein, that the
sheriff of the county of Kent, be and he hereby is
authorized in his discretion to give to the Kent Cornet
Band the use of the grand jury room in the court
house at East Greenwich, for the purpose of practising therein, when said room is not otherwise in use.

---

RESOLUTION in regard to the use of State property. No. 25.

*Resolved,* That in any case in which the use of the
state's property has been or shall hereafter be, granted

to any society, organization or company, the said property shall be and remain, as to the proper use thereof, under the control of the lawful custodian thereof.

---

No. 26. JOINT RESOLUTION relative to an exhibition by the Deaf and Dumb.

*Resolved,* That the superintendent of the American asylum for the deaf and dumb, at Hartford, be invited to give an exhibition, by his pupils before the members of the general assembly, on Wednesday the fourteenth day of February, instant, at 12 o'clock, M., and that the use of the hall of the house of representatives be given for that purpose.

---

No. 27. RESOLUTION relative to an exhibition by pupils from the Perkins Institution for the Blind at South Boston.

*Resolved,* That the superintendent of the Perkins institution for the blind at South Boston, be invited to give an exhibition by his pupils before the members of the general assembly, on Tuesday, March 6, 1877, at 12 o'clock M., and that the use of the hall of the house of representatives be given for that purpose.

---

No. 28. RESOLUTION authorizing the appointment of certain deaf semi-mutes as State Beneficiaries.

*Resolved,* That the governor is authorized to appoint for a term not exceeding one year, such indigent deaf semi-mutes being inhabitants of this state as he shall deem proper as state beneficiaries, to receive instruction at their homes or at some suitable place in the city of Providence, for the more special purpose of training in spoken language ; provided the expense for each person shall not exceed the sum of one hundred and fifty dollars, and the governor is authorized to draw on the general treasurer from time to time for the purpose aforesaid, his drafts therefor, provided however, that the sum authorized to be expended under the provisions of this resolution shall not exceed the sum of seven hundred and fifty dollars.

---

RESOLUTION authorizing the continuance of Henry A. Herrick, a State Beneficiary at the Perkins Institution for the Blind at South Boston.                    No. 29.

*Resolved*, That the governor is authorized in his discretion to continue Henry A. Herrick as a state beneficiary at the Perkins institution for the blind at South Boston, and he is hereby authorized to draw upon the general treasurer for the expense thereof, not to exceed the amount allowed by sec. 2, chapter 1 of the General Statutes, for blind beneficiaries of the state.

---

RESOLUTION relative to moneys received by the Board of State Charities and Corrections.                    No. 30.

*Resolved*, That the board of state charities and corrections shall cause to be paid into the state treasury, as provided in section 14, chapter 25 of the General Statutes, all moneys received by them for board of inmates, labor and materials, and from all other sources; which sums, so paid into the treasury, shall be added to the appropriation already made or to be made for the use of said board for the fiscal year ending April 30, 1878.

---

RESOLUTION making an appropriation for the State Farm for the fiscal year ending April 30, 1878.                    No. 31.

*Resolved*, That the sum of sixty-four thousand dollars, be and the same is hereby appropriated for the use of the board of state charities and corrections for the fiscal year ending April 30, 1878, for the state farm, and the state auditor is hereby authorized to draw his orders on the general treasurer for such portions thereof as may be required from time to time, upon the receipt by him of properly authenticated vouchers ; provided, however that no part of this sum shall be used for the erection of a school house or building for children.

---

No. 82.

RESOLUTION to settle claims of Job Wilbur against the State.

*Resolved*, That the board of state charities and corrections be and they hereby are directed to proceed and without unnecessary delay to erect so much of the stone wall as has not been built between land of Job Wilbur, and the highway in Cranston, and to reset the wall on the north side of the said highway as agreed with the said Wilbur and to fulfill the contract of the state with the said Wilbur in all respects in reference to said walls, and that the sum of four hundred dollars be and the same is hereby ordered to be paid to the said Job Wilbur, from the general treasury upon the order of the state auditor, provided that upon the receipt thereof the said Job Wilbur shall execute a release to the state of all claims and demands which he may have against the state for or on account of any non-fulfillment of the agreement of the state to erect said walls according to its contract.

---

No. 83.

RESOLUTION making an appropriation for educational purposes.

*Resolved*, That the sum of three hundred dollars be, and the same is hereby appropriated to the use of the board of education for the purpose of providing lectures and addresses in the different parts of the state, of distributing documents relating to public education and otherwise promoting the interests of education ;

and the governor is hereby authorized to draw his
order on the general treasurer in favor of the board of
education for the said sum of three hundred dollars as
the same may be required.

---

RESOLUTION making an appropriation for the support No. 34.
and maintenance of evening schools.

*Resolved*, That the sum of twenty-five hundred
llars be and the same is hereby appropriated for
e support of evening schools, to be expended under
e direction of the state board of education, provided
wever that no portion of this appropriation shall be
for any other purpose than the division of the
ey to the towns entitled to receive the same in
manner as the said board may see fit, and the
auditor is hereby authorized to draw his orders
uch portion thereof as may be required from time
ne upon the receipt by him of properly authenti-
vouchers.

LUTION appropriating ten thousand dollars for the No. 35.
new State Prison.

*Resolved*, That the sum of ten thousand dollars be
d the same is hereby appropriated for the new state
n, out of any money in the treasury not other-
e appropriated, and the state auditor is hereby
horized to draw his orders for such portion thereof
may be required from time to time, upon the re-
pt by him of properly authenticated vouchers, said
ropriation being in lieu of appropriation for same
mount included in appropriation bill passed the
house of representatives on the 7th day of February,
1877.

17

RESOLUTION making an appropriation for the State Prison Commission.

*Resolved*, That the sum of one hundred and twenty thousand dollars, be and the same is hereby appropriated for the use of the " commission for the purpose of building a new prison for the state," in carrying out the purposes of their appointment, and for completing the erection of said prison, kitchens, mess-rooms, hospital, keeper's house and officers' quarters, and for heating and furnishing same, and the state auditor is hereby authorized to draw his orders on the general treasurer for such portions thereof as may be required from time to time, upon the receipt by him of properly authenticated vouchers.

RESOLUTION for the purchase and distribution of 200 copies of Clapp's Index to the Opinions of the Supreme Court of this State.

*Resolved*, That the sum of four hundred and fifty dollars is hereby appropriated for the purchase of two hundred copies of William H. Clapp's Index to the decisions and opinions of the supreme court of this state, and that the state auditor is directed to draw his order on the general treasurer for said sum in favor of N. Bangs Williams, the publisher of said Index, upon the certificate of the secretary of state of the delivery to him of said two hundred copies.

*Resolved*, That the secretary of state is directed to distribute one copy of said Index to each justice of the supreme court, one copy to the state libraries of each of the states and territories; one copy to the secretary of state of the United States, one copy to the United States district judge for the district of Rhode Island; three copies to the state law library. He shall also distribute to be by them transmitted to their successors in office, one copy of said Index to each clerk of the supreme court and court of common pleas, to the attorney general, and the assistant attorney general,

the secretary of state, the reporter of the decisions of the supreme court, the commissioner of
public schools, to each town clerk, to the justice
courts of Newport, Providence, Pawtucket and Woonsocket, to the clerks of the senate and house of representatives, to each trial justice, and the residue he shall
retain in his office for sale at the cost price thereof,
except that the governor is authorized to transmit
copies of the same, as provided in section 9, of chapter
19 of the General Statutes.

RESOLUTION to appropriate $400,00 for the purpose of No. 38.
aiding in the distribution of the History of the 1st
R. I. Cavalry throughout the State.

*Resolved*, That the secretary of state be and hereby is instructed to purchase a sufficient number of
copies of Denison's history of the Rhode Island cavalry volunteers, to furnish each and every public
library in the state with one copy ; also to distribute
other copies as directed in section 5, chapter 19 of
the General Statutes ; and he is hereby authorized to
draw upon the state treasurer for an amount not to
exceed four hundred dollars, out of any money not
otherwise appropriated, said sum of four hundred dollars to be in full payment for said history.

RESOLUTION relative to the binding and repairing of No. 39.
books in the State Law Library.

*Resolved*, That the sum of not over one hundred and
fifty dollars be and the same is hereby appropriated
out of the general treasury to be expended under the
direction of the justices of the supreme court in binding and repairing such volumes in the state law library
as may need binding or repairing ; and that the
further sum of one hundred dollars be appropriated to
be expended in the same manner in supplying deficiencies in said library.

No. 40.    RESOLUTION making an additional appropriation for
repairs on the Soldiers' Cemetery on Dutch Island.

*Resolved,* That the sum of one hundred and fifty
dollars, or so much thereof as may be necessary, is her
by added to the appropriation for repairs on th
soldiers' cemetery on Dutch Island for the purpose o
completing the necessary repairs on the grounds of sai
cemetery, for grading and re-todding the same, fo
making a suitable gate to the enclosure and for la
quering the fence ; to be expended under directio
of the committee appointed by resolution No. 16, Ma
session, 1876 ; and that so much of said sum as sh
be unexpended shall remain a fund to be expende
under direction of the secretary of state or such oth
officer as the governor for the time being may desi
nate, to cause said fence to be annually lacquered, an
if need be, the grass to be cut.

---

No. 41.    RESOLUTION making an appropriation for the compl
tion of the new Providence county Court House, an
furnishing the same.

*Resolved,* That the following sums be and the
are hereby appropriated for the use of the commissio
ers of the new Providence county court house, viz :
For the completion of the court house, forty-fi
thousand dollars.
For furniture and fixtures, twenty-seven thousai
five hundred dollars ; and the governor is directed
draw his order on the general treasurer for such p
tions of said sums as may, from time to time, be nee
ed by said commissioners for the purposes herein men
tioned.

---

No. 42.    RESOLUTION upon the petition of Charles T. Northup,
late State Constable, for relief in certain liquor
cases.

*Resolved,* That the prayer of said petition be and
the same is hereby granted ; and the state auditor is
hereby directed to draw his order on the general treas-

urer for the sum of thirteen hundred and fifty-six 40-100 dollars, in full satisfaction of a judgment obtained against said Northup, and for costs and expenses incurred by him in defending said suits, the same being in full for all demands against the state.

---

RESOLUTION appropriating money for the purchase of No. 43. a bust of the late chief Justice Staples.

*Resolved,* That the sum of one hundred dollars be and the same is hereby appropriated for the purchase of a bust of the late chief justice William R. Staples, said bust to be placed in the supreme court room of the new Providence county court house, when completed, and the state auditor is hereby authorized to draw his order on the general treasurer for said sum in favor of C. H. Hemenway.

---

RESOLUTION to pay William M. Goldthwait $500, on ac- No. 44. count of reward offered for apprehension of the murderer of Catherine E. J. Weaver.

*Resolved,* That the state auditor be directed to draw his order on the general treasurer to the amount of five hundred dollars to be paid out of any money unappropriated in the treasury to William M. Goldthwait, in full for all claims against the state for giving the information that led to the arrest and conviction, and the apprehension of Merchant H. Weeden, for the murder of Catherine E. J. Weaver.

---

RESOLUTION upon the petition of Edmonds E. Anth- No. 45. ony and George Anthony, devisees under the last will and testament of James Chace, late of Middletown, deceased, for leave to sell real estate.

*Resolved,* That the prayer of said petition be and hereby is granted, and that said petitioners be and hereby are authorized and empowered to sell by

public or private sale, together or in parcels, that
tract of land containing about sixty acres, more or
less, situated in Portsmouth in this state, bounded
northerly on lands of Thomas G. Hazard and of Gould
Anthony, easterly on lands of William M. Rogers and
of                    Murphy, southerly on the highway,
sometimes called Bramans lane, and westerly on lands
of Peleg Albro and of John Lawton, with the buildings and improvements thereon, and to convey the
same to the purchaser or purchasers thereof in fee simple ; provided that every such sale be made under the
advice and direction of the court of probate of said
Middletown, and that all proceeds of sale be paid to
the Rhode Island Hospital Trust Company, to be held
by said company in trust so that the same shall take
the place of said farm under said will in all respects ;
that is to say, to pay the income of said proceeds to
and for the use of said petitioners respectively for
their respective lives, and upon their decease respectively to pay the principal funds absolutely to the persons entitled to the reversion of said farm in fee under
said will, in the same shares and proportions in which
such persons would have taken said reversion if said
farm had not been sold, provided further that the
petitioners give bond to said probate court, with sureties satisfactory to said court conditioned for the faithful payment of said proceeds to said Rhode Island
Hospital Trust Company for the uses and trusts aforesaid.

---

No. 46.    RESOLUTION upon the petition of Mary O. Richmond,
S. Dana Greene, S. Dana Greene, guardian of the
persons and estates of his three minor children, viz.:
S. Dana Greene, Jr., Mary R. Greene, and George D.
B. Greene ; and Charles H. Norris and Anna A.
Norris his wife, and A. A. Bradford, for leave to
sell real estate.

*Resolved*, That the prayer of the said petition be
and the same is hereby granted, and that the said petitioners be and they hereby are authorized and empower-

ed to sell the one undivided third part of the estate
situate in Bristol, and bounded easterly on High street,
on which it measures about two hundred and ninety-
seven feet, southerly on land of Lemuel C. Richmond,
on which it measures about eighty-six feet, westerly,
partly on land of A. O. Bourn, trustee, and partly on
land of Charles F. Herreshoff and wife, on which it
measures about two hundred and ninety-eight feet,
northerly on land of devisees of Francis L. Waldron,
deceased, on which it measures about eighty-eight feet,
th all the buildings thereon and appurtenances
ereto, and to convey the same to the purchaser therein *fee simple* ; *provided*, however, that the said sale
made under the advice and direction of the court of
bate of the said town of Bristol, and that the pro-
s of the said sale be paid over to the Rhode
nd Hospital Trust Company to be held by said com-
y upon the trusts and for the uses under which
said one undivided third of said estate was held
the said petitioners, that is to say, to pay the in-
e of the proceeds from said sale during her life to
l for the use of said Mary O. Richmond ; and upon
decease to hold said proceeds upon the same trusts
l for the same uses as the said undivided third of
l estate is held under the last will and testament of
y Willis Greene, that is to say, to pay the income
the said proceeds during his life to and for the use
S. Dana Greene, and at his decease to pay the said
ncipal fund to the persons entitled to the same under
will aforesaid in the shares and proportions in which
d persons would have been entitled to the said one
divided third of said estate had the same not been
d ; and provided further that the said S. Dana
ne give bond to said court of probate of Bristol
th satisfactory sureties to pay over to the said Rhode
nd Hospital Trust Company the proceeds of the
e of said estate, to be by said company held for the
and purposes aforesaid.

No. 47.

RESOLUTION upon the petition of Warren J. Crosby, of Drownville, in the town of Barrington, for leave to build a wharf.

*Voted and Resolved,* That the prayer of the petition be and the same is hereby granted, and that the said Warren J. Crosby be and he hereby is authorized and empowered to erect a wharf into the waters of Narragansett bay from his land at Drownville, in the town of Barrington, not exceeding thirty feet in width and two hundred and fifty feet in length ; provided that the said wharf be located at a place, to be approved by the harbor commissioners and that the same be erected under and according to their directions.

No. 48.

RESOLUTION upon the petition of Buel Buckingham, of Barrington, for leave to build a wharf.

*Voted and Resolved,* The honorable senate concurring, that the prayer of the petition be and the same is hereby granted, and that the said Buel Buckingham be and he is hereby authorized and empowered to erect a wharf from his own land into the waters of Narragansett bay, at Drownville, in said town of Barrington, not exceeding twenty-five feet in width and two hundred and fifty feet in length ; provided that the said wharf be located at a place to be approved by and be erected under the direction of the harbor commissioners.

No. 49.

RESOLUTION upon the petition of James Lawless, for leave to build a wharf at Bristol.

*Voted and Resolved,* That the prayer of said petition be, and the same is hereby granted and that the said petitioner be and he is hereby authorized and empowered to build or cause to be built a wharf not more than two hundred and fifty feet long and forty feet wide, extending from the shore land of the said 'tioner known as " Fort Rounds," in said Bristol, the waters of Bristol harbor ; provided the same constructed under the direction and in a manner to approved by the board of harbor commissioners.

No. 50. LUTION to print report of Commissioners of Inland sheries.

*ved*, That five hundred copies of the report of )mmissioners of inland fisheries, presented at the nt session of the general assembly, in addition to usual number for the schedules, are ordered printed the use of the general assembly and the commis-ers.

For report, see Appendix, document No. 18.]

No. 51. LUTION upon the petition of Patrick J. Carty, and Ann M. Carty his wife (both of the city and county of Providence, and state of Rhode Island, residing at No. 60 Seymour street, in said city,) for change of names to Patrick J. McCarthy and Ann M. McCarthy.

*Resolved*, That the prayer of said petitioners be and same is hereby granted, and that the name of said Patrick J. Carty be and the same is hereby ged to that of Patrick J. McCarthy and that the e of the said Ann M. Carty be and the same is by changed to that of Ann M. McCarthy, and that he latter names they be respectively entitled to the rights and privileges, and subject to all the es and liabilities they would have been subject to, their names not been changed.

No. 52. LUTION to change the name of Abby Ann Mun-roe to Abby Ann Greene.

WHEREAS, by resolution of the general assembly passed April 16, 1872, to change the name of Abby

18

Ann Munroe, of Providence, it was voted and resolved
that the name of the said Abby Ann Munroe be
changed to the name of Mary Ann Greene, whereas
the said name should have been changed to Abby Ann
Greene—

Now therefore it is

*Voted and Resolved,* That the name of the said
Abby Ann Munroe be and the same hereby is changed
to Abby Ann Greene, and that by the latter name she
be entitled to all the rights and privileges and be subjected to all the duties and liabilities to which she
would have been entitled or subjected, had her name
not been changed, and that this vote shall take effect
from and after said 16th day of April, A. D. 1872.

---

No. 53.

RESOLUTION upon petition of Fredrica W. Bouvard to
change her name to Fredrica W. Worch.

*Resolved,* That the prayer of the said petition be
and the same is hereby granted ; and that the name of
the said Fredrica W. Bouvard be and hereby is
changed to Frederica W. Worch, and that by the latter name she be entitled to all the rights and privileges and be subjected to all the duties and liabilities
to which she would have been subjected had her name
not been changed.

---

No. 54.

RESOLUTION upon the petition of John McGuinness for
change of name to John Patrick McGuinness.

*Resolved,* That the prayer of said petition be and
the same is hereby granted, and that the name of the
said John McGuinness be and the same is hereby
changed to that of John Patrick McGuinness, and that
by the latter name he be entitled to all the rights,
and subjected to all the duties and liabilities he would
have been entitled and subject to had his name not
been changed.

RESOLUTION upon the petition of Edward Kearins of No. 55. the city and county of Providence, for confirmation and change of name.

*Voted and Resolved,* That the prayer of the said person be and the same is hereby granted, and that the of the name of the said Edward Kearins from ck Kearins is hereby ratified and confirmed, and the said Edward Kearins shall be hereafter known called by the name of Edward Patrick Kearins, that the title to all estate, real or personal, acquired him in the name of Edward Kearins is hereby conned to him and he shall by the latter name be ended to all of the rights and privileges and be subto all the duties and liabilities to which he d have been entitled or subject had not his name changed.

---

RESOLUTION upon the petition of David Fitts for No. 56. change of name to David B. Fitts.

*Resolved,* That the prayer of said petition be and same is hereby granted, and that the name of the David Fitts be and the same is hereby changed to of David B. Fitts, and that by the latter name he entitled to all the rights and subjected to all duties liabilities he would have been entitled and subto, had his name not been changed.

RESOLUTION upon the petition of Abel Slocum, of No. 57. Warwick, praying for release of recognizance defaulted in the court of common pleas for the county of Providence for the appearance in court of Albert A. Slocum.

*Voted and resolved,* That the prayer of the said petiof the said Abel Slocum be and the same is hereby ted, and that the said Abel Slocum hereby is refrom the said recognizances, and that the attorgeneral be and he hereby is directed to disconue the actions brought upon the said recognizances.

RESOLUTION upon the petition of Ellen Cunningham, of Burrillville, for remission of fine and liberation from jail.

[Passed March 23, 1877.]

*Resolved*, That the prayer of said petition be and the same is hereby granted, and that the fine of one hundred dollars, and costs amounting to eighty dollars, upon which the said Ellen Cunningham is now in jail in the county of Providence, be, and the same is hereby remitted, and that the keeper of the said Providence county jail be, and he hereby is authorized and directed to release the said Ellen Cunningham from her said imprisonment.

---

RESOLUTION upon petition of Henry C. Cook, of Providence, for leave to take the poor debtor's oath.

[Passed March 28, 1877.]

*Voted and Resolved*, That the prayer of said petition be and the same is hereby granted, and that the said Henry C. Cook be, and he is hereby authorized to have issued a citation to his committing creditor upon the writ of return and restoration against him in replevin, and to have the same served upon such creditor in the same way as if the said Cook was committed upon execution upon a simple contract debt, and upon the return of such citation before any justice authorized to administer the poor debtor's oath, under the provisions of chapter 215 of the General Statutes, if it shall be made to appear to the satisfaction of the said justice that the said Cook has no estate, real or personal, wherewith to support himself in jail, or to pay prison charges, said justice shall admit the said Cook to take the poor debtor's oath upon the like conditions and with the like effect, in all respects, including his discharge from jail, as if he were committed on simple contract debt.

RESOLUTION upon the petition of the Inspectors of the No. 60.
State Prison, praying for a pardon and release from
imprisonment in the State Prison of Shubael Baker.

*Voted and Resolved*, That the senate do hereby advise and consent to the granting of the prayer of
the petition for the pardon of the said Shubael
Baker, as recommended by his excellency the
governor, and that the warden of the state prison be
directed to release said Shubael Baker from his said
imprisonment, to take effect on the first day of May,
1877.

RESOLUTION upon the petition of the Inspectors of the No. 61.
State Prison, praying for a pardon and release from
imprisonment in the State Prison of William T.
Hackett.

[Passed March 21, 1877.]

*Voted and Resolved*, That the senate do hereby advise
and consent to the granting of the prayer of said petition for the pardon of the said William T. Hackett,
as recommended by his excellency the governor, and
that the warden of the state prison be directed to release said William T. Hackett from his said imprisonment, to take effect immediately.

RESOLUTION upon the petition of William W. Potter, No. 62.
praying for reasons therein stated, to be restored to
his privileges.

[Passed February 20, 1877.]

*Voted and Resolved*, That the prayer of said petition be, and the same is hereby granted, and the said
William W. Potter is hereby restored to all his civil
rights and privileges, including the right of voting, if
otherwise qualified, and shall hereafter be entitled to
have and enjoy the same in like manner as if he had
never been deprived thereof.

No. 63.

RESOLUTION upon the petition of William Webb, for restoration of the right to vote.

[Passed February 28, 1877.]

*Resolved*, That the prayer of said petition be, and the same hereby is granted, and said William Webb is hereby expressly restored to the right to vote, if otherwise qualified.

---

No. 64.

RESOLUTION upon the petition of George W. Allen for restoration of the right to vote.

[Passed March 27, 1877.]

*Resolved*, That the prayer of said petition be, and the same is hereby granted, and said George W. Allen is hereby expressly restored to the right to vote, if otherwise qualified.

---

No. 65.

RESOLUTION to pay the bill of William Binney and others, Special Commissioners on the City Savings Bank.

*Resolved*, That the bill of William Binney, Royal C. Taft, and Alex. Farnum against the state, for services in examining into the condition of the City Savings Bank, by authority of a special commission issued by his excellency the governor, amounting to five hundred dollars, be, and the same is hereby allowed and ordered to be paid ; and the state auditor is directed to give his order on the general treasurer for the same, to be paid out of any money unappropriated in the treasury, and the general treasurer is hereby directed to collect the amount so paid from the above named City Savings Bank.

RESOLUTION to pay witnesses before Committee on No. 66. Fisheries.

*Resolved,* That the state auditor be, and is hereby instructed to draw his order in favor of the following named persons for the amounts placed opposite their several names, they having attended as witnesses before the committee on fisheries at the present session : Geo. Case, $2 10 ; John Case, $2 10 ; Anthony Case, $2 00 ; Charles Chickering, $2 00 ; Thomas Cameron, $2 10 ; John Mew, $2 10 ; Smith Shaw, $2 10 ; John Flagg, $2 10 ; John Miller, $2 20; J. E. Johnson, $2 00 ; Joseph Harris, $1 60 ; Geo Doane, $1 60 ; John W. Vars, $1 60 ; Richard Newcomb, $1 60 ; Buel Buckingham, $1 60 ; Frederick N. Goff, deputy sheriff, serving summons $3 40 ; L. Upham, deputy sheriff, serving summons, 30 cents.

---

RESOLUTIONS for the payment of sundry accounts against the State.

*Resolved,* That the following accounts against the state be, and the same are, hereby allowed and ordered to be paid ; and the state auditor is directed to draw his order on the general treasurer for the said several amounts out of any money unappropriated in the treasury :

| | | |
|---|---:|---|
| Angell, Burlingame & Co., for state printing for the senate............... | $82 33 | No. 67. |
| Angell, Burlingame & Co., for state printing for the house of representatives.. | 41 55 | |
| Angell, Burlingame & Co., for plats of the house...................... | 25 00 | No. 68. |
| Angell, Burlingame & Co., for printing for general assembly.................. | 172 55 | No. 69. |
| Angell, Burlingame & Co., for same...... | 42 03 | No. 70. |
| Lycurgus Sayles, for services as assistant attorney general................. | 100 00 | No. 71. |
| William Knowles, coroner, for services in justice court, city of Providence...... | 15 00 | |
| Tillinghast & Mason News Co., for newspapers furnished general assembly... | 668 50 | |

Tillinghast & Mason News Co., for stationery for use of the senate........    110 50
Tillinghast & Mason News Co., for stationery for use of the house of representatives.....................    299 11

No. 72.  Christopher Holden, sheriff of Providence county, for warning members of the general assembly, from Providence county, to attend special session, Dec. 1, 1876. ....................    87 20

No. 73.  Thomas J. Tilley, sheriff of Kent county, for serving warrants, convening legislature at special session............    4 30
Charles E. Potter, dep. sheriff, Kent county for same........................    5 05
Charles N. Martin, dep. sheriff, Kent county, for same....................    7 95
Lowell Pitcher, dep. sheriff, Kent county, for same........................    4 50
Charles A. Greene, sheriff of Bristol county, for same.........  .............    8 25

No. 74.  Henry Whipple, sheriff of Washington county, for warning members of the general assembly from Washington county, for special session.........    30 45

No. 75.  George Manchester, sheriff of Newport county, for warning members of the general assembly, for special session...    29 65

No. 76.  George Manchester, sheriff of Newport county, for service of sundry writs and for traveling fees.... ........    7 25

No 77.  Charles W. Wilcox, jailer of Washington county jail, for board &c. of sundry prisoners......................    30 82

No. 78.  J. Aborn Gardiner, for service of *scire facias* writs.....................    130 50

No. 79.  Henry Barnard, for the American Journal of Education and other books ......    149 50

No. 80.  Thomas A. Jenckes, for legal services....    1,250 00

No. 81.  Harrison H. Richardson, for attendance at a meeting of the joint committee on printing during the recess of the general assembly..................    5 00

William H. Angell, for the same.........        5  00
John Warner, for the same..............        5  00
Frederick A. Pratt, for the same.........        5  00
George H. Pettis, for the same..........        5  00
Wm. E. Gilmore, for the same...........        5  00
Alvord O. Miles, for the same...........        5  00
John A. Wood, for the same,...........        5  00
Samuel H. Cross, for traveling expenses as       No. 82.
  member of the state board of education
  for year ending March 7th, 1877.....       14  60
Charles H. Fisher, for the same,.........      10  00
omas H. Clarke, for the same..........      10  15
eo. L. Locke, for the same.............        5  00
ira K. Parker, for the same............      10  40
eleg Brown, for fees in criminal cases be-       No. 83.
  fore the justice courts in Warwick and
  West Greenwich...................      30  50
L. Freeman & Co., for printing plans             No. 84.
  for senate chamber...............      15  00
ha C. Clarke, for services as committee          No. 85.
  on repairs of the Washington county
  court house.....................     175  00
hn G. Perry, for services as committee on        No. 86.
  repairs of the Washington county
  court house.....................     175  00
erick A. Pratt, for services on state            No. 87.
  house and jail at Newport, and
  soldiers' cemetery at Dutch Island...      82  50
oulton & Ingraham, for labor and                 No. 88.
  materials at laying of corner-stone of
  Prov. county court house...........      64  55
S. Read and C. S. Richards, for extra            No. 89.
  work and expenses incurred in conse-
  quence of laying corner-stone of Prov.
  county court house...............      70  00
.Benjamin Greene, for visits and medi-           No. 90.
  cine &c. to R. L. Casey............      50  00
19

RESOLUTIONS authorizing disabled soldiers and citizens
to peddle without cost for license.

*Resolved*, That the general treasurer be and he
hereby directed to issue to the following disabled sol
diers:

| | |
|---|---|
| No. 91. | George W. Burrows, |
| No. 92. | Jeremiah Cassidy, |
| No. 93. | Robert Charnley, |
| No. 94. | Frank P. Chase, |
| No. 95. | Caleb W. Colvin, |
| No. 96. | James Craig, |
| No. 97. | William Diamond, |
| No. 98. | Daniel Falvey, |
| No. 99. | Richard Hayden, |
| No. 100. | David Hollingworth, |
| No. 101. | Daniel Kelly, |
| No. 102. | John Kendall, |
| No. 103. | James Langley, |
| No. 104. | James McCann, |
| No. 105. | Henry C. Newell, |
| No. 106. | Lafayette G. Nicholas, |
| No. 107. | Patrick Oates, |
| No. 108. | Elisha O. Sherman, |
| No. 109. | George L. Vibbert, |
| No. 110. | Owen Walsh, |
| No. 111. | William Wardell, |

licenses to personally peddle any merchandise, exce
watches, jewelry, gold, silver, and German silver w
for the term of one year, without cost to the said
sons, and that said licenses be not transferable.

No. 112.　RESOLUTION suspending Joint Rule No. 9.

[Passed March 30, 1877.]

*Resolved*, (If the honorable senate concur,) Tha
joint rule No. 9 be suspended so far that all publi
laws passed Friday, March 30, A. D., 1877, shall be

engrossed after the passage thereof, and the secretary
of state is hereby authorized to certify the same and
place them on file in his office.

---

RESOLUTION of thanks to His Excellency Henry Lip-   No. 113.
pitt.

[In Senate, Passed March 30, 1877.]

*Resolved,* That the thanks of this senate be, and
they are hereby tendered to his excellency Henry Lippitt, for the able and impartial manner in which he
has presided over the deliberations of this senate during the past year.

---

RESOLUTION of thanks to the Lieutenant–Governor.   No. 114.

[In Senate, Passed March 30, 1877.]

*Resolved,* That the thanks of this senate be and
they are hereby tendered to his honor Henry T. Sis-
on, for the able manner in which he has discharged
the duties of lieutenant-governor the past year, and
for his uniform courtesy to us, as senators.

---

RESOLUTION of thanks to Hon. Nelson W. Aldrich,   No. 115.
Speaker of the House of Representatives.

[In House of Representatives, Passed March 30, 1877.]

*Resolved,* That the thanks of this house be and they
hereby are tendered to the speaker, the Hon. Nelson
W. Aldrich, for the able and impartial manner in
which he has presided over this body, and for the
courtesy and affability which have distinguished his
intercourse with the members of the house.

No. 116. RESOLUTION to pay officers and attendants of the
General Assembly at the special session, December
1, 1876, and January session, A. D. 1877.

*Resolved,* That the following sums be paid to the
following persons, officers and attendants of the
general assembly at the special session, December 1,
A. D. 1876, and the January session, A. D. 1877 :

| | |
|---|---:|
| Nathaniel P. S. Thomas | $395 00 |
| Charles F. Ballou | 395 00 |
| Henry T. Braman | 395 00 |
| Nathan F. Dixon, Jr | 395 00 |
| Christopher Holden | 237 00 |
| J. Aborn Gardiner | 158 00 |
| Lyman Upham | 158 00 |
| Frederick N. Goff | 158 00 |
| Phineas Fairbrother | 158 00 |
| S. Arnold Aplin, Jr | 152 00 |
| Hollis D. Holden | 152 00 |
| Salmon W. Davis | 154 00 |
| Sullivan Ballou | 154 00 |
| Edwin B. Kingsbury | 154 00 |
| Otto Munroe | 152 00 |
| Burnett Rider | 2 00 |
| Clarence Kingsbury | 2 00 |

and the state auditor is directed to draw his order on
the general treasurer for the said several amounts out
of any money unappropriated in the treasury.

---

RESOLUTIONS of adjournment.

The general assembly by concurrent vote adjourned:
No. 117.   From Wednesday, February 21, to Tuesday, February 27 ;
No. 118.   From Tuesday, March 6, to Tuesday, March 13.

JOINT Resolution of adjournment. No. 119.

[Passed March 26, 1877.]

*Resolved,* The honorable senate concurring herein, that when this general assembly adjourns on Friday the 30th day of March, 1877, it adjourn to meet according to law.

---

RESOLUTION continuing all unfinished business to the No. 120. next May Session of the General Assembly.

[Passed March 30, 1877.]

*Resolved,* The honorable senate concurring herein, that all petitions and unfinished business pending before either house of this general assembly at the time of adjournment, are hereby continued to the next May Session of the general assembly.

---

SECRETARY OF STATE'S OFFICE,
Providence, Rhode Island.

I certify the acts, resolutions, record of officers elected, and reports contained in this volume to be true copies of the originals on file in this office.

IN TESTIMONY WHEREOF, I have hereto set my hand and affixed the seal of the state, this          day of
A. D.

# APPENDIX.

At the General Assembly of the State of Rhode Island and Providence Plantations, begun and holden by adjournment, at Providence, on the second Tuesday in January, (being the ninth day of the month,) in the year of our Lord one thousand eight hundred and seventy-seven, and of independence the one hundred and first.

### PRESENT.

His Excellency HENRY LIPPITT, Governor, and *ex-officio* President of the Senate.

His Honor HENRY T. SISSON, Lieut. Governor, and *ex-officio* senator.

### SENATORS FROM THE SEVERAL TOWNS.

| | |
|---|---|
| Newport, | JAMES M. DRAKE. |
| Providence, | BENJAMIN N. LAPHAM. |
| Portsmouth, | ALFRED SISSON. |
| Warwick, | JONATHAN BRAYTON. |
| Westerly, | SAMUEL H. CROSS. |
| New Shoreham, | RAY S. LITTLEFIELD. |
| North Kingstown, | JOHN REMINGTON. |
| South Kingstown, | WILLIAM G. CASWELL. |
| East Greenwich, | HENRY A. THOMAS. |
| Jamestown, | THOMAS CARR WATSON. |
| Smithfield, | SAMUEL W. FARNUM. |

| | |
|---|---|
| Scituate, - - | JEREMIAH H. FIELD. |
| Glocester, - - | ZIBA O. SLOCUM. |
| Charlestown, - | GEORGE C. JAMES. |
| West Greenwich, | JOHN T. LEWIS. |
| Coventry, - - | JOHN WARNER. |
| Exeter, - - | DANIEL L. MONEY. |
| Middletown, - | ROBERT S. CHASE. |
| Bristol, - - | AUGUSTUS O. BOURN. |
| Tiverton, - - | GIDEON H. DURFEE. |
| Little Compton, | NATHANIEL CHURCH. |
| Warren, - - | CHARLES H. HANDY. |
| Cumberland, - - | HENRY B. METCALF. |
| Richmond, - | DANIEL C. KENYON. |
| Cranston, - - | WILLIAM ELSBREE. |
| Hopkinton, - | OLIVER LANGWORTHY. |
| Johnston, - - | SAMUEL A. IRONS. |
| North Providence, | WILLIAM H. ANGELL. |
| Barrington, - | HARRISON H. RICHARDSON. |
| Foster, - - | JOSHUA PAINE. |
| Burrillville, - - | WILLIAM H. CLARKE. |
| East Providence, | OLIVER CHAFFEE. |
| Pawtucket, - - | WILLIAM F. SAYLES. |
| Woonsocket, - | NATHAN T. VERRY. |
| North Smithfield, | WILLIAM H. SEAGRAVE. |
| Lincoln, - - | JONATHAN CHACE. |

JOSHUA M. ADDEMAN,

Secretary of State, and *ex-officio* Secretary.

NATHANIEL P. S. THOMAS, Clerk.

---

## REPRESENTATIVES OF THE SEVERAL TOWNS.

| *Newport.* | *Providence.* |
|---|---|
| William P. Sheffield, | Allen Greene, |
| Henry H. Fay, | Henry W. Gardner, |
| Augustus P. Sherman, | Henry J. Spooner, |
| William C. Townsend, | James W. Blackwood, |
| Frederick A. Pratt. | Isaac M. Potter, |

Henry H. Ormsbee,
Gorham P. Pomroy,
Nelson W. Aldrich,
Harvey E. Wellman,
Edmund S. Hopkins,
George H. Pettis,
Joseph F. Brown.

*Portsmouth.*

Jonathan A. Sisson.

*Warwick.*

Christopher R. Greene,
Stephen W. Thornton,
John H. Collingwood,
J. Torrey Smith.

*Westerly.*

Nathan F. Dixon.
J. Alonzo Babcock.

*New Shoreham.*

Joshua T. Dodge,

*North Kingstown.*

Thomas C. Peirce.

*South Kingstown.*

John G. Clarke.

*East Greenwich.*

Thomas A. Pierce, Jr.

*Jamestown.*

Isaac B. Briggs.

*Smithfield.*

Andrew B. Whipple.

*Scituate.*

Benjamin Wilbur.

*Glocester.*

Raymond P. Colwell.

*Charlestown.*

Charles Cross.

*West Greenwich.*

John Tillinghast.

*Coventry.*

Thomas C. Peckham,
Dexter B. Potter.

*Exeter.*

Nathan B. Lewis.

*Middletown.*

Nathaniel Peckham.

*Bristol.*

William H. Spooner,
Samuel P. Colt.

*Tiverton.*

Holder N. Wilcox.

*Little Compton.*

Jediah Shaw.

*Warren.*

George Lewis Cooke.

*Cumberland.*

Dexter Clark,
James C. Dexter.

*Richmond.*

Reynolds C. Phillips.

*Cranston.*

Henry Whitman,
John Beattie.

*Hopkinton.*

Thomas H. Greene.

*Johnston.*

Alfred A. Williams,
George W. White.

*North Providence.*

Benjamin Sweet.

*Barrington.*

Earl C. Potter.

*Foster.*

Thomas E. Phillips.

*Burrillville.*

John A. Wood,
David Mathewson.

*East Providence.*

Alvord O. Miles.

*Pawtucket.*

Claudius B. Farnsworth,
William E. Gilmore,
Almon K. Goodwin,
Pardon E. Tillinghast,
Joseph E. Dispeau,
Oren S. Horton.

*Woonsocket.*
William E. Hubbard,
Nathaniel Elliott,
John A. Bennett,
Amos Sherman.
*North Smithfield.*
Arlon Mowry.

*Lincoln.*
Thomas Moies,
Alfred H. Littlefield,
Elisha S. Aldrich,
Edward L. Freeman.

NELSON W. ALDRICH, Speaker.

CHARLES F. BALLOU,
y T BRAMAN, } Clerks.

---

# PROCEEDINGS IN GRAND COMMITTEE.

---

TUESDAY, January 16, 1877.

The two houses met in grand committee for the se of counting the votes cast at the late election r representatives from this state to the 45th congress the United States, and for nominating candidates r state scholarships in Brown University, and the elec- n of notaries public and justices of the peace.

The ballots for candidates for representatives in gress cast at the election held on the 7th of Novem- last, were handed in by the secretary of state.

A committee, consisting of three from Providence unty and two from each of the other counties and e secretary and clerks of the two houses, was ap- inted to count the ballots and declare the result of d election.

The following candidates for state scholarships in Brown University were nominated, viz. :

*City of Providence.*—Friend P. Carpenter, Oliver
20

P. Clarke, Richard B. Esten, Zenas L. Leonard, Sidney
Putnam, Walter G. Webster.
*South Kingstown.*—George E. Perry.

NOTARIES PUBLIC, ELECTED.

*Providence County.*—Samuel P. Cook, Walter
Fieldhouse, Myron H. Fuller, John McCann, Clinton
R. Weeden.
*Washington County.*—Samuel W. K. Allen, Robert
Thompson.

JUSTICES OF THE PEACE, ELECTED.

*City of Providence.*—Byron H. Arnold, T. Paige
Dodge, Thomas Murphy, Addington D. Welch.
*North Kingstown*—Benjamin Baker.

The grand committee took a recess until Wednesday morning at 11 o'clock.

WEDNESDAY, January 17, 1877.

The grand committee re-assembled at 11 A. M.

The committee appointed to count the votes for
representatives in congress presented the following
report :

To the honorable the general assembly of the state
of Rhode Island, &c., at its January session A. D.
1877.

The committee appointed to count the votes for representatives in the forty-fifth congress, beg leave to
report as follows, viz :

In the FIRST DISTRICT, the whole number of electors
voting was 13,629 ; necessary for a choice 6815 ; that
8523 electors voted for BENJAMIN T. EAMES, of Providence ; that 5068 electors voted for EDWARD W.
BRUNSEN, of Bristol ; that 29 electors voted for BENJAMIN G. CHACE, of Providence ; and that 9 electors
voted scattering ; and that BENJAMIN T. EAMES is
elected by a majority of 3417 votes over all others.

In the SECOND DISTRICT, the whole number of electors
voting was 12,528 ; necessary for a choice 6265 ; that

7177 electors voted for LATIMER W. BALLOU, of Woonsocket; that 5303 electors voted for CHARLES H. PAGE,
of Scituate; that 25 electors voted for JOHN M. BAILEY,
of Woonsocket; and that 23 electors voted scattering; and that LATIMER W. BALLOU is elected by a
majority of 1826 votes over all others.

Your committee therefore recommend the passage of
the following resolutions:

*Resolved*, That BENJAMIN T. EAMES, of Providence,
be, and he is hereby declared to have been duly
elected a representative from the First Congressional
district of this State, in the forty-fifth congress of the
United States.

*Resolved*, That LATIMER W. BALLOU, of Woonsocket,
and he is hereby declared to have been duly
elected a representative from the Second Congressional
district of this State, in the forty-fifth congress of the
United States.

For the Committee,<br>
JAMES M. DRAKE,<br>
Chairman.

The foregoing report was received and the accompanying resolutions were adopted.

### NOTARIES PUBLIC, ELECTED.

*Providence County.*—Henry W. Hayes.
*Kent County.*—Benjamin C. Allen.

### JUSTICES OF THE PEACE, ELECTED

*City of Providence.*—Robert B. Chambers, Richard
Comstock, Robert Cook, Henry W. Hayes.
*Little Compton.*—Asa R. Howland.

TUESDAY, February 6, 1877.

Edmund S. Hopkins, of Providence, was elected
assistant attorney general, for one year from the nine-
th day of March next.

WEDNESDAY, February 14, 1877.

The two houses met in grand committee for the
purpose of electing notaries public and justices of

the peace, and nominating candidates for state scholarships in Brown University.

*Providence County.*—William H. Baker, Walter H. Barney, John A. Bennett, Edward R. Dawley, William F. Holland, James Moran, Richard B. Winsor.
*Newport County,* John D. Dennis, Jr.
*Washington County.*—Azel Noyes.

*City of Providence.*—James Moran, Richard B. Winsor.
*Coventry.*—George L. Card.
*Richmond.*—Nelson K. Church.

Prescott O. Clarke, of Providence, James Clay Starkweather, of Pawtucket, and Arthur B. Corthell, of Bristol, were nominated as candidates for state scholarships in Brown University.

THURSDAY, March 15, 1877.

The two houses met in grand committee for the purpose of electing a commissioner of sinking funds, and a clerk of the court of common pleas for the county of Washington, and for the nomination of candidates for state scholarships in Brown University.

Samuel S. Sprague, of Providence, was elected a commissioner of sinking funds for the term of two years from April 16th, 1877.

Benjamin W. Case, of South Kingstown, was elected clerk of the court of common pleas for Washington county, to fill vacancy caused by the resignation of J. Henry Wells.

Samuel R Simmons, and James D. Simmons, of Providence, were nominated as candidates for state scholarships in Brown University.

# REPORTS MADE TO THE GENERAL ASSEMBLY, AT ITS JANUARY SESSION, A. D. 1877.

Governor's message.

Eighth annual report of the board of state charities and corrections.

Seventh annual report of the board of education, and thirty-second annual report of the commissioner of public schools.

Semi-annual report of the railroad commissioner.

Annual report of the adjutant general.

Annual report of the quartermaster general.

Annual report of the inspectors of the state prison.

Annual statement of the condition of the banks and institutions for savings.

Seventh annual report of the commissioners of in-d fisheries.

Report of the inspector of the Hartford, Providence and Fishkill Railroad Company.

Seventh annual report of the state board of pharacy.

Twenty-third annual report upon the registration of irths, marriages and deaths, in the state.

Annual report of the commissioners of shell fish-eries.

Thirty-ninth annual report of the New York, Providence and Boston Railroad Company, of receipts and expenditures.

Semi-annual report of the general treasurer.

Semi-annual report of the state auditor.

Report of the pilot commissioners.

Report of the joint standing committee on printing.

Fourteenth annual report of the corporation of Brown University in reference to the United States land scrip grant for agricultural college.

Third annual report of the commissioners to build a new state prison.

Second report of the license commissioners in and for the city of Providence.

First annual report of the harbor commissioners.

Report of the women's board of visitors to the penal and correctional institutions of the state.

Report of special committee on the subject of a state industrial school.

Reports of house committee on education on the subject of the industrial arts in the public schools; also, on the proposition to reduce the number of the school committee in Providence and to change the mode of election.

Report of special committee on the subject of woman suffrage.

Report of the commissioners of sinking funds.

Report of the commissioner of public schools as to what means are used to inculcate principles of morality and virtue in the minds of the children in the public schools.

Report of committee on repairs of state house in Newport.

Report of committee on repairs of Washington County court house.

Report of special commission to examine the City Savings Bank.

Report of joint special committee in regard to verbatim reports of General Assembly proceedings.

Reports of committees on transfer of seals, books and papers in the clerks' offices of the supreme court and court of common pleas in the county of Kent, and in the clerk's office of the court of common pleas in the county of Washington.

---

## PETITIONS FOR ACTS OF INCORPORATION ETC., CONTINUED TO THE MAY SESSION WITH ORDER OF NOTICE.

---

Petition of James T. Downing and others, for An Act to incorporate the American Hardware and Butt Company.

Petition of Scott W. Mowry and others, for An Act

to incorporate the American Mutual Fire Insurance Company.

Petition of George F. Verry and others, for An Act to incorporate the Boston, Wrentham and Providence Railroad Company.

Petition of Edwin Darling and others, for An Act to incorporate the East Pawtucket Horse Railroad Company.

Petition of Thomas J. Hill and others, for charter for the Elizabeth Mill.

Petition of William S. Granger and others, for An Act to incorporate the Granger Foundry and Machine Company.

Petition of Benjamin F. Greene and others, for An Act to incorporate the Greene & Daniels Manufacturing Company.

Petition of Leonard M. Blodgett and others, for An Act to incorporate the Jackson Mill Company.

Petition of Stephen N. Mason and others, for An Act to incorporate the Mason Manufacturing Company.

Petition of Benjamin F. Thurston and others, for An Act to incorporate the Nayatt Brick Company.

Petition of George E. Waring Jr., and others, for An Act to incorporate the Ogden Farm Association.

Petition of the Pawtuxet Valley Railroad Company for amendment of Charter.

Petition of John G. Perry and others, for An Act to incorporate the Perry Harvester Company.

Petition of Truman A. Cunliff and others, for An Act to incorporate the Providence Stove Knob Company.

Petition of George A. Davis and others, for An Act to incorporate the Reversible Heel Company.

Petition of Augustus Hoppin and others, in relation to property of the Rhode Island Society of the Cincinnati.

Petition of Timothy Earle and others, for An Act to incorporate the Valley Falls Fire District.

Petition of Asa B. Waite and others, for An Act to amend Charter of the Fire Engine Company of Wickford in North Kingstown.

# MESSAGE

OF

# HENRY LIPPITT,

Governor of Rhode Island,

TO THE

# GENERAL ASSEMBLY,

AT ITS

## JANUARY SESSION, 1877.

PROVIDENCE:
ANGELL, BURLINGAME & CO., PRINTERS TO THE STATE.
1877.

# ANNUAL MESSAGE.

*To the Honorable General Assembly at its January Session, A. D. 1877:*

SENATORS AND REPRESENTATIVES :—In accordance with a custom which has prevailed for several years at the opening of the January Session of the Legislature, I have the honor to invite your attention to the general condition of the State, and to some of the objects which will probably call for legislative action :—

## THE STATE FINANCES.

| | |
|---|---:|
| Balance in Treasury, April 30, 1876 | $396,185 53 |
| Receipts from May 1, 1876, to November 30, 1876 | 259,396 55 |
| Total | $655,582 08 |
| Payments from May 1, 1876 to November 30, 1876 | 671,853 29 |
| Amount overdrawn at the R. I. Hospital Trust Co. Nov. 30, 1876. | $16,271 21 |
| Estimated Receipts from November 30, 1876 to April 30, 1877. | 550,000 00 |
| Estimated Expenses from November 30, 1876 to April 30, 1877 | 350,000 00 |
| Amount overdrawn November 30, 1876 | 16,271 21 |
| Total | $366,271 21 |
| Estimated balance on hand April 30, 1877 | $183,728 79 |
| Amount actually in the Treasury on the 4th of January, 1877, | $296,442 83 |
| The Bonded Debt of the State amounts to | $2,563,500 00 |
| From which may be deducted the amount paid to the Sinking Fund, $362.000.00 and accrued interest | $380,745 90 |
| Leaving the present indebtedness | $2,182,754 10 |

## STATEMENT OF SINKING FUNDS.

| | | |
|---|---|---|
| Received from the General Treasurer, June 1875 and 1876.... | | $362,000 00 |
| Interest received on Loan to January 1st, 1877,.... | $10,739.65 | |
| Interest on City Bonds, Gold...................... | 7,500.00 | |
| Premium on Gold............................... | 506.25 | |
| | | $18,745 90 |
| Total amount Sinking Fund..................... ..... | | $380,745 90 |

## INVESTMENTS.

| | |
|---|---|
| Bonds of the City of Providence, par value $300,000, costing | $324,000 00 |
| Bonds of the Town of Burrillville, par value $22,000, costing | 22,880 00 |
| Registered Bond, State of Rhode Island, par value, $5,000, costing........ .... ................................ | 5,400 00 |
| Registered Bonds, State of Rhode Island, par value $3000, costing................................. | 3,255 00 |
| Coupon Bonds, State of Rhode Island, par value $4000, costing | 4,372 00 |
| Registered Bonds, State of Rhode Island, par value $6000, costing  .................................. .. .... | 6,654 41 |
| Total.......... ..................................... | $366,561 41 |
| Balance on hand not invested............................. | $14,184 49 |

From these statements it will be observed that the large payments during the past year for the new Court House, the new State Prison, the State Farm, and the Sinking Fund, have drawn out the surplus previously existing in the Treasury, and reduced the funds to a low point. The requirements for these institutions will hardly be as large for the present year as during the past, and in their present incompleted state, it would not be a wise policy to cease work upon the buildings. If found necessary in order to continue the work during the Summer, it would be better to authorize temporary loans to a limited amount, which could be paid off from the regular income of the

State in a short time after their completion. The state of the Treasury, however, should compel a rigid economy in all appropriations for the present year.

### DEPARTMENT OF EDUCATION.

The following statistics, relative to our Public Schools, have been taken from the report of the Commissioner:—

Number of children, 5 to 15 years of age, Census, June, 1875........53,316

#### DAY SCHOOLS.

| | |
|---|---|
| Number of different pupils enrolled............................ | 39,328 |
| Average number belonging to the schools.................... | 30,516 |
| Average attendance......................................... | 27,021 |
| Number of schools (graded, 466 ; ungraded, 291)........... | 757 |
| Average length of schools................................... | 9 months. |
| Number of teachers regularly employed...................... | 861 |
| Amount paid male teachers.................................. | $97,138 33 |
| Average wages paid male teachers per month............... | $81 49 |
| Amount paid female teachers............................... | $310,425 37 |
| Average wages paid female teachers per month ............. | $46 73 |

#### EVENING SCHOOLS.

| | |
|---|---|
| Number of different pupils enrolled........................ | 3,179 |
| Average attendance ....................................... | 1,585 |
| Number of schools........................................ | 28 |
| Average length of schools................................. | 13 weeks. |

#### RECEIPTS.

| | |
|---|---|
| State appropriation for day and evening schools........... | $91,568 31 |
| Town appropriation for day and evening schools............ | 358,586 86 |
| Town appropriations for land, buildings and furniture........ | 151,370 69 |
| District taxation, individual and corporations................ | 69,255 18 |
| Registry taxes and all other sources ...................... | 63,335 26 |
| Total................................................... | $734,116 30 |

**EXPENDITURES.**

| | |
|---|---|
| Teachers' wages and other current expenses, day schools...... | $473,283 33 |
| "    "    "    "    " evening schools. | 15,732 33 |
| School supervision................... ...............······.... | 11,788 50 |
| Land, buildings, furniture and apparatus.................... | 208,662 53 |
| Total ........ ...... ........ ..........................··· | $709,466 69 |
| Current expenditure for day schools per capita of school population, five to fifteen years of age ...... .............. | $9 10 |
| Ditto       per capita of pupils enrolled ............. | 12 33 |
| "  "  "  "  " average attendance........ | 17 95 |

The facts here presented in regard to the attendance, taken in connection with those revealed by the State Census call for your immediate and careful attention. Illiteracy, the bane of all good government, is making rapid advances in our midst, and will soon bequeath a series of evils for our children to contend with, unless we take decisive and effectual measures to overcome it. A movement has already been inaugurated looking to such practical co-operation of the manufacturers and employers of the State with the school authorities, as shall render the existing provisions of the law relative to the schooling of minors, vital and effective. Should any change be deemed necessary in the details of that law, I hope the subject will receive your earnest and sympathetic consideration.

I desire, in this connection, to reiterate my conviction, as expressed last year, that the first step to be taken for the eradication of this evil from our State, is the establishment of an Industrial School. The Board of Education have considered this whole question very fully, and have, in every scheme proposed, been met by the unanimous conviction, that no law, or system of laws, can be made effectual which does not have such an institution at its base. It alone will furnish the leverage by means of which the necessary force can be applied to bring the penurious and the indifferent into compliance with the law. The present year should not close before the necessary steps are taken to found this school.

Another subject that has been before the Board of Education, and one that will be found treated at length in the report of the Commissioner, is that of equalizing the school tax of the State. It will there be seen that the rate of *local* taxation for school purposes varies from *five* cents on the hundred dollars, to *twenty-two*, where the amount raised in each town was just enough to enable it to draw its share of the public money. It certainly seems to me, that a scheme should be devised whereby the cost of education may be more evenly borne, and the benefits thereof more impartially distributed. The imposition of a specific tax for school purposes has been found in many of the States to serve this purpose.

In accordance with the vote of the General Assembly accompanying the Centennial Appropriation, an allowance of two thousand dollars was made to the Board of Education for their use in preparing a Centennial history of education in the State, and also in making an educational exhibit at Philadelphia. A full and detailed account of that exhibit will be found in the pages of the Commissioner's report. Of the history, its extent, character and value, you have already become personally acquainted. It is believed to be of permanent value, and a work that will be considered years hence as not the least of the mementos of this Centennial year.

For further information relating to this department, I would refer you to the Annual Reports of the Board of Education and the Commissioner of Public Schools.

### STATE NORMAL SCHOOL.

The Normal School is one of the most efficient means of promoting the interests of education throughout the State. The great work of our public schools is to furnish thorough instruction in the English branches and sound moral training. Such instruction and training is essential to success in any honorable employment, and to the discharge of the duties of citizenship. The necessity of teachers in our schools who have the requisite knowledge, skill in imparting it, and moral force, is evident. The Normal School is furnishing the State with such teachers. It is steadily raising the intellectual and moral standard of the teacher. It is unobtrusively, through its graduates, and in other ways, securing in many sections of the State a better appreciation of the value of good common schools.

By reference to the reports accompanying the reports of the Commissioner of Public Schools and the Board of Education, it will be seen that a good proportion of those who have been pupils in the Normal School since it was established, have taught before entering the school. This is one of the many evidences that this school, while furnishing the means of thorough preparation for teaching, has also

impressed very many of our teachers with the value and
the necessity of professional training.

I hope the day is not distant when every teacher
who enters upon the difficult and delicate duties of the
school-room, will first prepare by honorably completing
the course of study and training at our Normal School.

Without disparaging the large success of the school
hitherto, I yet feel assured, that as soon as a building adequate to its needs is provided, its usefulness will greatly
increase. I therefore earnestly recommend that the plans
devised by a previous assembly for securing a building be
consummated at an early date, or that other measures be
taken during in the present session to this end.

### THE MILITIA.

At the commencement of my administration, nearly two
years since, the new code of laws for the Militia had but
lately been enacted, the assignment under it, of companies
to Battalions, and Battalions to Brigades, being one of the
last official acts of my predecessor, Governor Howard.
As is generally well known, a radical change was effected
in the organization of the Militia; almost all the companies
that were officered upon the skeleton regimental plan were
obliged to elect such officers as are allowed to companies
in the regular army and were required to be assigned to
Battalions, thereby apparently losing old privileges.

Such a transformation could not of course be effected
easily, and my last annual message gave some evidence of

2

the difficulties that were encountered, and the opposition
made to the new system by some of the commands.

The execution of the duty falling upon me, as Commander-in-Chief, was quite unpleasant in many cases.
Time and association with the new order of things under
the law, have remedied these difficulties, and it gives me
pleasure to state, that all evidences tend to strengthen me
in the belief, that the new system is an improvement, and
that the Militia, generally, are all very well satisfied
with it.

Perhaps the system did not go quite far enough, and
make the Battalions as large as they should be, yet I think
it would be well to give the present arrangement a trial
for a year or two longer, and then change the law to provide for a consolidation of some of the small Battalions.

The Centennial season covering the past two years,
has given me opportunities to witness parades of large
bodies of Militia from different sections of the country,
and the appearance of strength and solidity as presented
by some of the distinguished regiments from other States,
tends to throw into the back-ground our organizations, by
reason of their deficiency in numbers. We have the
material in the city of Providence, by a union of three
prominent commands, which would make a regiment with
few, if any, superiors in the country. It is to be hoped
that time will effect this union.

Three of the Independent organizations still remain
"outside of the line;" their acceptance of the law and
assignment to Battalions would add greatly to the Militia

organization, and I think would not only be no detriment, but rather an advantage to them.

It is gratifying to know that for the past two years, under the workings of the present law, the expenses of the Militia have been materially less than for many years previous.

## THE STATE FARM.

The institutions at the State Farm are believed to be in excellent condition. The number of inmates differs but little from that of last year. In the asylum for the insane, there are 196 against 170 at this time last year; in the alms-house, 137 against 132 last year; and in the work-house and house of correction, 229 against 284 last year,—in all, 572 against 584 at this time last year. The accommodations and provisions for the insane are all that could be desired, with the exception of the dining-rooms con-nected with the cottage for excited patients, which are of insufficient size, and should be enlarged. The number in this building has materially increased since the last year. The accommodations of the alms house—the old work-house re-arranged and fitted up for its present use—are not so satisfactory. The original construction of the building, its comparatively small rooms, and the low ceilings, make thorough ventilation—so important for this class of occu-pants—a thing of difficult attainment. At no distant day, this cheap wooden structure will undoubtedly give place to one of stone, properly arranged, and of sufficient size, not only for the State, but for such of the towns as may choose to support their poor at the State Institution, in which they would find a large economy.

In May last, Mr. Samuel L. Blaisdell, of Providence, was elected Superintendent of the State Farm, in place of Mr. Norman Eayres, resigned; and immediately after entered upon the discharge of the duties pertaining to the office. During the brief period of his administration, he has shown high organizing power combined with rare executive ability. Under his firm and steady hand a wholesome discipline, so essential to the success of every reformatory institution, has been maintained. There have been comparatively few escapes, and those that have occurred, have been quickly followed by recapture. Besides the labor on the farm, a large amount of work has been done in grading, in constructing roads, in building walls, and in quarrying and delivering stone for the new Prison. Soon after Mr. Blaisdell entered upon the duties of Superintendent, the Rev. James P. Root was appointed Chaplain to the State Farm. In addition to holding a most acceptable service at the work-house on Sundays, he attends all funerals, and from his interest in the evening school, extends a voluntary supervision over it.

I would again call your attention to the necessity of some permanent provision for the children of the alms-house, and under proper legislation, for the neglected and exposed children on the street, who, if left to the influences surrounding them, are sure to become a charge to the State in some of its institutions. In Massachusetts, New York, and other leading States, schools have been estab-

lished for this class of children. The maintenance of such
schools is believed to be a matter of economy no less than
of humanity. It is much cheaper to educate and train a
child, and fit him by habits of industry, economy and self-
government, to become a useful member of society, than to
allow him to grow up in ignorance and vice, and afterwards to provide for him in reformatories and prisons.
A suitable building with all the necessary accommodations
for a hundred children, would require an appropriation of
not more than twenty-five thousand dollars. The structures required for the safe keeping and employment of the
same number of adult convicts would cost little short of
two hundred thousand dollars. The sum of twenty
thousand dollars expended annually by the State in supporting its juvenile delinquents at the Reform School,
would be sufficient to take care of at least an equal number of youthful candidates for that institution with far
greater chances of their turning out good citizens. But
the economical considerations are of little weight in comparison with the moral and social. The best growth of a
State, is brave, wise and good men, and noble and true
women; its worst product, ignorant and vicious citizens.
It is the highest function of Legislatures to encourage and
promote the one, and to reduce within the narrowest possible limits the other.

I am of the opinion that during the present session of
the Assembly, steps should be taken looking to the establishment at the State Farm of a school for children of the
dependent and vicious classes, where they may be kept and

cared for as wards of the State, until they arrive at a suitable age to be placed in families, or transported to industrial schools, as may be deemed most desirable. I also think that the necessary legislation should be initiated for securing the beneficent ends of such an institution.

### THE OLD STATE PRISON.

The State Prison has been administered as usual, and there is nothing requiring special remark. The numbers, both in Prison and Jail, have been largely in excess of those reported last year, and the crowded condition of the premises makes the speedy completion of the new Prison a matter of imperative necessity. As this is probably the last year of the occupancy of the old Prison, the Inspectors have prepared an account of the Jails and Prisons of the State, from the early times of our history, which will be, in due time, laid before the General Assembly. It will be necessary for the Legislature, at the present session, to take some action relative to the government of the Prison and Jail, when the institution shall have been removed to the State Farm. Whether it be advisable to continue the two Boards—of Inspectors of the State Prison and of State Charities and Corrections—in existence, with separate duties and functions, as at present, or to place the State Prison, closely connected, as it will necessarily be, with the other institutions upon the State Farm, under the charge of the latter, or to abolish both and form a new Board of Commissioners of Prisons, Peni-

tentiaries and Charities, with power to inspect the County
Jails, and all other institutions which the bounty of the
State fosters or over which its authority extends, is for the
General Assembly to determine. The subject should
receive an early attention and a thorough and judicious
consideration, and I would earnestly advise the appointment of a Commission for that purpose.

The finances of the Prison show a deficiency. The contract with Wm. Sweeney for the labor of 50 men expired
on the 8th of September, and as soon thereafter as could
be arranged, the labor of finishing furniture was continued
on account of the State. Some sales have already been
made, but the depression of business must necessarily
affect the financial condition of the Prison. It is quite
certain that no better work is anywhere done than within
the Prison work-shop, and it is hoped the quality of the
manufactured goods will attract purchasers. The usual
statistics will appear in the report of the Inspectors.

## NEW STATE PRISON.

Work began upon the new State Prison on the 18th of
April, and closed about the 1st of December. All the
main building was erected, roofed and slated, with the
exception of about one-third of the central portion. The
front yard-wall was finished and the sentry-turrets built.
Very fine and compact stone was found upon the State
Farm, and was furnished to the Commissioners by the
Board of State Charities and Corrections under contract.

It is believed that, when completed, the structure will be
in every way creditable to the State.   The whole amount
expended to the present time is as follows: —

Expended in 1874........................................ ...... $7,106.31
    "     " 1875..........................................................129,604.12
    "     " 1876...................................... about 117,700.00

    Total....................... ....................... . ... $254,410.43

Of this amount about forty thousand dollars have been
paid to the Board of State Charities and Corrections.

The buildings yet to be erected are workshops, kitchen,
mess-room, hospital, boiler-house and engine-house, and
the house for the warden.   It is desirable to build gas-
works for the supply of all the institutions upon the State
Farm.   It may also become necessary to make some
arrangement with the Providence Water Works, or to enlarge the facilities already existing upon the Farm, to ensure a full and constant supply of water.   The Commissioners will need an appropriation of at least one hundred thousand dollars to complete the Prison premises.
The old Prison and Jail are crowded more than ever
before, and it is greatly to be desired that the new Prison
shall be finished by the beginning of the next winter.
Prompt and liberal action on the part of the Legislature
will enable the Commissioners to finish the work they
have thus far carried on with great thoroughness, and as
much dispatch as the circumstances have permitted.

### LADIES' BOARD OF VISITORS.

The Ladies' Board of Visitors to the Penal and Correctional Institutions of the State has power to make recommendations only, and is not authorized to carry out the reforms that the investigations of its members may indicate as necessary. This fact has occasioned considerable difficulty in securing members of this Board. The number of females in the reformatory institutions of the State renders it proper that women should have some power in the various State boards controlling them. Women only can fully understand the peculiar necessities and characteristics of the female inmates, or can thoroughly investigate their actual condition, and the treatment they receive from those entrusted with their immediate control. There cannot well be two bodies, one of men and the other of women, having an equal voice in the management of the same institution. In a Board of men and women, chosen for their fitness for such service, the aid of the latter would be of great value. It would therefore seem advisable that the Legislature should make some provision whereby women shall be appointed on each of the following boards: State Charities and Corrections, Inspectors of the State Prison, and Trustees of the Reform School.

### THE PROPOSED AMENDMENTS TO THE CONSTITUTION.

The propositions of Amendment to the Constitution of the State, which had been approved by two successive Legislatures, and ordered to be submitted to the electors

3

for their approval or rejection, at their meeting on the first
Tuesday in November, 1876, were duly submitted, as directed by the act, and resulted in the rejection of all of
the proposed amendments, none of them having been approved by three-fifths of the electors of the State present
and voting thereon.   The vote was as follows :—

For Article V, 9,187, approved ; 9,418, reject.

" Article VI, 10,700, approved ; 11,432, reject.

" Article VII, 11,038, approved ; 10,956, reject.

I accordingly on the 12th of December, 1876, issued my
proclamation as provided by law, notifying the electors of
this result, which will be found in the Appendix.

Our people are very conservative, and justly so, in their
action on any amendments to the Constitution, but these
amendments had been carefully considered by the Legislature, and I think were worthy of a vote of approval.
That relating to the Registry Tax particularly, if it had
been adopted, would have enabled the Legislature, to provide for a tax in some other form, and thereby remove
from our State politics a source of corruption which has
increased wonderfully of late years.

### PROVIDENCE COUNTY COURT HOUSE.

The work on this fine building is progressing very satisfactorily.  As it approaches completion, the appearance
fully justifies the anticipation of its projectors.  The site
upon which it stands is a commanding one, and the beauty
of the architecture and fine proportions of the tower merit,

as they have received, the universal approval of our citizens. The exterior, walls, roof and main tower are now completed, and the building covered in. The steam heating apparatus is partially completed, and now in use, to enable the contractors to prosecute the work inside, during the winter. The construction will be forwarded with all the speed consistent with a thorough execution of the work.

The Commissioners have drawn from the Treasury the sum of one hundred and fifty-five thousand dollars, and have expended about one hundred and forty-five thousand dollars, a detailed account of which will be presented to the General Assembly at its present session.

The Commissioners are of the opinion that the cost of the building will not exceed the original estimate of two hundred and twenty-five thousand dollars.

As the Court House will probably be finished and ready for occupation before another winter, the rooms now occupied by the Courts in the State House will be available for other purposes. I therefore again call your attention to the necessity of providing for such changes and repairs upon the State House as will render it more suitable and convenient for transacting the public business. A moderate sum laid out in enlarging the building and changing the interior would furnish ample accommodation for all the State officers, and save the rent now paid for other premises. Committee rooms are required for both houses. The present Senate chamber is entirely too small, and should be enlarged so as to afford reasonable accommodation to the citizens who wish to be present to listen to debates

upon topics which affect their interests, a privilege which
they have a right to demand of their public servants. The
necessity of providing, without further delay, for the security and safety of the valuable public documents, which
have been accumulating for two centuries or more,
must be apparent to all. They are now subject to destruc-
tion any day, by even a slight fire, and their loss would be
irreparable. I trust this matter will receive your careful
consideration before the end of the present session.

## THE STATE CENSUS.

The census of the State, taken in 1875, has been completed. Since the last sesssion of the General Assembly,
the preparation of the tables has been finished, and a complete copy of the returns of the population in each town
has been made. This copy, suitably bound, has been deposited in the office of the Secretary of State, and the
original returns have been sent to the Town Clerks of
the several towns.

A pamphlet containing the tables prepared, was distributed in September last, to the Town Clerks of every
town and to each newspaper in the State. The report
upon the census, with numerous additional explanatory
and comparative tables, has been prepared, and the printing is nearly completed. It will be distributed to the
members of the General Assembly, and others, within a
short time. Including the tables, the complete report will
make a volume of 800 pages, and will present a much

more complete statement of the statistics of the population, the fisheries and shore farms, the agriculture, and the manufactures of the State, than was ever before presented in any census.

The aggregates of the four divisions are as follows:— Population of the State, 258,239; value of the Farm and Forest Products for the year, $5,028,329; value of the products of Fisheries and Shore Farms, $1,837,087; value of the products of Manufactures, $126,659,875.

The value of the products of some of the most important of the manufactures of the State is as follows:— Cotton manufactures, $22,430,860; Woolen manufactures, $17,463, 240; Print Works, $16,497,100; Iron manufactures, $10, 666,491; Jewelry and Silver ware, $7,077,651.

The total cost of the census, including the copying of the returns, and the printing of the report, will be less than the appropriation.

### THE LICENSE LAW.

This law went into effect on the first of July, 1875. The intent of the law was to regulate and restrain the sale of intoxicating liquors, so as to reduce the traffic to the smallest possible amount. For the previous year the so-called "Prohibitory Law" had been in force. Many of the provisions of this law were harsh, tyrannical, and unpopular, and the attempt to execute it by a body of paid officers, known as the State Constabulary, after a year of trial, proved an utter failure.

Many of the proceedings were unwise, and resulted in
one instance at least, in nearly bringing our State authorities into violent conflict with those of the United States.
This proceeding, by a recent decision of the Supreme Court,
was declared to have been illegal, and a verdict for damages was given against the officers.   The attempts to enforce
the law filled our Courts with hundreds of what were called
"liquor cases," and to such an extent, as to practically ex-
clude for a time the other business interests of the State
from obtaining a hearing.   It was, at this time, that the
"Board of License Commissioners," under the License Law,
were appointed in the city of Providence, and I am informed by them, that on entering upon their duties, they
found over 700 places in the city where intoxicating
liquors were sold openly and in defiance of law.   Thus
proving by a year of active and energetic trial, what is now
generally conceded, that a strictly Prohibitory Law cannot
be enforced in large and compact towns or cities.   During
their first year of office the Commissioners issued 664 Licenses of all classes, but at the commencement of the second year, profiting by the experience gained, and acting
under the discretionary clause in the law fixing the price
of different classes of licenses, they have been able to reduce
the number, so that not more than 450 are now issued.   It
is gratifying also to be able to state that the number of
arrests for drunkenness in the city, have been steadily on
the decline for the past three years, and are about 900 less
for 1876 than in 1875.

The amount paid into the State Treasury for licenses under this law for the year 1876 is as follows :—

| | | | |
|---|---|---|---|
| From the City of Providence | | | $51,666 06 |
| " | " | Newport | 6,150 00 |
| " | Town of East Providence | | 1,340 33 |
| " | " | East Greenwich | 75 00 |
| " | " | Warren | 780 00 |
| " | " | North Providence | 275 00 |
| " | " | Johnston | 450 00 |
| | | | $60,736 39. |

The other towns in the State have either not granted licenses, or as yet made no returns.

### HARBOR COMMISSION.

In accordance with the bill passed at the last session of the Legislature, I appointed, June 14th, 1876, J. Herbert Shedd, Jedediah Williams, and Nathaniel F. Potter, Harbor Commissioners. They organized on the 28th of the same month. The matters entrusted to them are of the deepest concern to our community. Providence is the natural port of New England, and the other cities and towns on Narragansett Bay occupy an important position in this respect. The time is not distant when our connections with the West will be completed, and a portion of the grain shipped from that section will seek Providence as a port. Its advent will be the beginning of a new period of prosperity for the State. To prepare for it, is a duty that we owe to ourselves and to our successors. The first object is to

preserve our excellent water communications. No harbor
upon our coast has the natural advantages of Narragansett
Bay. Two broad and deep entrances, that at all tides can
be navigated without a pilot by the largest ships afloat,
are supplemented by several commodious harbors, sur-
rounded by thriving cities and towns. At the head of the
bay stands the second city of New England. Providence
can easily prepare a resting place for the largest Atlantic
steamers, and in return receive the benefit of their teeming
freights. Within the past few years lines of ocean steamers have brought us into semi-weekly connection with
Philadelphia, Norfolk and Baltimore. This year, two of
the finest passenger steamers traversing Long Island Sound
will begin their daily trips to New York. Lines of Steamers
from Savannah and New Orleans are only waiting the
completion of improvements now in progress, to make
Providence the water terminus of their New England business. To secure others quite as important, the legislature
should give to this subject prompt and judicious consideration. Much has already been accomplished. It should
be followed by the energetic prosecution of the work, and
such changes in the act creating the Commissioners as will
better enable them to accomplish this end.

The Commissioners have given the subject a careful
study. The valuable maps of our inland waters made by
the U. S. Coast Survey, those in possession of the city of
Providence, and others, have been collected, copied and collated. They have consulted with the Commissioners of
Shell Fisheries relative to the respective duties of the two

boards. They have advised with the Harbor Committee of the City Council of Providence, as to the most desirable points of expending the amount appropriated by the city for harbor improvement, and the dredging now going on will undoubtedly result in giving good accommodations to the heavy coast-wise steamers frequenting this port. The commisioners have also designated a dumping ground, have prohibited steamers throwing over ashes above certain points in our bay, and have ordered the removal of some obstructions to navigation in the harbor. They have advised the cutting of passage-ways for water through certain railroad embankments, by which more than three million cubic feet of tidal flow will be retained, and have examined into certain injuries to the harbor of Pawtucket, and notified the president of the town council to the end that a remedy may be provided. Meetings have been held in Bristol and East Greenwich to awaken the interest of the people, and to give them an opportuinity of offering suggestions relative to the public waters. At the suggestion of the Commissioners, I have officially requested the President of the United States to appoint as an advisory board, the Chief of Engineers of the U. S. Army, the Superintendent of the U. S. Coast Survey, and the Chief of the Bureau of Navigation of the Navy Department. The Commissioners suggest the repeal of the act creating the present harbor line of East Providence, which they find to be unsuitable, and wish to change. It is desirable that the ship channels of the harbors of Newport and Washington Counties be plaaed in their charge, and that their du-

4

ties in reference to improvements within harbor lines be more fully defined. Their appeals to Congress for aid in improving the harbor, would have greater weight if a clause conferring the authority to act for the State in such matters were added to the act. Additional legislation may be required to insure suitable wharf accommodations for transient shipping. The desirability of requiring compensation for the tidal space occupied by permanent structures, as is done in some other States, should be considered. It will be the duty of the Commissioners to foster and develop the rights and interests of the State in the public waters, as well as to prevent direct injury. To this end an amendment of the act creating the Commission empowering them to make such examinations and observations as they may deem necessary is advisable. At the present session of the legislature, the Commissioners will present an extended report of the matters entrusted to their care, to which I earnestly request your careful attention.

In taking leave of this subject, I cannot too strongly impress upon you the great importance it bears to the prosperity of your constituents. A large majority of the people of our State dwell upon the shores of Narragansett Bay. No business they are engaged in can be unfavorably affected by judiciously pushing the improvement of our harbors. Commerce is necessary to the development and to the future welfare of our manufacturing interests. In itself it is a noble industry, and its possession cannot fail to materially benefit all the interests of Rhode Island.

## STATE BENEFICIARIES.

The pressure of my public and private duties, during the past few months, has prevented my visiting the various institutions in other States, at which our beneficaries are maintained. At my request, the Secretary of State has very acceptably performed this duty, and I respectfully call your attention to his report, which will be found in the appendix.

## CENTENNIAL.

Since my last Message, the Centennial Exhibition has been held at Philadelphia. It resulted in a marked success. The number of visitors exceeded that of any other exhibition. This event has brought together people from all parts of our great country, and has tended to obliterate sectional feeling. The various State exhibits have made known the resources and the products of the most distant parts of the country to one another. The good order that has prevailed, particularly on the great days of the exhibition, has well illustrated the influence of republican institutions upon our people. The hundreds of thousands that assembled to witness the celebration of the third and fourth of last July, and to take part in the exercises of Pennsylvania day at the exhibition, maintained order and decorum without the intervention of the military. Few events could better indicate the general intelligence and the law abiding character of our people.

The exhibition of American manufactures and products
of all kinds has favorably introduced them to the notice of
the world. The effect is already seen in the largely increased foreign demand for our textile fabrics and for our
other products. This export trade has assumed proportions, and is increasing with a rapidity that indicates an
extended traffic in the not-distant future. It cannot fail to
benefit the interests of Rhode Island.

Invitations to be present at the public ceremonies of the
exhibition have at various times been received from the
Centennial Commissioners, and on several occasions I have
visited Philadelphia with my staff for this purpose. An
opportunity was thus had of viewing the Rhode Island
exhibits. The industries of the State have, with one or
two exceptions, been very generally represented, and have
given a good impression of the intelligence and skill of our
artisans. Prominent among our exhibits was the Corliss
Engine. This great machine was completed and started at
the time agreed upon in the contract, and during the exhibition furnished all the power required for Machinery Hall.
It was a triumph of engineering and mechanical skill.
Rhode Island may well be proud that so important a
feature of the exhibition was contributed by her mechanics.
Notwithstanding the small size of the State, it appears from
the journal of the Commission, that the number of applications for space from Rhode Island was two hundred and
eighteen. Only seven other States sent a greater number
of applications for space  The awards to American exhibitors are not as yet fully completed, but the best informa-

tion at hand indicates that Rhode Island exhibitors have received over eighty awards. Our citizens may well congratulate themselves that the products of the State have received such favorable notice.

Rhode Island, as one of the thirteen original States, having been invited to hold a reception at the Centennial grounds, I appointed the first week in October as Rhode Island week, and Thursday, October 5th, as the reception day. During the week several thousand of our people visited the exhibition. On Thursday I was received at the grounds, with the personal and general staffs, and the general officers of the State militia with their staffs, by the Centennial Commission, and escorted to the Rhode Island State building at George's Hill. Citizens of the State to the number of eight hundred joined the procession. The reception at the State building was successful, and furnished an opportunity for a pleasant meeting of Rhode Islanders and their descendants from all parts of the country.

The Rhode Island State building was erected with a part of the fund appropriated by the last legislature for the State exhibit. It was designed as an head-quarters for our people at the Centennial, and was well adapted for the purpose. The register indicates that during the exhibition it was visited by about sixteen thousand Rhode Islanders.

The hundredth anniversary of our independence has been most appropriately remembered. Rhode Island has labored to do her part, and has succeeded in placing her name in an honorable position by the side of other States of much larger extent.

## CONCLUSION.

I do not consider it my province, and it is certainly not my intention, to discuss at length, in a Message of this kind, the condition of National affairs, despite their present uncertainty.

I have not so far, lost my faith in the intelligence, patriotism, and respect for law, of the American people, as to anticipate any violent rupture of our Government or its institutions. That some hot-headed partisans may see in the very close results of the Presidential contest, a circumstance that may lead to another civil war, is apparent. It is equally so, that the solid common sense of the mass of our people, entirely irrespective of party, would instantly crush any overt act in this direction.

The time has not yet come, and this is not the generation, to pull down the Temple of Liberty erected by our fathers. I think I can answer for our own State, limited as she is in numbers and influence, that no such attempt would for a moment, receive the support of any considerable number of her inhabitants.

I have faith that the representatives of the people having this matter in charge, will succeed in adjusting the difficulty. Whoever is found by them to have been legally elected, will be inaugurated, and receive the united support of the American people.

The cares of a largely increased private business, will compel me to devote my entire time in other directions, after my present term of office expires. I do not therefore intend to be a candidate for any further political honors.

The past two have been eventful years 'n our history. They have covered the Centennial celebrations of many of the most important events, that occurred in our early career as a nation, and have necessarily imposed many additional duties upon the Executives of the States.

I can only hope that my efforts to worthily represent my fellow citizens on these occasions, have met with their approval, and I may be permitted to take this opportunity to thank them for the honors conferred, and the support they have accorded me during my official career.

HENRY LIPPITT.

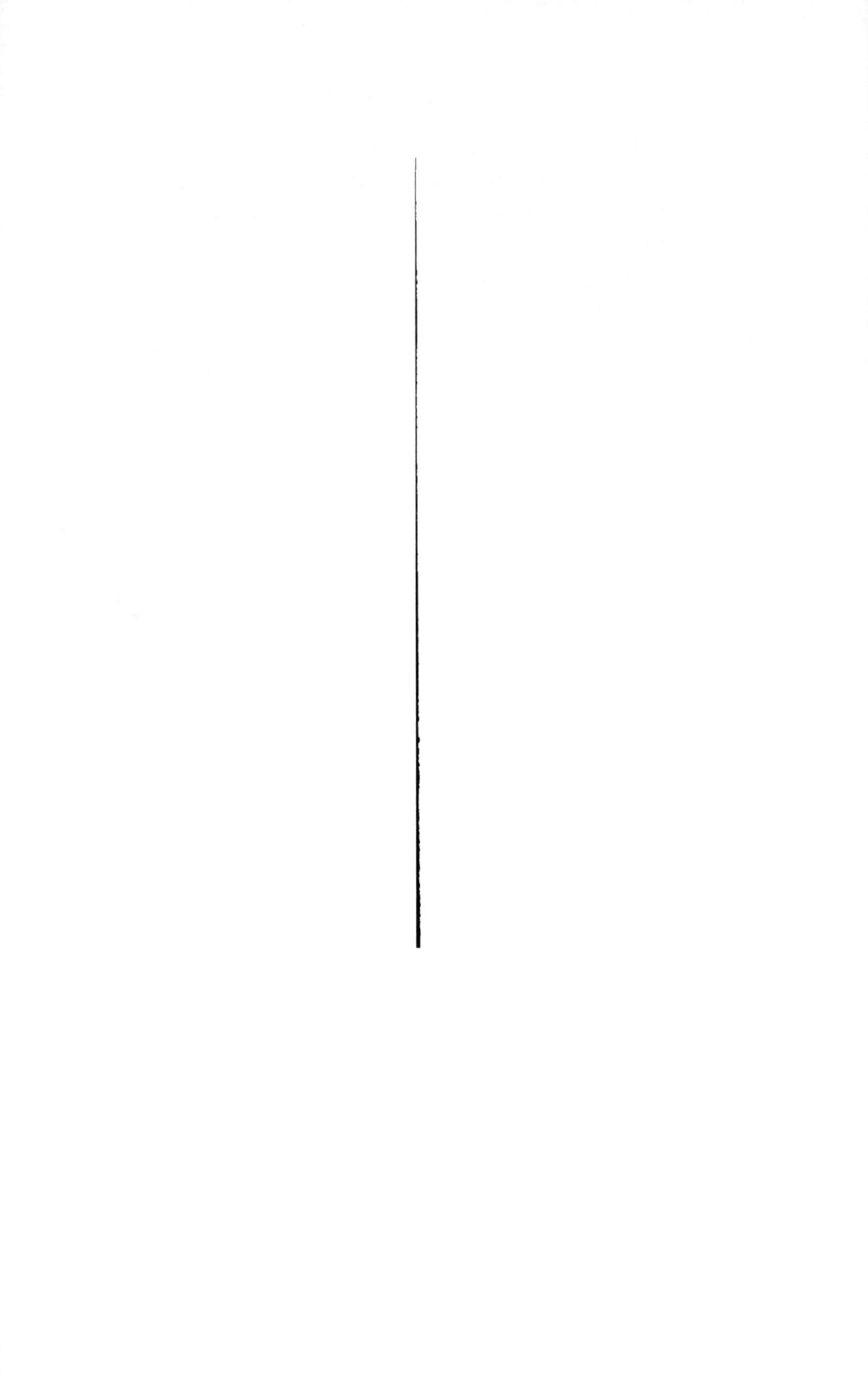

# 𝕻roclamation:

WHEREAS, By the provisions of Chapters 577, 578 and 579 of the Public Laws, severally passed on the 14th day of June, 1876, certain propositions of amendment to the Constitution of the State were declared approved, and for the purpose of submission to the electors, were severally designated as Article V, Article VI, and Article VII ; and

WHEREAS, Pursuant to the provisions of the Chapters aforesaid, the said propositions of amendment were duly published and submitted to the electors for their approval or rejection, at meetings of the electors held on the first Tuesday in November, 1876, and the ballots on said propositions given in at said meetings, were duly returned to the Secretary of State, and by the Governor and Secretary of State counted, with the following result, viz. :

For Article V.—9187 approved ; 9418 reject.

For Article VI.—10,700 approved ; 11,432 reject.

For Article VII.—11,038 approved ; 10,956 reject.

Now, therefore, I, HENRY LIPPITT, Governor of the State of Rhode Island and Providence Plantations, do hereby pursuant to said Chapters issue this my proclamation, that none of said propositions of amendment having been approved by three-fifths of the electors of the State present and voting thereon, in the Town, Ward and District meetings, on said first Tuesday in November, they were all rejected.

{ L. S. } In testimony whereof, I have hereunto set my hand and caused the seal of the State to be affixed, at Providence, this twelfth day of December, A. D. 1876.

HENRY LIPPITT.

By the Governor,

JOSHUA M. ADDEMAN, Secretary of State.

# Report of the Secretary of State on the State Beneficiaries.

To His Excellency Henry Lippitt, Governor:—

Sir:—I have the honor to report, that pursuant to your request to visit the several institutions where beneficiaries of the State are cared for, I have performed that duty, and submit the following statement as the result of my observations :—

Since the former visits made by me at your request to the State institutions, very few changes have been made. Experience suggests some improvements, but the general plan of instruction and discipline remains the same.

At the American Asylum for the Deaf and Dumb, Hartford, the following beneficiaries from this State were in attendance, on the 21st of December last :—

| NAMES. | Residence. | Date of Admission. |
|---|---|---|
| Frank J. Brown | Greene | September 1, 1871. |
| Enmund E. Dwyer | Providence | September 9, 1871. |
| Walter A. Eddy | Chepachet | September 4, 1873. |
| Joseph D. Hagerty | North Providence | September 7, 1871. |
| Burrill Lancaster | Providence | September 4, 1873. |
| James McGinn | Providence | September 5, 1874. |
| Ida Nicholas | Olneyville | September 4, 1874. |
| John Trainor | Providence | September 4, 1876. |

None of the beneficiaries at this institution have been discharged during the past year. One, the last named in the above list, was appointed during the year. This boy has made marked progress since entering the school, having learned to read some and to write simple sentences.

The others are continuing to make satisfactory progress. At my request, they have written letters to your Excellency, which appear on the face to be what was intended, original compositions, and which could compare favorably with the attainments of children in the public schools, who had been under instruction no greater length of time. These beneficiaries were sent to the institution without previous instruction or training whatever, and have studied the branches usually taught in the lower grades of schools. In addition to these, two of them have received instruction in the shoe shop, two in the cabinet shop, and three in the tailor's shop, connected with the school ; and judging from specimens of their handiwork, I should feel confident of their becoming self-supporting on leaving the school.

Three of these beneficiaries have been at the school the time allowed by law. They are recommended by their teachers for continuance. Some additional instruction will be needed to make their present acquirements serviceable for their maintenance and self-support. They are so young, and their infirmity is so great a disadvantage, that to stop at the present point might result in their losing the advantages already gained. The approval of the legislature will be needed for the continuance of these beneficiaries.

At the Perkins Institution and Massachusetts Asylum for the Blind, in South Boston, there were in attendance on the 3d of January inst., the following beneficiaries from this State :—

| NAMES. | Residence. | Date of Admission. |
|---|---|---|
| Henry A. Herrick............. | Pawtucket ......... | June, 1872. |
| Fremont Jefferson ............ | Providence ...... .. | October, 1873. |
| James H. Stirling............. | Providence. ..... | April, 1873. |
| Joanna Burke ............... | Woonsocket . ... | May, 1872. |
| Katie Downing................ | Providence.. ....... | June, 1871. |
| Sarah A. Hamson............. | Newport............ | September, 1873. |
| Fannie Kimball .............. | Providence ......... | March, 1868. |

One other, who is under appointment, is temporarily absent on account of ill health.

Of the beneficiaries in attendance a year ago, five have been discharged, two of whom will be able to support themselves. The others, being feeble in mind and body, will necessarily be objects of charity.

Those who remain in the school are among the best of the inmates of the institution. They appear intelligent and well-informed. I carefully examined the record of their conduct and scholarship, and found some of them standing at the head of their respective classes in a portion of the studies pursued ; and very rarely in any study was any beneficiary of the State below the average of the class to which he or she belonged.  The girls are also instructed in household work ; the boys, in addition to the studies they pursue, are taught the trades of making brooms and cane-seating chairs. All the children, who show any aptitude for it, are taught music, and with marked success.  Some of the beneficiaries will probably earn a good livelihood by this profession.

At the Massachusetts School for Idiotic and Feeble Minded Youth, located in South Boston, about a mile from the Institution for the Blind, this State had in attendance on the third of January inst., three beneficiaries.  One of these has made some progress, can read and write a little, and can do some simple kinds of handiwork, such as braiding mats.  Of the others, one is a boy of very feeble mind, in whose case there is not much hope of improvement, and who should be discontinued at an early day. The third is a little girl, who has been placed there for special medical treatment.  A short time will determine the value of the experiment.  In this case insanity seems to be the form of development, and for this class of cases the school makes no provision.  It is a very pitiable case, and one appealing strongly to the sympathies of the charitable, but having no claim upon the Executive discretion.

During the year, this institution, and that for the blind, have sustained a great loss in the death of Dr. Samuel G. Howe, the founder and life-long friend of both.  Probably no man living has labored more faithfully and unselfishly for the care and development of these two classes of unfortunates. His philanthropical labors have established the schools on sound foundations, and, under the care of their able officers and instructors, they will continue to do the very beneficent work which has for nearly half a century been the mission of the school for the blind, and for nearly thirty years that of the school for the feeble minded.

The public exhibitions, given during the last January session, by pupils from the American Asylum for the deaf and dumb, and by pupils from the institution for the blind, illustrated the character of the work pursued, and the success attained.  The interest shown by the large audiences present will be remembered; and if it is deemed advisable by the legislature, the officers of those schools have expressed their readiness to give other exhibitions during the coming session, at such time as may be designated.

In addition to the beneficiaries above named, the State contributes liberally for the indigent insane at the Butler Hospital.  There are twenty beneficiaries, who each receive state aid to the amount of $100 per annum; the remainder of their expense being paid by their friends.

There are forty-four city or town paupers at the same institution. For the support of these, the State contributes $30 per quarter each, the city or town sending them, paying the balance of the expense. When these cases are decided to be incurable, the person is sent to the State Farm.

The commission on complaints of the insane, of which the undersigned is one, have had no case brought to their knowledge during the year in which there was any reason to suspect improper treatment.

Respectfully submitted,

JOSHUA M. ADDEMAN,

*Secretary of State.*

# SEMI-ANNUAL REPORT

OF THE

# Railroad Commissioner,

MADE TO THE

# GENERAL ASSEMBLY

AT ITS

## JANUARY SESSION, 1877.

PROVIDENCE:

ANGELL, BURLINGAME & CO., PRINTERS TO THE STATE.

1877.

# REPORT.

*To the Honorable General Assembly of the State of Rhode Island,
at their January Session, A. D.* 1877 :—

The Railroad Commissioner has the honor of presenting the following report.

While the accidents during the time since my last report have materially decreased, in number, as compared with former years, the proportion of fatal cases have increased.

The following is an account of the various accidents since May 1:

June 15. CHARLES SMITH, a Swede, was found injured on the track of the New York, Providence and Boston Railroad Company, near Norwood station. He was sent to the Rhode Island Hospital, where I found him about 10 o'clock A. M., in an unconscious state. He remained so and died about noon. This corporation has a double track, always using the right hand one. When Mr. Smith was first discovered, about 4. 15 A. M., he was laying with his head so close to the rail of the *easterly* track (the up track), that the man who found him, hearing a train coming up, moved him, in order that the train might pass without hitting him. The last train that came over *this* track, was nearly two hours before this. If that train had hit him, it could *not* have left him in the position in which he was found. If that train had flung him off, some marks would have been discovered on the ground, and some one on the train must have seen him ; neither could he have been left by the down train, on the other track, as no marks could be found there. He was a man of intemperate habits, and when last seen, the evening before, he was evidently in a very excited state of mind. My own impressions are, that he received his injuries by either jumping or falling from the bridge.

June 15.  Mrs. JULIA A. GOLDTHWAITE was almost instantly killed, near Albion, by the cars of the Providence and Worcester Railroad Company, while walking upon the track. All the employés on the train, properly and promptly did all they could to avoid the accident, but, in my judgment, the whole cause of the accident is directly chargeable to the corporation for the ill arranged and dangerous location of their station. According to the testimony of the Station Agent, the station is by measurement, three hundred and sixty-three feet from the carriage road. Within the enclosures of the Railroad Corporation are a double track, a turnout, and a spur. All, or nearly all, the passengers to and from this station, drive on to the carriage road, then are compelled to walk this three hundred and sixty-three feet, to the station. The heavy baggage is transported on barrows. The numerous regular passenger and freight trains, in addition to the frequent extra trains, which their large business compels them to run, renders this place one of very great danger. I had called their attention to this matter over a year previous to the accident, and immediately after it, I renewed the suggestion relative to a new location for their station, but everything now remains the same as before the accident occurred.

July 5.  HENRY SIMIKIN, injured by cars of the Providence, Warren & Bristol Railroad Company, near Ocean Cottage, while standing upon the track talking with a friend. Owing to a curve in the road, neither he or the trainmen could see each other, until quite near together. Immediately upon being seen, the whistle was blown and the air brake applied. He received injuries on his leg, and also on his arm. He was promptly conveyed to the Rhode Island Hospital, and although he remained there some time, and I made frequent inquiries about him, yet immediately upon his coming out, he left the state before I had an opportunity of having a formal investigation.

July 21.  NICHOLAS RILEY, a man 65 or 70 years of age, was instantly killed near Greenwich station, by the cars of the New York, Providence and Boston Railroad Co. This man's eyesight was very defective, and he was also hard of hearing. He was in the habit of frequently crossing the track in this vicinity, and had often been cautioned by the station agent to take care of himself when near the depot. This time he stood near the track, and then started to cross it apparently looking down, and almost directly in front of the coming shore line noon express train.    There was several quite near him, some of whom shouted to him, but as the train was so near and coming so fast, none could help him.    A curve in the road prevented those on the engine from seeing him until they were almost on to him.    The power brake was promptly applied, but the breast beam of the engine hit him, and killed him.    The bell was ringing at the time, and the whistle had been blown but a few seconds before for the crossing.

August 16.  THOMAS COOK, killed near Lonsdale, on Providence and Worcester Railroad.    When first seen by the engineer, he was about a quarter of a mile off, walking between the two tracks, and going the same direction as the train was.    He was then in a safe position, but when the train was within about one hundred feet of him, without looking back, he stepped directly on to the track of the coming train.    The whistle was immediately blown, promptly followed by the signal for brakes, and the engine was reversed, but the man was hit and instantly killed.

September 2.  ANN MURRAY, killed near Olneyville, by cars of the Hartford, Providence and Fishkill Railroad Company, while attempting to walk across the track.    The whistle had just been blown for a crossing, and the bell was rung at the same place, which was about twenty-five rods from the place of accident. The woman suddenly appeared, and when the engineer first perceived her, she was so near he could not tell whether he had hit her or not.    The power brake was instantly applied, but the accident was inevitable.

In examining the surrounding grounds near the place of this accident, I found well trodden foot paths, and well worn places on the fence on each side, unmistakably showing that persons frequently make this one of their convenient walking places.    When I considered, that within these fences, there were two tracks of the New York, Providence & Boston Railroad Company, and one each of the Hartford, Providence and Fishkill and the Providence and Springfield Railroad Company there, with such a large number of regular trains, with frequent extra trains, running at almost all hours of the day and night, that it would be utterly impossible to know the time when trains were due, that I recommended the Hartford, Providence & Fishkill Railroad Company, in connection with the other corporation, to procure painted notices, to be placed on each side of the track, informing persons of danger, and forbidding them entering the enclosure.

October 14. WILLIAM HEENEY was slightly injured, near the Gaspee street crossing, Providence, by an engine of the Hartford, Providence & Fishkill Railroad Company, used for switching in the yard. Mr. Heeney was driving in a wagon, and had been to the freight depot. On returning from the depot, his attention was attracted by some work going on near by, and he was driving in one direction, and looking in an opposite one, his wagon was hit by the engine, he was flung out and injured. The engine was moving only some four or five miles per hour; the bell had been ringing for some time, and was ringing at the time of the accident, and the engineer reversed the engine as soon as possible. Mr. Heeney was carried home in a hack, by a policeman, to whom he admitted the accident was his own fault, and in which decision I fully concur.

September 27. An unknown man was instantly killed on the Providence and Worcester Railroad, near the slaughter house, in Providence. When first seen, he was walking between the two tracks, about one-fourth of a mile off, going same direction as the train. The whistle was blown, and the man turned twice and looked towards the coming train, and then stepped one side where he would have been perfectly safe. He then jumped over on to the other track immediately in front of the engine, and within twenty or thirty feet of it. He dropped a bundle: stopped to pick it up, was hit in the head, and was instantly killed. The whistle was sounding all the time after he was first seen, until the accident, and the engine was reversed. It was either a deliberate suicide, or the result of the grossest carelessness on the part of the man.

November 16. FRANK LOVELL, a brakeman in the employ, of the Providence and Worcester Railroad Company, was instantly killed between Lonsdale and Ashton. It was a freight train, and when he was last seen alive by either of the employés, he was at his post, on the top of the car. He had before been seen climbing from the door of the freight car to the top, by help of a rope, when the train was in motion. He had been cautioned against it and also been informed that it was in direct violation of one of the rules of the corporation. As a piece of broken rope was found fastened to the top of the car, it is presumed that his life was lost by the breaking of the rope. The car did not belong to this corporation but came with freight from another line.

November 23. JOHN SULLIVAN was fatally injured on the Providence, Warren and Bristol Railroad, in East Providence, near the Wilkes-Barre Coal Company wharf. It was a freight train, and on time, and as it was moving very slow, this boy and one other ran along by the side of it, and this boy caught hold of the side of the car, fell underneath it, and some of the wheels went over one of his feet. There has for a long time been a very conspicuous painted notice near the place of the accident forbidding boys from coming there. The train was stopped as soon as possible, and after the accident, this corporation did for him all they could. The cause of the accident rests solely on the fact that the boy was where he ought not to be, and doing what he had no right to do.

November 23. JOHN FOGERTY, a boy, was injured in Cranston, on Hartford, Providence and Fishkill Railroad Company. I have made great efforts in regard to this accident, to ascertain just how it was caused, but have not been able to find any one that saw it. This was a freight train, and was standing near the station, and the probabilities are, that this boy attempted to go between the cars, and that before he had got across the track, the train started, and the wheel went over one of his feet.

November 26. JOHN HENRY, killed near the slaughter houses, in North Providence, by the steamboat train of the Boston and Providence Railroad Company. When first seen by the engineer, he was only about one hundred feet off, laying on the track. Steam was shut off, power brake applied, train stopped as soon as possible, but all without avail. The train was nearly on time, being some two or three minutes late, running at the usual speed, and the head light was lighted. The evening before the accident, this John Henry, in company with two others, drank very frequently and at various places. This drinking commenced in the evening, and was kept up all night, in fact his companions testified to being with him up to nearly 4, A. M., and the accident occurred very shortly after that time, and the cause of it can be very properly charged to the intoxication of the man.

One other quite serious accident has occurred on the Providence, Warren and Bristol Railroad, but the man is not yet able to attend to his business, and I postponed the investigation so that I can be able to have the testimony of the man himself. One other accident, on the Union Railroad, reported December 27th, the investigation of which is also postponed.

There were one or two other accidents reported, but upon inquiring into the cause of them, I did not deem any further investigation necessary.

This closes the list of accidents, but one thing is very noticeable in regard to them. In my last January report, eleven accidents on the Union Railroad were reported, one of which was fatal and several of which were very serious, while in this report, covering the same length of time, with a material addition to the length of their track, only one accident is reported. In my last report I stated, that I had recommended to this corporation, to place a notice on each end of each car, warning people not to enter, or leave the car by the front platform, and also not to allow any person under the influence of liquor to ride in the cars. My own judgment is, that by the strict enforcement of these suggestions, and the extraordinary care and caution of the employés of this corporation, this gratifying result has been attained.

I now submit a detailed statement of the business, and financial position of all the Railroad Corporations, with a recapitulation of the prominent items of the same, with a corresponding table of the previous year.

| | New York, Boston and Providence Railroad Co. year ending Sept. 30, 1876. | Providence and Worcester Railroad Company, year ending Sept. 30, 1876. | Boston & Providence Railroad Co. Year ending Sept. 30, 1876. | Hartford, Providence and Fishkill Railroad Co. Sept. 30, 1876. | Providence and Springfield Railroad Company, year ending Sept. 30, 1876. |
|---|---|---|---|---|---|
| Capital stock actually paid in | $3,000,000 00 | $2,000,000 00 | $4,000,000 00 | $2,037,939 98 | $517,150 00 |
| Total amount of funded debt | 1,163,000 00 | 500,000 00 | 500,000 00 | 2,055,500 00 | 500,000 00 |
| Total amount of floating debt | None. | 1,490,000 00 | 794,000 00 | 291,648 83 | 8,838,33 00 |
| Interest due within the year | 81,650 00 | 106,529 20 | 100,023 86 | 174,061 12 | 81,227 66 |
| Interest paid within the year | 81,650 00 | 106,529 20 | 100,028 86 | 174,061 12 | 81,227 66 |
| Total amount of receipts from passengers | 516,272 43 | 840,231 51 | 880,468 40 | 470,982 14 | 40,866 84 |
| Total amount of receipts from freight | 399,743 79 | 587,197 47 | 568,648 87 | 417,059 81 | 42,952 64 |
| Total amount of receipts from all other sources | 149,211 92 | 21,675 52 | 68,642 29 | 62,702 53 | 3,248 69 |
| Total running expenses | 600,026 58 | 679,103 28 | 1,049,450 13 | 784,150 05 | 45,409 11 |
| Total net earnings | 465,201 56 | 113,472 02 | 418,309 48 | 166,594 48 | 9,931 40 |
| Rate of dividend paid to stockholders | 2½ per cent. quarterly | 8 per cent. | 8 per cent. | None. | None. |
| Surplus after paying dividend | 96,051 56 | 28,676 64 | None. | None. | None. |
| Surplus at commencement of the year | None. | 70,204 62 | 459,178 02 | None. | None. |
| Expended during the year in purchase or repairs of rolling stock | a 31,075 32 | 126,101 75 | 96,253 83 | 151,063 76 | 2,508 61 |
| Expended during the year for maintenance of way | 190,979 61 | 181,257 28 | c 861,481 89 | 234,601 04 | 42,900 50 |
| Total number of passengers | 769,764 | 1,585,893 | 3,475,378 | 1,389,733 | 115,366 |
| Tons of merchandise transported | 271,907 | 555,960 | 589,634 | 302,597 | 81,181 |
| Number of locomotives owned | 26 | 30 | 42 | 35 | 3 |
| Number of passengers cars owned | 31 | k 41 | 92 | 37 | 4 |
| Number of all other cars | 248 | 1,280 | 527 | 433 | 77 |

a.  For purchase and *not* for repairs.    c.  Including buildings.    k.  Including mail and baggage cars.

| | New York, Boston and Providence Railroad Co. year ending Sept. 30, 1876. | Providence and Worcester Railroad Company, year ending Sept. 30, 1876. | Boston & Providence Railroad Co. year ending Sept. 30, 1876. | Hartford, Providence and Fishkill Railroad Co. year ending Sept. 30, 1876. | Providence and Springfield Railroad Company, year ending Sept. 30, 1876. |
|---|---|---|---|---|---|
| Average number of regular passenger trains per day | b 9 | b 17 | b 13 | b 6 | 4 |
| Number of passenger trains equipped with Miller platform | All. | None. | d 91 | All. | 1 |
| Number of passenger trains equipped with power brake | All. | None. | d 89 | All. | None. |
| Total length of road—miles | 62¼ | l 51.41/100 | 44 | 122.88/1000 | 23 |
| Miles of track in this State | 45⅞ | 24.40/100 | 6 | 26.88/1000 | 23 |
| Number of passengers killed during the year | None. | None. | 1 | None. | None. |
| Number of passengers injured during the year | None. | 1 | 2 | 1 | None. |
| Number of persons walking on the track killed | 5 | 5 | 3 | 4 | None. |
| Number of persons walking on the track injured | None. | 7 | None. | 2 | None. |
| Number of employes killed | 2 | None. | 1 | 2 | None. |
| Number of employes injured | None. | 1 | 1 | 2 | None. |
| Average rate of fare per mile (exclusive of season tickets) | .0284 | 2 47/100 | 2 5/10 | 3 32/100 | .04 |
| Average rate of fare per mile for season ticket passengers, reckoning one round trip per day to each ticket | .0078 | 69/100 | 1.1 | 1½ | ? |

b. From Providence.    d. Cars.    l. Including branches.

| | Warwick Rail road Company, from Dec 1st, 1876, to July 1st, 1876. | Newport and Wickford Rail road and Steamboat Co., year ending Aug. 31, 1876. | Narragansett Pier Railroad Co., from July to Sept. 30, 1876. | Wood River Branch Railroad, year ending Nov. 30, 1876. | Old Colony Rail road Company, year ending Sept 30, 1876. |
|---|---|---|---|---|---|
| Capital stock actually paid in | $39,205 00 | $101,000 00 | $93,620 00 | $47,140 86 | $6,733,800 00 |
| Total amount of funded debt | 200,000 00 | 70,000 00 | 90,000 00 | 57,500 00 | 4,989,500 00 |
| Total amount of floating debt | 164,307 29 | None. | ........ | 21,642 55 | 1,101,808 41 |
| Interest due within the year | 11,501 51 | 4,830 00 | ........ | 4,841 07 | 323,518 88 |
| Interest paid within the year | ........ | 4,830 00 | ........ | 528 57 | 323,518 33 |
| Total amount of receipts from passengers | 1,630 47 | 39,053 90 | 7,797 58 | 4,177 40 | 1,310,234 23 |
| Total amount of receipts from freight | 90 74 | 1,910 48 | 644 52 | 6,526 93 | 712,929 09 |
| Total amount of receipts from all other sources | ........ | 7,445 48 | 40 00 | 490 75 | 183,717 05 |
| Total running expenses | 7,784 81 | 35,035 34 | 2,161 18 | 8,738 41 | f1,476,083 61 |
| Total net earnings | None. | 1,181 60 | 5,280 97 | 2,447 67 | 730,358 02 |
| Rate of dividend paid to stockholders | None. | None. | None. | None. | 6 per cent. |
| Surplus after paying dividend | None. | None. | None. | None. | 4,027 69 |
| Surplus at commencement of the year | None. | 1,181 60 | None. | None. | 677,947 48 |
| Expended during the year in purchase or repairs of rolling stock | 28 92 | 6,845 23 | 17,000 00 | 274 28 | 232,641 57 |
| Expended during the year for maintenance of way | 1,563 71 | 517 69 | 1,700 00 | 4,687 25 | 321,958 90 |
| Total number of passengers | 7,569 | 59,000 | 19,094 | 19,520 | 4,150,457 |
| Tons of Merchandise transported | 83 | 1,729 | 800 | 7,612 | 619,663 |
| Number of locomotives owned | e 1 | None. | 1 | 1 | 69 |
| Number of passenger cars owned | e 4 | 1 combined with engine | 2 | 1 | 147 |
| Number of all other cars | e 1 | 3 | 7 | 1 | 1,302 |

e. All hired.　f. Including taxes.

| | Warwick Railroad Company, From Dec. 1st, 1875, to July 1st, 1876. | Newport and Wickford Railroad and Steamboat Co., year ending Aug. 31, 1876. | Narragansett Pier Railroad Co., from July 1, to Sept. 30, 1876. | Wood River Branch Railroad, year ending Nov. 30 1876. | Old Colony Railroad Company, year ending Sept. 30, 1876. |
|---|---|---|---|---|---|
| Average number of regular passenger trains per day........... | 2 | 6 | 6 | 10 | $g$ 6 |
| Number of passenger trains equipped with Miller platform........ | 2 | 2 | 1 | None. | All. |
| Number of passenger trains equipped with power brake......... | None. | 2 | 1 | None. | All. |
| Total length of road, miles....... | $9\frac{4}{10}$ | $8\frac{8}{10}$ | $8\frac{1}{10}$ | $5\frac{7}{10}$ | $269\frac{44}{100}$ |
| Miles of track in this State....... | $9\frac{4}{10}$ | $3\frac{4}{10}$ | $8\frac{1}{10}$ | $5\frac{7}{10}$ | $16\frac{31}{100}$ |
| Number of passengers killed during the year................... | None. | None. | None. | None. | None. |
| Number of passengers injured during the year................ | None. | None. | None. | None. | 1 |
| Number of persons walking on the track killed................. | None. | None. | None. | None. | 3 |
| Number of persons walking on the track injured............... | None. | None. | None. | None. | 7 |
| Number of employes killed......... | None. | None. | None. | None. | 8 |
| Number of employes injured....... | None. | None. | None. | None. | 1 |
| Average rate of fare per mile (exclusive of season tickets)..... | $3\frac{1}{4}$ cts. | 4 cts. | $6\frac{3}{4}$ cts. | 5 cts. | .026 |
| Average rate of fare per mile for season ticket passengers reckoning one round trip per day to each ticket.... | | 4 cts. | $3\frac{1}{4}$ cts. | $2\frac{.68}{100}$ cts. | .009 |

$g$. In Rhode Island.

| | Fall River, Warren and Providence Railroad Co., year ending Sept. 30, 1876. | Providence, Warren, and Bristol Railroad Co., year ending Nov. 30, 1876. | New York and New England Railroad Co. year ending Sept. 30, 1876. | Pawtuxet Valley Railroad Co., year ending July 13, 1876. | Union, year ending Dec. 31, 1876. |
|---|---|---|---|---|---|
| Capital stock actually paid in | $150,000 00 | $437,917 49 | j $20,000,000 00 | $100,300 00 | $820,000 00 |
| Total amount of funded debt | 300,000 00 | 50,000 00 | 316,000 00 | 100,000 00 | 75,000 00 |
| Total amount of floating debt | 19,438 51 | None. | 680,479 67 | None. | None. |
| Interest due within the year | 21,000 00 | 4,000 00 | 63 956 59 | 7,000 00 | 7,275 00 |
| Interest paid within the year | 7,650 42 | 4,000 00 | 63,956 59 | 7,000 00 | 7,275 00 |
| Total amount of receipts from passengers | 21,184 16 | 69,613 85 | 436,637 53 | 6,212 28 | 387,131 28 |
| Total amount of receipts from freight | 3,017 35 | 27,671 19 | 447,385 27 | 8,629 39 | None. |
| Total amount of receipts from all other sources | 3,019 15 | 4,285 46 | 116,459 46 | None. | 10,244 06 |
| Total running expenses | 19,822 58 | m 99,587 84 | 737,469 92 | None. | 307,139 93 |
| Total net earnings | 7,650 42 | 1,982 96 | 22,575 68 | 14,841 67 | 90,235 41 |
| Rate of dividend paid to stockholders | None. | None. | None. | 6 per cent. | 6 per cent. |
| Surplus after paying dividend | None. | None. | 22,575 63 | 3,490 43 | 47,224 41 |
| Surplus at commencement of the year | h 150,792 67 | 13,487 05 | 39,475 44 | None. | None. |
| Expended during the year in purchase or repairs of rolling stock | None owned. | 21,240 87 | 161,806 47 | | 25,269 24 |
| Expended during the year for maintenance of way | 9,320 07 | 28,563 68 | 218,040 62 | | 23,931 96 |
| Total number of passengers | 96,349 | 249,349 | 1,794,597 | | 6,788,917 |
| Tons of merchandise transported | 11,965 | 30,805 | 330,667 | | None. |
| Number of locomotives owned | None. | 5 | 31 | | n 595 |
| Number of passenger cars owned | None. | 10 | 60 | | 98 |
| Number of all other cars | None. | 25 | 452 | | 5 |

*h.* Deficit.   *j.* And to be paid in Berdell Bonds.   *m* Including interest.   *n.* Horses.

| | Fall River, Warren and Providence Railroad Co., year ending Sept. 30, 1876. | Providence, Warren and Bristol Railroad Co., year ending Nov. 30, 1876. | New York and New England Railroad Co., year ending Sept. 30, 1876. | Pawtuxet Valley Railroad Co., year ending July 18, 1876. | Union, year ending Dec. 31, 1876. |
|---|---|---|---|---|---|
| Average number of regular passenger trains per day | 8 | b 5 | b 6 | | |
| Number of passenger trains equipped with Miller platform | All. | All. | 6 | | |
| Number of passenger trains equipped with power brake | All. | All. | 6 | | |
| Total length of road, miles | 5 794/1000 | 13 8/10 | 139 | 8 100/1000 | 37 1/4 |
| Miles of track in this State | 2 98/1000 | 13 4/10 | 1 | 3 100/1000 | 37 1/4 |
| Number of passengers killed during the year | None. | None. | None. | | None. |
| Number of passengers injured during the year | None. | None. | None. | | 7 |
| Number of persons walking on the track killed | None. | 1 | 5 | | |
| Number of persons walking on the track injured | None. | 2 | None. | | |
| Number of employes killed | None. | None. | 2 | | |
| Number of employes injured | None. | None. | None. | | |
| Average rate of fare per mile (exclusive of season tickets) | .039 | 3 1/4 | 2 44/100 | | |
| Average rate of fare per mile for season ticket passengers, reckoning one round trip per day to each ticket | None. | .01 | 957/1000 | | |

b. From Providence.

|  | 1876. | 1875. |
|---|---|---|
| Capital stock............................ | $40,078,073 33 | $37,247,313 35 |
| Total indebtedness...................... | $15,488,158 09 | $15,427,385 83 |
| Total receipts........................... | $8,288,584 20 | o $8,371,922 88 |
| Total earnings.......................... | $2,050,058 19 | $2,131,002 62 |
| Number of passengers................... | 20,520,486 | 20,575,973 |
| Total tons of merchandise............... | 2,754,603 | 2,748,267 |
| Total number of locomotives............ | 244 | 229 |
| Total number of cars.................... | 4,889 | 4,823 |
| Number of passengers killed............. | 1 | 6 |
| Number of passengers injured............ | 12 | 13 |
| Number of all others killed............. | 36 | 29 |
| Number of all others injured............ | 23 | 25 |
| Total miles of track in Rhode Island..... | 225 68/10 | 220 33/10 |

o.　Corrected from my last report

## WORK FOR THE YEAR.

### NARRAGANSETT PIER RAILROAD.

This road was completed and opened for travel in July last, and previous to the opening I went over it, and gave it a thorough examination.　The work is well done, and the masonry unusually well.　There are several bridges on the road, and I suggested the lengthening of the ties, so that they should extend eight or ten feet outside of the rails, on each side, and that an additional rail should be added to each bridge, to be placed between the other rails, and securely fastened to the ties.　I believe this would materially add to the safety of the bridge, and would be almost a thorough protection against a train going off.

This road has some of the most dangerous crossings that can be found, and I made suggestions in regard to them.

This road opens up another portion of our State, hitherto neglected by railroad facilities, and as it now completes an unbroken route, from the great cities to the fashionable summer resort of Narragansett Pier, its success in every respect is almost beyond a doubt.

### NEW YORK, PROVIDENCE AND BOSTON RAILROAD COMPANY.

This corporation has expended for maintenance of way $190,-979.61, including $52,707.88 for new steel rails, and for purchase of new rolling stock $81,075, and for repairs of the same, $42,-233.55. They charge to expense account $600,026.58, and to construction account $186,976.83, the last item including new rails, and new engine and cars.

### PROVIDENCE AND WORCESTER RAILROAD COMPANY.

Superintendent Hilton writes, " we have completed the stone work connected with Branch Avenue bridge, and also lengthened the abutments to bridge over highway near Horton's grove.

The piece of land along the road next north of Branch Avenue, known as the Hartshorn land, we have commenced to utilize, by laying some two miles of sidings, and have found them very valuable for handling, and distributing freight consigned to Providence.

The steady increase of business at Valley Falls, the junction of our main line, and East Providence Branch, has received attention by the addition of new sidings and with the opening of the road to Franklin there will be additional call for tracks at that point.

The necessary track has been laid at Lonsdale to connect with the new road built by the Lonsdale Company, connecting the old village with the main line of the railroad. We have rebuilt the bridge in Woonsocket known as the old Maid's bridge, involving the reconstruction of the abutments throughout.

The road and all apurtenances have been kept up in good working order ready for the revival of business."

They have expended during the year for maintenance of way $181,257.28, including $18,900.07 for new steel rails, and $10,637.02 for new iron rails, and for purchase, or repairs of rolling stock $126,101.75, including one new locomotive, one new passenger mail and baggage car combined, and new freight cars, amounting in all to $21,140, making the total of these expenditures $307,359.03, of which was charged to expenses $251,464.01, and to construction account $55,895.02.

### BOSTON AND PROVIDENCE RAILROAD COMPANY.

This Corporation has expended during the year $96,253.83 for purchase, or repairs of rolling stock, and for maintenance of way, including buildings, $351,481.89. Included in this amount, is $58,-910.19 for new steel rails, $64,604.92 for buildings, $21,863.50 for sleepers, $32,714.73 for bridges. These total expenditures amount to $447,785.72, all of which was charged directly to expenses.

### HARTFORD, PROVIDENCE AND FISHKILL RAILROAD COMPANY,

Have during the year expended $151,063.76 for purchase, or repairs of rolling stock, which amount includes $44,950.86 for new rolling stock, and for maintenance of way $234,601.04, including $56,587.40 for new steel rails, and $25,919.69 for stations. These aggregate amounts of $385,664.80, were charged to Profit and Loss account.

They have extended their side tracks 1 $\frac{401}{1000}$ miles; have added to their equipment two new locomotives, twenty-six freight cars, two baggage, and one derrick car.

### PROVIDENCE AND SPRINGFIELD RAILROAD COMPANY.

During the year have expended for purchase or repairs of rolling stock $2,508.61, and for maintenance of way $42,900.50, making an aggregate of $45,409.11, which was charged to expenses.

### WARWICK RAILROAD COMPANY.

Their report is as follows: " Owing to the non-payment of the sub scribers to the stock—leaving no money in the treasury, and while the operating expenses were in excess of the receipts, from both passengers and freight, it was determined by the Board of Directors to discontinue the operating of the road on the 31st of July, 1876.

Operations it is expected will be resumed when the negotiation for compromise, now pending, shall have been completed and fulfilled. Had the stockholders met their first obligation, and paid for their stock as agreed to when signed, this corporation might have been in strong hands ; its line completed to Cranston ; the road fully equipped for the transport of coal, passengers and freight. It is to be hoped that wiser counsels will prevail, and that the subscribers will come forward, and liquidate their just obligations, which will place the road in a condition to command the necessary capital for its completion, and active operations."

### WOOD RIVER BRANCH RAILROAD COMPANY.

During the year they have expended for purchase, or repairs of rolling stock $274.28, and maintenance of way $4,687.25, making a total expenditure of $4,961.53, which was charged to expenses.

### OLD COLONY RAILROAD COMPANY,

Have expended for purchase, or repairs of rolling stock $232,-641.57, which includes four new locomotives $30,490.01, two new passenger cars $9,887.01, fourteen new merchandise cars $11,-765.00, for maintenance of way $321,958.90, including eight hundred and forty-two tons new steel rails, and six hundred and fifty-nine tons new iron rails, costing together $69,699.57. This total amount of expenditures of $544,600.47, was all charged to expenses.

### PROVIDENCE, WARREN AND BRISTOL RAILROAD.

During the year they have expended for purchase, or repairs of rolling stock $21,240.87, and for maintenance of way $26,563.68, making an aggregate of $47,804.55, all of which was charged to expenses.

### NEW YORK AND NEW ENGLAND RAILROAD COMPANY.

This corporation has expended during the year for purchase, or repairs of rolling stock $151,806.47, including for two new locomotives, nine new passenger cars, one new baggage, and ten new freight cars $41,916.21, and for maintenance of way $218,040.62, making total expenditures $369,847.09, of which amount $325,-508.72, was charged to expenses, leaving a balance of $44,338.37 which was charged to Equipment Account.

### UNION RAILROAD COMPANY.

During the year they have added three and one half miles to their track, and also added eight new cars, and ten horses. They have expended during the year for maintenance of way $23,931.96, and for purchase and repairs of rolling stock $25,269.24, making an aggregate expenditure of $49,201.20, all of which was charged to expenses, except the amount required for the purchase of the new cars. If these new cars are required for the additional track laid during the year, their division of the charges was correct, but if these cars were for other routes, then the whole aggregate should have been charged to expenses.

I now make another classification in regard to the expenditures of these coporations, because these accounts are variously kept. I am aware that I shall lay myself open to criticism, nevertheless my views being so entirely different from the views of some of the corporations, I now proceed to place them, under two heads, as follows :

| ALL RIGHT. | ALL WRONG. |
|---|---|
| Boston & Prov. R. R. Co. | New York, Prov. & Boston R. R. Co. |
| Hartford, Prov. & Fishkill R. R. Co. | Providence & Worcester R. R. Co. |
| Providence & Springfield R. R. Co. | New York & New England R. R. Co. |
| Wood River Branch R. R. Co. | |
| Old Colony R. R. Co. | |
| Providence, Warren & Bristol R. R. Co. | |

I classify those as all right, because each of those corporations have directly charged to expenses, *all* their expenditures of the year, for maintainance of way, and for purchase, or repairs of rolling stock. I classify those as all wrong, that have charged *any proportion* of those expenditures either to construction, or to equipment account. When a road is thoroughly completed the construction account shows the cost of the grading, rails, sleepers, bridges, stations, turnouts, &c., and the equipment account shows the cost of all the rolling stock. The value of all these, except perhaps the investments in land, necessarily from constant use, are daily depreciating in value. These accounts are all allowed to stand, as first made up, and this being so, I maintain that all other expenditures should be charged to expenses. If a road was chartered, built and finished from Providence to Woonsocket, and after operating it for some time, it was extended to Worcester, in that case, it certainly would be proper to add both to con-struction and equipment account the additional expenditure, but this is the only case in my judgment, when such charges can be

justifiable. No one would claim that repairs made to replace worn
out rails, bridges or stations ought to be charged to construction,
and I cannot see why expenditures for new stations, double tracks,
new bridges, new cars or engines should be charged any other way,
because, commencing with what was then required,—all these
other expenditures are either to replace worn out material, or else
the natural result of an increased business. I regard these investments somewhat similar to the fixtures required to transact other
kinds of business. Some maintain that the ordinary repairs
made from time to time on rolling stock, keeps up fully the original value of that stock, but I cannot admit it. Take an entirely
new car that has been in use for a few months only, sell it to day,
and it must be sold as a second hand car and priced accordingly.
Should there be a certain per centage of the original cost, both of
construction, and equipment charged to expenses each year, to
equal the actual depreciation of it, then perhaps these accounts
might be increased by the new expenditures. To illustrate still
farther, the Boston & Providence Railroad Co., have been doing
business over forty years, their average expenditures per year for
for the last three years for purchase, or repairs of rolling stock
has been $122,914.88, and for maintainance of way, including
buildings, $364,235.40. Now if we take half of this as the
average for the past forty years, *leaving out the amount they
originally commenced with as charged these two accounts*, their
construction account would now stand $7,284,708.00 and their
equipment account at $2,458,297.60, thus after sinking all
the amount originally invested, these accounts would represent
nearly double the amount of their capital and their indebtedness.
Sales of stock made on this basis, would show a wonderful shrink-
age should the road be foreclosed. I am aware that in some years,
direct charges to expenses, of all these expenditures, might perhaps
entirely dispense with the payment of dividends, still I believe that
the stockholders would be better satisfied, because they would then
know the solid basis, and actual value of their stock.

# WORK PROPOSED FOR THE COMING YEAR.

### PONTIAC BRANCH RAILROAD COMPANY,

Report as follows :

"Contracts were awarded, and work of grading this road was commenced November, 1875. The road bed is nearly completed, work was discontinued waiting to arrange proper connections with connecting roads. As soon as these arrangements are completed, we hope to be able to complete the road."

### MOSHASSUCK VALLEY RAILROAD COMPANY,

report as follows :

"The road is nearly completed as far as the bleacheries of W. F. & F. C. Sayles, and they are receiving their freight on it.

The road will not be built, at present, further than to the south line of the branch road, so called, that crosses at the south end of Scott's pond, $1\frac{00}{100}$ miles from the point where it intersects with the Providence and Worcester road at Wood Lawn Station.

We expect before Spring, to run a passenger car over the road several times a day to connect with what are called short trains from Valley Falls to Providence."

### RHODE ISLAND AND MASSACHUSETTS RAILROAD COMPANY.

They report : "This road is to run from Valley Falls, R. I., to Franklin, Mass., connecting at Valley Falls with the Providence and Worcester Railroad, and at Franklin with the New England Railroad Company. The distance is about fourteen miles, about half of which is in Rhode Island and the remainder in Massachusetts.

We are now building that portion in Rhode Island, under a charter and amendments granted by the general assembly of this State. About one-third of the grading has been done, but the time for completion of the road will depend very much upon the severity of the weather this winter.

The amount of stock subscribed is 892 shares of $100 each. We have not proposed to issue bonds at present.

That portion of the road in Massachusetts is now being built by a Massachusetts Company, under their general railroad law.

The road is to have iron rails. The number of stations have not yet been determined upon. There are no bridges in Rhode Island, but there will be about three hundred feet of tressle work. The estimated cost of the road is about $100,000."

### NEWPORT HORSE RAILROAD COMPANY.

This road has not yet been commenced, and I should judge from the best information that I can obtain, I think they have abandoned, at least for the present, any idea of building it.

On the 6th of September, I attended a meeting in Boston, when there were present most of the Railroad Commissioners of the New England States, and the representatives of a few of the railroad corporations.

The object of the meeting was to devise a plan, whereby a uniformity in the railroad reports of the various States might be made.

This certainly would be very desirable, and I earnestly hoped that a plan might be devised, whereby the desired end would be attained, but when the result of the meeting showed, that the accepted plan would require the printing of twenty-six full pages of questions, for each corporation to reply to, including two hundred and sixty-three questions, many of which necessarily must have extended replies, besides requiring a transcript of the balance sheet of each corporation, I did not assent.

I do not consider that a very large proportion of the information thus sought is of any value, either to the public or the corporations, and the only object to be attained, is the gathering and compiling of statistics of no value to any one.

I doubt very much, whether the corporations themselves compare many of the details of their own statistics, with the others, or even glance at them after their completion, and the very size, and extent of them most assuredly would drive many from looking at them, even if they were desirous of obtaining information on some particular point.

The United States bank officials in obtaining information as to the condition of the various banks of the country, submit to each banking institution a series of twenty-two questions, and the State of Massachusetts in gathering information relative to sundry manufacturing corporations, submits a series of eleven questions, both of which are considered ample, and each of which represent a huge capital, and a vast number of stockholders. It is certainly very unfortunate, that the stockholders of our New England railroad corporations, should be deemed so incompetent to manage their own funds, or that the directors and superintendents of these railroad corporations should be classed so much under the average business ability as to require them to make oath to the correct replies of two hundred and sixty-three questions. I cannot imagine, whether the information thus sought for on such an extended plan, is for the benefit of the traveling public, that they might know the probabilities of recovering in cases of accidents, or is it for the investing public, who after having waded through an interminable mass of statistics and understanding but a very small portion of them, or is it for the benefit of the curious public, that they may be gratified to know, how much is sought for, and how little is really necessary.

I propose, and desire to present all such items in regard to each of these railroad corporations, as in my judgment will be of general interest, and I respectfully submit, that the thirty-three questions which I propounded to these corporations do contain all that is desired.

By my non-assent to the plans and questions adopted, the railroad reports of this State will not be in conformity with those of the other New England States, and while I have not the least objection to adopting that form, as far as the labor is concerned, I will collect and collate precisely the same as the other New England States, if your honorable body so desire it, but the expenses of the publication of it will undoubtedly be more than ten fold the present cost.

On the 20th of June I addressed a communication to the Honorable City Council of the City of Providence, in relative to a grade crossing at Greenland street, in the north part of the City of Providence. The tracks of the Boston and Providence, and Providence and Worcester Railroad Companies, each crossed this street, and as I could not see the least particle of necessity, for having the crossing, I petitioned to have the street closed. After various meetings of the Committee, and the necessary delays, the vote was finally passed, declaring that portion of Greenland street unnecessary as a highway, and the following day I had both sides of the track protected by a substantial fence, and now have the satisfaction of saying, there is one dangerous crossing less.

I subsequently addressed the same body relative to two grade crossings on the westerly side of the City, where a double track of one corporation, and a single track of two others cross it. One of them, I think, might be closed without any detriment to any one, and the other one bridged, the expenses of which, I think, should be proportionately borne, by the City, and each of the three railroad corporations.

This petition was referred to a Committee which has been essentially changed since the reception of the petition, but I propose to renew the matter immediately after the organization of the new City government.

In August I received an appeal from the Honorable Town Council of Warren, in relation to two grade crossings in that town. I immediately wrote the Superintendents of the two Railroad Corporations, appointing an early meeting on the ground. Previous to meeting these gentlemen there, I examined the location, and was prepared to make recommendations to the Superintendents immediately upon meeting them. The result was, that the corporations filled in on one side of the track, upon my purchasing for them a small piece of land, so as to extend and widen a highway upon the side of the track, and thereupon the grade crossing was closed. In regard to the other crossing, I suggested that the highway should be made under the track, but upon a careful survey and measurement, the land would not allow it, therefore the highway was improved in accordance with the wishes of the Honorable Town Council.

The law passed at the last January session, relative to carrying water on the trains, has received the unqualified approval of the whole traveling public. The words of the law are, " carry on each passenger car a suitable quantity of good drinking water." Immediately upon the passage of the law, I had it printed, and forwarded a copy to each corporation. At the same time, I forwarded a circular to them, giving my construction of the law, which, in regard to water, was as follows : " That water shall be carried through *each* train, say every thirty minutes, when the running time is over an hour, but through *every train*, however short the running time may be." This plan met the letter of the law, and is far preferable to having tanks of water kept in each car, because it is a difficult mat· ter, for ladies and children, to go to the extreme end of a car when the train is in motion, to say nothing of finding the floor wet when they get there, and the drinking vessels covered with cinders and dust. By having the water carried through, the drinking vessels are at all times inviting, and all other objections are entirely removed.

The subject of lighting cars is one that is receiving the earnest attention of our prominent railroad corporations through our whole country. Our January law provides that nothing except gas or candles shall be used in this State. The practical results of using gas show that some very serious accidents have arisen from its use, and is now in great disfavor. Corporations that have used it are now using candles, and in fact, candles are now generally used on the most important roads of our land. Almost everything has been tried, no one thing however resulting in such a large loss of life as from the use of kerosene oil, and I hope never again to see the time when it can be used in our State.

The adoption of candles is not a popular one with some of our corporations, on account of their cost, and I have heard unfavorable comments on their use by some of the travelling public. I believe that generally these complaints come from those passengers who have but a few miles to travel, while invariably those who have long distances to travel, especially in the late hours of the night, approve their use. The opposition to their use seems to come from those corporations, who I believe seeking to make them unpopular, use but two candles for a long car. This of course makes a very dim light, altogether too little to read by, and scarcely enough to discern any thing by. They reluctantly put in even those two, because there is no penalty in the law for using anything else, still I imagine in case an accident should occur, which might have been prevented by a strict compliance with the law, or proof con-

4

clusive to show that the accident was aggravated by the use of something else except gas, or candles, that the corporation would not find any surplus sympathy at the hands of a jury.

I did not propose to carefully examine the different cars to ascertain the quantity of light they had, or to specially invite the dissatisfied travelers to send a protest to me against the insufficiency of light, but should those protests be received, I think the present law gives me ample power to remedy the fault.

If I had preserved all the notices of accidents that have been caused by kerosene oil on cars, that have been in my possession, the number would be perfectly astounding. Kerosene oil when up to the standard, is a safe light for ordinary purposes, but to be used in cars, the lamps must be made of metal, and that lamp has never yet been made, that will remain tight against the constantly jostling moving of the cars. Glass would never answer, because it is so easily broken. To obtain a safe light we must be prepared to see these cars overturned, and then on fire, and lamps filled with kerosene, or even with sperm oil, having before the accident saturated well that portion of the floor under them, now break and materially add fuel to the flames. I therefore most earnestly hope that the present law may be allowed to remain. If any amendment is to be made, I would recommend the same penalty for section 3, as is now a part of section 2.

The matter of warming cars is another thing that engages my serious thoughts. In the recent fearful accident at Ashtabula, undoubtedly by far the largest number of lives were lost by burning, than from all other causes combined, and although no material now known used for stoves, could withstand that fearful plunge of over seventy feet, on to the rocks, still it seems to me that we should make every precaution against such accidents as might occur. These stoves should be made materially different from most of those now in use. The door should be the only opening in them, and that should be fastened by a lock and key. It should be firmly fastened through the floor, and so strongly made that when a car is overturned, it would retain its position, and not scatter the red hot coals. I have frequently called the attention of your honorable body to the matter, and do believe that legislation is necessary on this point to make travelling as safe as possible.

## SUGGESTIONS.

The only suggestions that I propose now to make, are upon only two matters, and are almost a repetition of what I have made before. The first is in relation to

## PRIVATE GRADE CROSSINGS.

This matter I have given my earnest attention to for a long time past, and while I have been successful in many instances in having crossings closed, yet new ones are made much faster than I can close the old ones. These are made by Commissioners appointed by the Courts for the lay out of a new road, and they have not the faintest shadow of the first particle of authority given them by the laws of our State, by the Courts, or by their commissions to grant any such applications. The only excuse they can possibly render, is that a similar authority has been previously exercised by other commissioners : a matter of precedence only. A large proportion of these crossings are entirely unnecessary, entirely uncalled for,and while the lives of the travelling public are constantly placed in jeopardy by these crossings, it seems to me a matter of the utmost importance that legislation should be promptly made to arrest the astounding growth of these crossings. There is another source of evil on this same subject, and that is after a railroad has been located, and the corporation doing business, then to have the various Town Councils authorized to lay out new roads, crossing at grade these railroad tracks.

In the first place this is an act of great importance to the whole travelling community, who would view it in altogether a different light, from what the members of a Town Council would, as they would be looking exclusively to the benefit of their own town. Second, it is an act of great injustice to the railroad corporation. Their right of way had already been secured, and had they known that a road at grade, was contemplated across their tracks they would in many instances, have changed their location in preference to having it. Again, the benefits, and advantages of the highways are exclusively for those not travelling on the railroad, while the whole responsibility and liability, in case of an accident, is thrown on to the railroad corporation, and finally as there is nothing among us, that possesses equal danger to all, that a grade crossing does, I would recommend that the authority to lay out new highways, or private crossings, at grade, across any railroad track, shall be placed only subject to the decision of our Courts, when due notice shall be given, and all parties can be fully represented and heard.

The other remaining suggestion that I make, is prompt legislation in reference to stoves used in cars.

All of which is respectfully submitted.

HENRY  STAPLES,

*Railroad  Commissioner.*

PROVIDENCE, DECEMBER 30, 1876.

# REPORT

OF THE

## Board of Inspectors

OF THE

# STATE PRISON,

### With the Accompanying Documents,

FOR THE YEAR 1876.

*MADE TO THE GENERAL ASSEMBLY OF THE STATE OF RHODE ISLAND AT ITS JANUARY SESSION, A. D. 1877.*

PROVIDENCE:

ANGELL, BURLINGAME & CO., PRINTERS TO THE STATE.

1877.

# OFFICERS.

| | | |
|---|---|---|
| T. PAIGE DODGE, | - | *Deputy Warden.* |
| THOMAS W. HAYWARD, | - | *Clerk.* |
| FRANK C. VIALL, | - | *Overseer.* |
| CHARLES W. DAVIS, | | " |
| ELIJAH R. TEFFT, | - | .. |
| CHESTER H. BLOOD, | | " |
| FREDERIC A. DANIELS, | - | *Watchman.* |
| WELCOME U. FOYE, | | " |
| ALONZO M. ROWE, | | .. |
| WILLIAM H. SHERMAN, | | " |
| Miss GRACE E. VIALL, | | *Matron.* |

# Report of the Board of Inspectors

# RHODE ISLAND STATE PRISON.

The Inspectors of the State Prison present their report for the year 1876, to the General Assembly. But in view of the fact, that the work of building the new Prison will doubtless be completed before the end of another year, and the present building will pass beyond their control, they have thought proper, in yielding their trust, to prepare a brief sketch of the action of the State, in reference to the provisions made for the imprisonment of offenders against its laws.

The building now occupied is of comparatively recent construction, and the system of which it is the exponent, dates back less than forty years. But the need of this method of restraint for those who violate law—as manifest within the limits of our State —is as old as the beginning of our colonial history. It was found necessary, at the very start, to provide a place of confinement for those who could not live at peace with their neighbors. As early as the Summer of 1638, the town of Portsmouth directed, in general meeting of the inhabitants, that a house "for a Prison containing twelve foote in length and tenn foote in breadth and tenn foote studd be forthwith built of sufficient strength." William Brenton was appointed to oversee the work. It was finished at some time during the subsequent Winter or Spring, and Henry Bull—chosen town Sergeant—was appointed keeper. On the 28th of February, 1639, the people who lived on the southwest part of the Island of Aquidneck formed a body politic by themselves, and

on the 16th of March following, they called their "Plantation".by
the name of Newport. Among these persons was Henry Bull,
"near" or "joyned unto" whose house the prison had been built.
A regular organization of all the inhabitants of the island was
effected in January, 1640, the "Plantation" at the other end of
the island was called Portsmouth, and a Governor, Deputy Governor and other officers were elected. In 1643, commissioners
were appointed by Parliament, who in 1647, granted a patent or
charter of incorporation, uniting the towns of Providence, Portsmouth and Newport. The town of Warwick makes its first record,
under date of August 8, 1647, although there seems to have been
some organization previous to this time. A "General Court of
Election" was held at Warwick, May 22d, 1649, at which the
general officers of the colony—now the colony of Providence
Plantations—were regularly chosen. At this session, it was
ordered, that "each town within this collonie shall provide a prison
with a chimneye and necessaries for any offender that shall be
committed, within nine months; and, in the meanwhile, it was
ordered "that the Prison in Newport"—doubtless the structure
at first ordered—"shall be the collonie Prison and Richard Knight
shall be the keeper of it." This was afterwards amended by
ordering a prison for Warwick, and a cage for each of the towns
of Providence and Portsmouth. The dissensions which arose
between the northern and southern towns prevented obedience to
the order directing the building of a prison in each place. But
upon the resumption of united counsels, the subject was agitated
anew. In the session of March, 1656, it was again enacted, that
the work should go on, and the 20th of September was fixed as
the date of its completion. But from some cause not sufficiently
apparent, no prison was built.

The only decisive action that was taken in the premises seems
to have been at Newport, where the town ordered the construction
of a new building, or possibly the enlargement of the old one.
Accordingly, at the session of May, 1658, "the Court, fynding by
experience,how difficult it will be to procure two prissons according
to former order, as alsoe two cages &c.; and alsoe the great uncertainty and difficulty as will from time to time arise in the using

such prissons and cages for want of sufficient keepers; and furthermore, taking into consideration the direct and absolute way and course that the towne of Newport have lately taken for the present furnishinge the prisson in their towne, which prisson is already in a good forwardness—upon the consideration of the aforesayd, the Court do therefore order and declare that the sayd prisson house at Newport, accordingly finished as the sayd towne have lately agreed to doo, shall be accounted to be the prisson for the occasions that may arise in any part of the collony to make use of the same." For defraying the expense of building the prison, Providence was to pay thirty pounds, Warwick twenty pounds, and Portsmouth ten pounds, besides what it had already paid. The former order relating to the construction of a prison at Warwick and cages at Providence and Portsmouth, was revoked. The building at Newport thus became the Colony Prison, and the General Sergeant was to "take care, that the prison be not voyd of a sufficient keeper." The town of Newport, moreover, was to be at the cost of keeping the building in repair, Richard Knight of Newport, was the General Sergeant for that year, and to him the care of the prison was committed. But at the next election, James Rogers, of Newport succeeded to the place, which he filled, by annual election, till his decease in the Autumn of 1676, when Thomas Frye was chosen to the office.

Whether Sergeant Knight or Sergeant Rogers was the keeper of the prison in person is somewhat doubtful, for on the accession of Sergeant Frye, one Robert Taylor is recorded as keeper. He is deprived of his office by special vote of the General Assembly, at the May session of 1677, and Henry Lilly is appointed "keeper of his Majesty's Prison or Jail in Newport." But at the October session of the same year, both Sergeant Frye and keeper Lilly are found among the grantees of the tract of land in the Narragansett country, to which was given the name of East Greenwich. Mr Frye was chosen General Sergeant in 1678, but was succeeded in 1679 by Edmund Calverly, who held the office till 1681, when Mr. Frye was again elected. At the May election of 1682, Mr. Calverly was once more chosen to the office, which he filled, by successive elections, until 1686, when the colony lost its independent government in the troublous times of Dudley, Randolph and Andros. It seems, however, that Calverly was continued as Jailor. Upon the recovery and restoration of the charter of 1663, under the government of Henry Bull, now "more than octogenarian," Thomas Frye was elected General Sergeant, and held the office till 1691, when Charles Tillinghast was chosen. A hiatus in the Colonial Records here occurs, and when, in 1696, they again appear, Frye is found as a deputy from East Greenwich, and the office of General Sergeant is lost in that of Sheriff, to which Captain Thomas Townsend is chosen.

Calverly does not seem to have been very efficient in his position. He at one time had a serious trouble with the General Attorney, John Pocoke, in which the Assembly judged the Sergeant to be wrong, but excused him, as his negligence of duty was "not through wilfulness, but through ignorance." He also permitted the escape of some of his prisoners, "by leaving the prison doore open," which also the Assembly excused, in part, at least—this time on account of "his poverty." Sheriff Townsend also came under the censure of the Assembly, for allowing, by "connivance or wilful neglect," the escape of a prisoner held on a charge of piracy. He did not get off so easily as his predecessor, for the matter came up afterwards in the Royal Council, and was made the subject of special investigation. From this time onward, the Jail at Newport—until 1778 the Colony Prison—was under the charge of the sheriff of Newport County, annually elected at the May session of the General Assembly.* At the June session of 1729, an act was passed, dividing the Colony into three counties, Newport, Providence, (first incorporated, June, 1703,) and King's, and at the May session of 1730, sheriffs of these counties were chosen.

---

*The successors of Townsend, while the Newport Jail continued to be the Colony Prison, were Jireh Bull (1698-'99), Thomas Mallet (1699-1703), Francis Pope (1703-'05) William Coddington(1705-'07), Nicholas Lang (1707-'15), William Coddington(1715-'21), Jahleel Brenton (1721-'33), John Coddington (1733-'38), Jonathan Nichols (1738-'40), Thomas Potter (1740-'45), Joseph Scott (1745-'46), Peleg Brown (1746-'47), Joseph Scott (1747-'56), George Gardner (1756-59), Joseph Wanton, jr. (1759-'60), George Gardner (1760-'61) Joseph Wanton (1761-'63), Samuel Brenton (1763-65), Joseph Wanton (1765-'67), Walter Chaloner (1767-'68), Joseph Wanton (1768-'69), Walter Chaloner (1769-'75), Jabez Champlin (1775-'81).

Various attempts had already been made to build prisons and jails, or cages, in different parts of the colony. The General Assembly, June, 1663, ordered a cage to be built at Warwick, with the necessary accompaniment of a pair of stocks. In June, 1686, the Royal Commissioners, (having taken the power from the Colonial Government and established a new Province in the Narragansett country,) ordered a prison to be built and stocks erected at Rochester, [Kingstown,] and appointed Daniel Vernon marshal of the Province and keeper of the prison. The expense of this erection was to be defrayed by seizing thirty wild or unmarked horses, and selling them under the direction of the justices of the peace. In November, 1695, the General Assembly, " sensible of the want of a prison upon the main land,"—by which it would seem that the order of the Commissioners had not been obeyed—directed a prison to be built in Providence, at the expense of the town. It is doubtful, indeed, if either structure was built, for the authority which the Assembly exercised over the towns was not of a very stringent kind. Judge Staples, in his Annals of Providence, tells the story: " At a town meeting in February, 1696, the town agreed to erect a jail 'near the water's side, next Gideon Crawford's warehouse.' The prison was to be ten feet by twelve. Judging from the contentious spirit manifested in their town meetings, one cannot imagine that a prison of these dimensions afforded very ample and roomy accommodations for such a community. At the April town meeting, the town voted to change the location, but, says the record, ' whilst the matter was in propagating by the town, obstruction was made by Samuel Windsor against the same, thereby raising such a tumult among the people that the moderator was put upon to dissolve the meeting.' " And thus ended the matter for the time. The jail of Newport was evidently the only building worthy the name, and this was found to be insecure and insufficient.

Accordingly, at the May session of 1702, the Assembly ordered that the " Governor and Council, or any four of them, shall have full power to cause to be erected in the town of Newport, a good and sufficient jail, and to cause the same to be fully completed

2

and finished, as they in their wisdom shall see meet." To meet
the expense of this building, the government did not resort to
the doubtful expedient of catching and selling wild horses, or
possibly the equally doubtful one of assessing the town treasury,
but wisely directed the Governor and Council "to take and
receive from the general treasury of the colony, so much as shall be
sufficient to finish and complete said jail." At the February session, 1708, a tax was levied to pay sundry expenses of the colony,
among which was the sum of £150, "for the building a jail." At
the April session of the same year, the work on the jail is spoken
of as repairs. There had, however, been built at Providence, in
1698-'99, a prison of some kind, but that it was at all suited to its
purpose is hardly to be supposed. Its cost is stated to be £21,
17s., exclusive of the locks. It had but a short existence, for it
was burnt before February, 1705. At the session of the General
Assembly held at that time, Joseph Latham and John Scott are
declared to be bound to build a jail at Providence, "in as good
manner as that was that was burnt." But the Assembly were to
judge whether they were to be allowed to do it, or pay £33.
The latter course was decided upon, and the two men were
ordered to pay the money, of which £30 were appropriated to
build a new jail. It is supposed to have been built on the west side
of Benefit street, nearly opposite the old Grammar School House
in that district. It was not a building large enough for a colonial
prison. Newport was then the chief town in the colony, with a
population nearly twice as large as Providence, and was the place
where most of the business, criminal and otherwise, was
dispatched. Its jail was estimated at £150, and within its walls,
"pirates" and "privateersmen" from abroad, as well as domestic
offenders, found a temporary, and not always a secure, habitation.

Whatever was done at the Newport jail in 1702-'08 must have
been of an imperfect character. It was doubtless found difficult
to raise the needful money, and the building was kept along from
year to year, with only sufficient repairing to make it barely
habitable. For at the June session of 1714, the sheriff protested
against its condition, and the Deputy Governor, Major Nathaniel
Sheffield, and Col. William Wanton, were appointed a committee

to consider the subject and decide what was best to be done.   At the June session of 1715, the subject came up again for consideration, and His Majesty's jail was declared to be in "ruinous condition, and daily growing worse,"  There was "no securing any person who was there committed—the which" it was thought might "prove to the unspeakable loss of creditors," and would "greatly encourage malefactors."  The keeper's house, also, was "not tenantable."  It was therefore enacted, that "Lieut. Col. John Wanton and Mr. John Odlin be a committee to repair, rebuild, augment and enlarge the house and jail aforesaid, so as to make it substantial and firm, and fit for the use intended."  They were also "to build or cause to be built a good and sufficient yard, adjoining and contiguous" to the jail; and, as before, the "charges were to be paid out of the general treasury."  At this time Ezekiel Bull is mentioned as keeper.  At the July session of the same year, an act was passed emitting £30,000 in bills of credit, and the necessary funds having been thus secured, the long desired object was at last attained.  It was easier to print money than to catch wild horses.  At the June session of 1717, Messrs. Wanton and Odlin presented their accounts.  The cost of building the jail was £426, 19s. 5d., and the two gentlemen were allowed £3 each for their services.  The addition to the yard, if made at this time, was not paid for till 1728, when the sum of £20 was appropriated for the purpose.  Newport having become "metropolitan," now had a jail corresponding to its consequence, and, while the towns on the main land were permitted—as in 1725—to "build and erect a house of correction" and "a small jail" in addition, if they were so disposed, it was yet especially enacted, that "all offenders" who were to be brought to trial, should not be kept in these places "longer than till they" could be "conveniently transported to Newport Jail."

But when the Counties were established, in 1729, it became necessary to provide for the more speedy and convenient trial of offenders, and the court-house and jail became needful structures. Those for King's county were ordered to "be set upon the hill "— Tower Hill—"near Robert Case's dwelling house in South Kingstown."  In 1731, Major William Smith seems to have been engaged in building a "county court-house and jail in Providence," for which he received the sum of £664, 9s.  But the latter structure must have been of little value or importance, for in January, 1733, it was found that Providence County required that a new jail should be built.  The building which had been used for the purpose, and the land which belonged to it, were to be sold, and the amount thus obtained was to be applied, "as far as it would go," to the new structure.  It was suggested, that possibly some public spirited citizens would give a lot of land near the county-house for the purpose.  But at all events, a new jail was to be built, "in some suitable and convenient place in Providence, of the same bigness of that in King's County."  Col. Nicholas Power, John Angell, Jr., and Daniel Abbott, sheriff of the county, were appointed to carry on and finish the work.  A piece of land was bought on the north side of what is now called Meeting street—giving to that thoroughfare the name of Jail Lane.  But this was only a temporary structure.  The stirring events which soon followed—the Spanish war, the war with France, the capture of Louisburg, the invasion of Canada, and the like—drew public attention to matters outside the colony limits.  In the meantime, paper money had increased in volume to an enormous extent, and, in 1753, the General Assembly was ready to set about the matter of the new Jail in Providence in earnest.  By an appropriation of £1000, in June, followed in October by an additional sum to an equal amount, the prosecution of the work was assured.  The old building and land on which it stood were to be sold, and the new jail was finally built under the direction of Messrs. Daniel Jenckes and Elisha Brown.  The proprietors of Providence gave the lot of land, on which it stood—" a lot adjoining the cove and west of the lot on which the court-house now stands."

Possibly, the action taken in King's County may have stimulated the people of Providence to move more effectively in this matter.  In February, 1752, the citizens of South Kingstown and others interested in the subject, decided that the court-house and jail on Tower Hill had gone to decay,—" being miserably built at first,"—and would be a perpetual tax upon the people to "keep them fit for use;" that they were in an inconvenient position, and that new buildings were imperatively necessary. Messrs. Elisha Reynolds, William Potter and Latham Clarke, stood ready to give the land and erect the buildings at their own cost, provided they were placed on Little Rest Hill, nearer the centre of the county. The Tower Hill people protested, but the offer was too generous to be declined, and the "court-house, jail and jail house" were ordered to be built—the three gentlemen giving bonds to the amount of £20,000 for the "performance of the conditions," and agreeing to complete the work in a year's time. The colony had by this time been divided into five counties. The County of Bristol had been incorporated in February, 1747, and the County of Kent in June, 1750. Court-houses and jails followed as a matter of course—those in the latter county having been built by the free contributions of the people, but aided in their "furnishing" by a lottery. The King's County Jail, without doubt, served well for a time the purpose of its erection. But on the night of October 8, 1770, a successful attack was made upon it from without, by persons in disguise, who broke it open and liberated four prisoners. One of these, Samuel Casey, was under sentence for counterfeiting. Another, by a curious coincidence, bore the name of Elisha Reynolds. They all made good their escape, fleeing upon horses—which seem to have played a somewhat prominent part in the history of this jail. The court-house required rebuilding in 1774–'76.

The jail at Newport was also falling out of repair, and it was accordingly decided at the October session of the year 1771, to sell the "old prison house," and to build anew in the place best suited to the purpose. Messrs. Oliver R. Warner, Thomas Freebody, Walter Chaloner, Job Bennett and John Wanton, were appointed a Committee, with full power to act in the premises. The new structure was to be 38 feet wide and not exceeding 45 feet in length. The jail passed out of the hands of the colonial government during the occupation of the town by the British forces, from December 8, 1776, to October 25, 1779. It was used, in connection with prison-ships anchored in the harbor, for the confinement of prisoners of war. Offenders against the colonial laws were distributed among the jails of the other counties. In the Autumn of 1778, the jail at Bristol was burnt in a bombardment of that town by the British forces, and in December of the same year, the General Assembly ordered that the sheriffs of Newport and Bristol counties should deliver their prisoners to the custody of the sheriffs of Providence County, to be kept in the Providence Jail. From that time until 1839, this jail was the place of confinement for the chief offenders in the State, and thus belongs to the history of the State Prison.* The British occupation of Newport was destructive to its prosperity. The inhabitants were left in great poverty and distress. "Hundreds of buildings had been destroyed, the vessels and wharves had gone to decay altogether. The war had destroyed" the town, "and taken from its population the means of rebuilding it." Thereafter, Newport lost, in a measure its metropolitan position in domestic affairs, as also its foreign trade, and Providence soon began to assume the controlling place in all affairs of State.

During the Revolution, the jail in Kent County required some repairs, which were made in the autumn of 1779. At the October session of 1781, the name of Kings County was changed to Washington, "in perpetual and grateful remembrance of the eminent and most distinguished services and heroic actions of the illustrious commander-in-chief of the forces of the United States." Had the County of Kent received the name of Greene at the same time, it would have been a grateful and appropriate act of commemoration of Rhode Island's own distinguished son. Washington County required a new jail. At the March session of 1789, a committee was appointed, consisting of Messrs. Rowse J. Helme, Samuel J. Potter, John Gardner, and Rowland Brown, to find a suitable lot on Little Rest Hill, and to report plans and estimates. The Com-

---

*A list of the Sheriffs of Providence County, from 1778 to the time of building the State Prison, is given, as they were the persons responsible for the care of the Jail. A list of the jail-keepers cannot be given. William Rhodes (1778-'80), John Beverly (1780-'83), Ephraim Bowen, jr. (1783-'87), Nehemiah Knight (1787-1800), William Allen (1800-'01), John Manning (1801-'04), Jeremiah Knight (1804-'08), Alpheus Billings (1808-'10) David Bartlett (1810-'11), William Foster (1811-'14), Andrew Waterman (1814-'18), Richard M. Field (1818-'21), Alpheus Billings (1821-'31), Henry G. Mumford (1831-'33), Richard Knight, jr. (1833-'36), William B. Mann (1836-'38), Roger W. Potter (1838-'51).

mittee reported at the January Session of 1790, that they had "contracted with Col. Thomas Potter for a suitable lot of land on the south side of the road opposite the old jail." They also submitted plans. Messrs. Samuel J. Potter, Jonathan J. Hazard, and Rowland Brown were appointed to purchase the lot and build thereon a jail two stories in height and " of the dimensions of forty feet by thirty-two." " Two thousand one hundred pounds in bills of credit " were appropriated for the "purposes aforesaid." This jail was finished in 1798, and cost £694, 7s. 10 8 4d.—of which £90 were paid for superintendence. Rhode Island became an integral part of the Federal Union in the Spring of 1790, and at the September session of that year, an act was passed allowing the use of the county jails to the United States, for the imprisonment of offenders against the national laws, " at the rate of fifty cents per month for each prisoner." In the Spring of 1782, some repairs were made upon the jail in Providence, of which at this time Jesse Whitmore is recorded as keeper. This building continued in use till 1799.

When the State government had become fairly established, there began to be some question as to the necessity of a State Prison. Up to the time of the occupation of Newport by the British forces, the jail in that town had been the Colonial Prison, as has already been stated. But that arrangement could no longer continue. In December, 1778, the Providence Jail, as has been said, became the principal jail in the Colony. The common punishments in vogue at this date, were flogging, confinement in the pillory and stocks, branding, fine and imprisonment for periods of comparatively short duration. The death penalty was inflicted by the code of 1647, for the crimes of " high treason, murder, petit treason, manslaughter, witchcraft, burglary, robbery, arson, rape, and the crimes against nature." In the revision of the laws which was made in 1718, arson and rape were omitted from the list of capital crimes. In 1767, witchcraft was omitted. In the digest of 1797, according to Judge Staples's enumeration, arson and rape were again added to the list, and high treason, petit treason, and the crimes against nature were taken from it. From that time till 1838 the list remained unaltered. But in January of that year, "imprisonment was substituted for the death penalty for all crimes except murder and arson." The latter was punishable by death or imprisonment, at the discretion of the Court. In January, 1852, capital punishment was abolished, and the penalty for murder was imprisonment for life. In the revision of 1872, the death penalty was affixed to murder committed by one "under sentence of imprisonment for life."

The gradual mitigation of the criminal code was due mainly to the increased attention given to the subject of prison discipline, both in this country, and in Europe, in the latter part of the last century. The custom of inflicting cruelties, torture, mutilation and death, was found to be ineffectual for the prevention of crime. Imprisonment came to be regarded as a punishment in itself, and it began to be thought, that, under proper regulations as to labor and discipline, there might be some hope even for the reformation of the offender. But the jails and prisons everywhere were in wretched condition. No labor was provided, prisoners were crowded into the cells, the buildings were comfortless and insecure, and the entire system of treating criminals was, in fact, if not in design, directed to making them worse than they had been before. Within our own limits, as has been set forth, it was necessary, at short intervals, to repair or rebuild the structures, used for purposes of imprisonment, in the different counties. Besides, it was easier to whip, brand or hang a man, than to take care of him in jail.

Judge Staples, writing as late as 1853, speaks thus: "In the county jails no means are provided by the State, and no pains taken to reform criminals. In only one [Providence] are the inmates obliged to labor. In all others, they are left to brood over their fancied wrongs, and to plan deeper schemes of villainy." The condition of things half a century before that time, may be imagined rather than described. The note of reform, however, had been sounded, and it was beginning to dawn upon the public perception, that men, even if they were criminals, were fitted for something better than hanging. How was it best to treat them, so that they might be improved in character, and returned, if possible, to society, prepared to become useful members thereof? At the close of the last century, the objects proposed were the following: "Safe keeping, moderate expense, determent from crime, maintenance of health, and the reformation and moral and intel·lectual improvement of the prisoners." The first requisite was to give the prisoners occupation. It was thought, that these objects could best be attained by complete isolation of the convict, and his confinement in a cell large enough to give him room to labor, as well as to live by day and sleep by night. While here, he was to have no sight of his fellow prisoners, scarcely of any visitor, and was to be known only by a certain number—that of the cell he occupied, or the number of his committal. The plan is said to have been first adopted in the prison connected with the hospital of San Michele, at Rome, in 1703. It was introduced into this country in 1786, in the construction and management of the Walnut street Prison in Philadelphia. It has since been carried to its perfection in the Eastern Penitentiary in Pennsylvania, where both its merits and its defects can profitably be studied. The evils of the congregate system had been so glaring as to make the separate system highly acceptable at first to the public mind.

The discussion of the subject had its influence in Rhode Island. As has been stated, a new jail had been built in Washington County. In Bristol County, also, a new jail was built at Bristol in 1793, at a cost of £109, 3s. 1½d. The jail in Kent County was repaired in 1794. The Providence County Jail claimed especial attention. Providence had become by this time the principal place for the confinement of prisoners, and for the transaction of the business of the Courts. In June, 1792, a movement was made toward putting the building in proper order. Messrs. Welcome Arnold, Nicholas Easton and Edward Smith were appointed a Committee to examine the condition of the Jail, that it might be repaired at a cost of £30. In February, 1793, they reported that the building was not worth repairing, and recommended that the lot be filled out to the channel and a new Jail be built. The object in view was to combine, if possible, a State Penitentiary with a Jail for the County, so that both State and County prisoners could aid in their maintenance by their own labor. In June, 1794, the project had secured so much favor and support, as to induce

3

the General Assembly to make a grant of £2,000, and to appoint a committee to erect a building, three stories in height, 53 feet in length and 42 feet in width. Messrs. Charles Lippitt, John Smith and Jason Newell were empowered to build.

An active opposition to the plan was immediately encountered. There was a strong feeling on the part of many persons, that the connection of the two institutions was not advisable. The State should have a prison by itself, which should have an independent system of management. But, on the other hand, it was urged, that an institution of this kind would involve great expense, and, with the small number of prisoners, would fail of its intended purposes. Possibly, the plans themselves were not thoroughly matured. At all events, the movement proved abortive, and in January, 1795, the action of the Assembly was revoked. The grant, however, was continued, and the same gentlemen were appointed a committee to build, but now, according to such plans and of such dimensions as the Representatives from Providence should agree upon. A small grant of £200 was added in June. The whole matter remained in abeyance for a year and more. The subject was felt to be of such importance, as to preclude any hasty action in the same premises. Perhaps there was the same reluctance to proceed as was manifested when the proposition to rebuild a jail was submitted to the freemen of Providence, a century before. But in October, 1796, the matter began to assume a more practical form. Messrs. Moses Brown, Simeon Martin, Thomas Holden, Rowse Babcock and Ichabod Cole were appointed a committee to prepare and report a plan of jail in Providence, " together with a plan for the confinement of criminals to labor, to be connected therewith, and also a plan of discipline." In May, 1797, the committee reported a general plan for a building to cost $12,000, and added to their report a printed list of the regulations adopted for the government of the prison for the city and county of Philadelphia—the Walnut Street jail, before referred to. In June, the report was so far acted upon, as to order the lot to be filled up and preparations to be made for laying a suitable foundation—the work to be done under the direction of Mr. Lippitt and his associates. In October, the foundations were ordered to be laid, and an appropriation of $1000 was made by the General Assembly.

But the adverse influences which had previously hindered the enterprise were still powerful enough to frustrate the prosecution of the work—so far as a State Prison was concerned. The foundations were laid. So much at least had been accomplished. But the plans for a State Prison must be laid aside for a new generation to execute. In January, 1798, it was finally decided by the General Assembly, that " a County Prison should be built in Providence on the foundation laid for the erection of a State Prison and Penitentiary House." Messrs. Lippitt, Smith and Allen were empowered, as before, " to receive proposals for building " the Prison. But it was to be built with "such alterations in the Prison and apartments from those contained in the plan for building a State Prison and Penitentiary House, reported to the Assembly in June, 1797, as are necessary, in consequence of the rejection of that part of said plan which related to the State Prison." Joshua Lindley had prepared the plans, and still retained them in his possession, but now it appears, that, as a portion of them had been rejected, he declined to allow the use of them to the Committee. Caleb Howard had contracted to do the work, and he prepared his own plans for a brick structure. The work now proceeded in earnest. Appropriations were made from time to time,— at this date, of $700 ; in October, $3000 ; in June, 1799, of $4000. At the session of the last mentioned time, Messrs. Edward Manton, Richard Mathewson, Ichabod Cole, Caleb Williams and Henry Spencer, were appointed to examine the work and settle with the contractor. In October, they reported that with a slight deduction, they had agreed to accept the building, and it was accordingly declared to be completed, and was delivered into the charge of Nememiah Knight, sheriff of the County. But Howard still had a claim of $1200, which the Assembly allowed, and a further sum of $200 was granted to Mr. Smith, of the building committee, for his services as superintendent. In February, $70.00 were paid to Lindley, and Howard received $226.00, as a final payment. Judge Staples, says that the cost of the building was $8,500.00. It was a little more than $9,000.00.

After the jail was built, it continually needed repairs. Almost every year, for thirty years, an appropriation was made for the purpose of putting it in proper order. But all to no purpose. Its condition and character were continually growing worse. Irregularities of all kinds prevailed. Many persons now living remember the method of communication and trade employed by the prisoners. All authorities agree, that it became, in the later years of its existence, "a disgrace to the State and a nuisance to the town." Its memory excites mingled emotions of ridicule and horror. Meanwhile, the building, of which it took the place, after being used in 1799 for the temporary confinement of a few French prisoners and for barracks for troops, was condemned in 1820 as a building unfit to stand, and after being demolished, by order of the General Assembly, the materials of which it was composed, were granted to the town of Providence—for what purpose it does not sufficiently appear. The jail-yard had been enlarged by the purchase of land east of the building in 1809, and now, in 1820, the lot was filled up west of the Jail wharf. Two years later, and the jail was supplied with medical attendance at the cost of the State—Drs. P. and Richmond Brownell being appointed physicians.

The project of a State Prison had only been slumbering. Public attention was again drawn to the subject of Prison Discipline by the experiment made by the keeper of the New York State Prison at Auburn, in 1823. The defects which appeared in the solitary system had induced those who were moving in this matter to attempt some other plan. The silent system, as it was once called, was tried at Auburn, with such flattering success as to excite the greatest interest. It is needless to describe it now, as it has become established, with some modifications suggested by experience, in most of the prisons in this country, and has passed over into one or two of the prisons of Europe. It is said to have been tried at Ghent as early as 1772, but for some reason was soon abolished. It may therefore be considered as essentially the American system of Prison Discipline, although the managers of the Eastern Penitentiary still cling to the separate system, and assert its supremacy over all others. It may be expressed in two simple phrases—separate confinement by night ; congregate but silent work by day. With this, permission is granted to converse with the Inspectors, officers. and visitors in the presence of an officer, as also to join in singing in public worship, at stated times to engage in social religious exercises, and in one prison at least, to eat together in the same mess room. The System, differing entirely from former methods, thus challenged scrutiny and awakened the attention of the most thoughtful minds.

In October, 1825, therefore, the matter was brought up in the General Assembly, on a motion to appoint a committee to examine the Providence Jail, and to ascertain on what terms the property could be sold and a new jail built. Messrs. Samuel W. Bridgham, Edward Carrington, and Judge Samuel Randall, were appointed the committee, with power to report plans and estimates. The opposition—for opposition there was—took alarm. But the matter could not well be dropped altogether. In May, 1826, by what seems to have been a compromise, a new committee was appointed, consisting of Messrs. Elisha R. Potter, Samuel W. Bridgham, Eleazar Trevett, John R. Waterman, and Joshua Bicknell, to report on the subject of a State Prison, with reference to similar establishments in other States. Massachusetts on one side, Connecticut on the other, were moving, and Rhode Island could not well remain still. The Committee thought it inexpedient to report plans without visiting other prisons, especially that at Auburn. Accordingly, Messrs. Bridgham and Waterman were directed, in January, 1827, to visit Auburn and such other prisons, as they judged best, and after proper deliberation to report. For some reason, however, this movement, which seemed so promising, came to a premature end, and nothing more appears to have been done.

In October, 1828, the General Assembly, again obliged to take action upon the subject, appointed a committee, consisting of Messrs. Joseph L. Tillinghast, Zachariah Allen and Christopher Rhodes, to examine the Jail and lot. These gentlemen reported in January, 1829, that a new jail was very greatly needed, and recommended that a tract of land of four or five acres at Great Point, so called, be purchased. The project was again killed—or at least put into a state of suspended animation—by continuing the committee, and adding to it Mr. Nathan Brown of the Senate. But the friends of the measure now determined to carry the subject to the people. A petition was prepared, circulated for signatures, and presented to the General Assembly—a form of procedure not then very common in Rhode Island legislation— asking that a State Prison be built. The Assembly, this time, met the appeal by appointing Governor John Brown Francis, James F. Simmons, and William R. Staples, to consider the whole sub- ject, and report the best method of answering the request of the petitioners. To this Committee were added, in January, 1834, Messrs. Rensellaer B. Smith and Elisha Mathewson. There was evidently a disposition, on the part of the General Assembly, to take the matter seriously in hand, and with a view to come to some definite conclusion. The result, to which the Committee and the Assembly came, was eminently characteristic. With that recognition of the power of the people and that deference to the popular will, which are to be noticed in the legislation of Rhode Island, the question was referred to the freemen of the State. Shall a State Prison be built, to be paid for by a tax on the ratable polls and estates ? The third Wednesday in April, 1834, was the day fixed " for the freemen to vote upon the question. Four thousand four hundred and thirty-three (4433) voted yes; five hundred and two (502) voted no. The subject had been so thor- oughly canvassed, that the vote may be taken as the voice of the citizens of the State, acting intelligently and deliberately upon a matter which they deemed of great importance.

At the June session of 1834, Messrs. John Stevens of Newport, R. B. Smith of Glocester, John H. Cross of Westerly, Oliver G. Waterman of Coventry, William R. Staples, of Providence, and James F. Simmons of Johnston, were appointed to select a site, report estimates of cost, and such other preliminary arrangements for the work. In the following January, (1835,) they reported that Great Point, in Providence, seemed the most suitable place, and they were ordered to purchase the land at a cost not exceed- ing $500.00. Messrs. Smith, Waterman, Staples, George D. Cross, Christopher Spencer and Christopher Rhodes, were appointed a committee to receive proposals for building at Great Point, where the land was bought of the city of Providence for two hundred dollars. Messrs. Staples, Rhodes and Zuriel Potter were chosen Commissioners, and they were ordered to go on and build, without departing from the plan of separate confinement at labor with instructors. In the comparison between the Philadelphia and Auburn systems, the former had thus been preferred. Mr. Staples, having been elected as associate justice of the Supreme Court in June, 1835, resigned his position, and Mr. Edward S. Williams was appointed in his place.

It was soon found that more land would be required, and two acres more were added to the area of the premises. In October, 1835, a contract was made with James Lewis, but, owing to some mistake in his estimates, this was rescinded in June, 1836, and a new contract was made. Mr. James M. Warner was appointed superintendent of the work. With the new contract and the new superintendent, there seemed to be a disposition to have new commissioners. In January, 1837, Messrs. Asa Pierce and Elisha O. Angell were appointed commissioners to complete the work. Mr. Angell was to be at all times present, and give to it a continual oversight, with a compensation of three dollars per day. Mr. Pierce was to visit the scene of labor at least once a week, and receive " a reasonable compensation " for his services. Perhaps it was found by the General Assembly, that work of this kind could receive a stricter attention from those who were able to give their entire time to it with an adequate compensation—or what was thought so—than if it were merely a labor performed gratuitously, or with an uncertain amount of payment. The work from this time was prosecuted with vigor, and though it was thought, that the building should have been placed farther away from the cove, upon higher ground, it was still accepted, as, on the whole, well and properly situated. Yet there was still considerable dissatisfaction, which found expression in the appointment of Messrs. Simmons, John H. Clarke, Asa Winsor, and Christopher Spencer, by the General Assembly, in May, 1837, to consider the expediency of continuing the work. These gentlemen were also empowered, if they thought best, to convert the building into a jail for the County, or even to stop the work altogether. But they decided, that the enterprise should be carried out. The Prison was finally completed in the Summer or early Autumn of 1838, and on the 16th of November, of that year, four convicts were committed to its cells.

That Prison is the building, which, now used for a House of Correction, has been repeatedly condemned by the Board of Inspectors who have been appointed to the charge of the institution. Built of huge granite blocks, clamped with iron, it is indeed, a pile of massive masonry, which, at the time of its erection, might well have been thought "impregnable from within." The original plan. it is said, "embraced a keeper's house, two stories high, 48 feet square, fronting the cove, adjoining this on the north a small building uniting it with the State Prison, and the Prison, 48 feet by 93 feet, two stories high. A corridor, ten and a half feet wide passes through the centre of the prison, on each side of which are the cells " Of the cells there were 40, those on the lower story 8 feet wide, 15 feet long, and 9 feet high, those on the upper story of the same width and height, but of only 12 feet in length. The light is admitted through a narrow aperture at the top of the cell, the ventilation is attempted through a still narrower aperture at the bottom. With inadequate means of heating, with no lining of brick or plaster to the outside walls, it is, in the winter season, the most comfortless place imaginable. The frost can be scraped from the inside wall of the cell upon any day when the temperature is low, and it is difficult to understand how the inmate, who has succeeded in avoiding suffocation for want of air, can escape being frozen by excess of cold. By what means the Commissioners or the General Assembly could have become convinced that this was the best method of construction at the time, it is impossible to perceive. But taken captive by the glowing accounts of the results attained by the Pennsylvania system, they built a structure which, in five years' use, was found to be unsuited for its uses, and which, for thirty years, has been thought to be a disgrace to the State. Its cost was $51,501.69, or an average of about $1300 per cell.

During the progress of the building, it was thought best by the General Assembly to construct and connect with the State Prison

a new Jail for the County of Providence. The work was ordered
at the January session of 1838, and was completed in the Spring of
1839. Mr. Asa Pierce superintended its construction, and its cost
was $7,894.41. This was built on a somewhat different plan from
the other, and was a smaller and more compact structure. It ad-
joined the keeper's house on the east. It was 27 feet wide, 66
feet long, and two stories in height. It was divided into 18 cells,
7 feet wide by 9 feet in length, and 4 rooms for persons committed
for debt. Unlike the State prison, the cells occupied the centre
of the building, "the corridor being between them and the walls."
Water was supplied to both prison and jail by a tank in the upper
part of the small building, occupying the central space between
them and the keeper's house, and both buildings were warmed by
hot water pipes, running through the different cells and corridors.
The Jail, as well as the Prison, seemed to have proved itself unfit.
Judge Staples, writing in 1848, declared that it had, even in that
short period, "gained for itself anything but an enviable reputation."

But for better or for worse, the Prison and Jail had been built
and joined together. The question of management had already
engaged the attention of the General Assembly, and at the January session of 1838, an act was passed for the government and
discipline of the Prison. A board of seven Inspectors was to be
annually elected by the General Assembly at the May session,
and these gentlemen were to have the supervision and control
of officers and convicts. The appointment of warden, under-
keepers and physician, was placed in their hands, but the compensation of these officers was fixed by the General Assembly.
They could arrange and contract for the labor of the prisoners,
and fix upon the style and fashion of the prison uniform, according to their discretion. They were to serve gratuitously, and
were to report in October of each year to the General Assembly.
At the May session of 1838, Messrs. Samuel W. King, William
R. Staples, William S. Patten, Christopher Rhodes, Henry G.
Mumford, Isaac Thurber, and George B. Holmes, were elected to
constitute the first Board of Inspectors. Messrs. Thurber and
Holmes declined to accept the appointment. On the 26th of May,

4

the Board was organized. Mr. King was chosen chairman, and
Mr. Staples, clerk, but upon Mr. Staples declining the office, Mr.
Patten was elected. The Inspectors elected Dr. Thomas Cleveland, warden, and Dr. Isaac Hartshorn, physician, their terms of
office beginning on the 1st of November. The General Assembly, in October, 1838, directed that the warden of the State Prison
should also be keeper of the Providence County Jail, and both
institutions, in 1841, were placed in charge of the Inspectors. Before the term of the first Board had expired, a third vacancy
occurred by the resignation of Judge Staples, and Messrs. John J.
Stimson, John L. Hughes, and Roger W. Potter, then sheriff of
the County, were elected, in January, 1889, to fill the places.
The Board, in full working order, was thus enabled to begin its
administration.

The first and second reports of the Inspectors are very com-
mendatory of the separate system, thus fairly inaugurated. They
find some difficulty in heating the cells, but, on the whole, they
seem satisfied with the arrangements, both for the punishment
and the instruction of the convicts. " Of the effect of the discipline and regimen of the State Prison upon the convicts," they
express " a very favorable opinion. Experience shows it to be
beneficial rather than injurious. The cells are commodious, well
ventilated and cleanly. The prisoners were anxious for employment, and solicited it," and deprivation of labor would be considered a hardship. " Their docility and contentment are remarkable.
They have sufficient food, which is simple and healthful ; they are
treated with all proper kindness; they are instructed in the value
of good conduct and good principles. Perhaps no condition can
be imagined in which they could be placed, all circumstances considered, more advantageously for society and themselves." The
Inspectors anticipate " successful results from the methods,
which the State had thus adopted to diminish crime and to reform
criminals. " Perhaps the contrast between the new building and
the old jail was so great as to make the former assume qualities
which it did not really possess. The principal labor carried on at
this time was the making of shoes. To this was afterwards added
the painting and finishing of fans. Matters were thus conducted

till 1840, when Messrs. Patten, Stimson, Hughes, and Mumford, left the Board, and Messrs. Samuel Y. Atwell, Gideon Spencer, Martin Stoddard and Amherst Everett were appointed to the position. Mr. Everett was elected clerk in place of Mr. Patten. In 1841, Mr. King, having been elected governor in 1840, retired, and Mr. Thomas M. Burgess was chosen Inspector in his place. Messrs. Atwell and Spencer also retired, and their places were filled by the appointment of Messrs. Barzillai Cranston and George Rice. At the regular meeting in May, 1841, Mr. Burgess was elected chairman of the Board. In the internal direction, warden Cleveland remained in office; but two changes were made in the sanitary department, Dr. Hartshorn retiring and Dr. Henry W. Rivers receiving the appointment, November 1, 1840, and Dr. Rivers giving place, July 14, 1841, to Dr. Richmond Brownell.

By this time, there had grown up a very strong feeling of disapprobation of the system which the first Board of Inspectors had regarded so favorably. A committee was appointed by the General Assembly, in June, 1841, consisting of Messrs. Samuel Y. Atwell, Alfred Bosworth, and E. S. Wilkinson, to examine the Prison and Jail, and ascertain if any reduction of the expenditures could be made, and if any abuses existed which might call for further legislation. The Inspectors, in their report of October, 1841, find that the "labor in the Prison is not a source of profit to the State." They also declare, that "many of the prisoners are inclined to be idle," and that "the cases in which the taking away of labor would be considered a hardship are very rare." They "further report, that the experiment of solitary confinement has not, since the Prison has been in operation, proved perfectly satisfactory. They fear the effect is to injure strong minds, and to produce imbecility in those that are weak."

The report of 1842 is no better. The number of convicts had increased to 37, of whom 6 had become insane, and several others had shown symptoms of derangement. The year 1843 brought a slight alleviation in the form of a law allowing the prisoners to work together in the corridors of the Prison. But the Inspectors deemed that a workshop would be a desirable addition, and earnestly and successfully pressed the subject upon the attention of

the General Assembly.  In response to their appeal, a shop was
built, 42 feet wide, 54 feet long, 10 feet high to the eaves, with a
steep roof, and lighted from the top, the cost of which was
$2,897.20.  They appeared to think in those early days, that the
State might derive from the Prison labor a certain profit.  But it
is evident that they were working at a disadvantage.  The separate system was in danger of breaking down.  The warden, in
his report for 1844, gave the finishing stroke to it, by enlarging
at considerable length and with great vigor upon " the injurious
and alarming effects of solitary imprisonments upon those who
are subjects of it. "  He also defended the administration of the
Prison, from the charge brought against it by some " foreign writer
of distinction," who had declared, that the " system had failed
in this State, through the mismanagement of those charged with
the duty of carrying it into effect. "  Dr Cleveland discusses the
subject with considerable ability, and he comes to the conclusion
that " it is impossible for " him " to hesitate in condemning the
penal system of solitary confinement. "  It is needless in this
place to speak of the comparative merits or demerits of the system.  It simply suffices at present to record its utter failure in
the early management of the Rhode Island State Prison, and its
consequent abandonment.  Some changes were made at this time
in the Board of Inspectors, by the retirement of Mr. Stoddard in
1843, and Messrs. Rice and Potter in 1844.  Mr. Stoddard's place
was filled by Mr. Rufus W. Kimball, and the other two gentlemen
were succeeded by Messrs. James Y. Smith and Isaac Thurber.

The year 1844 was signalized by the passage of a stringent set
of rules and regulations by the Inspectors, the chief penalty for
the violation of which was the deprivation of food and water to
the offender.  Jail prisoners were also set to work, and an addition to the jail itself was begun, which was completed in 1845.
In their report for the last named year, the Inspectors impress
upon the General Assembly that the reduction of the prison expenses should not be the chief object of the managers.  The
Prison and Jail " were rather to be maintained as places for the
safe confinement of criminals, where, under wholesome restraints,
proper efforts may be made to give them habits of industry, and

to teach those who are to return to society, correct ideas of their duties to their fellow-men."

This period of the history of the State Prison is memorable in being marked by the incarceration of a political prisoner—the first, and it is hoped the last, in our State—Thomas W. Dorr. It is needless to recall here the incidents of that peculiar political convulsion of the years 1841 and 1842, in which Mr. Dorr acted a conspicuous part. It is difficult at the present day, to appreciate the intensity of feeling which arrayed the citizens of the State in two opposing camps, and which threatened at one time to bring upon our community the horrors of a civil war. Mr. Dorr, who had been elected governor by those who were opposed to the charter government, succeeded in escaping from the State, immediately upon the failure of the movement of which he was the head. But on returning, in the year 1844, he was arrested, tried, and convicted for treason, for which he was sentenced to imprisonment for life. He was committed, June 27, 1844. The records of the Inspectors at the time show that there was considerable apprehension that some improper communication might be had between him, his parents and counsel. The rules of the Prison were enforced with great strictness, not to say severity, and were not relaxed till the spring of 1845. The question of a general amnesty to those who had been engaged in "the rebellion" entered largely into the canvass for the election of that year. By the Constitution, which, in 1842, took the place of the old charter, the obnoxious restrictions to suffrage were removed, and the result of the election was favorable to those who desired Mr. Dorr's release. The General Assembly, at the June session of 1845, although declining to make a special case of releasing Mr. Dorr, yet enacted a law granting complete amnesty, and providing that no person was to be thereafter prosecuted for treason against the State. All persons in custody were to be discharged. The law was passed June 26, and Mr. Dorr was accordingly set at liberty June 27, having passed exactly a year in the Prison. He occupied, for a large part of the term, what is now cell No 17, and it is even at this day an object of curiosity and interest to visitors. The experience through which he had passed impaired his health, and he died

on the 27th day of December, 1854, at the age of 49 years. But
the last year of his life was soothed by the passage of an act
in January, 1854, annulling the judgment of the Supreme Court
in his case. That judgment was "repealed, reversed, annulled,
and declared in all respects to be as if it had never been rendered,"
and the clerk of the Court at Newport was ordered to write
across the face of the record—"reversed and annulled by order
of the General Assembly, January, A. D. 1854."

The year 1847 was marked by the death of warden Cleveland.
He was a physician by profession, and had undertaken the duties
of a prison official, with the sincere desire to carry out the system
adopted at the first. But he soon became convinced that it was
not conducive either to the good health or the good morals of the
prisoners, and while he endeavored to do the best possible in the
circumstances, he felt that success was of very difficult attainment. His physical strength gave way, and on the 1st of May,
1847, he resigned the office of warden, and the charge of the
Prison passed by law into the hands of the sheriff of the county,
Roger W. Potter, who had been Inspector from 1839 to 1844. Dr.
Cleveland died September 29, 1847, aged 45 years, leaving behind
him the memory of a true and faithful man. Mr. Thomas W.
Hayward, who had been underkeeper and clerk in the prison for
a considerable time, was elected warden on the 11th of August, to
enter upon his duties on the 1st of October. In May, 1847, the
election of Inspectors was relinquished by the General Assembly,
and the appointment was placed in the hands of the Governor.*
The Board was now entirely changed. Messrs. Burgess, Everett,
Rhodes, Cranston, Kimball, Smith and Thurber retired. The
Governor appointed to their places, Messrs. Edward S. Williams,
Daniel Wilkinson, Adnah Sackett, Abner Peckham, Edward Potter, William Sheldon and Ariel Ballou. Mr. Williams was
elected chairman, and Mr. Wilkinson, clerk. The Board continued unbroken until May, 1849, when Messrs. Sheldon and Ballou retired, and Messrs. Alfred Wright and Thomas Davis were
appointed. On the 13th of July, of the same year, the chairman,

---

*A full list of Inspectors is given at the end of this Report.

Mr. Williams, died, and the Board put on ~cord their estimate of his service in the following resolution, passed August 8th: "*Resolved*, That this Board have received, with deep regret, the announcement of the death of their late chairman, Edward S. Williams, whose industry, fidelity and experience they have highly appreciated." Beyond this, there is little to record besides the changes which took place in the Board and administration by appointment. Mr. Wright succeeded Mr. Williams as chairman. Dr. Isaac Hartshorn was added to the Board. Mr. Wright retired in 1850, and the Reverend Dr. Francis Wayland, succeeding, was elected chairman, which position he held till 1854. In 1851, Messrs. Wilkinson, Potter and Hartshorn left the Board, and were succeeded by Messrs. George L. Clarke and Zachariah Allen, the latter of whom was soon succeeded by Mr. Amasa Manton. Mr. Clarke was chosen clerk. Mr. Hayward resigned his position as warden, June 5, 1851,* and Mr. Francis B. Lee, of Norwich, Conn., was elected as his successor. Dr. Brownell resigned in October, 1848, and Dr. Salmon Augustus Arnold was chosen as Prison Physician, holding the post till October, 1852, when Dr. E. V. Hathaway was elected. Dr. Hathaway retired, April 12, 1854, and Dr. George P. Baker was chosen. Mr. Lee held the position of warden till July 1, 1852, when he was succeeded by Mr. William Willard, who in turn was succeeded by Mr. Samuel L. Blaisdell, August 1, 1854. During this period some additions were made to the workshop, and attempts were made to improve the ventilation, both of the Prison and Jail. The labor was carried on under the direction of instructors and officers, and on account of the State.

The year 1852 was notable for the abolition of capital punishment. It was also signalized by a work, whose necessity had for some time been evident, the erection of a new wing on the west side of the premises, to be used thenceforward for a State Prison. The "impregnability" of the first structure had been disproved

---

*Mr. Hayward has been connected with the prison for at least twenty-five years, in different positions, lately as clerk and accountant. While these pages were passing through the press, he died, on the 2d of January, 1877, in the sixty-fifth year of his age. He was a very faithful, conscientious and pains-taking official, and his thorough knowledge of the prison and its affairs, made him a public servant whose place it will be extremely difficult to fill.

by escapes from time to time, and the crowded condition of the buildings had required the occupancy of some of the cells by two or more persons each. The defects of the construction had become obvious, and the system generally had become extremely distasteful to all concerned. Indeed, it had been virtually abandoned at the date of the erection of the workshop. A new prison had become necessary, and the General Assembly, in June, 1851, made an appropriation of $16,000.00 for the purpose of supplying the need. The work was very properly and wisely put into the hands of the Inspectors, who chose Messrs. Sackett, Peckham, and Allen, a committee to prepare plans. It was decided that the dimensions of the cells should be in the clear, four feet wide, seven feet high, and seven and a half feet long. Mr. Clarke was added to the building committee, and the work was immediately taken in hand. Mr. Thomas A. Tefft furnished the plans, and Mr. Allen, of the Inspectors, invented the door and lock; Mr. Peckham superintended the entire construction, which was completed—a block of 88 cells—in the Autumn of 1852, at a cost of $18,143.71—an average of about $200.00 to a cell—"a sum," as the Inspectors might well say, "much lessthan has generally been expended upon prisons of this description." The separate system of labor was thus in the construction completely set aside. The new wing of the prison was built with the cells in the centre, and the corridor upon the outside—the method of construction now generally adopted in our country. In building, one cell in each story, and on each side of the old prison, was removed where connection was made with the new wing.

At this time, also, a change was made in the time of presenting the annual report of the Inspectors, from October to January—caused by the amendment of the constitution in 1854. The contract system of employing the prisoners was introduced in 1852, and the State gave up the business of manufacturing on its own account. The first contractor was Mr. James H. Field, and the price of labor was fixed at "25 cents a day for the first year, 30 cents for the second, and 35 cents for the third year." But the most important improvement made was the establishment of a library for the prisoners. The Inspectors, in 1851, asked for a

grant of $200.00 for the purchase of books, and also desired au-
thority to allow the warden to admit visitors at his discretion,
upon the payment of a small fee—the proceeds to be devoted to
the continuance of the library.  The authority was given, and
Messrs. Wayland and Davis were appointed to select and buy the
books.  From that time to the present, the sums received yearly
from visitors have been sufficient to give an annual increase to the
library, creditable both as to the number and quality of the books
purchased.  The library now numbers about 1,250 volumes.  In
their report for the year 1853, the Inspectors say: " The library
of the Prison contains at present four hundred well-selected volumes, and abundant means of enlargement are provided for devoting to this purpose the fees received for the admission of visitors.
Free access to the library is granted to the prisoners, and as a lamp
is allowed to each cell, opportunity is afforded for intellectual improvement, after the labors of the day are ended.  It will then be
seen," adds the report, " that it has been the design of the Board to
render the Rhode Island State Prison not only a place of confinement and useful labor, but especially a school of reformation, and
to do this at the least possible expense to the State."

At the end of the year 1853, the number of convicts in the State
Prison was 49; in the County Jail, 84, of whom several were women.  While the Inspectors were hopeful for the former class of
prisoners, they regarded the condition of the latter as something
requiring the attention of the General Assembly.  At the end of
the year 1854, there were 51 convicts in the State Prison, and 117
prisoners in the County Jail.  For the first time in its history, the
Prison accounts exhibited an excess of income to the amount of
$125.65.  But the Jail, as nearly always before and since, showed
still, that the expense was greater than the receipts.  In 1854, this
excess was $1,442.85.  As has been already stated, Mr. Willard
retired from the office of warden, and was succeeded by Mr. Blaisdell.  Mr. Willard resigned for the purpose of taking charge of
the Connecticut State Prison as its warden.  The Inspectors, in
parting with him, expressed their " high estimation " of his personal character and the value of his service.

The success which had attended the efforts of the Inspectors in

5

procuring the construction of the new wing, encouraged them to
still another attempt to improve the premises.  In the course of a
few years, under the personal direction and oversight of Dr. Arnold,
the unsightly sand hill immediately outside the wall became a
smiling garden.  The wall was covered with vines, and various
kinds of fruit trees contributed their product to the dietary of the
Prison.  In 1854, a special statement was made to the General Assembly, covering the expression of the necessity—1.  Of the erection of a wing on the side of the prison opposite to the last new
structure, upon the same plan, and with " sufficient capacity for
two hundred prisoners, with an hospital, chapel, bath-room and
suitable apartments for female convicts."  2. Of the erection of
workshops of a sufficient size to employ all the prisoners.  3. Of
the extension of the wall that the new shops might be enclosed.
The statement was referred in the Assembly to a committee,
consisting of Messrs. John Boyden, Jr., A. M. Gammell, N. C.
Peckham, George Manchester and Simon H. Greene, who reported
favorably, and the Inspectors were authorized to proceed at once
to the work.  Immediately upon the grant of a sufficient sum, the
work was begun, and was carried forward with such expedition
as to complete, by the end of the year 1855, the new wing, with
chapel, the extension of the wall, the construction of a boiler-
house with engine, and other necessary additions, a force-pump
and drains.  A new workshop was so nearly built as to promise
its completion in the Spring of 1856.  The total cost of these new
works was $47,143.37, of which about $25,000.00 was expended
in the construction of the new wing and chapel.  In the new building there was sufficient accommodation for thirty six male and
thirty-six female prisoners, with hospital-cells upon each side.
The work was done under the superintendence of Messrs. Sacket,
Amasa R. Tourtellot and James G. Anthony.  The last two gentlemen had been appointed to the Board in May, 1854.  Mr. Tourtellot gave to the construction a special supervision.

An additional improvement was now made in the appointment
of a chaplain.  The Inspectors in their reports had, for several
years, called the attention of the General Assembly to the necessity of making this appointment, and at this time a petition, nu-

merously signed by some of the best and most influential citizens
of the State, supported their recommendation. In 1856, the Assembly passed the requisite act, and the Rev. William Douglas
was appointed chaplain. It is appropriate at this point to give
an account of the manner in which the department of religious
instruction has been administered. In the act creating the Board
of Inspectors, authority was granted to them, to "license any
proper person who will serve without compensation, to visit the
convicts, as a moral and religious instructor." The further provision was made, for holding "public religious services in the corridor, measures being taken to prevent the convicts from seeing
each other, or communicating." Preaching to stone walls, with,
perhaps, the application of the ear of a convict to a small aperture in the cell door, or even to the open door itself, cannot be
regarded as a spiritual exercise, stimulating to the preacher, or
calculated to excite devotion, or strengthen the moral sense of the
listener. But notwithstanding the unfavorable surroundings, there
were still found men and women who were moved to the benevolent, but not always hopeful work of religious instruction. Prayer
books and Bibles from the first were furnished to the convicts—
the former through the liberality of Mr. John B. Chace. But it
needed the living voice and the personal presence of a wise coun-
sellor, to give direction to the reading and study of those devo-
tional manuals.

In May, 1839, the Reverend Messrs. John Maxcy and William
Douglas, and Mr. Gilbert Congdon, were authorized to visit the
prisoners as religious instructors, to converse with them and teach
them in their cells. The following persons were also authorized
from time to time to perform this duty: September, 1840, Mr. T.
Salisbury; May, 1841, Messrs. R. M. Field, Jr., and Abner Gay, Jr.;
March, 1842, the Reverend Henry F. Harrington; August, 1842,
Mr. John B. Chace; September, 1842, Mr. Healy; December,
1842, the Rev. Henry Bacon; October, 1843, Mr. Carpenter; June,
1844, the Rev. Doctor Alva Woods; April, 1848, Mrs. Anna Jen-
kins, and Mrs. John Maeder, June, 1848, Mrs. Adnah Sackett,
and January, 1851, Mrs. Alva Woods, as instructors of the female
prisoners. It will thus be seen, that Mr. Douglas, who now holds

the position of chaplain, has been connected with the Prison from
the beginning, and has the satisfaction of looking back over a continuous and faithful service of 38 years, as "moral and religious
instructor" in our State Penitentiary.   There could be no preaching in the corridor of the State Prison, it is true, but in July,
1844, the public services on Sunday for the State prisoners, were
held in the new building, then erected—a portion of which now
remains, and is incorporated with the Chapel at present in use.
Here a better opportunity for preaching and for Sunday School
instruction was presented, and the religious instructor was cheered
by the collective presence of his congregation.   The labors of a
preacher in this place were performed by the Reverend Doctor
Woods, from 1844 to 1854, when religious exercises were inter-
rupted by the alterations of the buildings.   In 1856, the new chapel was fitted up, and Mr. Douglas was elected chaplain.   Doctor
Woods was also largely instrumental in procuring funds for the
establishment of a library for the prisoners.   He remarks, as a
gratifying circumstance, the presence of the Chairman of the Board,
Mr. Burgess, during his administration of the Prison, at the preaching service on Sundays.   The Inspectors in their reports from year
to year, make mention, with deserved commendation, of this kind
and gratuitous service.

Mr. Douglas, even before his connection with the Prison, had
been laboring with the prisoners in the old jail on Meeting street,
and, like other pastors, he followed his flock, when they were
transferred to their new fold.   The jail prisoners were brought
from their cells into their own corridor, and Mr. Douglas preached
to them in the open space.   When the west wing of the Prison
was built, he preached to all the prisoners in the corridor.
Upon his appointment as chaplain of the State Prison, and
the erection of the Chapel, the Sunday school, which three
years previously had been formed, was more thoroughly organized.
Dr. Wayland, Professor George I. Chace, Mr. Stephen Atwater
and Warden Willard are mentioned as having taken part in the
school, and given great assistance to the chaplain in his labor.
Singing was introduced, and became a very important part of the
services.   The library soon came into constant use, and its influence

was beneficial to a marked degree.    But the chapel was found to be too small, as scarcely more than two thirds of the prisoners could attend divine service.

In December, 1867, the Inspectors ordered the upper story of the old workshop to be fitted as a chapel, and ample accommodations for the Sunday exercises were thus secured.   The old chapel is now used for the sewing-room of the female prisoners.   Mr. Douglas says, " we now have a well organized Sunday school, an efficient and intelligent corps of teachers, and a well selected library.   No person, unless an eye witness to the facts, can form any adequate conception of the improvement in the deportment and appearance of the inmates, which we have reason to believe has been effected, to a great extent, by the religious and moral influences exerted upon them."   The Inspectors say in their report of the year 1857—a year also marked by the removal of the last vestige of the separate system, in the restoration of the prisoner's personality, by the substitution of his name for his number—" the proportion of the discharged convicts, who are becoming reputable members of society, furnishes evidence that the Prison is accomplishing the purpose of a house of reformation, and thus realizing the benevolent design of the General Assembly."   Certainly it can be added, that too much commendation cannot be given to those faithful men and women, who, through many years of oftentimes discouraging labor, have given their time and strength to the duty of instruction in the Prison and Jail.   It has been mostly gratuitous, and had its source in a genuine christian sympathy for the unfortunate and the vicious, and in the sense of obligation to help the weak and wanting to a better knowledge and a stronger and higher life.   It is impossible, and it will not be considered necessary, even by those most interested, to give the names of all who have taught in the Sunday school.   It is enough that they have done their work well and faithfully, and such labor does not ask for the poor reward of an earthly record.   Two men are especially mentioned in the reports—Mr. Varnum J. Bates, who died in 1868, and Mr. Benjamin White, who died in 1875, both of whom have left the memory of devoted and self-sacrificing labor.   During the last year, the Sunday school has suffered a loss by the death of Rev. Thomas Vernon, and of Mr. Joseph W. Beynon, who for several years have been faithful and earnest instructors. Mr. and Mrs. James W. Goodwin are also commended for the essential and valuable aid they have rendered in conducting the music.

But it is not too much to say, that in making the changes and improvements apparent at this period, the personal influence of Dr. Wayland was largely exercised. That he was ably seconded and cordially supported by such men as Messrs. Sackett, Peckham, Davis, Allen, Clarke, Tourtellot, S. A. Arnold and Thomas P. Shepard—all men of positive opinions—is as much to the credit of their good judgment and sound policy as to his own executive ability. They and their associates would doubtless all agree, that, if his mind did not furnish the guiding impulse of their administration, they still relied upon the assurance, that the remarkable power which had been displayed in other fields of labor would be applied—even in this, unpromising as at first sight it might appear—to make it fruitful unto good results. He might not have originated these movements and plans, which gave an essentially new direction to the government of the Prison; but he contributed, in no small measure, to their successful prosecution. Doctor Wayland was a member of the Board from 1850 to 1864. He was chairman from 1850 to 1854, and again in 1860–61. Retiring in 1861, he was re appointed in 1863, and served as chairman for one year. Mr. Sackett was chairman from 1854, to his death, February 15, 1860. He served as Inspector from his appointment in May, 1847, to the time of his death—a term of nearly 13 years—the longest continuous term of any Inspector from the construction of the Prison. It was a very faithful and conscientious labor, and its results remain to this day. Mr. Wilkinson was clerk from 1847 to 1851, when he retired from the Board to be re-instated in 1854, and to be re-appointed to his clerkship, which he held till 1860. Mr. Clarke was clerk from 1851 to 1854, when he retired from the Board. The Inspectors, during all this period, speak in terms of high appreciation of the services of the warden, Mr. Samuel L. Blaisdell. In 1859, for the first time since their establishment, the Prison and Jail united showed a balance of income. The Prison alone, since the 1st of August, 1854, had more than paid for its maintenance; but now the Inspectors were able to report a surplus from both of $635.07—the expenses of the Jail, which had been always in excess, being more than counterbalanced, by the returns from its labor, increased by the income from the Prison. In 1860, the entire surplus was $2,583.29. In 1861, the net profit was $76.68. In 1862, the Jail accounts showed an excess of income of $143.16, and the Prison accounts the handsome income of $3,194.95. In 1863, the Jail income was $13.33, and the Prison income $1,177.90. In 1864, the last year of Mr. Blaisdell's wardenship, the Jail income was $79.60, and the Prison income $1,186.42.* Through all the years in which Mr. Blaisdell had the immediate direction of affairs, the results, both financially and morally, were very creditable to his skill and spirit. In every Report, the Inspectors bear cheerful and united testimony to the excellence of his discipline, the humane yet firm character of his government, the strict integrity which characterized his business transactions, and the general efficiency of his administration.

Besides the changes already noted in the Board, there are now to be recorded the following : Mr. Davis retired in 1853, and Messrs. Clarke and Peckham in 1854; Messrs. William P. Bullock and Walter S. Burges served from 1852 to 1854; Mr. William Sheldon from 1854 to 1855; Mr. Amasa R. Tourtellott from 854 to 1865, being clerk in 1860-'61; Dr. S. A. Arnold from 1854 to 1861; Mr. James G. Anthony from 1854 to 1861; Mr. Zachariah Allen from 1855 to 1861 ; Dr. Thomas P. Shepard from 1860 to 1864, being chairman from 1861 to 1863; Mr. Byron Sprague from 1860 to 1865 ; Bishop Thomas M. Clark from 1861 to 1863; Mr. William E. Hamlin from 1861 to 1863, being clerk during that time ; Mr. Horatio N. Slater from 1861 to 1863 ; Mr. George H. Whitney, also as clerk, 1863–64; Mr. Thomas Brown from 1863 to 1866, clerk for the last two years ; Mr. Thomas K.

---

*A table containing an account of the receipts and expenditures of the Prison and the Jail from the time of building the Prison, with the surplus, deficit, expense per capita of each year, &c., has been prepared, and is given at the end of this Report. It will be seen that the average net cost per year has been about $2,357.02

King, also as chairman, from 1864 to 1866; the Reverend A. Huntington Clapp, 1864–'65; Messrs. Hiram H. Thomas and George L. Clarke from 1864 to 1866.

There were two objects dear to the heart of Dr. Wayland, and those longest associates with him: 1. The completion of the Prison buildings, by the demolition of the oldest wing—what was now the old Jail with its "dungeon"—and the construction of a new wing upon the site and 2. The prolongation of the sentences of those committed for petty offences and drunkenness. The two really belonged together, for it would be an added inhumanity to doom any human being to a long imprisonment in the old Jail. Let a new jail be built, substantially on the same plans as the other wings had been, and then let these offenders be confined long enough within its walls to wean them from their bad habits and vices, and instil into them some good and useful principles of conduct. For the furtherance of the first object, the efforts of the warden and Inspectors to make the Prison profitable to the State, were mainly directed. They hoped to accumulate a sufficient amount to partially defray the cost of the new erection, and then, having the money at their own disposal, they could easily obtain, as they thought, a grant of authority from the General Assembly, with whatever additional sum was necessary to do the work. Plans were prepared by Mr. James C. Bucklin, and everything was got in readiness to begin the structure, and to press it to completion without unnecessary delay. More than $7,000 had been saved by the end of the year 1868, and the subject was pressed upon the attention of the Legislature. Indeed, for at least ten years previous to this time, the matter had been brought up for consideration. Year by year, the Inspectors had urged, with ever increasing warmth, the need of the new structure. But it was found impossible to make the General Assembly believe that the first State Prison which the State had built, had become, in less than thirty years, "a hideous remnant of barbarism," a collection of "cheerless dungeons" and "noisome cells," and a disgrace and scandal to the good name of our community. But this was not all. In May, 1863, the General Assembly authorized the Inspectors, at their discretion, to deposit the surplus earnings of the Prison and Jail with the General Treasurer, at an interest of 5 per cent., and in May, 1864, directed them to do so—leaving them no discretion in the premises. Dr. Wayland, seeing no prospect of carrying out his plan for rebuilding, resigned on the 12th of July, 1864, and Dr. Shepard accompanied him in his retirement from the Board.

The second object which Dr. Wayland had in view—the prolongation of sentences—was afterwards partially attained by the organization of the institutions on the State Farm. But Dr. Wayland did not live to see the day. Meanwhile, although the subject was, year after year, pressed upon the General Assembly, in connection with the administration of the Jail, it was impossible to accomplish any satisfactory result. It was either treated with indifference, or rejected when the measure was proposed in practical form. It is needless now to urge the subject anew. It would seem that any candid mind would readily perceive, that in order to accomplish any beneficial results from prison discipline, a longer detention than a week or ten days is imperative. The provisions of the charters of the cities of Providence and Newport, and the town ordinances, which apply to this subject, work only mischief. They are bad for the community, bad for the towns and cities, and bad for the persons subject to restraint. One thing has been accomplished—imprisonment for debt has been abolished, in name at least, though not actually in fact. It is hoped that not many years will pass, when the Legislature will see the necessity of providing some place where petty offenders, and those committed for drunkenness, will have an opportunity to free themselves from habits of intemperance and vice. Wholesome discipline for three months at least, would accomplish good results.

On the 18th of February, 1865, Warden Blaisdell resigned, and was succeeded by his brother, Richard W. Blaisdell, who had been acting as deputy warden for a considerable portion of the previous year. It was hardly to be expected that he would prove as successful an administrator as the former warden had been. But, in 1865, the accounts showed a net surplus of $347.80, and the Inspectors speak of him as judicious and efficient. The Board at this time consisted of Messrs. King, Brown, Clarke, Thomas, Stephen R. Weeden and Stephen C. Arnold.      6

In May, 1866, the Board was very materially changed. Messrs. Weeden and Arnold remained, but the places of the other gentlemen were supplied by Messrs. Augustus Woodbury, Samuel L. Caldwell, Lewis Fairbrother, Edwin M. Snow and Moses B. Lockwood. Mr. Woodbury was elected chairman, and Mr. Weeden, clerk. Mr. Lockwood resigned in the autumn, and Dr. George L. Collins was appointed in his place. Dr. Collins remained but a few months, and upon his resignation, Mr. William Binney was appointed, in April, 1867. The new Board, upon entering on their duties, found that the contract for labor, which had been held by the East New York Boot, Shoe and Leather Company, had expired, about three weeks previous to their appointment, and the male prisoners were entirely idle. A new contract could not be made until the 1st of September, when the labor was let at a considerable reduction from former rates. The financial exhibit of the year was, consequently, not so favorable as in previous years. The expenditures exceeded the income to the amount of $1,594.25. Nearly four months of enforced idleness made a considerable difference in the financial condition of the Institution. But the year was occupied by the Inspectors in an attempt to give a more thorough organization to the Prison and its concerns. The government was divided into six departments,—1, general management; 2, sanitary; 3, religious instruction; 4, labor and finance; 5, subsistence and clothing, and 6, repairs. The first was placed in charge of the chairman and one Inspector, and to each of the others, one Inspector was assigned. A new set of regulations was prepared, by which each officer was specially informed of his station and its duties. A new catalogue of the library was prepared, and the library itself revised under the particular direction of Dr. Caldwell. The Inspectors recommended the construction of a new Prison, upon some site properly selected, or if found more feasible a partial reconstruction upon the present site. Public sentiment in the State was already drifting toward the establishment of some reformatory institution, to be connected with a State asylum for the insane, a State alms-house and other kindred institutions. The General Assembly, in January, 1867, appointed a committee to inquire into the matter, and in 1868 and 1869, other committees were appointed, with power to select a site and purchase the land. In the summer of 1869, a farm, finely situated on a commanding elevation in the town of Cranston, was bought, and the "State Farm," under the direction of the Board of State Charities and Corrections, was duly and legally constituted. The act of establishment, as passed by the General Assembly, contemplated the erection of a State workhouse, a house of correction, a State asylum for the insane, and a State almshouse, and these departments are now fully organized. The concentration of all the penitentiary establishments of the State gradually became the policy of the authorities, sustained by the sentiment of the people. The construction of a new Prison upon the State Farm was soon to be expected.*

Meanwhile, the Inspectors of the State Prison endeavored to make the institution, under their immediate charge, serve its purposes, as well as the circumstances would permit. The equipment was found to be low, and the buildings somewhat out of repair. In 1867, Mr. Arnold retired, and Dr. Benoni Carpenter was appointed to the place. Some changes in the internal administration had already been found necessary, and on the 1st of May, Warden Blaisdell resigned, and General Nelson Viall, previously elected by the Board, entered upon his duties. General Viall had served for a year or two as Chief of the Providence Police, and at once commended himself to the favor of the authorities. The parti-colored uniform of the prisoners was thrown aside, and neat and serviceable clothing was received from the Quartermaster's Department of the State. The upper story of the old workshop, which had been mainly used of late for a lumber-room, was cleansed and fitted up for a chapel. The room used for this purpose had always been too small for the accommodation of all the prisoners on Sunday. The lower hall was used for a time, and found to be inadequate. But the fitting of the room in the workshop at once supplied the need, and an airy, commodious and capa-

---

*An account of the Providence Reform School hardly comes within the scope of this report, as it is more of a municipal, than a State institution, and is under the charge of Trustees elected by the City Council of Providence. The school was formally opened, November 1, 1850, and has been instrumental in saving a large number of boys and girls from the harmful influence of street life, and the contamination of the Jail.

cious chapel was furnished. Two years afterwards, in 1869, the kitchen was removed from the basement below the central hall to the lower story of the old workshop, and the change was felt to be in every way an improvement. Changes could not thus be made without an increase of expense. In 1867, the sum of $1,799.40 was spent for repairs, $1,596.58 for clothing and bedding, and $398.48 for furniture. The excess of expenses for the first four months was $3,242.81, for the remaining eight months, from May 1st, $3,418.14. The Inspectors recommended the passage of a law authorizing a commutation of imprisonment for good behavior, and the General Assembly at once acted upon their advice. The law has proved to be a most efficient agency for promoting good conduct among the convicts. In the early part of 1868, the small pox appeared in the Prison and continued for two or three months, notwithstanding the efforts of the physician to check its progress. Happily, but one prisoner died, but the presence of the disease was sufficient to cause a hindrance to labor, a reduction of income and increase of expense. The balance against the Prison and Jail was $3,829.03. Dr. Baker, after a service of fourteen years, resigned on the 14th of July, and Dr. George W. Carr was elected to the position. A relaxation of the rules was permitted, allowing the prisoners to enjoy an hour or two of comparative freedom in the yard and chapel on the public holidays. Dr. E. M. Snow retired from the Board in 1869, and Mr. Jesse Metcalf was appointed to fill the vacancy.

In 1869, the excess of expenditures was $5,078.54, of which, $3,005.95 were paid for new steam boilers, pumps, &c., for ventilators for shop, for new gas pipe, and burners for lighting each cell in the Prison wing and other extraordinary expenses. The balance against the Institution for ordinary expenses was a little over $2,000.00. During the winter of 1868–69 a course of lectures was delivered in the Prison chapel by different gentlemen of the city of Providence, and an evening school was opened for the instruction of such prisoners as desired to obtain some familiarity with the common English branches of knowledge. At the end of the year, the chaplain was able to say in his report: "At no time since my connection with the Prison as a religious teacher, extending over a period of more than thirty years, has the institution been in a better condition than at the present, to accomplish the design of its establishment—the protection of society and the reformation of offenders." In 1870, a board of women to visit the correctional and penal institutions in the State, was established by the General Assembly, and the female prisoners—few in number since the organization of the State Farm—were encouraged by the presence and counsels of members of their own sex, officially appointed to consider their needs. During this year, the amount expended for repairs—in fitting up a bath-room, building an oven in the kitchen, finishing the attics of the warden's house and making other improvements of the premises, was $1,765.60, and the deficiency for ordinary expenditures was $347.19. A new and more favorable contract for labor was made on the 1st of August.

In 1871, the buildings still needed repairs to the amount of $1,101.11, but the accounts of the Prison and Jail showed a balance of income over all expenses of $3,018.46. The Inspectors recommended the appointment of a special commission for building a new State Prison. They also adopted a system of classification and gradation of prisoners, which went into effect January 1st, 1872. They suggested to the General Assembly the feasibility of providing, that a portion of the earnings of the prisoners should be paid to them at their discharge, or applied to the assistance of their families during their imprisonment. In 1872, the subject was again brought to the attention of the Legislature in the form of a recommendation, and an act embodying the principle was soon after passed. The balance of income for this year was $4,518.90. The Prison school began to show unexpected results. One or two convicts went beyond " the rudiments " to engage in higher studies, and one made considerable progress in the study of both ancient and modern languages.

In May, 1873, Mr. Weeden was re-elected clerk of the Board, but was obliged, in the following November, to resign the office, on account of feeble health, and Mr. Metcalf was chosen to fill the vacancy. Mr. Weeden received the thanks of the Inspectors for his faithful service. In September, Doctor Caldwell resigned his position on the Board, having removed from the State. His retirement was a source of sincere regret [to his associates, and they placed on record a minute, expressing their grateful appreciation of his fidelity and usefulness. The Reverend Doctor Alexis Caswell was appointed to fill the vacancy. During this year a change of labor was made, by reason of the expiration of the contract held by the former parties. The manufacture of boots and shoes had been the chief branch of industry pursued in the Prison since 1858, when the contract with Mr. Field expired. Contracts were made in September for finishing furniture and weaving wire. Chair seating was also carried on to a considerable extent. The loss of a month's labor, incurred during these changes, and the subsequent depression of business, which prevented any remunerative occupation, seriously affected the receipts, and the balance of income fell to $2,365.02. A fire, which occurred in the workshop, on the morning of January 15, 1874, caused a damage which required an expenditure of $5,109.89 to repair. The balance of income over the ordinary expenditures fell to $461.47. The Inspectors endeavored, by a thorough investigation, to ascertain the origin of the fire, but without arriving at any satisfactory results. They immediately took measures to provide against a similar misfortune, by the introduction of Pawtuxet water, with the necessary hose, upon each floor of the workshop.

In January, 1874, the General Assembly began to move, preliminary to the erection of a new Prison for the State. A Commission, consisting of Messrs. Edwin M. Snow, William B. Lawton, and William D. Brayton, was appointed to select a site, to be approved by the Board of State Charities, and to prepare plans to be approved by the Inspectors of the State Prison. This commission, after consultation with the two Boards, reported to the Assembly in May. A site was selected on the State Farm near the Pontiac road, and plans, combining recent improvements in Prison architecture, prepared by Messrs. Stone and Carpenter, Architects, were submitted to the Inspectors and received their approval. A new Commission was appointed, consisting of the same gentlemen, with whom were associated the Chairman of the Inspectors, and Mr. George I. Chace, Chairman of the Board of State Charities, ex officiis. The foundations were laid in the Autumn of 1874, and the work has been pushed forward as rapidly as possible. The estimate of the cost for a prison of 252 cells was $334,000.00—an average per cell very nearly the same as that for the first State Prison, built forty years ago. The Inspectors congratulate themselves and their fellow citizens, that the old Prison will soon be known only in memory. Public sentiment, directed at last into the right channel, has decided upon the demolition of a structure which had become a reproach and scandal to our good name.

The year 1875 was not marked by any event of special importance. A new branch of industry was introduced in the manufacture or repairing of cotton ties, but it was found impossible to obtain employment for scarcely more than half the inmates of the Prison and Jail, except at prices ridiculously small. Nevertheless, the men were kept at work, for idleness is especially demoralizing in Prison life. The excess of expenditures was $5.68, and the reserved fund—encroached upon largely by the fire—amounted to $4,431.20. An enumeration of the different branches of labor pursued during the existence of the Prison may not be without interest. It is as follows: Boot and shoe making, and finishing of fans, on account of the State; manufacture of furniture, boot and shoe making, broom-making, finishing of furniture, upholstery, wire-weaving, chair-seating, manufacture of cotton-ties, and preparation of shoddy, under contract; finishing and manufacture of furniture on account of the State. From the beginning, the Inspectors have been mindful of the necessity of furnishing for the prisoners constant employment. The want of occupation is a prolific source of trouble and irregularity, both within and without the Prison walls. No prisoner, who has been committed for any length of time to the Rhode Island State Prison, has gone forth without having learned some useful employment, by which he might, if so he chose, gain an honest livelihood. At this day, there are as good workmen in the Prison as can be found anywhere, and many of them have become skilful artisans by the occupation afforded them in the Prison workshops. The knowledge of a trade is in itself a certain restraining influence from crime. In the case of convicts, it helps to prevent a relapse after

they are discharged.  And thus, while steady work is one of the
best aids to good government within the Prison, it is also a contribution to the instrumentalities which tend to promote the
safety of society and the preservation of public order.  To furnish
employment to discharged prisoners is a benefit to the community,
as well as to the individuals personally concerned ; and it is hoped
that the General Assembly, in its revision of the laws pertaining
to the direction of our penitentiary establishments, will find some
place for an agency, which will help in the attainment of so desirable an end.

For the year 1876, the Inspectors have to report a decided
increase of numbers, both in the Prison and Jail.  The buildings
have been crowded more than ever before—the number of inmates
rising upon some days as high as 270, while there are but 214 cells
that are available for the confinement of prisoners.  The new
State Prison will be finished none too soon, and it certainly is
gratifying to feel, that the present winter will be the last in which
the old Jail will be occupied by human beings.  Fortunately, no
serious disease has prevailed among the prisoners.  Indeed, through
the entire period of the existence of the Prison, there has been a
somewhat remarkable continuance of good health within the walls.
With the exception of the cases, when the small pox gained an
entrance—happily with but little loss of life—the premises have
been exempt from epidemic dieases.  Sanitary regulations have
been well observed, and the prison physicians have faithfully performed their duty.  In this connection, the Inspectors would make
grateful acknowledgment of the kindness of the ladies connected
with the Union for Christian Work, for gifts of flowers, which, for
several years, have brightened the life of the Prison, and especially
of the hospital.

With careful attention to the physical health of the prisoners,
there has been the same diligent labor for their moral well-being.
The evening school, which was opened in 1869, has been continued
with results, which, with every succeeding year, have given
renewed satisfaction.  To the regular religious instructions of
Sunday, a religious meeting of a more social character has been
held on the first Sunday of every month, and also during the week

on every Friday evening. In accordance with the request of the chaplain, the Inspectors authorized the warden to allow the State Prison convicts to eat their last Christmas dinner together. A table was spread in the old chapel, and they sat down in company, instead of taking their dinner to their cells. In some State Prisons this practice is followed daily, and a mess-room is as necessary an adjunct as a work-shop. The Commissioners for building the new State Prison, have proposed, in their plans, to make provision for its adoption in the management of that institution. On the occasion now referred to, the meal passed off in a manner gratifying to the officers, and, as an experiment for the day, was regarded as a success.

The continued derangement of labor and the depression, which has existed in all branches of industry, have naturally had their effect upon the Prison finances. Mr. William Sweeney's contract, for furnishing and upholstering furniture, expired on the 8th of September. The Inspectors advertised the labor of 50 men, thus deprived of employment, but no one seemed willing to enter into a contract, which would not be likely to continue for more than a year. It was, therefore, decided to carry on the business, with which the men had become familiar, on account of the State. As soon as the necessary preparations could be made, the prisoners were set to work. The results thus far are as satisfactory as could reasonably be expected in the circumstances, and it is believed that the State will suffer no loss. The contract heretofore made with Mr. H. H. Fenner for the manufacture of wire goods, was transferred to Mr. George Campbell, in May last, and is to continue in force till October 1st, 1877. Mr. Campbell employs 8 men, at the rate of 80 cents per day. The contract with the Providence Cotton Tie Company, for the labor of no less than 15 men, at the rate of 40 cents per day, was renewed for one year, on the 11th day of May. At least 8 men are employed by Mr. T. A. Cunliff, at the rate of 40 cents per day, in the cutting of woolen rags for the preparation of shoddy. The remainder of the men are employed in chair-seating for different parties in Massachusetts. The price paid for the last mentioned labor is very low, but the Inspectors have judged it best to keep the men steadily

employed, even if the returns would be no more than sufficient
to pay for the services of the supervising officer. During the year,
as during the period of his management of the Prison and Jail,
Warden Viall has performed his duties with efficiency and good
judgment. The internal administration has been conducted with
ability and accuracy, and both the Warden and his subordinate
officers have, in the main, exhibited a ready spirit of coöperation
and a commendable interest in promoting the success of the Institution.

The amount of receipts during the year 1876, is as fo ows:—

| | | |
|---|---|---:|
| From labor | | $11,662 61 |
| " | board | 7,204 27 |
| " | rent | 233 40 |
| .. | visitors | 256 00 |
| " | all other sources | 412 43 |
| | Total receipts | $19,768 71 |

The amount of expenditures during the year is as follows:—

| | | |
|---|---|---:|
| For salaries | | $12,023 77 |
| " | supplies | 7,048 43 |
| " | repairs and improvements | 398 44 |
| " | the library and kindred purposes | 496 79 |
| " | all other purposes | 2,808 33 |
| | Total expenditures | $22,775 76 |

The receipts and expenditures have been divided between the
Prison and Jail as follows:—

| | |
|---|---:|
| Receipts on Prison account | $4,173 82 |
| Expenditures on Prison account | 7,328 45 |
| Balance against the Prison | $3,154 63 |
| Receipts on Jail account | $15,594 89 |
| Expenditures on Jail account | 15,447 31 |
| Balance in favor of the Jail | $147 58 |
| Balance of expenditures against Prison and Jail | $3,007 05 |
| Amount owed Prison and Jail by towns and other parties consid- ered good | $694 22 |

Total receipts for the year 1875.............................$23,897 92  
Total expenditures for the year 1875............. ............$23,903 55  

Total receipts for the year 1876...................... .........$19,768 71  
Total expenditures for the year 1876.........................$22,775 76  

Decrease of receipts for the year 1876.......................... $4,129 21  
Decrease of expenditures for the year 1876....................$1,127 79  

The statistics of the Prison are as follows:—

Number of convicts in Prison, January 1, 1876........................ 56  
"     "     "     committed during the year..................... 56  
"     "     "     discharged................................... 22  
"     "     "     pardoned.................................. 4  

"     "     "     in Prison December 31, 1876.................. 86  
No death has occurred in the Prison or Jail during the year.

The statistics of the Jail are as follows:—

|  | | Males. | Females. | Total. |
|---|---|---|---|---|
| Number in Jail, January 1, 1876.................. | | 128 | 7 | 135 |
| " | committed during the year............ | 2,199 | 348 | 2,547 |
| " | discharged.......................... | 2,180 | 341 | 2,521 |
| " | pardoned............................ | 1 | . . | 1 |
| " | committed by the State.............. | 698 | 109 | 802 |
| | "     " city of Providence... | 1,262 | 218 | 1,480 |
| | "     " other towns... ..... | 195 | 19 | 214 |
| | "     — United States....... | 14 | 2 | 16 |
| " | of debtors committed................ | 35 | | 35 |
| " | in Jail, December 31, 1876............ | 147 | 14 | 161 |

Average number during the year :—  
By the State .......................................96$\frac{44}{111}$  
" the city of Providence.............................44$\frac{11}{111}$  
" other towns........................................15$\frac{44}{111}$  
" United States......................................1$\frac{10}{111}$  
Average number of debtors........................................ 5$\frac{44}{111}$  
Total average....................................................162$\frac{44}{111}$

Thus it will be seen, that while the number of prisoners has increased 29 per cent., the expenses have been reduced. The difficulty of obtaining work has materially reduced the receipts of the Institution, and in view of the continuance of the existing depres-

sion, the Inspectors, for the first time since 1870, are obliged to
ask for an appropriation.

During the year, there have been committed to the Prison,
under sentence of imprisonment of life for the crime of murder,
three convicts. It happened that the trials of these prisoners all
took place in the same week. The unusual circumstance attracted
attention, both in our own State and beyond our borders. The
question as to the effect of the abolition of capital punishment
upon the progress of crime came up anew for discussion. It is
not infrequently the case, that letters are received from students
of criminal jurisprudence in other States, asking for information
upon the practical influence of our policy. Since the institution of the State Prison, in 1838, 28 persons have been sentenced for murder, of whom 23 have been sentenced since
the abolition of the death penalty, in 1852. The population of the
State in 1850 was 147,545; in 1875, 258,239. It is doubtful
if considerations of the penalty enter largely into the calcula-
tions of the criminal. Crimes of violence are generally committed
under the influence of a sudden frenzy, or in the excitement of
passion, or from the impulse of angry provocation. Deliberate
murder, as the result of a systematic plan, induced by cupidity or
revenge, or as proceeding from the murderous disposition, is somewhat rare. But it is by no means clear, that, when thus induced
to crime, the murderer thinks of the consequences of his deed. If
the thought should occur, there is still the hope of escaping detec-
tion. A case in point was presented a few years ago, by the murder of a man in Worcester, by two brothers, belonging to Rhode
Island. The victim was frequently in Providence, and opportunities for killing him in Rhode Island were not wanting. But his
enemies, actuated by the spirit of revenge for some real or fancied
wrong, dogged his steps for a considerable time, and finally des-
patched him in Massachusetts, where they knew that the penalty
of their crime was death. It appears, that they were so absorbed by
their desire to gratify their enmity, as to think but little or
nothing of subsequent possibilities. The chief requisite in dealing with criminals of this class is to convince them that punishment—whether by imprisonment or death—will be sure and

speedy, and that no morbid or unhealthy sympathy with the criminal will prevent, or even hinder, the infliction of the penalty for
his crime.

During the period of the existence of the Prison, of 829 convicts committed, 132 have been pardoned, or about 15.9 per cent.
of the whole number—an average of 3.48 per year.  No more delicate function is the Executive called upon to discharge than this
exercise of the pardoning power, and none should be considered
with a clearer and more impartial judgment.  To pardon a convict, through sympathy with his misfortunes or the grief he has
brought upon his kindred, through the inclination to do an act of
clemency, or through a desire to secure the favor of any particular
class of citizens, is a proceeding not only of questionable propriety,
but, also, in some cases, of positive harm.  As a general rule, the
decisions of our courts,—the conclusions of judges and juries, may
be accepted as wise and just, and it is a matter of no small importance to undertake to pass them in review.  It is true, that an
instance may occasionally be found, when new evidence is discovered, or some extraordinary circumstance can be pleaded in extenuation of the offence or mitigation of the penalty, or when the
application of the statute may be necessarily of exceptional
severity, or when such proofs of sincere and thorough penitence
are adduced, as to make it clear that the ends of justice have been
attained, in the prevention of a repetition of the offence.  But
cases like these are exceedingly rare.  In the very large majority
of instances, it is humane and just, as well as politic, to let the
law take its course, and the crime meet its deserved penalty.
Generally, the pardoning power has been judiciously exercised.
But sometimes there seems to have been a lack of proper discrimi-
nation in conferring the boon of Executive clemency.  The largest
number pardoned in one year was 14—in 1853, when there were
26 convicts committed, 8 discharged, and but 49 left in the Prison
on the 1st of January, 1854.  In 1850, 11 were pardoned, leaving
42, and in 1851, 10, leaving 49.  It is impossible at this time to
state the reasons for such extraordinary generosity. but it bears the
appearance of a mistaken kindness.  Of course, it cannot be affirmed
that pardons are never to be granted.  But it should be fully under-

stood, both by the convict and the community, that the cases will be subjected to the keenest scrutiny, and favorably decided only upon grounds which can never be called in question.

The completion of the new State Prison will render necessary certain changes in the direction of the Institution, and a revision of Title XXXII of the General Statutes. The Inspectors, in 1875, urged the subject upon the attention of the General Assembly. The removal of the Prison to the site upon the State Farm will require special care in legislation, and it is hoped that the General Assembly will take the matter into consideration at the earliest possible date. It seems to be desirable that there be no divided authority in the administration of the institutions, which now are and will hereafter be established on the State Farm. It is possible, and even probable, that this is the last Board of Inspectors which will be recognized in the legislation of the State. Whether it be advisable to place the entire management of the penitentiary establishments of the State into the hands of the Board of State Charities and Corrections, or to abolish that board and the Board of Inspectors, and appoint a new board of Commissioners, who shall have charge of all the Prisons, Penitentiaries and Correctional and Charitable Institutions belonging to the State, is for the General Assembly to determine. In the former case, the authority of the Board of State Charities will require considerable enlargement. In the latter, the range of the inspection of the Commissioners should be extended, so as to include the County Jails and the Providence Reform School, so far as that is a beneficiary of the State, and indeed all institutions, which are the objects of the care of the State and receive its bounty. The subject requires a calm, careful and thorough consideration at the hands of the Legislature. But it does not become the Inspectors to make any recommendation in the premises.

The Inspectors, in common with their fellow citizens, keenly feel the loss which the entire community has suffered in the death of the Reverend Doctor Caswell, on the 8th of January, 1877. Since the time of his appointment upon the Board, he has had charge of the department of religious instruction, and with it the care of the library. Not infrequently he has conducted religious service—the

last time on Christmas day, at the table where the convicts dined,—
and has always shown great interest in the welfare of the prisoners.
Many valuable books have been added by his judicious purchases
to the Prison Library. As a member of the Board, a regular
attendant at the monthly meetings, his counsels were marked by
kindness and impartiality, and his personal intercourse, it is needless to say, was of the most genial and attractive character. At
the regular meeting in January, 1877, the Board ordered the following minute to be put on record : " The Inspectors of the Rhode
Island State Prison, receiving with unfeigned sorrow, intelligence
of the death of their associate, the Reverend Doctor Alexis Caswell, would express their grateful appreciation of the wisdom and
humanity of his personal counsels and the faithfulness of his public
service, and would tender to his bereaved family their cordial
sympathy." Mr Joseph C. Hartshorn was appointed to fill the
vacancy.

In closing this review of the past, a single personal allusion will
not, it is trusted, be deemed amiss. The present Board of Inspectors have nothing to say of themselves or their administration. But they may be permitted to speak in general terms of
the character of the past. The composition of the Board of
Inspectors has evidently been, with the appointing power, a
matter of considerable importance and moment. It certainly is not
an office to be sought. But it is an office, which requires, for the
proper and faithful discharge of its functions, wisdom, tact, humanity, knowledge of men and affairs, a careful attention to the interests
of the State, and a sincere desire for the welfare and improvement
of those who come under its direction. The philosophy of crime
and the treatment of criminals are subjects, which might well challenge the best thought of the most judicious and careful minds.
It is not enough to have a warm and sympathetic heart. There
must be combined with it a clear, well-balanced and well-adjusted
brain. The list of Inspectors for the last thirty-eight years com-
prises men of different professions and callings—clergymen, physicians, lawyers, manufacturers, and men of business. Two have
filled the office of President of Brown University; one, that of Bishop
of the Episcopal diocese of Rhode Island ; two, that of Judge of the

Supreme Court; two, that of Governor; three, that of Mayor of the city of Providence; one, that of representative in Congress. All, with but few exceptions, have been active participants in the affairs of the city and the State. In one respect, the Board of Inspectors has been especially fortunate, in being free from any political influences. The office has never been a reward in any sense for partizan service. Without a dollar of compensation, and claiming no conspicuous position, it has offered no temptation either to cupidity or ambition. The wisdom of the policy which has been pursued in the direction of our penitentiary institutions, can easily be appreciated, and it is believed, as it is hoped, that the State will long be enabled to command the willing service of wise and enlightened citizens, in the conduct of its charities and the care, discipline—and possibly—the reformation of its perishing and dangerous classes.

AUGUSTUS WOODBURY, *Chairman.*
JESSE METCALF, *Secretary.*
WILLIAM BINNEY,
BENONI CARPENTER,
LEWIS FAIRBROTHER,
JOSEPH C. HARTSHORN,
STEPHEN R. WEEDEN, *Inspectors.*

ERRATA.—On page 14, line 1, for Autumn read Spring.
    "    On page 23, line 1, for two, read five.

Page 14, 5th line from bottom, for Manning, read Mawney.
Page 23, line 11, after premises, read, at a cost of one thousand
Page 52, line 5, for three, read two, and strike out all at end

| | Rhode Island State Prison Deficit. | Providence County Jail Surplus. | Providence County Jail Deficit. | Construction. | Average Number of Prisoners for Each Year. | Per Capita. |
|---|---|---|---|---|---|---|
| ... | .......... | ...... | .......... | a$60,896 10 | ..... | ........ |
| ... | .......... | ...... | .......... | 1,283 88 | ...... | ........ |
| ... | .......... | ...... | .......... | .......... | ...... | ........ |
| ... | .......... | ...... | .......... | .......... | ...... | ........ |
| ... | .......... | ...... | ....... | 2,397 20 | ...... | ........ |
| ... | .......... | ...... | .......... | .......... | ...... | ........ |
| ... | $2,903 53 | .......... | 2,743 64 | .......... | 65. | $119.88 |
| ... | 2,421 31 | ...... | 2,666 60 | .......... | 85. | 102 91 |
| ... | 3,207 84 | ...... | 2,255 03 | .......... | 90. | 95.21 |
| ... | 3,029 74 | .......... | 4,060 12 | .......... | 112. | 87.96 |
| ... | 2,824 26 | ...... | 4,871 11 | 18,143 71 | 131. | 96.11 |
| ... | 404 58 | .......... | 1,988 43 | .......... | 110. | 81.29 |
| ... | 519 53 | .......... | 3,112 99 | .......... | 136. | 87.46 |
| 09 | ...... | ...... | 4,298 72 | 47,143 37 | 174. | 72.85 |
| 01 | ...... | ...... | 4,049 00 | .......... | 175. | 73.11 |
| 48 | ...... | ...... | 2,670 82 | .......... | 156. | 87.97 |
| 30 | ...... | ...... | 1,487 63 | .......... | 169. | 67.94 |
| 61 | ...... | ...... | 753 54 | .......... | 158. | 75.46 |
| 84 | ... | ...... | 234 59 | .......... | 189. | 71.37 |
| 48 | ... | ...... | 1,608 80 | .......... | 207. | 59.22 |
| 96 | ...... | $143 16 | ...... | .......... | 183. | 61.40 |
| 90 | ...... | 13 83 | .......... | .......... | 175. | 69.73 |
| 42 | ...... | 79 60 | .......... | .......... | 130. | 96.43 |
| 54 | ...... | ...... | 496 78 | .......... | 130. | 106.06 |
| 32 | ...... | ...... | 2,114 57 | .......... | 184. | 88.87 |
| | 866 57 | ...... | 5,794 38 | .......... | 186. | 123.74 |
| 57 | ...... | ...... | 4,150 60 | .......... | 155. | 118.86 |
| 10 | ...... | ...... | 2,926 69 | 3,005 95 | 184. | 121.71 |
| 74 | ...... | ...... | 2,739 98 | 1,765 60 | 171. | 119.49 |
| 37 | ...... | ...... | 1,775 91 | .......... | 160. | 119 52 |
| 60 | ...... | ...... | 576 70 | .......... | 165. | 110.75 |
| 04 | ...... | ...... | 1,435 02 | .......... | 205. | 102.44 |
| 88 | ...... | ...... | 3,159 41 | 5,345 06 | 242. | 94.91 |
| 90 | ...... | ...... | 3,670 53 | .......... | 215. | 111.18 |
| . | 3,154 63 | 147 58 | .......... | .......... | 233. | 97.75 |
| 72 | e$19,426 30 | $283 67 | $65,643 54 | $139,981 87 | f161.5 | $93.85 |

Su]
cit;
wit
of
has
infl
pai
no
cuț
pui
eas
Sta
wis
the
anc

E

# INSPECTORS OF THE STATE PRISON.*

SAMUEL W. KING, (Chairman, 1838–'41)................1838—1841.
WILLIAM S. PATTEN, (Clerk, 1838–'40)............ .....1838—1840.
WILLIAM R. STAPLES........... .................... ...1838—1839.
CHRISTOPHER RHODES........................... . ...1838—1847.
HENRY G. MUMFORD..................................1838—1840.
JOHN J. STIMSON................. .............1839—1840.
JOHN L. HUGHES... .................... ... ... ....1839—1840.
   GER W. POTTER..................................1839—1844.
   DEON SPENCER...... ...... .....................1840—1841.
    TIN STODDARD........ ........................1840—1843.
   HERST EVERETT, (Clerk, 1840–'47).................1840—1847.
   MUEL Y. ATWELL.................................1840—1841.
   OMAS M. BURGESS, (Chairman, 1841–'47).............1841—1847.
   ARZILLAI CRANSTON................................1841—1847.
   EORGE RICE.....................................1841—1844.
   UFUS W. KIMBALL............................. ...1843—1847.
   AMES Y. SMITH............... ......... .........1844—1847.
   AAC THURBER  ..............................1844—1847.
EDWARD S. WILLIAMS, (Chairman, 1847–'48; died, July 18,
                 1846)......................1847—1849.
DANIEL WILKINSON (Clerk, 1847–'51...................1847—1851.
ADNAH SACKETT, (Chairman,1854–'60; died, Feb. 15, 1860.) 1847—1860.
ABNER PECKHAM...................................1847—1854.
EDWARD POTTER...................................1847—1851.
WLLLIAM SHELDON...................... ............1847—1849.

*Elected by the General Assembly in May, till 1847; afterwards appointed by the Governor.

ARIEL BALLOU..................................    ....1847—1849.
ALFRED WRIGHT, (Chairman, Aug. 1849-'50)...........1849—1850.
THOMAS DAVIS.......................................1849—1853.
ISAAC HARTSHORN....................................1849—1851.
FRANCIS WAYLAND, (Chairman, 1850'-'54; 1860-'61)......1850—1861.
GEORGE L. CLARKE, (Clerk, 1851-'54)..................1851—1854.
ZACHARIAH ALLEN, (resigned, Sept. '51)..............1851—1851.
AMASA MANTON, (appointed, Sept. '51).................1851—1852.
WILLIAM P. BULLOCK................................1852—1854.
WALTER S. BURGES..................................   ...........1852—1854.
WILLIAM SHELDON.........   .....................  ..1854—1855.
AMASA R. TOURTELLOT, (Clerk, 1860-'61)...............1854—1865.
S. AUGUSTUS ARNOLD...............................1854—1861.
JAMES G. ANTHONY...  ...........................1854—1862.
DANIEL WILKINSON, (Clerk, 1854-'60).................1854—1860.
ZACHARIAH ALLEN...................................1855—1862.
THOMAS P. SHEPARD (Chairman, 1861-'63; resigned,
                        July 12, '64.)...  ...........1860—1864.
BYRON SPRAGUE.....................................1860—1865.
THOMAS M. CLARK....   .........................1861—1864.
WILLIAM E. HAMLIN, (Clerk, 1861-'63).................1861—1863.
FRANCIS WAYLAND, (Chairman, 1863; resigned,
                        July 12, 1864.).................1863—1864.
HORATIO N. SLATER.............  ..................1861—1863.
GEORGE H. WHITNEY, (Clerk, 1863-'64)...............1863—1864.
THOMAS BROWN, (Clerk, 1864-'66)....................  .1863—1866.
THOMAS K. KING, (Chairman, 1864-'66).............  1864—1866.
A. HUNTINGTON CLAPP, (appointed July, '64)...........1864—1865.
GEORGE L. CLARKE, (appointed July '64)..............1864—1866.
HIRAM H. THOMAS...........................  .........1864—1866.
STEPHEN R. WEEDEN, (Clerk, 1866-Nov. '73).........1865. In office.
STEPHEN C. ARNOLD.................................1865—1867.
AUGUSTUS WOODBURY, (Chairman, 1866. In office).....1866. In office.
SAMUEL L. CALDWELL, (resigned, Sept. '73)...........1866—1873.
MOSES B. LOCKWOOD, (resigned Dec. '66)......:.........1866—1866.
LEWIS FAIRBROTHER.........  ...................... 1866. In office.
EDWIN M. SNOW....................................  1866—1869.
GEORGE L. COLLINS (app. Dec. '66; resigned April '67).....1866—1867.
WILLIAM BINNEY, (appointed April '67)............. .1867. In office.

BENONI CARPENTER....................... ........1867. In office.
JESSE METCALF, (Clerk, Nov. '73. In office)..........1869. In office.
ALEXIS CASWELL, (app. Sept. '73; died Jan. 8, '77).....1873—1877.
JOSEPH C. HARTSHORN, (app. Jan. '77. In office)....1877. In office.

---

NOTE.—The following gentlemen have been appointed Inspectors, but declined the office : GEORGE B. HOLMES, 1838; ISAAC THURBER, 1838: GEORGE BAKER, 1841; ALFRED ANTHONY, 1862 and 1865.

---

## WARDENS OF THE STATE PRISON.

---

THOMAS CLEVELAND........ ......November 1, 1838—May 1, 1847.
SHERIFF ROGER W. POTTER...........May 1, 1847—October 1, 1847.
THOMAS W. HAYWARD.............October 1, 1847—June 5, 1851.
FRANCIS B. LEE.....................June 5, 1851—June 30, 1852.
WILLIAM WILLARD..................July 1, 1852—August 1, 1854.
SAMUEL L. BLAISDELL............August 1, 1854—February 1,1865.
RICHARD W. BLAISDELL...........February 1, 1865—May 1, 1867.
NELSON VIALL.............................May 1, 1867—In office.

---

NOTE.—Mr. JAMES M. TALCOTT was elected Warden April 9, 1867, but declined the office.

---

## PHYSICIANS.

---

ISAAC HARTSHORN.................November 1, 1838—Nov. 1,1840.
HENRY W. RIVERS.................November 1,1840—July 14,1841.
RICHMOND BROWNELL.... .........July 14, 1841—October 1, 1848.
SALMON AUGUSTUS ARNOLD.........October 1, 1848—October 1,1852.

E. V. HATHAWAY,................. October 1, 1852—April 12, 1854.
GEORGE P. BAKER................April 12, 1854—July 14, 1868.
GEORGE W. CARR............. ............July 14, 1868—In office.

---

## CHAPLAIN.

---

REV. WILLIAM DOUGLAS......................June 1856—In office

# WARDEN'S REPORT.

*To the Honorable, the General Assembly of the State of Rhode Island.*

The undersigned, Warden of the Rhode Island State Prison, respectfully presents the following account of receipts and expenditures for the year ending December 31st, 1876.

## PROPERTY ON HAND, AS PER INVENTORY, JANUARY 1st, 1876.

| | | |
|---|---:|---:|
| Books and stationery.................................................... | $20 00 | |
| Bedding and clothing.................................................. | 1,085 00 | |
| Building on Gaspee St.................................................. | 1,300 00 | |
| Fuel and lights........................................................ | 923 11 | |
| Furniture.............................................................. | 1,176 18 | |
| Library................................................................ | 729 00 | |
| Miscellaneous.......................................................... | 569 00 | |
| Provisions and groceries............................................... | 215 87 | |
| Cash on library account............................................... | 569 12 | |
| Cash on general account............................................... | 6,112 87 | |
| Debts due............................................................. | 286 62 | |
| | | $12,986 72 |

## PROPERTY ON HAND, AS PER INVENTORY, DECEMBER 31st, 1876.

| | | | |
|---|---:|---:|---:|
| Books and stationery.................................................... | | $30 00 | |
| Bedding and clothing.................................................. | | 1,065 30 | |
| Building on Gaspee st.................................................. | | 1,300 00 | |
| Fuel and lights....................................................... | | 975 00 | |
| Furniture.............................................................. | | 1,248 57 | |
| Library................................................................ | | 777 00 | |
| Miscellaneous.......................................................... | | 592 00 | |
| Provisions and groceries............................................... | | 384 36 | |
| Cash on library account............................... | $331 36 | | |
| Cash borrowed from library account................. | 155 12 | 176 24 | |
| Cash on general account............................... | | 3,431 20 | |
| | | | $9,979 67 |
| Balance of expense for the year............................................ | | | $3,007 05 |

## EXPENSE AND INCOME DECEMBER 31st, 1876.

### Dr.

| | | |
|---|---:|---:|
| Books and stationery... | $117 98 | |
| Bedding and clothing | 595 84 | |
| Discharged Convicts.... | 195 00 | |
| Expenses | 686 25 | |
| Fuel and lights | 1,029 35 | |
| Furniture | 6 66 | |
| Library | 378 81 | |
| Miscellaneous | 295 23 | |
| Provisions and groceries | 7,048 43 | |
| Repairs and improvements | 398 44 | |
| Salaries of Officers | 12,023 77 | $22,775 76 |

### Cr.

| | | |
|---|---:|---:|
| Building on Gaspee street | $233 40 | |
| Cane shop | 746 67 | |
| Cotton tie shop | 2,540 29 | |
| Furniture shop | 6,189 86 | |
| Interest on deposits | 39 77 | |
| Jail Board | 6,736 27 | |
| Jail fees | 354 66 | |
| Jail labor | 70 38 | |
| Prisoners' board | 468 00 | |
| Prisoners' fees | 18 00 | |
| Visitors' fees | 256 00 | |
| Wire shop | 2,115 41 | $19,768 71 |
| Balance of expense, as above | | $3,007 05 |

## ABSTRACT OF ACCOUNTS FOR THE YEAR, 1876.

### BOOKS AND STATIONERY.

| | | |
|---|---:|---:|
| Amount on hand January 1, 1876 | $20 00 | |
| " since purchased | 127 98 | $147 98 |
| " on hand December 31, 1876 | | 30 00 |
| Balance being expense | | $117 98 |

### BEDDING AND CLOTHING.

| | | |
|---|---:|---:|
| Amount on hand January 1, 1876 | $1,085 00 | |
| " since purchased | 617 94 | $1,702 94 |
| " credited | 41 80 | |
| " on hand December 31, 1876 | 1,065 30 | $1,107 10 |
| Balance being expense | | $595 84 |

### DISCHARGED CONVICTS.

Cash and clothing for same.......................... $195 00

### EXPENSES.

Cash paid for sundry expenses...... ......... ..... $686 25

### FUEL AND LIGHTS.

| | | | |
|---|---|---|---|
| Amount on hand January 1, 1876... ... .......... | $923 11 | | |
| "  since purchased . ....................... | 1,089 55 | $2,012 66 | |
| "  credited ............................. .... | 8 31 | | |
| "  on hand December 31, 1876.............. . | 975 00 | 983 31 | |
| Balance being expense ................. ....... | | | $1,029 35 |

### FURNITURE.

| | | | |
|---|---|---|---|
| Amount on hand January 1, 1876................. .... | $1,176 13 | | |
| "  since purchased.................... ..... | 79 10 | $1,255 23 | |
| "  on hand December 31, 1876 .............. | | 1,248 57 | |
| Balance being expense........................... | | | $6 66 |

### LIBRARY.

| | | | |
|---|---|---|---|
| Amount on hand January 1, 1876................. | $729 00 | | |
| "  since charged........................... | 426 81 | $1,155 81 | |
| "  on hand December 31, 1876...... ........ | | 777 00 | |
| Balance being expense................... ........ | | | $378 81 |

### MISCELLANEOUS.

| | | | |
|---|---|---|---|
| Amount on hand January 1, 1876................. | $569 00 | | |
| "  charged to this account.................. | 320 23 | $889 23 | |
| "  credited........................... ...... | 2 00 | | |
| "  on hand December 31, 1876.............. | 592 00 | 594 00 | |
| Balance being expense............ ............. | | | $295 23 |

### PROVISIONS AND GROCERIES.

| | | | |
|---|---|---|---|
| Amount on hand January 1, 1876................. | $215 87 | | |
| "  since purchased................... ....... | 7,427 49 | $7,643 36 | |
| "  credited........... ................ | 210 57 | | |
| "  on hand December 31, 1876.............. | 384 36 | 594 93 | |
| Balance being expense...... .................... | | | $7,048 43 |

### BUILDING ON GASPEE STREET.

| | | | |
|---|---|---|---|
| Inventory January 1, 1876........................ | $1,300 00 | | |
| Received for rent................................ | 252 00 | $1,552 00 | |
| Paid for insurance................................ | 18 60 | | |
| Inventory December 31, 1876..................... | 1,300 00 | 1,318 60 | |
| Balance being income.............................. | | | $233 40 |

Abstract of furniture account manufactured by the State from November 1, 1876, to December 31, 1876:

| | |
|---|---:|
| Furniture bills for material in the wood. | $553 10 |
| Paint stock purchased for finishing same. | 220 53 |
| Hardware purchased    "      "      " | 75 50 |
| Glass plate           "      "      " | 69 40 |
| Wooden ware and lumber used in     " | 34 07 |
| Freight bills for the above purchases. | 26 49 |
| | $994 09 |

| | | |
|---|---:|---:|
| Valuation of finished furniture since November 1, 1876, to December 31, 1876. | $784 50 | |
| Valuation of paint stock as per inventory. | 91 59 | |
| Debts due from sundry accounts for furniture sold to December 31, 1876. | 344 00 | $1,220 09 |
| Balance being gain from November 1, to December 31, 1876. | | $226 00 |

The expenses and income are divided between the State Prison and County Jail, as follows:

### EXPENSE.

| | Prison. | Jail. | Total. |
|---|---:|---:|---:|
| Books and stationery. | $35 89 | $82 09 | $117 98 |
| Bedding and clothing | 181 27 | 414 57 | 595 84 |
| Discharged convicts | 195 00 | .. .. | 195 00 |
| Expenses. | 208 78 | 477 47 | 686 25 |
| Fuel and lights. | 313 25 | 716 11 | 1,029 35 |
| Furniture. | 2 03 | 4 63 | 6 66 |
| Library. | 378 81 | . .... | 378 81 |
| Miscellaneous.. | 89 82 | 205 41 | 295 23 |
| Provisions. | 2,144 36 | 4,904 07 | 7,048 43 |
| Repairs. | 121 22 | 277 22 | 398 44 |
| Salaries. | 3,658 03 | 8,365 74 | 12,023 77 |
| | $7,328 45 | $15 447 31 | $22,775 76 |

### INCOME.

| | Prison. | Jail. | Total. |
|---|---:|---:|---:|
| Building on Gaspee street. | $71 09 | $162 31 | $233 44 |
| Board. | 468 00 | 6,736 27 | 7,204 27 |
| Cane shop. | 227 16 | 519 51 | 746 67 |
| Cotton tie shop. | 772 84 | 1,767 45 | 2,540 29 |
| Furniture shop. | 1,883 16 | 4,306 70 | 6,189 86 |
| Visitors' fees. | 77 89 | 178 11 | 256 00 |
| Interest. | 12 10 | 27 67 | 39 77 |
| Jail labor. | ........ | 70 38 | 70 38 |
| Jail fees. | 18 00 | 354 66 | 372 66 |
| Wire shop. | 643 58 | 1,471 83 | 2,115 41 |
| | $4,173 82 | $15,594 89 | $19,768 71 |

## BALANCES OF EXPENSE AND INCOME FOR THE YEAR.

Prison expenses..................................... $3,154 63
Jail income.... . ...................................    $147 58
Balance of Prison expense over Jail income . .....                $3,007 05

Current expenses, *per capita*, of prisoners for the year 1876.

For salaries of officers...... ...........................................................$51 60
" provisions and groceries...................................................... ... 30 25
" fuel and lights  :...... ............................................ ...................... 4 42
" bedding and clothing.................... ....................... .....······.. 2 56
" miscellaneous expenses ...................................................,..... 8 92
                                                                   $97 75

The undersigned have examined the account of receipts and expenditures of the Rhode Island State Prison and Providence County Jail, for the year ending December 31, 1876, as presented in the foregoing statement, have compared the same with the books and vouchers, and find the same correct.

AUGUSTUS WOODBURY,
JESSE METCALF.

PROVIDENCE, January 9, 1877.

9

*Number of convicts in Prison, Committed, Discharged, Pardoned, Deceased, Escaped and Returned, in each year, since the establishment of the Institution in 1838.*

| YEAR. | In Prison. | Committed. | Discharged. | Pardoned. | Died. | Escaped. | Returned. |
|---|---|---|---|---|---|---|---|
| 1838. | ...... | 5 | ...... | ...... | ...... | ...... | ...... |
| 1839. | 5 | 6 | 2 | ...... | ...... | ...... | ...... |
| 1840. | 9 | 9 | 3 | ...... | ...... | ...... | ...... |
| 1841. | 15 | 13 | 2 | ...... | ...... | ...... | ...... |
| 1842. | 26 | 7 | 6 | 2 | 1 | ...... | ...... |
| 1843. | 24 | 13 | 10 | 3 | 1 | ...... | ...... |
| 1844. | 23 | 6 | 5 | 2 | 2 | 1 | ...... |
| 1845. | 19 | 8 | 5 | 2 | 1 | ...... | ...... |
| 1846. | 19 | 8 | 5 | 3 | ...... | ...... | ...... |
| 1847. | 19 | 11 | 5 | 3 | 1 | ...... | ...... |
| 1848. | 21 | 8 | 2 | ...... | ...... | ...... | ...... |
| 1849. | 27 | 14 | 4 | 5 | 2 | 3 | 3 |
| 1850. | 30 | 29 | 6 | 11 | ...... | 1 | ...... |
| 1851. | 42 | 21 | 2 | 10 | 1 | 1 | ...... |
| 1852. | 49 | 17 | 17 | 4 | ...... | ...... | ...... |
| 1853. | 45 | 26 | 8 | 14 | ...... | ...... | ...... |
| 1854. | 49 | 23 | 13 | 4 | 3 | ...... | 1 |
| 1855. | 52 | 27 | 13 | 2 | 1 | ...... | ...... |
| 1856. | 63 | 14 | 20 | 2 | 1 | ...... | ...... |
| 1857. | 54 | 34 | 19 | 2 | ...... | ...... | ...... |
| 1858. | 67 | 26 | 20 | ...... | 3 | 1 | 1 |
| 1859. | 70 | 23 | 18 | 3 | 5 | ...... | ...... |
| 1860. | 67 | 29 | 27 | 1 | 1 | ...... | ...... |
| 1861. | 67 | 39 | 18 | 3 | ...... | ...... | ...... |
| 1862. | 85 | 18 | 38 | 5 | ...... | ...... | ...... |
| 1863. | 60 | 12 | 20 | 4 | 1 | ...... | ...... |
| 1864. | 47 | 10 | 13 | 2 | 1 | ...... | ...... |
| 1865. | 41 | 22 | 11 | 3 | 1 | 1 | 1 |
| 1866. | 48 | 40 | 9 | 7 | ...... | ...... | ...... |
| 1867. | 72 | 25 | 27 | 9 | 2 | ...... | ...... |
| 1868. | 59 | 26 | 20 | 6 | ...... | ...... | ...... |
| 1869. | 59 | 42 | 16 | 8 | 2 | 1 | 1 |
| 1870. | 80 | 25 | 25 | 5 | ...... | ...... | ...... |
| 1871. | 75 | 26 | 31 | 2 | 3 | ...... | ...... |
| 1872. | 65 | 30 | 16 | 5 | 1 | 2 | ...... |
| 1873. | 71 | 33 | 26 | 1 | ...... | ...... | 1 |
| 1874. | 77 | 24 | 29 | 3 | 2 | ...... | ...... |
| 1875. | 67 | 24 | 29 | 3 | 3 | ...... | ...... |
| 1876. | 56 | 56 | 22 | 4 | ...... | ...... | ...... |
| 1877. | 86 | ...... | ...... | ...... | ...... | ...... | ...... |

*The Ages, Sexes, Complexions and Nativities of persons committed to the State Prison, since its first institution in 1838.*

| | | | |
|---|---|---|---|
| Under 20 years of age | 162 | Males | 805 |
| From 20 to 30 years | 417 | Females | 24 |
| " 30 " 40 " | 145 | Natives of the United States | 589 |
| " 40 " 50 " | 72 | Foreigners | 240 |
| " 50 " 60 " | 20 | White | 730 |
| " 60 " 70 " | 11 | Colored | 99 |
| Over 70 years | 1 | | |

The places of nativity are:

| | | | |
|---|---|---|---|
| Rhode Island | 321 | Ireland | 149 |
| Massachusetts | 100 | England | 39 |
| New York | 48 | Canada | 14 |
| Connecticut | 31 | Germany | 9 |
| Maine | 18 | France | 6 |
| Pennsylvania | 12 | Nova Scotia | 4 |
| Virginia | 12 | Scotland | 3 |
| New Hampshire | 9 | New Brunswick | 3 |
| New Jersey | 7 | Sweden | 3 |
| District of Columbia | 7 | Italy | 3 |
| Vermont | 6 | Wales | 1 |
| Kentucky | 3 | Gibraltar | 1 |
| Maryland | 3 | New Foundland | 1 |
| Ohio | 3 | Bermuda | 1 |
| Illinois | 1 | Santa Cruz | 1 |
| Delaware | 1 | Peru | 1 |
| North Carolina | 1 | Turkey | 1 |
| Florida | 1 | | |
| Mississippi | 1 | | |
| Louisiana | 1 | | |
| Texas | 1 | | |
| Wisconsin | 2 | | |
| California | 1 | | |
| | **589** | | **240** |

*The Crimes for which persons have been committed to the State Prison since its institution in 1838.*

| | | | |
|---|---|---|---|
| Assault and Larceny | 2 | Bigamy | 9 |
| " " Battery | 8 | Burglary | 62 |
| " " with intent to kill | 27 | Breaking into a bank | 5 |
| " " with a dangerous w'pon. | 24 | " " church | 2 |
| " " intent to commit rape | 25 | " " school-house | 1 |
| " " " " " sodomy | 1 | " " vessel | 4 |
| " " " " rob | 11 | " " engine-house | 1 |
| " on the warden | 2 | Conspiracy | 2 |
| Adultery | 2 | Counterfeiting | 2 |

| | | | |
|---|---|---|---|
| Destroying a Dam | 1 | Murder | 28 |
| Embezzlement | 5 | Manslaughter | 20 |
| Escape from Prison | 2 | Mingling poison with drink | 1 |
| False pretences | 1 | Obstructing Railroad | 2 |
| Forgery | 27 | Obtaining goods by false pretences | 2 |
| Fraudulently taking a letter from the the Post Office | 1 | Perjury | 12 |
| | | Rape | 8 |
| House breaking | 34 | Receiving stolen goods | 1 |
| Having and passing counterfeit money | 33 | Rescuing a Jail prisoner | 1 |
| Inciting another to commit larceny | 1 | Robbery | 48 |
| " " " perjury | 1 | Setting fire | 27 |
| Incest | 1 | Store breaking | 174 |
| Indecent exposure | 1 | Sodomy | 1 |
| Larceny | 191 | Treason | 1 |

Average number of convicts in 1874...................................... $71\frac{5}{111}$

There are in Prison December 31, 1876............................................ 86

| | | | |
|---|---|---|---|
| Males | 82 | Colored | 10 |
| Females | 4 | Natives of the United States | 64 |
| White | 76 | Foreigners | 22 |

NELSON VIALL, *Warden.*

PROVIDENCE, December 31, 1876.

# JAILER'S REPORT.

## DECEMBER 31, 1876.

*There are in Jail January 1, 1876:*

|  | Males. | Females. | Total. |
|---|---|---|---|
| Committed by the State ........................... | 69 | 2 | 71 |
| "          the City of Providence...... ......... | 39 | 5 | 44 |
| "          the Town of Johnston ........  ........ | 1 | ............ | 1 |
| "          the Town of Burrillville................... | 2 | .......... | 2 |
| "          the Town of Lincoln..... | 2 | .......... | 2 |
| "          the Town of Pawtucket....... ........ | 2 | .......... | 2 |
| "          the Town of Woonsocket................. | 4 | .......... | 4 |
| "          the United States....................... | 4 | .......... | 4 |
| Debtors in Jail....... ............... .......... .. ..... | 5 | .. ........ | 5 |
|  | 128 | 7 | 135 |

*There have been committed since:*

|  | Males. | Females. | Total. |
|---|---|---|---|
| By the State sentenced....................................... | 323 | 29 | 352 |
| "       "        "      for want of bail.................... | 370 | 80 | 450 |
| "       City of Providence, sentenced...  ................... | 1247 | 198 | 1445 |
| "       "      "      for want of bail.............. ...... | 15 | 20 | 35 |
| "       Town of North Providence................. ...... | 2 | 1 | 3 |
| "       Town of Johnston............................... | 8 | 2 | 10 |
| "       Town of Cumberland...............   ........... | 15 | 1 | 16 |
| "       Town of Burrillville............................ | 13 | ............ | 13 |
| "       Town of East Providence....................... | 25 | 4 | 29 |
| "       Town of Lincoln.................. ........... | 48 | 5 | 53 |
| "       Town of Pawtucket. ........................... | 37 | 3 | 40 |
| "       Town of North Smithfield...................... | 2 | ............ | 2 |
| "       Town of Scituate.............................. | 1 | ............ | 1 |
| "       Town of Warren............................... | 3 | ............ | 3 |
| "       Town of Woonsocket.......................... . . | 41 | 3 | 44 |
| "       United States.............................. ..... | 14 | 2 | 16 |
|  | 2164 | 348 | 2512 |
| Debtors committed....................................... | 35 | ......... | 35 |
|  | 2199 | 348 | 2547 |
| Total in Jail during the year............................. | 2327 | 355 | 2682 |

*Discharged during the year:*

| | Males. | Females. | Total. |
|---|---|---|---|
| By the State..... ...................................... | 617 | 101 | 718 |
| "    "    sentenced to State Prison.... ............... | 42 | 2 | 44 |
| "    City of Providence............................. | 1273 | 219 | 1492 |
| "    Town of Burrillville.... .  ........... .......... | 15 | ...... | 15 |
| "    Town of North Providence..................... | 2 | 1 | 3 |
| "    Town of Cumberland............................ | 13 | 1 | 14 |
| "    Town of East Providence..................... | 25 | 4 | 29 |
| "    Town of Johnston ..... ....................... | 8 | 1 | 9 |
| "    Town of Lincoln.... ........................... | 47 | 5 | 52 |
| "    Town of North Smithfield...................... | 2 | ......... | 2 |
| "    Town of Pawtucket............................. | 39 | 2 | 41 |
| "    Town of Scituate...................... .  ...... | 1 | ......... | 1 |
| "    Town of Warren............................  .. | 3 | ......... | 3 |
| "    Town of Woonsocket...... ............ ......... | 40 | 3 | 43 |
| "    United States................................... | 16 | 2 | 18 |
| Debtors discharged................................ ....... | 37 | .......... | 37 |
| | 2180 | 341 | 2521 |

*Leaving in Jail, December 31, 1876:*

| | Males. | Females. | Total. |
|---|---|---|---|
| Committed by the State. ...................... | 103 | 8 | 111 |
| "    "    City of Providence ................... | 28 | 4 | 32 |
| "    "    Town of Cumberland................. | 2 | .......... | 2 |
| "    "    Town of Johnston................... | 1 | 1 | 2 |
| "    "    Town of Lincoln.................. ..... | 3 | .......... | 3 |
| "    "    Town of Pawtucket. ................... | ...... | 1 | 1 |
| "    "    Town of Woonsocket........... ...... | 5 | .......... | 5 |
| "    "    United States.............. ..... ...... | 2 | .......... | 2 |
| Debtors in Jail........................................ | 3 | .......... | 3 |
| | 147 | 14 | 161 |

*Average number in Jail in 1876:*

| | Males. | Females. | Total. |
|---|---|---|---|
| At the suit of the State........................ | 88 | 7 | 96.44 |
| "    "    City of Providence................... | 39 | 4 | 44 |
| "    "    Various towns ,  .................... | 13 | 2 | 15 |
| "    "    United States....................... | .340 | .45 | 1.30 |
| Debtors in close jail .................................. | 5.65 | .......... | ........ |
| | 147.353 | 14.160 | 162.148 |

*Committed on sentence by the State for:*

|  | Males. | Females. | Total. |
|---|---|---|---|
| Assault | 92 | 5 | 97 |
| Assault with a dangerous weapon | 6 | .......... | 6 |
| Adultery | 1 | .......... | 1 |
| Breaking and entering | 4 | .......... | 4 |
| Cruelty to animals | 2 | .......... | 2 |
| Contempt of Court | ..... | 1 | 1 |
| Common gambler | 5 | .......... | 5 |
| Defacing Building | 19 | 1 | 20 |
| Evading fare | 27 | 1 | 28 |
| Embezzlement | 2 | .......... | 2 |
| False pretences | 3 | .......... | 3 |
| Firing a pistol | 1 | .......... | 1 |
| Fornication | 1 | .......... | 1 |
| Keeping a dog without a license | 1 | .......... | 1 |
| Malicious mischief | 13 | .......... | 13 |
| Nuisance | 1 | .......... | 1 |
| Obstructing an officer | 4 | .......... | 4 |
| Peddling without license | 3 | .......... | 3 |
| Sabbath breaking | 1 | .......... | 1 |
| Selling liquor without license | 6 | 1 | 7 |
| Selling lottery tickets | 1 | .......... | 1 |
| Theft | 129 | 20 | 149 |
| Threats | 1 | .......... | 1 |
|  | 323 | 29 | 352 |

*State Sentences:*

| Fines. | Males. | Females. | Total. | Imprisonment. | Males. | Females. | Total. |
|---|---|---|---|---|---|---|---|
| 1.00 | 7 | 2 | 9 | 10 days | 3 | 2 | 5 |
| 2.00 | 6 | 1 | 7 | 15 " | 3 | .......... | 3 |
| 3.00 | 11 | 1 | 12 | 30 " | 44 | 4 | 48 |
| 5.00 | 74 | 8 | 82 | 60 " | 10 | .......... | 10 |
| 10.00 | 47 | 5 | 52 | 3 months | 32 | 4 | 36 |
| 15.00 | 11 | .......... | 11 | 4 " | 11 | .......... | 11 |
| 20 00 | 42 | 1 | 43 | 5 " | 1 | .......... | 1 |
| 25.00 | 1 | .......... | 1 | 6 " | 12 | .......... | 12 |
| 100.00 | 1 | 1 | 2 | 8 " | 3 | .......... | 3 |
|  |  |  |  | Sureties to keep the peace | 2 | .......... | 2 |
|  |  |  |  | 7 months | 1 | .......... | 1 |
|  |  |  |  | 10 " | 1 | .......... | 1 |

*Committed on sentence by the City for:*

|  | Males | Females. | Total. |
|---|---|---|---|
| Drunkenness | 1142 | 186 | 1328 |
| Revelling | 103 | 12 | 115 |
| Bathing unsuitably dressed | 1 | .......... | 1 |
| Driving carriage without license | 1 | .......... | 1 |
|  | 1247 | 198 | 1445 |

*City Sentences:*

| Fines. | Males. | Females. | Total. | Fines. | Males. | Females. | Total. |
|---|---|---|---|---|---|---|---|
| 1.00............ | 12 | 4 | 16 | 10.00.......... | 13 | 2 | 15 |
| 2.00.. ....... | 754 | 115 | 869 | 15.00····..... | 5 | .......... | 5 |
| 3.00........... | 309 | 52 | 361 | 20.00.......... | 10 | .......... | 10 |
| 5.00 ......... | 137 | 25 | 162 | Imprisonment | | | |
| 7.00 ......... | 1 | ....... | 1 | 10 days....... | 6 | ....... ... | 6 |
| | 1213 | 196 | 1409 | | 34 | 2 | 36 |

*Committed on sentence by the various towns for:*

| | Males. | Females. | Total. |
|---|---|---|---|
| Drunkenness........................................... ... .... | 122 | 11 | 133 |
| Revelling................................................ | 69 | 8 | 77 |
| Allowing horse to go at large............................... | 1 | .......... | 1 |
| Allowing goat to go at large............................... | 1 | .......... | 1 |
| Assault.............. ..... ....... ............ ........ | 2 | .......... | 2 |
| | 195 | 19 | 214 |

*Sentences by the towns:*

| Fines. | Males. | Females. | Total. | Imprisonment. | Males. | Females. | Total. |
|---|---|---|---|---|---|---|---|
| 1.00........ ... | 37 | 7 | 14 | 10 days | 26 | 1 | 27 |
| 2.00... ....... | 96 | 6 | 102 | 30 days | 1 | .......... | 1 |
| 3.00.... ...... | 14 | 3 | 17 | | | | |
| 5.00........... | 13 | 2 | 15 | | | | |
| 8 00........ · | 1 | .......... | 1 | | | | |
| 10.00.. ....... | 5 | .......... | 5 | | | | |
| 20.00.... ...... | 2 | .......... | 2 | | | | |
| | 168 | 18 | 186 | | 27 | 1 | 28 |

*Committed on sentence by the Unites States for:*

| | Males. | Females. | Total. |
|---|---|---|---|
| Selling liquor without a license.......................... | 1 | | |
| Illegally voting ................................. ........ | 1 | | 2 |
| | 2 | | 2 |

*Sentences by the United States:*

|  | Males. | Females. | Total. |
|---|---|---|---|
| Imprisonment for six months and fined $1,000.......... | 1 | ............. |  |
| "            " fifteen months..... .......... ...... ... | 1 | ... ...... | 2 |
|  | 2 |  | 2 |

*The nativities of persons committed to jail on sentence:*

| | | | |
|---|---|---|---|
| Rhode Island.... ............... . | 523 | Ireland. ........................... | 687 |
| Massachusetts....................... | 197 | England ...................•......... | 148 |
| New York........................ ... | 128 | Scotland............................ | 39 |
| Connecticut....................... | 47 | Canada....................... ....... | 18 |
| New Hampshire.................... | 16 | Nova Scotia........................ | 41 |
| Maine.............. ...... .......... | 35 | Germany.......... ............... | 16 |
| Maryland........................... | 13 | Sweden .. ... .......... ..... | 5 |
| Pennsylvania................. ...... | 16 | South America . ............. .. .. | 4 |
| New Jersey........................ | 12 | Russia ...................•..... | 1 |
| Virginia ....................... ......... | 10 | Holland..... .................... | 3 |
| Vermont....................... .. | 10 | Austria . .......... . . ........ .. | 1 |
| Louisiana........................... | 1 | Prussia...... ...... ... .......... | 1 |
| Ohio...... ........................ | 9 | Africa ............................ | 1 |
| Delaware........................... | 8 | | |
| District of Columbia ............... | 11 | | |
| North Carolina.......... ..... .... | 1 | | |
| South Carolina..................... | 2 | | |
| Tennessee........... .......... ...... | 1 | | |
| Missouri........... ............. . ........ | 1 | | |
| Indiana................................. | 2 | | |
| Georgia ............ ............. ..... | 4 | | |
| Michigan .............. ............. | 1 | | |
| | 1048 | | 965 |

*Age of persons committed on sentence:*

| | | | |
|---|---|---|---|
| Under 20 years of age................ | 169 | From 50 to 60 years of age....... | 114 |
| From 20 to 30 years ... .............. | 768 | From 60 to 70 years of age...... | 41 |
| From 30 to 40 years.................. | 586 | Over 70 years.......... ......... | 2 |
| From 40 to 50 years.................. | 833 | | |

| | | | | | |
|---|---|---|---|---|---|
| Males.... ........ ...1731 | Whites ......... . | 1894 | Married......... ... | 730 |
| Females............. 282 | Colored............. | 119 | Single.............. | 1283 |

Read and write........ 1442  Read, but not write  153  Neither read nor write 418

Total number of criminal commitments.................................... 2547
"      "      sentenced..... ...................................... ........ 2013

NELSON VIALL.

PROVIDENCE, December 31, 1876.                                    *Jailer.*
10

## STATE PRISON CONVICTS FOR YEAR ENDING DECEMBER 31st, 1876.

| Number. | Name. | Age. | Nativity. | Crime. | Time of Commitment. | Term of Sentence. | Discharged. | Manner of Discharge. |
|---|---|---|---|---|---|---|---|---|
| 252 | Shubael Baker | 38 | Massachusetts | Murder | Mh. 21, 1856 | Life. | | |
| 384 | Patk Robinson | 52 | Island | " | April 15, 1861 | " | | |
| 385 | Lydia Phetteplace | 67 | Rhde Island | " | Mh. 1, 1867 | " | | |
| 519 | Robert Crowe, U.S. | 35 | rhland. | " | April 20, 1867 | " | | |
| 525 | John White | 40 | " | " | Aug. 21, 1867 | " | | |
| 532 | Charles Hozie | 30 | Connecticut | Assault with intent to commit rape | Mch. 17, 1860 | 15 years | May 1, 1876 | Pardoned. |
| 581 | Did Peters | 25 | Rhode Island | Robbery | Oct. 19, 1860 | 10 " | Sept. 5, 1876 | 410 days deducted for good conduct. |
| 598 | John nally | 25 | | Burglary | Oct. 19, 1869 | 8 " | | |
| 600 | George Calamity | 36 | New York | lny | Feb. 10, 1871 | 1 year | | |
| 638 | John W. Andrews | 21 | Massachusetts | Mingling Poison with Drink | Sept. 9, 1871 | 8 years ad | | |
| 645 | Eliab E Peck. | 26 | | imeny | Sept. 6, 1871 | 8 " | | |
| | Same. | | | Shop B eaking | Sept. 25, 1871 | 6 " | | |
| | Same. | | | Robbery | May 2, 1873 | ad | Jan'y 17, 1876 | 286 days deducted for good conduct. |
| 649 | Clarence Thurber | 24 | Rhode Island. | Burglary | Sept. 9, 1871 | 5 | May 4, 1876 | 148 " |
| 655 | Edward Wilson | 31 | | Robbery | Sept. 21, 1871 | 5 | | |
| 671 | illss Wilkinson | 44 | Pennsylvania | Burglary | April 8, 1872 | 7 | | |
| 672 | Patrick Saxton | 24 | Pennsylvania | Burglary | April 10, 1872 | 5 | April 12, 1876 | Pardoned. |
| 673 | Patrick Hackett | 24 | Ohio | Burglary | April 29, 1872 | 5 | Aug. 18, 1876 | 255 days deducted. |
| 680 | Henry Thomas | 25 | igla. | Burglary | Dec. 2, 1872 | 5 | | |
| 686 | Ics Gillease | 33 | Ireland | Manslaughter | Dec. 3, 1872 | 5 | | |
| 688 | Henry Johnson | 28 | Connecticut | Burglary | Bc. 3, 1872 | 5 | | |
| 697 | Francis Hughes | 42 | Ireland | Murder | April 22, 1873 | Life. | | |
| 698 | Patrick F. D mahy | 29 | Connecticut | Perjury | May 1, 1873 | 4 years | | |
| 704 | Joseph Perry, U.S. | 60 | | Shop Breaking | June 24, 1873 | 3 | July 21, 1876 | 50 days deducted for good conduct. |
| 707 | Hugh Burns | 19 | Rhod lnd | Larceny | Sept. 8, 1873 | 3 | July 23, 1876 | 60 " |
| 709 | Andrew Connors | 30 | Ireland. | Burning a Barn | Sept. 22, 1873 | 3 | Aug. 7, 1876 | 98 " |
| 713 | Amherst A. Bliven | 45 | Connecticut | Shop Breaking | Nov. 10, 1873 | 3 | Feb. 6, 1876 | 40 " |
| 720 | e Robinson | 100 | Virginia | Robbery | Oct. 16, 1873 | 2 | | |
| 731 | John Ryan | 38 | Ireland | Robbery | May 11, 1874 | 5 | | |
| 732 | James W. Arnold | 30 | Rhode Island | House Breaking | May 12, 1874 | 5 | May 3, 1876 | 44 days deducted for good conduct. |
| 733 | Ellis B. Manchester | 90 | Massachusetts | | June 15, 1874 | 2 | Aug. 16, 1876 | 33 " |
| 734 | Levi Coney | 27 | Canada | Forgery | June 15, 1874 | 2 | Mch. 5, 1876 | 21 " |
| 740 | Charles Dillon | 40 | France | Larceny | Sept. 15, 1874 | 1 year | | |
| 744 | Wss A. Leary | 31 | Virginia | Larceny | Sept. 29, 1874 | 1 year | | |
| 746 | ma M. O'Brien | 37 | Connecticut | Burglary | Nov. 20, 1874 | 7 years | | |

## STATE PRISON CONVICTS FOR THE YEAR ENDING DECEMBER 31st, 1876.—CONTINUED.

| Number | Name | Age | Nativity | Crime | Time of Commitment. | Term of Sentence. | Discharged. | Marks or Discharges. |
|---|---|---|---|---|---|---|---|---|
| 748 | John Malbone | 21 | Connecticut | Rape | Dec. 17, 1847 | 15 years | Nov. 24, 1876 | 44 days deducted. |
| 752 | George T. St. Aubin | 55 | Rhode Island | Shop Breaking | Jan. 6, 1875 | 2 " | Oct. 19, " | 35 days deducted for good conduct. |
| 753 | Henry M. Pollard | 50 | Massachusetts | Inciting to perjury | " 26, " | 2 " | Jan. 27, " | Expiration of time. |
| 754 | John Smith | 21 | Wisconsin | Shop breaking | " " | 1 year. | | |
| 755 | Henry A. Steere | 35 | Rhode Island | Forgery | Feb. 5, " | 2 years | | |
| | Same | | | Larceny | Mch. 15, " | 2 " | | |
| 756 | Thomas McCabe | 22 | New Hampshire | House breaking and larceny | " 11, " | 1 year | Mch. 5, " | 7 days deducted for good conduct. |
| 757 | James Frackleton | 20 | New York | Larceny | " 10, " | 1 " | April 12, " | 9 " " |
| 758 | John H Sanders | 24 | Ohio | Shop breaking | April 20, " | 1 " | " 12, " | 9 " " |
| 759 | William M. Sanders | 22 | Massachusetts | | " 20, " | 1 " | " 21, " | Expiration of time. |
| 760 | Shaman Sanders | 20 | New York | | " 20, " | 1 " | | |
| 761 | Stephen Northup | 36 | Rhode Island | | June 14, " | 2 years | | |
| 762 | James Smith | 29 | | Burglary | " 28, " | 6 " | | |
| 763 | Edward O. Cole | 26 | Massachusetts | False pretence | " 29, " | 2 " | | Pardoned. |
| 764 | Edwin A. Hall | 31 | New Hampshire | Shop breaking | July 3, 1876 | 2 " | " 13, " | 7 days deducted for good conduct. |
| 765 | James Berrigan | 18 | New York | Assault with a dangerous weapon | Sept. 27, 1875 | 1 year. | Sept. 21, " | 8 " " |
| 766 | Patrick Smith | 28 | Ireland | Larceny from person | " 28, " | 1 " | " 20, " | 7 " " |
| 767 | Patrick L. Cunningham | 36 | England | Murder | Oct. 1, " | Life. | " 22, " | |
| 768 | Robert L. Casey | 42 | New Jersey | Larceny, breaking and entering | " 1, " | 2 years | | |
| 769 | John Cogens | 26 | Rhode Island | | | | | |
| 770 | Geo. E. Butterworth, U. S. | 25 | England | Passing counterfeit currency | Nov. 15, " | 5 " | | |
| 771 | Daniel D. Carpenter | 32 | Massachusetts | Larceny | Dec. 21, " | 1 " | Dec. 11, " | 11 " |
| 772 | John McCarty | 20 | Rhode Island | Shop breaking | " 21, " | 2 years | | |
| 773 | Geo. H. Arnold | 21 | | Forgery | " 21, " | 2 " | | |
| 774 | William Grimes | 23 | Virginia | Shop breaking | Jan. 3, 1876 | 2 " | June 15, " | Pardoned. |
| 775 | Terrence Prior | 29 | Massachusetts | | " 4, " | 2 " | | |
| 776 | Thomas Collins | 24 | New York | | " 4, " | 2 " | | |
| 777 | Philip McLaughlin | 41 | Ireland | Manslaughter | " 4, " | 1 year. | | |
| 778 | Henry N. Jastram | 34 | Rhode Island | Embezzlement | " 29, " | 1½ " | | |
| 779 | Edward S. Jordan | 25 | Hopkinton | Assault and larceny | Feb. 25, " | 3 years | | |
| 790 | Albert Wright | 21 | | | " 25, " | 1½ " | | |
| 781 | John Robinson | 24 | East Greenwich | House breaking and larceny | Mch. 11, " | 1½ " | | |
| 782 | Patrick Verdon | 19 | Providence | | " 11, " | 1 year. | | |
| 783 | John Falvon | 17 | | Shop breaking | " 11, " | 1½ " | | |
| 781 | Carrington P. Slade | 31 | Rhode Island | Larceny | " 11, " | 1 " | | |
| 785 | William T. Hacket | 18 | Rhode Island | Shop breaking | " 11, " | 2 years | | |

## STATE PRISON CONVICTS FOR THE YEAR ENDING DECEMBER 31st, 1876.—CONTINUED.

| Number. | Name. | Age. | Nativity. | Crime. | Time of Commitment. | Term of Sentence. | Discharged. | Manner of Discharge. |
|---|---|---|---|---|---|---|---|---|
| 786 | Oscar Reynolds | 43 | Vermont | Larceny | Mch. 13, 1876 | 1 year. | | |
| 787 | Thomas Burns | 39 | New York | House breaking | Mch. 13, | 1½ years. | | |
| 788 | Theophilus Medbury | 39 | Rhode Island | Larceny | Mch. 15, | 2 years. | | |
| 789 | John Fleming | 21 | | House Breaking and Larceny | " 21, | 16 moe. | | |
| 790 | Mary Hancock | 32 | Ireland | Larceny from person | " 21, | 1 year. | | |
| 791 | Charles H. Lillibridge | 22 | New Hampshire | Robbery | May 10, | 5 years. | | |
| 792 | James Ennis | 43 | Ireland | Shop Breaking | " 10, | 3 " | | |
| 793 | Jesse D Mitchell | 22 | Rhode Island | Robbery and assault with a dangerous weapon | June 8, | 20 " | | |
| 794 | Edwin Westgate | 32 | " | Burglary | " 8, | 5 " | | |
| 795 | Peter Gardner | 24 | Canada | " | " 19, | 5 " | | |
| 796 | Elisha Jones | 19 | Washington D C | " | " 19, | 1 year. | | |
| 797 | James Adams | 23 | Massachusetts | Larceny | " 19, | 1 " | | |
| 798 | James Keeney | 18 | Rhode Island | " | " 19, | | | |
| 799 | William F. Potter | 30 | " | Uttering forged policies of insurance | " 24, | 2 years. | | |
| 800 | Fred H. Angell | 29 | " | Forgery | " 24, | 3 " | | |
| 801 | John Smith | 21 | Wisconsin | Assault and battery | " 24, | 1 year. | | |
| 802 | Thomas Breenahoo | 16 | New York | Shop breaking | " 25, | 3 years. | | |
| 803 | David M. Johnson | 48 | Rhode Island | Forgery | " 25, | 3 " | | |
| 804 | Mayo Linn | 35 | Massachusetts | Larceny | " 26, | 1 " | | |
| 805 | Thomas Cogan | 19 | Ireland | Shop breaking | " 26, | 1½ " | | |
| 806 | Albert W. Farnam | 35 | Rhode Island | Larceny | " 26, | 1½ " | | |
| 807 | Ellen McGlynn | 24 | Ireland | " | " 27, | 2 " | | |
| 808 | Clifford B. Pease | 26 | Massachusetts | Uttering forged policies of insurance | " 27, | 3 " | | |
| 809 | William Bender | 22 | Germany | Shop breaking | " 27, | 1 year. | | |
| 810 | William Arnold | 33 | Maine | Larceny | " 27, | 1 " | | |
| 811 | George Foster | 19 | England | Shop breaking | Aug. 15, | 1 " | | |
| 812 | Andrew E. Bowers | 19 | Massachusetts | " | Sept. 15, | 18 moe. | | |
| 813 | Frank Fletcher | 21 | England | " | " 15, | 1½ years. | | |
| 814 | William Turner | 20 | " | Larceny | " 19, | 1 year. | | |
| 815 | Archibald Wood | 21 | New York | " | " 19, | 1 " | | |
| 816 | James Collins | 21 | Rhode Island | Shop breaking | " 19, | 1 " | | |
| 817 | Frank Mason | 34 | Canada | Larceny | " 23, | 1 " | | |
| 818 | Patrick O'Donnell | 25 | Ireland | Assault with intent to ravish | " 27, | 1 " | | |

## STATE PRISON CONVICTS FOR THE YEAR ENDING DECEMBER 31ST, 1876.—CONTINUED.

| Number. | Names. | Age. | Nativity. | Crime. | Time of Commitment. | Term of Sentence. | Discharged. | Manner of Discharge. |
|---|---|---|---|---|---|---|---|---|
| 819 | James O'Donnell | 19 | Rhode Island | Burning a barn | Sept. 30, 1876 | 3 years | | |
| 820 | Clinton Smith | 36 | Canada | Manslaughter | Oct. 30, " | 8 " | | |
| 821 | Caesare Pacini | 31 | Italy | Murder | Nov. 1, " | Life | | |
| 822 | Merchant H. Weeden | 36 | Rhode Island | Murder | Nov. 2, " | Life | | |
| 823 | Emily F. Roberts, U. S. | 27 | Massachusetts | Fraudulently taking a letter from Post Office | Dec. 19, " | 1 year | | |
| 824 | Moses Barling | 24 | Canada | Shop Breaking | Dec. 21, " | 5 years | | |
| 825 | George M. Ross | 19 | Rhode Island | Larceny | Dec. 21, " | 1 year | | |
| 826 | Thomas Robinson | | " | Burglary, two cases | Dec. 21, " | 5 years | | |
| | Same. | | | Shop Breaking | | | | |
| 827 | Henry Allen | 19 | " | Burglary | Dec. 21, " | 5 " | | |
| 828 | Frank Smith | 22 | Ohio | Burglary | Dec. 21, " | 5 " | | |
| 829 | Michael Dwyer | 18 | England | Setting Fire | Dec. 30, " | 15 months | | |

PROVIDENCE, December 31st, 1876.

NELSON VIALL, *Warden.*

# PHYSICIAN'S REPORT.

*To the Honorable the General Assembly of the State of Rhode Island, at its January Session, A. D. 1877.*

The undersigned, physician to the Rhode Island State prison, respectfully presents the following report for the year ending December 31, 1876 :

A fair degree of health has attended the prison during the year past. There has been a falling off in the number of chronic complaints, and a small increase of cases of acute disease. The average number in the Hospital Ward has been somewhat larger than during the previous year, owing, in part, to the gravity of the cases treated, and in part to increased efforts to promote the comfort of the sick. We have endeavored to make the best of circumstances, and to do all in our power, consistent with prison discipline, that would conduce to their restoration to health. The Hospital Ward, though scarcely worthy of the name, is better heated than the ordinary cells, and also affords a fair opportunity for exercise.

No deaths have occurred either in the State Prison or the County Jail during the year. All the sick, with the exception of a few chronic cases, still under treatment, have recovered or are convalescent.

Fifty-five professional visits were made to the prison during the year, and seven hundred and thirty-four applicants received medical or surgical treatment.

The following is a list of diseases treated during the year, with the corresponding number of applications :

| | | | |
|---|---|---|---|
| Scrofula | 29 | Gonorrhœa | 18 |
| Indigestion | 27 | Dyspepsia | 15 |
| Coryza | 26 | Dysuria | 15 |
| Rheumatism | 25 | Pneumonia | 15 |
| Bronchitis | 21 | Stricture | 15 |
| Phthisis | 20 | Constipation | 15 |
| Syphilis | 18 | Debility | 15 |

| | | | |
|---|---|---|---|
| Ascarides | 14 | Abscess | 6 |
| Bubo | 14 | Enuresis | 6 |
| Laryngitis | 13 | Contusion | 6 |
| Orchitis | 12 | Sprain | 6 |
| Eczema | 12 | Ecthyma | 6 |
| Ague | 12 | Pyrosis | 6 |
| Gastritis | 11 | Hæmoptysis | 6 |
| Cystitis | 9 | Herpes | 6 |
| Leucorrhœa | 9 | Otitis | 6 |
| Diarrhœa | 9 | Urticaria | 6 |
| Heart Disease | 9 | Onanism | 6 |
| Injury | 9 | Insanity | 5 |
| Condylomata | 9 | Colic | 5 |
| Epilepsy | 8 | Erythema | 5 |
| Onychia | 8 | Neuralgia | 5 |
| Hernia | 8 | Conjunctivitis | 5 |
| Toothache | 8 | Nephritis | 5 |
| Whitlow | 8 | Ingrowing Nail | 5 |
| Acne | 8 | Convulsions | 5 |
| Anœmia | 8 | Miscarriage | 5 |
| Pleurodynia | 7 | Gastrodynia | 5 |
| Dropsy | 7 | Prurigo | 5 |
| Catarrh | 7 | Gastric Catarrh | 5 |
| Urethretis | 7 | Emissions | 5 |
| Ulcer | 7 | Tonsillitis | 5 |
| Hæmorrhoids | 7 | Myalgia | 4 |
| Fistula | 7 | Keratitis | 4 |
| Dysentry | 7 | Pediculi | 4 |
| Lumbago | 6 | Necrosis | 4 |
| Sleeplessness | 6 | Other Diseases | 36 |
| Ephemeral Fever | 6 | | — |
| Total | | | 734 |

Respectfully submitted,

GEORGE W. CARR, M. D.,

*Physician.*

PROVIDENCE, R. I., December 31, 1876.

# CHAPLAIN'S REPORT.

*To the Honorable the General Assembly of the State of Rhode Island, at its January Session, A. D. 1877:—*

We have, during the past year, continued our usual efforts for the intellectual, moral and religious improvement of the inmates of the State Prison and County Jail. These efforts consist in Sunday school instruction and preaching the Gospel.

Our Sunday school is well organized, and has an intelligent and devoted band of teachers. We still continue to use the "International Sunday School Lessons" and find that the prisoners take increasing interest in their study. We also continue our Sunday school concert with profit, and many of the inmates take part by reciting passages on the topic assigned them. As the number of prisoners has increased we have a larger number of classes and teachers than formerly. The teachers have been generally prompt and regular in their attendance although many of them come from quite a distance. The school has, during the year, suffered a great loss in the death of two of our faithful teachers. Mr. Joseph W. Beynon was connected with the school for somewhat more than ten years. He earnestly sought the reformation and spiritual interest of those he taught and gave personal counsel and encouragement to many a discharged convict. The Rev. Thomas Vernon, M. D., was for five years connected with the school as an efficient, able and devoted instructor. He oftentimes addressed us on the Sabbath with great acceptance and profit. He was much beloved by the prisoners and was always listened to respectfully. So greatly was he interested in the work, that he brought with him his son and daughter who are still laboring with us in this Christian work. The memory and instructions of Dr. Vernon will be cherished by us.

After the session of the Sunday school, we hold our regular religious service, the order of which is similar to that observed by the churches of the city. At times during the past year, these exercises have been deeply solemn and impressive. Some of the clergymen of the city have occasionally preached here on the Sabbath, whose appropriate discourses we hope will prove to have made lasting impressions.

We have held a weekly prayer and conference meeting on Friday evenings, at which a number of the prisoners are present and take part, and as many of the Sunday school teachers as can attend. At these meetings, several of the convicts have professed to have received new light from on High, and that they are striving after a purer and nobler life, day by day. Some that have gone out are giving good evidence that the discipline of their prison life has not been in vain.

Mr. and Mrs. James W. Goodwin continue to lead the singing and train the choir. All the inmates take a deep interest in this part of the service, and its influence is very beneficial in preparing the mind for the reception of the truth presented to them in the sermon.

Our conference meetings, held on the first Sunday of the month, are still seasons of special interest to all. When some of these men tell, simply, their own story of sin and suffering, their fellow prisoners are deeply affected. They often with great emotion describe the various influences which have led them, step by step, to their present miserable condition. They often speak of the resolutions they had formed to change their course of life. Many of them speak of maternal influences thrown around them in their youth, and how they were led by evil associations to break away from these counsels and restraints. The liberty granted them at these meetings and also the indulgences of the holidays and especially the opportunity afforded them on Christmas Day, of dining together at the same table, has had a pleasant and happy effect, in relieving to some extent, the tediousness of prison life.

The evening school is still doing its quiet yet efficient work for the mental improvement of the inmates. The progress made by most of them is very encouraging.

During the past year many valuable additions have been made to the library. It is kept in a good and available condition, and contains the works best adapted to the needs of the inmates.

I have had the cheerful and ready co-operation of General Viall and his subordinate officers in all my efforts to benefit the prisoners, for which I wish to return them my sincere thanks.

Respectfully submitted,

WILLIAM DOUGLAS, *Chaplain.*

January 1st, 1877.

# ANNUAL REPORT

OF THE

# Quartermaster General,

MADE TO THE

## GENERAL ASSEMBLY

OF THE

## STATE OF RHODE ISLAND,

AT ITS

January Session, A. D. 1877.

PROVIDENCE:

ANGELL, BURLINGAME & CO., PRINTERS TO THE STATE.

1877.

# REPORT.

STATE OF RHODE ISLAND,
QUARTER MASTER GENERAL'S OFFICE,
PROVIDENCE, JANUARY 2, 1877.

*To His Excellency Henry Lippitt, Governor and Commander-in-Chief:*

GOVERNOR,—I have the honor to present to you, this, my Annual Report, with the inventory of State property in the possession of the militia and this department, as required by law.

## ARMS, EQUIPMENT, &C.

The arms, equipment, and other military property owned by the State are the same as reported by inventory of January 1876, no change having been made.

The effort to exchange some old arms (and other property) for those of a more recent invention and manufacture, is still being made, and, I trust, will yet meet with success.

The muskets, equipments, cannon, carriages, and other property in the hands of the militia are well cared for, and in most excellent order, generally; while a considerable interest is shown by those having them in charge to acquire a better knowledge of the proper method of cleaning them, amounting to a spirit of rivalry, among some of the companies.

Although it is quite difficult for all of the companies to engage the services of men competent to hold the position of an armorer and fulfil the duties properly, many of them have succeeded in securing the services of such persons, and the present condition of their muskets show great improvement over that of previous years. Some of the armorers employed are very skilful in their work, and I have no hesitation in asserting that the condition of the arms in this State is not equaled by that of any other State, while the arms of some companies cannot be excelled, being absolutely perfect in their condition.

The loss of property during the past year has been much less than formerly, but any loss is hardly pardonable, and generally results from a lack of system making all the men accountable to their commanding officer for the property placed in their hands ; but very few companies, however, have such system, or any books showing inventory of either State, or private property. One organization has lost during the past year *another* B. L. musket, making three of these fine arms lost since they received them, and for which no excuse can be offered. I again respectfully recommend that the law be so revised, that an amount equal to the cost thereof, be retained from the pay or allowance of any company failing to satisfactorily account for any property of the State lost or damaged while in their possession.

The amount of clothing owned by the State is very meagre, and yearly decreasing, the only portion of any value being a few overcoats of various kinds, and they, much worn  A supply of good servicable overcoats, sufficient to protect at least one battalion, should be kept on hand for case of any sudden call to duty in cold or inclement weather, such as the militia are at all times liable to perform. The overcoats now on hand are used mostly for the Light Battery men and drivers.

I again call attention to the fact that the State owns no camp equipage of any description. It would be economy, as it may at any time be a necessity, to have a small amount on hand.

The cost of hiring tents for the muster of the two Brigades for 1875, was $175; for the muster of October, 1876, it was $222.25.

I would respectfully ask and recommend that authority be granted by the General Assembly at the coming session, to procure a certain, or necessary, amount of tents, sufficient to shelter at least one battalion, and also suitable headquarter tents for the brigades. I am earnestly urged by the Division and Brigade Commanders and the officers of the Battalions to bring this petition before you. The present time would be a favorable one to procure good tents at a reasonable price.

The amount of ammunition furnished for Artillery has been larger than for previous two years by reason of the many Centennial salutes. The buck and ball cartridges, &c., so long on hand have been taken from the inventory, as they are in process of exchange for other ammunition.

### ARMORIES AND ARSENAL.

The armories owned by the State, four in number, are in fair order, requiring but little immediate outlay.

The windows upon two sides of the Armory at Woonsocket require to be protected by wire screens, as many of them have been broken by stones thrown from the school house yard adjoining, and the windows are now covered with boards, which obstruct the light.

The roof of the Armory occupied by Battery A., at Providence, is again leaky, and will require repairs, a want that seems to be chronic with this building. The magazine under this armory, intended for the use of the State, is totally unfit for storage of ammunition, by reason of the dampness, and I have removed the metallic cartridges to a more proper place of deposit, before they become unfit for service, as was the case with the carbine cartridges, furnished to the Cavalry last summer, and which were taken from this magazine.

The want of a proper building for an Arsenal in which to store the property of the State, and to supply a hall of sufficient dimensions for the drill of a battalion, is every day more apparent. No better investment could be made for the militia, and its good results would be quickly manifested. Within the past few years many occasions have occurred when a number of our companies from outside the city have been exposed to the sun or rain, or waiting in streets and depots for the time of their departure, for want of a suitable place of shelter, such as this building might afford.

The cost of a suitable building would be but little if any more than by the present system of armories in Providence and vicinity, while its advantages are greater than can be imagined by those who are not conversant with the Militia and its needs.

### "ANNUAL INSPECTION."

The last annual inspection was commenced and completed earlier than usual, but every armory has been visited, and all the arms and equipments of every description have been carefully inspected.

Previous to entering upon the duty, I issued the following circulars, and the inspections were held upon the days and hours appointed.

(CIRCULAR.)

STATE OF RHODE ISLAND, ETC., }
QUARTERMASTER GENERAL'S OFFICE, }
PROVIDENCE, NOVEMBER 9, 1876. }

To ....................................................................................

Commanding .................................................................

SIR:—I shall visit your Armory on ...........................................
at      o'clock, P. M., for the purpose of inspecting the arms, equipments
and other military property in your possession, and to execute such orders
as may be received from His Excellency the Governor and Commander-in-
Chief.  Please forward your complete inventory of State property at once,
with a statement of the cause of any difference (if there be any) from the
one last rendered.

The attention of all officers is respectfully called to paragraphs Nos. 183-786
to 790 inclusive, and to the forms for inspection, page 357, of Upton's Infantry Tactics.

Yours, very respectfully,
C. R. DENNIS,
*Quartermaster General.*

## Annual Inspection by the Quartermaster General, Rhode Island, 1876:

1876.
November 23.—Providence, Co's A, B and C, 6th Battalion of Infantry.
November 24.—Pawtucket, Co. C, 1st Battalion of Cavalry.
November 25.—Apponaug, Co. D, 3d Battalion of Infantry.
November 25.—East Greenwich, Co. C, 3d Battalion of Infantry.
November 27.—Newport, The Newport Artillery Company.
November 28.—Bristol, The Bristol Artillery Company.
November 28.—Bristol, Co. C, 2d Battalion of Infantry.
December  4.—Westerly, Co's A and B, 3d Battalion of Infantry.
December  5.—Providence, Co. B, 4th Battalion of Infantry.
December  6.—Woonsocket, Co. A, 4th Battalion of Infantry.
December  6.—Woonsocket, Co. E, 5th Battalion of Infantry.
December  8.—Newport, Co. B, 2d Battalion of Infantry.

December 8.—Newport, Co. D, 6th Battalion of Infantry.
December 11.—Providence, Co's A, B, C and D, 1st Battalion of Infantry.
December 12.—Pawtucket, Battery B, 1st Battalion of Light Artillery.
December 13.—Providence, Co's A and B, 1st Battalion of Cavalry.
December 14.—Providence, The United Train of Artillery.
December 18.—Warren, Co. A, 2d Battalion of Infantry.
December 19.—Providence, Co. A, 5th Battalion of Infantry.
December 19.—Providence, Co. F, 5th Battalion of Infantry.
December 20.—Central Falls, Co. C, 5th Battalion of Infantry.
December 21.—Providence, Co. D, 5th Battalion of Infantry.
December 22.—Pawtucket, Co. B, 5th Battalion of Infantry.
December 27.—Providence, Battery A, 1st Battalion of Light Artillery.
December 29.—Providence, Mowry & Goff's School Battalion.

The inspection of the First Battalion of Infantry was held in Howard Hall, their present armory rooms being entirely inadequate. Several hundred ladies and gentlemen had gathered here to witness the ceremonies, which were conducted with that admirable precision and steadiness for which this battalion is noted. The brilliancy of their uniforms, arms, and accoutrements, flashing under the gas light, together with the stirring music of the drum corps, and the soft strains from the orchestra, made the scene one of unusual attraction. The absence of Col. Goddard, by reason of sickness, was much regretted. The ceremonies opened with a Review, tendered me by the Lieut. Colonel in command, which was well performed, and followed by the inspection in form, which was well executed, the men standing firmly, and handling their pieces handsomely.

The muskets were found to be in perfect order, and were favorably commented upon by all who saw them. Your Excellency can vouch for the condition of many that you inspected personally. The cartridge boxes, belts and scabbards worn are the property of the Battalion.

After the inspection, the ceremony of dress parade was performed, in all its details with admirable style and precision, the fine drum corps of 17 drums, under Drum Major Lewis, sounding off in a splendid manner. In the orders published by the Adjutant, the announcement was made of the resignation of Lieut. Col. E. B. Bullock, who has so long been identified with the "First Light Infantry," and proved himself to be an able and efficient officer. His resignation and removal from the city, is not only a source of regret to the Battalion and his many friends, but a positive loss to the Militia. Company D, of this Battalion, reported as present, the largest number of any Company in the Division, Company B, being the second largest.

The pleasure of the evening was much enhanced by the presence of your Excellency, and your words of advice and commendation to the Battalion. Dancing was in order after the ceremonies, the National Orchestra furnishing fine music.

The inspection of the Second Battalion, showed a marked improvement had been made during the past year, the most noticeable being that of Company A, (Warren Artillery) both officers and men, showing decided advancement in their knowledge of the tactics, and the drill. The property in their possession was in its usual excellent order. The company paraded in much larger force than usual, notwithstanding the severe storm. After the inspection they, with their guests, and a large number of ladies and gentlemen, adjourned to a neighboring hall and partook of a fine supper, which was accompanied by speeches from several of the officers, and others.

Company B, at Newport, presented everything in fine order, with a good company present, who gave a drill showing considerable proficiency in the manual.

Company C, at Bristol, was large in numbers, and gave a good exhibition of drill. The muskets were in good order, even better than they were last year.

The Third Battalion paraded Companies A and B, at

2

Westerly. The battalion of two companies under the command of Capt. J. A. Brown, of Co. B., and accompanied by the Westerly Band, escorted the inspecting officer, with Generals Walker and Chace, from the Hotel to the Armory, where the inspection was held in the presence of an audience of ladies and gentlemen. The muskets and equipments were found to be in very fine order, much improvement having been made since last inspected. These companies are composed of fine young men, Company A men being particularly stalwart, and above the average height. The armory is large, well lighted and in good order.

Companies C and D were excused from parade, their arms, equipment and armory being inspected in presence of their officers and proved to be in fair condition only. The muskets are the old pattern ($_{1847}^{year}$) smooth bore, much used before they received them.

The Fourth Battalion evinced a decided advancement in their drill, discipline and general appearance.

Company A, at Woonsocket, appeared with double the number usually present, its drill and discipline so much improved, I should have failed to have recognized it but for the uniform. The members are certainly deserving of great credit for their efforts in resuscitating this old command, that once held so prominent a place in the militia. The captain commanding would do well to confine himself to the tactics, and leave out fancy movements. The muskets were in the best order I have yet seen them, and I hope to find them placed in a good case or rack before the spring parade. The re-introduction of gas makes the armory more cheerful and attractive for the members at their drill meetings.

Company B, at Providence, gave a fine exhibition of its drill, and is not excelled in the manual of arms by any company in the division The muskets appeared well, but the armorer was too profuse with his oil. The equipments are used only for drill purposes. The present fine quarters of this command prove an attraction for the ladies, who grace it frequently on social occasions.

The Fifth Battalion appeared in good numbers, with much better discipline than usual. The men in line were better set up, more tidy in dress and general appearance, with less of the inclination to swagger, that pervaded some portions of the command. The drill is generally good in the manual of arms, but there is a want of better instruction on the part of the officers and guides, there being a variety of interpretations of the tactics prevailing. This want is not confined to this Battalion, but is quite general. The muskets were found to be in very good order with few exceptions, and these did not appear to be caused by neglect, but from oversight. In one company there was a want of the requisite knowledge of properly cleaning the arms, but the *intention* to have everything in fine order was well manifested throughout the Battalion.

Companies A, D and F are the largest and best drilled, being quite proficient in the manual.

Company E has made most marked improvement during the past six months both in numbers and drill, while the discipline was shown to be excellent, and the captain commanding seems competent to enforce it.

Companies C and B have the difficulty to encounter of a scattered command, but the records of members attending drills, give evidence of their interest in them. Company B turned out a large company, in spite of the severe snow storm prevailing.

The Sixth Battalion (colored) paraded a battalion of three companies at Providence, in a fair state of drill and appearance, with their muskets and equipments in good order for the class of arms. The armory is not suited to their purposes, and the officers are in quest of better quarters, of which they are in much need.

Company D, at Newport, has just occupied a fine, large and well lighted hall on Bellevue avenue, where it was inspected. The numbers were much larger than at previous inspections, the drill much improved, and the muskets and equipments in better order than any other of their class of arms, viz.: the smooth bore muzzle loading cal. 69. The improvement in the "order arms," was particularly noticeable in this Battalion.

The Battalion of Cavalry presented their property and that of the State, in good order as usual, the saddles being in especial good order, and well arranged in the Quartermaster's rooms. The bridles and sabres were in as good order as before reported. Company C, at Pawtucket, gave a fine exhibition in the manual of the sabre, and in marching.

Companies A and B, at Providence, under the command of the Major, passed in review, and performed the ceremony of dress parade.

The Battalion of Light Artillery paraded in fair numbers, and all their property is well cared for.

Battery A, at Providence, have a large amount of valuable property which requires much labor to keep in order, but the harnesses, saddles, &c., were in unusual fine order and well placed in the harness room. The guns were nicely polished, and the carriages, limbers, caissons, wagon and forge were in good order, having been recently thoroughly repaired and painted. Two detachments gave the numerous visitors an opportunity to witness their proficiency in the manual of the piece, dismounting and mounting guns, carriages, &c.

Battery B, at Pawtucket, had all the property in fine

order, guns well cleaned, all the iron and wood work in proper order, the harnesses and saddles properly hung up, and in usual condition. A detachment gave an exhibition of the drill in the manual of the piece, dismounting and mounting guns and carriages, which was very creditably performed.

The Newport Artillery Company appeared at inspection, with very full ranks, accompanied by the Newport Brass Band. The appearance of the armory on entering it, presents the most military aspect of any in the State; the muskets arranged in fine cases with glass fronts, the three colors spread to view in their cases, the cartridge boxes, belts, &c., hung on the wall, each one the same, the knap-sacks placed around the hall above the cases, the swords of officers and non-commissioned officers, bright as gold, placed in a conspicuous place, in fact everything having a place, and in perfect order in its place. The muskets of this command are the first in point of condition; under the superintendence of Col. Powel, and the skilful hands of Sergeant Lawton, they have become models of beauty in their finish. The accoutrements were in unusually fine order, and the cannon marvellously bright.

Through the generosity of its friends, and the citizens of Newport, the Company has during the past year, pur. chased 114 overcoats, 100 pair of trowsers, 100 hats and pompons, 100 knapsacks, 100 fatigue blouses and caps, 100 canteens and 100 gun covers, at an expense of about $5,-500, and made an excursion to Philadelphia, costing $3,500.

The command paraded at inspection as a battalion of 4 companies, executing the forms of inspection, a series of movements in the school of the Battalion, and the manual of arms, with great promptness and precision, under the command of Lieut. Col. Sherman, who never seemed more in his element than on this occasion.

The officers and non-commissioned officers gave sufficient evidence of the immense benefit derived from a school of instruction. Colonel Powel's absence was regretted by all present.

The United Train of Artillery, inspected as a battalion, with two companies, small in numbers, and a drum corps with 7 drums.

The brilliant uniforms of this command with the large numbers of visitors present, made an animated scene. The inspection ceremonies were well performed, and the muskets shown to be in very fine order, (with the exception of those lost or broken). State equipments are not used. Company D gave an exhibition of its drill, in which it has no superior. The ceremonies closed with a dress parade, in which most of the officers and sergeants gave evidence of a want of drill in the school of the Battalion, and of more familiarity with the tactics. The location of this Armory, as before reported, is unfit as a place for deposits of arms and equipment

The Bristol Artillery Company appeared in fair numbers, but in an indifferent state of drill. The muskets were in very good order, and a decided improvement has been made in their appearance since last inspected. The equipments not in use had received but little care. The two small cannon, though worthless probably for service, could be improved in their condition, inside especially. The armory is probably the property of the Company, appears to be in good order, and a source of revenue to the company.

The Mowry & Goff School Battalion inspection has been postponed to a later date, by the reason of the day assigned occurring during a vacation. The arms are in fine order, being under the constant care of an armorer, employed for that purpose.

## TABLE OF ATTENDANCE AT THE ANNUAL INSPECTION, OF 1876.

| COMPANY,—BATTALION. | Field Officers | Staff Officers | Non-Commissioned Staff | Company Officers | Musicians | Non Commissioned and Privates | Total |
|---|---|---|---|---|---|---|---|
| First Battalion of Infantry | 1 | 5 | 2 | ... | 17 | ... | |
| Co. A, " | ... | ... | ... | 2 | ... | 32 | |
| Co. B, " | ... | ... | ... | 3 | ... | 39 | |
| Co. C, " | ... | ... | ... | 3 | ... | 31 | |
| Co. D, " | ... | ... | ... | 2 | ... | 41 | |
| | | | | | | | 178 |
| Second Battalion of Infantry, " | 1 | 3 | ... | ... | 6 | ... | |
| Co. A, " | ... | ... | ... | 3 | ... | 35 | |
| Co. B, " | ... | ... | ... | 3 | ... | 31 | |
| Co. C, " | ... | ... | ... | 3 | ... | 30 | |
| | | | | | | | 115 |
| Third Battalion of Infantry, " | ... | 1 | ... | ... | 4 | ... | |
| Co. A, " | ... | ... | ... | 2 | ... | 33 | |
| Co. B, " | ... | ... | ... | 2 | ... | 28 | |
| Co. C, "  ..( excused from parade) | ... | ... | ... | ... | ... | ... | |
| Co. D, "  "     "     " | ... | ... | ... | ... | ... | ... | |
| | | | | | | | 70 |
| Fourth Battalion of Infantry | 2 | 2 | ... | ... | 2 | ... | |
| Co. A, " | ... | ... | ... | 3 | ... | 38 | |
| Co. B, " | ... | ... | ... | 3 | ... | 33 | |
| | | | | | | | 83 |
| Fifth Battalion of Infantry | 3 | 2 | ... | ... | 5 | ... | |
| Co. A, " | ... | ... | ... | 3 | ... | 38 | |
| Co. B, " | ... | ... | ... | 3 | ... | 31 | |
| Co. C, " | ... | ... | ... | 3 | ... | 3' | |
| Co. D, " | ... | ... | ... | 2 | ... | 35 | |
| Co. E, " | ... | ... | ... | 3 | ... | 28 | |
| Co. F, " | ... | ... | ... | 3 | ... | 30 | |
| | | | | | | | 219 |
| Sixth Battalion of Infantry | 2 | 3 | ... | ... | 5 | ... | |
| Co. A, " | ... | ... | ... | 3 | ... | 23 | |
| Co. B, " | ... | ... | ... | 3 | ... | 24 | |
| Co. C, " | ... | ... | ... | 2 | ... | 26 | |
| Co. D, " | ... | ... | ... | 3 | ... | 33 | |
| | | | | | | | 127 |
| 1st Battalion of Cavalry | 2 | 4 | 1 | ... | ... | ... | |
| Co. A, " | ... | ... | ... | 2 | ... | 21 | |
| Co. B, " | ... | ... | ... | 2 | ... | 25 | |
| Co. C, " | ... | ... | ... | 3 | ... | 27 | |
| | | | | | | | 87 |
| 1st Battalion of Light Artillery | ... | ... | ... | 1 | 1 | ... | |
| Battery A, " | ... | ... | ... | 3 | ... | 29 | |
| Battery B, " | ... | ... | ... | 3 | ... | 40 | |
| | | | | | | | 77 |
| Newport Artillery Company, paraded as a Battalion of 4 Companies | 2 | 5 | 1 | 1 | ... | 86 | 95 |
| United Train of Artillery as a Battalion of 2 companies | 3 | 8 | 1 | 5 | 7 | 49 | 73 |
| Bristol Artillery Company | 2 | 1 | ... | 1 | ... | 29 | 33 |
| Total | 18 | 34 | 6 | 77 | 47 | 975 | 1157 |

The Armories throughout the State appear clean and in good order, and many of the companies have good sized rooms for drill, but the exceptions are the infantry companies in the city of Providence, who are unable to lease halls or rooms of suitable size and desirable location without incurring an expense they are unable to meet. The allowance by the State for Armory rent is the same for a company in the city of Providence as in the small towns, viz.: $100. The companies in this city should and ought to be allowed $250 each at least. The members of these commands are deserving of much credit for their interest in sustaining the militia in these depressed times, paying as they do a considerable sum for their uniforms and equipments, and a monthly or quarterly tax to defray the expenses of rents, &c., besides giving liberally of their time for drills and parades.

The wide difference in discipline, drill, and the care of the arms, that always existed between some of the companies, has been somewhat lessened, and the new organization is doing much towards bringing the poorer companies up to a better standard; but it will never reach the uniformity desirable, neither will the battalions or companies arrive at that degree of excellence and efficiency that should be requisite for them to attain, until the officers and sergeants are better and more properly instructed in the tactics, and their duties in the field and drill room.

A school of instruction is as much needed and required by the officers and non-commissioned officers as their swords and muskets for drill; many of them have expressed a desire for it to be organized under proper authority.

Any candid observer of the condition of the militia

must admit, that although a gain has been made during the past three years in the organization and general appearance of the commands, the men in the ranks have made more improvement than the officers and guides. Very few officers give their orders full and proper, or handle their swords as well as their men handle their muskets, or even seem to suspect they are required to draw, carry, or return them properly, and in accordance with the tactics; while the salutes are most of them ill-timed and ungraceful.

An officer should never be careless of his dress and accoutrements, or tolerate carelessness by his men while on duty. Wherever I find an officer with his coat only partly buttoned, his belt or hat put on loosely and unbecoming, there I find the men careless in their dress and accoutrements.

### CONCLUSION.

It is my duty and pleasure to report, that so far, during the performances of the duties of an inspector, any orders I have given, have been received with a spirit of obedience, and any suggestions made, have been adopted willingly and readily, and whenever I have sought to derive information concerning the management of the different companies, the inquiries have been met and answered fully and courteously by the officers, with the exception of one single instance, and I doubt if this one would again occur.

The presence of the Adjutant General, the Division and Brigade Commanders and other officers of the Militia at many of the inspections, has been a pleasure to me and gratifying to the commands visited.

My sincere thanks are tendered to the officers and members of all the companies, for their great interest mani-

R

fested in making the inspection   not only pleasant, but
interesting and profitable.    My especial thanks are due to
the officers of the Newport Artillery Company; Company
A. 2d Battalion, at Warren ; Company C. 2d Battalion, at
Bristol ; Company A. and B., third Battalion, at Westerly;
Company C., 5th Battalion, at Central Falls ; and Commis-
sary George, of the 6th Battalion, for their hospitalities
and courtesies.

My staff officer, Capt. F. S. Arnold, has been constant in
attendance, rendering valuable and necessary assistance,
with a knowledge of his duties as an officer.

Respectfully submitted.

C. R. DENNIS.
*Brigadier and Quartermaster General.*

# APPENDIX.

---

A.—Inventory of arms, equipments, &c., in hands of the Militia.

B.—Inventory of arms, equipments &c., received into the storehouse.

C.—Inventory of property issued from storehouse.

D.—Issues of ammunition for artillery.

E.—Inventory of the whole of the arms, equipments, ammunition clothing, &c., owned by the State in hands of Militia, storehouse &c.

F.—List of armories, where located, how owned or leased. with the amount of rent paid by the Militia and the amount allowed by the State.

G.—List of bills certified by this department to State Auditor.

Schedule A.—Property of the State in the hands of the Militia.

| NAME OF COMPANY. | Springfield breech-loading rifles, Cal. .50. | Springfield muskets, Cal. .69. | Muzzle-loading R. Cal. .69. | Bayonets. | Gun Slings. | Carbines, "Burnside." | Carbine Slings. | Pistols, (Revolvers.) | Tumbler Punches. | Screwdrivers. | Spring Vices. | Tompions. | Metallic Cartridges, Cal. .50. | Cartridge Boxes. | Cartridge Box Plates. | Crossbelts. | Crossbelt Plates. | Waist Belts. | Waist Belt Plates. | Bayonet Scabbards. | Cap Pouches. | Canteens. | Drums. | Colors. |
|---|---|---|---|---|---|---|---|---|---|---|---|---|---|---|---|---|---|---|---|---|---|---|---|---|
| Co. A, First Battalion of Infantry, | 220 | | | 220 | 200 | | | | 5 | 20 | 5 | 220 | | | | 50 | | 50 | 50 | 50 | 50 | | | |
| Co. B, " " " | 50 | | 60 | 55 | 55 | | | | 8 | 10 | 2 | 50 | 700 | 55 | | | | 50 | 55 | 55 | 40 | | | |
| Co. C, " " " | 55 | | | 55 | 55 | | | | 3 | 10 | 2 | 55 | 330 | 55 | 55 | | | 45 | 49 | 55 | 47 | | | |
| Co. D, " " " | | | | 55 | 55 | | | | | 1 | 1 | | | 55 | | 50 | | 49 | 49 | 50 | 47 | | | |
| Co. A, Second Battalion of Infantry. | 50 | | 50 | 50 | 50 | | | | 8 | 10 | 1 | 100 | 100 | 50 | 50 | 50 | | 47 | 47 | 50 | 44 | | | |
| Co. A, Third Battalion of Infantry. | | | 50 | 50 | 50 | | | | 8 | 10 | 1 | 100 | 100 | 50 | 50 | | | | 25 | | | | | |
| Co. B, " " " | 55 | | | 55 | 58 | | | | | | | 41 | | 53 | | | | 48 | 48 | | 51 | | | |
| Co. C, " " " | | | | | | | | | | | | | 200 | | | | | 47 | 47 | | 47 | | | |
| Co. D, " " " | | | | | | | | | 3 | 10 | 1 | 28 | | 40 | 40 | | | 40 | 40 | 40 | 40 | | 2 | |
| Co. A, Fourth Battalion of Infantry | 53 | | 60 | 49 | 50 | | | | 6 | 17 | 2 | 60 | | 40 | 40 | | | 47 | 47 | 50 | 40 | | | |
| Co. B, " " " | 60 | | | 35 | 35 | | | | 5 | 10 | 1 | 35 | | | | | | 40 | 15 | 51 | 40 | | | |
| Co. A, Fifth Battalion of Infantry | 50 | | | 40 | 40 | | | | 3 | 10 | 1 | 14 | | | | | | 40 | 11 | | 40 | | | |
| Co. B, " " " | 35 | | 50 | 40 | 42 | | | | 3 | 10 | 1 | 40 | | 40 | 40 | | | 38 | 38 | 36 | 34 | | | |
| Co. C, " " " | 40 | | 50 | | | | | | | | | | | | | | | | | | 34 | | | |
| Co. E, " " " | | | | | | | | | | | | | | | | | | | | | | | | |
| Co. F, " " " | | | | | | | | | | | | | | | | | | | | | | | | |
| Co. A, Sixth Battalion of Infantry | | | | | | 28 | 17 | 8 | 5 | 20 | 5 | 120 | 1500 | | | | | | | | 46 | | | |
| Co. B, " " " | | | | | | 28 | 17 | 8 | 5 | 20 | 1 | 600 | | 53 | 55 | 80 | 80 | 46 | 46 | 50 | 59 | | | |
| Co. C, " " " | 120 | | 60 | 60 | 60 | | | | 8 | 10 | 3 | 22 | | 50 | 55 | 80 | 80 | 40 | 40 | 50 | 40 | | | |
| Co. D, " " " | 97 | | 0 | 60 | 60 | | | | | | | | 1000 | 55 | 53 | 80 | 80 | 45 | 44 | 45 | 34 | | | |
| Co. A, First Battalion of Cavalry... | 50 | | 50 | 50 | 50 | | | | 2 | 10 | 2 | | | 40 | | | | 50 | 44 | 40 | 34 | | | |
| Co. B, " | | | | | | | | | | | | | | | | | | | 15 | | | | | |
| Co. C, " | | | | | | | | | | | | | | | | | | | 70 | | | 60 | | |
| Battery A, First Battalion Artillery | 120 | | | 120 | 120 | | | | 5 | 20 | 5 | 120 | 1500 | 120 | | 120 | | 120 | 120 | 120 | 100 | | | |
| Battery B, " | 97 | 150 | | 97 | 100 | | | | 5 | 20 | 1 | 600 | | 120 | | 100 | | 100 | 100 | 100 | 100 | | | |
| " | 53 | | | 50 | 50 | | | | 2 | 10 | 2 | 22 | | 60 | | | | 68 | 58 | 68 | 100 | | 1 | |
| Bristol Artillery | | | | | | | | | | | | | | | | | | | | | | | | 1 |
| State Prison | 5 | | | | | | | | | | | | | | | | | | | | | | | |
| Mowry & Goff School | | 150 | 50 | 150 | 150 | | | | | | | | | | | 120 | | 150 | 150 | 180 | 180 | 60 | | |
| Totals | 975 | 150 | 450 | 1067 | 1022 | 46 | 34 | 6 | 51 | 1188 | 271 | 835 | 4630 | 1005 | 403 | 550 | 190 | 1134 | 1387 | 1140 | 841 | 60 | 8 | 1 |

*Two breech loading muskets lost since 1872.　†One breech loading musket lost in 1876, and two previously.

*Schedule A.—Property of the State in the Hands of the Militia.—Continued.*

| NAME OF COMPANY. | Swords or Sabres. | Sabre Belts. | Saddles, (Artillery.) | Saddles, (Cavalry.) | Bridles, (Artillery.) | Bridles, (Cavalry.) | Knapsacks. | Overcoats. | Frock Coats. | Jackets, (Artillery.) | Trowsers, (Artillery.) | Blouses. | Caps. | Shoulder Scales, (pair.) | Arms Chests. | Accoutrement Cases. | Field Guns, 6 pounder bronze. | Field Guns, 4 pounder bronze. | Field Gun Carriages and Limbers. | Field Gun Caissons and Limbers. | Battery Wagons. | Battery Forge. | Baggage Wagon two wheel. |
|---|---|---|---|---|---|---|---|---|---|---|---|---|---|---|---|---|---|---|---|---|---|---|---|
| Co. A, First Battalion of Infantry | | | 2 | | | | | 24 | | | | 16 | 16 | | 3 1 | 1 | 2 | | | | | | |
| Co. B, " " " | 5 | | | | | | | | | | | | | | | | | | 2 | | | | |
| Co. C, " " " | | | | | | | | | | | | | | | | | | | | | | | |
| Co. D, Second Battalion of Infantry | | | | | | | | 16 | | | | | | | 3 | | | | | | | | 1 |
| Co. A, " " " | | | | | | | | | | | | | | | 3 3 | | | | | | | | |
| Co. B, Third Battalion of Infantry | | | | | | | | | | | | | | | 3 | | | 3 | 3 | | | | |
| Co. C, " " " | | | | | | | | | | | | | | | | | | | | | | | |
| Co. H, " " " | | | | | | | | | | | | | | | | | | | | | | | |
| Co. D, " " " | | | | | | | | | | | | | | | 3 | | | | | | | | |
| Co. A, Fourth Battalion of Infantry | | | | | | | | | | | | | | 45 | | 1 | | | | | | | |
| Co. B, Fifth Battalion of Infantry | | | | | | | | | 45 | | | | | | | | | | | | | | |
| Co. A, " " " | | | | | | | | | | | | | | | | | | | | | | | |
| Co. B, " " " | | | | | | | | 35 | | 30 | | | 35 | | | | 4 | | 4 | 6 | | | |
| Co. C, " " " | | | | | | | | | | | | | 16 | | 6 | 2 | 4 | | 4 | | | | |
| Co. D, " " " | 44 | 44 | | 36 | | 98 | | 75 | | 30 | 16 | | | | | 2 | 3 | | 3 | 2 | | | |
| Co. E, " " " | 44 | 44 | | 37 | | 28 | | 27 | | 14 | 16 | | | | 5 | 2 | 3 | | 3 | 2 | | | |
| Co. F, Sixth Battalion of Infantry | 55 | 15 | | 60 | | 60 | | | | | | | | | | | | | | | | | |
| Co. A, " " " | 12 | 70 | | | | | 75 | | | | | | | | | | | | | | | | |
| Co. B, " " " | 12 | 11 | 14 | | 15 | | | | | | | | | | | | | | | | | | |
| Co. C, First Battalion of Cavalry | | | | | | | | | | | | | | | | | | | | | | | |
| Co. A, " " " | | | | | | | | | | | | | | | | | | | | | | | |
| Co. B, " " " | | | | | | | | | | | | | | | | | | | | | | | |
| Co. C, " " " | | | | | | | | | | | | | | | | | | | | | | | |
| Battery A, First Battalion Artillery | 3 | 3 | | | | | | | | | | | | | | | | | | 10 | 1 | 1 | |
| Battery B, " | | | | | | | | | | | | | | | | | | | | | | | |
| Newport Artillery Company | | | | | | | | | | | | | | | | | | | | | | | |
| United Train of Artillery | | | | | | | | | | | | | | | | | | | | | | | |
| Bristol Artillery Company | | | | | | | | | | | | | | | | | | | | | | | |
| State Prison | | | | | | | | | | | | | | | | | | | | | | | |
| Mowry & Goff's School | | | | | | | | | | | | | | | | | | | | | | | |
| Total | 175 | 191 | 16 | 133 | 15 | 116 | 75 | 186 | 45 | 46 | 16 | 16 | 67 | 45 | 27 | 6 | 16 | 4 | 30 | 10 | 1 | 1 | 1 |

*Schedule A.—Property of the State in the Hands of the Militia.—Continued.*

| NAME OF COMPANY | Spare Wheels. | Spare Poles. | Water Buckets. | Sponge Buckets. | Tar Buckets. | Sponge and Rammer. | Hand Spikes. | Tube Pouches. | Cannoneer's Haversack. | Harness. (Artillery) complete. | Paulins. | Worms. | Tow-hooks. | Prolonges. | Priming Wires. | Priming Gimlets. | Thumb Stalls. | Shovels and Spades. | Vent Covers. | Tompions. | Axes. | Round Shot 6 pounders. | Rifle projectile 6 pounders. |
|---|---|---|---|---|---|---|---|---|---|---|---|---|---|---|---|---|---|---|---|---|---|---|---|
| Co. A, First Battalion of Infantry | | | | 3 | 2 | 2 | 4 | | | | | | | | | | | | | | | | |
| Co. B,    "         "         " | | | | | | | | | | | | | | | | | | | | | | | |
| Co. C,    "         "         " | | | | | | | | | | | | | | | | | | | | | | | |
| Co. D,    "         "         " | | | | | | | | | | | | | | | | | | | | | | | |
| Co. A, Second Battalion of Infantry | | | | | | | | | | 4 | | | | | | | | | | | | | |
| Co. C,    "         "         " | | | | | | | | | | | | | | | | | | | | | | | |
| Co. A, Third Battalion of Infantry | | | | | | | | | | | | | | | | | | | | | | | |
| Co. B,    "         "         " | | | | | | | | | | | | | | | | | | | | | | | |
| Co. C,    "         "         " | | | | | | | | | | | | | | | | | | | | | | | |
| Co. D,    "         "         " | | | | 2 | | 2 | | | | | | | | | | | | | | | | | |
| Co. A, Fourth Battalion of Infantry | | | | | | | | | | | | | | | | | | | | | | | |
| Co. A, Fifth Battalion of Infantry | | | | | | | | | | | | | | | | | | | | | | | |
| Co. B,    "         "         " | | | | | | | | | | | | | | | | | | | | | | | |
| Co. C,    "         "         " | | | | | | | | | | | | | | | | | | | | | | | |
| Co. D,    "         "         " | | | | | | | | | | | | | | | | | | | | | | | |
| Co. F,    "         "         " | | | | | | | | | | | | | | | | | | | | | | | |
| Co. A, Sixth Battalion of Infantry | | | | | | | | | | | | | | | | | | | | | | | |
| Co. B,    "         "         " | | | | | | | | | | | | | | | | | | | | | | | |
| Co. C,    "         "         " | | | | | | | | | | | | | | | | | | | | | | | |
| Co. D,    "         "         " | | | | | | | | | | | | | | | | | | | | | | | |
| Co. A, First Battalion of Cavalry | | | | | | | | | | | | | | | | | | | | | | | |
| Co. B,    "         "         " | | | | | | | | | | | | | | | | | | | | | | | |
| Battery A, First Battalion Artillery | 6 | 6 | 12 | 6 | 6 | 12 | 12 | 12 | 12 | 70 | 12 | 6 | 12 | 6 | 12 | 12 | 6 | 8 | 6 | 2 | 6 | 150 | 40 |
| Battery B,    "         "         " | 4 | 4 | | 6 | 6 | 6 | 8 | 4 | 4 | 32 | | 4 | | | | | | | 1 | | | | |
| Newport Artillery Company | | | | 2 | 2 | 4 | 4 | 4 | 4 | | | 1 | | | | | | | | | | | |
| United Train of Artillery | | | | | | 2 | 4 | | | | | 2 | | | | | | | | | | | |
| Bristol Artillery Company | | | | | | 2 | 2 | | | | | | | | | | | | | | | | |
| State Prison | | | | | | | | | | | | | | | | | | | | | | | |
| Mowry & Goff's School | | | | | | | | | | | | | | | | | | | | | | | |
| Total | 10 | 10 | 12 | 18 | 12 | 30 | 34 | 20 | 90 | 106 | 12 | 13 | 12 | 6 | 12 | 12 | 6 | 8 | 7 | 2 | 6 | 150 | 40 |

## Schedule B.—Property Received into Storehouse, 1876.

| NAME OF COMPANY, &c. | Springfield, Muskets, Rifle Cal., .58. | Smooth Bore Muskets, Cal., .69. | Bayonets. | Gun Slings. | Cartridge Boxes. | Cartridge Box Plates. | Cross Belts. | Waist Belts. | Waist Belt Plates. | Cap Pouches. | Met. Cartridges, Cal. .69 | Overcoats. | Trowsers. | Hats and Caps. |
|---|---|---|---|---|---|---|---|---|---|---|---|---|---|---|
| First Battalion of Infantry | 100 | | 100 | 100 | | | | | | | | | | |
| Company A, Second Battalion of Infantry | | | | | | | | | | | | | | |
| Company A, Fourth Battalion of Infantry | | 26 | 26 | | | | | | | | | | | |
| Company C, Fifth Battalion of Infantry | | | | | | | | | | | | | | |
| Company D, Sixth Battalion of Infantry | | | | | | | | | | | | | | |
| Newport Artillery Company | | | | | 8 | 8 | 52 | 8 | 8 | 60 | | | 50 | 50 |
| Purchased of C. F. Pope | | | | | | | | | | 8 | 2000 | 97 | 5 | |
| Totals | 100 | 26 | 126 | 100 | 8 | 8 | 52 | 8 | 8 | 68 | 2000 | 97 | 55 | 50 |

C.—*Property delivered from Storehouse* 1876.

To First Battalion of Infantry—14 Overcoats, 1,000 Metallic Cartridges, Cal .50, for Breech Loading Muskets.

To Fourth Battalion of Infantry—500 Metallic Cartridges, Cal. .50 for Breech Loading Muskets.

To Fifth Battalion of Infantry—1,520 Metallic Cartridges, Cal. .50 for Breech Loading Muskets.

To the State Board Charities &c.—50 caps, 8 frock coats, 12 trowsers.

---

D.—*Artillery Ammunition made and delivered during year* 1876.

| DATE. | COMPANY. | Blank Cartridges. | Primers. |
|---|---|---|---|
| 1876. | | | |
| Jan. 1.. .. | Battery B, Pawtucket......................... | 100 | 150 |
| Feb. 23..... | Battery B. Pawtucket ........................ | 100 | 150 |
| " ..... | Battery A. Providence........... ...... | 100 | 150 |
| March 22..... | Newport Artillery Company Newport ........ | 150 | 100 |
| May 29 . | Battery B. Pawtucket........................ | 75 | 100 |
| June 2..... | Battery A. Providence .... ................. | 200 | 275 |
| " 29 .... | Town of East Greenwich.... ................. | 100 | 150 |
| " . | Kentish Artillery, Apponaug.................. | 70 | 100 |
| " 30..... | Battery B. Pawtucket ....... .............. | 175 | 250 |
| " ..... | Warren Artillery, Warren.................. | 75 | 100 |
| " ..... | Battery A. Providence ......... .......... | 175 | 200 |
| July 1..... | Newport Artillery Company, Newport... ...... | 200 | 200 |
| " 3..... | Bristol Artillery Company, Bristol............ | 100 | 150 |
| " 3..... | Town of Woonsocket....... ................. | 100 | 150 |
| Aug 23..... | Battery A. Providence.. ................. ... | 175 | 225 |
| " ..... | Battery B. Pawtucket........... ......... ... | 175 | 225 |
| " | Battery B. Pawtucket ⎱ 400 round shot | | |
| " | Battery A. Providence ⎰ 2,600 pounds.......... | | |
| Oct. 16.... | Battery B. Pawtucket..... . .. ............ | 175 | 175 |
| " | Battery A. Providence .................... | 75 | 100 |
| Nov. 2..... | Battery A. Providence........... ........... | 100 | 150 |
| | Total Cost....$1,033 43 | 2,421 | 3,100 |

E.—*Inventory of the whole of the Arms, Equipments, Cannons, Clothing, Ammunition and other military property owned by the State.*

| In the hands of the Militia, &c. | In the Storehouse and Magazines. | NAMES OF ARTICLES. | Total of Property. |
|---|---|---|---|
| 975 | 20 | Breech loading muskets, "Springfield, Cal. 50". | 995 |
| 150 | 100 | Muzzle-loading muskets. "Springfield, Cal. 58". | 250 |
| 450 | 473 | Muzzle-loading smooth bore muskets, Cal. 69. | 923 |
| ...... | 40 | Whitney rifles, Cal. 54. | 40 |
| 1,567 | 633 | Bayonets. | 2,200 |
| 1,522 | 1,060 | Gun Slings. | 2,582 |
| 46 | ...... | Carbines, "Burnside". | 46 |
| 34 | ...... | Carbine slings. | 34 |
| 6 | ...... | Pistols, "Revolvers". | 6 |
| 51 | 147 | Tumbler punches. | 198 |
| 268 | 672 | Screwdrivers. | 940 |
| 29 | 50 | Spring Vises | 79 |
| ...... | 217 | Camlatch springs. | 217 |
| ...... | 247 | Main springs. | 247 |
| ...... | 253 | Sear springs. | 253 |
| ...... | 189 | Ejector springs. | 189 |
| ...... | 171 | Firing pin springs. | 171 |
| ...... | 219 | Firing pin screws. | 219 |
| ...... | 219 | Firing p ns. | 219 |
| ...... | 217 | Breech block cap screws. | 217 |
| ...... | 229 | Tumbler screws. | 229 |
| ...... | 97 | Extractors. | 97 |
| 835 | 120 | Tompions. | 955 |
| 4,530 | 15,300 | Metallic cartridges, Cal. 50. | 19,830 |
| ...... | 150 | Screwdrivers for Cal. .58. | 150 |
| 1,005 | 1,540 | Cartridge boxes. | 2,545 |
| 403 | 1,125 | Catridge box plates. | 1,528 |
| 550 | 1,824 | Cross belts. | 2,374 |
| 180 | 1,369 | Cross belt plates. | 1,549 |
| 1,134 | 1,142 | Waist belts. | 2,276 |
| 1,347 | 1,237 | Waist belt plates. | 2,584 |
| 1,140 | 1,137 | Bayonet scabbards. | 2,277 |
| 841 | 1,466 | Cap pouches. | 2,307 |
| 60 | ...... | Canteens. | 60 |
| 3 | 2 | Drums. | 5 |
| 1 | ...... | Colors. | 1 |
| 175 | 14 | Swords or Sabres | 189 |
| 187 | 84 | Sabre belts. | 271 |
| 16 | 10 | Saddles, "Artillery Officers". | 26 |
| 133 | ...... | Saddles for Cavalry. | 133 |
| 116 | ...... | Bridles for Cavalry. | 116 |
| 15 | 10 | Bridles for "Artillery Officers". | 25 |
| 75 | ...... | Knapsacks. | 75 |
| 186 | 150 | Overcoats | 336 |
| 45 | ...... | Frock coats. | 45 |
| 46 | ...... | Jackets, Artillery. | 46 |
| 16 | 40 | Trowsers, Artillery. | 56 |
| 16 | ...... | Blouses. | 16 |
| 67 | ...... | Caps. | 67 |
| 45 | 70 | Pairs of shoulder scales, "brass". | 115 |
| 27 | 47 | Arms chest. | 74 |
| 6 | 30 | Accoutrement cases. | 36 |
| 16 | ...... | Field guns, "bronze 6 pounder rifled". | 16 |
| 4 | ...... | Field guns, "bronze 4 pounder smooth". | 4 |
| ...... | 4 | Field guns, "Howitzers 12 pounder bronze". | 4 |

E.—*Account of Arms, Equipments, Clothing, &c.—Continued.*

| In the hands of the Militia, &c. | In the Storehouse and Magazines | NAMES OF ARTICLES. | Total of Property. |
|---|---|---|---|
| 20 | 4 | Field gun carriages and limbers............................ | 24 |
| 10 | 4 | Field gun caissons..".....".".............................. | 14 |
| 1 | 1 | Battery wagons, "complete"............................... | 2 |
| 1 | 1 | Battery forge "complete"................................. | 2 |
| 1 | ...... | Baggage wagon, "two wheel"............................. | 1 |
| 10 | 4 | Spare wheels............................................. | 14 |
| 10 | 3 | Spare poles.............................................. | 13 |
| 12 | 8 | Water buckets........................................... | 20 |
| 18 | .. | Sponge buckets.......................................... | 18 |
| 12 | 4 | Tar buckets............................................. | 16 |
| 30 | 8 | Sponge and rammers..................................... | 38 |
| 34 | 8 | Hand spikes............................................. | 42 |
| 20 | 9 | Tube pouches........................................... | 29 |
| 20 | 9 | Cannonier's haversacks.................................. | 29 |
| 106 | 40 | Harness' "Artillery complete".......................... | 146 |
| 12 | .... | Paulins................................................. | 12 |
| 13 | 6 | Worms.................................................. | 19 |
| 12 | ...... | Tow-hooks.............................................. | 12 |
| 6 | 4 | Prolongs................................................ | 10 |
| 12 | ...... | Priming wires........................................... | 12 |
| 12 | ...... | Priming gimlets......................................... | 12 |
| 6 | ...... | Thumb stalls........................................... | 6 |
| 8 | ...... | Shovels and spades..................................... | 8 |
| 7 | ...... | Vent covers............................................ | 7 |
| 2 | ...... | Tompions, "Artillery".................................. | 2 |
| 6 | ...... | Axes................................................... | 6 |
| ...... | 1 | Enfield rifle............................................ | 1 |
| ...... | 1 | Carbine, "old, smooth bore"............................ | 1 |
| ...... | 53 | Marine Short swords.................................... | 53 |
| ...... | 38 | Wheel traces, with chains............................... | 38 |
| ...... | 36 | Lead traces, with chains................................ | 36 |
| ...... | 7 | Long lead traces........................................ | 7 |
| ...... | 13 | Girths, "poor"......................................... | 13 |
| ...... | 7 | Trace hook, extra...................................... | 7 |
| ...... | 4 | Tripods, for Sibley tents............................... | 4 |
| ...... | 25 | Tent poles.............................................. | 25 |
| ...... | 2 | Wipers, "for muskets"................................. | 2 |
| ...... | 11 | Fifes................................................... | 11 |
| ...... | 5 | Spurs.................................................. | 5 |
| ...... | 1 | Flag, "large United States, for Quartermaster General,"... | 1 |
| ...... | 1 | Armorer's chest......................................... | 1 |
| ...... | 1 | Quartérmaster's chest................................... | 1 |
| ...... | 1 | Camp desk, "with drawers"............................. | 1 |
| ...... | 4 | Regimental chests, "containing papers and books of regiment during the war"...................................... | 4 |
| ...... | 2 | Boxes of     do     do     do     do     do     do | 2 |
| ...... | 2 | Cases of books and papers, Q. M. Gen. Department.......... | 2 |
| ...... | 1 | Pair of box hooks with chain............................. | 1 |
| ...... | 1 | Set blocks, (2) with rope for hoisting..................... | 1 |
| ...... | 1 | Hand saw............................................... | 1 |
| ...... | 1 | Hand truck............................................. | 1 |
| ...... | 1 | Hammer................................................ | 1 |
| ...... | 1 | Hatchet................................................ | 1 |
| ...... | 1 | Scraper................................................ | 1 |
| ...... | 1 | Work bench............................................. | 1 |

E.—*Account of Arms, Equipments, Clothing, &c.—Continued.*

| In the hands of the Militia, &c. | In the Storehouse and Magazines. | NAMES OF ARTICLES. | Total of Property. |
|---|---|---|---|
| ...... | 1 | Bench vise....... ............................ ..... ...... | 1 |
| ...... | 1 | Bench anvil ......... ................................ .............. | 1 |
| ...... | 1 | Screw driver......... ........................ ............. | 1 |
| ...... | 1 | Chisel.... ............................................. | 1 |
| ...... | 1 | Mallet...... ........................................... | 1 |
| ...... | 1 | Brace for bits... ..................................... | 1 |
| ...... | 1 | Lot of stencil plates...... ........................ .. | 1 |
| ..... . | 1 | Lot of letters for caps, "brass " ..................... | 1 |
| ...... | 1 | Lot of figures for caps, "silver " ................... | 1 |
| ...... | 60 | Eagle oruaments for caps, "brass " ................... | 60 |
| ... .. | 30 | Bugle ornaments for caps, "brass ".................. | 30 |
| ...... | 235 | Artillery cap cords. .. ........... ........... .......... | 235 |
| . .... | 20 | Cavalry cap cords... ..................................... | 20 |
| . ... | 270 | Crossed cannon for caps, "brass ". ... ..... ..... . ........ | 270 |
| ...... | 310 | Crossed sabres for caps, "brass " .    ............ | 310 |
| ...... | 750 | Metallic cartridges for "Burnside Carbine"............. | 750 |
| . . . | 1 | Box of loaded shells, "Cal. unknown " ..... ........ | 1 |
| ..... | 29 | Rounds of shot with sabots for 12 pounder.......... .... | 29 |
| ..... | 32 | Rounds of canister for 12 pounder. ... ..... . .......... | 32 |
| .. ... | | Rounds of canister for 6 pounder............. ......... .. | 280 |
| 150 | .. 330 | Round shot for 6 pounder .. ........ .. .... ......... | 150 |
| 40 | ...... | Rifle projectile for 6 pounder .. ................... | 40 |
| ..... | 125 | Cones for Cal .69 musket.......................... . | 125 |
| ...... | 13 | Ball screws for Cal. .69 musket.... ... .............. .......... | 13 |
| ...... | 138 | Worms for Cal. .69 musket ................. .. .......... | 138 |
| . .... | 3 | Chairs   ............................................ | 3 |
| . .... | 10 | Packing boxes ... .................................... | 10 |
| ...... | 1 | The Gettysburg gun, 12 pounder bronze, "with carriage " ..... | 1 |
| 1 ...... | | Silk American flag | 1 |
| 3 ...... | | " Field " } At First Brigade Headquarters. ...... | 3 |
| 1 ...... | | " Brigade Standard, } ............................... | 1 |
| ...... | | First Brigade | |
| 1 ...... | | Silk American flag | 1 |
| 6 ..... | | " Field " } At Second Brigade Headquarters... .. | 6 |
| 1 ...... | | " Brigade Standard, } ............................ | 1 |
| .... .. | | Second Brigade | |

F—*Armories in the State, where located, how owned, rent paid, &c.*

| LOCATION. | LETTER OR NAME OF COMPANY. | HOW OWNED OR LEASED. | State mortgage | Company pays | State pays |
|---|---|---|---|---|---|
| Providence | Battery A, Light Artillery | Building and land owned by the State | | 6¼ cts. | |
| " | United Train of Artillery | Building owned by State, land by City of Prov. | | | |
| " | Cos. A, B, C and D, First Battalion of Infantry | Leased | | 1,500 | 400 |
| " | Co. B, Fourth Battalion of Infantry | Leased | | 500 | 100 |
| " | Co. A, Fifth Battalion of Infantry | Leased | | 500 | 100 |
| " | Cos. D, and F, Fifth Battalion of Infantry | Leased | | 500 | 200 |
| " | Cos. A, B and C, Sixth Battalion of Infantry | Leased | | 300 | 300 |
| " | Cos. A, and B, Battalion of Cavalry | Leased | | 1,300 | 200 |
| Newport | Newport Artillery | Owned by the Company | | | |
| " | Co. B, Second Battalion of Infantry | Leased | | 150 | 100 |
| " | Co. D, Sixth Battalion of Infantry | Leased | | 200 | 100 |
| Warren | Co. A, Second Battalion of Infantry | Owned by the company | | | 100 |
| Bristol | Co. C, Second Battalion of Infantry | Owned by the company | | 100 | 100 |
| Apponaug | Bristol Artillery Company | Building owned by company, land owned by town | | | |
| East Greenwich | Co. D, Third Battalion of Infantry | Building owned by company, land owned by town | | | |
| Westerly | Co. C, Third Battalion of Infantry | Owned by State | 3,775 | | 200 |
| Pawtucket | Cos. A and B, Third Battalion of Infantry | Owned by company | 4,000 | | 200 |
| " | Battery B, Light Artillery | Owned by the company | | | 100 |
| " | Co. C, Battalion of Cavalry | Leased | | | 200 |
| Central Falls | Co. B, Fifth Battalion of Infantry | Leased | | 400 | 100 |
| Woonsocket | Co. C, Fifth Battalion of Infantry | Leased | | 150 | 100 |
| " | Co. A, Fourth Battalion of Infantry | Owned by the State | | 300 | |
| Pawtucket | Co. E, Fifth Battalion of Infantry | Owned by the State | | | |
| " | Armory of Pawtucket Light Guard | Owned by company, (now disbanded) | 6,000 | | |
| | | Total | 18,755 | 5,950 | 2,400 |

G.—*Account of Bills certified by the Department to the State Auditor.*

| | |
|---|---|
| I. A. Sherman, bill carting................................................................ | $3 40 |
| E. M. Hunt, forage for artillery horses............................... ...... | 14 00 |
| B. Bardeen, painting gun carriages caissons Battery wagon forge &c ..... | 250 00 |
| G. M. Grant, repairs of carriages caissons &c............................... | 50 25 |
| I. A. Sherman, freight, carting &c..... ..................................... | 6 00 |
| G. W. Eastabrook, repairs Artillery harness... ........ .......... . ...... | 11 55 |
| M. H. Sullivan,       "       " &c................................. | 53 05 |
| Angell, Burlingame & Co., printing.............................. ...........…… | 6 60 |
| Builders Iron Foundry, shot for Artillery... ........... ................ | 117 00 |
| C. F. Pope, ammunition &c.for Artillery.................................... | 1075 93 |
| J. H. Welch, hire of tents, for the Division Fall Muster of 1876............ | 150 00 |
| Fred. Miller,       "          ".................. ...... | 20 00 |
| B. B. Martin,       "       ............. . ............".................. | 11 00 |
| 1st. Battalion of Cavalry, hire of tents.................".................. | 12 00 |
| 1st. Battalion of Infantry       "       ..............".................. | 10 00 |
| A. A. White,       "          ".................. | 12 00 |
| L. F. Pease,       --          ".................. | 2 25 |
| Amos Sherman,       "          ".................. | 5 00 |
| L. A. Tillinghast, rations...........................".......… ........ | 654 00 |
| E. M. Hunt, forage for horses.............................".......… | 11 05 |
| A. C. Eddy & Studly, pipe....................... .. ".................. | 2 64 |
| Geo. C. Jencks, carting &c...... .........................".................. | 25 00 |
| Jas. F. Williams, damage.............................".................. | 5 00 |
| Heirs Asa Messer, use of lot....................... " .. ............. ... | 30 00 |
| American Steamboat Co., transportation.... ........"....... .......... | 51 00 |
| Providence & Worcester R. R. Co. "    ..............".................. | 92 60 |
| Providence, Warren & Bristol R. R., transportation..".................. | 27 70 |
| Providence & Stonington R. R.,       "    ..".................. | 191 10 |
| R. Waterman, rent of storehouse to Jan. 1st 1877......................... . | 191 67 |
| C. R. Dennis, sundries and postage........... ................ .......... | 26 17 |

# THIRD ANNUAL REPORT

OF THE

# RHODE ISLAND

MADE TO THE

General Assembly of the State of Rhode Island,

AT ITS

*JANUARY SESSION, A. D. 1877.*

PROVIDENCE:
ANGELL, BURLINGAME & CO., PRINTERS TO THE STATE.
1877.

# THIRD ANNUAL REPORT

#### OF THE

# RHODE ISLAND STATE PRISON COMMISSION.

PROVIDENCE, January 9, 1877.

*To the Honorable the General Assembly of the State of Rhode Island,
at its January Session, A. D.* 1877 :—

The State Prison Commission herewith presents its Third Annual Report, in accordance with the resolutions of the General Assembly passed at the May Session, A. D. 1874, authorizing the building of a new State Prison at the State Farm.

The second report of the Commission was for the year ending December 31, 1875 ; the present report is for the calendar year, 1876.

During the year 1876, the Commission has held twenty-five stated meetings; but this represents only a small portion of the time devoted to the work by different members of the Commission. Besides the regular meetings of the Commission, the different members have spent seventy-two days during the year, in attending to the business of building the prison.

The first meetings of the year were devoted to the examination of the plans for the prison, and to the final decision upon some points not previously decided. At the meeting, February 8, 1876, it was voted to advertise for proposals for granite for the trimmings of the prison buildings. At the same meeting, Mr. Horatio

L. Briggs was employed as Superintendent, and Mr. Isaac Walker as Assistant Superintendent, of    ason Work on the prison buildings, for the ensuing season.

At the meeting, February 23d, the proposal of the "Smith Granite Company" of Westerly, was accepted, to furnish the granite according to the plans and specifications for the prison buildings, delivered at the site of the prison, for the sum of twenty-two thousand, eight hundred and twenty-eight $\frac{25}{100}$ dollars, ($22-828$\frac{25}{100}$).

At the meeting, March 3, 1876, Mr. James C. Plant was appointed clerk and time keeper of the work at the prison, his duties having been defined previously.

The appropriations for the work on the prison, for the year, having been made, and not being sufficient to do all the work necessary to complete the prison and other buildings, at a meeting April 10th, it was

*Voted,* That we proceed to build the main centre building, and the wings of the prison, this year.

*Voted,* That the upper portion of the centre building be built in an octagon form, and of stone, like the rest of the building, instead of iron, as had been proposed.

At the same meeting, an additional contract for the granite for the cornices and quoins of the centre building, was awarded to the Smith Granite Company for the sum of eighteen hundred and thirty-nine dollars ($1,839).

At the same meeting, it was voted to advertise for proposals to furnish lime and cement, and also iron gratings for the windows, window frames, sash, etc.

At the next meeting, April 17th, the proposal of Messrs. Hopkins & Pomroy was accepted, to furnish one thousand barrels, more or less, of best Dexter Lime, delivered at the Prison, for two dollars and fifteen cents per barrel; also to furnish six hundred barrels, more or less, of the Newark Lime and Cement Company's Cement, at one dollar fifty-two and one-half cents per barrel, delivered at the State Prison.

April 27, 1876, the proposal of the "Pawtucket Lumber and Builders' Supply Company." to furnish window frames, sash, glazing, &c., according to specifications, was accepted for $5,987$\frac{40}{100}$.

At a meeting, June 8, 1876, the proposal was accepted, of the Watson Manufacturing Company of Paterson, N. J., to furnish Wrought Iron Window Guards, Iron Window Sills, &c., according to specifications, for the sum of $7,950.

In the month of June, by vote of the State Prison Commission, a copper box was prepared, and placed in the corner stone, at the northeast corner of the north wing of the prison building. The box contains the following articles :

"1. Rhode Island Manual, for 1875–76; 2. Annual Report of the Inspectors of the State Prison for the year 1875; 3 and 4. Annual Reports of the Board of State Charities and Corrections for the years 1870 and 1875; 5. Preliminary Report of the Commissioners to select a site and prepare plans for a new State Prison, in 1874; 6. First Annual Report, 1874, and 7. Second Annual Report, 1875, of the Commissioners appointed to build a new State Prison; 8. Rules and Regulations of the Rhode Island State Prison printed in 1867; 9. Sheet containing the General Statistics of the State Census of 1875; 10. One copy each of the Providence Daily Journal, the Evening Bulletin, the Evening Press, and the Morning Star; 11. A List of the Commissioners for building the new State Prison, with their Autographs, and the names of the Architects, and the Superintendent of the work; 12, An Envelope containing one each of 50 cent, 25 cent, and 10 cent Fractional currency; also one each of half dollar, quarter dollar, two dime, and one dime silver currency, and one five cent, one three cent, and one one cent coins."

At the meeting, August 7, 1876, the proposal of Jerome Patterson to furnish lumber and do the work for the roofs of the prison building, was accepted for $3,485.

At the next meeting, August 31st, it was voted to accept the proposal of the Danforth Locomotive and Machine Company of Paterson, N. J., to furnish the iron work needed in the roof and floors of the central building according to plans and specifications, for the sum of $20,700, and the contract was signed by the members of the Commission.

Monday, September 4th, a contract was voted to be made with Michael Golrick to furnish the slate and do the slating of the prison building and the wings for the sum of $5,875.

At the meeting December 4, 1876, it was voted to discontinue the work on the prison, as soon as the buildings can be properly protected for the winter.

The work on the buildings was commenced for the year, on Monday, April 3d, and finally closed on Wednesday, December 13, 1876, the buildings and other property having been carefully secured so far as possible for the winter, and an exact inventory of all the moveable property having been made.

Mr. Woodbury and Mr. Ballou have acted as Superintending Committee of the work at the Prison, on the part of the Commission, during the past year, and have given much time and care to the work.

## THE WORK DONE THE PAST YEAR.

The work accomplished during the year 1876, has been as follows :—

1. The foundations of the prison buildings have been completed.

2. The sentry turrets, and the walls around the prison yard have been completed, except one gateway in the west wall, which has been left for convenience in the work.

3. The wings of the prison building, covering the blocks of cells, have been built and roofed over, and the roofs have been covered with slate.

4. The walls of the centre, or main prison building, have been carried up about eight feet above the chapel floor, and all the iron beams for all the floors have been placed in position.

The above work protects the blocks of cells, and the centre building has been covered over with a temporary covering, so that all the work is protected for the winter. It was the expectation of the Commission to put on the roof of the centre building the past year, but it was found to be impossible.

All the work has been done that was possible, with the reduced eppropriation made by the General Assembly. All the work upon the buildings, and all the mason work of the past year, has been done by day's work, under the immediate direction of Mr. Horatio L. Briggs as Superintendent, and Mr. Isaac Walker as Assistant Superintendent, and the Commission is satisfied that everything has been done in a most faithful and workmanlike manner.

The rough stone for all the work has been furnished by the Board of State Charities and Corrections, from the State Farm.

In the work of the year 1876, there were laid 766 cubic yards of foundation not completed in 1875, also 3,559 cubic yards of super-structure, of which 2,981 yards were of State Farm stone, and 578 yards of Westerly granite, also 223 yards to complete the yard wall and the cut granite for the two East gateways ; making a total of 4,548 cubic yards of stone work laid in 1876, besides the erection of three granite sentry turrets.

There were also laid, 587,600 bricks, which were used in backing up the stone work of the walls, and to make an inside finish to all parts of the building that are not to be plastered.

The cost of the labor in the whole year 1876, was divided as follows :—

| | |
|---|---:|
| Excavation | $403 70 |
| On account, Board of S. C. & C. excavating, &c. | 700 55 |
| Blacksmiths | 1,236 00 |
| Brick Masons | 12,607 95 |
| Stone Masons | 24,578 63 |
| Total, labor account | $39,526 83 |

There remain 246 yards of State Farm stone, and 101 yards of granite, to be laid in 1877, to complete the stone work of the centre building.

### CONTRACTS OF THE PAST YEAR.

The condition of the contracts made by the State Prison Commission, during the year 1876 and previously, is as follows :—

The contract with the "Oneco Quarry Company," for granite for the coping of the yard walls, the sentry turrets, and the gateways, was completed, and they were paid in full, July 7, 1876.

"The Architectural Iron Works," of New York, have delivered all the iron work, under their contract, that could be used during the past season, and have been paid $31,500. The whole amount of their contract is $43,000.

Messrs. William Hall & Co., of Boston, have delivered all the locks for cell doors, under their contract, and have been paid $1,621 45. A balance due them of $311 39 is reserved until the ocks are placed upon the doors of the cells.

By a contract agreed to at the meeting of the Commission, February 28, 1876, and with additions at a subsequent meeting, the "Smith Granite Company," of Westerly, agreed to furnish and deliver on the ground, all the granite required in the centre building and wings of the prison, for quoins, belt courses, cornices, &c., &c., for the sum of $24,667 25. The granite has all'been delivered, and the most of it set in the buildings, and they have been paid nearly in full, only reserving a small balance until the granite is all laid.

The contract made April 17th, 1876, with Messrs. Hopkins & Pomroy, to furnish Dexter lime and Rosendale cement, has been fulfilled satisfactorily, and they have been paid in full.

A contract was voted by the Commission, April 27, 1876, with the "Pawtucket Lumber and Builders' Supply Company," to furnish window frames, sash, glazing, &c. The window frames are nearly all set, and the glazed sash has been delivered, and they have been paid $4,025 72 on account, towards contract.

The contract agreed to by the Comnission, June 3, 1876, with the "Watson Manufacturing Company," of Paterson, N. J.,to furnish the wrought iron window gratings and the iron work connected with them, for the sum of $7,950, has been completed, and they have been paid $7,600, the balance to be paid when the work is all set.

A contract was agreed to by the Commission, August 31, 1876, with the "Danforth Locomotive and Machine Company," of Paterson N. J., to furnish iron beams for floors, iron trusses, the guard room iron cage, &c., for the sum of $20,700. The iron beams have been delivered and set, and other iron work has been delivered,except with slight delays, as fast as it could be used,and they have been paid $5,000 on account, towards the contract.

A contract was made August 7, 1876, with Jerome Patterson, to furnish the material and frame and board the roofs of the prison building and wings,for the sum of $3,485. This contract has been completed except the framing and boarding the roof of the centre building, and the contractor has been paid the sum of $2,350 on account.

A contract was voted, September 4, 1876, with Michael Gol-rick, to furnish the slate and do the slating of the prison building and the wings for the sum of $5,875. The work has been done, except the roof of the centre building, and the contractor has been paid $3,500 on account, towards the contract.

The contract in 1876, with the Board of State Charities and Corrections, was similar in character to those of the previous years, and was, that they should " furnish the stone needed for the prison buildings, as needed during the year; the amount called for not to exceed fifty cubic yards per day, at $1,75 per cubic yard, or at the actual cost of the same, if that should prove to be less; said cost being estimated upon the following basis, namely : $4.00 per day for a pair oxen, horses, or mules and cart, and $1.00 per day for the inmates of the Work House and House of Correction, including drivers, or for the price actually paid for men and teams, if necessary to hire them; and all other expenses, such as powder, wear and tear of tools, &c., &c., incurred in doing the work."

In accordance with this contract, the State Prison Commission, during the year 1876, paid the Board of State Charities and Corrections the sum of $10,298 06. This amount was divided as follows :—

Labor of inmates of the Work House, excavating and grading......$796 00
Labor of inmates and teams, quarrying..........................6,176 14
Laborers and Teamsters hired, quarrying .................. ......2,049 11
Materials furnished............................................ 880 38
Use of Derricks............................................... 396 43
                                                              _____
Whole amount paid to Board of State C & C..................$10,298 06

The stone furnished by the Board of State Charities and Corrections under this contract, not having all been laid, cannot be measured. It is, therefore, impossible to tell at this time the exact cost per cubic yard, of the stone furnished.

The stone that has been brought to light on the State Farm, by the demands for the State Prison, proves to be of a most excellent quality for building, and in quantity more than sufficient for all the present and future wants of the State Farm and State

2

Prison. If the quality and quantity of the stone had been earlier discovered, the Work House building on the State Farm, and the wall of the prison yard, might have been much improved in appearnce, and the granite corners and trimmings in the prison buildings might have been dispensed with.

### WORK REMAINING TO BE DONE.

For the completion of the new State Prison, there yet remains:

1. To finish the centre main building, including its annexes, the kitchen, mess room, and hospital.

2. To build the Warden's house, including offices.

8. To build the work-shops.

4. To put in steam heating apparatus, and provide the necessary furniture.

It is for the General Assembly to decide, by the amount of the appropriation for this object, how much shall be accomplished the present year. On many accounts it is extremely desirable that the prison should be completed at as early a day as possible. The present State Prison and Jail connected with it, are crowded to excess, and on this account, as the reports of the Inspectors show every year, they have long been a disgrace to the State. The cry of the Inspectors for relief has been long continued and urgent.

Again, it has been fully settled as the policy of the State to concentrate its institutions of charities and of correction at the State Farm. It is, therefore, desirable both, for economy and for the best results, that this policy should be carried out as soon as convenient—the sooner the better. The whole work on the State Prison can be completed during the present year, if the General Assembly so directs, and furnishes the necessary means to do it.

### PLAN PROPOSED BY THE COMMISSION.

For the sake of economy, it is desirable that, if possible, some of the work on the prison should be done by the prisoners themselves. It is thought by the State Prison Commission, that if provision can be made for feeding the prisoners, and for the accommodation of the officers, the prisoners might be safely employed inside of the prison yard, in building the work-shops and other necessary buildings. The cells for the accommodation of the prisoners could be made ready in a very short time.

If this arrangement should be made, the prisoners can be removed to the new prison *before the first day of January next*, and can be employed in building the workshops and other buildings, probably with greater profit to the State than in their present employment. This will relieve the old prison at the earliest date now possible, and during the time required for building the work-shops, the necessary arrangements can be made for the permanent employment of the prisoners.

The State Prison Commission would, therefore, suggest that provision be made for completing, during the present year, the centre building, including the kitchen and mess room; for building the Warden's house; and for providing the necessary furniture and heating apparatus for the prison.

It is understood that the necessary furniture for the prison, and Warden's house, can all be made at the present State Prison, and if the proposed plan be approved by the General Assembly, the work on the furniture can be commenced immediately.

### ESTIMATES.

To accomplish the work, in accordance with this plan, it is estimated by the architects, that the sum of one hundred thousand dollars ($100,000) will be needed during the present year, and the State Prison Commission would hereby respectfully ask for an appropriation of that amount.

A portion of the above sum is now due to the contractors for material already delivered. While the subject is under consideration in the General Assembly, the Commission would ask that a special appropriation of ten thousand dollars ($10,000), from the above sum, may be placed at their disposal for immediate use.

### RAILROAD TO THE PRISON.

The railroad passing near the new State Prison, which was commenced and worked to a considerable extent at the date of our last report, has been abandoned for some months. The State

Prison Commission has had no communication with the projectors of the road, and has no information in relation to their plans. We would, however, repeat the opinion expressed in our last report, that the construction of a railroad connecting the city with the State Prison and State Farm is a matter of great importance to the State, and it is desirable that such a means of communication should be provided. Had the railroad been available for the transportation of freight to the State Prison and State Farm, during the past year, several thousands of dollars would have been saved to the State. It is to be hoped that some plan will be devised for completing the road without delay.

### RECEIPTS AND EXPENDITURES.

The total receipts and expenditures, on account of the new State Prison, from the first day of May, 1874, to the last day of December, 1876, inclusive, have been as follows :—

#### RECEIPTS.

| | |
|---|---:|
| Appropriation, May Session, 1874 | $25,000 00 |
| Appropriation, January Session, 1875 | 150,000 00 |
| Appropriations, January Session, 1876 | 80,000 00 |
| Interest on Deposits, in 1875 | 421 96 |
| Interest on Deposits, in 1876 | 44 80 |
| Check for expense returned, in 1876 | 8 40 |
| Total receipts to January 1, 1877 | $255,475 16 |

#### EXPENDITURES

| | |
|---|---:|
| Total expenditures in 1874 | $7,106 31 |
| Total expenditures in 1875 | 129,604 12 |
| Total expenditures in 1876 | 117,666 36 |
| Charged to this Appropriation in 1875, by State Auditor | 214 97 |
| Total expenditures to January 1, 1877 | $254,591 76 |
| Balance in State Treasury, January 1, 1877 | 883 40 |
| Total | $255,475 16 |

Of the total expenditures from the commencement of the prison to the present time, the sum of $43,080 47, has been paid to the Board of State Charities and Corrections.

A detailed statement of the receipts and expenditures, during the year 1876, will be found in the Appendix.

Respectfully submitted

EDWIN M. SNOW, *Chairman.*
WILLIAM D. BRAYTON,
OREN A. BALLOU,
GEORGE I. CHACE,
AUGUSTUS WOODBURY,
          *State Prison Commission.*

# APPENDIX.

## RECEIPTS AND EXPENDITURES.

The receipts and expenditures on account of the new State Prison, during the year 1876, were as follows :—

### RECEIPTS.

| | |
|---|---:|
| Balance January 1, 1876, on deposit in R. I. Hospital Trust Co. | $1,711 53 |
| Balance in State Treasury of former appropriation, not drawn. | 36,785 03 |
| Special appropriations, January session, 1876 | 40,000 00 |
| General appropriation, January session, 1876 | 40,000 00 |
| Check, Watson Manufacturing Co., expense returned | 8 40 |
| Interest on the deposit in the R. I. Hospital Trust Co. | 44 80 |
| Total receipts during the year 1876 | $118,549 76 |

### EXPENDITURES.

| | |
|---|---:|
| Labor pay-rolls for the season of 1876 | $39,526 83 |
| Granite from Westerly | 24,672 17 |
| Granite from Oneco Quarry in full | 3,098 00 |
| Building stone from the State Farm | 10,298 06 |
| Iron work, window gratings, floor beams, truss work, &c | 15,906 97 |
| Lime, cement, bricks and coal | 7,236 49 |
| Window frames, sash, glazing, &c., on account | 4,025 72 |
| Frame and boarding roofs, on account | 2,350 00 |
| Drawing sand and expressage | 1,294 73 |
| Services of architects, on account | 1,000 00 |
| Lumber | 1,322 04 |
| Hardware | 750 53 |
| Locks, on account towards contract | 821 45 |
| Blacksmithing | 467 68 |
| Slate roofing, on account towards contract | 3,500 00 |
| Plumbers' material and labor | 217 25 |
| Horse hire | 156 50 |

| | |
|---|---:|
| Staging poles............................................................ | 265 00 |
| Iron and steel. .......................................... ............... | 246 48 |
| Testing cement.................................... ................... | 51 00 |
| Freight........................................... ................. | 70 00 |
| Derrick.................................... .......... .............. .. .... | 98 00 |
| Damaged hay to protect foundations........................... | 93 75 |
| Advertising..................................................... ....... | 61 29 |
| Powder................,............................ ............... | 42 50 |
| Wooden ware, brooms, stove and stove furniture...... ...... | 27 90 |
| Wharfage, (returned by Watson Manufacturing Co.)......... | 8 40 |
| Stationery..................................... .. ............. | 4 35 |
| Miscellaneous expenses.......... .. ............. ......... | 53 27 |

| | |
|---|---:|
| Total expenditure in 1876 ...... ................ ...... | $117,666 36 |
| Balance January 1, 1877, in State Treasury.................. | 883 40 |
| Total..... ............... ..................... ........ | $118,549 76 |

The above account of receipts and expenditures for the year, includes the account for the balance on deposit, January 1, 1876, with the R. I. Hospital Trust Co. That amount has been paid out directly by the Chairman of the Commission, and the account is as follows :—

| | |
|---|---:|
| Balance, January 1, 1876, on deposit........................ | $1,711 53 |
| Interest on the same........ ......................... | 44 80 |
| Check, from Watson Manufacturing Co...................... | 8 40 |
| Total receipts................................. | $1,764 73 |

### PAID OUT.

| 1876. | | | |
|---|---|---|---:|
| March | 18. | Paid Wm. Hall & Co.. towards locks.......... | $821 45 |
| July | 12. | Paid Capt. Hammer freight of iron........... | 70 00 |
| December 27. | | Paid Board of State C. & C. on account....... | 873 28 |
| | | Total paid out.... ............................ | $1,764 73 |

With the exception of this amount, all the bills for expenditure of the year 1876, have been certified by the Chairman of the State Prison Commission, to the State Auditor for payment, in accordance with the resolution of the General Assembly, at the January session, 1876.

EDWIN M. SNOW,

*Chairman, State Prison Commission.*

## DETAILED STATEMENT OF EXPENDITURES.

The following shows the dates and the amounts of all the sums paid out, or certified to the State Auditor for payment, and the names of the parties to whom they were paid, during the year 1876, on the account of the new State Prison :—

EXPENDITURES

| 1876. | | | |
|---|---|---|---|
| March | 18. | William Hall & Co ........................ | $821 45 |
| May | 2. | William H. Miller & Co ............ ........ | 64 27 |
| " | 2. | Knowles, Anthony & Danielson . ........ ... | 24 25 |
| " | 2. | Pay-roll for labor in April.... ........ ...... | 1,499 42 |
| | 2. | Moses L. Watson ... ... · ...... ........ | 188 00 |
| | 2. | Augustus Woodbury........................ | 19 08 |
| | 3. | Hopkins & Pomroy........... ............ .. | 396 25 |
| " | 8. | A. J. Goff.......... ............ ..... ... | 42 50 |
| June | 3. | Pay-roll for labor in May . .............. | 4,066 06 |
| " | 3. | Providence Press Company ..... ..... ..... | 20 26 |
| " | 3. | Board of State Charities and Corrections...... | 796 00 |
| | 3. | Moses L. Watson...................... ..... | 259 00 |
| | 3. | *L. Upham & Co ......................... | 98 00 |
| | 3. | Hopkins & Pomroy......................... | 574 00 |
| | 3. | Barker, Whitaker & Co .................... | 169 65 |
| | 3. | William H. Miller & Co.......... .......... | 46 75 |
| | 3. | Nightingale & Kilton ...................... | 117 95 |
| | 3. | John H. Eddy & Co........................ | 14 75 |
| | 3. | Providence Sewer Department .............. | 51 00 |
| | 3. | Henry D. Griswold.................... | 42 50 |
| | 3. | Smith Granite Co...................... | 4,596 58 |
| | 5. | Stone & Carpenter.... ............ ...... .... | 500 00 |
| " | 16. | Architectural Iron Works ... ..... ......... | 3,300 00 |
| " | 16. | William G. R. Mowry & Co.................. | 96 00 |
| July | 5. | Pay-roll for labor in June................. .. | 4,735 79 |
| " | 5. | Moses L. Watson......... .............. | 293 05 |
| " | 5. | Hopkins & Pomroy........................ | 614 00 |
| | 5. | Barker, Whitaker & Co................. ..... | 51 20 |
| | 5. | B. F. Greene, Assignee............ ...... | 115 91 |
| | 5. | Nightingale & Kilton........................ | 13 79 |
| | 5. | Crowell & Sisson.......................... | 45 00 |
| " | 5. | Tuttle & Hobbs............................ | 57 00 |
| " | 5. | Augustus Woodbury........................ | 6 88 |
| " | 7. | Oneco Quarry Co.......................... | 3,098 00 |
| " | 10. | Smith Granite Co.......................... | 4,575 67 |

*Two dollars returned and credited in labor account.

3

| July | 12. | Capt. [John M. Hammer... .................... | 70 00 |
|---|---|---|---|
| " | 24. | Pawtucket Lumber & Builders' Supply Co...... | 2,000 00 |
| " | 27. | Providence Press Company.................. | 5 40 |
| " | 29. | Thomas Phillips & Co........................ | 93 92 |
| August | 4. | Pay-roll for labor in July.................... | 4,191 76 |
| " | 4. | Crowell & Sisson............................ | 145 12 |
| " | 4. | William H. Miller & Co........ ............ | 40 10 |
| " | 4. | Nightingale & Kilton..................... .... | 34 44 |
| " | 4. | Barker, Whitaker & Co....................... | 61 27 |
| " | 4. | John H. Eddy & Co.......................... | 3 25 |
| " | 4. | B. F. Greene, Assignee...................... | 428 92 |
| " | 4. | Smith Granite Co............................ | 3,149 40 |
| " | 4. | Hopkins & Pomroy.......................... | 357 15 |
| " | 4. | Job Wilbur................................. | 175 25 |
| " | 4. | Moses L. Watson............................ | 105 95 |
| " | 4. | Point Street Iron Works.................... | 8 40 |
| " | 8. | Watson Manufacturing Co................... | 6,600 00 |
| " | 9. | Pawtucket Lumber & Builders' Supply Co...... | 525 72 |
| September | 4. | Pay-roll for labor in August.... ........ .... | 6,837 58 |
| " | 4. | Smith Granite Co............................ | 4,056 01 |
| " | 4. | B. F. Greene, Assignee...................... | 253 68 |
| " | 4. | Hopkins & Pomroy.......................... | 421 70 |
| " | 4. | Providence Builders' Association.............. | 385 00 |
| " | 4. | William H. Miller & Co...................... | 40 10 |
| " | 4. | Barker, Whitaker & Co...................... . | 81 63 |
| " | 4. | Nightingale & Kilton........................ | 37 62 |
| " | 4. | Moses L. Watson............................ | 107 30 |
| October | 4. | Pay-roll for labor in September.............. | 6,746 62 |
| " | 4. | Smith Granite Co............................ | 3,343 46 |
| " | 4. | Hopkins & Pomroy.......................... | 1,396 23 |
| " | 4. | Stone & Carpenter...................... .... . | 500 00 |
| " | 4. | Barker, Whitaker & Co...................... | 145 54 |
| " | 4. | Moses L. Watson............ .. ... ........ | 133 20 |
| " | 4. | Job Wilbur................................. | 89 75 |
| " | 4. | B. F. Greene, Assignee...................... | 83 35 |
| " | 4. | Tuttle & Hobbs.............................. | 72 00 |
| " | 4. | Winsor & Brown............................ | 63 09 |
| " | 4. | William H Miller & Co...................... | 39 88 |
| " | 4. | Nightingale & Kilton........................ | 22 43 |
| " | 4. | Tucker Swan & Co.......................... | 13 00 |
| " | 4. | Augustus Woodbury......................... | 8 35 |
| " | 4. | Sidney S. Rider............................. | 4 35 |
| " | 21. | Providence Water Works........ .......... | 139 54 |
| November | 2. | Pay-roll for labor in October.................. | 6,734 11 |
| " | 2. | Providence Press Co......................... | 6 13 |

| | | | |
|---|---|---|---|
| November | 2. | Smith Granite Co........................... | 1,351 05 |
| " | 2. | Barker Whitaker & Co...................... | 215 09 |
| " | 2. | Nightingale & Kilton....................... | 12 95 |
| " | 2. | Hopkins & Pomroy......................... | 1,489 40 |
| " | 2. | Winsor & Brown.................... ........ | 205 77 |
| " | 2. | Providence Builders' Association............ | 629 85 |
| " | 2. | Moses L. Watson........................... | 135 40 |
| " | 2. | E. Ward, Agent ........................... | 6 15 |
| " | 2. | Oren A. Ballou............................. | 10 45 |
| " | 2. | Board of State Charities and Corrections...... | 7,000 00 |
| " | 2. | Watson Manufacturing Company............. | 1,000 00 |
| " | 6. | Jerome Patterson.......................... | 1,000 00 |
| December | 5. | Pay-roll for labor in November.............. | 4,275 69 |
| " | 5. | William H. Miller & Co........ ............. | 40 10 |
| " | 5. | Barker, Whitaker & Co...................... | 18 00 |
| " | 5. | John H. Eddy & Co......................... | 3 75 |
| " | 5. | Nightingale & Kilton......................... | 7 30 |
| " | 5. | Hopkins & Pomroy......................... | 687 38 |
| " | 5. | James C. Plant.... ....................... | 22 86 |
| " | 5. | Builders' Iron Foundry..................... | 6 97 |
| " | 5. | Union Ice Company......................... | 93 75 |
| " | 5. | Jerome Patterson........................... | 850 00 |
| " | 5. | Moses L. Watson........................... | 110 65 |
| " | 5. | Pawtucket Lumber and Builders' Supply Co. | 1,500 00 |
| " | 5. | Smith Granite Company.................... | 3,300 00 |
| " | 5. | Danforth Locomotive Works................. | 5,000 00 |
| " | 5. | Board of State Charities and Corrections...... | 672 20 |
| " | 12. | Pay-roll for labor in December, in part........ | 197 52 |
| " | 13. | Pay-roll for labor in December, in part........ | 199 78 |
| " | 26. | Smith Granite Company... ................. | 300 00 |
| " | 26. | Hopkins & Pomroy......................... | 132 99 |
| " | 26. | Winsor & Brown .......................... | 75 32 |
| " | 26. | Moses L. Watson........................... | 12 18 |
| " | 26. | Augustus Woodbury........................ | 2 98 |
| " | 26. | Board of State Charities and Corrections...... | 956 58 |
| " | 26. | Barker, Whitaker & Co...................... | 2 18 |
| " | 26. | Jerome Patterson.......................... | 500 00 |
| " | 26. | Michael Golrick........ .................... | 3,500 00 |
| " | 26. | Thomas Phillips & Co...................... | 123 83 |
| " | 27. | Tuttle & Hobbs............................ | 27 50 |
| " | 27. | Knowles, Anthony & Danielson.............. | 5 25 |
| " | 27. | Board of State Charities and Corrections...... | 873 28 |
| | | | $117,666 36 |

# ANNUAL REPORT

OF THE

# ADJUTANT GENERAL,

OF THE

## STATE OF RHODE ISLAND,

FOR THE YEAR 1876.

---

PROVIDENCE:

ANGELL, BURLINGAME & CO., PRINTERS TO THE STATE,

1877.

# REPORT.

STATE OF RHODE ISLAND,
ADJUTANT GENERAL'S OFFICE, Providence, Dec. 31st, 1876. }

*To his Excellency Henry Lippitt, Governor and Commander-in-Chief:*

GOVERNOR :—In accordance with law, I have the honor to transmit through you to the Honorable General Assembly, an abstract of the Active Militia, together with a report of this department for the past year.

## THE MILITIA ORGANIZATION.

The active militia of this State is now organized in one division of two brigades, which are divided into small battalions, of which there is one battalion of six, three of four, one of three and one of two companies of Infantry, together with one battalion of Light Artillery, composed of two light batteries of four guns each, and one battalion of Cavalry having three companies.

This organization, while not the most desirable, seemed best fitted to meet the situation at the time the law was framed, and was intended to accommodate many of the commands as they then existed without making too radical a change in their composition. Formerly the battalion was the exception, rather than the rule. The force as now constituted, was not supposed to be permanent, but was calculated as a stepping stone from the old time of the skeleton regiment formation, when a command with scarcely men enough for a company, had all the elements of a regimental organization.

The old system has given place to the new; both officers and men have accustomed themselves to the change, and the general feeling is tending towards an increase of the number of companies in a battalion.

At the Centennial Anniversaries of Lexington, Bunker Hill, Philadelphia and elsewhere, large numbers of the militia from different States congregated, and the exhibition of so many large and celebrated regiments, has created a desire on the part of our military, that the superior material our State possesses, should be organized into regiments, as well equipped and effective as those of our sister States.

There are various reasons why an immediate change in the law, or a re-arrangement of battalions is not desirable, it should be kept steadily in mind, however, and when this depressed condition of the business interest of the State and country shall have given place to an era of prosperity, a movement should be made towards the increase in the size of the battalions, by a decrease of their number, or rather by consolidation. There is still a portion of the uniformed militia who do not feel it a duty to unite with the majority of the active Militia. These companies number more than one fifth as many as the others, and in our small force, this proportion of " Independents " is larger than it should be. They are composed of the best of our old companies, and ought to see it for their own interest as well as obligation, to unite with those who certainly would be, and have been, their comrades in cases of emergency. Their union with the others, would augment to a great degree, the efficiency of the whole. In fact, their separate action, as I have often expressed, is one of the *most serious* impediments in the way of our State Militia taking a position second to that of no State in the Union in point of efficiency. I have seen no reason to change my former judgment, that their claims to independent privileges under their charters, are not what was granted them by the General Assembly when they were chartered.

## MUSTER.

The annual muster required by law, occurred on the 18th day of October. The past year having been one of anniversaries, in which the Commander-in-Chief and Staff, the General and Staff Officers, together with some of the commands had taken part, it was thought advisable, in order to save time and expense, to have both brigades muster on one day, and the time having passed when the Major General could order the Division to assemble, an order was issued from this department, directing Major General Walker, commanding the Division, to assemble his command on the day above named, at Dexter Training Ground, for the purposes required by law.

Brigadier General Thomas W. Chace, commanding the First Brigade, assembled his command on the field south of Cranston street, occupied by the second brigade last year. The Second Brigade, Brig. Genl. Frederick Miller commanding, formed in line on Exchange Place, at 9 a. m., and marched to the Dexter Training Ground. The morning was occupied by both commands in the usual exercises of muster, inspection and drill. At 12 m., both brigades being in line, the Commander-in-Chief accompanied by his Staff was received with appropriate honors.

In the afternoon, the Division was reviewed by His Excellency Gov. Lippitt, the Commander-in-Chief, when it proceeded through the streets of Providence to Exchange Place, where it was dismissed.

The appearance of the troops was very fine indeed, and their drill under the circumstances was creditable, and especially so, in view of the fact that so little opportunity is attainable for the assembly of the companies by battalion, in consequence of which some of the commands have no other occasion than this for battalion drill. It certainly would be greatly to the advantage of the militia, if there could be an encampment for a period of a week at least; if this cannot be done I think the old custom of assembling for muster for one day only, is of sufficient benefit to the Militia, to have it continued. In this connection, I have to say, that an additional appropriation to defray the expenses of a School of instruction for officers, would produce better results than any thing else that could be done for the militia.

PAY.

From a special report of the General Treasurer, dated February 14, 1874, on the expenses of the militia for a period of six years, I make the following extracts, viz. :

| | |
|---|---:|
| Paid Militia for services................................. | $107,034 |
|     Staff   "    "   .............................. | 922 |
|     Bands "    "   ............................. | 1,250 |
|     Rent of Armories.............. ................. | 14,455 |
|     Transportation, subsistence, repairs of property, (not including repairs of Armories,) and miscellaneous expenses,............................. | 10,439 |

| | |
|---|---:|
| Paid for six years.................................. | $134,100 |
| Average payment per year......................... | $ 22,350 |

This amount does not include the total expense of the Militia for that period, as rendered by the General Treasurer. The expenses for the last two years covering the same items as enumerated above, do not exceed per year.............................. $ 18,000

The above statement does not cover appropriations for erection and repairs of armories, special appropriations to companies for uniforms, &c., nor the expenses of the Adjutant, Quartermaster, and Paymaster General's Departments.

The total amount paid during this period of six years, (which covers these items,) averaged per year..... $ 32,710
The total expenditure for the last two years, has averaged per year less than.................................. $ 19,500

As the bills for the past year have not all been rendered, I do not give the exact figures, but have allowed enough (and probably more than enough) to cover the case. A careful comparison will show that there has been a reduction in the running expenses of the Militia of forty-five hundred dollars, ($4,500) a year, for the past two years, or twenty per cent.

A comparison of the *total* amounts expended, shows that including special appropriations for armories, uniforms, &c., the Militia have cost thirteen thousand dollars a year less, than the average for the term of six years above cited.

It is believed that no other department in the service of the State can show such a proportionate reduction of expenses.

At the close of the last January session of the General Assembly, the law was hurridly amended, so that but one thousand men could be paid for duty performed. In view of the above, showing of reduction of expenses, it certainly would be an act of justice if the Assembly would voluntarily remove this restriction.

### INSPECTIONS.

The inspections of Armories, Military property and of such commands as voluntarily appeared for that purpose, has lately been made by Brig. Genl. Chas. R. Dennis, Quartermaster General, assisted by Capt. Frank S. Arnold, Assistant Quartermaster General.

Occasional reports from General Dennis show, that the Militia is at least in as good, if not better condition than it has been for years, and in consideration of the effect of the general business depression, it is remarkable that such should be the case.

I have heretofore attested to the value of these annual inspections, and it shows that the companies appreciate its value, by their voluntary appearance in line, and by their general interest on these occasions.

### OFFICE BUSINESS.

For various reasons, and partly as the result of amendments made to the law at the January session of the past year, the duties of this office have been less complicated than for the year preceding my last report. Nevertheless, receiving and making reports and returns, and attending to the many requirements of the Militia, together with the large number of cases of varied character, arising from details of the late war, makes the daily routine of business very much larger in the aggregate than is generally supposed to be the case.

### CONCLUSION.

Two years duty has now been performed since the adoption of the present law, and although the system never was claimed to have been such as was supposed to be wanted, yet it cannot be denied that the organization is more efficient than formerly. It certainly has effected a reduction in the expenses. If for no other reasons, these would amply repay the expense and trouble incident to the change. So far as I can learn, the Militia are generally satisfied with the law as it is; the principal point made in objection to it being this, that the battalions should be less in number, with more companies to the battalion.

I recommend no material change at present, but look forward to the time (in the near future, I trust,) when we can show a model Militia organization, second to that of no other State.

Respectfully submitted,

HEBER LeFAVOUR,<br>*Adjutant General.*

# RETURNS OF THE MILITIA.

The following returns of the militia in detail is made chiefly from the Field, Staff and Company parade returns for the "Muster" parade, on the 18th of October, 1876, and shows the aggregate "present and absent" of the uniformed Militia:—

| | Commissioned Officers. | Non Commissioned Officers. | Privates, Musicians, Drivers, &c. | Aggregate. |
|---|---|---|---|---|
| Governor's Personal Staff.................. | 6 | ...... | ...... | 6 |
| General Staff............................. | 11 | ...... | ...... | 11 |
| Major General and Staff.................. | 8 | ...... | ...... | 08 |
| **FIRST BRIGADE.** | | | | |
| Brigadier General and Staff.............. | 7 | ...... | ...... | 7 |
| Second Battalion of Infantry, Field and Staff......... | 6 | 1 | ...... | 7 |
| Co. A.—Warren Artillery ..................... | 3 | 10 | 41 | 54 |
| Co. B.—Newport Light Infantry............. | 3 | 10 | 43 | 56 |
| Co. C.—Bristol Light Infantry......... | 2 | 9 | 44 | 55 |
| Third Battalion of Infantry, Field and Staff............. | 8 | 2 | ...... | 10 |
| Co. A.—Westerly Rifles ............... | 3 | 10 | 50 | 63 |
| Co. B.—Westerly Rifles ............... | 3 | 10 | 53 | 66 |
| Co. C.—Kentish Guards...... | 2 | 9 | 37 | 48 |
| Co. D.—Kentish Artillery....... | 2 | 11 | 61 | 74 |
| Sixth Battalion of Infantry, Field and Staff............. | 9 | 2 | ...... | 11 |
| Co. A.—Burnside National Guards........... | 3 | 10 | 44 | 57 |
| Co. B.—Burnside National Guards..... | 2 | 10 | 31 | 43 |
| Co. C.—Burnside National Guards....... | 3 | 10 | 33 | 46 |
| Co. D.—Burnside Guards....... | 3 | 10 | 41 | 54 |
| First Battalion of Cavalry, Field and Staff.............. | 7 | 2 | ...... | 9 |
| Co. A.—Providence Horse Guards ............ | 2 | 9 | 36 | 47 |
| Co. B.—Providence Horse Guards .. ......... | 3 | 9 | 35 | 47 |
| Co. C.—Pawtucket Horse Guards............. | 3 | 8 | 48 | 59 |
| Total First Brigade................. | 74 | 142 | 597 | 813 |

| | Commissioned Officers. | Non Commissioned Officers. | Privates, Musicians, Drivers, &c. | Aggregate. |
|---|---|---|---|---|
| **SECOND BRIGADE.** | | | | |
| Brigadier General and Staff.................... | 6 | ...... | ...... | 6 |
| First Battalion of Infantry, Field and Staff............. | 9 | 2 | ...... | 11 |
|     Co. A.—First Light Infantry................. | 3 | 10 | 46 | 59 |
|     Co. B.—First Light Infantry.................. | 3 | 10 | 49 | 62 |
|     Co. C.—First Light Infantry................. | 3 | 10 | 44 | 57 |
|     Co. D.—First Light Infantry................. | 3 | 10 | 48 | 61 |
| Fourth Battalion of Infantry, Field and Staff............ | 7 | 1 | ...... | 8 |
|     Co. A.—Woonsocket Guards. ............... | 3 | 10 | 53 | 66 |
|     Co. B.—Slocum Light Guards................ | 3 | 10 | 49 | 62 |
| Fifth Battalion of Infantry, Field and Staff......... | 9 | 1 | ...... | 10 |
|     Co. A.............................. | 3 | 10 | 43 | 56 |
|     Co. B.............................. | 3 | 7 | 32 | 42 |
|     Co. C.............................. | 3 | 8 | 33 | 44 |
|     Co. D.............................. | 3 | 10 | 41 | 54 |
|     Co. E.............................. | 3 | 13 | 38 | 54 |
|     Co. F.............................. | 3 | 10 | 42 | 55 |
| First Battalion of Light Artillery, Field and Staff........ | 8 | 2 | ...... | 10 |
|     Co. A.—Providence Marine Corps of Artillery. | 3 | 10 | 66 | 79 |
|     Co. B.—Tower Light Battery................ | 4 | 10 | 66 | 80 |
| Total Second Brigade........................ | 82 | 144 | 650 | 876 |
| **AGGREGATE OF THE DIVISION.** | | | | |
| Major General and Staff............................ | 8 | ...... | ...... | 8 |
| First Brigade....................................... | 74 | 142 | 597 | 813 |
| Second Brigade..................................... | 82 | 144 | 650 | 876 |
| | 164 | 286 | 1,247 | 1,697 |
| **INDEPENDENT COMPANIES.** | | | | |
| Newport Artillery Company ...................... | 13 | 15 | 111 | 139 |
| United Train of Artillery, three companies.............. | 18 | 35 | 98 | 151 |
| Bristol Train of Artillery.. ........................... | 9 | 8 | 57 | 74 |
| | 40 | 58 | 266 | 364 |
| **RECAPITULATION.** | | | | |
| Governor's Personal Staff and the General Staff.......... | 17 | ...... | ...... | 17 |
| Division of Militia...................... | 164 | 286 | 1,247 | 1,697 |
| Independent Companies ...................... | 40 | 58 | 266 | 364 |
| | 221 | 344 | 1,513 | 2,078 |

ABSTRACT *of the Annual Returns of the Uniformed Militia of the State of Rhode Island and Providence Plantations, for the year* 1876.

| | General and Staff. | Cavalry. | Artillery. | Infantry. | Total of all Arms. |
|---|---|---|---|---|---|
| Major General | 1 | ... | ... | ...... | 1 |
| Brigadier General | 2 | ... | ... | ...... | 2 |
| Aides-de-Camp | 10 | .. | ... | ...... | 10 |
| Adjutant General's Department | 3 | ... | ... | ...... | 3 |
| Judge Advocates | 3 | ... | ... | ...... | 3 |
| Quartermaster's Department | 5 | ... | ... | ...... | 5 |
| Subsistence Department | 3 | ... | ... | ...... | 3 |
| Medical Department | 6 | .. | ... | . ... | 6 |
| Pay Department | 5 | ... | ... | . ... | 5 |
| Colonels | ... | 1 | ... | 9 | 10 |
| Lieutenant Colonels | ... | 1 | 1 | 8 | 10 |
| Majors | ... | 1 | 1 | 8 | 10 |
| Regimental surgeons | .. | ... | ... | 7 | 7 |
| Regimental Assistant Surgeons | ... | ... | 1 | 1 | 2 |
| Adjutants | ... | 1 | 1 | 9 | 11 |
| Regimental Quartermasters | ... | 1 | 1 | 9 | 11 |
| Regimental Paymasters | ... | 1 | 1 | 7 | 9 |
| Regimental Commissaries | ... | 1 | 1 | 8 | 10 |
| Captains | ... | 2 | 1 | 28 | 31 |
| First Lieutenants | ... | 3 | 4 | 28 | 35 |
| Second Lieutenants | ... | 3 | 2 | 25 | 30 |
| Chaplains | ... | ... | 1 | 7 | 8 |
| Total Commissioned | 38 | 15 | 15 | 154 | 222 |
| | | | | | |
| Sergeant Majors | ... | 1 | 1 | 7 | 9 |
| Quartermaster Sergeants | ... | 1 | 1 | 6 | 8 |
| Commissary Sergeants | ... | ... | ... | 2 | 2 |
| Principal Musicians | ... | ... | ... | 1 | 1 |
| Sergeants | ... | 13 | 12 | 117 | 142 |
| Corporals | ... | 12 | 8 | 161 | 181 |
| Musicians | ... | 1 | 4 | 54 | 59 |
| Artificers, Blacksmiths, Farriers, &c. | ... | 2 | 3 | .. | 5 |
| Wagoners and Drivers | ... | 1 | 32 | ...... | 33 |
| Privates | ... | 116 | 93 | 1,207 | 1,416 |
| Total enlisted | ... | 147 | 154 | 1,555 | 1,856 |
| | | | | | |
| Aggregate (this year) | 38 | 162 | 169 | 1,709 | 2,078 |
| Aggregate (last year) | 39 | 140 | 158 | 1,782 | 2,119 |

## ENROLLED MILITIA.

The enrolled militia, comprising all persons between the ages of eighteen and forty-five, liable to be enrolled by the laws of the United States, numbers 39,966, and is distributed as follows:   .

### NEWPORT COUNTY.

| Names of Towns. | Number Enrolled. | Names of Towns. | Number Enrolled. |
|---|---|---|---|
| City of Newport. .......... | 2,670 | Little Compton............... | 130 |
| Portsmouth ......... .... | 283 | Middletown................... | 172 |
| Tiverton ... . .......... | 358 | | |

### PROVIDENCE COUNTY.

| | | | |
|---|---|---|---|
| City of Providence........... | 21,717 | East Providence.......... .. | 602 |
| North Providence............ | 166 | Smithfield.... .. .......... | 296 |
| Cranston..................... | 574 | Pawtucket............. .. | 1,877 |
| Burrillville.... ............ | 226 | Cumberland.................. | 282 |
| Johnston............. .... | 747 | Woonsocket......... .... | 880 |
| Foster..... ................ | 174 | North Smithfield............. | 269 |
| Scituate.. .. . .. ..... | 453 | Lincoln .................... | 1,030 |
| Glocester....... ............ | 430 | | |

### WASHINGTON COUNTY.

| | | | |
|---|---|---|---|
| North Kingstown............ | 639 | Hopkinton........... . ... | 517 |
| South Kingstown ........... | 790 | Westerly. ................. | 653 |
| Exeter.. ............ ....... | 243 | Charlestown.......... ...... | 141 |
| Richmond.. .... ..... .. | 255 | | |

### KENT COUNTY.

| | | | |
|---|---|---|---|
| Coventry.... ............... | 471 | East Greenwich............. | 281 |
| Warwick.......... .......... | 1,001 | West Greenwich............. | 120 |

### BRISTOL COUNTY.

| | | | |
|---|---|---|---|
| Bristol........ ............... | 829 | Barrington................... | 147 |
| Warren...... .......... . | 443 | | |

### RECAPITULATION.

| County. | Number Enrolled. | County. | Number Enrolled. |
|---|---|---|---|
| Newport..................... | 3,713 | Kent.... ...... ............ | 1,873 |
| Providence........... ...... | 29,723 | Bristol...................... | 1,419 |
| Washington........... ...... | 3,238 | | |
| Total.................................................. .................... | | | 39,966 |

# ROSTER OF THE RHODE ISLAND MILITIA,

## 1876.

### GOVERNOR AND PERSONAL STAFF.

| NAMES. | RANK. | DATE OF RANK. | P. O. ADDRESS. |
|---|---|---|---|
| Henry Lippitt............ } | Gov. & Com.- in Chief...... | Inaug. May 30, '76 | Providence. |
| *Aids-to-Com.-in-Chief.* | | | |
| Charles Warren Lippitt........ | Colonel........ | May 26, 1876........ | " |
| Edward C. Ames....... ....... | " ......... | " " ......... | " |
| Henry J. Spooner............. | " ......... | " " ......... | " |
| Theodore M. Cook... ... .... | " ........ | " " ........ | Woonsocket. |
| Samuel P. Colt................ | " ......... | " " ........ | Bristol. |
| James Fludder... ... ........ | " ......... | " " ........ | Newport. |

### GENERAL OFFICERS AND STAFF.

| | | | |
|---|---|---|---|
| *Adjutant General.* | | | |
| Heber LeFavour............... | Brig. General.. | Jan. 29, 1875........ | Providence. |
| *Quartermaster General,* | | | |
| Charles R. Dennis.... ........ | " " | March 26, 1874..... | " |
| *Asst. Quartermaster General,* | | | |
| Frank S. Arnold............... | Captain........ | May 8, 1875....... | " |
| *Paymaster General,* | | | |
| Jabez C. Knight.............. | Colonel........ | June 26, 1856....... | " |
| *Asst. Paymaster General,* | | | |
| Wm. A. Knight............... | Captain.... ... | Oct. 22, 1862........ | " |
| *Commissary General,* | | | |
| Wm. Gilpin ................ | Colonel........ | June 26, 1856..... | Newport........ |
| *Surgeon General,* | | | |
| John C. Budlong.............. | " .... | March 24, 1875...... | Centredale..... |
| *Asst. Surgeons General,* | | | |
| Walter E. Anthony............ | Captain........ | May 26, 1873........ | Providence..... |
| Wm. Howard King.... ........ | " .. .... | July 1, 1874...... | " |
| *Judge Advocate General,* | | | |
| John Turner............ ...... | Colonel........ | March 26, 1869..... | " |
| *Asst. Judge Advocate General,* | | | |
| A. J. Cushing........ ...... | Captain........ | Oct. 13. 1874........ | " |

## MAJOR GENERAL AND STAFF.

| NAMES. | RANK. | DATE OF RANK. | P. O. ADDRESS. |
|---|---|---|---|
| Wm. R. Walker................. | Maj. General. | March 26, 1874..... | Providence. |
| *Inspector,* | | | |
| Jo n J. Jencks................. | Colonel..... ... | April 14, 1875... ... | " |
| *Surgeon,* | | | |
| Geo. H. Stanley.............. | Lieut. Colonel. | June 22, 1875 ....... | Pawtucket. |
| *Quartermaster,* | | | |
| John W. Tillinghast........... | Major........... | April 14, 1874....... | Providence. |
| *Paymaster,* | | | |
| Almon K. Goodwin........... | " ......... | June 29, 1870. ..... | " |
| *Commissary,* | | | |
| Richard H. Deming............ | " ......... | April 14, 1874 ....... | Pawtucket. |
| *Aids-de-Camp,* | | | |
| Henry A. Pierce, } ............ | " ......... | " " ...... | " |
| Stephen F. Fisk, } | | | |

## BRIGADIER GENERAL AND STAFF—FIRST BRIGADE.

| Thomas W. Chace............. | Brig. General. | Dec. 2, 1872........ | Providence. |
|---|---|---|---|
| *Inspector,* | | | |
| J. Alonzo Babcock............. | Lieut. Colonel. | July 30, 1875....... | Westerly. |
| *Surgeon,* | | | |
| Geo. T. Perry................. | Major.......... | " " ........ | Natick. |
| *Quartermaster,* | | | |
| Geo. G. Stillman.............. | Captain........ | Dec. 3, 1872.... . | Westerly. |
| *Paymaster,* | | | |
| Charles H. Sprague........... | " ........ | July 30, 1875 ...... | Providence. |
| *Commissary,* | | | |
| William J. Dyer.. ............ | -- ........ | " " ........ | " |
| *Aid-de-Camp,* | | | |
| Clarence I. Anthony.......... | " ........ | " " | " |

## BRIGADIER GENERAL AND STAFF—SECOND BRIGADE.

| Frederick Miller ............. | Brig. General.. | March 27, 1874..... | Providence. |
|---|---|---|---|
| *Inspector,* | | | |
| Robert Grosvenor.............. | Lieut. Col..... | May 27, 1875....... | " |
| *Surgeon,* | | | |
| George W. Carr............... | Major.......... | June 7, 1875....... | " |
| *Quartermaster,* | | | |
| ............. | Captain........ | | |
| *Paymaster,* | | | |
| Albert E. Green.. ........... | Captain........ | May 5, 1874........ | Woonsocket. |
| *Commissary,* | | | |
| .............. .. | " ........ | | |
| *Judge Advocate,* | | | |
| Walter B. Vincent ............ | ::  . .... | May 5, 1874........ | Woonsocket. |
| *Aid-de-Camp,* | | | |
| Charles A. Hopkins........... | " .. ..... | Sept. 17, 1874 ..... | " |

FIRST BATTALION OF INFANTRY,

Organized May 1, 1875.

*First Light Infantry, Chartered* 1818.

| NAME. | RANK. | DATE OF RANK. | P. O. ADDRESS. |
|---|---|---|---|
| Robert H. I. Goddard. ........ | Colonel ...... | April 27, 1874....... | Providence. |
| ................. | Lieut. Colonel.. | ................. .... | |
| James E. Chace................ | Major........: | Sept. 28, 1874...... | " |
| *Adjutant,* | | | |
| C. Henry Barney............... | Captain..... .. | May 10, 1875........ | " |
| *Surgeon,* | | | |
| Clarence T. Gardner............ | " ....... | " ........ | .. |
| *Quartermaster,* | | | |
| William H. Teel............ | 1st Lieut....... | April 29, 1872..... | " |
| *Paymaster,* | | | |
| Thos. F. Fessenden............. | 1st Lieut...... | Sept. 20, 1876 | " |
| *Commissary,* | | | |
| Henry L. Parsons............... | 1st Lieut...... | April 28, 1873...... | " |
| *Chaplain,* | | | |
| Samuel H. Webb.......... | 1st Lieut. .... | " 29, 1872.. ... | " |

*Company A.*

| | | | |
|---|---|---|---|
| John H. Kendrick.. ........... | Captain........ | Aug. 13, 1872....... | Providence. |
| ............... | 1st Lieut....... | ....... | |
| Greenwood E. Soule.......... | 2d Lieut.... | April 18, 1876..... | 40 Common st. |

*Company B.*

| | | | |
|---|---|---|---|
| R. Frank Annable............. | Captain........ | June 17, 1872...... | Providence. |
| John B. Cook, Jr...... ......... | 1st Lieut........ | May 3, 1875........ | 100 Lockw'd st. |
| Henry B. Franklin............. | 2d Lieut...... | May 3, 1875 ....... | 50 Canal st. |

*Company C.*

| | | | |
|---|---|---|---|
| Wm. Frankland......... ...... | Captain........ | Sept. 13, 1872........ | Providence. |
| Nathaniel Grant................:... | 1st Lieut....... | April 28, 1873....... | " |
| George J. Knutton............ | 2d Lieut ........ | Aug. 14, 1873....... | " |

*Company D.*

| | | | |
|---|---|---|---|
| Edwin Draper ................ | Captain........ | May 3, 1875........ | Providence. |
| Linus A. Webster........ .... | 1st Lieut...... | " " ........ | " |
| George B. Hale................ | 2d Lieut........ | June 30, 1875....... | " |

SECOND BATTALION OF INFANTRY,

Organized May 1st, 1875.

| NAME. | RANK. | DATE OF RANK. | P. O. ADDRESS. |
|---|---|---|---|
| Benjamin B. Martin... ........ | Colonel. .... | July 21, 1875... .... | Warren. |
| ................ | Lieut. Colonel. | .... ............. | " |
| ............... | Major......... | ................... | |
| *Adjutant,* | | | |
| Joshua C. Drown, Jr.......... | Captain........ | April 10, 1876. ...... | " |
| *Quartermaster,* | | | |
| Frank E. Dana ... ........ | 1st Lieutenant. | Sept. 29, 1876....... | " |
| *Paymaster,* | | | |
| William J. McCaw............ | " | Oct. 16, 1876........ | " |
| *Commissary.* | | | |
| Frank J. Sherman.... .. ...... | " | Sept. 29, 1875....... | " |
| *Chaplain,* | | | |
| Sidney Dean .............. | " | " " ....... | " |

### Company A.

Warren Artillery, Chartered 1842.

| | | | |
|---|---|---|---|
| Benj. M. Bosworth Jr.......... | Captain........ | May 4, 1875 .. ..... | Warren. |
| Charles D. Kelley.............. | 1st Lieut....... | May 10, 1876........ | " |
| Frank J. Gladding............. | 2nd Lieut ..... | " " ....... | " |

### Company B.

Newport Light Infantry, Chartered 1866.

| | | | |
|---|---|---|---|
| James M. Jaques.............. | Captain........ | April 27, 1874....... | Newport |
| John P. Steele .............. | 1st Lieut....... | " " ...... | " |
| Thomas Chambers ........ .... | 2nd Lieut...... | " " ....... | " |

### Company C.

Bristol Light Infantry, Organized 1866.

| | | | |
|---|---|---|---|
| Thomas F. Cahill.............. | Captain........ | Aug. 5, 1875....... | Bristol. |
| Thomas H. Brown............. | 1st Lieut....... | " " .. .... | " |
| Thomas Dwyer................ | 2nd Lieut...... | Nov. 13, 1876....... | " |

THIRD BATTALION OF INFANTRY,

Organized May 1st, 1875.

| NAMES. | RANK. | DATE OF RANK. | P. O. ADDRESS. |
|---|---|---|---|
| Albert N. Crandall.... ....... | Colonel ....... | April 20, 1874....... | Westerly. |
| Stephen T. Arnold............. | Lieut. Colonel. | Aug. 6, 1875........ | Apponaug. |
| Alvah A. Crandall............. | Major...... ... | May 10, 1875........ | Westerly. |
| *Adjutant,* | | | |
| C. C. Maxson... .... ......... . | Captain........ | "    "    ........ | " |
| *Surgeon,* | | | |
| A. N. Lewis.................. . | "    . ......| July 2, 1875........ | " |
| *Quartermaster,* | | | |
| J. Clark Barber.... ............ | 1st Lieut....... | April 21, 1873...... | " |
| *Paymaster,* | | | |
| E. H. Knowles ... ...... .....| "    ...... | April 15, 1872...... | " |
| *Commissary,* | | | |
| Samuel H. Cross.............. | "    ...... | April 21, 1873...... | " |

## Company A.

### Westerly Rifles, Chartered 1854.

| | | | |
|---|---|---|---|
| Daniel Champlin.... ........... | Captain........ | Sept 21, 1875........ | Westerly. |
| Joseph H. Crandall ............ | 1st Lieut...... | May 3, 1875 ........ | " |
| Joseph Taylor..................... | 2nd Lieut...... | Sept. 18, 1876....... | " |

## Company B.

### Westerly Rifles, Chartered 1854.

| | | | |
|---|---|---|---|
| J. Albert Brown................ | Captain ....... | Aug. 29, 1872 ...... | Westerly. |
| G. E Stillman................... | 1st Lieut....... | Oct. 8, 1873. ....... | " |
| Eugene B. Pendleton...... . | 2nd Lieut...... | April 20, 1874 ..... | " |

## Company C.

### Kentish Guards, Chartered 1774.

| | | | |
|---|---|---|---|
| Lyman Himes ............. | Captain........ | April 29, 1874..... | E. Greenwich. |
| William E. Brown.......... | 1st Lieut. .....| "    "    ...... | " |
| ............ ...| 2nd Lieut......|... ................|.............. |

## Company D.

### Kentish Artillery, Chartered 1797.

| | | | |
|---|---|---|---|
| William H. Baker............. | Captain........ | April 26, 1876.. ... | Apponaug. |
| ............ ..../ | 1st Lieut ......|..................... |............. |
| John G. Browning.... . .....| 2nd Lieut...... | April 26, 1876    ...| " |

3

FOURTH BATTALION OF INFANTRY,
Organized May 1st, 1875.

| NAME. | RANK. | DATE OF RANK. | P. O. ADDRESS. |
|---|---|---|---|
| Amos Sherman . ............ | Colonel ... .. | May 10, 1875......... | Woonsocket. |
| Henry M. Howe... ...... | Lieut. Colonel.. | " " ........ | Providence. |
| George A. Mason............... | Major... ...... | April 17. 1871...... | Pawtucket. |
| *Adjutant,* Sanford W. Grant............. | Captain........ | Sept. 24, 1875....... | 120 Dorrance St |
| *Surgeon,* D. M. Edwards.... .... .... | " ........ | " " ...... | Woonsocket. |
| *Quartermaster,* ....,............... | 1st Lieut...... | .. ............. ....... | ............ ........ |
| *Paymaster,* Jefferson Aldrich....... ...... | " ....... | Sept. 24, 1875....... | Woonsocket. |
| *Chaplain,* Joseph S. Miller ........ .... | " ....... | " " ....... | " |

*Company A.*
Woonsocket Guards, Chartered 1842.

| | | | |
|---|---|---|---|
| John R. Waterhouse........... | Captain........ | June 19, 1876....... | Woonsocket. |
| Frank M. Cornell...... ........ | 1st Lieut....... | July 10, 1876 ...... | " |
| Fred. W. Jencks.............. | 2d Lieut........ | June 26, 1876...... | " |

*Company B.*
Slocum Light Guards—Chartered 1854.

| | | | |
|---|---|---|---|
| Wm. B. W. Hallett............ | Captain... ... | April 20, 1874....... | Providence. |
| Bartholomew McSoley......... | 1st Lieut....... | " " ....... | " |
| Joseph Stringer... ............ | 2d Lieut........ | May 3, 1875........ | " |

FIFTH BATTALION OF INFANTRY.
Organized May 1, 1875.
*Rhode Island Guards Regiment—Organized, 1865.*

| NAMES. | RANK. | DATE OF RANK. | P. O. ADDRESS. |
|---|---|---|---|
| James Larkin............ .... | Colonel........ | June 8, 1876....... | Pawtucket. |
| Hugh Hammill... ............ | Lieut. Col..... | " " ........ | Providence. |
| John McManus................ | Major ......... | " " ........ | Providence. |
| *Adjutant,* James H. McGann............. | Captain........ | Sept. 1, 1876....... | 6 Polk st. |
| *Surgeon,* Stephen H. King............... | " .... .. | " " ........ | 334 Broad st. |
| *Quartermaster,* Patrick Farrell...... . ........ | 1st Lieut........ | " " ........ | Pawtucket. |
| *Paymaster,* Patrick H. Edgerton............ | 1st Lieut........ | " " ....... | Central Falls. |
| *Commissary,* James H. Kelly .... .. | 1st Lieut..... | " " ........ | Pawtucket. |
| *Chaplain,* Robert J. Sullivan ............ | 1st Lieut. . ... | " " ........ | 264 Broadway. |

## FIFTH BATTALION OF INFANTRY.—*Continued.*

### *Company A.*

| | | | |
|---|---|---|---|
| Thomas H. Powers | Captain | July 24, 1876 | 10 Benefit st. |
| Michael E. O'Brien | 1st Lieut | " " | 34 " |
| John Quinn | 2d Lieut | " " | 51 Carroll st. |

### *Company B.*

| | | | |
|---|---|---|---|
| John Cullen | Captain | July 21, 1873 | Pawtucket. |
| Owen Goodwin | 1st Lieut | May 5, 1871 | " |
| William Driscoll | 2d Lieut | April 13, 1874 | " |

### *Company C.*

| | | | |
|---|---|---|---|
| Patrick A. Cosgrove | Captain | Sept. 7, 1874 | Central Falls. |
| John Donohue | 1st Lieut | July 15, 1873 | " |
| Bernard McLoughlin | 2d Lieut | Sept. 7, 1874 | " |

### *Company D.*

| | | | |
|---|---|---|---|
| ..... | Captain | | |
| Anthony Mungiven | 1st Lieut | Sept. 30, 1875 | R. 110 Pr'le av |
| Charles A. Garvin | 2d Lieut | " " | 118 So. Main st. |

### *Company E.*

| | | | |
|---|---|---|---|
| James W. Smith | Captain | January 17, 1876 | Woonsocket. |
| Phillip Whaland | 1st Lieut | May 3, 1875 | " |
| Michael H. Butler | 2d Lieut | January 17, 1876 | " |

### *Company F.*

| | | | |
|---|---|---|---|
| Wm. McPherson | Captain | Sept. 7, 1874 | 235 So. Main st. |
| Bernard McEntee | 1st Lieut | " " | 23 Governor st. |
| John J. Dwyer | 2d Lieut | May 9, 1876 | 9 Trenton st. |

SIXTH BATTALION OF INFANTRY.

Organized May 1, 1875.

| NAMES. | RANK. | DATE OF RANK. | P. O. ADDRESS. |
|---|---|---|---|
| John H. Monroe...... ........ | Colonel......... | May 10, 1875........ | Providence. |
| Albert E. Smith............... | Lieut. Col.. ... | "    "    ........ | " |
| Aaron C. Buchanan........... | Major.......... | "    "    ........ | Newport. |
| *Adjutant,* George T. Smith................ | Captain........ | "    "    ........ | Providence. |
| *Surgeon,* Andrew A. Jackson... ........ | "    ........ | June 1, 1874........ | " |
| *Quartermaster,* Ezra J. Morris................ | 1st Lieut....... | June 1, 1868........ | " |
| *Paymaster,* Charles H. Burrill.... .......... | "    ...... | June 1, 1874........ | " |
| *Commissary,* Thomas George....... ........ | ..    ...... | June 22, 1875...... | " |
| *Chaplain,* William Jackson............... | "    | June 3, 1872....... | " |

### Company A.

Burnside National Guards—Organized, 1867.

| Andrew M. Terrence.......... | Captain ...... | Aug 10, 1875........ | 54 Bates st. |
|---|---|---|---|
| William T. Jackson ,.......... | 1st Lieut....... | "    "    ........ | Providence. |
| George Mills.................. | 2d Lieut........ | May 3, 1875........ | " |

### Company B.

Burnside National Guards—Organized, 1867.

| Thomas Brinn................. | Captain........ | May 12, 1873....... | 60 Westm'trst. |
|---|---|---|---|
| Stephen J. West............... | 1st Lieut....... | May 19, 1875....... | |
| Carrington P. Slade........... | 2d Lieut........ | "    "    ....... | |

### Company C

Burnside National Guards—Organized. 1867.

| Lewis Kenegee................. | Captain........ | May 12, 1873....... | 29 M'Don'gh st |
|---|---|---|---|
| Benjamin Bryan............... | 1st Lieut....... | May 13, 1872....... | |
| Wm. H. Becket................ | 2d Lieut........ | May 12, 1873....... | |

## SIXTH BATTALION OF INFANTRY.—*Continued.*

### *Company D.*

Burnside Guards—Organized, 1867.

| | | | |
|---|---|---|---|
| James W. Johnston | Captain | Aug. 3, 1875 | Newport. |
| John P. Easton | 1st Lieut. | " " | " |
| Charles H. Roberts | 2d Lieut. | " " | " |

### FIRST BATTALION OF LIGHT ARTILLERY,

Organized May 1, 1875.

| NAMES. | RANK. | DATE OF RANK. | P. O. ADDRESS. |
|---|---|---|---|
| Elisha Dyer, Jr. | Lieut. Col. | May 10, 1875 | Providence. |
| Lyman B. Goff. | Major | " " | Pawtucket. |
| *Adjutant,* Stephen F. Brownell | Captain | Nov. 30, 1875 | Providence. |
| *Surgeon,* George B. Peck, Jr. | " | Aug. 23, 1876 | " |
| *Quartermaster,* John B. Hull | 1st Lieut. | " " | " |
| *Paymaster,* Frank D. Fisk | " | Aug. 5, 1875 | Pawtucket. |
| *Commissary,* William A. Beatty | " | " " | " |
| *Chaplain,* David H. Greer | " | " " | Providence. |

### *Company A.*

Providence Marine Corps of Artillery—Chartered, 1801.

| | | | |
|---|---|---|---|
| Robert Grosvenor Brigade Inspector on Detached Service | | Aug. 15, 1876 | Providence. |
| Calvin A. Burr | Sen. 1st Lieut. | July 8, 1876 | " |
| James A. Abbott | Jun. 1st Lieut. | " " | " |
| Clinton Mauran | 2d Lieut. | " " | " |

### *Company B.*

Tower Light Battery—Organized, 1864.

| | | | |
|---|---|---|---|
| Eugene B. Crocker | Captain | May 8, 1876 | Pawtucket. |
| Henry H. Sager | Sen. 1st Lieut. | " " | " |
| David W. Briggs | Jun. 1st Lieut. | " " | " |
| Elmer R. Curtis | 2d Lieut. | " " | " |

## FIRST BATTALION OF CAVALRY.

Organized May 1, 1875.

| NAME. | RANK. | DATE OF RANK. | P. O. ADDRESS. |
|---|---|---|---|
| J. Lippitt Snow ...... ....... | Colonel......... | March 31, 1874..... | Providence. |
| John W. Leckie........ ....... | Lieut. Col..... | May 10, 1875...... | Pawtucket. |
| Henry V. A. Joslin........ .. | Major........... | "      "  ....... | Providence. |
| *Adjutant,* | | | |
| Reginald O. Brown............ | Captain........ | "      "  ....... | " |
| *Quartermaster,* | | | |
| Michael H. Sullivan ........... | 1st Lieut...... | April 21, 1873...... | 19 No. Main st. |
| *Paymaster,* | | | |
| Henry W. Weaver............. | 1st Lieut...... | Oct. 23, 1874........ | Crary st.cMary |
| *Commissary,* | | | |
| Herbert L. Gates............. | 1st Lieut... .. | May 17, 1875..... | 76 Westmin'r st |

### Company A.

Providence Horse Guards—Chartered 1842.

| NAME. | RANK. | DATE OF RANK. | P. O. ADDRESS. |
|---|---|---|---|
| ............ | Captain ...... | ......... | |
| Martin L. Cary..... ......... | 1st Lieut...... | April 21, 1873...... | Providence. |
| Benjamin Martin........... .. | 2d Lieut...... . | April 20, 1874...... | Watchemoket. |

### Company B.

Providence Horse Guards—Chartered 1842.

| NAME. | RANK. | DATE OF RANK. | P. O. ADDRESS. |
|---|---|---|---|
| David Lester. ................. | Captain........ | April 20, 1874 ..... | Providence. |
| Peleg A. Weeden.............. | 1st Lieut...... | "      "  ...... | " |
| Louis E. Davis................. | 2d Lieut...... . | May 3, 1875........ | " |

### Comapny C.

Pawtucket Horse Guards—Organized 1864.

| NAME. | RANK. | DATE OF RANK. | P. O. ADDRESS. |
|---|---|---|---|
| Alexander Strauss............. | Captain........ | April 20, 1574...... | Pawtucket. |
| Jubal P. Perrin................ | 1st Lieut.. .— | Oct. 11, 1875........ | " |
| Squire F. Fisk................. | 2d Lieut........ | "      "  ....... | " |

## NEWPORT ARTILLERY COMPANY,

### Chartered 1741—*Independent.*

| NAMES. | RANK. | DATE OF RANK. | P. O. ADDRESS. |
|---|---|---|---|
| John Hare Powel | Colonel | Dec. 3, 1864. | Newport. |
| Augustus P. Sherman | Lieut. Col. | April 28, 1868. | " |
| Thomas S. Burdick | Major | April 24, 1866. | " |
| Thomas S. Nason | Captain | April 26, 1870 | " |
| *Quartermaster,* George H. Vaughn | 1st Lieut. | April 25, 1871 | " |
| *Adjutant,* Henry T. Easton | " | April 28, 1868 | " |
| *Paymaster,* William G. Stevens | " | April 27, 1869 | " |
| *Commissary,* George A. Simmons | " | April 25, 1871 | " |
| *Surgeon,* Nathaniel G. Stanton | " | April 27, 1869 | " |
| *Assistant Surgeon,* James H. Taylor | " | April 24, 1866 | " |
| *Chaplain,* Thatcher Thayer | " | April 25, 1876 | " |

## UNITED TRAIN OF ARTILLERY.

### Chartered 1775—*Independent.*

| NAMES. | RANK. | DATE OF RANK. | P. O. ADDRESS. |
|---|---|---|---|
| William E. Clarke | Colonel | Oct. 6, 1874. | Providence. |
| George A. Dodge | Lieut. Col. | April 24, 1876. | " |
| Elisha H. Rockwell | Major | April 26, 1875. | " |
| *Adjutant,* Thomas E. Adams | 1st Lieut. | April 24,1876. | " |
| *Quartermaster,* Walter E. White | " | April 24, 1876 | " |
| *Commissary,* Horace E. Metcalf | " | April 26, 1869 | " |
| *Surgeon,* Robert Hall | " | April 24, 1876 | " |
| *Paymaster,* Benj Frank Pabodie | " | April 26, 1869 | " |

### Company A.

| | | | |
|---|---|---|---|
| Allen T. Johnson | Captain | April 24, 1876. | Providence. |
| Andrew J. Cartwright | 1st Lieut. | " " | " |
| Louis E. Cady | 2d Lieut. | April 26, 1875 | " |

## UNITED TRAIN OF ARTILLERY.—*Continued.*
### *Company C.*

| | | | |
|---|---|---|---|
| Fred. S. McCausland........... | Captain...... | April 28, 1873 ..... | Proidence. |
| Albert G. Carpenter............ | 1st Lieut....... | April 28, 1873..... | " |
| James F. Downing............. | 2d Lieut....... | April 24, 1876...... | " |

### *Company D.*

| | | | |
|---|---|---|---|
| Edwin L. Eddy............... | Captain ....... | April 24, 1876...... | Providence. |
| | 1st Lieut....... | | |
| Oliver S. Alers. ............... | 2d Lieut........ | April 24. 1876...... | " |

### BRISTOL TRAIN OF ARTILLERY.
#### Chartered 1794.—*Independent.*

| NAMES. | RANK. | DATE OF RANK. | P. O. ADDRESS. |
|---|---|---|---|
| ........ | Colonel.... ... | ........ | ... .. |
| ........ | Lieut. Col. | ........ | ...... |
| James Coggeshall...... ........ | Major........... | April 4, 1872. ..... | Bristol. |
| Lyman B. Bosworth........... | Captain ....... | " 19, 1875........ | " |
| *Lieutenan,t*<br>John H. Adams................ | 1st Lieut....... | " 6, 1876........ | " |
| *Adjutant,*<br>Alonzo U. Pierce............. | " ....... | " 6, 1876...... | " |
| *Quartermaster,*<br>Benj. M. Lincoln.............. | " | " 6, 1876 ...... | ". |
| *Paymaster,* | " | ....... | |
| *Commissary,*<br>Samuel Taylor. ............. . | " ...... | " 6, 1876........ | " |
| *Surgeon,*<br>George A. Pike................ | " ....... | " 6, 1876........ | " |

### RESIGNED.

| | | | | | | |
|---|---|---|---|---|---|---|
| Capt. H. C. Armstrong .......... | Brig. Commissary 2d Brigade..... | | | | | Nov.10,1876 |
| Lieut. Col. E. B. Bullock........ | 1st Battalion of Infantry........ .. | | | | | Dec.11, 1876 |
| Quartermaster F. J. Sheldon...... | 1st | " | " | | .... | Sept. 10 " |
| First Lieut. Joseph T. Snow....... | 1st | " | " | Co. A. | .... | Nov. 8, " |
| Adjutant Walter A. Day........... | 2d | " | " | | .... | Feb. 10, " |
| First Lieut. John Livesey ......... | 2d | " | " | " A.... | .... | May 8, " |
| Second Lieut. Gerald Downey. .. | 2d | " | " | " C...... | .... | Oct. 2, " |
| Second Lieut. Thomas D. Edwards | 3d | " | " | " A .... | | June 6, " |
| Captain Henry Adams........... | 4th | " | " | " A...... | | Jan. 18, " |
| First Lieut. Arnold A. Jencks..... | 4th | " | " | " A...... | | " " |
| Colonel Jeremiah Costine.......... | 5th | " | " | " A .... | .... | May 20, " |
| Captain Peter McHugh.... ........ | 5th | " | " | " A...... | | June 30, " |
| Second Lieut. James H Collins.... | 5th | " | " | " F..... | | May 20, " |
| Chaplain Samuel R. Fuller.... | 1st | " | of Cavalry ............ | | | " " |
| Captain John D. Lewis ; ......... | 1st | " | of Lt. Artillery, Co. A. | | .... | Aug. 15, " |
| Captain Edward Thayer.......... | 1st | " | " " " B. | | .. | April 17, " |
| Colonel Charles A. Greene | ... | Bristol Train of Artillery, Ind. | | | .... | Nov. 17, " |
| Lieut. Colonel Thomas F. Usher.. | " | " " " | | " | ... | Dec. 29, " |

### DIED.

| | |
|---|---|
| Captain James E. Curran.... ...... | Co. D. Fifth Batt. of Infantry...... |

# GENERAL ORDERS.

---

STATE OF RHODE ISLAND.

ADJUTANT GENERAL'S OFFICE,
Providence, August 8, 1876.

GENERAL ORDERS.
## No. 1.

The Examining Board, organized by General Orders No. 6, from this office, dated May 12th, 1875, is hereby dissolved.

An examining Board is hereby organized to consist of the following named officers :

Brig. General FREDERICK MILLER, Commanding 2d Brigade R. I. Militia.

Lt. Colonel ELISHA DYER, JR., Commanding 1st Battalion Light Artillery, R. I. Militia.

Captain C. H. BARNEY, Adjutant, 1st Battalion Infantry, R. I. Militia.

The Board will hold its sessions, at the call of the Senior officer thereof, at such times and places as candidates for examination may be notified from this office to appear.

By order of the Commander-in-Chief,

HEBER LeFAVOUR,
*Adjutant General.*

## STATE OF RHODE ISLAND.

ADJUTANT GENERAL'S OFFICE,
Providence, August 15, 1876.

GENERAL ORDERS.
No. 2.

An addition is hereby made to the Examining Board organized by General Orders No. 1, from this office, dated August 8th, 1876, and the Board as constituted will consist of the following named officers :

Brig. General FREDERICK MILLER, Commanding 2d Brigade, R. I. Militia.

Col. BENJAMIN B. MARTIN, Commanding 2d Battalion Infantry, R. I. Militia.

Lt. Colonel ELISHA DYER, JR., Commanding 1st Battalion Light Artillery, R. I. Militia.

Captain J. ALBERT BROWN, Commanding Co. B. 3d Battalion Infantry, R. I. Militia.

Captain C. H. BARNEY, Adjutant, 1st Battalion Infantry, R. I. Militia.

By order of the Commander-in-Chief,

HEBER LEFAVOUR,
*Adjutant General.*

---

## STATE OF RHODE ISLAND.

ADJUTANT GENERAL'S OFFICE,
Providence, September 16, 1876.

GENERAL ORDERS.
No. 3.

On the occasion of the Annual Fall Parade, by Brigade, for this year, the ceremony of Muster will be duly carried out as prescribed on page 361, of the Infantry Tactics, page 383 for the Artillery, and page 436 for the Cavalry.

Each company commander will provide himself with two complete rolls of his command, made upon the " Parade Return " blank which will be issued from this office. These rolls will contain the name of every active member of the command, but the column of " Present and Absent " will be left vacant for the Inspecting Officer, who will fill it in a manner to show who was present or absent at the muster.

The Rolls, (at the time of muster,) will be delivered to the Inspector, who will forward one copy to this office and the other to Brigade Headquarters.

These Rolls will take the place of those required by Section 4, Chapter 253, of the Militia Law.

The respective brigade commanders are charged with execution of this order; and they will cause as thorough an inspection to be made in connection with the muster as is practicable.

The "list of absentees alphabetically arranged," as mentioned in the tactics, will not be required.

The Adjutant of each Battalion will also be provided with two rolls of the Field and Staff of their respective Battalions.

Fifty cents will be allowed as the price of the Ration for that day, to be paid for each man that is mustered as present. The Brigade commanders will arrange for the furnishing of the Ration in such manner as they may deem best.

By order of the Commander-in-Chief,

HEBER LeFAVOUR,
*Adjutant General.*

---

## STATE OF RHODE ISLAND.

ADJUTANT GENERAL'S OFFICE,
Providence, September 23, 1876.

GENERAL ORDERS.
NO. 4.

Major General WILLIAM R. WALKER, is hereby directed to order the Division of Rhode Island Militia to assemble on Dexter Training Ground in this city, on Wednesday, the 18th day of October, 1876, for the Annual Muster and Review.

The First Brigade, Brig. General THOMAS W. CHACE, Commanding, will rendezvous on the field occupied by the Second Brigade at the Muster last year, (corner of Harrison and Cranston streets,) and the Second Brigade, Brig. General FREDERICK MILLER, Commanding, on the Dexter Training Ground.

By order of the Commander-in-Chief,

HEBER LeFAVOUR,
*Adjutant General.*

## STATE OF RHODE ISLAND.

ADJUTANT GENERAL'S OFFICE,
Providence, November 13, 1876.

GENERAL ORDERS.
No. 5.

At the Annual Inspection of Armories, Arms, Equipments, &c., soon to be made by Brigadier General C. R. DENNIS, Quartermaster General, an inspection will be made by him of the books and papers of each command

Commanding officers are hereby directed to present the same for inspection.

General Dennis will report to this office from time to time the condition thereof.

By order of the Commander-in-Chief,

HEBER LeFAVOUR,
*Adjutant General.*

# EIGHTH ANNUAL REPORT

OF THE

# Board of State Charities and Corrections

OF

# RHODE ISLAND,

# 1876.

OFFICE, 104 NORTH MAIN STREET, (ROOM NO. 10,) PROVIDENCE.
OFFICE HOURS FROM 9 A. M., TO 2 P. M.

PROVIDENCE:
ANGELL, BURLINGAME & CO., PRINTERS TO THE STATE.
1877.

## PAST AND PRESENT MEMBERS OF THE BOARD.

Names of past members in SMALL CAPITALS, of present members in Italics. *Deceased.

| NAME. | RESIDENCE. | DATE OF APPOINTMENT. | DATE OF RE-APPOINTMENT. | DATE OF RESIGNATION. | TERM EXPIRES. |
|---|---|---|---|---|---|
| JONATHAN BRAYTON | Warwick | May Session, 1869 | | March 18, 1871 | |
| THOMAS A. DOYLE, Chairman | Providence | " " | | April 11, 1871 | |
| JAMES M. PENDLETON | Westerly | " " | | April 19, 1871 | |
| HENRY H. FAY | Newport | " " | June 1, 1870 | April 20, 1871 | |
| *HENRY W. LOTHROP | Providence | " " | | May 11, 1874 | |
| Samuel W. Church | Bristol | " " | June 1, 1871 | | June 1, 1877 |
| EDWIN M. SNOW, Secretary | Providence | June 1, 1869 | | November 30, 1872 | |
| EDWARD D. PEARCE, Chairman | East Providence | May Session, 1871 | | | |
| Job Kenyon | Warwick | " " | June 1, 1873 | | June 1, 1879 |
| Thomas Coggeshall | Newport | " " | June 1, 1876 | | June 1, 1882 |
| HORACE BABCOCK | Westerly | " " | June 1, 1872 | May, 1876 | |
| William H. Hopkins | Providence | May Session, 1874 | June 1, 1875 | | June 1, 1881 |
| George I. Chace, Chairman | Providence | " " | | | June 1, 1880 |
| James M. Pendleton | Westerly | May Session, 1876 | | | June 1, 1882 |
| William W. Chapin, Secretary | Providence | January 1, 1878 | | | |

The Secretary is appointed by the Board, and is ex officio a member thereof. His term of office has no specified limit, depending upon the pleasure of the Board.

# Board of State Charities and Corrections

OF

# RHODE ISLAND.

The regular meetings of the Board are held on the first and third Fridays of each month.

Office of the Board, No. 104 North Main Street, Room No. 10, Providence. Office hours from 9 A. M. to 2 P. M.

# CONTENTS.

----●----

# EIGHTH ANNUAL REPORT

OF THE

# Board of State Charities and Corrections.

--------

*To the Honorable General Assembly of the State of Rhode Island,*
*etc., at its January Session,* 1877 :—

The Board of State Charities and Corrections respectfully present their report for the year ending Dec. 31, 1876, as required by the General Statutes.

In May, Mr. Horace Babcock, of Westerly, resigned his position on the Board, on account of continued ill-health ; and at the May session, Hon. James M. Pendleton, of Westerly, was appointed his successor. Mr. Pendleton had previously been a member of the Board, from its organization in June, 1869, to April, 1871.

Mr. Thomas Coggeshall, of Newport, was re-appointed at the May session, for a term of six years.

The members of the Board desire to express their regret for the temporary loss of the valuable services of two of their number ; Dr. Job Kenyon, who is absent in Europe ; and Mr. William H. Hopkins, who has been confined to the house by illness since September.

Mr. Norman W. Eayrs, who entered upon the duties of the office of Superintendent of the State Farm in January, tendered his resignation, February 18, to take effect May 1. He remained a few weeks after the latter date, until his successor was appointed. Mr.

Eayrs, in his letter of resignation, says: "I believe that it was the expectation of the Board, that, if a young man was appointed super-intendent, he would grow up with the institution, and devote a large portion of his life to it. My appointment for three months was, I think, to give me a chance to try the work and life, and also to give you an opportunity to try me.    *    *    *    *
I thank the Board most heartily for the cordial support they have given me. Every aid that I could ask for has been given me, and almost more authority than I cared to receive. It is not from any want of harmony between us, that I have determined to resign. My reason is simply this,—that I do not like the situation well enough to retain it for a number of years."

Mr. Samuel L. Blaisdell was appointed Superintendent of the State Farm, at a meeting of the Board held May 17, and assumed the office, May 22.

Mr. William L. Roberts gave up the position of Deputy of the Workhouse and House of Correction in the latter part of January, and Mr. Ira B. Wilson was appointed Acting Deputy by the Sup-erintendent.

Miss Naomi Thompson was promoted to be matron of the Work-house and House of Correction, January 7.

Mr. and Mrs. Fred. W. Perry continue in charge of the Asylum for the Insane, and Mr. and Mrs. William G. Ward in charge of the Almshouse.

Mr. George H. Snow resigned the place of farmer and engineer of the State Farm, October 31. No one has been appointed in his stead.

### CONSTRUCTION.

But little building has been done during the year. The sum of $1515.96 has been expended upon the new barn since January 1, 1876, in preparing the interior for occupation; and the sum of $150.50, received from the Prison Commission for staging plank and poles, charged to the barn last year, has been credited to it; making the net expenditure for the year $1365.46. This amount, added to the cost reported a year ago, $28,034.33, makes a total to date of $29,399.79. Of the above amount, the sum of $369.91

was for plumbing. Water is brought through the barn in a three-inch cast-iron pipe; and is distributed through one-inch lead pipes to seven cast-iron troughs, placed in different parts of the building, and to a trough in the yard. Two-inch lead waste-pipes lead from the troughs to the drains in the cellar. This work has been done in the most thorough manner, and the pipes are so arranged that the water may be shut off from any one of them, or from the entire barn, to prevent freezing in extremely cold weather.

To complete the barn and the piggery, which is greatly needed, together with the sheds and fences, will require $3,000. This sum we include in the estimate of expenses for the coming year.

The extension of the cottage for excited patients at the Insane Asylum, described in the report of 1875, has been completed at a cost of $1142.54. This includes an additional boiler for heating, 11 feet long by 36 inches in diameter; and a steam water-heater for the bath-rooms, 6 feet long by 20 inches in diameter; costing together, with the necessary connections, etc., $727.

The cottage for the deputy of the Insane Asylum and his family, referred to as finished in the last report, was found to require an additional outlay of $127.60.

The Almshouse improvements, spoken of the report of 1875 as in process of construction, have been completed at an expense of $711. This includes the cost of converting the old blacksmith's shop into a sitting-room for the men, and a small wash-room for the women. The actual cost of completing the Insane Asylum extension and the Almshouse improvements is considerably less than the estimate given in the last report.

In the summer, when work ceased in many of the mills in the State, it was thought that there might be a large number of poor persons sent the Almshouse the coming winter. To provide for this contingency, the old storehouse was moved a short distance into the Almshouse yard, and placed where it might be used, if needed. Nothing has been done towards preparing the interior for use, the condition of the poor indicating later in the season, that there would be no unusual demand for admittance to this institution.

An old barn, used for carriage horses, which stood beside the storehouse, was pulled down when the storehouse was moved.

The old basket shop has also been taken down. It was in the way of the grading and road-making in front of the workhouse. and, standing outside of the workhouse yard, had ceased to be of use as a shop. The roof was saved, and was moved to the rear of the new barn to be used as a shed. The cost of moving the old storehouse and the basket shop roof was $225.

### LAYING OUT THE WORKHOUSE GROUNDS.

In June, the Board voted to adopt the plan which had been prepared by Messrs. Bowditch & Copeland, of Boston, of laying out the roads and grounds in front of and around the Workhouse. This work has been pushed forward during the summer and autumn, and a great improvement is already apparent. The roads have been laid with large stone to the depth of two feet; broken stone and gravel have then been spread upon them and thoroughly rolled. A large area has been graded and prepared for turfing and the planting of shade and ornamental trees the coming spring. A considerable portion of the earth taken from the roads has been carried into the women's yard of the Workhouse, which will soon be in condition to lay down to grass and be made more suitable for an exercise and recreation ground for the inmates.

Before the main avenue through the farm, to which the name of " Howard" has been given, can be completed, the old barn will have to be removed. The old farm wall in front of the Insane Asylum also encroaches upon the avenue, and must be taken down. The Board think it desirable, instead of replacing this, to begin along the line of Howard avenue the building of a high stone wall, to enclose the entire Asylum grounds. This work, which will occupy several years, can doubtless be done mostly by the inmates, and can be carried forward to completion as time and opportunity allow. But a small outlay will be needed for material.

### WORK FOR THE NEW STATE PRISON.

An agreement was made in December, 1875, to furnish the stone for the new prison during the season of 1876, at $1.75 per cubic yard, or at the actual cost, should it be less. This has been done, we believe, to the satisfaction of all concerned. The amount delivered and laid is 3,970 cubic yards. The cost has exceeded the price agreed upon by eleven cents per yard, as a better kind of stone was furnished than any heretofore quarried upon the farm. To procure this stone, which lies in detached masses, it has been necessary work over a large area, at an increased expense of digging, moving derricks, etc. A quantity of stone delivered, but not laid, was not considered in calculating the cost. This will enter into the account the coming season, should a similar contract be made with the Prison Commission in 1877. The experience of the past year has proved, that there exists upon the farm a considerable quantity of stone, suitable for the trimmings of any building that may hereafter be erected there.

The Board have also furnished to the Prison Commission, at prices agreed upon, in addition to the contract work, several of the farm teams, the labor of some of the inmates, the use of derricks, staging plank and poles, and other material.

The whole amount received from the Prison Commission during the year was $10,298.06,

| | |
|---|---:|
| Of which 3970 cubic yards x $1.75 | $6,947.50 |
| (Less material and labor furnished by Prison Commission) | 374.05 |
| Was on account of the contract | $6,573.45 |
| And the balance was for additional labor and material | 3,724.61 |
| | $10,298.06 |

Of this amount there were:

| | |
|---|---:|
| For teams | 4,160.96 |
| For labor of inmates | 2,591.45 |
| For hired labor | 2,268.84 |
| For material, etc. | 1,276.81 |
| | $10,298.06 |

| | |
|---|---:|
| The total amount received from the Prison Commission for work done for them in 1874, 1875 and 1876, is | 43,080.47 |
| Of which, for labor hired, material purchased and the use of tools | 29,344.98 |
| And for labor of inmates and teams, and material from the farm | 13,735.49 |

WORKHOUSE AND HOUSE OF CORRECTION.

There has been no great change in the number and condition of the persons sent to this institution during the past year, as compared with previous years. The statistics show that the number of commitments for vagrancy and for prostitution were somewhat larger, and the number for drunkenness somewhat smaller, than in 1875. Against the vagrant or "tramp" class, the authorities of some of the towns have taken, at times, unusually vigorous action. Eleven persons were committed as vagrants from one town of about 4,000 inhabitants within ten days; seven were committed from another town of about the same population, within fourteen days; and from another five were committed as vagrants in one day.

It would be an advantage to the State, if the town authorities would refrain from committing to the Workhouse aged and disabled persons, who are more fit to be inmates of the Almshouse than of the former institution, and who, in many cases, could be sent away from the State by the Superintendent of State Charities and Corrections, at a less cost than is incurred for court and commitment expenses.

The labor of the inmates has been employed mostly out of doors, upon the farm, in digging stone for the state prison and for farm walls, in grading, and in the various employments which the institutions and the extended area of the farm afford. Basketmaking was carried on during the winter and up to July, by those of the inmates who could not be trusted in the fields. After the first of July, these men were employed in the Workhouse yard breaking stone for the roads.

The basket shop will be in operation again about the first of January, and, under the energetic supervision of the present superintendent, will doubtless show better results than heretofore, although the price which the product brings in the market is but slightly remunerative.

The men, by weaving wire, and the women, by picking over cotton, have earned small sums.

The following tables show the kinds of labor upon which the in-

mates, both men and women, have been employed since July 1st,
when the record was begun, and the number of days devoted to
each:

*Labor of Men.*                                                          **Days.**
Farming, building farm walls, etc..................... ..... .....   2,841
Quarrying and getting pasture stone...........................   2,304
Breaking stone for roads in Workhouse yard....................   3,419
Grading and road-making in front of Workhouse and in Work-
    house yard............... ..... ................:.............   2,146
Driving teams............. ..... ......................... ...... ...   1,654
Building wall on Oaklawn Road and repairing the road..........     318
Building foundation of old storehouse in Almshouse yard .......     117
Cutting and getting in ice.......................................     152
Taking care of the Workhouse ..................... ............   1,578
Barn work.. ..... ................. ...............................     416
Carpentering... ........... ........... ......................... ....     492
Painting..... ........... ......... ......... ......... ......... ...     218
Blacksmithing............................................. ..........     363
Taking care of boilers......... .....................................     360
Tailoring... ............. ......... ... .......................... ....     472
Repairing shoes........................................ ..........     157
Repairing harnesses................................ .................      27
Whitewashing............................... ......... ..........     104
Barber's work................ .. ..................... ........     140
Miscellaneous work ......................... ....................     459

      Total................................. ............ ...  17,737

*Labor of Women.*                                                       **Days.**
Sewing and knitting.........................................   2,255
Work in the laundry.................................. ..........   2,575
Work in the cookhouse.... .................. ..... ............   1,649
Picking over cotton.............................................   1,567
Miscellaneous work................................... ........     484

      Total............. ................... ............ .........   8,530

Under existing circumstances, it has been thought best, as was
stated in the report of 1874, to employ as many of the men as possible upon the farm, and in improving the land and grounds around
the buildings. To convert the entire area of the State Farm into a
series of smooth, well-cultivated, and thoroughly-drained fields and
meadows, properly divided by evenly-built and solid stone walls,

with stone-laid roads and tasteful grounds around the institutions, will furnish an abundance of employment for many years to come. A number of the Workhouse men, however, must always be confined within walls. For these it is the earnest desire of the Board and of the Superintendent to obtain paying employment, either by letting the labor on contract or otherwise; and measures have already been taken, but thus far without success, towards the accomplishment of this end.

Employment of some kind, they are quite aware, is important beyond its mere economic results. It is necessary for the good of the inmates themselves. The first condition of improvement is honest labor;—steady, earnest, faithful work. This, if not voluntarily rendered, must be enforced. So long as laziness and shamming are tolerated, moral appliances are of little avail. The habit of industry and useful occupation is the only basis upon which right character can be built up. For the vagrant and tramp, work is the specific remedy; and there is little danger of its being too liberally administered. Those who are too indolent or too selfish to provide for their families, must not complain, if they do not find the service of the state an easy or agreeable one. And for all classes; even for those who are weak rather than depraved; who deserve our pity more than our censure; over whose wills appetite and passion have gained a fatal mastery, so that the firmest resolve give way before temptation;—even for these, constant employment is indispensable. Its drudgery, however, should be relieved as much as possible by kindness, sympathy, and encouragement. Something may then be hoped from more direct moral agencies; from the lessons of the school, from good books, and from earnest Christian appeals.

The statistics of the Workhouse are as follows:

|  | Men. | Women. | Total. |
|---|---|---|---|
| Number of inmates January 1, 1876 | 206 | 73 | 279 |
| " committed during the year. | 368 | 132 | 500 |
| " of escaped inmates recommitted | 45 | | 45 |
| " discharged during the year | 361 | 148 | 509 |
| " escaped during the year | 57 | | 57 |
| " died during the year | | | .. |
| " of inmates January 1, 1877 | 201 | 57 | 258 |

The average numbers in the Workhouse, taken from the monthly reports, were :

|  | Men. | Women. | Total. |
|---|---|---|---|
| In 1872.... | 108 | 48 | 156 |
| 1873 | 146 | 62 | 208 |
| 1874.... | 139 | 69 | 208 |
| 1875 | 159 | 64 | 223 |
| 1876 | 166 | 66 | 232 |

In this connection, we take pleasure in calling attention to the decrease in the number of escapes, as an evidence of the more watchful care exercised under the present management. Forty-four occurred in the first half of the year, and only thirteen in the second ; a total of fifty-seven, which is twenty-three less than the total of 1875.

|  | Escaped. | Returned. |
|---|---|---|
| 1874. | 83 | 37 |
| 1875 | 81 | 72 |
| 1876 | 57 | 45 |

The health of the inmates has been excellent, and no deaths are reported. Of 3459 persons committed to the Workhouse since it was established in 1869, only eighteen have died ; a trifle over one half of one per cent. of the whole number, and an average of less than three per annum.

### STATE ASYLUM FOR THE INCURABLE INSANE.

The extension of the cottage for excited patients, begun in 1875, was finished and occupied early in the year ; as was also the house built for the use of Mr. and Mrs. Fred W. Perry, who continue to have charge of this institution.

The new rooms were provided none too soon, the statistics showing an increase of twenty-three in the number of patients since January 1, 1876. Several of these were brought from the Butler Hospital, where they had been kept on account of want of room at the state institution.

An enlargement of the dining-rooms at the cottage for excited patients is made necessary by the increase of the number of inmates ;

and additional rooms for the attendants in this building are also
needed. These improvements can be effected by extending the
projection from the cottage, at an expense of about $1000.

The same amount of liberty has been allowed the patients as
heretofore. The greater part of them are free to roam at will
through the grounds, and derive from this treatment great benefit;
being made happier and more tractable than when under restraint.

The garden was cultivated by the inmates with almost the usual
success, notwithstanding the dryness of the season.

The statistics for the year are as follows:

|  | Men. | Women. | Total. |
|---|---|---|---|
| Number of inmates January 1, 1876 | 86 | 87 | 173 |
| "        received during the year | 51 | 25 | 76 |
| "        discharged | 20 | 10 | 30 |
| ··      died | 9 | 11 | 20 |
| ··      escaped | 3 | 0 | 3 |
| "        remaining January 1, 1877 | 105 | 91 | 196 |

The average numbers were:

|  | Men. | Women. | Total. |
|---|---|---|---|
| In 1872 | 70 | 78 | 148 |
| " 1873 | 78 | 84 | 162 |
| " 1874 | 84 | 82 | 166 |
| " 1875 | 86 | 84 | 170 |
| " 1876 | 101 | 87 | 188 |

### STATE ALMSHOUSE.

Until the State provides a better building for the inmates of the
Almshouse, the Board can never give a satisfactory report of the
condition of this institution.

The joint select committee, in their report, speaking of the Almshouse buildings, say: "These are not what they should be. They
are all built of wood, are low-studded, and the ventilation is anything but the best."

Owing to the manner in which the buildings are constructed,
they cannot be properly ventilated. Everything possible has been
done to improve them in this respect and the master and matron
are indefatigable in their efforts to bring about the greatest degree
of cleanliness, and to keep the air pure and healthful; but, not-

withstanding the efforts of the Board and of its officers, complete
success has not been attained.

The health of the inmates, however, has been as good as in ordinary institutions of this kind; and, when we consider that in 1873
these buildings, which were then used as a workhouse; and were
less commodious than they now are, contained at times over two
hundred and fifty persons; with less than the usual amount of sickness incident to such institutions, we cannot but conclude that,
although the rooms are low and the ventilation deficient, the institution is not an unhealthful one. It has been occupied—at times
crowded—during seven years, and no epidemic has occurred there.

It is true, however, as the committee say, that the accommodations for the state poor are not what they should be; and it is the
opinion of the Board that, before many years pass by, the present
wooden buildings of the Almshouse should be replaced by a suitable stone structure. The location of the institution also should be
changed, as it is at present too near the residence of the Superintendent.

The statistics are as follows:

| | Men. | Women. | Boys. | Girls. | Total. |
|---|---|---|---|---|---|
| Number remaining January 1,1876.. | 61 | 62 | 20 | 21 | 164 |
| " received during the year... | 107 | 98 | 33 | 41 | 279 |
| " born during the year..... | | | 7 | 8 | 15 |
| Total......................... | 168 | 160 | 60 | 70 | 458 |
| Number discharged during the year. | 85 | 91 | 50 | 57 | 283 |
| " died during the year...... | 15 | 9 | 4 | 5 | 33 |
| Total ...................... | 100 | 100 | 54 | 62 | 316 |
| Number remaining January 1, 1877 | 68 | 60 | 6 | 8 | 142 |

The average number were:

| | Men. | Women. | Boys. | Girls. | Total. |
|---|---|---|---|---|---|
| In 1875......................... | 46 | 55 | 17 | 14 | 132 |
| " 1876......................... | 55 | 66 | 13 | 12 | 146 |

In our report of last year, we urged the importance of making,
at an early day, some suitable provision for the children of the
Almshouse. This remains still a pressing need. Since the opening of the Almshouse, in August, 1874, a little more than two

years ago, 173 different children have been admitted to it. Of these, seventeen have been admitted a second, and two a third time. In addition to the 173 children received into the Almshouse, 34 have been born in it, making a total of 207. Of the children born in the Almshouse, 18 were illigitimate; and of six the mothers were under twenty. What proportion of the whole number of children are from families in the habitual receipt of public or private assistance, the Superintendent of State Charities is unable to ascertain with precision, as they come to him from all parts of the state. He is of the opinion, however, that more than one-half, perhaps three-fourths, of them belong to the permanently dependent class.

These children have been removed from the debasing influences of pauper association, as fast as suitable places could be found for them. Five, and only five, have been placed in families. While children, especially girls, from a well-conducted orphan house, are always in demand, there is great reluctance among all classes to receive them from a poorhouse. Ten have been bound to the managers of the Providence Children's Friend Society, who become responsible for their maintenance and instruction, until they can be placed in suitable families. After they are put out, they are still watched over, and frequently heard from, each child being under the special care of some one of the managers, until they arrive at majority.

This society has been in existence forty-one years, and of the 1050 children,—largely the offspring of pauper parents—which it has reared, not a single one is known to have become a charge to the State in any of its institutions.

Forty-five have been taken from the Almshouse by the St. Aloysius Orphan Asylum. They are simply received into this charitable institution, and cared for until their parents or relatives, desire to take them, or consent to their being put out to service, or indentured to some trade, or adopted into families. There is no restriction upon the number of times which children may enter and leave the Asylum. They come and go, as the ability and circumstances of those upon whom they are naturally dependent may vary.

While affording present relief, therefore, which is most acceptable, it offers but a slender guarantee against future burdens. Five of the number taken by it have since come back to us.

Thirty children who had no residence in the state, have been removed to other states and communities justly chargeable for their support. Fifteen have died. Eighty-eight have returned to such homes as their parents, or other relatives, were able to provide for them. " A large number of these," says the Superintendent of State Charities, Mr. George W. Wightman, " will, in all probability, become sooner or later, dependents upon the state ; for their parents are, in many cases, intemperate and shiftless, and entirely unfit to rear a family. There is little hope that those who are born paupers, and pass their early years amid the debasing and enervating influences of an almshouse, will ever become self-supporting citizens. My experience is decided on this point." Such, also, is the experience of all who have had to do with this unfortunate portion of the community. Pauperism, like vice and crime, with which it is so often associated, tends to run in families. The children of paupers, if left to their surroundings, rarely rise above the condition of their parents. It is thus that an hereditary pauper class comes at length to be formed. Freed from the restraints of virtue, prudence, and self-respect, they increase in a ratio quite out of proportion to the rest of the population. This rapidly-growing class of dependents upon society, is constantly receiving, through various causes, additions from the classes above it ; so that as communities grow older, unless the evil is in some way checked, the burden of its support becomes, every year, greater and greater.

" The special investigation, which this Board (the New York State Board of Charities) has made during the past year," says President Anderson, " has proved, beyond question, that the great mass of our pauperism is hereditary. The fecundity of this class, in spite of all those conditions that would seem naturally likely to increase the death-rate among them, is something frightful. Frequently, three generations of paupers have been found in one almshouse. Nothing is more unfounded than the common idea, that the inmates of our poorhouses, in general, are the victims of unavoidable misfortunes. Of those who have reached adult age, and

are not idiotic, probably more than two-thirds of those supported
by the State, at a cost of nearly $3,000,000, are paupers by their
criminal acts; and, worse than all, this voluntary degradation
tends, by a natural law, to reproduce itself in all their descendants.
This atavism of poverty and crime, unless broken in upon by the
separation of children from their parents, and their absorption into
the healthy portion of the community, will go on, in an increasing
ratio, through all time." Examples of hereditary pauperism will
be found sufficiently numerous in all almshouses, of considerable
size, which have been long in existence. Hon. William P.
Letchworth, Vice-President of the State Board of Charities, met
with them frequently, in his late examination of the county poorhouses of New York. In one of these, containing only nineteen
children, he found three who had pauper grandfathers; three
who had pauper grandmothers; ten who had pauper fathers; sixteen who had pauper mothers; six who had pauper uncles; five
who had pauper aunts; ten who had pauper brothers; and eleven
who had pauper sisters. One of the little girls had been three
years in the poorhouse. Her father, mother, and younger sister,
were then inmates. Six brothers and sisters had been, at different times, there. The father was seventy years of age, of intemperate habits, and had been several times in jail for vagrancy. "In
this old man," Mr. Letchworth remarks, " is seen a type of debased
humanity, fruitful in progeny, who are likely to follow in his foot-
steps."

The same tendency of vice and crime to become hereditary has
also been shown by recent investigations. This is remarkably illustrated in the case of the Juke family, whose disgraceful history has
lately come before the public. Within the present century were
living in an obscure part of Ulster County, New York, six sisters
—the best known of them bearing the name of Margaret,—from
whom there have been traced between six and seven hundred descendants. In this shameful lineage are found seventy-six criminals,
whose terms of imprisonment aggregate one hundred and sixteen
years; one hundred and sixty-four prostitutes, of whom seventeen
kept brothels, and sixty-three were notoriously diseased; and two
hundred and six, who had received out-door and almshouse relief,

equal, in the aggregate, to seven hundred and thirty-four years of individual relief. What an amount of injury to society, and of loss to the state, would have been prevented, had this foul current of vice, pauperism and crime, been arrested at its source.

Families that have been reared in the debilitating atmosphere of an almshouse, go out from it indolent and weak of purpose. By a natural law, they seek to obtain a living "in the direction of the least resistence." The sisters become prostitutes, and corrupt the communities in which they live ; the brothers, being debarred from that vocation, turn thieves, and prey upon property. Hence the affiliation, so commonly observed, of pauperism with vice and crime.

The \$3,000,000 referred to by Dr. Anderson, is the sum expended annually, in maintaining the State charitable institutions and county poorhouses. Besides this, one and a quarter millions are expended in supporting seven city almshouses, and \$3,000,000 in supporting one hundred and thirty-four orphan asylums, and homes for the friendless. The value of the grounds and buildings belonging to these noble institutions, public and private, is estimated at \$22,000,000 ; the interest of which, added to the cost of maintaining them, will swell the expenditure of the Empire State, in organized charities, to about \$9,000,000 annually.

But the cost of supporting the dependent classes in New York, large as it is, is small in comparison with what is expended for their maintainance in some of the older cities of Europe, where the causes at work here have been in operation a much longer time, and have worked out, without check, their legitimate results. In London, with a population differing not greatly from that of the state of New York, the poor rates alone, amount to \$10,000,000. Besides this large sum, no less than \$35,000,000 are supposed to reach the same class, through innumerable benevolent institutions, and an abounding private charity. And, notwithstanding all this profuse almsgiving, pauperism is continually increasing. One-eighth of the entire population, it is said, are in the habitual receipt of public or private charity. Moreover, the blood of the pauper class has become so tainted, that the consequences appear in the children.

Twenty per cent. of these are said to be affected with opthalmia and diseases of the skin, originating in transmitted syphilitic virus. The contagious character of the diseases, with which so many are affected, opposes an insuperable barrier to gathering the children into large communities. It is only in small asylums, where they may receive individual attention and treatment, that they can be properly cared for. So great are the difficulties in the way of reaching the pauper class of the great Metropolis, and lifting it from its degradation and misery. But the best men of England, backed by a nation's wealth, are bravely encountering them.

It is now generally recognized, that mere almsgiving does but increase pauperism ; that the only way to check it is to take care of the children, and leave the parents to experience, to a certain extent, at least, the natural consequences of idleness and vice. Most of the states are acting on this principle. They are removing the children from their parents, and gathering them into primary schools and orphan asylums, where they may receive a kindly nurture and training. When they have reached the proper age, they are either transferred to industrial schools, or, what is better, if it can be done, placed in families, where they may grow up under healthy influences, and become respectable and respected citizens.

In New York, as early as 1868, the State Board of Charities urged upon the county superintendents of the poor, the importance of removing the children from the county poorhouses, to places more suitable for them. As the Board had only advisory powers, their recommendation, though in many cases heeded, was not generally carried out. Finding their continued remonstrances unavailing, they recommended, in their report of 1875, " that the commitment of children of intelligence over two years of age, to the county poorhouses, be prohibited by statute ; and that the proper authorities be required to remove all such children now there, and provide for them otherwise, within a reasonable and specified time." That same year, the following law was enacted by the Legislature : " It shall be the duty of the county Superintendents of the Poor, or other proper officers, charged with the support and relief of indigent persons, of the several counties

of the State, in which there are county poorhouses, to cause the removal of all children between the ages of three and sixteen years,
not idiotic, epileptic, or paralytic; or otherwise defective, diseased,
or deformed; from their respective poorhouses, on or before the first
day of January, 1876 ; and, also, to cause the removal of all those
who may hereafter come under their care and control, or hereafter be
born in such poorhouses, before they shall arrive at the age of three
years, and to provide for their support and care, in families, orphan
asylums, and other appropriate institutions." Thi law, it is
understood, has been carried into execution throughout the State.
Many of the children have been transferred to institutions under
private control, but receiving, from time to time, generous aid from
the state. Others have been sent, largely through the agency of
the Children's Aid Society, of New York city, to homes provided
for them in the Western States. This society, during the last
twenty-three years, has placed in families, chiefly in the West,
" some 35,000 boys and girls, a very large portion of whom have
turned out well."

The charities of Massachusetts,—quite as large, in proportion to
the population, as the charities of New York—are more thoroughly
organized than those of any other state. This is due, in a great
degree, to the labors of her Board of Charities, which has numbered
among its members, some of her ablest and best citizens, and
whose supervision extends over the State Prison and State Reformatories, as well as the institutions more distinctively charitable.
So careful is she to remove the children of her dependent and
vicious classes from parental influence, that, after having exhausted
the accommodations specially provided for them in the State Primary School at Monson, in the Farm School on Thomson Island, and
in several industrial schools, she boards them in private families in
the rural districts, under proper local supervision, until they are
able to repay by their work the cost of keeping them. For the
last six years she has supported, at an annual cost of more than
$15,000, a visiting agency; whose business it is to find places for the
children from the various state establishments, and to visit them
from time to time afterwards, and see that they are properly cared
for; with " results in the highest degree gratifying." She prefers to

3

support and educate her poor children, and turn them into productive citizens, rather than to send them out of her territory. " She does not think it her business to depopulate the Commonwealth, to increase the population of Illinois and Wisconsin. She does not feel that she has a right to extradite her own children."

The right of the state to take the children of paupers and vicious parents, and educate them and train them to habits of industry and virtue, admits of no question. Nor is it merely a right. It is a duty, which it alike owes to them and to society ;—a duty which cannot be evaded or disregarded without the entailment of the greatest evils.

The Board are of the opinion that the time has come when a separate house for the children should be added to the buildings at the State Farm. The cost would be comparatively small, and the results to the community, to be hoped from it, greater than from all the other institutions. It would be the one bright spot in a moral landscape painfully sombre. The labors of philanthrophy, under the most favorable circumstances, are apt to be disappointing. With a population, such as is gathered at the State Farm, they are peculiarly discouraging. " Set thyself to do good, and thou shalt have sweet moments and bitter hours ; nevertheless, do good to thy neighbor. or thou art not worthy of God's gifts."

The Board will be happy to procure plans and estimates of cost, and to furnish any further information that may be desired, should their earnest recommendation meet the approval of your honorable body. The erection of the building, should it be decided upon, might, with advantage, extend over two years. This would afford opportunity for employing the labor of the inmates, as far as practicable, in its construction. An appropriation of ten thousand dollars would be sufficient for the first year.

### CHAPLAIN AND RELIGIOUS SERVICES.

In August. the Board appointed Rev. James Pierce Root, of Pettaconsett, Chaplain of the State Farm. Up to that time, services had been held almost every Sunday by clergymen and others, procured by Mr. George H. Slade, and by the Chairman of the Board.

As this work was performed gratuitously, it was often difficult to find a person disengaged and willing to undertake it. Moreover, during the heat of summer, and the severe weather of winter and spring, a drive to the State Farm was, at times, attended with so much discomfort, and risk of health, that some hesitancy was felt in extending invitations to clergymen to go there.

Mr. Root now holds service regularly in the chapel on Sunday, and the Board are no longer under obligations to any one for the performance of this branch of labor.

Besides the usual Sunday services, the duties of the Chaplain include, reading the burial service, when an interment takes place at the Farm; furnishing the consolations of religion to the sick and the dying, and such other Christian work as time and opportunity may allow.

Mr. Root has taken an active interest in organizing and carrying on the school, which is held in the chapel, four evenings in the week. Miss Coe, of Pettaconsett, and Miss Root, daughter of the Chaplain, have also lent their aid to the matrons, in the school for the women of the workhouse.

The members of the Roman Catholic Church continue to be ministered to by clergymen of their faith when they desire it.

To clergymen and others, who have kindly given their services in helping to improve the moral condition of the inmates of the State Farm, and to Mr. George H. Slade, especially, the Board desire to express their most sincere gratitude.

### FARM.

The Superintendent, Mr. Blaisdell, entered upon his duties too late in the season to effect any very decided change in the condition of the farm this year. Enough has been done, however, to give great promise of success in the future; and with the economy, good judgment, and earnestness of purpose, everywhere apparent in the present management, the farm may soon be expected to contribute largely to the support of the institutions established upon it.

The yield of potatoes was good, considering the dryness of the season, and a vigorous attack of the Colorado beetle. The hay crop was about the same as in 1875 ; but was supplemented by the planting of fodder corn and turnips, wherever there was a piece of land suitable, and manure at hand for the purpose.

Some of the Stockbridge fertilizer was tried upon potatoes, and a field of five acres was prepared, one-half with the Stockbridge, and one-half with Darling's Animal Fertilizer, and sown with millet. In both experiments, the drought prevented a satisfactory result. In the field of millet, no difference could be detected in the effects of the two manures.

The side hill, in the rear of the Almshouse, to the brow of which the sewage pipe from two of the institutions had been brought, as mentioned in the last report, was laid down to grass, and the sewage distributed over the surface. This land will need to be underdrained, before the full effects of the sewage can be realized; but, as men and teams were not available for the purpose the past season, the work had to be postponed.    There will, doubtless, be a good yield of grass here the coming summer.

A table of the amounts of produce raised is given in another place.

### INSURANCE.

At the January session, 1876, the following resolution was passed by the General Assembly :

*Resolved*, That it is inexpedient to insure the buildings belonging to the State at the State Farm, and that the Board of State Charities and Corrections are hereby so instructed.

The insurance upon the Workhouse and other stone buildings, expired January 20, 1876, and was renewed for another year, for the amount of $70,500.    This was done previous to the passage of the above resolution, and the premium paid, $1,024.70, appears in the expenditures of the year.

The insurance upon the wooden buildings, amounting to $64,700, expired October 15, 1876, and was not renewed.    After January 20, 1877, there will be no insurance upon the buildings at the State Farm.

The insurance account stands, January 1, 1877, as follows:

Paid for insurance to date.................................... $9,751 98

Received for loss of chapel, laundry and cookhouse, destroyed by
    fire, April 6, 1872....................................... 7,833 47

## FINANCES.

Previous to the January Session, 1876, the appropriations for the use of the Board were special appropriations, made payable "from time to time upon the order of the chairman of the Board, countersigned by the Secretary," and having no limitation as to time of payment. The money so received was deposited in the R. I. Hospital Trust Co., and disbursed and accounted for by the Board.

At the January Session, 1876, the amount appropriated "for the support of the State Farm" was included in the general appropriation act.

At the May Session, 1876, no provision having been made at the January Session for the disposition of the various sums, which are paid to the Board for the board of the insane, for labor, sale of produce, &c., &c., the following resolution was passed:

Resolved. That the Board of State Charities and Corrections shall cause to be paid into the State Treasury, as provided in Section 14, Chapter 25 of the General Statutes, all moneys received by them for board of inmates, labor and materials, and from all other sources ; which sums, so paid into the Treasury, shall be added to the appropriations already made for the use of said Board for the fiscal year, ending April 30, 1877.

Appropriation made for the support of the State Farm at the
    January session, 1876...... ....... ..................... $70,000 00

Received previous to the change in the method of making payments:

Balance of appropriation of 1875 ...................5,000 00

For board of insane, &c., &c......... $13,984 91

Less balance returned to the Treasury,
    June 8, 1876.................... ... 3,286 28, 10,698 63    15,698 63

After the passage of the above resolution the amounts received and paid into the Treasury, including the balance, 3,286 28, as above, were (See statement of State Auditor in report of the Secretary,)...... ....... ................... 24,785 29

                                                       $110,483 92

Payments, for expenses, made by the Board previous to May 1, 1876.... ..................... $15.098 63
Payments for the Board by the Treasury ....... 76,044 51    91,743 14

Available balance to the credit of the appropriation for the
"support of the State Farm" Jan 1, 1877, (See statement
of State Auditor,) .............. ..... .......... .........:.    $18,740 78

The amounts charged to the various expense accounts, &c., including indebtedness (that is, these amounts include all purchases
and debts incurred) are as follows :

For Construction ............................... $3,346 60
"   Material and hired labor for State Prison....   3,515 65
"   Removal of paupers, salary and expenses of
      office of Sup't of State Charities and Cor-
      rections............................. . ...   2,436 41
"   Paid indebtedness of 1875.................   5,867 33
                                                            $15,165 99
"   Expenses of the farm, purchase of stock,
      farm implements, &c., current expenses....  $11,793 89
"   Subsistence,            "        "     ....  25,709 65
"   Salaries, exclusive of Supt.
      of S. C. & C.,        "        --    ....  19,322 67
"   Fuel,                   --       --    ....   5,964 13
"   Furniture,              "        --    ....   2,894 10
"   Repairs and improvements "       "     ....   2,817 76
"   Clothing and bedding,   "        "     ....   5,957 05
"   Insurance,              --       --    ....   1,024 70
"   Other expenses,         --       --    ....   3,665 34,   79,149 29
                                                            $94,315 28

Following the calculation of the Joint Select Committee on the
State Farm, (see their report, page 7,) we find the gross
amount of expenditure, for the current expenses of the
State Farm, for the year, to be..........................    79,149 29
Deducting receipts for labor, for farm produce, baskets, &c.,
&c., that is for earnings, as follows, (see Secretary's report),
For labor of inmates and teams......................7,044 21
"   Sale of farm produce............. ........... ....873 05
"     "   " baskets................. ...............918 95
"     "   " old junk, &c.,....... ....... ...........288 17

                                                             9,124 38

We have a net expenditure of .............. ..................    $70,024 91

The average numbers in the institutions during the past two years were as follows:

|  | 1875, | 1876. |
|---|---|---|
| Workhouse and House of Correction | 228 | 232 |
| Asylum for the Insane | 170 | 188 |
| Almshouse | 132 | 146 |
| Total | 525 | 566 |

Dividing the net current expenses, as above, by 566, the average number of inmates, the result shows a cost of $123 72 for each inmate for the year, which is at the rate of $2 88 per week.

In 1875, as shown in the report of the Joint Select Committee, the net expenditure was $71,689 24, for an average of 525 inmates; being at the rate of $136 55 per annum, or $2 62 per week for each.

### ESTIMATE OF EXPENDITURES.

The Board estimate that their available resources, which are herewith given approximately, are sufficient to pay current expenses until May 1, 1877, the beginning of the State fiscal year:

| | |
|---|---|
| Balance available in treasury, January 1, 1877, say | $18,700 00 |
| Less indebtedness | 2,500 00 |
| | $16,200 00 |
| Add receipts for board of insane | 4,600 00 |
| | $20,800 00 |

For the fiscal year, ending April 30, 1878, the estimates of expenditure are as follows:

| | | |
|---|---|---|
| For the same number of inmates and at the same rate of net cost as in 1876, say | | $70,000 00 |
| For removal of paupers, say | | 2,500 00 |
| For construction : | | |
| Building for children | $10,000 00 | |
| Completion of barn, etc | 3,000 00 | |
| Plastering workhouse yard wall, storehouse, etc | 2,500 00 | |
| Enlargement of cottage for excited patients at Insane Asylum, etc., etc | 1,500 00 | 17,000 00 |
| | | $89,500 00 |
| Deduct estimated receipts for board of insane | | 15,500 00 |
| And, to carry out what has been proposed in the foregoing report, the Board will require an appropriation of | | $74,000 00 |

All of which is respectfully submitted by the Board of State
Charities and Corrections.

GEORGE I. CHACE,
WILLIAM H. HOPKINS,
JAMES M. PENDLETON,
THOMAS COGGESHALL,
SAMUEL W. CHURCH,
WILLIAM W. CHAPIN.

*January* 1, 1877.

# REPORT OF THE SECRETARY.

*To the Board of State Charities and Corrections:*

The Secretary respectfully presents the following report :

Twenty-three regular, and two special meetings have been held during the year; of these, thirteen were at the State Farm, and twelve in the city of Providence.

The attendance of members of the Board has been as follows ;

George I. Chace .. ....... ........ ........ ...Present at 25 meetings
Samuel W. Church. .............................    "   25    "
Job Kenyon.................................····· .    "   14    "
Thomas Coggeshall .........................................    "   21    "
Horace Babcock (resigned, May, 1876)......... ..    "   4    "
William H. Hopkins.............................    "   19    "
James M. Pendleton (appointed at May session)...    "   10    "
William W. Chapin.................·······.......    "   25    "

As the method of disbursing the appropriation, made for the use of the Board, was changed at the January session, it will be necessary to make the statement of the receipts and expenditures in two parts.

The first will cover the period from January 1, to May 1, 1876, when the payments were made directly by the Board; and the second, the period from May 1, 1876, to January 1, 1877, when the payments were made through the offices of the Auditor and Treasurer of the State.

At the May session, a resolution was passed by the General Assembly, directing the Board to pay into the State Treasury, "all moneys received by them for the board of inmates, labor,

material, and from all other sources," and authorizing the sums so
paid into the Treasury to be added to the appropriations, already
made for the use of said Board. for the fiscal year, ending April
80, 1877.

The following account gives the amounts received and paid by the
Secretary from January 1, to June 8, 1876.

RECEIVED,

1876.

| | | | |
|---|---|---|---|
| January 1. | Balance on deposit in R. I. Hospital Trust Co.,... | $6,690 | 04 |
| 11, | From George H. Snow............. .... ...... | 10 | 00 |
| 26, | " George W. Wightman, Supt. S. C. & C.... | 2,154 | 57 |
| 8, | " R. I. Hospital Trust Co., interest.......... | 17 | 14 |
| Feb.  3, | " George W. Wightman...... ... ......... | 363 | 37 |
| 5, | " Norman W. Eayrs, Supt. State Farm...... | 169 | 55 |
| " | " George W. Wightman.................. | 13 | 00 |
| 7, | " General Treasurer..................... | 5,000 | 00 |
| 9, | " R. I. Hospital Trust Company., interest... | 12 | 49 |
| 15, | " Johnson & Whaley..................... | 10 | 00 |
| 19, | " Moses L. Watson... ................... | 28 | 00 |
| 29, | " George W. Wightman........... ........ | 792 | 09 |
| March  6, | " Norman W. Eayrs....................... | 33 | 95 |
| 8, | " R. I. Hospital Trust Co., interest.......... | 9 | 51 |
| 30, | " George W. Wightman.................... | 545 | 83 |
| April  3, | " Norman W. Eayrs....................... | 216 | 75 |
| " | " George Grover...................... | 2 | 48 |
| 10, | " R. I. Hospital Trust Co., interest......... | 5 | 25 |
| " | " Pinniger & Manchester................. | 4 | 50 |
| 17, | " George W. Wightman.................... | 2,043 | 75 |
| 25, | " Moses L. Watson..................... ...... | 20 | 00 |
| " | " C. Sherman & Co...................... | 2 | 50 |
| 29, | " W. S. Burgess........................... | 12 | 00 |
| May  2, | " W. S. Fifield............ ............ | 30 | 90 |
| 3, | " Norman W. Eayrs...................... | 26 | 75 |
| " | " J. W. Sherman & Co........··........... | 5 | 00 |
| 6, | " R. I. Hospital Trust Co., interest......... | 4 | 33 |
| 16, | " Cary Bros............................. | 29 | 00 |
| " | " Charles Spooner........ ................ | 20 | 50 |
| " | " Bateman & Gardner.................... | 60 | 50 |
| " | " William E. Dennis.................. .... | 11 | 50 |
| " | " George Weaver..................... ......... | 8 | 00 |
| " | " John Green............................ | 9 | 00 |
| " | " Batchelor & Pitman.................... | 6 | 50 |

| May  | 16, | "  | J. W. Sherman............................ | 67 |
|------|-----|----|-------------------------------------------|----|
|      | 27, | "  | Daniel Brown............ ............. | 8 00 |
|      | 29, | "  | Julius Sayer............................ | 34 00 |
|      | "   | "  | George W. Wightman................... | 564 19 |
| June | 8,  | "  | R. I. Hospital Trust Co., interest........ | 9 20 |

$18,984 91

PAID.

| January 8. | Tuttle & Hobbs............................... | $193 50 |
|------------|----------------------------------------------|---------|
| " " | Thomas J. Tilley. ......... .............. | 1,018 51 |
| " 10. | George T. Perry ......... ............... | 150 00 |
| " 13. | Wm. G. R. Mowry & Co..................... | 526 03 |
| " " | Hartford, Prov. & Fishkill R. R............. | 73 91 |
| " " | Builders' Iron Foundry...................... | 310 40 |
| " 15. | Wood & Winsor............................. | 500 00 |
| " " | William Sweeney.......... . ....... | 78 88 |
| " 18. | Moulton & Ingraham. ..................... | 4 50 |
| " " | A. & W. Sprague.......................... ... | 42 50 |
| " 21. | James M. Pendleton & Co......... .......... | 1,024 70 |
| " 22. | George E. Sammis........ .... . ........... | 76 50 |
| " " | Chambers. Calder & Co......... ........... | 186 70 |
| " " | George M. Griffin & Co...................... | 40 33 |
| " " | Greene, Brayman & Co . ....... ........... | 16 95 |
| " " | R. E. Hamlin & Co ......................... | 25 06 |
| " " | D. D. Bucklin ........ ................. | 35 05 |
| " " | Henry T. Root.............................. | 15 03 |
| " " | Congdon, Carpenter & Co.... .. ...... ...... | 14 91 |
| " " | Mason, Chapin & Co........................ | 48 50 |
| " " | Thomas W. Sprague........................ | 23 75 |
| " " | Winsor & Brown............... ............. | 82 09 |
| " " | Rice & Hayward............................ | 28 34 |
| " " | S. D. Andrews.............................. | 7 80 |
| " " | Spicers & Peckham.......................... | 99 61 |
| " " | T. W. Rounds & Co.... ................... | 21 00 |
| " " | A. J. Sanborn ......................... .. | 63 49 |
| " " | E. Allen & Co.............................. | 54 00 |
| " " | A. Burgess & Co........................ ....... | 30 02 |
| " " | Colwell & Winsor........................... | 8 86 |
| " " | L. D. Anthony & Co......................... | 14 75 |
| " " | Waldron, Wightman & Co..................... | 230 58 |

| | | | |
|---|---|---|---:|
| January | 22. | George L. Claflin & Co..... ................... | 45 75 |
| " | " | Tucker, Swan & Co............................ | 61 00 |
| " | " | Calef Bros............................ ............. | 9 60 |
| " | " | Brownell & Barrows........................... | 22 90 |
| " | 24. | Day, Sprague & Co........................... | 333 25 |
| " | 20. | Bristol (Mass·) Co. House of Correction........ | 78 00 |
| " | 28. | D. F. Burlingame..................... ....... | 12 00 |
| " | " | C. P. Lobdell............................ ....... | 18 50 |
| " | 31. | William L. Roberts............................ | 79 16 |
| Feb'y | 1. | Pay-roll of Carpenters &c.  January............ | 613 51 |
| " | " | do  "  officers &c.  "  ............. | 1,525 74 |
| " | 3. | J. A. Budlong & Son........................... | 18 00 |
| " | 7. | Thomas J. Tilley................................ | 1,066 47 |
| " | " | Providence Board of Trade..................... | 10 89 |
| " | 8. | Hartford, Prov. & Fishkill R. R............... | 247 27 |
| " | 12. | Wood & Winsor............................... | 100 00 |
| " | " | E. M. Thurston, Agt........................... | 188 80 |
| " | " | F. E. Turner.................................. | 83 90 |
| " | " | George H. Snow... .  ......... .......... | 11 45 |
| " | " | Mrs. Moses Wightman........................ | 47 40 |
| " | 14. | Hill & Morse................................. | 38 37 |
| " | " | Lincoln Mf'g Co......... ............ | 57 38 |
| " | 15. | Johnson & Whaley............ ............ | 179 53 |
| " | " | H. H. Fenner................................. | 172 80 |
| " | " | Wm. G. R. Mowry & Co..................... | 112 96 |
| " | 17. | Alexander Mc Teer........................... | 43 49 |
| " | " | Browning. Capron & Co....................... | 7 02 |
| " | 19. | Wm. E. Langley & Co............... ...... ..... | 102 80 |
| " | 21. | Hartford, Prov. & Fishkill R. R................ | 31 10 |
| " | 16. | Lincoln Mf'g Co........................ :..... | 56 81 |
| " | " | Bugbee & Hall............................... | 49 66 |
| " | " | Somerset Potters' Works..................... | 21 02 |
| " | " | Allen & Thompson........................... | 84 45 |
| " | " | Parsons, Bugbee & Co......................... | 289 69 |
| " | " | W. Congdon & Sons........................... | 70 22 |
| " | " | Taylor, Symonds & Co.................... .... | 302 17 |
| " | " | Dewing & Monsell.... ........................ | 21 15 |
| " | " | Congdon & Aylsworth......................... | 112 85 |
| March | 1. | Pay-roll of officers, carpenters &c......... ..... | 1,800 34 |
| " | 7. | C. P. Burlingame........................... .. | 104 41 |
| " | " | Wm. H. Mason... ........................ | 22 15 |
| " | 8. | A. M. Hawkins & Co........................... | 8 49 |
| " | 11. | Hartford, Prov. & Fishkill R. R......... ...... | 49 96 |
| " | 31. | Goodwin '& Allen............................. | 32 50 |

| | | | |
|---|---|---|---:|
| April | 1. | Pay-roll of officers &c.......... .................. | 1,664 88 |
| " | 4. | J. S. Gallup............................. ....... | 58 62 |
| " | " | George H. Copeland & Co........................ | 9 00 |
| " | " | Hartford, Prov. & Fishkill R. R................. | 17 92 |
| " | 5. | Akerman & Co...................... ............ | 5 25 |
| " | 6. | Daniel Smith................................. | 16 00 |
| " | 14. | J. S. Budlong............................. ..... | 30 30 |
| " | 17. | Tucker Man'f'g Co. Boston, Mass.............. | 115 00 |
| " | 22. | Hartford, Prov. & Fishkill R. R................. | 50 00 |
| " | 25. | Wm. W. Chapin......................... ....... | 40 12 |
| " | " | Hopkins & Sears............................. | 12 00 |
| " | " | James H. Munroe............................. | 12 00 |
| " | " | Daniel Tillinghast........ ..................... | 34 50 |
| " | " | D. N. Graffum....................:........ | 2 50 |
| " | " | William Rowson....:....... ................. | 14 44 |
| " | " | George A. Leete ................... ......... | 8 54 |
| " | " | F. Coggeshall............................. ..... | 3 50 |
| " | " | Wm. B. Blanding........................... | 2 00 |
| " | " | Daniels & Cornell............................. | 3 84 |
| " | " | F. B. Hodges................................. | 1 20 |
| " | " | N. Thornton................................. | 5 00 |
| " | " | Cory Bros................................... .. | 1 00 |
| " | " | F. A. Paige & Co............................. | 10 00 |
| " | " | T. C. Holloway............................. | 14 00 |
| " | " | Providence Press Co...... ................. | 3 32 |
| " | " | James Smith................................. | 13 50 |
| " | " | Providence Post office........................ | 5 22 |
| " | " | E. L. Valentine. ............................. | 21 00 |
| " | " | George H. Snow............................. | 33 11 |
| " | " | Preston & Brown............................. | 3 00 |
| " | 29. | Wood & Winsor............................. | 101 71 |
| June | 8. | General Treasurer of Rhode Island............. | 3,286 28 |

$18,984 91

We have examined the vouchers from January 1. to June 8. 1876, and find them correct.

Signed.    SAMUEL W. CHURCH, } *Finance Committee.*
          THOMAS COGGESHALL,

The second statement is as follows:

*Rhode Island State Treasury in account with Board of State Charities and Corrections.*

DR.

Appropriation made at the January Session, 1876,..$70.000 00
Money paid into the Treasury, as directed by
   Resolution passed at the May Session, 1876........24,785 29

                                                   $94,785 29

CR.

Payments for the Board of State Charities and Corrections,
  from May 1, to Dec. 31, 1876.............................. $76,044 51

Balance available for the use of the Board of State Charities
  and Corrections, January 1, 1877........................ $18,740 78

                         STATE AUDITOR'S OFFICE,
                    Providence, R. I. January 6, 1877.

   I hereby certify that the sum of Twenty-four thousand, seven hundred, eighty-five, and $\frac{29}{100}$ dollars, ($24,785 29) has been credited to the appropriation for support of the State Farm, for present fiscal year ending April 30, 1877, in accordance with law ; being moneys paid to the General Treasurer from May 1st. to Dec. 31, 1876, by Board of State Charities and Corrections. I also certify that the Books of this office show an unexpended balance on account of said appropriation January 1, 1877, amounting to eighteen thousand, seven hundred, forty and $\frac{78}{100}$ Dollars.

                         JOEL M. SPENCER,
                              *State Auditor.*

The sums collected, and paid into the Treasury are, in detail, as follows :

|  |  |  |  |  |
|---|---|---|---|---:|
|  |  | Cash balance, as above............ ............... | 3,286 28 |
| June | 3. | From Norman W. Eayrs, Sup't. State Farm ..... | 44 60 |
| " | 6. | " Moses L. Watson........................ | 20 00 |
| " | " | " James Tucker Jr ...... .................. | 20 00 |
| " | 8. | " State Prison Commission.... .......... | 796 00 |
| " | 9. | " Rose & Walker.......................... | 56 20 |
| " | " | " Thomas J. Tilley.......... ...........·····. | 40 30 |
| " | 12. | " Sherman & Crosby... ............. ······ | 10 00 |
| " | " | " Lincoln M'f'g Co........................ | 43 00 |
| " | 26. | " Hopkins & Pomroy...... .. ........ .... | 40 00 |
| " | 27. | " George W. Wightman, Supt. S. C., & C ... | 1,116 24 |
| July | 1. | " Jno. Mc Carrick. .. .................... | 5 00 |
| " | " | " N. W. Eayrs............. .............. | 25 |
| " | " | " James Murphy........................... | 12 39 |
| " | " | " H. F. Gaines........................... | 1 25 |
| " | " | " James Oatley............ ........... | 3 59 |
| " | " | " Wm. F. Hayden..................... .... . | 3 59 |
| " | " | " S. L. Blaisdell..................... ....... | 2 00 |
| " | 15. | " W. E. Barrett & Co ................... ... | 22 50 |
| " | 17. | " George W. Wightman.............. ...... | 2,012 35 |
| " | 24. | " F. J. Sheldon ··· ............... .... | 17 89 |
| " | 29. | " George W. Wightman........... .... ... | 921 40 |
| Aug't | 1. | " Moses L. Watson............. .... .. | 30 00 |
| " | " | " James L. Murphy................. .... . | 8 74 |
| " | " | " John Mc Carrick............. ........... | 6 00 |
| " | " | " William O. Towne............. .......... | 1 00 |
| " | " | " B. F. Tefft... ........ ............... | 1 00 |
| " | " | " Austin Bugbee........................... . | 1 00 |
| " | " | " George H. Snow............ ........... | 1 00 |
| " | " | " S. B. Goffe ......................... | 1 00 |
| " | " | " Sarah J. Derby......................... | 75 |
| " | " | " S. L. Blaisdell .................. ....... | 2 75 |
| " | " | " —— Jennison.. ......................... | 1 25 |
| " | " | " —— Murphy..................... .......... | 55 |
| " | " | " —— Quinlan............. ......... ........ | 50 |
| " | 10. | " Thomas J. Tilley........ ............ ··· . | 69 96 |
| " | 12. | " James Tucker, Jr......................... | 9 00 |
| " | 22. | " George W. Wightman.... ............. .. | 447 29 |
| Sept | 2. | " F. Potter ............................. | 1 25 |
| " | " | " Watson M'f'g Co ......... .............. | 38 |
| " | " | " Moses L. Watson............. .......... | 14 00 |
| " | " | " Eliza J. Ryan ........ ................. | 11 40 |
| " | " | " John T. Mc Donald .... ................. | 5 00 |

| Date | | | Name | Amount |
|---|---|---|---|---|
| Sept. | 2. | From | George W. Thomas | 5 00 |
| " | " | " | George W. Sherman | 5 75 |
| " | " | " | Bateman & Gardner | 8 00 |
| " | " | " | Joshua Sayer | 9 00 |
| " | " | " | Thomas Hanly | 1 00 |
| " | " | " | S. L. Blaisdell | 8 00 |
| " | 4. | " | George W. Wightman | 199 76 |
| " | 8. | " | Thomas J. Tilley | 46 53 |
| " | 15. | " | George W. Wightman | 456 92 |
| " | 23. | " | do | 119 45 |
| Oct. | 4. | " | O. A. Hodges | 2 50 |
| " | " | " | B. B. & R. Knight | 26 68 |
| " | " | " | Moses L. Watson | 7 00 |
| " | " | " | John Clark | 7 00 |
| " | " | " | George H. Grover | 75 |
| " | " | " | Richard Welch | 1 00 |
| " | " | " | Charles G. A. Peterson | 1 00 |
| " | 11. | " | S. P. Taylor | 1 00 |
| " | 12. | " | Thomas J. Tilley | 48 00 |
| " | 16. | " | Chambers, Calder & Co | 4 25 |
| " | 14. | " | George W. Wightman | 1,914 43 |
| " | 17. | " | O. A. Hodges | 7 50 |
| " | " | " | Sweet & Arnold | 33 13 |
| " | 20. | " | William Elsbree | 3 50 |
| " | " | " | B. A. Jackson | 5 00 |
| " | 25. | " | George W. Wightman | 683 80 |
| " | 26. | " | Rose & Walker | 60 59 |
| Nov. | 1. | " | O. A. Hodges | 65 |
| " | " | " | S. L. Blaisdell | 6 00 |
| " | " | " | Julia O'Rourke | 6 60 |
| " | " | " | Ira B. Wilson | 75 |
| " | " | " | Caleb B. Parker | 1 00 |
| " | " | " | Wm. G. Ward | 1 00 |
| " | 3. | " | Hiram F. Gaines | 15 18 |
| " | 4. | " | Nelson Titus | 68 00 |
| " | 8. | " | George Bowen | 9 00 |
| " | " | " | Chas. G. A. Peterson | 25 |
| " | 10. | " | Lincoln M'f'g Co | 167 69 |
| " | 11. | " | State Prison Commission | 7,000 00 |
| " | " | " | R. I. Hospital Trust Co | 10 15 |
| " | " | " | George W. Wightman | 483 81 |
| " | 18. | " | John H. Eddy & Co | 159 97 |
| " | 20. | " | W. E. Barrett & Co | 66 50 |
| " | 21. | " | James Tucker Jr | 14 50 |

| | | | | | |
|---|---|---|---|---|---:|
| Nov. | 21. | From | W. S. Fifield | | 57 75 |
| " | 23. | " | Samuel W. Church | | 17 42 |
| " | " | " | Sweet & Arnold | | 1 20 |
| " | 25. | " | George Campbell | | 33 35 |
| " | 28. | " | G. & C. P. Hutchins | | 62 25 |
| " | " | " | Chas. H. Hunt | | 16 00 |
| " | " | " | Mary Barnes | | 6 65 |
| " | " | " | William Thurber | | 11 40 |
| " | " | " | Peter Moriarty | | 5 00 |
| " | " | " | Sarah Simmons | | 5 00 |
| " | 29. | " | George W. Wightman | | 842 87 |
| Dec. | 1. | " | H. F. Gaines | | 7 00 |
| " | " | " | Ira B. Wilson | | 1 00 |
| " | " | " | John Ryan | | 1 00 |
| " | " | " | William F. Hayden | | 1 00 |
| " | " | " | Caleb B. Parker | | 25 |
| " | " | " | James Cook | | 25 |
| " | " | " | C. G. A. Peterson | | 25 |
| " | 13. | " | Michael Golrick | | 107 00 |
| " | " | " | George W. Wightman | | 176 50 |
| " | 16. | " | Jessie Nelson | | 10 70 |
| " | 19. | " | F. J. Sheldon | | 5 83 |
| " | 27. | " | Prison Commission | | 873 28 |
| " | 27. | " | " " | | 672 20 |
| " | " | " | " " | | 956 58 |
| " | 29. | " | Michael Golrick | | 16 00 |
| " | " | " | Esek. B. Tallman | | 5 00 |
| " | " | " | George Cutting | | 6 00 |
| " | " | " | George Marcy | | 5 00 |
| " | " | " | Isaac Walker | | 16 00 |
| " | " | " | Daniel Kenyon | | 16 00 |
| " | " | " | Hugh O. Donnell | | 3 25 |
| " | " | " | Page Grover | | 50 |
| " | " | " | S. L. Blaisdell | | 75 |
| " | 30. | " | B. B. & R. Knight | | 72 64 |
| " | " | " | R. I. Hospital Trust Co | | 6 20 |

5

$24,785 29

The payments for the Board are, in detail, as follows :—

1876.

| | | | |
|---|---|---|---|
| May | 1. | Thomas J. Tilley | 1,824 98 |
| " | " | Pay-roll for April | 1,682 81 |
| " | 2. | R. E. Hamlin & Co | 13 75 |
| " | " | W. S. Fifield | 100 54 |
| " | " | Brownell & Barrows | 86 19 |
| " | " | Morse & Sons | 16 37 |
| " | 3. | J. H. & J. B. Sweet | 851 91 |
| " | " | Popkins & Pomroy | 5,122 90 |
| " | 4. | L. D. Anthony & Co | 52 15 |
| " | " | Tillinghast &. Sherman | 134 80 |
| " | " | Day, Sprague & Co | 1,808 00 |
| " | " | E. M. Aldrich & Co | 62 19 |
| " | " | L. Brayton & Co | 63 05 |
| " | " | J. B. Barnaby & Co | 222 00 |
| " | " | Spicers & Peckham | 63 64 |
| " | " | Rice, Draper & Co | 54 00 |
| " | " | F. L. Gould | 9 90 |
| " | " | Tibbitts & Randall | 12 00 |
| " | " | D. D. Sweet & Co | 128 20 |
| " | 5. | Franklin Society | 10 00 |
| " | " | Winsor & Brown | 110 98 |
| " | " | J. L. Slocum & Son | 5 60 |
| " | 6. | Morse & Sons | 18 82 |
| " | 8. | J. H. & J. B. Sweet | 307 80 |
| " | " | Builders' Iron Foundry | 60 20 |
| " | " | Johnson & Whaley | 368 60 |
| " | " | George M. Griffin & Co | 38 64 |
| " | " | Thomas J. Tilley | 1,064 07 |
| " | 9. | Colwell & Winsor | 87 15 |
| " | " | W. Morlock & Co | 42 46 |
| " | " | Michael Golrick | 47 38 |
| " | " | Sweet & Arnold | 194 60 |
| " | " | N. W. Eayrs | 12 75 |
| " | " | Hartford, Providence & Fishkill R. R. | 505 58 |
| " | 10. | Tuttle & Hobbs | 180 75 |
| " | 11. | Anna Tuman | 50 00 |
| " | " | Lincoln M'f'g Co | 111 27 |
| " | 12. | C. P. Burlingame | 51 00 |
| " | " | Taylor, Symonds & Co | 973 73 |
| " | " | Wm. G. R. Mowry & Co | 120 70 |
| " | " | Barker, Whitaker & Co | 107 69 |
| " | " | Charles H. George & Co | 208 99 |
| " | " | C. Farnum & Co | 27 76 |

| May | 12. | Congdon, Carpenter & Co | 68 16 |
| " | " | Whitford, Aldrich & Co | 261 85 |
| " | " | Waldron, Wightman & Co | 748 92 |
| " | " | T. W. Sprague | 49 50 |
| " | " | Chambers, Calder & Co | 398 84 |
| " | " | Greene, Brayman & Co | 84 00 |
| " | 13. | Parsons, Bugbee & Co | 320 70 |
| " | " | Wm. H. Fenner & Co | 9 34 |
| " | " | A. J. Sanborn | 119 44 |
| " | " | Comstocks & Co | 197 68 |
| " | " | O. C. Williams | 46 05 |
| " | 16. | Dutee Wilcox, Assignee | 325 00 |
| " | " | Hill & Morse | 19 88 |
| " | 17. | Hartwell, Richards & Co | 62 92 |
| " | " | George L. Claflin & Co | 135 34 |
| " | " | Sweet & Arnold | 557 37 |
| " | " | A. Burgess & Co | 160 79 |
| " | 20. | Congdon, Carpenter & Co | 110 62 |
| " | " | W. Congdon & Sons | 45 62 |
| " | 22. | Congdon & Aylesworth | 137 59 |
| " | " | J. S. Gallup | 15 75 |
| " | " | Mason, Chapin & Co | 92 78 |
| " | " | Bugbee & Hall | 67 06 |
| " | " | Henry T. Root | 16 86 |
| " | 23. | Solomon Harrington | 11 81 |
| " | 26. | Rice & Hayward | 25 75 |
| " | 27. | Charles H. West | 150 00 |
| " | " | Charles H. George & Co | 340 64 |
| " | " | Taylor, Symonds & Co | 96 57 |
| " | " | Comstocks & Co | 110 66 |
| " | " | W. S. Fifield | 22 20 |
| " | 29. | Adams Bros | 699 07 |
| " | " | Bugbee & Hall | 20 42 |
| " | " | Greene, Brayman & Co | 54 20 |
| " | " | Chambers, Calder & Co | 150 23 |
| " | " | Whitford, Aldrich & Co | 956 72 |
| " | " | Tucker, Swan & Co | 215 88 |
| " | " | Waldron, Wightman & Co | 679 44 |
| " | " | A. Burgess & Co | 68 59 |
| " | " | Parsons, Bugbee & Co | 148 40 |
| " | " | T. W. Sprague | 54 50 |
| " | 31. | Calef Bros | 39 09 |
| " | " | Waldo Tillinghast | 6 49 |
| " | " | H. C. Maine | 20 41 |

| June | 1.  | Cory Bros | 14 50 |
|------|-----|-----------|-------|
| "    | 2.  | Hartwell, Richards & Co | 33 62 |
| "    | 3.  | Pay roll for May | 1,833 48 |
| "    | "   | E. L. Valentine | 6 00 |
| "    | "   | Barden & Keep | 4 62 |
| "    | "   | D. N. Graffum | 1 50 |
| "    | "   | Allen & Thompson | 1 00 |
| "    | "   | Clapp & King | 1 67 |
| "    | "   | J. H. Atwater | 1 80 |
| "    | "   | W. S. Allen | 3 50 |
| "    | "   | Wm. W. Chapin.  Cash items | 23 17 |
| "    | "   | Mc Crillis, Harris & Co | 235 19 |
| "    | "   | Wood & Winsor | 24 40 |
| "    | "   | Congdon & Aylesworth | 12 00 |
| "    | "   | Job Kenyon | 16 29 |
| "    | 5.  | Barker, Whitaker & Co | 56 99 |
| "    | "   | George T. Perry | 75 00 |
| "    | 6.  | Day, Sprague & Co | 625 00 |
| "    | "   | Charles Whitford | 73 80 |
| "    | "   | Auldis Borden | 19 82 |
| "    | "   | Samuel W. Church | 51 65 |
| "    | 7.  | James Tucker, Jr | 191 58 |
| "    | 9.  | Rose & Walker | 122 48 |
| "    | "   | Hartford, Prov. & Fishkill R. R. | 53 07 |
| "    | "   | Thomas J. Tilley | 849 69 |
| "    | 10. | Johnson & Whaley | 228 69 |
| "    | "   | J. H. & J. B. Sweet | 208 84 |
| "    | 12. | Thomas H. Rhodes | 94 15 |
| "    | 15. | Mc Crillis, Harris & Co | 202 63 |
| "    | 16. | George W. Wightman | 339 98 |
| "    | 17. | Taylor, Symonds & Co | 75 05 |
| "    | "   | L. D. Anthony & Co | 6 00 |
| "    | "   | Cleveland Bros | 50 07 |
| "    | "   | Wood & Winsor | 21 14 |
| "    | "   | Parsons, Bugbee & Co | 160 36 |
| "    | "   | E. M. Aldrich & Co | 17 12 |
| "    | "   | Charles H. George & Co | 260 48 |
| "    | "   | Chambers, Calder & Co | 119 28 |
| "    | "   | Barker Whitaker & Co | 57 30 |
| "    | "   | Greene, Brayman & Co | 79 20 |
| "    | "   | Whitford, Aldrich & Co | 199 11 |
| "    | "   | Bugbee & Hall | 19 35 |
| "    | "   | Wm. G. R. Mowry & Co | 172 17 |
| "    | "   | Congdon, Carpenter & Co | 46 36 |

| June | 17. | W. Congdon & Sons | 86 06 |
|---|---|---|---|
| " | " | R. E. Hamlin & Co.. . | 30 24 |
| " | " | Thomas Phillips & Co. | 93 37 |
| " | " | Thomas W. Sprague | 15 50 |
| " | " | Greene M'f' g Co. | 33 49 |
| " | 19. | Hartwell, Richards & Co. | 48 92 |
| " | " | T. P. Shepard & Co. | 17 50 |
| " | 20. | J. B. Barnaby & Co. | 402 25 |
| " | 21. | Waldron, Wightman & Co. | 103 86 |
| " | 26. | William Rowson | 40 54 |
| " | 16. | Samuel W. Church | 1,331 66 |
| " | 30. | William H. Hopkins | 415 00 |
| " | " | Pay-roll of officers & workmen | 2,492 04 |
| July | 1. | F. B. Hodges | 1 75 |
| " | " | H. M. Coombs | 1 00 |
| " | " | Samuel M. Gray | 1 20 |
| " | " | E. L. Valentine | 6 00 |
| " | " | George Jones | 3 00 |
| " | " | Wm. W. Chapin. Cash items | 80 20 |
| " | " | E. M. Thurston, Ag't. | 73 80 |
| " | " | G. C. Luther | 89 00 |
| " | 3. | Morse & Sons | 41 59 |
| " | " | H. A. Burlingame | 87 55 |
| " | 6. | T. C. Holloway | 34 00 |
| " | 8. | Tuttle & Hobbs | 181 00 |
| " | " | N. W. Eayrs | 242 32 |
| " | 10. | Thomas J. Tilley | 619 58 |
| " | " | D. C. Wood | 9 00 |
| " | 13. | Job Kenyon | 10 10 |
| " | 14. | N. E. Butt Co. | 10 50 |
| " | 15. | Pawtucket Lumber & Builders' Supplies Co. | 57 00 |
| " | " | H. C. Maine | 14 00 |
| " | " | Hartford, Prov. & Fishkill R. R. | 51 86 |
| " | " | J. H. & J. B. Sweet | 247 34 |
| " | " | Thomas H. Rhodes | 47 81 |
| " | " | W. E. Barrett & Co. | 511 12 |
| " | 17. | Hartford, Prov. & Fishkill R. R. Co. | 50 00 |
| " | 18. | W. C. Burlingame | 13 33 |
| " | " | Wm. H. Reynolds. Carriage trimmer | 8 00 |
| " | " | Fisk & Thompson | 33 57 |
| " | " | G. G. Hicks | 11 84 |
| " | " | Charles H. George & Co. | 32 87 |
| " | " | S. D. Andrews | 4 70 |
| " | " | Taylor, Symonds & Co. | 46 07 |

| July | 18. | Bugbee & Hall | 13 50 |
| " | " | R. E. Hamlin & Co | 13 10 |
| " | " | Samuel H. Bullock & Co | 234 85 |
| " | " | Mason, Chapin & Co | 21 83 |
| " | " | Congdon, Carpenter & Co | 9 22 |
| " | " | Day, Sprague & Co | 1,185 00 |
| " | " | Colwell & Winsor | 15 39 |
| " | " | Greene, Brayman & Co | 67 72 |
| " | " | C. Farnum & Co | 6 55 |
| " | " | Spicers & Peckham | 9 18 |
| " | " | Whitford, Aldrich & Co | 212 28 |
| " | " | Thomas W. Sprague | 41 30 |
| " | " | Henry T. Root | 78 09 |
| " | " | Hartwell, Richards & Co | 108 47 |
| " | " | W. Congdon & Sons | 20 00 |
| " | " | Waldron, Wightman & Co | 412 66 |
| " | " | Albert Dailey & Co | 8 70 |
| " | " | E. M. Aldrich & Co | 165 67 |
| " | " | Winsor & Brown | 158 90 |
| " | " | Hopkins & Pomroy | 34 55 |
| " | " | D. D. Sweet & Co | 30 25 |
| " | " | Chambers, Calder & Co | 45 10 |
| " | " | Dewing & Monsell | 39 06 |
| " | " | Coventry Company | 150 00 |
| " | " | F. Olds | 5 25 |
| " | " | H. C. Bishop & Co | 85 60 |
| " | " | A. Burgess & Co | 35 60 |
| " | 19. | Barker, Whitaker & Co | 37 45 |
| " | 20. | Somerset Potters' Works | 38 66 |
| " | 21. | A. Burgess & Co | 22 75 |
| " | " | Sayles & Greene | 25 00 |
| " | " | H. M. & A. A. Kimball | 6 40 |
| " | " | B. A. Whitcomb & Co | 36 00 |
| " | " | Comstocks & Co | 21 62 |
| " | " | D. D. Bucklin | 5 74 |
| " | " | Calef Bros | 13 58 |
| " | " | Rice, Draper & Co | 290 47 |
| " | " | Cairns & Williams | 25 00 |
| " | " | Rice & Hayward | 14 58 |
| " | " | George L. Claflin & Co | 102 84 |
| " | " | Alexander Mc Teer | 17 25 |
| " | 25. | Parsons, Bugbee & Co | 21 90 |
| " | 27. | Clapp & King | 8 43 |
| " | " | H. C. Burgess | 11 07 |
| " | " | Brownell & Barrows | 5 50 |

| | | | |
|---|---|---|---:|
| Aug't | 1. | George T. Perry | 75 00 |
| " | " | Pay-roll | 1,967 92 |
| " | 10. | Sweet & Arnold | 195 53 |
| " | " | Prov. Post Office | 2 53 |
| " | " | A. S. Potter | 1 50 |
| " | " | Wm. E. Clarke | 85 |
| " | " | Moulton & Ingraham | 96 |
| " | " | William Rowson | 4 37 |
| " | " | Builders' Iron Foundry | 1 56 |
| " | " | F. Coggeshall | 75 |
| " | " | Sampson, Davenport & Co | 3 00 |
| " | " | Tibbitts & Randall | 3 00 |
| " | " | Wm. W. Chapin. Cash items | 8 13 |
| " | " | Thomas.J. Tilley | 544 28 |
| " | " | Thomas W. Sprague | 15 50 |
| " | " | Chambers, Calder & Co | 37 89 |
| " | " | Waldron, Wightman & Co | 224 81 |
| " | " | Taylor, Symonds & Co | 330 75 |
| " | " | Parsons, Bugbee & Co | 149 21 |
| " | " | Morse & Sons | 17 46 |
| " | " | Barden & Keep | 17 46 |
| " | " | Greene, Brayman & Co | 50 40 |
| " | " | Congdon, Carpenter & Co | 21 58 |
| " | " | Charles H. George & Co | 18 10 |
| " | " | Whitford, Aldrich & Co | 110 73 |
| " | " | T. C. Holloway | 5 00 |
| " | " | Thomas H. Rhodes | 22 89 |
| " | " | Wm. H. Haskell & Co | 5 70 |
| " | " | James Tucker, Jr | 33 41 |
| " | " | William Sweeney | 35 00 |
| " | 11. | Cleveland Bros | 96 00 |
| " | 12. | J. H. & J. B. Sweet | 244 99 |
| " | 15. | Hartford, Prov. & Fishkill R. R. | 30 67 |
| " | " | George H. Copeland & Co | 6 00 |
| " | 22. | Charles E. Kennedy | 36 75 |
| " | " | George Chatterton | 19 61 |
| " | " | Johnson & Whaley | 156 03 |
| " | " | A. Shackford | 90 00 |
| " | " | A. G. Shippee | 69 75 |
| " | " | H. M. Blaisdell | 67 00 |
| " | 30. | George W. Wightman | 895 20 |
| Sept. | 2. | Pay-roll | 1,896 75 |
| " | 6. | Henry T. Brown & Co | 3 75 |
| " | " | E. L. Valentine | 6 00 |

| | | | |
|---|---|---|---:|
| Sept. | 6. | L. Upham & Co | 75 |
| " | " | Albert G. Shippee | 5 00 |
| " | " | A. J. Sanborn | 4 42 |
| " | " | Estate of Almoran Harris | 3 50 |
| " | " | Wm. G. Ward | 1 00 |
| " | " | Wm. W. Chapin. Cash items | 3 04 |
| " | 8. | Thomas J. Tilley | 695 44 |
| " | 12. | Taylor, Symonds & Co | 217 60 |
| " | " | Day, Sons & Co | 144 75 |
| " | " | Samuel H. Bullock & Co | 204 84 |
| " | " | Congdon & Aylsworth | 77 50 |
| " | " | Thomas W. Sprague | 15 50 |
| " | " | Geo. Hawes & Sons | 12 00 |
| " | " | R. I. Cement Drain Pipe Co | 42 00 |
| " | " | H. M. & A. A Kimball | 8 01 |
| " | " | Wm. Barstow & Co | 88 80 |
| " | " | Charles H. West | 200 00 |
| " | " | Waldron, Wightman & Co | 158 73 |
| " | " | B. G. Chace & Co | 28 92 |
| " | " | Parsons, Bugbee & Co | 103 93 |
| " | " | Edward F. Curtis | 16 75 |
| " | " | E. M. Aldrich & Co | 15 56 |
| " | " | Congdon, Carpenter & Co | 32 37 |
| " | " | J. H. & J. B. Sweet | 186 86 |
| " | " | Whitford, Aldrich & Co | 82 71 |
| " | " | Greene, Brayman & Co | 53 60 |
| " | " | Barker, Whitaker & Co | 45 15 |
| " | " | Hartford, Prov. & Fishkill R. R | 35 23 |
| " | 13. | Wm. B. Blanding | 99 73 |
| " | 30. | George W. Wightman | 231 06 |
| Oct. | 2. | Charles H. Scrutton | 15 00 |
| " | " | Henry D. Griswold | 78 00 |
| " | 4. | Pay-roll | 1,881 44 |
| " | 3. | Barden & Keep | 46 08 |
| " | " | Field & Cory | 256 25 |
| " | " | Samuel H. Bullock & Co | 209 00 |
| " | " | Thomas J. Wardwell | 12 90 |
| " | " | W. Morlock & Co | 20 86 |
| " | " | Rob't Hogg | 14 12 |
| " | 12. | Thomas J. Tilley | 714 26 |
| " | 13. | Hartford, Prov. & Fishkill R. R | 24 39 |
| " | 14. | Tuttle & Hobbs | 178 00 |
| " | 18. | Clapp & King | 12 01 |
| " | " | George H. Copeland & Co | 9 00 |

| | | | | |
|---|---|---|---|---|
| Oct. | 18. | Congdon, Carpenter & Co.............. ......... | 41 | 12 |
| " | " | Parsons, Bugbee & Co.......................... | 38 | 73 |
| " | " | Thomas W. Sprague......... .................... | 22 | 58 |
| " | " | Hartwell, Richards & Co........................ | 11 | 57 |
| " | " | J. H. & J. B. Sweet.... ...................... | 248 | 88 |
| " | " | E. M. Aldrich & Co.......................... .. | 105 | 30 |
| " | " | R. E. Hamlin & Co....................,........ | 36 | 07 |
| " | " | Henry T. Root................................ | 16 | 05 |
| " | " | Charles H. George & Co............. ........... | 33 | 52 |
| " | " | Barker, Whitaker & Co............... .......... | 7 | 78 |
| " | " | Wm. B. Blanding. ,........................... | 27 | 04 |
| " | " | Tillinghast & Sherman......................... | 177 | 56 |
| " | " | Bugbee & Hall.... ................... ............. | 10 | 08 |
| " | " | Adams Bros........................,........... | 18 | 25 |
| " | " | Brownell & Barrows.......................... | 5 | 25 |
| " | " | Congdon & Aylesworth............... ......... | 72 | 00 |
| " | " | B. G. Chace & Co.... ......................... | 36 | 99 |
| " | " | Edward F. Curtis............................. | 69 | 50 |
| " | " | Waldron, Wightman & Co.... ... ... . ........ | 30 | 12 |
| " | " | Henry M. Angell & Co...................... .... | 131 | 54 |
| " | " | Comstocks & Co......................,......... | 91 | 01 |
| " | " | Whitford, Aldrich & Co........................ | 165 | 32 |
| " | " | D. D. Sweet & Co....,........................ | 31 | 00 |
| " | " | Greene, Brayman & Co......................... | 85 | 06 |
| " | " | Taylor, Symonds & Co .. ... ................... | 124 | 67 |
| " | " | E. L. Freeman & Co ......................... | 7 | 88 |
| " | " | Chambers, Calder & Co........................ | 34 | 50 |
| " | 19. | James B. Tallman.... ............... .. ...... | 25 | 00 |
| " | " | A. Burgess & Co............................... | 94 | 09 |
| " | " | George L. Claflin & Co. ...................... | 23 | 90 |
| " | " | A. Shackford.................................. | 15 | 96 |
| " | 20. | Prov. Post Office...., . .................... | 2 | 50 |
| " | " | L. D. Anthony & Co. ......................... | 4 | 50 |
| " | " | Henry Hardon............................... | 3 | 00 |
| " | " | E. L. Valentine............................. | 9 | 00 |
| " | " | Adams Express Co.... .. ... ........... | | 50 |
| " | " | L. Upham & Co............................... | 1 | 75 |
| " | " | C. Farnum & Co.......................... .. ... .... | 1 | 91 |
| " | " | A. A. White................................ | 3 | 47 |
| " | " | Wm. W. Chapin. Cash items........ ......... | | 24 |
| " | " | Anna Inman.......... ................. | 50 | 00 |
| Nov. | 2. | Pay-roll...................................... | 1,811 | 94 |
| " | 3. | Hartford, Prov. & Fishkill R. R.............. ... | 29 | 11 |
| " | 4. | Nelson Titus.... ........................... | 225 | 00 |
| " | " | Thomas J. Tilley............................. | 671 | 39 |

6

| Nov. | 4.  | Henry W. Ellis, Ag't .......................... | 23 50 |
|------|-----|------------------------------------------------|--------|
| "    | 6.  | George H. Snow.................................. | 112 50 |
| "    | "   | James P. Root.................................... | 35 55 |
| "    | "   | Lincoln M'f'g Co................................ | 191 28 |
| "    | 13. | S. S. Sprague & Co.............................. | 931 09 |
| "    | 17. | George W. Wightman............................. | 224 57 |
| "    | "   | Charles H. Hunt. ............................. | 43 00 |
| "    | 18. | Hartwell, Richards & Co......................... | 28 69 |
| "    | "   | Edward F. Curtis................................ | 96 63 |
| "    | "   | Waldron, Wightman & Co......................... | 300 91 |
| "    | "   | Thomas W. Sprague.............................. | 18 50 |
| "    | "   | Parsons, Bugbee & Co............................ | 53 76 |
| "    | "   | J. H. & J. B. Sweet............................. | 266 32 |
| "    | "   | Wm. B. Blanding................................ | 59 76 |
| "    | "   | Charles H. George & Co.......................... | 40 54 |
| "    | "   | Barker, Whitaker & Co........................... | 6 19 |
| "    | "   | E. M. Aldrich & Co.............................. | 64 87 |
| "    | "   | Taylor, Symonds & Co........................... | 384 77 |
| "    | "   | S. D. Andrews.................................. | 160 77 |
| "    | "   | Rose & Walker.................................. | 91 25 |
| "    | "   | Whitford, Aldrich & Co.......................... | 136 81 |
| "    | "   | John H. Eddy & Co.............................. | 166 26 |
| "    | "   | Colwell & Winsor .............................. | 89 95 |
| "    | "   | Wm. E. Barrett & Co............................ | 162 27 |
| "    | "   | W. S. Fifield................................... | 39 50 |
| "    | "   | Congdon & Aylesworth........................... | 60 00 |
| "    | "   | Congdon, Carpenter & Co........................ | 14 41 |
| "    | "   | N. W. Eayrs.................................... | 20 00 |
| "    | "   | George I. Chace................................ | 34 95 |
| "    | "   | Thomas Coggeshall............................. | 31 90 |
| "    | "   | Samuel W. Church.............................. | 5 25 |
| "    | "   | Peckham, Ralph & Co............................ | 217 78 |
| "    | "   | J. B. Barnaby & Co.............................. | 139 13 |
| "    | "   | Wm. H. Fenner & Co............................ | 26 58 |
| "    | "   | Hopkins & Pomroy .............................. | 65 40 |
| "    | 21. | Perkins & Tucker............................... | 996 53 |
| "    | 25. | George Campbell................................ | 39 88 |
| "    | 29. | Preston & Brown................................ | 54 |
| "    | "   | E. L. Valentine................................. | 9 00 |
| "    | "   | Calendar, McAuslan & Troupe.................... | 2 80 |
| "    | "   | D. D. Bucklin................................... | 25 |
| "    | "   | Morse & Sons................................... | 4 00 |
| "    | "   | A. A. White.................................... | 60 |
| "    | "   | J. T. Walker & Hammond, N. York ............... | 3 25 |

| Nov. | 29. | Wm. W. Chapin. Cash items.................... | 1 | 78 |
|---|---|---|---|---|
| " | " | G. & C. P. Hutchins............................ | 77 | 59 |
| " | " | Adams Bros.................................... | 459 | 90 |
| " | " | Thomas Phillips & Co......................... | 528 | 22 |
| " | " | Pay-roll.... ................................. | 1,643 | 96 |
| Dec. | 2. | Hartford, Prov. & Fishkill R. R................. | 67 | 26 |
| " | 7. | Day, Sons & Co......... ..... | 157 | 25 |
| " | " | A. Shackford................................. | 10 | 00 |
| " | " | R. I. Cement Drain Pipe Co.................... | 65 | 06 |
| " | " | Edward F. Curtis. ........................... | 110 | 50 |
| " | " | J. B. Barnaby & Co............................. | 245 | 50 |
| " | " | Hartwell, Richards & Co...................... | 7 | 83 |
| " | " | Congdon, Carpenter & Co..................... | 4 | 22 |
| " | " | Chambers, Calder & Co....................... | 13 | 75 |
| " | " | Dexter Asylum............................... . | 8 | 00 |
| " | " | Thomas J. Tilley............................. | 280 | 87 |
| " | 9. | F. Coggeshall.............................,..... | 12 | 75 |
| " | " | Greene, Brayman & Co ....................... | 28 | 08 |
| " | " | J. H. & J. B. Sweet........................... | 259 | 95 |
| " | " | Congdon & Aylesworth....................... | 76 | 00 |
| " | " | E. M. Aldrich & Co........................... | 193 | 42 |
| " | " | Barker, Whitaker & Co......... .............. | 21 | 11 |
| " | " | R. E. Hamlin & Co............................ | 41 | 89 |
| " | " | A. Burgess & Co............................. | 72 | 48 |
| " | " | Whitford, Aldrich & Co................. .. .... | 203 | 70 |
| " | " | Parsons, Bugbee & Co........................ | 60 | 85 |
| " | " | Waldron, Wightman & Co........... .......... | 154 | 28 |
| " | " | George L. Claflin & Co............... . ...... | 49 | 35 |
| " | " | Taylor, Symonds & Co........ ............... | 324 | 34 |
| " | " | Charles H. George & Co.................. ... | 9 | 69 |
| " | " | Thomas W. Sprague........................... | 80 | 25 |
| " | " | Barden & Keep............................... | 5 | 72 |
| " | 13. | James Tucker, Jr............................ | 83 | 04 |
| " | " | Dudley, Parkhurst Co.................. ... | 53 | 78 |
| " | " | Charles F. Pope.............................. | 14 | 83 |
| " | " | Builders' Iron Foundry.............. .. ....... | 9 | 13 |
| " | " | Samuel H. Brayton.. .. ..................... | 150 | 00 |
| " | 14. | Walker, Pratt & Co. Boston, Mass.....,....,.. | 781 | 60 |
| " | " | L. Brayton & Co.............................. | 253 | 82 |
| " | 18. | George E. Wright & Co. Boston, Mass.......... | 25 | 60 |
| " | 21. | D. N. Davis & Co............................. | 50 | 28 |
| " | " | Prov. Steam & Gas Pipe Co................. . | 12 | 30 |
| " | " | W. Congdon & Sons... ..................... | 18 | 38 |
| " | " | Dewing & Monsell............................. | 92 | 35 |
| " | 23. | Rice & Hayward........................... | 57 | 52 |

| Dec. | 26. | Henry D. Griswold............................ | 20 75 |
| " | 27, | Charles S. Hoyt.................... ............ | 20 50 |
| " | 30. | Anna Inman.................................. | 25.00 |
| " | " | George T. Perry.............................. | 150 00 |
| " | " | George W. Wightman........ .. ............ . .. | 800 65 |
| " | " | Charles H. Hunt.............................. | 49 85 |
| " | " | F. W. Perry.............................. ... | 20 05 |
| " | " | W. W. Chapin................................ | 86 05 |
| " | " | Providence Board of Trade ..................... | 9 36 |
| " | " | Pay-roll for December......................... | 1,387 50 |
| | | | $76,044 51 |

### RESOURCES.

The following statement is a classification of the Resources and Expenditures for the year ending Dec. 31, 1876.

| | |
|---|---|
| Balance on deposit in R. I. Hospital Trust Co., January 1, 1876 | 6,690 04 |
| Balance of appropriation of 1875 ........................... | 5,000 00 |
| Appropriation of 1876........................................ | 70,000 00 |
| From board of insane.... ................................. | 15,759 68 |
| " " " poor in Almshouse.......................... | 79 04 |
| " interest on deposits in R. I. Hospital Trust Co........... | 74 27 |
| " costs collected.................................... | 164 20 |
| " sale of farm produce............................... | 843 05 |
| " " " old junk &c........................... | 246 09 |
| " rent.................................................... | 172 66 |
| " sale of baskets...................................... | 918 95 |

| | | | |
|---|---|---|---|
| " Prison Commission for materials bought, labor hired, &c.......... . . ..................... | 3,515 65 | |
| material from farm......................... | 80 00 | |
| labor of inmates & teams.................. | 6,752 41 | |
| | | 10,298 06 |
| " labor of inmates & teams on other work................ | | 291 80 |
| " sundries.... ...................................... | | 42 08 |
| | | $110,579 92 |

### EXPENDITURES.

Construction.

| | | | |
|---|---|---|---|
| Insane Asylum. | Completion of cottage for excited patients...................... | 1,142 54 | |
| " " | Completion of cottage for Deputy. | 127 60 | |
| Almshouse. | Completion of improvement........ | 711 00 | |
| Barn ... ................................. .... | | 1,365 46 | |
| | | | 3,346 60 |
| Subsistence... ...........................,,............. | | | 25,709 65 |

Farm expenses

| | | |
|---|---:|---:|
| Live stock purchased............................. | 2,238 66 | |
| Vehicles, harness, farming implements, &c., &c ... | 1,796 48 | |
| Marure.............................. ............. | 988 25 | |
| Grain for stock........... .................... | 3,116 28 | |
| Hay................................... ........... | 2,721 31 | |
| Straw......................... ................... | 310 76 | |
| Seeds, including potatoes........................ | 461 40 | |
| Sundries................................... ..... | 160 75 | |
| | | 11,793 89 |

| | |
|---|---:|
| Fuel, including freight to Oaklawn............... ......... | 5,964 13 |
| Furniture ...................................... | 2,894 10 |
| Repairs and improvements..,..,................... | 2,817 76 |
| Clothing and bedding..................................... | 5,957 05 |
| Insurance ...................................... ........ | 1,024 70 |
| Salaries .................................. ....... | 19,322 67 |
| Removal of paupers and expenses of Superintendent of State Charities and Corrections, including salary and travelling expenses of Superintendent . .............................. | 2,436 41 |
| Travelling expenses of the Board...................... ....... | 141 00 |
| Rewards for returning escaped inmates................... .. | 141 60 |
| Legal expenses............................................. | 25 00 |
| Freight, exclusive of coal................................. | 460 53 |
| Postage and telegraphing ................................ | 99 68 |
| Transportation of inmates and officers on duty................ | 224 42 |
| Lights...................... ................. ............... | 548 06 |
| Medical supplies........................................... | 388 41 |
| Stationery....... ........................................ | 264 29 |
| Basket timber, and supplies................................ | 450 37 |
| Fire apparatus........... . .......................... ............. | 654 24 |
| Miscellaneous......................................... ..... | 267 74 |
| Material and hired labor for Prison Commission.............. | 3,515 65 |
| Paid indebtedness of 1875................................. | 5,867 33 |
| | 94,315 28 |

| | | |
|---|---:|---:|
| Balance due from the Treasury................... | 18,740 78 | |
| Less balance of book accounts. (Net indebtedness.) | 2,476 14 | |
| Available balance after settling all accounts.................. | | 16,264 64 |
| | | $110,579 92 |

Respectfully submitted,

WILLIAM W. CHAPIN, *Secretary.*

# Statistics of the State Workhouse.

|  | 1876 | Previously. | Total. |
|---|---|---|---|
| Committed | 545 | 2914 | 3459 |
| Discharged | 509 | 2238 | 2747 |
| Escaped | 57 | 379 | 436 |
| Died | 0 | 18 | 18 |

|  | Males. | Females. | Total. |
|---|---|---|---|
| Number of inmates Jan. 1, 1876 | 206 | 73 | 279 |
| Committed during 1876 | 368 | 132 | 500 |
| Escaped inmates recommitted during 1876 | 45 | 0 | 45 |
| Total | 619 | 205 | 824 |
| Discharged during 1876 | 361 | 148 | 509 |
| Escaped during 1876 | 57 | 0 | 57 |
| Total | 418 | 148 | 566 |
| Remaining Jan. 1st, 1877 | 201 | 57 | 258 |

## STATISTICS OF PERSONS COMMITTED.

|  | 1876. | Previously. | Total. |
|---|---|---|---|
| **SEX** | | | |
| Males | 413 | 2112 | 2525 |
| Females | 132 | 802 | 934 |
| **RACE.** | | | |
| White | 524 | 2784 | 3308 |
| Colored | 21 | 127 | 148 |
| Indians | 0 | 3 | 3 |
| **BIRTH PLACE.** | | | |
| United States | 295 | 1407 | 1702 |

Foreign Countries :—

| | 1876. | Previously. | Total. |
|---|---|---|---|
| Ireland | 183 | 1129 | 1312 |
| England | 39 | 199 | 238 |
| Scotland | 8 | 78 | 86 |
| Canada | 3 | 27 | 30 |
| Nova Scotia | 6 | 26 | 32 |
| New Brunswick | 0 | 17 | 17 |
| France | 3 | 4 | 7 |
| Germany | 2 | 9 | 11 |
| Sweden | 1 | 2 | 3 |
| Prussia | 0 | 3 | 3 |
| East Indies | 0 | 3 | 3 |
| Spain | 0 | 2 | 2 |
| Italy | 0 | 2 | 2 |
| Mexico | 0 | 1 | 1 |
| New Foundland | 0 | 1 | 1 |
| St. Helena, Island of | 0 | 1 | 1 |
| Western Islands | 0 | 1 | 1 |
| Calcutta | 1 | 0 | 1 |
| At Sea | 1 | 0 | 1 |
| Unknown | 3 | 2 | 5 |
| Total | 545 | 2914 | 3459 |

### BIRTH PLACE OF PARENTS.

| | 1876. | Previously. | Total. |
|---|---|---|---|
| United States | 134 | 745 | 879 |
| Ireland | 340 | 1775 | 2115 |
| England | 40 | 217 | 257 |
| Scotland | 12 | 88 | 100 |
| France | 1 | 10 | 11 |
| British America | 7 | 53 | 60 |
| Germany | 3 | 10 | 13 |
| Prussia | 0 | 3 | 3 |
| Sweden | 1 | 2 | 3 |
| Italy | 0 | 2 | 2 |
| East Indies | 1 | 1 | 2 |
| West Indies | 0 | 1 | 1 |
| Mexico | 0 | 1 | 1 |
| South America | 0 | 1 | 1 |
| Unknown | 6 | 5 | 11 |
| Total | 545 | 2914 | 3459 |

| AGE. | 1876. | Previously. | Total. |
|---|---|---|---|
| Under      20 years | 22 | 185 | 207 |
| From 20 to 30    " | 191 | 841 | 1032 |
|     "    30 to 40    " | 171 | 812 | 963 |
|     "    40 to 50    " | 102 | 613 | 715 |
|     "    50 to 60    " | 42 | 311 | 353 |
|     "    60 to 70    " | 13 | 108 | 121 |
|     "    70 to 80    " | 3 | 37 | 40 |
| Over        90    " | 1 | 6 | 7 |
| Unknown | 0 | 1 | 1 |
| Total | 545 | 2914 | 3459 |

| OCCUPATION. | | | |
|---|---|---|---|
| Bakers | 4 | 18 | 22 |
| Barbers | 5 | 24 | 29 |
| Basket maker | 0 | 1 | 1 |
| Bell hanger | 0 | 1 | 1 |
| Blacksmiths | 4 | 47 | 51 |
| Bleachers | 0 | 5 | 5 |
| Boiler makers | 4 | 7 | 11 |
| Bookkeepers | 5 | 10 | 15 |
| Boot fitters | 1 | 1 | 2 |
| Box makers | 2 | 4 | 6 |
| Brakemen | 8 | 9 | 17 |
| Brass workers | 0 | 3 | 3 |
| Brokers | 0 | 1 | 1 |
| Butchers | 1 | 15 | 16 |
| Confectioner | 1 | 0 | 1 |
| Cabinet makers | 3 | 9 | 12 |
| Carpenters | 5 | 99 | 104 |
| Cigar makers | 0 | 8 | 8 |
| Clerks | 4 | 21 | 25 |
| Clothes cleaner | 0 | 1 | 1 |
| Comb maker | 0 | 1 | 1 |
| Cooks | 8 | 46 | 54 |
| Coopers | 2 | 4 | 6 |
| Curriers | 1 | 4 | 5 |
| Cutler | 0 | 1 | 1 |
| Draughtsmen | 1 | 3 | 4 |
| Dress makers | 5 | 18 | 23 |
| Dyers | 0 | 11 | 11 |
| Engineers | 5 | 14 | 19 |
| Farmers | 5 | 45 | 50 |

| OCCUPATION (*Continued.*) | 1876. | Previously. | Total. |
|---|---|---|---|
| File cutters | 1 | 2 | 3 |
| Firemen | 0 | 2 | 2 |
| Gardeners | 0 | 12 | 12 |
| Gas fitters | 0 | 11 | 11 |
| Grocers | 0 | 2 | 2 |
| Hair drawer | 0 | 1 | 1 |
| Hair dresser | 0 | 1 | 1 |
| Harness makers | 2 | 9 | 11 |
| Hatter | 0 | 1 | 1 |
| Hostlers | 10 | 73 | 83 |
| House servants | 61 | 181 | 242 |
| Housewives | 14 | 139 | 253 |
| Jewelers | 18 | 66 | 84 |
| Laborers | 179 | 1186 | 1365 |
| Lawyers | 1 | 1 | 2 |
| Leather japanner | 0 | 1 | 1 |
| Machinists | 16 | 89 | 105 |
| Marble workers | 0 | 5 | 5 |
| Masons | 7 | 67 | 74 |
| Mender of china ware | 0 | 1 | 1 |
| Merchants | 0 | 3 | 3 |
| Mill hands | 20 | 35 | 55 |
| Moulders | 5 | 36 | 41 |
| Musicians | 0 | 7 | 7 |
| Music teacher | 1 | 1 | 2 |
| Painters | 17 | 76 | 93 |
| Pedlers | 4 | 17 | 21 |
| Photographers | 2 | 2 | 4 |
| Physicians | 0 | 3 | 3 |
| Plumbers | 0 | 2 | 2 |
| Preacher | 0 | 1 | 1 |
| Printers | 1 | 18 | 19 |
| Quarrymen | 3 | 0 | 3 |
| Sailors | 6 | 31 | 37 |
| Saloon keepers | 0 | 2 | 2 |
| Sail makers | 1 | 7 | 8 |
| School teachers | 2 | 0 | 2 |
| Seamstresses | 5 | 14 | 19 |
| Servants and waiters | 18 | 27 | 45 |
| Ship carpenters | 0 | 6 | 6 |
| Ship riggers | 0 | 3 | 3 |
| Shoe makers | 11 | 58 | 69 |

|  | 1876. | Previously. | Total. |
|---|---|---|---|
| **OCCUPATION** (*Continued.*) | | | |
| Silver polishers | 0 | 6 | 6 |
| Soldier | 0 | 1 | 1 |
| Spinners | 10 | 39 | 49 |
| Steam pipe workers | 0 | 2 | 2 |
| Stone cutters | 6 | 6 | 12 |
| Stucco worker | 0 | 1 | 1 |
| Tailors | 9 | 41 | 50 |
| Tanner | 0 | 1 | 1 |
| Teamsters | 11 | 63 | 74 |
| Tinsmith | 1 | 5 | 6 |
| Trader | 0 | 2 | 2 |
| Washers and Ironers | 6 | 25 | 31 |
| Weavers | 18 | 46 | 64 |
| Wheelwrights | 0 | 2 | 2 |
| White washers | 3 | 6 | 9 |
| Wool sorters | 0 | 4 | 4 |
| Wool spinner | 0 | 1 | 1 |
| Unknown | 2 | 33 | 35 |
| Total | 545 | 2914 | 3459 |

| **TIME OF COMMITMENT.** | | | |
|---|---|---|---|
| January | 50 | 169 | 219 |
| February | 32 | 122 | 254 |
| March | 46 | 183 | 229 |
| April | 36 | 146 | 182 |
| May | 47 | 240 | 287 |
| June | 52 | 282 | 334 |
| July | 44 | 325 | 369 |
| August | 51 | 343 | 394 |
| September | 43 | 332 | 375 |
| October | 41 | 293 | 334 |
| November | 46 | 251 | 297 |
| December | 57 | 228 | 285 |
| Total | 545 | 2914 | 3459 |

**OFFENCES FOR WHICH COMMITTED.**

| | 1876 | Previously | Total |
|---|---|---|---|
| Being common drunkards | 292 | 1920 | 2212 |
| "　vagrants | 127 | 498 | 625 |
| "　common prostitutes | 50 | 167 | 217 |
| "　railers and brawlers | 3 | 48 | 51 |
| "　sturdy beggars | 17 | 43 | 60 |
| "　common cheats and swindlers | 2 | 0 | 2 |

|  | 1876. | Previously. | Total. |
|---|---|---|---|
| **OFFENCES FOB WHICH COMMITTED, (*Continued.*)** | | | |
| Neglect to support families | 7 | 51 | 58 |
| Larceny | 1 | 13 | 14 |
| House breaking | 0 | 5 | 5 |
| Revelling | 0 | 4 | 4 |
| Assault | 0 | 4 | 4 |
| Night walking | 0 | 4 | 4 |
| Obstructing officer | 0 | 1 | 1 |
| Maintaining common nuisance | 0 | 1 | 1 |
| Intent to commit rape | 0 | 1 | 1 |
| Transfer'd from Prov. Reform school | 0 | 1 | 1 |
| Wilfully escaping | 45 | 153 | 198 |
| Malicious Mischief | 1 | 0 | 1 |
| **Total** | 545 | 2914 | 3459 |

**PLACES FROM WHICH COMMITTED.**

|  | 1876. | Previously. | Total. |
|---|---|---|---|
| Providence | 365 | 1885 | 2250 |
| North Providence | 0 | 271 | 271 |
| Pawtucket | 23 | 145 | 168 |
| Newport | 33 | 126 | 159 |
| Woonsocket | 15 | 124 | 139 |
| Johnston | 8 | 60 | 68 |
| Bristol | 4 | 43 | 47 |
| East Providence | 20 | 41 | 61 |
| Cranston | 8 | 40 | 48 |
| Lincoln | 11 | 35 | 46 |
| Warwick | 4 | 23 | 27 |
| Burrillville | 7 | 24 | 31 |
| Smithfield | 1 | 23 | 24 |
| Westerly | 9 | 17 | 26 |
| Coventry | 0 | 12 | 12 |
| Warren | 13 | 11 | 24 |
| East Greenwich | 2 | 8 | 10 |
| West Greenwich | 0 | 1 | 1 |
| South Kingstown | 18 | 8 | 26 |
| North Kingstown | 1 | 4 | 5 |
| Scituate | 1 | 4 | 5 |
| Glocester | 0 | 2 | 2 |
| Tiverton | 0 | 2 | 2 |
| Exeter | 0 | 2 | 2 |
| Barrington | 0 | 1 | 1 |
| Foster | 0 | 1 | 1 |
| Richmond | 2 | 1 | 3 |
| **Total** | 545 | 2914 | 3459 |

| TERMS OF SENTENCE. | 1876. | Previously. | Total. |
|---|---|---|---|
| Three months..................... | 0.............. | 2.......... | 2 |
| Six        "        .................... | 439............. | 2139......... | 2578 |
| Eight    "        .................... | 0............. | 109..... | ...109 |
| Nine      ..      .................... | 0............. | 65.......... | 65 |
| Ten        ..      .................... | 5............. | 45.......... | 50 |
| Eleven    .      .................... | 0............. | 1.......... | 1 |
| Twelve    '        .................... | 77............. | 455......... | 532 |
| Fifteen    '        ...........·....... | 0............. | 3.......... | 3 |
| Sixteen    "        ....... ........... | 0 ............ | 1.......... | 1 |
| Eighteen "        .................... | 3............. .. | 14......... | 17 |
| Two years...................... | 16............. | 28.......... | 44 |
| Two years five months and six days. | 0............. | 1.. ........ | 1 |
| Two years and six months........... | 0............. | 1.......... | 1 |
| Three years ...................... | 5............. | 49 ........ | 54 |
| Three years and six months........ | 0............. | 1.......... | 1 |
| Total..................... | 545............. | 2914......... | 3459 |

### RECOMMITMENTS.

| Had been previously committed once........................... ...... | 94 |
|---|---|
|    "       "       "     twice ............................. | 50 |
|    "       "       "    three times.  .............  .....  .... | 41 |
|                  "    four times...........  ............ | 22 |
|                  "    five times........................... | 16 |
|                  "    six times......................... | 7 |
|                  "    seven times........................ | 3 |
|                  "    eight times.. ....................... | 3 |
|    "       "       "    nine times........ ... ............ | 2 |
| Never before committed................................. ............ | 307 |
| Total............................................... | 545 |

### EDUCATIONAL STATISTICS.

| Number of inmates who can read and write........................... | 361 |
|---|---|
|    "       "       "    read only.............................. | 71 |
|    "       "       "    neither read nor write.................. | 113 |
| Total................................................. | 545 |

### SOCIAL CONDITION.

| Married........... ............. ............................. | 212 |
|---|---|
| Single............................................. | 333 |
| Total................................................. | 545 |

## RELIGION.

Protestant............................................................187
Catholic..............................................................358
_____

Total...............................................................545

## STATE FARM.

### CROPS, 1876.

Apples.................................................. ..... 572 bbls.
Beef.................................. ........................ 23,596 lbs.
Beans, white........ . .................................... 6 bushels.
   "   string............................................... 18   "
   "   shell..................................... ............... 9½   "
Beets .................................................... ......... 252   "
   "   Mangel Wurzel ....................... ................ 13 tons.
Corn, in the ear....................................... ....... 300 bushels.
   "   green ···································· 7,092 ears.
Cabbage............................................... ..... 9,333 lbs.
Carrots................................................... 21 tons.
Cucumbers ............................................... 50 bushels.
Corn fodder.............................................. 5 tons.
Hay...................................................... 40 "
Hides............... ..................................... 2,881 lbs.
Melons.................. ................................. 400.
Millet .............................................. ............. 3 tons.
Milk. .. ................................... .............. ...... 8,186 gals.
Onions................................................... 79 bushels.
Peas....... ................................................. 37½   "
Pigs,—sold for $520 50..... .............................. 78.   .
Pork........ ...... ...................................... 8,038 lbs.
Potatoes............................................ .... ............ 1,647 bushels.
Pumpkins .......................................... ...... 6,764 lbs.
Rye...................................................... ... ................ 140 bushels.
Rye straw................................................ ..... 5 tons.
Tallow ....................................................... . 1,688 lbs.
Turnips, round ......................................... 607 bushels.
   "   French.. ........................... ......... ........ 984   "
Tomatoes .............................................. 150   "
Squash...................................... .............. 10,000 lbs.
Veal.... ................................. .............. 871   "

# Chaplain's Report.

---

*To the Board of State Charities and Corrections :*

GENTLEMEN :—The following report is offered by the Chaplain :

For the larger part of the past year, religious worship and instruction at the State Farm were conducted by various clergymen and laymen who were secured through the persevering efforts of Mr. George H. Slade, and the Chairman of the Board.

During the brief period since my appointment as Chaplain, it has been my privilege to hold a stated religious service on Sundays in the chapel of the House of Correction. The attendance of all the inmates able to be present, is made obligatory by the Superintendent, for the general welfare of the institution as well as the good of each one. The large company assembled has been orderly and attentive, and there has been a marked increase of apparent interest in the exercises. The singing has improved very greatly, and especially since the efficient service in the playing of the organ afforded by an inmate, formerly an organist in one of the larger city churches.

It is sad to contemplate the work of desolation which intemperance and its associated vices have wrought, and the impressions upon the minds of those who are called to address such an audience are necessarily in a degree painful. Yet the possibility of the reformation of some, is a sufficient motive for earnest and constant endeavor to secure that result. The steady discipline pursued here, is highly favorable to the forming of right habits, and the religious instruction given in the chapel and at other times is intended to communicate higher ideas of life, to stimulate courage to do right, to inspire a hopeful feeling with the discouraged, and especially to strengthen the moral principle of the many, who on their return to society, are to be exposed once more to trying temptations. The recognized presence of a Higher Power, and the helpful love of a Saviour have been enforced as the best reliance,—the only sure help—of those so liable to fall again from the place of safety, and drift away from the responsibilities of life, becoming still more hardened and reckless. The inefficiency of mere resolutions and good desires have been so frequently illustrated in the experience of numbers who have repeatedly returned to the institution, that the need of a radical change of character can be demonstrated without much argument. It is hoped that the time may soon come when it will be practicable to sustain a Sabbath School as well as preaching and singing services. The evening schools, operated under the supervision of the officers, and taught by inmates of the institution, have proved valuable aids to many, who, though commencing late in life, are making good progress in their studies.

I have been called upon to attend several funerals in the Alms-house, and other religious services have been held there. As much time as could be spared from parish duties has been devoted to visits among the sick and feeble in that building.

Respectfully submitted,

JAMES PIERCE ROOT,

*Chaplain.*

# Report of the Physician.

To the Board of State Charities and Corrections :

GENTLEMEN :—The undersigned respectfully submits the following report for the year 1876 :

The health of the male inmates of the Workhouse and House of Correction has been remarkably good, and no deaths have occurred in the institution during the year. One hundred and thirty-three have been under treatment for the following complaints :—

| | | | |
|---|---|---|---|
| Abscess | 1 | Inflammation of the stomach | 1 |
| Bronchitis | 6 | Lumbago | 2 |
| Chills | 1 | Neuralgia | 3 |
| Delirium Tremens | 9 | Nervous and general debility | 19 |
| Diarrhœa | 9 | Ophthalmia | 3 |
| Dysentery | 1 | Palpitation of the heart | 2 |
| Ear ache | 1 | Phthisis | 1 |
| Eczema | 1 | Rheumatism | 24 |
| Gonorrhœa | 7 | Sore throat | 6 |
| Hemorrhoids | 3 | Syphilis | 3 |
| Hemorrhage of the lungs | 2 | Syphilitic sore throat | 2 |
| Headache | 9 | Vertigo | 1 |
| Indolent ulcer | 4 | Wounds | 3 |
| Indigestion | 9 | | |
| Total | | | 133 |

In the Asylum for the Insane fifty-four patients have been treated, of whom twenty died. Their diseases were as follows :—

| Recovered, or still under treatment. | | Died. | |
|---|---|---|---|
| Abscess | 2 | Chronic Diarrhœa | 1 |
| Asthma | 1 | Diarrhœa | 3 |
| Bronchitis | 1 | Dropsy | 1 |
| Chronic Diarrhœa | 1 | Epilepsy | 3 |
| Diarrhœa | 8 | General debility | 4 |
| Eczema | 2 | Maniacal exhaustion | 2 |
| Epilepsy | 2 | Old age | 3 |
| General debility | 5 | Paralysis | 2 |
| Jaundice | 1 | Softening of the brain | 1 |
| Paralysis | 3 | | |
| Rheumatism | 7 | | |
| Softening of the brain | 1 | | |

In the Almshouse I have had one hundred and sixty-three patients, whose diseases are given herewith. Thirty-three have died.

Recovered, discharged, or still under treatment.      Died.

| | | | |
|---|---|---|---|
| Asthma | 3 | Aneurism | 1 |
| Bronchitis | 5 | Bronchitis | 1 |
| Cancer | 2 | Convulsions | 2 |
| Chills | 1 | Delirium tremens | 1 |
| Cancrum oris | 2 | Dysentery | 1 |
| Child-bed | 17 | Diarrhœa | 8 |
| Chronic diarrhœa | 2 | Dropsy | 1 |
| Constipation | 3 | General debility | 4 |
| Delirium tremens | 2 | Heart disease | 1 |
| Diarrhœa | 6 | Marasmus | 2 |
| Dyspepsia | 5 | Old age | 2 |
| Dropsy | 1 | Paralysis | 1 |
| Eczema | 2 | Phthisis | 7 |
| Gonorrhœa | 2 | Syphilis | 3 |
| Hemorrhoids | 2 | Softening of the brain | 1 |
| Indolent ulcer | 4 | Uterine cancer | 1 |
| Indigestion | 4 | Whooping cough | 1 |
| Influenza | 8 | | |
| Inflammation of the stomach | 1 | | |
| Leucorrhœa | 1 | | |
| Lumbago | 3 | | |
| Nervous and general debility | 8 | | |
| Neuralgia | 3 | | |
| Ophthalmia | 3 | | |
| Palpitation of the heart | 1 | | |
| Paralysis | 2 | | |
| Paralysis agitans | 1 | | |
| Phthisis | 11 | | |
| Rheumatism | 14 | | |
| Sore throat | 2 | | |
| Softening of the brain | 2 | | |
| Sprained ankle | 1 | | |
| Syphilis | 3 | | |
| Typhoid fever | 1 | | |
| Uterine hemorrhage | 2 | | |

Seventeen children have been born : fifteen of which—eight girls and seven boys,—were born alive.

GEORGE T. PERRY, M. D.

NATICK, R. I., January 1, 1877.

8

# Report of the Female Physician.

---

*To the Board of State Charities and Corrections :*

GENTLEMEN :—In conformity with your regulations, I submit the following annual report for 1876.

The number of cases which have come under my care, among the women of the Workhouse, during the year, is 249. The diseases are as follows :—

Uterine and urinary diseases, 115 ; Rheumatism and Neuralgia, 25 ; Coughs and Colds, 22 ; Dyspepsia and Indigestion, 35 ; General and Nervous Debility, 31 ; Miscellaneous, 21.

Number of prescriptions, 418.

> Very Respectfully,
>
> ANNA INMAN, M. D.

PROVIDENCE, January 1, 1877.

# ANNUAL REPORT

## OF THE

# Superintendent of State Charities and Corrections.

OFFICE OF THE SUPERINTENDENT OF STATE }
CHARITIES AND CORRECTIONS,
PROVIDENCE, January 1, 1877. }

*To the Board of State Charities and Corrections :*

GENTLEMEN :—The undersigned, in accordance with your regulations, submits the annual report of his department for the year 1876 :

### THE STATE ASYLUM FOR THE INCURABLE INSANE.

|  | Men. | Women. | Total. |
|---|---|---|---|
| Number of inmates January 1, 1876 | 86 | 87 | 173 |
| Received during the year | 51 | 25 | 76 |
|  | 137 | 112 | 249 |
| Discharged during the year | 20 | 10 | 30 |
| Died     "     "     " | 9 | 11 | 20 |
| Escaped  "     "     " | 3 | 0 | 3 |
|  | 32 | 21 | 53 |
| Remaining January 1, 1877 | 105 | 91 | 196 |

The amount received for board of the insane was $15,759 68—a decrease of $409 07 since 1875, and was paid as follows :

| | |
|---|---|
| Providence | $3,738 83 |
| Newport | 1,151 34 |
| Pawtucket | 697 01 |
| Foster | 637 53 |

| | | |
|---|---:|---:|
| Coventry............................................................ | 741 | 13 |
| Johnston........................................................... | 698 | 12 |
| Warwick........................................................... | 506 | 37 |
| Bristol............................................................. | 606 | 07 |
| Glocester.......................................................... | 607 | 56 |
| Jamestown......................................................... | 461 | 30 |
| Exeter............................................................. | 447 | 56 |
| South Kingstown.................................................. | 360 | 76 |
| Portsmouth........................................................ | 412 | 69 |
| Cumberland........................................................ | 446 | 05 |
| North Kingstown.................................................. | 423 | 83 |
| Cranston.......................................................... | 460 | 10 |
| East Greenwich................................................... | 345 | 02 |
| Lincoln............................................................ | 385 | 69 |
| Little Compton.................................................... | 15 | 00 |
| East Providence................................................... | 198 | 87 |
| Tiverton........................................................... | 115 | 58 |
| Woonsocket........................................................ | 125 | 58 |
| North Smithfield.................................................. | 115 | 33 |
| Westerly........................................................... | 116 | 68 |
| West Greenwich................................................... | 203 | 55 |
| Charlestown....................................................... | 67 | 26 |
| Barrington......................................................... | 112 | 78 |
| Sundry persons.................................................... | 1,562 | 09 |
| | 15,759 | 68 |

The following amounts were received for each quarter of the year:

| | | | | | |
|---|---|---|---|---:|---:|
| For the quarter ending Dec. 31, 1875............................ | $3,855 | 86 |
| "       "       " March 31, 1876....................... | 3,724 | 28 |
| "       "       " June 30, 1876......................... | 4,126 | 13 |
| "       " Sept. 30, 1876........................ | 4,053 | 41 |
| | $15,759 | 68 |

There is now due for the quarter ending Dec. 31, 1876..........$4,601 17

Of the 196 inmates of the Asylum, January 1, 1877, the board of 106 is paid as follows:

| | | |
|---|---:|---|
| Eight.......................................................... | $4 00 | per week. |
| Fifty-four .................................................... | 3 00 | "     " |
| Forty-four.................................................... | 2 00 | "     " |

Ninety are supported by the State.

### STATE ALMS HOUSE.

|  | Men. | Women. | Boys. | Girls. | Total. |
|---|---|---|---|---|---|
| Remaining January 1, 1876........ | 61 | 62 | 20 | 21 | 164 |
| Received during the year..........| 107 | 98 | 88 | 41 | 279 |
| Born during the year.... ......... .. | .. | 7 | 8 | 15 |
| Total.....................| 168 | 160 | 60 | 70 | 458 |
| Discharged during the year........ | 85 | 91 | 50 | 57 | 283 |
| Died.............................| 15 | 9 | 4 | 5 | 33 |
| Total..................... ...| 100 | 100 | 54 | 62 | 316 |
| Remaining January 1, 1877........ | 68 | 60 | 6 | 8 | 142 |

The numbers received from the cities, towns, &c., were as follows :

| From Providence....... .. .. ..... ............... .................. | 146 |
|---|---|
| " Pawtucket................................. ........................ | 26 |
| " Woonsocket.............., ............................ ....... | 16 |
| " Lincoln.......... ............ ........................ | 15 |
| " Newport. .. ................................. .................... | 13 |
| " Bristol.... .... ......................... ..... . ................. | 10 |
| " Warwick........................................... .... ........ | 9 |
| " Scituate.........................,............................... | 7 |
| " East Greenwich ................................................. | 7 |
| " Burrillville................. ... ........................... | 6 |
| " Warren ...............,.,................................ ..... | 4 |
| " Johnston..... ............................................... | 2 |
| " Smithfield................................... ......... | 1 |
| " Westerly ...................................... ..... | 1 |
| " East Providence........................................... | 1 |
| " North Providence................................... .........•... | 1 |
| " Glocester.......................................... | 1 |
| " Tiverton..................... .............................. | 1 |
| " Barrington.... .................................... .. ..... | 1 |
| " Massachusetts............... ............. .. ........... | 1 |
| " Workhouse and House of Correction........................... | 10 |
|  | 279 |

The ten received from the Workhouse and House of Correction were committed from the following places :

| Providence........................................................ | 8 |
|---|---|
| East Providence.... ............................. .........1 |
| Lincoln...... ........................ .......................... | 1 |
|  | 10 |

The sum of $79 04 was collected during the year for the board of the inmates of the Almshouse.

## REMOVAL OF PAUPERS.

Notwithstanding the continued depression of business, the policy of removing dependents to their places of settlement, when liable to became a public charge, has kept down the number of admissions to the Almshouse, so that there has been an increase of only two in the year. The number of removals from the State is considerably in excess of that of any previous year, reaching a total of 456, against 329 in 1875, and 299 in 1874. Of the persons removed, 52 were from the Almshouse and 35 from the Workhouse.

The total of 456 includes 28 insane persons, of whom 10 were removed from the State Asylum, 6 from the Butler Hospital, 5 from the Workhouse and 2 from the Almshouse ; the other five were sent away before entering any institution.

|  | Total. | Insane. |
|---|---|---|
| Removed in 1874, . . . . . | 299 | 26 |
| Removed in 1875, . . . . . | 329 | 23 |
| Removed in 1876, . . . . . | 456 | 28 |
| Since the organization of the Board, . . . | 1,743 | 177 |

There is another subject deserving consideration. The practice of sending to the Workhouse, on a charge of vagrancy, insane persons who have wandered from home, and inmates of almshouses, who are legally settled in the towns, is a needless cause of expense to the State. In many instances I am called upon to send to their homes insane persons committed to the Workhouse, the State being obliged in such cases to pay the expenses of trial and commitment, and for their support while at the institution.

If in these cases the towns were compelled to share in the expense by paying board, it would tend to discourage such prosecutions, and the paupers would be disposed of at much less cost. Those who have a legal settlement in a town and become dependent upon charity, should not on any pretence be made a charge to the State. If, however, it becomes desirable, from any cause, to sentence town paupers to the Workhouse, the least any town can expect to do is to pay the board of such paupers, or a reasonable share of the cost of their support.

## COMPLAINTS UNDER THE BASTARDY ACT.

During the year twenty-two complaints have been made under this act, and have been disposed of as follows :

Settled by marriage, . . . . . . . 7
Settled by paying a specified sum of money, . . . . 2
Discharged on account of defect in warrant, . . . . 2
Defendants adjudged not guilty, . . . . . . 2
Defendants not yet arrested, . . . . . . 5
Now pending in Court, . . . . . . . 4
—
22

## BUTLER HOSPITAL.

In obedience to the provisions of the Act of the General Assembly, passed at the May session, 1874, requiring me to visit all places in the State, where insane persons are confined, I have made frequent inspections of the Butler Hospital. I can only reiterate what I have said in former reports, that the institution is ably managed, and is well fulfilling the intention of its founders.

The following is a statement of the number of paupers sent to, and discharged from the Butler Hospital during the year:

Remaining January 1, 1876, . . . . . . 25
Admitted during the year, . . . . . . . 37
—
Total, . . . . . . . . . 62
Discharged during the year, . . . . . 30
Died " " " . . . . . 3
— 33
—
Remaining January 1, 1877, . . . . . . 29

Of the thirty discharged, eleven had recovered, eight had improved, and eleven had not improved ; eighteen were taken by their friends, and twelve were sent to the State Asylum, or away from the State.

The whole expenditure for their board and clothing was.......$6,817 07
of which the towns paid...........................$3,166 61
and the State.................................. ....3,650 46
——— 6,817 07

Respectfully submitted,

GEORGE W. WIGHTMAN,

*Superintendent of State Charities and Corrections.*

# 'ANNUAL REPORT

OF THE

# 𝔏icense 𝔆ommissioners

## IN PROVIDENCE,

MADE TO THE

## GENERAL ASSEMBLY OF THE STATE OF RHODE ISLAND,

AT ITS

### January Session, A. D. 1877.

### PROVIDENCE:

ANGELL, BURLINGAME & CO., PRINTERS TO THE STATE.

1877.

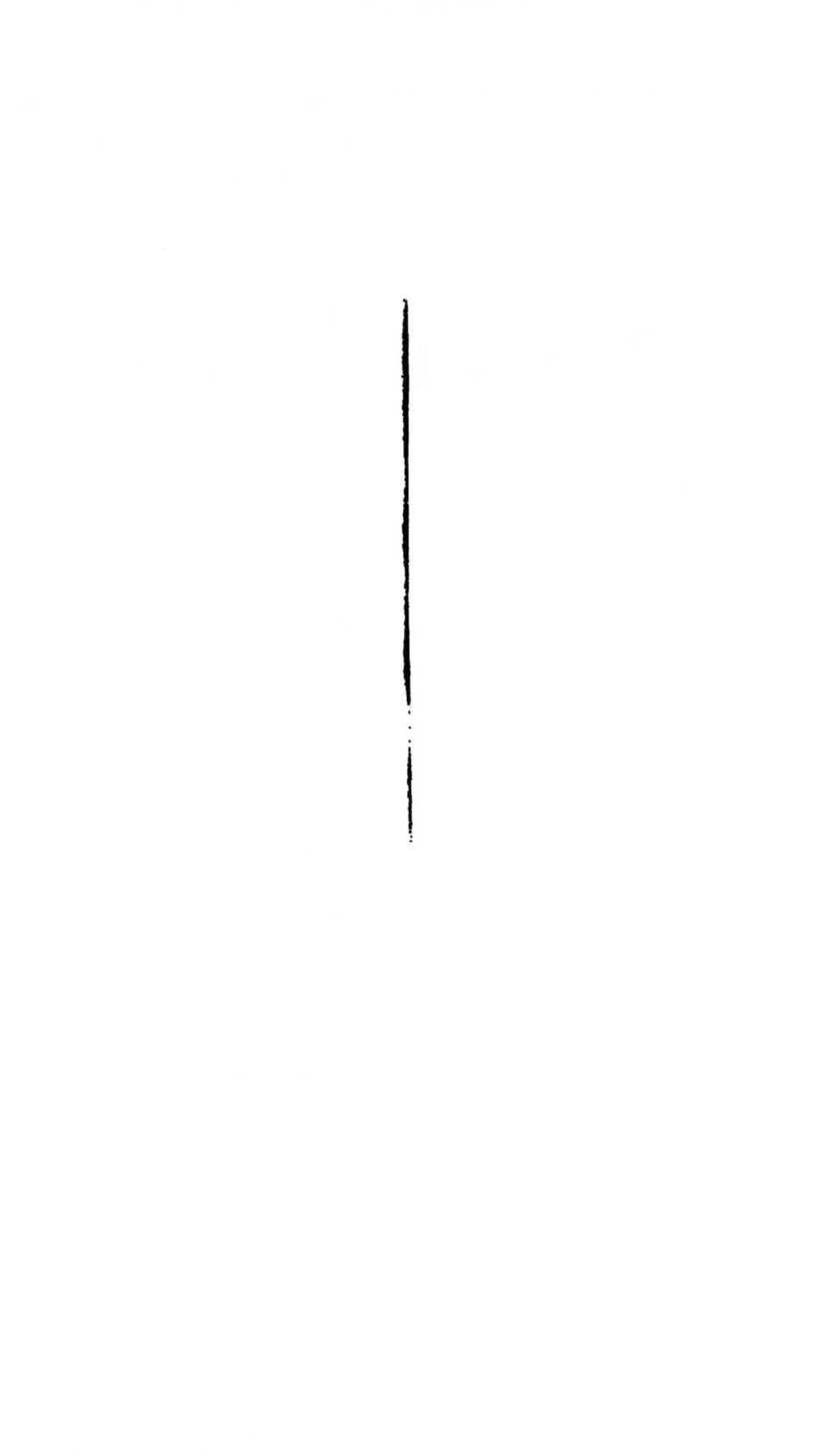

# REPORT

To the Honorable General Assembly of the State of Rhode Island,
at its January Session, A. D. 1877: —

The License Commissioners, in and for the city of Providence,
State of Rhode Island, in compliance with an amendment to Section 1 of Chapter 508 of the Public Laws, made by your honorable
body, in February, 1876, hereby respectfully submit their second
annual report.

By reference to our report made March 15th, 1876, it will be
seen that many of the predictions as to results that might be accomplished by pursuing the course we had adopted for the regulating and restraining the sale of intoxicating liquors in this city, have
been verified.

The law has been strictly enforced. We have sought to administer it, in a business like manner, entirely free from radicalism, and
have now to reiterate the statement made by us one year since, viz. :
that *no* illegal sales of liquors are made in this city *openly.*

We granted from the 15th July, 1875, to the 15th July, 1876,
664 licenses of all classes, the fees for the same amounting to one
hundred and sixteen thousand, six hundred dollars, ($116,600.)

Of these licenses, a majority were of the " fourth class, " entitling
the holder to sell lager beer, ale and other malt liquors only, for a
fee of fifty dollars, ($50.00.)

Of the violations of the conditions of license, nearly all were
made by these fourth class licensees.

The penalty for violation was light, comparatively, and we discovered (what was really of prime importance) that persons took

this license who were unsuitable to be clothed with authority of any kind.

In casting about for a remedy, we decided this difficulty could be overcome by making the fee for the fourth class license $150.00. This price was adopted at the commencement of our second year and the result we sought has been gained.

In lieu of more than 300 of these fourth class licenses issued last year, we have now 68, and of those persons who last year intended to violate the law, but very few now are the holders of license.

Commencing with the 15th, July, 1876, we have granted 443 licenses of all classes, (in number one-third less than last year) the fees amounting to one hundred thousand three hundred and fifty dollars, ($100,350.)

The entire issue for our second year will not exceed probably 450 and we shall have collected in fees in eighteen months, the very large sum of two hundred and seventeen thousand dollars, ($217,-000.)

The whole expense for collecting the fees for license in this city, including salaries of the Commissioners, amounts to about three per cent. on the sum collected.

The average cost of a license last year was about $175.00. This year the average cost is nearly $227.00.

When we assumed our official duties on the first of July, 1875, there were more than 700 persons engaged in the sale of liquors in this city unmolested. There are now engaged in the traffic some 450, and we believe this number will be materially reduced another year.

Some attribute the falling off in the number of licenses issued to "hard times." It must be that advancing the fee for the fourth class license made "hard times" for those intending to invest in that for the total of licenses of the other classes issued, already exceeds largely the number issued during the entire year ending in July, 1876.

### THEORY OF EXTREMISTS.

It is a favorite theory of extremists that the amount of revenue derived from what they term immoral business, is of no importance.

That if the collections from such a source are of some magnitude, this only proves that crime is on the increase and that such revenue will compensate but partially for the support of the convicts in our reformatory institutions, largely increased by illicit traffic.

We invite the attention of all such to the statistics relating to our business and to an examination of the police records for the two years just passed, and urge them to compare the figures now with those of 1875, when license was not the law and because these figures may not be easily obtainable we are induced to reproduce them here.

Fees collected for license in the city of Providence, for the eighteen months ending in January, 1877, $217,000.

Decrease in arrests for drunkenness, in the year 1876, 900.

### THE PROBLEM BEING SOLVED.

According to the real friends of prohibition, all sincerity in their belief, we desire to remind them that the heretofore difficult problem, "How can drunkenness be checked?" is rapidly approaching a solution in our city, and we can assure those of our citizens, the friends of temperance, who are prepared to advocate the best measures for its promotion, that the weapons we are using are most potent for the advancement of the cause.

Taking the population for a basis, and Providence has now a smaller number of legalized drinking places than any of our large cities, with but one or two exceptions.

### CLUB ROOMS.

Rooms furnished with all the requirements for drinking and gambling, with the social evil attached and born of prohibition. Establishments answering the above description, were discovered in different localities in this city. They were situated in the upper stories of buildings and entrance could only be gained by those holding keys, doing business ostensibly with members alone, with all the transactions of the habitues subjected to secrecy. It is only necessary to draw the attention of that portion of our community (who really desire the advancement of temperance and good morals) to these and kindred establishments, for them to condemn such professed reformatory measures as induce young men to frequent such rooms and allow them to be continued undisturbed. By persistent effort, most of these establishments have been closed and our citizens relieved of their pernicious influence.

### HOUSES OF ILL FAME.

We have granted no license to keepers of these places this year. It is well known that the proprietors and inmates are plying their vocation without let or hindrance, as it were, for notwithstanding the well directed efforts of the police and the summary disposition of this class of offenders when arraigned before the Justice Court of this city, they are driven from their abodes, only to appear again in some other locality, or if removed from the city, their places are soon filled by characters of the same stripe. The query naturally arises, why are they not made to take license and so obliged to disgorge a part of their ill gotten gains?

Our reply is, a large number of our citizens are opposed to lending these people any authority, and from deference to their opinions, we have omitted obliging those engaged in this nefarious business, to take license. Making it obligatory for the keepers of bagnios to take a liquor license, would, in our opinion, decrease the numbers now in existence in this city, would effectually close the vilest in a few weeks, and would add thousands of dollars to the State's exchequer.

These significant invitations, " Rooms to let furnished," and " Machine Stitching to order," would not be so frequently displayed upon houses on our principal streets.

### WAITERESSES AND WAITER GIRLS.

As nothing is more meritorious than honorable employment, so nothing is more censurable than the want of refinement in females.

It is for this reason, we would make a distinction between the former, who are employed in the respectable restaurants and saloons in this city, and the latter who may make a lodgement for a few weeks in those not altogether reputable.

It is not possible for the attachés of these latter places to enjoy a long lease, for armed with the authority of license, the officers make arrests, that would require greater provocation under other circumstances.

The employés in saloons are not enlisted by the License Commissioners, nor does the law provide that either sex shall be employed to the exclusion of the other in this business, but utilizing the discretionary powers vested in us, which we have always endeavored to administer judiciously, we have exacted promises from the keepers of many of these saloons, to the end that abandoned girls should not be employed by them or allowed to frequent their establishments, and those proprietors who failed to fulfill this condition have become ensnared in the meshes of the law.

### DESECRATION OF THE SABBATH.

Licensees were given to understand fully and unequivocally, that any attempt at business by them on Sunday, would receive the unqualified condemnation of the Commissioners, and that performing labor of their ordinary calling on that day, breaking as they would both the law of God and man, would surely bring themselves and their business into disrepute.

These admonitions were disregarded in some instances.

We were advised that sales were being made covertly, very quietly, but certainly, on Sunday.

To obtain evidence to convict persons who will take such chances is difficult, for they are usually as sagacious as they are unscrupulous, but while they were using their cunning devices to make sales, and congratulating each other upon their success, the officers were weaving a net which at the appointed time gathered in these desecrators, astounded and abashed.

The means used by the police to bring about these particular arrests and the disposition of their cases by the Courts, had a salutary effect.

Sunday selling, which was the rule, is now the exception in this city.

### SUITS ARE INSTITUTED.

Suits are now as heretofore promptly instituted against all violators of the law.

With the means of discovery at our command, it is next to an impossibility for the law to be transgressed in any part of the city for any length of time. It is a matter of surprise to those arrested that we are so conversant with their business, residing as they do in partial retirement.

We believe, however, we know all the persons in this city, and are familiar with their abodes, who are desirous of engaging in the illegal traffic in liquors, and who are deterred only by the enforcement of the present law.

### AMENDMENTS.

Opposed to tinkering laws generally, nevertheless, we believe an amendment giving authority to the officers to arrest without warrant, every one detected in making sales on Sunday, would make the law more effective, and if appeals could be more speedily reached, we think they would be fewer in number. These suggestions may be worthy of your consideration.

### ACKNOWLEDGMENTS.

We appreciate the favors extended to us by John M. Knowles, Chief of Police, and William H. Ayer, Deputy Chief of Police. Always ready, as they have been, to lend us their experience, their aid has proved invaluable.

Captains and Sergeants of Police, with all the Patrol, will accept our acknowledgments for ready attention to all our suggestions.

### LICENSEES, WITH THEIR LOCATIONS.

The names of Licensees, alphabetically arranged under their respective classes, with their locations, are to be found in the accompanying appendix.

Respectfully submitted,

WILLIAM H. BOWEN,
JABEZ C. KNIGHT,
SAMUEL H. WALES,

License Commissioners, in and for the City of Providence, State of Rhode Island.

PROVIDENCE, January 24th, 1877.

# APPLICANTS FOR LICENSE.

## FIRST CLASS.

Armstrong John..........................184 Canal street.
Blanding William B...............54 and 58 Weybosset street.
Claflin George L. & Co ............56 to 66 South Main street.
Cooney John P.....................143 and 144 Canal street.
Chorlton Edmund.........................112 Pine street.
Campbell Owen..........................158 Eddy street.
Doyle Philip A................... ...........135 Canal street.
Eddy Jesse G. & Co..................14 Custom House street.
Furlong Thomas.......................177 North Main street.
Greene John W . ....... ......44, 45 and 46 Exchange Place.
Greene & Co............. ..................58 Orange street.
Gorman Hugh & Co........ ......14 and 16 Wickenden street.
Grimes Thomas.......... ................. 125 Pine street.
Harvey George P... ..... ..................24 Peck street.
Hennessey John B.....................151 and 153 Canal street.
Hanley James.......................166 North Main street.
Keily & Sullivan. ............ ..Corner Cedar and Barney streets.
Keily & Sullivan......Northwest Corner of Peck and Pine streets.
Kennedy & Gough..........................58 Chaffee street.
Kiess Brothers................................44 Peck street.
MacNamara Michael B...............145 and 146 Canal street.
McArdle John............ ...........196 North Main street.
Mason, Chapin & Co ................83 to 87 Canal street.
Merchants Brewery..........Cor. Jackson and Fountain streets.
M. O'Hara & Co....................... .....29 Peck street.

2

Molter Nicholas...........................115 and 117 Pine street.
Paige F. A. & Co.........................9 South Main street.
Palmer & Madigan.......................17 to 21 Pine street.
Proctor Walter R..........................1077 High street.
Reid Owen...............    ......156 to 158 Randall Square.
Ryan Michael E.....................50 and 52 Orange street.
Stearns Frank N.....................37 and 39 Union street.
Wesson Samuel A........  ..................45 Dyer street.
Young Charles F.......    ............38 South Main street,
Young & Lyon........................22 North Main street.

### SECOND CLASS.

Austin George R.............................95 Eddy street.
Ashton William Y..........................9 Middle street.
Adams Thomas.......................1 Hardenburgh street.
Aiken Orris R..........................82 Dorrance street.
Adshead Joseph....................... 77 Weybosset street.
Aldrich Hiram A......................8¼ Weybosset street.
Aldrich Charles..........................163 Broad street.
Anness William W.....................Matilda street.
Ainscough Henry.........................15 Market Square.
Baggott Thomas.......    ..........224 India street.
Baxter Patrick W............   .........Lippitt street.
Booth Richard...................11 and 13 Union street.
Brackett Byron M......................115 North Main street.
Brady Philip...........................153 Richmond street.
Brady James...............................288 Eddy street.
Brannegan Daniel....   ....................327 Broadway.
Brannegan Peter J........................919 High street.
Brennan James...........................21 Martin street.
Bligh Andrew W. ..  ...............88 Weybosset street.
Bligh Andrew W....  .........................10 A street.
Butler Thomas M.........................169 High street.
Brady John J.............................96 Spruce street.
Barton Richard T............   .........1 Otis street.
Burns John...............................261 Eddy street.
Bamford John...............................315 Broadway.

Brown Salurvan R . ...........80 and 84 North Main street.
Bannon John...........................107 Prairie Avenue.
Bannon Patrick..........................20 Darling street.
Bradley John.........................106 Richmond street.
Bannon John....... ..................202 West River street.
Bannon Joseph..........................80 Summer street.
Boyd John A.............. ..........107 Weybosset street.
Brown Elisha M. & Co.....................477 High street.
Booth Thomas........ ............ ......11 Delaine street.
Bennett George W.........................65 Eddy street.
Cosgrove Michael......................898 South Main street.
Carberry Pierce ....................180 South Main street.
Caulfield Michael............................553 Eddy street.
Charnley William H .......................11 Orange street.
Cooney James.........................537 Eddy street.
Carroll Andrew T .........................206 India street.
Carroll Andrew T...........................96 India street.
Careher Patrick................. .............60 High street.
Cox Francis.......................... ......249 Dyer street.
Coleman Thomas. ...............................Dale street.
Checkley Edward.......................98 North Main street.
Connolly Peter...........................803 High street.
Connelly John......................... . 280 Eddy street.
Coyle John..............................7 Fountain street.
Carlin Daniel...........................163 Fountain street.
Courtney James.........................37 Chaffee street.
Campbell William A.............. ......75 and 77 Eddy street.
Connoll Gilbert....... ..............569 North Main street.
Campbell Edward... ......................525 Eddy street.
Carr Samuel...........................Pawtucket Avenue.
Carroll Hugh.......... ...............776 Eddy street.
Cooney Timothy S.......................309 Broad street.
Casey John........... ...................65 Putnam street.
Carpenter Thomas S..............Cor. of Board and Fifth streets.
Crohen James...............................Admiral street.
Crane George Jr............Corner of Acorn and Spruce streets.
Corcoran Dominick. .................... ....522 Valley street.

Connolly & Martin...................... .......56 Pond street.
Dailey Andrew.............................208 Plane street.
Doyle Edward L........   ..................128 Charles street.
Darling Samuel.....................2 and 6 Post Office Court.
Doyle Michael.......................661 North Main street.
Doyle Thomas F........................98 Wickenden street.
Doyle Peter...........................145 Douglas Avenue.
Doyle Michael........................724 North Main street.
Drury John............. ....................331 Broadway.
Drake Charles V...........................50 Union street.
Devitt Michael..........................4 Wickenden street.
Dorman Charles K......... ......Rear 155 Westminster street.
Dolan Michael............................43 Codding street.
Delaney Joseph..........................148 Charles street.
Doyle Peter.............................140 Charles street.
Duffy William....................73 and 77 Douglas Avenue.
Darcy William W...........................355 Eddy street.
Degnan Patrick........................104 Richmond street.
Dolan James....... .....................38 Diamond street.
Dunbar Thomas........................ 8 McKenna street.
Degnan Thomas............. ..............118 Plane street.
Doonan Michael.........................48 Diamond street.
Doheny Edward...........................925 High street.
Donovan Thomas, Agent................114 Douglas Avenue.
Driscol Morty............................54 Acorn street.
Darcy Edward H.......... .............195 Canal street.
Doherty James..........................121 Square street.
Daley Charles H..........................25 Gaspee street.
Dougherty James........................49 Atwell's Avenue.
Dodd William H........................81 Weybosset street.
Dorman Charles K.....................40 Washington street.
Drury Peter........................ .Valley Street Hotel.
Devine Edwin..................... ...........307 High street.
Dwyer Edward........................32 South Main street.
Dwyer Edward........................248 North Main street.
Early Daniel.............................12 Evans street.
Eyre & Gammon............................128 Pine street.

Eichhorn Henry.... . ...............257 South Main street.
Enos Joseph S.........................458 South Main street.
Flemming John.........................40 Whelden street.
Fenner Steary A................... ...46 Washington street.
Ferguson George......... .........21 Hardenburgh street.
Furlong Thomas...........................218 India street.
Furlong Thomas.........................281 Fountain street.
Foran John....... .In basement, junction High and Broad streets.
Fournier John M. & Co......................47 Middle street.
Foley John.................................78 Brook street.
Flannagan & Gallagher.....................132 Charles street.
Fanning Bartholomew.................59 South Main street.
Fogarty & Edmonds....................69 South Main street.
Foley Michael ......Southwest corner of Peck and Pine streets.
Flynn Matthew............................58 Langley street.
Farrell James...................................10 B street.
Gray Thomas ............................132 Canal street.
Gamble Joseph W........................191 Martin street.
Gainor John..........................468 North Main street.
Galligan Peter.........................190 Wickenden street.
Gorman Michael.................109 and 111 Prairie Avenue.
Greenhalgh James, Jr....................118 North Main stroet.
Gravlin William B........................ ...60 Ship street.
Gallagher William...........................79 Eddy street.
Greene Arthur................................Hoyle Hotel.
Gorman Michael...........................349 High street.
Gormley Patrick.......................222 Branch Avenue.
Gseller John Frederick...Corner of Putnam and Amherst streets.
Goyette Joseph........................68 Wickenden street.
Gannon John................................8 Mill street.
Humphreys Lewis H..............................City Hotel.
Heller Gelles............. .... ............183 Orms street.
Heslin Edward J......................... 61 Clifford street.
Heslin Edward J........................131 Richmond street.
Hardy Thilesphore...........................194 Fountain street.
Hoyle Joshua..............................126 Canal street.
Hemmingway George........................1 McNeal Lane.

Hopkins John D..............................3 Peck street.

Holden Charles C......................66 Wickenden street

Hellman David..............................18 Snow street

Hart Norman L........................47 South Main street.

Hanley Michael.......................... ..877 High street

Hughes Thomas............................75 Martin street.

Hackett Peter........................... 29 Putnam street.

Harrop Abraham........................85 Manton Avenue.

Hardman Samuel G..................... ...28 Orange street.

Hines Terrence.... ....................263 Atwell's Avenue.

Hanley Thomas G...........................341 High street.

Hanoway Francis......................118 Prairie Avenue.

Hoch Christian............................ ....10 Union street

Haebel Theodore A....... .......49 and 53 Washington street

Healey Edward..... ................ ......129 Canal steeet.

Higgins Patrick.........................464 Cranston street.

Hunt Roderick............................2 Susan street

Hill Job W.................................470 High street.

Hawksmith Robert S.....................23 Fulton street.

Huntoon Frank W...................261 Westminster street.

Horton John F.......................532 North Main street.

Heslin Patrick............................537 Eddy street.

Holden Charles C.................. .....66 Wickenden street.

Haig Robert J........................... .27 Fulton street

Kiernan Bryan...............................68 Back street

Kennedy Lawrence......................27 South Main street

Kavanagh James...... ...................285 Valley street

Kenney Michael........................880 Potter's Avenue

Kenney Patrick........ .........288 Potter's Avenue.

Kiernan Edward............................495 Eddy street.

Kerwick Dennis............................126 Orms street.

Keefe Michael............................ Douglas Avenue

Keefe John... .........................290 North Main street.

Knott Benjamin...........................267 Smith street.

Kennedy Samuel......................26 South Water street.

Kelley John..............................238 India street.

Kiernan Bryan...... ............... .......81 Charles street.

Keach Seth & Co..........................441 High street.
Kelley William E.............. ........311 Wickenden street.
Kraus Fritz...............................199 Broad street.
Kirwin Thomas........................83 Manton Avenue.
Leary Cornelius.......................279 South Main street.
Link John S...........................2½ Post Office Court.
Lord Thomas.................... ......91 Westminster street.
Ladd Thomas.... .....................89 Cranston street.
Lewis Job...............................56 Charles street.
Lindsey Benjamin F.......................25 Fulton street.
Ludowicy John P....................333 North Main street.
Lawton Jonas...........................53 Manton Avenue.
Leigh George.........................160 Canal street.
Luby Joseph....... .... ............18 Smithfield Avenue.
Lyons William...........................163 Martin street.
Lynch Patrick. .......................278 Potter's Avenue.
Leach James................................13 B street.
Macomber George A.....................1 North Main street.
Milmon Patrick..............10th Ward House, Charles street.
Moroney Patrick......................28 South Water street.
Markey Peter.........................236 South Main street.
McGovern Patrick.........................84 Spruce street.
Martin Owen ....... ..............497 North Main street.
McCabe Patrick.............................33 Julian street.
Mahn Lawrence........ .................271 Orms street.
MacNamara Michael P. .......... .........103 Charles street.
McHale Michael........................112 Douglas Avenue.
McHale Michael........................110 Charles street.
McHale Michael......................100 South Water street.
Munroe Joseph S....... ............153 South Main street.
Murphy James......... ............161 South Water street.
McCusker James H..........................88 Plane street.
McCarron Henry.......................35 Atwell's Avenue.
McKenna Michael F.........................94 Plane street.
Mitchell Benjamin....................233 South Main street.
Morrin Patrick.......................665 North Main street.
Marchant Edmund E.......................12 Canal street.

Menard Abraham..........................434 Cranston street.
Mello Emanuel C.......................468 South Main street.
McCulla Bernard.......................89 West River street.
McElroy Henry........................316 North Main street.
Mueller Casper.........................239 South Main street.
Montague Michael..........................10 Darling street.
McQuaid Daniel................. ..........127 Charles street.
Murphy Owen........................850 South Main street.
McManus Patrick...........................199 Canal street.
McManus Hugh...........................273 Eddy street.
McKenna James...........................405 High street.
Mullen Patrick.............................89 Pond street.
Medbury Charles....................874 and 876 Eddy street.
McKenna Patrick...........................19 Sexton street.
McGarty John.....................:.....509 High street.
McQueeney James.........................128 Hospital street.
McElroy John.......... ..............33 Dyer street.
McQueeney Patrick.........................489 Eddy street.
McGarty James...............................988 High street.
Murray Owen...........................100 Federal street.
Murphy Michael........................20 Wickenden street.
McMahon James.............................901 High street.
Mahoney Patrick..............corner Ives and Williams streets.
Mahoney Frank.......................125 South Water street.
Mann Robert..............................86 Martin street.
Mulholland Arthur..........................68 Canal street.
Maguire Brothers..........................82 Brook street.
McCusker Michael.......................177 Atwell's Avenue.
McNally Alfred.........................834 North Main street.
Murray Terrance.......................188 Prairie Avenue.
McCartin John..............................1 Pond street.
McCarron John.........................75 West River street.
McKenna John.........................818 Atwell's Avenue.
McCardell Dennis.......................135 Atwell's Avenue.
McMaugh Stephen.....corner Valley street and Atwell's Avenue.
Murrey John...................................64 Ives street.
McGarty John H......... corner Branch Av. and Veazie street.

McCusker Thomas.......................17 Washington street.
Nolan Patrick W...........................169 Broad street.
Nichols Frank O.........................85 Weybosset street.
Nugent Michael H..........................44 Orange street.
Naylor Judah...........................207 Manton Avenue.
Neaf John...........................117 Wickenden street.
O'Byrne Bernard...........................102 Plane street.
O'Beirna Hugh...........................202 India street.
O'Neill John...................................2 Otis street.
O'Neil Cornelius...........................106 India street.
O'Neil Thomas.................................Veazie street.
Osborne Obadiah P....................72 South Water street.
O'Farrell John...........................79 Martin street.
O'Reilly John.......................113 South Water street.
O'Connor John............Corner of Ives and Fremont streets.
O'Reilly John..........................104 Putnam street.
O'Reilly Edward...........................72 Traverse street.
Pond Charles W...........................478 Broad street.
Proctor Walter R....................286 North Main street.
Proctor Walter R...........................30 Orange street.
Pierce Charles F.......................145 Weybosset street.
Pinder Benjamin.......................62 Thurber's Avenue.
Perry Marsden J...........................9 Fountain street.
Palmer Henry.............................432 Eddy street.
Palmer Henry...........................102 High street.
Palmer Henry...........................127 Plane street.
Payne John C.........................92 North Main street.
Proctor Walter R.......................29 South Main street.
Proctor Walter R.......................45 South Main street.
Parker Samuel.............................96 Martin street.
Quinn Michael...........................20 Printery street.
Quinn Patrick...........................100 Douglas Avenue.
Quinn Thomas.............................31 Smith street.
Ryan John F.........................205 Atwell's Avenue.
Rogers Brothers.............................67 Ives street.
Raleigh Walter.........................110 Prairie Avenue.
Reilly Bernard...............corner Vinton and Gesler streets.

Revens John . . . . . . . . . . . . . . . . corner Point and Richmond streets.
Ralph Albert R . . . . . . . . . . . . . . . . . .3 and 4 Post Office Court.
Rounds Charles A . . . . . . . . . . . . . . . . . .8 North Main street.
Reynolds George R . . . . . . . . . . . . . . . 94 and 95 Weybosset street
Rielly Daniel . . . . . . . . . . . . . . . . . . . . . . . . . . . . . .503 High street.
Riewold Julius . . . . . . . . . . . . . . . . . . . . . . .33 Greenwich street.
Schwab John C . . . . . . . . . . . . . . . corner Eddy and Fulton streets.
Salisbury Leroy H . . . . . . . . . . . . . . . . . . . . . .18 Weybosset street.
Sheldon George W . . . . . . . . . . . . . . . . . . . . . .203 Broad street.
Smith Joseph . . . . . . . . . . . . . . . . . . . . . . . . . . . .80 Back street.
Sperry Henry . . . . . . . . . . . . . . . . . . . . . .161 Thurber's Avenue.
Stearns Frank N . . . . . . . . . . . . . . . . . . . .46 and 48 Union street.
Schofield John . . . . . . . . . . . . . . . . . . . . . . . . . . .154 Eddy street.
Sullivan Jeremiah J . . . . . . . . . . . . . . . . . . . . . .426 Cranston street.
Sullivan Patrick J . . . . . . . . . . . . . . . . . . . . . . . . . . . .1 Peck street.
Simmons Michael . . . . . . . . . . . . . . . . . . . . . .257 Atwell's Avenue.
Smith Martin . . . . . . . . . . . . . . . . . . . . . . . . . . . .12 Martin street.
Smith & Furnam . . . . . . . . . . . . . . . . . . . . . . . . . .78 Eddy street.
Stahl Charles A . . . . . . . . . . . . . . . . . . . . . . . . . . .411 High street.
Sherry James . . . . . . . . . . . . . . . . . . . . . . . . . . .47 Diamond street.
Sherry James . . . . . . . . . . . . . . . . . . . . . . . .300 Potter's Avenue.
Stanz John . . . . . . . . . . . . . . . . . . . . . . . . . .45 Mathewson street.
Sullivan Daniel . . . . . . . . . . . . . . . . . . . . . . . .219 Cranston street.
Salisbury Edward S . . . . . . . . . . . . . . . . . . . . . . . . .2 Canal street.
Swallow George S . . . . . . . . . . . . . . . . . . . . . . . .8 Weybosset street.
Sykes John . . . . . . . . . . . . . . . . . . . . . . . . . . . .76 Weybosset street.
Thornton John W . . . . . . . . . . . . . . . . . . . . . . . . . . . .Branch Avenue.
Taft David . . . . . . . . . . . . . . . . . . . . . . . . . . . . .16 Richmond street.
Turbitt Francis . . . . . . . . . . . . . . . . . . . . . . .324 Atwell's Avenue
Tinker Edward W . . . . . . . . . . . . . . . . . . . . . . .8 Fountain street.
Teehan Michael F . . . . . . . . . . . . . . . . . . . . .309 Westminster street.
Tummin Stephen A . . . . . . . . . . . . . . . . . . . . 278 South Main street.
Thayer Lucius M . . . . . . . . . . . . . . . . .31 and 33 Washington street.
Taft George . . . . . . . . . . . . . . . . . . . . . . . . . . . . . .49 Superior street.
Tilly William . . . . . . . . . . . . . . . . . . . . . . . . .7 Hardenburgh street.
Tillinghast Samuel W . . . . . . . . . . . . . . . . . . . . . . .9 Market Square.
Vallily James . . . . . . . . . . . . . . . . . . . . . . . . . . .144 Richmond street.

Whipple Albert L....................104 Westminster street.
Wilcox & Brownell...............rear 155 Westminster street.
Wilson Joseph B......................272 South Main street.
Walsh Richard..........................237 Broad street.
Walsh Robert F.........................112 Charles street.
Whipple Frank...........................  Hopkins Hotel.
Watts John..............................Manton Avenue.
Webb William............................830 Eddy street.
Ward John P...........................121 Richmond street.
Walsh James..............................248 Eddy street.
Walsh John...........................101 South Main street.
Whipple Daniel A..........................78 Canal street.
Watson John H...........................881 Broad street.
Wright James H...........................258 India street.
Wood George L..........................182 Smith street.

## THIRD CLASS.

Blanding William B...............68 and 70 North Main street.
Burgess Horace C....................155 Westminster street.
Chambers, Calder & Co...................10 Exchange Place.
Eddy Thomas W. & Son....................375 High street.
Gladding Charles A....................223 Greenwich street.
Hale & Burrough.....................32 South Water street.
McWilliams Owen.........................78 Spruce street.
Preston & Spalding..............29 and 81 North Main street.
Remington & Sessions..................247 Westminster street.
Sumner Ossian & Son.....................260 Broad street.

## FOURTH CLASS.

Arnold William E......................12 Weybosset street.
Aldrich & Gardner.........................281 Broad street.
Amann Jacob...............................23 Eddy street.
Buffum Frederick T......................41 Hospital street.
Becker Jacob........................264 North Main street.
Bogman & Wilbur...........Railroad Saloon, Exchange Place.
Brug Philip...............cor. Dorrance and Pine streets, }
                              Opera House Building.   }

Brucker Peter......................16 Custom House street.
Dietrich Gustav.............................30 Market Square.
Drury James F............................111 Spruce street.
Duffy William...............................20½ B street.
English Mathew...........................78 Langley street.
Freeman William H.....................71 Richmond street.
Finck & Hainbach..........................188 Pine street.
Fox John.................................7 Appleton street.
Fitzgerald James............................1 Gaspee street.
Gauch Charles.......................109 North Main street.
Gauch John E..............................45 Ives street.
Gorman Hugh...........................43 Whelden street.
Geary Michael.............................45 Smith street.
Hertha William F.......................40 Richmond street.
Hausenstein Hubert........................198 Eddy street.
Hopkins John D.........82 Weybosset street, Theatre Comique
Hickey Timothy E.......................10 Planet street.
Herrick Albin...................................Joslin street.
Hines Henry F.....................rear of 160 Canal street.
Hogan Michael...........................11 Fillmore street.
Higney Patrick............................23 Canal street.
Harvey Isaac J...............317 and 319 Westminster street.
Jones Henry C...........................211 Broad street.
Keily Bartholomew...................rear Old Brewery, ⎫
          corner of Pine and Richmond streets. ⎭
Kennedy Michael..........................498 Valley street.
Martin Henry..............................4 Wayne street.
McNulty William.........................57 Appleton street.
Maryott Thomas S.........................5 Fountain street.
McGuire Thomas.........................Smithfield Avenue.
McGeo John..............corner of Polk and Hedley streets.
Matthes Herman...........................102 Pine street.
Meyer John.................................69 Eddy street.
McLaughlin Michael...................100 Pavillion Avenue.
Maguire John J............................3 Bergen street.
Maxcy William H. H..................401 Potter's Avenue.
McGrath Thomas..........................42 Miner street.

Murphy Michael........................183 Williams street.
Newcomb Calvin & Co....................45 Dorrance street.
Newcomb Seth...........................581 High street.
O'Hara Michael.........................3 Hicks street.
Pettis John W .........................241 Broad street.
Pettis Robert..........................5 and 7 Orange street.
Pohle Theodore.....................1 and 2 Jackson Court.
Reidel John............................25 Eddy street.
Reichenbach John.......................30 South Main street.
Roberts George.........................124 North Main street.
Schmidt Frederick......................58 Pine street.
Scheminger John........................333 High street.
Sperry Henry...........................6 Chapel street.
Schoenleber John L.....................209 Broad street.
Steere Joshua H .......................461 Pine street.
Schuman Binnhard...................295 Westminster street.
Thoene Fritz........................... 274 Broad street.
Tierney Martin.........................156 Prairie Avenue.
Thurston Peleg.........................6 High street.
Vanetti Cæsar..........................19 Cedar street.
Woelfel Andrew.........................165 Broad street·
Weber Edward...........................52 Richmond street.
Young Charles F..................55 South Main street.
Waterman Benjamin.....................8 Union street.
Zuleger Edward.........................906 High street.

# ANNUAL STATEMENT

### EXHIBITING THE CONDITION OF THE

# State Banks of Rhode Island,

##### ON

### *TUESDAY, THE 28th DAY OF NOVEMBER,*

## 1876.

PREPARED BY
JOEL M. SPENCER, STATE AUDITOR.

PROVIDENCE:
ANGELL, BURLINGAME & CO., PRINTERS TO THE STATE.
1877.

# INDEX TO STATE BANKS.

# INDEX TO THE INSTITUTIONS FOR SAVINGS.

The Cashiers of State Banks and Treasurers of the Savings Institutions transacting business in the State, were requested, within the time fixed by our laws, to render a sworn statement of their condition on Tuesday, November 28, 1876, in compliance with the requirements of Chapter 141 of the General Statutes and Chapter 427 of the Public Laws A similar request was also made of the President of the Rhode Island Hospital Trust Company, in accordance with a provision in their charter, requiring an annual statement of condition to be made to this department, which was promptly given. An exhibit of the condition of the Cranston Savings Bank and Franklin Institution for Savings, both of Providence, was cheerfully furnished at my request, although no positive law is in force exacting similar statements from Receivers. The Cranston Savings Bank was placed in the hands of Alexander Farnum, Esq., as receiver, on the 17th day of December, 1873. Dividends amounting to $179,986 82, have been declared and paid to depositors during the year 1876. The aggregate of dividends thus far is $1,537,634 40, being sixty-eight per cent. of the deposits. Dividends amounting to about ten thousand dollars still remain unclaimed. The total disbursements of Winthrop De Wolf, Esq. receiver of the Franklin. to this date amount to $1,911,097, being seventy per cent. of its deposits. This report shows that thirty-seven savings institutions are actually transacting business in the State, the Bristol County Savings Bank of Bristol having commenced business in August, 1876.

The aggregate of deposits and number of depositors may be found on page 74 ; a summary of conditions on page 75 ; a table showing the largest amount due any one depositor on page 76 ; and a table giving amount of deposits and number of depositors for ten years, from 1867 to 1876 inclusive, on pages 78 and 79.

Fifteen State Banks are doing business in the State, twelve being located at Providence and three at Newport, showing same amount of capital as at the date of previous annual return A summary of resources and liabilities is given on page 24 ; a description of stocks in other Banks and other stocks and bonds owned by the Banks on page 25 ; and a description and amount of stocks held as collateral security for loans on page 26.

The location and post office address of these institutions are given in the index on preceding pages.

JOEL M. SPENCER,
STATE AUDITOR.

# BANK RETURNS.

# ATLANTIC BANK, PROVIDENCE.

C. M. STONE, *Cashier.*　　CALEB G. BURROWS, *President.*

### RESOURCES.

| | |
|---|---:|
| Debts due from directors.................................... | $4,350 00 |
| Debts due from other stockholders....................... | 4,825 00 |
| Debts due from all others................................. | 178,823 67 |
| Specie actually in Bank................................... | 300 00 |
| Bills of other Banks...................................... | 11,496 73 |
| Deposits in other Banks.................................. | 8,864 12 |
| Its own Stock held by the Bank........................... | 1,100 00 |
| Stock in other Banks...................................... | |
| Other stock owned by the Bank .......................... | |
| Real estate............................................... | |
| Other property ........................................... | 84 00 |
| Expense Account.......................................... | 295 15 |
| Total amount of resources.............................. | $205,138 67 |

### LIABILITIES.

| | |
|---|---:|
| Capital stock actually paid in............................. | $131,650 00 |
| Bills in circulation....................................... | |
| Deposits on interest...................................... | 3,000 00 |
| Deposits not on interest.................................. | 50,983 80 |
| Debts due to other banks................................. | 10,000 00 |
| Dividends unpaid......................................... | 546 00 |
| Net profits on hand....................................... | 8,958 87 |
| Total amount of liabilities............................. | $205,138 67 |

### ADDITIONAL PARTICULARS.

| | |
|---|---:|
| Increase of capital since last return..................... | |
| Par value of shares....................................... | $50 00 |
| Amount of last dividend.................................. | 3,949 50 |
| Date of last dividend.............................October 5, 1876. | |
| Rate per cent. of last dividend.....................3 pr. ct. 6 mo. | |
| Reserved profits at the time of last dividend............. | 7,454 94 |
| Debts due and not paid................................... | 8,542 62 |
| Amount of suspended paper considered bad or doubtful....... | 272 40 |
| Amount loaned on pledges of stock in Bank................ | 400 00 |
| Amount of stocks held as collateral security for loans..... | |
| Largest amount of indebtedness of any one person or firm..... | 18,000 00 |
| Amount of bills in circulation under five dollars.......... | |

## BANK OF AMERICA, PROVIDENCE.

A. C. TOURTELLOT, *Cashier.*                    ZECHARIAH CHAFEE, *President.*

### RESOURCES.

| | |
|---|---:|
| Debts due from directors.................................... | $11,323 00 |
| Debts due from other stockholders.......................... | 31,353 01 |
| Debts due from all others.................................. | 226,384 28 |
| Specie actually in Bank.................................... | 2,379 59 |
| Bills of other Banks....................................... | 15,043 11 |
| Deposits in other Banks ................................... | 4,726 59 |
| Its own stock held by the Bank............................. | |
| Stock in other Banks....................................... | |
| Other stocks owned by the Bank............................. | |
| Real estate................................................ | |
| Other property............................................ | |
| Expense account........................................... | 237 93 |
| Total amount of resources............................. | $291,447 51 |

### LIABILITIES.

| | |
|---|---:|
| Capital stock actually paid in............................. | $200,000 00 |
| Bills in circulation....................................... | 565 00 |
| Deposits on interest....................................... | |
| Deposits not on interest................................... | 49,977 64 |
| Debts due to other Banks................................... | 19,400 00 |
| Dividends unpaid........................................... | 1,058 50 |
| Net profits on hand........................................ | 20,446 37 |
| Total amount of liabilities........................... | $291,447 51 |

### ADDITIONAL PARTICULARS.

| | |
|---|---:|
| Increase of capital since last return...................... | |
| Par value of shares....................................... | $50 00 |
| Amount of last dividend................................... | 6,000 00 |
| Date of last dividend.....................................October 5, 1876. | |
| Rate per cent. of last dividend...........................3 pr. ct. 6 mo. | |
| Reserved profits at the time of last dividend.............. | 18,449 80 |
| Debts due and not paid.................................... | 22,875 49 |
| Amount of suspended paper considered bad or doubtful....... | 202 67 |
| Amount loaned on pledges of stock in Bank................. | |
| Amount and description of stocks held as collateral security for loans*................................................ | |
| Largest amount of indebtedness of any one person or firm.... | 19,658 46 |
| Amount of bills in circulation under five dollars.............. | 565 00 |

*See page 26.

## BUTCHERS AND DROVERS BANK, PROVIDENCE.

N. C. DANA, *Cashier.*

DANIEL REMINGTON, } *Directors.*
C. W. MOORE,

### RESOURCES.

| | |
|---|---:|
| Debts due from directors | $45,000 00 |
| Debts due from other stockholders | 2,055 00 |
| Debts due from all others | 189,226 25 |
| Specie actually in Bank | 381 27 |
| Bills of other Banks | 20,608 85 |
| Deposits in other Banks | 6,153 71 |
| Its own stock held by the Bank | 14,350 00 |
| Stock in other Banks | |
| Other stocks owned by the Bank | |
| Real estate | |
| Other property | |
| Expense account | 120 15 |
| Total amount of resources | $295,895 23 |

### LIABILITIES.

| | |
|---|---:|
| Capital stock actually paid n | $246,450 00 |
| Bills in circulation | 2,208 00 |
| Deposits on interest | |
| Deposits not on interest | 4,682 54 |
| Debts due to other Banks | |
| Dividends unpaid | 1,509 00 |
| Net profits on hand | 3,045 69 |
| Total amount of liabilities | $295,895 23 |

### ADDITIONAL PARTICULARS.

| | |
|---|---:|
| Increase of capital since last return | |
| Par value of shares | $50 00 |
| Amount of last dividend | 4,929 00 |
| Date of last dividend | October 7, 1876. |
| Rate per cent. of last dividend | 2 pr. ct. 6 mo. |
| Reserved profits at the time of last dividend | 2,006 81 |
| Debts due and not paid | 42,290 10 |
| Amount of suspended paper considered bad or doubtful | 40,940 10 |
| Amount loaned on pledges of stock in Bank | 21,550 00 |
| Amount of stocks held as collateral security for loans | |
| Largest amount of indebtedness of any one person or firm | 30,000 00 |
| Amount of bills in circulation under five dollars | |

## GROCERS AND PRODUCERS BANK, PROVIDENCE.

E. TALLMAN, *President.*

JOHN B. CALDER, *Cashier.*

### RESOURCES.

| | |
|---|---|
| Debts due from Directors.................................... | $8,000 00 |
| Debts due from other stockholders........................... | 13,400 00 |
| Debts due from all others................................... | 204,850 62 |
| Specie actually in Bank.................................... | |
| Bills in other Banks....................................... | 12,281 43 |
| Deposits in other Banks................................... | 6,477 76 |
| Its own stock held by the Bank............................. | 14,600 00 |
| Stock in other Banks...................................... | |
| Other stocks owned by the Bank........................... | |
| Real estate.............................................. | |
| Other property........................................... | |
| Expense account.......................................... | 3,633 31 |
| Total amount of Resources............................ | $263,243 12 |

### LIABILITIES.

| | |
|---|---|
| Capital stock actually paid in.............................. | $160,000 00 |
| Bills in circulation....................................... | 1,791 00 |
| Deposits on interest...................................... | |
| Deposits not on interest................................... | 74,761 40 |
| Debts due to other Banks................................. | 15,357 03 |
| Dividends unpaid......................................... | 657 75 |
| Net profits on hand...................................... | 10,675 94 |
| Total amount of liabilities.......................... | $263,243 12 |

### ADDITIONAL PARTICULARS.

| | |
|---|---|
| Increase of capital since last return........................ | |
| Par value of shares....................................... | $50 00 |
| Amount of last dividend................................... | 5,600 00 |
| Date of last dividend.............................September 4, 1876. | |
| Rate per cent. of last dividend........................3½ pr ct. 6 m. | |
| Reserved profits at the time of last dividend................ | 8.627 51 |
| Debts due and not paid.................................... | 23,333 14 |
| Amount of suspended paper considered bad or doubtful....... | 3,000 00 |
| Amount loaned on pledges of stock in Bank................. | 15,900 00 |
| Amount and description of stock held as collateral security for loans*............................................... | 11,300 00 |
| Largest amount of indebtedness of any one person or firm.... | 11,884 64 |
| Amount of bills in circulation under five dollars.............. | 1,541 00 |

* See page 26.

# HIGH STREET BANK, PROVIDENCE.

E. ALLEN, *Cashier.*

AARON B. CURRY, *President.*

### RESOURCES.

| | |
|---|---:|
| Debts due from directors | $16,600 00 |
| Debts due from other stockholders | 5,870 00 |
| Debts due from all others | 153,196 72 |
| Specie actually in Bank | 180 91 |
| Bills of other Banks, checks and currency | 4,458 79 |
| Deposits in other Banks | 15,579 57 |
| Its own stock held by the Bank | |
| Stock in other Banks | |
| Other stocks owned by the Bank | |
| Real estate | 5,200 00 |
| New building account | 9,870 27 |
| Furniture and fixtures | 1,292 66 |
| Expense account | 575 05 |
| Total amount of resources | $212,823 97 |

### LIABILITIES.

| | |
|---|---:|
| Capital stock actually paid in | $120,000 00 |
| Bills in circulation | |
| Deposits on interest | |
| Deposits not on interest | 67,094 40 |
| Debts due to other banks | |
| Dividends unpaid | 254 75 |
| Net profits on hand | 25,474 82 |
| Total amount of liabilities | $212,823 97 |

### ADDITIONAL PARTICULARS.

| | |
|---|---:|
| Increase of capital since last return | |
| Par value of shares | $50 00 |
| Amount of last dividend | 4,200 00 |
| Date of last dividend | Aug. 3, 1876. |
| Rate per cent. of last dividend | 3½ pr. ct. 6 mo. |
| Reserved profits at the time of last dividend | 23,769 04 |
| Debts due and not paid | 21,700 00 |
| Amount of suspended paper considered bad or doubtful | |
| Amount loaned on pledges of stock in Bank | 22,470 00 |
| Amount and description of stocks held as collateral security for loans | |
| Largest amount of indebtedness of any one person or firm | 21,000 00 |
| Amount of bills in circulation under five dollars | |

## JACKSON BANK, PROVIDENCE.

CHARLES A. BOYD, } *Directors.*
R. P. GLADDING, }

THEO. B. TALBOT, *Cashier.*

### RESOURCES.

| | |
|---|---|
| Debts due from directors..................................... | $48,100 00 |
| Debts due from other stockholders.......................... | 45,140 00 |
| Debts due from all others............... ................ | 356,638 78 |
| Specie actually in Bank.................................... | 690 42 |
| Bills of other Banks........................................ | 28,980 91 |
| Deposits in other Banks.................................... | 17,382 98 |
| Its own stock held by the Bank............................ | |
| Stock in other Banks...................................... | |
| Other stocks owned by the Bank.......................... | |
| Real estate................................................ | |
| Other property............................................ | |
| Expense account........................................... | |
| Total amount of resources............................. | $496,863 09 |

### LIABILITIES.

| | |
|---|---|
| Capital stock actually paid in............................. | $344,450 00 |
| Bills in circulation....................................... | 1,048 00 |
| Deposits on interest....................................... | 1,000 00 |
| Deposits not on interest................................... | 87,979 19 |
| Debts due to other Banks................................. | 40,706 50 |
| Dividends unpaid.......................................... | 1,182 25 |
| Net profits on hand....................................... | 20,497 15 |
| Total amount of liabilities............................ | $496,863 09 |

### ADDITIONAL PARTICULARS.

| | |
|---|---|
| Increase of capital since last return....................... | |
| Par value of shares....................................... | $50 00 |
| Amount of last dividend................................... | 12,055 75 |
| Date of last dividend..................................... | July 1st. 1876. |
| Rate per cent. of last dividend ........................... | 3½ pr. ct. 6 mo. |
| Reserved profits at the time of last dividend............... | 13,493 32 |
| Debts due and not paid.................................... | 69,514 63 |
| Amount of suspended paper considered bad or doubtful...... | 16,150 00 |
| Amount loaned on pledges of stock in Bank................ | 35,345 00 |
| Amount and description of stocks held as collateral security for loans...... | |
| Largest amount of indebtedness of any one person or firm.... | 35,700 00 |
| Amount of bills in circulation under five dollars........................... | |

## LIBERTY BANK, PROVIDENCE.

C. R. DROWNE, *Cashier.*     DUTY EVANS, *President.*

### RESOURCES.

| | |
|---|---:|
| Debts due from directors.................................... | $35,480 00 |
| Debts due from other stockholders.................... ....... | 5,650 00 |
| Debts due from all others ................................. | 118,908 95 |
| Specie actually in Bank.................................... | 333 00 |
| Bills of other Banks....................................... | 6,899 69 |
| Deposits in other Banks.................................... | 2,834 45 |
| Its own stock held by the Bank............................ | 1,142 00 |
| Stock in other Banks...................................... | |
| Other stocks owned by the Bank........................... | |
| Real estate................................................ | |
| Other property............................................ | |
| Expense account.......................................... | 360 50 |
| Total amount of resources........................... | $171,108 59 |

### LIABILITIES.

| | |
|---|---:|
| Capital stock actually paid in.............................. | $121,150 00 |
| Bills in circulation........................................ | 980 00 |
| Deposits on interest....................................... | 14.552 00 |
| Deposits not on interest................................... | 27,820 43 |
| Debts due to other Banks................................. | 2,300 00 |
| Dividends unpaid.......................................... | 997 50 |
| Net profits on hand........................................ | 3,308 66 |
| Total amount of Liabilities........................... | $171,108 59 |

### ADDITIONAL PARTICULARS.

| | |
|---|---:|
| Increase of capital since last return...................................... | |
| Par value of shares.......................................... | $50 00 |
| Amount of last dividend..................................... | 3,634 50 |
| Date of last dividend....................................October 2, 1876. | |
| Rate per cent of last dividend..............................3 pr. ct. 6 mo. | |
| Reserved profits at the time of last dividend.................. | 1,749 00 |
| Debts due and not paid....................................... | 12,910 94 |
| Amount of suspended paper considered bad or doubtful.................. | |
| Amount loaned on pledges of stock in Bank.................. | 5,850 00 |
| Amount and description of stocks held as collateral security for loans*................... ..................... | 20,500 00 |
| Largest amount of indebtedness of any one person or firm.... | 13,825 00 |
| Amount of bills in circulation under five dollars.............. | 700 00 |

\* See page 26.

## NORTHERN BANK, PROVIDENCE.

HENRY J. STEERE, *President.*
SULLIVAN FENNER, *Cashier.*

### RESOURCES.

| | |
|---|---|
| Debts due from directors................................... | $30,000 00 |
| Debts due from other stockholders......................... | 3,000 00 |
| Debts due from all others................................. | 322,015 66 |
| Specie actually in Bank................................... | 1,873 65 |
| Bills and checks of other Banks and Government scrip....... | 8,009 58 |
| Deposits in oth  Banks.................................... | 5,281 45 |
| Its own stock held by the Bank........................... | ............ |
| Bank call loan........................................... | 5,000 00 |
| Description of stock in other Banks...................... | ............ |
| Other stocks owned by the Bank.......................... | ............ |
| Real estate............................................. | ............ |
| Other property.......................................... | 816 61 |
| Expense account......................................... | ............ |
| **Total amount of resources**........................... | **$375,996 95** |

### LIABILITIES.

| | |
|---|---|
| Capital stock actually paid in............................. | $251,000 00 |
| Bills in circulation....................................... | ............ |
| Deposits on interest....................................... | ............ |
| Deposits not on interest................................... | 66,923 36 |
| Debts due to other Banks................................... | ............ |
| Suspense account.......................................... | 29,870 27 |
| Dividends unpaid.......................................... | 1,471 50 |
| Call loan................................................. | 375 00 |
| Bankrupt claim............................................ | 1,960 61 |
| Net profits on hand....................................... | 24,396 21 |
| **Total amount of liabilities**........................... | **$375.996 95** |

### ADDITIONAL PARTICULARS.

| | |
|---|---|
| Increase of capi  since last return....................... | ............ |
| Par value of shares....................................... | $100 00 |
| Amount of last dividend................................... | 7,530 00 |
| Date of last dividend..................................... | Dec. 6, 1875. |
| Rate per cent. of last dividend........................... | 3 pr. ct 6 m. |
| Reserved profits at the time of last dividend............. | 13,922 41 |
| Debts due and not paid.................................... | 119,356 00 |
| Amount of suspended paper considered bad or doubtful...... | 70,861 56 |
| Amount loaned on pledges of stock in Bank................. | 7,000 00 |
| Amount and description of stocks held as collateral security for loans†................................... | 10,000 00 |
| Largest amount of indebtedness of any one person or firm.... | 39,500 00 |
| Amount of bills in circulation under five dollars......... | ............ |

† See page 26.

# PAWTUXET BANK, PROVIDENCE.

A. M. KIMBALL, *President.*

S. D. GREENE, *Cashier.*

### RESOURCES.

| | |
|---|---:|
| Debts due from directors...................................... | $7,550 00 |
| Debts due from other stockholders ........................ | 5,850 00 |
| Debts due from all others.................................... | 135,581 15 |
| Specie actually in Bank..................................... | 185 77 |
| Bills of other Banks......................................... | 3,225 83 |
| Deposits in other Banks..................................... | 5,777 57 |
| Its own Stock held by the Bank.............................. | |
| Description of stock in other Banks......................... | |
| Other bonds owned by the Bank.............................. | 23,183 33 |
| Real estate................................................. | |
| Other property ............................................. | |
| Expense Account............................................. | 424 03 |
| Total amount of resources........................... | $181,777 68 |

### LIABILITIES.

| | |
|---|---:|
| Capital stock actually paid in.............................. | $150,000 00 |
| Bills in circulation....................................... | 2,260 00 |
| Deposits on interest....................................... | |
| Deposits not on interest................................... | 18,134 00 |
| Debts due to other banks................................... | |
| Dividends unpaid........................................... | 842 50 |
| Net profits on hand........................................ | 10,541 18 |
| Total amount of liabilities........................... | $181,777 68 |

### ADDITIONAL PARTICULARS.

| | |
|---|---:|
| Increase of capital since last return ...................... | |
| Par value of shares........................................ | $50 00 |
| Amount of last dividend.................................... | 4,500 00 |
| Date of last dividend...................................... | Aug. 6, 1876. |
| Rate per cent. of last dividend............................ | 3 pr. ct. 6 mo. |
| Reserved profits at the time of last dividend............... | 8,540 66 |
| Debts due and not paid..................................... | 32,326 70 |
| Amount of suspended paper considered bad or doubtful....... | 10,000 00 |
| Amount loaned on pledges of stock in Bank.................. | 5,700 00 |
| Amount of stocks held as collateral security for loans...... | |
| Largest amount of indebtedness of any one person or firm..... | 10,000 00 |
| Amount of bills in circulation under five dollars........... | |

## STATE BANK, PROVIDENCE.

GEORGE B. PECK,  
SAMUEL W. PECKHAM, } *Directors.*

SAMUEL KENNEDY, *Cashier.*

### RESOURCES.

| | |
|---|---|
| Debts due from directors..................................... | $700 00 |
| Debts due from other stockholders.......................... | 18,105 00 |
| Debts due from all others.................................... | 115,379 84 |
| Specie actually in Bank..................................... | 61 00 |
| Bills of other Banks........................................ | 9,681 72 |
| Deposits in other Banks .................................... | 155 03 |
| Its own stock held by the Bank.............................. | 5,101 10 |
| Stock in other Banks*....................................... | 960 00 |
| Other stocks owned by the Bank............................. | 11,335 00 |
| Real estate................................................. | |
| Other property............................................. | 3,000 00 |
| Expense account............................................ | 2,503 66 |
| Total amount of resources......................... | $166,982 35 |

### LIABILITIES.

| | |
|---|---|
| Capital stock actually paid in.............................. | $154,450 00 |
| Bills in circulation........................................ | 1,905 50 |
| Deposits on interest....................................... | |
| Deposits not on interest................................... | 7,896 79 |
| Debts due to other Banks................................... | |
| Dividends unpaid.......................................... | 1,895 75 |
| Net profits on hand........................................ | 834 31 |
| Total amount of liabilities........................ | $166,982 35 |

### ADDITIONAL PARTICULARS.

| | |
|---|---|
| Increase of capital since last return....................... | |
| Par value of shares........................................ | $50 00 |
| Amount of last dividend.................................... | 3,089 00 |
| Date of last dividend............................ | Oct. 1, 1876. |
| Rate per cent. of last dividend.................... | 2 pr. ct. 6 mo. |
| Reserved profits at the time of last dividend................ | 2,500 00 |
| Debts due and not paid..................................... | 45,815 57 |
| Amount of suspended paper considered bad or doubtful....... | 1,672 50 |
| Amount loaned on pledges of stock in Bank................ | 6,805 00 |
| Amount and description of stocks held as collateral security for loans†................................................. | 2,000 00 |
| Largest amount of indebtedness of any one person or firm.... | 26,300 87 |
| Amount of bills in circulation under five dollars.............. | 1,195 50 |

*See page 25.   † See page 26.

## UNION BANK, PROVIDENCE.

J. C. JOHNSON, *Cashier.*  
C. A. NICHOLS, *President.*

### RESOURCES.

| | |
|---|---:|
| Debts due from directors.................................... | $69,617 20 |
| Debts due from other stockholders........................... | 20,900 00 |
| Debts due from all others................................... | 1,084,592 45 |
| Specie actually in Bank..................................... | 1,742 00 |
| Bills and checks of other Banks....  ........................ | 11,977 47 |
| Deposits in other Banks.................................... | 61,835 48 |
| Its own stock held by the Bank............................. | 966 00 |
| Stock in other Banks...................................... | |
| Other stocks owned by the Bank........................... | |
| Real estate............................................... | 22,500 00 |
| Other property........................................... | |
| Expense account.......................................... | |
| **Total amount of resources........................** | **$1,274,180 60** |

### LIABILITIES.

| | |
|---|---:|
| Capital stock actually paid in.............................. | $800,000 00 |
| Bills in circulation....................................... | |
| Deposits on interest....................................... | 209,508 70 |
| Deposits not on interest .................................. | 165,400 77 |
| Debts due to other Banks.................................. | 68,246 00 |
| Dividends unpaid.......................................... | 1,280 75 |
| Net profits on hand....................................... | 29,694 38 |
| **Total amount of liabilities........................** | **$1,274,130 60** |

### ADDITIONAL PARTICULARS.

| | |
|---|---:|
| Increase of capital since last return....................... | |
| Par value of shares ...................................... | $50 00 |
| Amount of last dividend................................... | 24,000 00 |
| Date of last dividend.........................................July 1, 1876. | |
| Rate per cent. of last dividend...........................3 pr. ct. 6 mo. | |
| Reserved profits at the time of last dividend................ | 14,160 06 |
| Debts due and not paid.................................... | 57,760 91 |
| Amount of suspended paper considered bad or doubtful....... | 38,760 91 |
| Amount loaned on pledges of stock in Bank............. ... | 8,400 00 |
| Amount and description of stocks held as collateral security for loans†............................................. | 58,550 00 |
| Largest amount of indebtedness of any one person or firm.... | 110,000 00 |
| Amount of bills in circulation under five dollars................ | |

†See page 26.

## WESTMINSTER BANK, PROVIDENCE.

**ELI AYLSWORTH,** *President.*

A. W. SIMONS, *Cashier.*

### RESOURCES.

| | |
|---|---:|
| Debts due from Directors | $3,200 00 |
| Debts due from other stockholders | 11,885 00 |
| Debts due from all others | 307,773 71 |
| Specie actually in Bank, including nickels | 1,489 77 |
| Bills of other Banks and cash checks | 11,310 38 |
| Deposits in other Banks | 22,591 95 |
| Its own stock held by the Bank | |
| Stock in other Banks | |
| Other stocks owned by the Bank | |
| Real estate | 6,973 26 |
| Other property | 15 44 |
| Expense account | 209 80 |
| Total amount of resources | $365,449 31 |

### LIABILITIES.

| | |
|---|---:|
| Capital stock actually paid in | $200,000 00 |
| Bills in circulation | 1,051 00 |
| Deposits on interest | 33,921 53 |
| Deposits not on interest | 84,493 77 |
| Debts due to other Banks | |
| Dividends unpaid | 1,732 75 |
| Government dues | 678 94 |
| Profits on hand | 43,571 32 |
| Total amount of liabilities | $365,449 31 |

### ADDITIONAL PARTICULARS.

| | |
|---|---:|
| Increase of capital since last return | |
| Par value of shares | $50 00 |
| Amount of last dividend | 7,000 00 |
| Date of last dividend | Nov. 6, 1876. |
| Rate per cent. of last dividend | 3½ pr ct. 6 m. |
| Reserved profits at the time of last dividend | 42,693 69 |
| Debts due and not paid | 37,846 73 |
| Amount of suspended paper considered bad or doubtful | 2,890 61 |
| Amount loaned on pledges of stock in Bank | 510 00 |
| Amount and description of stock held as collateral security for loans† | 75,770 00 |
| Largest amount of indebtedness of any one person or firm | 48,000 00 |
| Amount of bills in circulation under five dollars | 500 00 |

† See page 26.

# MERCHANTS BANK, NEWPORT.

A. S. **SHERMAN**, *Cashier.*

**SILAS H. COTTRELL**, *President.*

### RESOURCES.

| | | |
|---|---:|---:|
| Debts due from directors | $14,000 | 00 |
| Debts due from other stockholders | 4,950 | 00 |
| Debts due from all others | 242,410 | 22 |
| Specie actually in Bank | 328 | 60 |
| Bills of other Banks, | 9,572 | 30 |
| Deposits in other Banks | 49,230 | 32 |
| Its own stock held by the Bank | 6,300 | 00 |
| Stock in other Banks | | |
| Other stocks owned by the Bank | | |
| Real estate | 10,000 | 00 |
| Other property | | |
| Expense account | | |
| Total amount of resources | $336,791 | 44 |

### LIABILITIES.

| | | |
|---|---:|---:|
| Capital stock actually paid in | $100,000 | 00 |
| Bills in circulation | | |
| Deposits on interest | 20,025 | 68 |
| Deposits not on interest | 212,213 | 15 |
| Debts due to other banks | 779 | 91 |
| Dividends unpaid | 156 | 00 |
| Net profits on hand | 3,616 | 70 |
| Total amount of liabilities | $336,791 | 44 |

### ADDITIONAL PARTICULARS.

| | | |
|---|---:|---:|
| Increase of capital since last return | | |
| Par value of shares | $100 | 00 |
| Amount of last dividend | 3,000 | 00 |
| Date of last dividend | July 1, 1876. | |
| Rate per cent. of last dividend | 3 pr. ct. 6 mo. | |
| Reserved profits at the time of last dividend | 117 | 41 |
| Debts due and not paid | | |
| Amount of suspended paper considered bad or doubtful | 1,050 | 00 |
| Amount loaned on pledges of stock in Bank | 2,150 | 00 |
| Amount and description of stocks held as collateral security for loans† | 12,100 | 00 |
| Largest amount of indebtedness of any one person or firm | 22,975 | 00 |
| Amount of bills in circulation under five dollars | | |

† See page 26.

## NEW ENGLAND COMMERCIAL BANK, NEWPORT.

GEORGE BOWEN, *President.*

N. UNDERWOOD, *Cashier.*

### RESOURCES.

| | |
|---|---:|
| Debts due from directors | $12,860 00 |
| Debts due from other stockholders | 1,175 00 |
| Debts due from all others | 40,141 07 |
| Specie actually in Bank | 1,148 66 |
| Bills of other Banks | 7,838 22 |
| Deposits in other Banks | 5,513 61 |
| Its own stock held by the Bank | 3,400 00 |
| Stock in other Banks* | 400 00 |
| Other stocks owned by the Bank* | 45,885 00 |
| Real estate | 5,500 00 |
| Other property | 131 22 |
| Expense account | |
| Total amount of resources | $123,992 78 |

### LIABILITIES.

| | |
|---|---:|
| Capital stock actually paid in | $75,000 00 |
| Bills in circulation | 2,752 00 |
| Deposits on interest | |
| Deposits not on interest | 32,059 27 |
| Debts due to other Banks | |
| Dividends unpaid | 291 00 |
| Net profits on hand | 13,890 51 |
| Total amount of liabilities | $123,992 78 |

### ADDITIONAL PARTICULARS.

| | |
|---|---:|
| Increase of capital since last return | |
| Par value of shares | $50 00 |
| Amount of last dividend | 3,000 00 |
| Date of last dividend | July 1st. 1876. |
| Rate per cent. of last dividend | 4 pr. ct. 6 mo. |
| Reserved profits at the time of last dividend | 12,466 57 |
| Debts due and not paid | 7,583 20 |
| Amount of suspended paper considered bad or doubtful | |
| Amount loaned on pledges of stock in Bank | 6,235 00 |
| Amount and description of stocks held as collateral security for loans† | 3,000 00 |
| Largest amount of indebtedness of any one person or firm | 12,000 00 |
| Amount of bills in circulation under five dollars | 1,296 00 |

* See page 25.    † See page 26.

## RHODE ISLAND UNION BANK, NEWPORT.

GEO. F. CRANDALL, *President, pro tem.*
J. S. COGGESHALL *Cashier.*

### RESOURCES.

| | | |
|---|---:|---:|
| Debts due from directors............................................. | $15,551 | 69 |
| Debts due from other stockholders................................ | 7,075 | 00 |
| Debts due from all others............................................ | 204,020 | 82 |
| Silver, fractional currency and cents............................. | 3,081 | 80 |
| Bills of other Banks and cash checks............................ | 18,758 | 74 |
| Deposits in other Banks............................................. | 26,839 | 12 |
| Its own stock held by the Bank................................... | | |
| Stock in other Banks................................................. | | |
| Other stocks owned by the Bank*................................ | 20,000 | 00 |
| Real estate............................................................. | | |
| Other property....................................................... | | |
| Expense account..................................................... | | |
| Total amount of resources........................... | $295,327 | 17 |

### LIABILITIES.

| | | |
|---|---:|---:|
| Capital stock actually paid in...................................... | $173,700 | 00 |
| Bills in circulation................................................... | 1,955 | 00 |
| Deposits on interest................................................. | | |
| Deposits not on interest............................................ | 88,189 | 13 |
| Debts due to other Banks.......................................... | | |
| Dividends unpaid..................................................... | 1,994 | 00 |
| Bank building account............................................... | 10,891 | 27 |
| Net profits on hand.................................................. | 18,597 | 77 |
| Total amount of liabilities........................... | $295,327 | 17 |

### ADDITIONAL PARTICULARS.

| | | |
|---|---:|---:|
| Increase of capital since last return............................. | | |
| Par value of shares.................................................. | $100 | 00 |
| Amount of last dividend............................................ | 6,948 | 00 |
| Date of last dividend................................................July 1, 1876. | | |
| Rate per cent. of last dividend.................................4 pr.ct. 6 mo. | | |
| Reserved profits at the time of last dividend.................. | 12,798 | 12 |
| Debts due and not paid............................................. | 20,270 | 35 |
| Amount of suspended paper considered bad or doubtful........ | 1,000 | 00 |
| Amount loaned on pledges of stock in Bank.................. | 5,010 | 00 |
| Amount and description of stocks held as collateral security for loans†...................... | 24,000 | 00 |
| Largest amount of indebtedness of any one person or firm.... | 26,953 | 38 |
| Amount of bills in circulation under five dollars.............. | 750 | 00 |

* See page 25.  † See page 26.

## SUMMARY OF RESOURCES AND LIABILITIES.

*of State Banks on Tuesday November 28, 1876.*

| | BANKS IN PROVIDENCE. | BANKS OUT OF PROVIDENCE. | ALL BANKS IN THE STATE. |
|---|---|---|---|
| **RESOURCES.** | | | |
| Debts due from directors......... | $279,920 20 | $42,411 69 | $322,331 89 |
| Debts due from other stockholders | 186,033 01 | 13,200 00 | 199,233 01 |
| Debts due from all others........ | 3,393,372 08 | 486,572 11 | 3,879,944 19 |
| Specie actually in Banks.......... | 9,547 38 | 4,559 06 | 14,106 44 |
| Bills of other Banks.............. | 148,974 49 | 36,169 26 | 185,143 75 |
| Deposits in other Banks.......... | 152,160 66 | 81,583 05 | 233,743 71 |
| Amount of own stock held by the Banks...................... | 37,259 10 | 9,700 00 | 46,959 10 |
| Amount of stock in other Banks.. | 960 00 | 400 00 | 1,360 00 |
| Amount of other stocks owned by the Banks.................... | 34,518 33 | 65,885 00 | 100,403 33 |
| Real estate...................... | 34,673 26 | 15.500 00 | 50,173 26 |
| Other property.................. | 15,078 98 | 131 22 | 15,210 20 |
| Expense account................ | 8,359 58 | None. | 8,359 58 |
| Total amount of resources.... | $4,300,857 07 | $756,111 39 | $5,056,968 46 |
| **LIABILITIES.** | | | |
| Capital stock actually paid in..... | $2,879,150 00 | $348,700 00 | $3,227,850 00 |
| Bills in circulation.............. | 11,808 50 | 4,707 00 | 16,515 50 |
| Deposits on interest.............. | 261,982 23 | 20,025 68 | 282,007 91 |
| Deposits not on interest.......... | 744,148 09 | 332,461 55 | 1,076,609 64 |
| Loans on call and cashiers' checks. | 375 00 | None. | 375 00 |
| Debt due to other Banks.......... | 156,009 53 | 779 91 | 156,789 44 |
| Dividends unpaid................. | 13,429 00 | 2,441 00 | 15,870 00 |
| Suspense account................ | 31,830 88 | None. | 31,830 88 |
| Bank building account............ | None. | 10,891 27 | 10,891 27 |
| Government taxes................ | 678 94 | None. | 678 94 |
| Net profits on hand.............. | 201,444 90 | 36,104 98 | 237,549 88 |
| Total amount of liabilities..... | $4,300,857 07 | $756,111 39 | $5,056,968 46 |
| **SUMMARY OF OTHER ITEMS.** | | | |
| Increase of capital since last return | ............ | ............ | N |
| Amount of last dividend.......... | $86,487 75 | $12,948 00 | $99,435 |
| Amount of suspended paper considered bad or doubtful........ | 184,750 75 | 2,050 00 | 186,800 75 |
| Reserved profits at time of last dividend.................... | 157,367 24 | 30,382 10 | 187,749 34 |
| Amount loaned on pledges of stock in Banks................ | 124,930 00 | 13,395 00 | 138,325 00 |
| Debts due and unpaid............ | 488,572 83 | 27,853 55 | 516,426 38 |

# DESCRIPTION OF STOCKS

## IN OTHER BANKS AND OTHER STOCKS AND BONDS OWNED BY THE BANKS.

---

### State Bank, Providence.

| | |
|---|---:|
| 16 shares Merchants Exchange National Bank, New York city, par value $50 per share, market value.......... .................. ...............… | $960 00 |

### Pawtuxet Bank, Providence.

| | |
|---|---:|
| Providence Water Loan Bonds and United States 6 per cent. Bonds 1881............ | $23,183 33 |

### New England Commercial Bank, Newport.

| | |
|---|---:|
| Four shares Merchants Bank, Newport............................................ | $400 00 |
| Chicago Park Loan Bonds......................................................... | $10,175 00 |
| Chicago River Improvement Bonds................................................ | 2,910 00 |
| City of Brooklyn Park Loan Bonds................................................ | 3,000 00 |
| Town of Osage, La Salle County, Illinois Bonds.. ............................... | 3,000 00 |
| Town of Cairo, Illinois Bonds.................................................... | 7,000 00 |
| Town of Vermont, Illinois Bonds................................................. | 975 00 |
| Town of Oswego, Illinois Bonds.................................................. | 4,950 00 |
| Town of Amity, Illinois Bonds................................................... | 4,950 00 |
| Town of Bushnell, Illinois Bonds... ............................................ | 2,625 00 |
| City of Covington, Ky., Water Loan.............................................. | 6,000 00 |
| | $45,885 00 |

### Rhode Island Union Bank, Newport.

| | |
|---|---:|
| United States 6 per cent. Bonds 1881 ........................................... | $20,000 00 |

# STOCKS

## HELD AS COLLATERAL SECURITY FOR LOANS.

---

### Bank of America, Providence.

| | |
|---|---:|
| 35 shares Commercial National Bank, Providence, par............................ | $1.750 00 |
| 24 shares Phenix National Bank, Providence, par.............................. | 1,200 00 |
| (Amount loaned $3,100)............ ................................. | $2,950 00 |

### Grocers and Producers Bank, Providence.

| | |
|---|---:|
| 226 shares Pawtucket Hair Cloth Company, par.................... .................. | $11,300 00 |
| (Amount loaned $500.) | |

### Liberty Bank, Providence.

| | |
|---|---:|
| St. Louis, Alton & Terre Haute Railroad Bonds, par.............................. | $3,000 00 |
| (Loan of $2,000.) | |
| A. & W. Sprague Mf'g Co. notes, (loan $4,000)............................ ......... | $10,000 00 |
| Savings Bank Books ..... ........................................................ | 7,500 00 |

### Northern Bank, Providence.

| | |
|---|---:|
| 200 shares American Ship Windlass Company, par.............................. | $30,000 00 |
| (Amount loaned $10,000.) | |

### State Bank, Providence.

| | |
|---|---:|
| 20 shares Nevada Reservoir Ditch Company, California, par.................... . | $2,000 00 |
| (Amount loaned $2,000.) | |

### Union Bank, Providence.

| | |
|---|---:|
| 20 shares Roger Williams National Bank, Providence, par........................ | $1,500 00 |
| 8 shares Providence  "  "  "  "  ............................ | 3,200 00 |
| 55 shares Merchants  "  "  "  "  .......................... | 2,750 00 |
| 20 shares First  "  "  "  "  ............................ | 2,000 00 |
| 36 shares United States Trust Company, New York  "  ............ ............ | 2,600 00 |
| 30 shares Mechanics Mills, Fall River, par.... .................................... | 3,000 00 |
| 45 shares West Providence Land Company, par.................... ................ | 7,500 00 |
| 5 shares Union Oil Company, Providence, par.............................. ..... | 5,000 00 |
| 12 Bonds Quicksilver Mining Company, par................... ...... .............. | 12,000 00 |
| 7 Bonds New York Central Railroad Company, par...................... .......... | 7,000 00 |
| 19 Bonds United States sixes, par.............................................. | 12,000 00 |
| (Amount loaned $60,000.)............................................. | $65,550 00 |

## Westminster Bank, Providence.

| | |
|---|---|
| 9 shares Old Colony and Newport Railroad Company, par......................... | $900 00 |
| 86 shares New York, Providence & Boston Railroad Company............... ..... | 8,840 00 |
| 6 shares Fall River Manufacturing Company, supposed value ................... | 4,800 00 |
| 12 shares Troy C. & W. Manufacturing Company, supposed value................. | 18,000 00 |
| 5 shares Annawan          "          "          "          " ............. | 4,000 00 |
| 250 shares R. Borden      "          "          "          " | 25,000 00 |
| 100 shares Flint Mills............................      "       " ................. | 10,000 00 |
| 4 shares American Screw Company.......................................... | 1,580 00 |
| 20 shares Shoe Mills, par................................................. | 2,000 00 |
| Savings Bank Books...................................................... | 650 00 |
| (Amount loaned $54,797 25.)...................................... | $75,770 00 |

## Merchants Bank, Newport.

| | |
|---|---|
| American Telegraph Company stock, par........................... | $6,750 00 |
| United States Bonds, par......................................... | 1,000 00 |
| Savings Bank Books........... ................................ | 350 00 |
| Paid up policy in life insurance Company............... ......... | 4,000 00 |
| (Amount loaned $5,100.). ...................................... | $12,100 00 |

## New England Commercial Bank, Newport.

| | |
|---|---|
| 2 shares Newport Gas Company stock, par ......... ................. | $200 00 |
| 10 shares Old Colony Railroad Company, par........................... | 1,000 00 |
| 20 shares Aquidneck National Bank, par............................. | 1,000 00 |
| 10 shares Newport    "       "       " ................................ | 600 00 |
| 2 shares Merchants  "       "       " ................................ | 200 00 |
| (Amount loaned $2,250.)............. ......................... | $3,000 00 |

## Rhode Island Union Bank, Newport.

| | |
|---|---|
| Atlantic and Gulf Railroad Bonds (loan $1,000)..................................... | $1,000 00 |
| Cedar Rapids and Missouri River Railroad Bonds (loan $10,000)........ ........... | 20,000 00 |
| United States Bonds (loan $200).................................. | 500 00 |
| Brooklyn N. Y. Water Loan Bond and United States Bonds (amount loaned $1,500) | 1,500 00 |

# ANNUAL STATEMENT

EXHIBITING THE CONDITION OF THE

# INSTITUTIONS FOR SAVINGS

—ON—

TUESDAY, THE 28TH DAY OF NOVEMBER, 1876,

FROM RETURNS MADE TO THE STATE AUDITOR.

## ASHAWAY SAVINGS BANK.

*G. N. LANGWORTHY, Treasurer.*

| | RESOURCES. | LIABILITIES. | MISCELLANEOUS. |
|---|---|---|---|
| Amount invested in mortgages on real estate............ ......... | $32,780 95 | ............ | |
| Amount invested in stocks..... | 4,613 50 | ............ | |
| Amount invested in bonds..... | 15,050 88 | .... ........ | |
| Amount loaned on personal security..................... | 25,655 86 | ............ | |
| Amount loaned on collaterals of personal property.......... | ............. | ............ | |
| Amount of cash on hand....... | 2 38 | ......... ... | |
| Amount of deposits............ | ............ | $75,889 67 | |
| Amount of profit on hand...... | ............ | 2,213 90 | |
| | $78,103 57 | $78,103 57 | |
| Number of depositors.......... | ............ | ............ | 393 |
| of $500 and $1,000........ | ............ | ............ | 17 |
| of $1,000 and upwards,.... | ............ | ............ | 17 |
| Largest amount due to any one depositor.................. | $3,442 84 | ............ | |
| Amount, date and rate per cent. of last dividend........... | 1,791 99 | July 1, 1876 5 pr. ct. pr. an. | |
| Average rate of dividend for the last three years............ | ............ | ............ 6¼ pr. ct pr.an. | |
| Amount of reserved profits at time of last dividend....... | 719 34 | ............ | |

Amount loaned on mortgages in State of Connecticut.... ...   $340 00

Description of stocks and bonds held by the Bank, names of the Institutions in which invested, with their several amounts:

Stocks—Ashaway National Bank............................. ........................   $3,433 50
  Merchants National Bank, Providence...... ...................... .........   1,180 00
Bonds—Burlington, Cedar Rapids and Minnesota Railroad .........................   8,850 88
  Moultrie County, Illinois......................................................   1,800 00
Notes—Town of Hopkinton.......................................................   4,400 00

                  $19,663 38

## BRISTOL COUNTY SAVINGS BANK.

*P. SKINNER, JR., Treasurer.*

| | RESOURCES. | LIABILITIES. | MISCELLANEOUS. |
|---|---|---|---|
| Amount invested in mortgages on real estate.............. | $5,000 00 | .............. | |
| Amount invested in stocks..... | .............. | .............. | |
| Amount invested in bonds..... | .............. | .............. | |
| Amount loaned on personal security ................ | .............. | .............. | |
| Amount loaned on collaterals of personal property ....,.... | 220 00 | .............. | |
| Amount of cash on hand....... | 833 96 | .............. | |
| Amount of deposits........,... | .............. | $6,025 89 | |
| Amount of profit on hand...... | .............. | 28 07 | |
| | $6,053 96 | $6,053 96 | |
| Number of depositors......... | .............. | .............. | 108 |
| of $500 and under $1,000, | .............. | .............. | 3 |
| of $1,000 and upwards..... | .............. | .............. | 1 |
| Largest amount due to any one depositor............... | | | $1,948 21 |
| Amount, date and rate per cent. of last dividend........... | .............. | .............. | |
| Average rate of dividend for the last three years........... | .............. | .............. | |
| Amount of reserved profits at time of last dividend....... | .............. | .............. | |

*The Bank commenced business in August, 1876.

## BRISTOL INSTITUTION FOR SAVINGS, BRISTOL.

*MARTIN BENNETT, Treasurer.*

| | RESOURCES. | LIABILITIES. | MISCELLANEOUS |
|---|---|---|---|
| Amount invested in mortgages on real estate.............. | $226,203 67 | ... ......... | |
| Amount invested in stocks..... | 24,583 46 | ... ......... | |
| Amount invested in bonds..... | 28,000 00 | ....,....... | |
| Amount loaned on personal security.................... | 75,617 06 | ... ...... | |
| Amount loaned on collaterals of personal property.......... | ............ | ... ........ | |
| Amount of cash on hand...... | 10,326 65 | ............. | |
| Premium..................... | 4,162 50 | ............. | |
| Amount of deposits............ | .... .... . | $349,361 20 | |
| Amount of profit on hand...... | ............ | 19,532 14 | |
| | $ 368,893 34 | $368,893 34 | |
| Number of depositors.. ...... | ............ | .... .. .... | 1,223 |
| of $500 and under $1,000. | ............ | .... ....... | 174 |
| of $1,000 and upwards..... | ............ | .... ....... | 73 |
| Largest amount due to any one depositor.................. | ............ | ............. | $3,135 60 |
| Amount, date and rate per cent. of last dividend............ | June 1, 1876. | 3 pr.ct. 6 mos. | 9,868 03 |
| Average rate of dividend for the last three years............ | ............ | ............. | 6¾pr.ct.pr.an. |
| Amount of reserved profits at time of last dividend...... | ............ | ............. | 9,491 59 |

Amount loaned on mortgages in State of Massachusetts..........$3,814 87

Description of stocks and bonds held by the Bank, names of the Institutions in which invested, with their several amounts :

Stock in National Bank of North America, Providence.... ........................ $5,192 50
   "  " National Bank of Commerce   "    ........................... ... 4.005 68
   "  " Commercial National Bank,   "    ...... ...................... .. 3,371 50
   "  " Third National Bank,    "    ...... ..... .................... 2.040 00
   "  " Merchants National Bank,   "    .. • ...................... ...... 2,623 73
   "  " First National Bank, of Bristol.... ........... ........................ 7,350 00

$24,583 46

United States 6 per cent. registered bonds, of 1881......................... .......... $18,000 00
United States 5 per cent. registered bonds.... ... ......... .. ....................... 10,000 00

$28,000 00

## CITIZENS SAVINGS BANK, PROVIDENCE

*E. ALLEN, Treasurer.*

| . | RESOURCES. | LIABILITIES. | MISCELLANEOUS. |
|---|---|---|---|
| Amount invested in mortgages on real estate............. | $499,357 48 | ............. | |
| Amount invested in stocks...... | 25,100 00 | ............. | |
| Amount invested in bonds...... | 10,000 00 | ...... ....... | |
| Amount loaned on personal security.................... | 24,300 00 | .... .. ..... | |
| Amount loaned on collaterals of personal property .. ...... | ............. | | |
| Amount of cash on hand ....... | 24,583 45 | ............. | |
| Premium.................... | 1,059 20 | ............. | |
| Real Estate............... ..... | 1,800 00 | ............. | |
| Amount of deposits................. | ............. | $565,838 11 | |
| Amount of profit on hand...... | ............. | 20,362 02 | |
| | $586,200 13 | $586,200 13 | |
| | | | |
| Number of depositors.......... | ............. | ............ | 756 |
| of $500 and under $1,000... | ............. | ............ | 100 |
| of $1,000 and upwards.... | ............. | ...... ..... | 133 |
| Largest amount due to any one depositor............... | ............. | ............ | $31,563 88 |
| Amount, date and rate per cent. of last dividend........... | $14,807 68 | July 1, 1876. | 3¹ pr.ct. 6 mos. |
| Average rate of dividend for the last three years........... | .. ........ | ........ .... | 7₁¹₂ per cent. |
| Amount of reserved profits at time of last dividend...... | 7,353¹⁰⁵⁄₁₀₀ | ...... ....... | |

Amount loaned on mortgage in State of Massachusetts................$7,800 00

Description of stocks and bonds held by the Bank, names of the Institution, in which invested, with their several amounts :

High Street Bank, Providence, R. I.................................................. ... .    $10,100 00
Commercial National Bank, Providence, R. I. ...... ........ .. .............. .......    5,000 00
National Bank of Commerce. Providence, R. I ......................................    10,000 00
                                                   $25,100 00

Town of Burrillville bonds.... ....... ... .... .......... ................ .......    $10,000 00

# CITIZENS SAVINGS INSTITUTION, WOONSOCKET.

*W. H. ALDRICH, Treasurer.*

| | RESOURCES. | LIABILITIES. | MISCELLANEOUS. |
|---|---|---|---|
| Amount invested in mortgages on real estate.............. | $150,435 00 | .......... | |
| Amount invested in stocks..... | 7,979 50 | .......... | |
| Amount invested in bonds..... | 8,000 00 | .......... | |
| Amount loaned on personal security.................. | 135,655 00 | .......... | |
| Amount loaned on collaterals of personal property......... | .......... | .......... | |
| Amount of cash on hand....... | 5,120 89 | .......... | |
| Real Estate................... | 5,700 00 | .......... | |
| Amount of deposits........... | .......... | $308,640 84 | |
| Amount of profit on hand..... | .......... | 4,249 55 | |
| | $312,890 39 | $312,890 39 | |
| Number of depositors......... | .......... | .......... | 556 |
| of $500 and under $1,000.. | .......... | .......... | 90 |
| of $1,000 and upwards..... | .......... | .......... | 100 |
| Largest amount due to any one depositor.................. | .......... | .......... | $8,259 52 |
| Amount, date and rate per cent. of last dividend........... | $9,602 48 | | July 16, 3 pr.ct. 6 mos. |
| Average rate of dividend for the last three years........... | .......... | .......... | 6½pr.ct.pr.an. |
| Amount of reserved profits at time of last dividend....... | .......... | .......... | 3,000 00 |

Amount loaned on mortgages in other States:—

Wisconsin ............................... $27,700 00

Description of stocks and bonds held by the Bank, names of the Institutions in which invested, with their several amounts :

| | |
|---|---|
| Stock in Liberty Bank, Providence............... | $1,500 00 |
| Stock in Butchers and Drovers Bank, Providence........... | 2,944 50 |
| National Bank of Commerce, " | 1,535 00 |
| Third National Bank, " | 2,000 00 |
| | $7,979 50 |
| Town Woonsocket bonds........ | $8,000 00 |

## CITY SAVINGS BANK, PROVIDENCE.

*JAMES E. CRANSTON*, Treasurer.

| | RESOURCES. | LIABILITIES. | MISCELLANEOUS. |
|---|---|---|---|
| Amount invested in mortgages on real estate.............. | $1,109,994 00 | ............ | |
| Amount invested in stocks...... | 173,300 00 | ............ | |
| Amount invested in bonds...... | 113,500 00 | ............ | |
| Amount loaned on personal security..................... | 458,840 33 | ............ | |
| Amount loaned on collaterals of personal property ......... | 65,300 00 | | |
| Amount of cash on hand......... | 59,643 75 | ............ | |
| Real Estate.................... | 35,000 00 | | |
| Amount of deposits............. | ............ | $1,981,282 20 | |
| Amount of profit on hand...... | ............ | 34,295 88 | |
| | $2,015,578 08 | $2,015,578 08 | |
| Number of depositors......... | ............ | ............ | 2,818 |
| of $500 and under $1,000... | ............ | ............ | 458 |
| of $1,000 and upwards..... | ............ | ............ | 613 |
| Largest amount due to any one depositor.................... | ............ | ............ | $25,806 02 |
| Amount, date and rate per cent. of last dividend............ | $60,161 14 | July 17, 1876. | 6 pr. ct. pr. an. |
| Average rate of dividend for the last three years............ | ............ | ............ | 6½ pr ct. pr. an. |
| Amount of reserved profits at time of last dividend...... | ............ | ............ | $1,942 52 |

Amount loaned on mortgages in other States:—

| | |
|---|---|
| Massachusetts................................ | $30,000 00 |
| Philadelphia, Penn............................ | 6,000 00 |

Description of stocks and bonds held by the Bank, names of the Institution, in which invested, with their several amounts :

| | |
|---|---|
| Merchants National Bank............ | $5,900 |
| Fourth National Bank............ | 24,000 |
| Manufacturers National Bank ............ | 2,400 |
| American National Bank... ............ | 15,900 |
| Old National Bank.... ............ | 103,206 |
| Lime Rock National Bank.... ............ | 10,000 |
| Continental National Bank. New York ............ | 7,500 |
| New York State Loan and Trust Company............ | 5,000 |
| City of Elizabeth, New Jersey, Street Improvement bonds............ | 25,000 |
| New Haven, New London and Stonington Railroad Company's bonds............ | 30,000 |
| Pawtuxet Valley Railroad bonds............ | 5,000 |
| Bernon Manufacturing Company's bonds............ | 10,000 |
| Union Pacific Railroad First Mortgage bonds... ............ | 26,500 |
| City of Providence bonds.... ............ | 27,000 |
| | $196,800 |

## CODDINGTON SAVINGS BANK, NEWPORT.

*BENJAMIN MUMFORD*, *Treasurer.*

|  | RESOURCES. | LIABILITIES. | MISCELLANEOUS. |
|---|---|---|---|
| Amount invested in mortgages on real estate............ | $186,915 00 | ............ | |
| Amount invested in stocks..... | 8,300 00 | ............ | |
| Amount invested in bonds...... | 371,992 16 | ............ | |
| Amount loaned on personal security.................. | ............ | ............ | |
| Amount loaned on collaterals of personal property.......... | ............ | ............ | |
| Amount of cash on hand........ | ............ | ............ | |
| Amount of deposits............. | ............ | $557,155 98 | |
| Bills payable.................. | ............ | 8,173 71 | |
| Amount of profit on hand...... | ............ | 1,877 47 | |
| | $567,207 16 | $567,207 16 | |
| | | | |
| Number of depositors.......... | ............ | ............ | 1,525 |
| of $500 and under $1,000... | ............ | ............ | 136 |
| of $1,000 and upwards..... | ............ | ............ | 170 |
| Largest amount due to any one depositor.... ............ | ............ | ............ | $12,815 52 |
| Amount, date and rate per cent. of last dividend........... | $16,718 74 | Oct. 18, 1876. | 3 pr. ct., 6 m. |
| Average rate of dividend for the last three years'........... | 6,₁₀₀⁸⁸ | ............ | |
| Amount of reserved profits at time of last dividend....... | $353 21 | ............ | |

Amount loaned on mortgages in other States—

Massachusetts............................ $4,500 00

Illinois.................................. 30,700 00

$35,200 00

Description of stocks and bonds held by the bank, names of the institutions in which invested, with their several amounts :

| United States 4½ per cent. bonds, gold................................. | $10,000 00 |
|---|---|
| State of Missouri 6 per cent. bonds.......... ......... ... ............ | 9,000 00 |
| State of Tennessee 6 per cent. bonds........... ......................... | 8,000 00 |
| State of North Carolina 6 per cent. bonds........... ................ ........... | 3,000 00 |
| Delaware and Hudson Canal Company 7 per cent ..................... | 20,000 00 |
| Western Pacific first 6 per cent. gold................... .............. ...... | 7,000 00 |
| Union Pacific first 6 per cent. gold................................. | 1,000 00 |
| Central Pacific first 7 per cent. gold .......... ..................... | 2,000 00 |

| | |
|---|---|
| City of Bath, Maine, 6 per cent | 5,000 00 |
| City of Chicago, Illinois 7 per cent | 31,000 00 |
| City of Chicago, Illinois 6 per cent | 1,000 00 |
| City of St. Louis, Missouri, 6 per cent | 14,000 00 |
| County of St. Louis, Missouri, 7 per cent | 6,000 00 |
| City of Brooklyn, New York, 6 per cent | 30,000 00 |
| City of Newport, Rhode Island, 6 per cent | 1,000 00 |
| City of Cincinnati, Ohio, 7 3-10 per cent | 10,000 00 |
| City of Portsmouth, New Hampshire, 6 per cent | 2,000 00 |
| City of Dover, New Hampshire, 6 per cent | 3,000 00 |
| Bay City, Michigan, 10 per cent | 10,000 00 |
| Town of Osage, La Salle County, Illinois 10 per cent | 2,000 00 |
| Town of Vermont, Fulton County, Illinois, 10 per cent | 6,000 00 |
| Town of Amity, Fulton County, Illinois, 10 per cent | 4,000 00 |
| Town of Bushnell, McDonough County, Illinois, 10 per cent | 3,000 00 |
| Town of Lacon, Illinois, 10 per cent | 5,000 00 |
| Town of Hardwick, Vermont, 6 per cent | 75,000 00 |
| Town of St. Johnsbury, Vermont, 6 per cent | 15,000 00 |
| Town of Sheldon, Vermont, 6 per cent | 18,000 00 |
| Town of Hyde Park, Vermont, 6 per cent | 6,100 00 |
| Town of Morristown, Vermont, 6 per cent | 9,000 00 |
| Town of Hyde Gate, Vermont, 6 per cent | 7,900 00 |
| Town of Bakersfield, Vermont, 6 per cent | 4,000 00 |
| Town of Greensboro', Vermont, 6 per cent | 3,000 00 |
| Town of Concord, Vermont, 6 per cent | 22,000 00 |
| Town of Elmore, Vermont, 6 per cent | 1,000 00 |
| Town of Walden, Vermont, 6 per cent | 6,000 00 |
| Town of Walcott, Vermont, 6 per cent | 10,000 00 |
| Town of Swanton, Vermont, 6 per cent | 20,000 00 |
| La Moisie Valley, Montpelier, St. Johnsbury and Essex County, First Mortgage 6 per cent gold | 60,000 00 |
| Chesapeake and Ohio Railroad, first mortgage, 6 per cent. gold | 25,200 00 |
| 28 shares Newport Gaslight Company stock, par $100 | 2,800 00 |
| 15 shares First National Bank of Newport, par $100 | 1,500 00 |
| 15 shares National Bank of Rhode Island, Newport par $100 | 1,500 00 |
| 10 shares Old National Bank of Providence, par $100 | 1,000 00 |
| 10 shares Globe National Bank of Providence par $50 | 500 00 |
| 10 shares Rhode Island Union Bank, Newport, par $100 | 1,000 00 |
| | $426,000 00 |
| The above stocks are charged on the books of the Bank, as in this account, at | 380,292 16 |
| Leaving a balance of | $45,707 84 |

applicable to depreciation, besides the premiums at which most of these securities are now selling in the market.

## COVENTRY SAVINGS BANK, ANTHONY.

*EDWARD B. WILLIAMS, Treasurer.*

| | RESOURCES. | LIABILITIES. | MISCELLANEOUS. |
|---|---|---|---|
| Amount invested in mortgages on real estate............. | $151,402 32 | ............. | |
| Amount invested in stocks..... | 4,021 50 | ............. | |
| Amount invested in bonds...... | ............. | ............. | |
| Amount loaned on personal security.................... | 87,240 00 | ............. | |
| Amount loaned on collaterals of personal property.......... | 4,875 00 | ............. | |
| Town notes................... | 5,000 00 | ............. | |
| Amount of cash on hand....... | ............. | ............. | |
| Amount of deposits........... | ............. | $244, 124 30 | |
| Due Coventry National Bank... | ............. | 707 58 | |
| Amount of profit on hand..... | ............. | 7,706 94 | |
| | $252,538 82 | $252,538 82 | |
| Number of depositors......... | 574 | ............. | |
| of $500 and under $1,000... | 52 | ............. | |
| of $1,000 and upwards...... | 60 | ............. | |
| Largest amount due to any one depositor.................. | ............. | $12,262 03 | |
| Amount, date and rate per cent. of last dividend........... | 7,182 25 | June16th1876 | 3 pr.ct. 6 mos. |
| Average rate of dividends for the last three years........ | 6⅜ pr.ct.pr.an. | ............. | |
| Amount of reserved profits at time of last dividend...... | ............. | 2,146 26 | |

Amount loaned on mortgages in other states................ .......None.

Description of stocks held by the Bank, names of the Institutions in which invested, with their several amounts:

20 shares Weybosset National Bank....................................... ........ $1,000 00
57 shares National Bank of Commerce................................ ......... 1,850 00
Premiums paid for stocks................................ ................ .... ............ 171 50

$4,021 50

## CRANSTON SAVINGS BANK, PROVIDENCE.

| | RESOURCES. | LIABILITIES. | MISCELLANEOUS. |
|---|---|---|---|
| Amount invested in mortgages on real estate............... | $92,153 71 | ............. | |
| Amount invested in stocks...... | 17,062 50 | ............. | |
| Amount invested in bonds...... | ............. | ............. | |
| Amount loaned on personal security................ ...... | 776,909 24 | ............. | |
| Amount loaned on collaterals of personal property........... | ............. | ............. | |
| Amount of cash on hand....... | 2,028 43 | ............. | |
| Amount of deposits............. | ............. | $715,646 51 | |
| Amount of profit on hand...... | ............. | 154,923 49 | |
| First National Bank overdraft.. | ............. | 17,583 88 | |
| | $888,153 88 | $888,153 88 | |
| Number of Depositors.......... | 4,400 | | |

# EAST GREENWICH INSTITUTION FOR SAVINGS.

*SAMUEL M. KNOWLES,* Treasurer.

| | RESOURCES. | LIABILITIES. | MISCELLANEOUS. |
|---|---|---|---|
| Amount invested in mortgages on real estate.............. | $182,807 15 | ............. | |
| Amount invested in stocks..... | 8,395 00 | ............. | |
| Amount invested in bonds..... | 8,500 00 | ............. | |
| Amount loaned on personal security.................... | 2,512 65 | ............. | |
| Amount loaned on collaterals of personal property.......... | 6,050 00 | ............. | |
| Amount of cash on hand....... | 3,418 21 | ............. | |
| Amount of deposits............ | ............. | $199,025 15 | |
| Amount of profit on hand...... | ............. | 12,657 86 | |
| | $211,683 01 | $211,683 01 | |
| Number of depositors......... | ............. | ............. | 528 |
| of $500 and under $1,000 .. | ............. | ............. | 58 |
| of $1,000 and upwards,.... | ............. | ............. | 46 |
| Largest amount due to any one depositor................. | ............. | ............. | $6,295 75 |
| Amount, date and rate per cent. of last dividend........... | 6,771 96 | June 1, 1876. | 3½ pr. ct. 6 m. |
| Average rate of dividend for the last three years............ | 7 pr. ct. | ............. | |
| Amount of reserved profits at time of last dividend....... | ............. | ............. | 6,345 33 |

Amount loaned on mortgages in other States:—

Massachusetts....................................$3,000 00

Illinois.........................................19,298 00

Description of stocks and bonds held by the Bank, names of the Institutions in which invested, with their several amounts:

National Bank of Commerce, Providence.............................................. $867 00
National Bank of North America, "  ............................................ 2,080 00
Greenwich National Bank, East Greenwich.......................................... 5,448 00

$8,395 00

United States five-twenty Bonds..................................................$7,500 00
Hartford, Providence and Fishkill Railroad Bond.................................... 1,000 00

$8,500 00

# FRANKLIN SAVINGS BANK, PAWTUCKET.

*GEORGE W. NEWELL, Treasurer.*

| | RESOURCES. | LIABILITIES. | MISCELLANEOUS. |
|---|---|---|---|
| Amount invested in mortgages on real estate............... | $1,411,886 94 | ............... | |
| Amount invested in stocks..... | 87,450 00 | ............... | |
| Amount invested in bonds..... | ............... | ............... | |
| Amount loaned on personal security................... | 122,351 87 | ............... | |
| Amount loaned on collaterals of personal property.......... | ............... | ............... | |
| Amount of cash on hand....... | 17,461 88 | ............... | |
| Amount of deposits............ | ............... | $1,588 981 70 | |
| Amount of profit on hand...... | ............... | 50,168 99 | |
| | $1,639 150 69 | $1,639 150 69 | |
| Number of depositors.......... | ............... | ............... | 2521 |
| of $500 and under $1,000... | ............... | ............... | 381 |
| of $1,000 and upwards..... | ............... | ............... | 469 |
| Largest amount due to any one depositor................. | ............... | ............... | $20,000 00 |
| Amount, date and rate per cent. of last dividend........... | 47,397 55 | July 19, 1876. | 6 pr. ct pr. an. |
| Average rate of dividend for the last three years............ | ............... | ............... | 7 pr. ct. |
| Amount of reserved profits at time of last dividend....... | ............... | ............... | 9,418 00 |

Amount loaned on mortgages in other States:—

Illinois.........................................$326,375 00
Missouri.............................................20,000 00
Massachusetts.......................................32,920 00

Description of stocks and bonds held by the Bank, names of the Institutions in which invested, with their several amounts:

Slater National Bank, Pawtucket,..........................................................$25,700 00
Pacific National Bank,        "         ................................................. ..........3,380 00
Pawtucket Gas Company       "         ...............................................21,050 00
First National Bank,  Providence,....................................................11,000 00
Second National Bank,       "         .....................................................5,000 00
Third National Bank,        "         ....................................................11,000 00
National Bank of North America, Providence................................................3,500 00
Commercial National Bank,        "         .......................................................2,450 00
City National Bank,        "         .....................................................600 00
Roger Williams National Bank,       "         ......................................................600 00
New York, Providence and Boston Railroad Company.............................3,200 00
                                                                                    $87,450 00

## FRANKLIN INSTITUTION FOR SAVINGS, PROVIDENCE.*

*WINTHROP DE WOLF, Receiver.*

| | RESOURCES. | LIABILITIES. | MISCELLANEOUS. |
|---|---|---|---|
| Amount invested in mortgages on real estate.............. | $230,000 00 | ............. | |
| Amount invested in stocks..... | | ............. | |
| Amount invested in bonds..... | 15,000 00 | ............. | |
| Amount loaned on personal security ................. | 653,956 03 | ............. | |
| Amount loaned on collaterals of personal property . ..,.... | 2,800 00 | ............. | |
| Amount of cash on hand....... | 14,388 65 | ............. | |
| Amount of deposits.........,... | ............. | $819,764 38 | |
| Amount of profit on hand...... | ............. | 96 380 30 | |
| | $916,144 68 | $916,144 68 | |
| Number of depositors........... | ............. | ............. | 5818 |

*In liquidation. See page 5.

## HOPKINTON SAVINGS BANK, HOPE VALLEY.

### J. B. POTTER, Treasurer.

| | RESOURCES. | LIABILITIES. | MISCELLANEOUS. |
|---|---|---|---|
| Amount invested in mortgages on real estate.............. | $162,448 80 | ............. | |
| Amount invested in stocks..... | 8,900 00 | ............. | |
| Amount invested in bonds..... | ............. | ............. | |
| Amount loaned on personal security.................... | 48,670 00 | ............. | |
| Amount loaned on collaterals of personal property.......... | ............. | ............. | |
| Amount of cash on hand....... | 3,363 23 | ............. | |
| Amount of deposits............ | ............. | $222,745 08 | |
| Amount of profit on hand:..... | ............. | 636 95 | |
| | $223,382 03 | $223,382 03 | |
| Number o depositors......... | ............. | ............. | 777 |
| of $500 and under $1,000.. | ............. | ............. | 80 |
| of $1,000 and upwards..... | ............. | ............. | 53 |
| Largest amount due to any one depositor.................. | ............. | ............. | $6,086 87 |
| Amount date and rate per cent. of last dividend.......... | 6,372 92 | Nov 20, 1876. | 3 per. ct. 6 m. |
| Average rate of dividend for the last three years............ | ............. | ............. | 6.58 per cent. |
| Amount of reserved profits at time of last dividend....... | ............. | ............. | $605 73 |

Amount loaned on mortgages in other States..................None.

Description of stocks held by the Bank, name of the Institutions in which invested, with their several amounts:

Stock in First National Bank of Hopkinton,........... .......... ......................$8,900 00

## ISLAND SAVINGS BANK, NEWPORT.

*STEPHEN H. NORMAN*, Treasurer.

| | RESOURCES. | LIABILITIES. | MISCELLANEOUS. |
|---|---|---|---|
| Amount invested in mortgages on real estate.............. | $202,032 00 | ............. | |
| Amount invested in stocks ..... | ............. | ............. | |
| Amount invested in bonds. ..... | ............. | ............. | |
| Amount loaned on personal security...................... | .......... ... | ............. | |
| Amount loaned on collaterals of personal property.. ....... | ............. | ............. | |
| Amount of cash on hand....... | 9,611 17 | ............. | |
| Amount of deposits............ | ............. | $205,716 12 | |
| Amount of profit on hand...... | ............. | 5,927 05 | |
| | $211,643 17 | $211,643 17 | |
| | | | |
| Number of depositors.......... | ............. | ............. | — |
| of $500 and under $1,000... | ............. | ............. | 408 |
| of $1,000 and upwards..... | ............. | ............. | 65 |
| Largest amount due to any one depositor................. | ............. | ............. | 52 |
| Amount, date and rate per cent. of last dividend............ | $6,359 30 | July 1876 | 12,161 63 |
| Average rate of dividend for the last three years........... | ............. | ............. | 3½ pr.ct.6 mos |
| Amount of reserved profits at time of last dividend...... | ............. | ............. | 7 pr.ct.pr.an. |
| | | | $416 82 |

Amount loaned on mortgages in other States:—

       In Massachusetts.....................................$3,300 00

## JACKSON INSTITUTION FOR SAVINGS.

*THEO. B. TALBOT, Treasurer.*

| | RESOURCES. | LIABILITIES. | MISCELLANEOUS. |
|---|---|---|---|
| Amount invested in mortgages on real estate............. | $381,850 00 | ............. | |
| Amount invested in stocks..... | 25,000 00 | ............. | |
| Amount invested in bonds...... | | | |
| Amount loaned on personal security.................... | 24,344 35 | ............. | |
| Amount loaned on collaterals of personal property.......... | ............. | ............. | |
| Amount of cash on hand....... | 13,164 42 | ............. | |
| Amount of deposits............ | ............. | $437,727 60 | |
| Amount of profit on hand...... | ............. | 6,631 17 | |
| | $444,358 77 | $444,358 77 | |
| Number of depositors.......... | ............. | ............. | 788 |
| of $500 and under $1,000... | ............. | ............. | 143 |
| of $1,000 and upwards....... | ............. | ............. | 131 |
| Largest amount due to any one depositor.... ............. | ............. | ............. | $10,000 00 |
| Amount, date and rate per cent. of last dividend............ | $12,258 36 | Aug. 16, 1876. | 3 pr. ct., 6 m. |
| Average rate of dividend for the last three years........... | ............. | ............. | 6 5-6 pr. ct. |
| Amount of reserved profits at time of last dividend....... | ............. | ............. | 2,788 32 |

Amount loaned on mortgages in other States..................None.

Description of stocks held by the bank, names of the institutions in which invested, with their several amounts :

500 shares stock in Jackson Bank, Providence, R. I........................ ............$25,000 00

# KINGSTON SAVINGS BANK, KINGSTON.

*THOMAS P. WELLS,* Treasurer.

| | RESOURCES. | LIABILITIES. | MISCELLANEOUS. |
|---|---|---|---|
| Amount invested in mortgages on real estate .... ...... | $115,219 92 | ............ | • |
| Amount invested in stocks. .. | 39,480 00 | .... ....... | |
| Amount invested in bonds..... | 35,815 00 | ............. | |
| Amount loaned on personal security ........ ......... | 70,281 08 | ............. | |
| Amount loaned on collaterals of personal property ......... | ............ | ............ | |
| Amount of cash on hand....... | ............ | ............ | |
| Amount of deposits...... .... | ............ | 247,445 21 | |
| Amount of profit on hand...... | ............ | 13,350 79 | |
| | $260,796 00 | $260,796 00 | |
| Number of depositors......... | ............ | ............ | 542 |
| of $500 and under $1000... | ............ | ............ | 89 |
| of $1000 and upwards...... | ............ | ............ | 64 |
| Largest amount due to any one depositor.............. | ............ | ............ | $16,096 89 |
| Amount, date and rate per cent. of last dividend...... ..... | 12,286 74 | July 1, 1876. | 5 pr. ct. pr. an. |
| Average rate of dividend for the last three years............ | 6¼ pr ct pr an. | ............ | |
| Amount of reserved profits at time of last dividend...... | ............ | ............ | 9,142 35 |

Amount loaned on mortgages in other States:—

In Illinois.................................... ....  ........$3,500 00

Description of Stocks and Bonds held by the Bank, names of the Institutions in which invested, with their several amounts :

STOCKS—50 shares Delaware and Hudson Canal Company, cost............................$5,850 00
    150   "    Stonington Railroad Company,    "   .........,....,.............20,635 00
    137   "    National Landholders' Bank,    "   ...........................4,795 00
    50   "    Commercial National Bank, Providence, par .......... ................2,500 00
    50   "    National Bank of Commerce   "   cost .......,.............2,850 00
    50   "    Merchants National Bank,    "   "   .............................. 3,050 00

                                                               $39,480 00

BONDS—United States five-twenty............. ....................................14,300 00
    Union Pacific Railroad Company,.... .......................................4,000 00

    Burlington, Cedar Rapids and Minnesota Railroad ........ .....................3,315 00
    Selma, Marion and Memphis Railroad......................... . ................3,000 00
    Northern Pacific Railroad.... ....... ............................ .........11,200 00

                                                               $35,815 00

# MECHANICS SAVINGS BANK, PROVIDENCE.

*WM. KNIGHT, Treasurer.*

| | RESOURCES. | LIABILITIES. | MISCELLANEOUS. |
|---|---|---|---|
| Amount invested in mortgages on real estate.............. | $5,404,021 23 | .............. | |
| Amount invested in stocks..... | 134,250 00 | .............. | |
| Amount invested in bonds..... | 304,000 00 | .............. | |
| Amount loaned on personal security...................... | 764,802 51 | .............. | |
| Amount loaned on collaterals of personal property.......... | 298,011 00 | | |
| Amount of cash on hand....... | 86,957 34 | | |
| Real estate................. .. | 97,941 53 | .............. | |
| Amount of deposits........... | .............. | $6,774,698 38 | |
| Certificates................... | .............. | 5,057 00 | |
| Amount of profit on hand, including surplus............. | .............. | 310,228 23 | |
| | $7,089,983 61 | $7,089,983 61 | |
| Number of depositors......... | .............. | .............. | 10,335 |
| of $500 and under $1,000.. | .............. | .............. | 1,580 |
| of 1,000 and upwards...... | .............. | .............. | 2,012 |
| Largest amount due to any one depositor.................. | .............. | .............. | 27,300 00 |
| Amount, date and rate per cent. of last dividend.......... | 196,233 82 | July 16, 1876. | 3 pr. ct. 6 m. |
| Average rate of dividend for the last three years......... .. | .............. | .............. | 7 pr. ct. pr. an. |
| Amount of reserved profits at time of last dividend....... | .............. | .............. | 155,000 00 |

Amount loaned on mortgages in other States:

Illinois.........................................376,100 00
Massachusetts.....  ...........................150,200 00
Connecticut....................................30,000 00

Description of stocks and bonds held by the Bank, names of the Institutions in which invested, with their several amounts:

Williamsport City, bonds.......................................$82,000 00
Providence and Worcester Railroad bonds..........  .............23,000 00
City of Cincinnati, bonds......................................200,000 00
Chicago, Wilmington and Vermilion Coal Company bonds. ...........50,000 00
National Bank North America stock...............................700 00
Mechanics National Bank stock..................................1,550 00
Second National Bank stock.....................................10,000 00
Fourth National Bank stock ....................................30,000 00
Merchants National Bank stock..................................15,000 00
City National Bank stock.......................................27,350 00
Lime Rock National Bank stock..................................5,000 00
Jackson Bank stock.............................................5,000 00
Westminster Bank stock.........................................15,000 00
Bank of America stock..........................................5,000 00
Commercial National Bank stock.................................4,650 00
Rhode Island Hospital Trust Company stock......................25,000 00

$438,250 00

## MECHANICS SAVINGS BANK, WESTERLY.

*HENRY FOSTER, Treasurer.*

|  | RESOURCES. | LIABILITIES. | MISCELLANEOUS. |
|---|---|---|---|
| Amount invested in mortgages on real estate............. | $249,476 55 | ............ |  |
| Amount invested in stocks..... | 4,306 00 | ............ |  |
| Amount invested in bonds...... | 11,823 75 | ............ |  |
| Amount loaned on personal security.................... | 60,405 00 | ............ |  |
| Amount loaned on collaterals of personal property.......... | 4,740 00 | ............ |  |
| Amount of cash on hand....... | ............ | ............ |  |
| Amount of deposits............. | ............ | $315, 743 85 |  |
| Due National Bank........... | ............ | 978 74 |  |
| Amount of profit on hand..... | ............ | 14,028 71 |  |
|  | $330,751 30 | $330,751 30 |  |
| Number of depositors.......... | ............ | ............ | 704 |
| of $500 and under $1,000... | ............ | ............ | 67 |
| of $1,000 and upwards...... | ............ | ............ | 92 |
| Largest amount due to any one depositor................. | 6,380 78 | ............ |  |
| Amount, date and rate per cent. of last dividend........... | 8,889 11 | Aug.1st, 1876. | 6 pr.ct. pr.an. |
| Average rate of dividend for the last three years....... | ............ | ............ | 6¾ pr.ct.pr.an. |
| Amount of reserved profits at time of last dividend...... | ............ | ............ | $10,005 89 |

Amount loaned on mortgages in other States:—

Illinois.............................................$84,000 00
Connecticut.........................................14,075 00
New Jersey........ ........----......................6,000 00
Massachusetts...................................3,000 00

Description of stocks held by the Bank, names of the Institutions in which invested, with their several amounts:

City of New Brunswick, New Jersey........................ ........................ ...$930 00
City of Cincinnati.............................................................................5,000 00
United States 1881 Bonds.......................... ................................ .........5,898 75
National Phenix Bank, Westerly, stock........................ ........................4,306 00
$16,129 75

# MECHANICS SAVINGS BANK, WOONSOCKET.

*R. P. SMITH, Treasurer.*

| | RESOURCES. | LIABILITIES. | MISCELLANEOUS. |
|---|---|---|---|
| Amount invested in mortgages on real estate............. | $36,225 00 | ............. | |
| Amount invested in stocks ..... | ............. | ............. | |
| Amount invested in bonds. .... | 10,000 00 | ............. | |
| Amount loaned on personal security...................... | 5,580 00 | ............. | |
| Amount loaned on collaterals of personal property.. ........ | ............. | ............. | |
| Amount of cash on hand....... | 2,813 55 | ............. | |
| Amount of deposits............. | ............. | $52,512 84 | |
| Amount of profit on hand...... | ............. | 2,105 71 | |
| | $54,618 55 | $54,618 55 | |
| | | | |
| Number of depositors.......... | ............. | ............. | 279 |
| of $500 and under $1,000... | ............. | ............. | 25 |
| of $1,000 and upwards..... | ............. | ............. | 16 |
| Largest amount due to any one depositor................. | ............. | ............. | 2,435 81 |
| Amount, date and rate per cent. of last dividend........... | $824 87 | June 1876. | 3 pr.ct. 6 mos. |
| Average rate of dividend for the last three years........... | ............. | ............. | |
| Amount of reserved profits at time of last dividend...... | ............. | ..•........ | $714 38 |

Amount loaned on mortgages in other States........ ............None.

Description of stocks and bonds held by the Bank.

Bonds secured by first mortgage to the Rhode Island Hospital Trust Company, as Trustee, on the real estate, mills and machinery of the Woonsocket Company, situated in the town of Woonsocket, R. I.

*Commenced business April 1, 1875.

## MERCHANTS SAVINGS BANK, PROVIDENCE.

*C. R. DROWNE, Treasurer.*

| | RESOURCES. | LIABILITIES. | MISCELLANEOUS. |
|---|---|---|---|
| Amount invested in mortgages on real estate............... | 252,267 40 | ...... ...... | |
| Amount invested in stocks...... | | | |
| Amount invested in bonds...... | 44,000 00 | ............ | |
| Amount loaned on personal security....... ............ | 25,686 90 | ............ | |
| Amount loaned on collaterals of personal property.......... | ............ | ... ......... | |
| Premium....................... | 2,246 25 | ..... ........ | |
| Amount of cash on hand....... | ............ | ....... .. | |
| Amount of deposits............. | ............ | $309,478 73 | |
| Due Liberty Bank............. | ............ | 1,823 25 | |
| Amount of profit on hand...... | ............ | 12,898 57 | |
| | $324,200 55 | $324,200 55 | |
| | | | |
| Number of depositors.......... | ............ | ....... ..... | 416 |
| of $500 and under 1,000.... | ............ | ............ | 90 |
| of $1,000 and upwards..... | ............ | ............ | 93 |
| Largest amount due to any one depositor............. .. | ............ | $10,552 95 | |
| Amount. date and rate per cent. of last dividend........... | $9,175 57 | July 16, 1876. | 3 pr. ct. 6 m. |
| Average rate of dividend for the last three years.... .. ...... | ......... .... | ............... | 7 1-2 per cent. |
| Amount of reserved profits at time of last dividend...... | $7,515 35 | .......... .. | |

Amount loaned on mortgages in other States.....................None.

Description of stocks and bonds held by the Bank, names of the Institutions in which invested with their several amounts.

City of Cincinnati bonds.... .......... ...............................................$20,000 00
Chicago Rock Island and Pacific Railroad Company, bonds..... ........................14,000 00
New York Central Railroad Company bonds ...............................................10,000 00

$44,000 00

## NIANTIC SAVINGS BANK, WESTERLY.

*HENRY P. MORGAN Treasurer.*

| | RESOURCES. | LIABILITIES. | MISCELLANEOUS. |
|---|---|---|---|
| Amount invested in mortgages on real estate............. | $238,160 73 | ............. | |
| Amount invested in stocks.... | 37,113 50 | ............. | |
| Amount invested in bonds..... | 76,412 50 | ............. | |
| Amount loaned on personal security .................. | 55,102 92 | ............. | |
| Amount loaned on collaterals of personal property........... | | | |
| Amount of cash on hand....... | 5,449 49 | ............. | |
| Amount of deposits...... ..... | ............. | 400,968 96 | |
| Amount of profit on hand..... | ............. | 11,270 18 | |
| | $412,239 14 | $412,239 14 | |
| Number of depositors......... | ............. | ............. | 910 |
| of $500 and under $1000... | ............. | ............. | 102 |
| of $1000 and upwards...... | ............. | ............. | 99 |
| Largest amount due to any one depositor................ | ............. | ............. | $12,067 92 |
| Amount, date and rate per cent. of last dividend...... ..... | 11,886 55 | Aug. 1, 1876. | 6 pr. ct. pr. an. |
| Average rate of dividend for the last three years............ | ............. | ............. | 6¼ pr.ct.pr.an. |
| Amount of reserved profits at time of last dividend...... | ............. | ............. | 8,065 94 |

Amount loaned on mortgages in other States:—

     Connecticut....................................$47,570 00
     Kansas........................................22,909 76
     Michigan......................................3,000 00
     Washington, D. C .............................4,000 00

Description of Stocks and Bonds held by the Bank, names of the Institutions in which invested, with their several amounts :

STOCKS—Bank of Commerce, New York..................................$6,000 00
     Bank of the Republic, New York............................5,700 00
     National Bank North America, Providence...................6,950 00
     National Bank of Commerce, Providence.....................5,500 00
     National Niantic Bank, Westerly, R. I.....................13,963 50

                    $37 113 50

BONDS—Burlington, Cedar Rapids and Minnesota Railroad ........12,750 00
     City of Boston, Mass............................11,820 00
     Chicago, Vermilion and Wilmington Coal Co.................16,000 00
     Town of Meriden, Conn....................................16,112 00
     Morris and Essex Railroad.................................6,480 00
     Lehigh and Wilkes Barre Consolidated Bonds...............4,595 00
     Douglass Township Ill....................................4,675 00
     Crawford County Ill......................................5,000 00
     School District No. 78, Montgomery County, Kansas........ 600 00

                    $76,412 50

# PASCOAG SAVINGS BANK, PASCOAG.

*JAMES S. COOK, Treasurer.*

|  | RESOURCES. | LIABILITIES. | MISCELLANEOUS. |
|---|---|---|---|
| Amount invested in mortgages on real estate............. | $436,736 42 | ............. | |
| Amount invested in stocks..... | 19,742 50 | ............. | |
| Amount invested in bonds..... | 11,700 00 | ............. | |
| Amount loaned on personal security.................... | 80,287 49 | ............. | |
| Amount loaned on collaterals of personal property.......... | ............. | ............. | |
| Amount of cash on hand....... | 14,239 93 | ............. | |
| Amount of deposits............. | ............. | $554,348 37 | |
| Amount of profit on hand...... | ............. | 8,357 97 | |
|  | $562,706 34 | $562,706 34 | |
| | | | |
| Number of depositors.......... | ............. | ............. | 1,110 |
| of $500 and under $1,000.. | ............. | ............. | 147 |
| of $1,000 and upwards..... | ............. | ............. | 156 |
| Largest amount due to any one depositor.................... | ............. | $8,811 23 | |
| Amount date and rate per cent. of last dividend.......... | 16,494 77 | Oct. 1, 1876. | 3 per. ct. 6 m. |
| Average rate of dividend for the last three years............ | ............. | ............. | 6¼ pr ct.pr.an. |
| Amount of reserved profits at time of last dividend....... | ............. | ............. | $6,098 75 |

Amount loaned on mortgages in other States:—

        Massachusetts.....................................$87,500 00
        Connecticut.......................................25,000 00

Description of stocks held by the Bank, name of the Institutions in which invested, with their several amounts:

Pascoag National Bank...................................................$19,742 50
Town of Burrillville Bonds...............................................11,700 00

                               $31,442 50

# PAWTUCKET INSTITUTION FOR SAVINGS.

*THOMAS MOIES, Treasurer.*

| | RESOURCES. | LIABILITIES. | MISCELLANEOUS. |
|---|---|---|---|
| Amount invested in mortgages on real estate............. | $2,009,809 00 | ............. | |
| Amount invested in stocks..... | 23,500 00 | ............. | |
| Amount invested in bonds..... | 2,000 00 | ............. | |
| Amount loaned on personal security.................... | 379,519 00 | ............. | |
| Amount loaned on collaterals of personal property......... | ............. | ............. | |
| Amount of cash on hand....... | 18,629 01 | ............. | |
| Amount of deposits........... | ............. | $2,347,512 28 | |
| Amount of profit on hand...... | ............. | 85,944 73 | |
| | $2,433,457 01 | $2,433,457 01 | |
| Number of depositors......... | ............. | ............. | 3973 |
| of $500 and under $1,000 .. | ............. | ............. | 463 |
| of $1,000 and upwards,.... | ............. | ............. | 728 |
| Largest amount due to any one depositor............. | ............. | $30,000 00 | |
| Amount, date and rate per cent. of last dividend.......... | 70,165 00 | July 15, 1876. | 6 pr. ct.pr. an. |
| Average rate of dividend for the last three years............ | ............. | ............. | 7 pr. ct.pr. an. |
| Amount of reserved profits at time of last dividend....... | ............. | ............. | |

Amount loaned on mortgages in other States:—

      Massachusetts...................... ..............$26,800 00

      Illinois.........................................278,000 00

Description of stocks and bonds held by the Bank, names of the Institutions in which invested, with their several amounts:

Pacific National Bank, Pawtucket............. ...............................10,500 00

Fourth National Bank, Providence............................................4,000 00

Weybossett National Bank, Providence..........................................3,000 00

National Bank of North America, Providence.....................................3,000 00

National Bank of Commerce, Providence........................................3,000 00

Hartford, Providence and Fishkill Railroad Bonds................................2,000 00

                                                               $25,500 00

## PEOPLES SAVINGS BANK, PROVIDENCE.

*A. C. HOWARD, Treasurer.*

| | RESOURCES. | LIABILITIES. | MISCELLANEOUS. |
|---|---|---|---|
| Amount invested in mortgages on real estate............ | $1,036,544 66 | ............ | |
| Amount invested in stocks..... | 285,000 00 | ............ | |
| Amount invested in bonds...... | 1,753,000 00 | ............ | |
| Amount loaned on personal security..................... | 874,336 54 | ............ | |
| Amount loaned on collaterals of personal property.......... | 211,600 00 | ............ | |
| Amount of cash on hand....... | 6,105 94 | ............ | |
| City of Providence loan on notes. | 125,000 00 | ............ | |
| Bank Estate.................. | 18,000 00 | ............ | |
| Real Estate................... | 47,363 13 | ............ | |
| Premium..................... | 42,800 00 | ............ | |
| Amount of deposits............. | ............ | $4,311,764 20 | |
| Amount of profit on hand...... | ............ | 87,986 07 | |
| | $4,399,750 27 | $4,399,750 27 | |
| Number of depositors.......... | ............ | ............ | 6,229 |
| of $500 and under $1,000... | ............ | ............ | 1,158 |
| of $1,000 and upwards...... | ............ | ............ | 1,333 |
| Largest amount due to any one depositor.... | ............ | ............ | $24,656 38 |
| Amount, date and rate per cent. of last dividend............ | $126,756 97 | July 17, 1876. | 3 pr. ct., 6 m. |
| Average rate of dividend for the last three years............ | ............ | ............ | 6 1-2 pr. ct. |
| Amount of reserved profits at time of last dividend...... | ............ | ............ | 45,874 90 |

Amount loaned on mortgages in other States:—

Sutton, Massachusetts ..........................$14,144 66

Description of stocks and bonds held by the bank, names of the institutions in which invested, with their several amounts :

Stock in National Bank, of Commerce of Providence, par value............. ...........$125,000 00
" American National Bank, of Providence, par value....................50,000 00
" Globe National Bank, of Providence, par value.....................20,000 00
" Old National Bank, of Providence, par value......................20,000 00
" Fourth National Bank, of Providence, par value....................10,000 00
" Merchants National Bank, of Providence, par value.................10,000 00
" Groceras and Producers Bank, of Providence, par value.............5,000 00
" Commercial National Bank, of Providence, par value................5,000 00
" Rhode Island Hospital Trust Company of Providence, par value .............,.... 40,000 00

Town of Pawtucket Bonds........... ............................$285,000 00
Water Loan of the City of Providence.....................................$100,000 00
United States six per cent. Registered Bonds of 1881 .......................30,000 00
Manville Company Coupon Bonds.........................................130,000 00
Social Manufacturing Company First Mortgage Bonds.... .................150,000 00
Narragansett Hotel Company Bonds.......................................100,000 00
Delaware and Hudson Canal Company Registered Bonds...................170,000 00
Providence and Worcester Railroad Company Bonds......................175,000 00
New York Providence and Boston Railroad Company Bonds...............100,000 00

$1,753,000 00

## PEOPLES SAVINGS BANK, WOONSOCKET.

*S. G. RANDALL, Treasurer.*

|  | RESOURCES. | LIABILITIES. | MISCELLANEOUS. |
|---|---|---|---|
| Amount invested in mortgages on real estate.............. | $291,177 04 | ............. | |
| Amount invested in stocks..... | 25,415 34 | ............. | |
| Amount invested in bonds..... | 139,500 00 | ............. | |
| Amount loaned on personal security...................... | 87,500 00 | ........ .... | |
| Amount loaned on collaterals of personal property......... | ............. | ............. | |
| Amount of cash on hand...... | ............. | ........... | |
| Amt. due First National Bank. | ............. | $1,464 60 | |
| Amount of deposits............ | ............. | 536,471 32 | |
| Amount of profit on hand...... | ............. | 5,656 46 | |
|  | $543 592 38 | $543 592 38 | |
| Number of depositors.......... | ..... ........ | ............. | 1055 |
| of $500 and under $1,000... | ............. | ............. | 201 |
| of $1,000 and upwards..... | ............. | ............. | 189 |
| Largest amount due to any one depositor................. | ............. | ............. | $4,734 68 |
| Amount, date and rate per cent. of last dividend............ | $15,726 57 | Oct. 1, 1876. | 3 pr. ct 6 mos. |
| Average rate of dividend for the last three years........... | ............. | ............. | 6¾ pr. ct. pr.an. |
| Amount of reserved profits at time of last dividend....... | ............. | ............. | 1,937 22 |

Amount loaned on mortgages in other States................None.

Description of stocks and bonds held by the Bank, names of the Institutions in which invested, with their several amounts:

Stocks—National Union Bank, Woonsocket cost........ ....................................$2,740 17
"     First National Bank, Woonsocket, cost ...............................................5,607 75
"     Eagle National Bank, Providence,cost..........................................1,043 50
"     Mechanics National Bank, Providence, cost.......................................3,904 42
"     National Bank of North America, Providence, cost............................3,112 56
"     Dry Goods Bank, New York, cost... ...........  ....................................10,000 00

                                                              $25,415 34
United States bonds..................................................................$46,500 00
Manville Company's bonds,.......................................................50,000 00
Woonsocket Company's bonds............. ..................................20,000 00
own of Woonsocket ............................................................23 ,000 00

                                                                $139,500 00

# PHENIX SAVINGS BANK, PHENIX.

### H. D. BROWN, *Treasurer.*

| | RESOURCES | LIABILITIES. | MISCELLANEOUS. |
|---|---|---|---|
| Amount invested in mortgages on real estate.............. | $177,845 00 | ............ | |
| Amount invested in stocks..... | 28,600 00 | ......... ... | |
| Amount invested in bonds..... | 20,000 00 | ............ | |
| Amount loaned on personal security..................... | 94,605 00 | ............ | |
| Amount loaned on collaterals of personal property.......... | .... ........ | ............ | |
| Town Notes................ .. | 25,500 00 | ............ | |
| Amount of cash on hand...... | 9,338 88 | ............ | |
| Amount of deposits.......... | ............ | $351,575 32 | |
| Amount of profit on hand.... | ............ | 4,313 56 | |
| | $355,888 88 | $355,888 88 | |
| Number of depositors........ | ............ | ............ | 745 |
| of $500 and under $1,000.. | ............ | ............ | 110 |
| of 1,000 and upwards...... | ............ | ............ | 94 |
| Largest amount due to any one depositor................. | ............ | ............ | 6,755 50 |
| Amount, date and rate per cent. of last dividend.......... | · 10,195 80 | Nov 13, 1876. | 6 pr. ct. pr.an. |
| Average rate of dividend for the last three years......... .. | ............ | ............ | 6½ pr. ct. pr an. |
| Amount of reserved profits at time of last dividend....... | .... ........ | ............ | 4,000 00 |

Amount loaned on mortgages in other States...................None.

Description of stocks and bonds held by the Bank, names of the Institutions in which invested, with their several amounts:

Stock—National Bank of North America, Providence.................................$5,000 00
National Bank of Commerce, Providence,........................................ 6,000 00
American National Bank.................... ............. .. ...................5,000 00
Manufacturers National Bank.................................................... ......1,500 00
State Bank....................................................... ..................500 00
Liberty Bank................................................................600 00
Northern Bank, Providence,........................................... ..........1,000 00
Rhode Island Hospital Trust Company................................................4,000 00
Phenix National Bank, Phenix, ........................................ ..............5,000 00
Pawtuxet Valley Railroad bonds,......................... ... ..............5,000 00
Social Manufacturing Company bonds..........................................5,000 00
Woonsocket Company bonds...........................................................10,000 00

8

$48,600 00

## PRODUCERS SAVINGS BANK, WOONSOCKET.

*THEO. M. COOK, Treasurer.*

| | RESOURCES. | LIABILITIES. | MISCELLANEOUS. |
|---|---|---|---|
| Amount invested in mortgages on real estate............... | $123,645 00 | ............. | |
| Amount invested in stocks..... | 11,920 00 | ............. | |
| Amount invested in bonds..... | 68,000 00 | ............. | |
| Amount loaned on personal security ................... | 62,750 00 | ............. | |
| Amount loaned on collaterals of personal property....,.... | 12,000 00 | ............. | |
| Amount of cash on hand....... | 4,409 26 | | |
| Amount of deposits.........,... | ............. | $270,412 66 | |
| Amount of profit on hand..... | ............. | 12 311 60 | |
| | $282,724 26 | $282,724 26 | |
| Number of depositors........... | ............. | ............. | 503 |
| of $500 and under $1,000,.. | ............. | ............. | 96 |
| of $1,000 and upwards..... | ............. | ............. | 103 |
| Largest amount due to any one depositor................... | ............. | ....... ..... | $2,793 86 |
| Amount date and rate per cent. of last dividend.......... .. | $8,205 55 | July 17, 1876. | 3 pr ct. 6 mos. |
| Average rate of dividend for the last three years............. | ............. | ............. | 6 2-3 per cent. |
| Amount of reserved profits at time of last dividend .... | ............. | ............. | $6,698 03 |

Amount loaned on mortgages in other States..... ...  ........None.

Description of stocks and bonds held by the Bank, names of the Institution in which invested, with their several amounts.

Producers National Bank, of Woonsocket..........................................  ........$11,920 00
Alabama State Bonds,..................................  ........................ ........ .5,000 00
Minneapolis City Bonds,...........................................................................10,000 00
Town of Woonsocket Bonds,..... ...........................................................23,000 00
Woonsocket Company Bonds....................................... ......................20,000 00
Social Manufacturers Company Bonds................... ................ .............10,000 00

$79,920 00

# PROVIDENCE COUNTY SAVINGS BANK, PAWTUCKET.

*OLNEY ARNOLD, Treasurer.*

| | RESOURCES. | LIABILITIES. | MISCELLANEOUS. |
|---|---|---|---|
| Amount invested in mortgages on real estate................ | $2,641,698 52 | ............. | |
| Amount invested in stocks..... | 171,380 00 | ............. | |
| Amount invested in bonds..... | ............. | ............. | |
| Amount loaned on personal security.................... | 205,434 47 | ............. | |
| Amount loaned on collaterals of personal property.......... | 311,556 07 | ............. | |
| Real estate..................... | 209,344 36 | ............. | |
| Furniture and fixtures... ..... | 6,250 00 | ............. | |
| Amount of cash on hand....... | 33,530 19 | ............. | |
| Amount of deposits............ | ............. | $3,495,849 86 | |
| Amount of profit on hand...... | ............. | 83,343 75 | |
| | $3,579,193 61 | $3,579,193 61 | |
| Number of depositors......... | ............. | ............. | 5841 |
| of $500 and under $1,000 .. | ............. | ............. | 730 |
| of $1,000 and upwards,.... | ............. | ............. | 1150 |
| Largest amount due to any one depositor............ | ............. | ............. | $48,092 87 |
| Amount, date and rate per cent. of last dividend........... | 108,667 46 | July 17, 1876. | 6 pr. ct. pr. an. |
| Average rate of dividend for the last three years........... | ............. | ............. | 6¼ pr.ct.pr.an. |
| Amount of reserved profits at time of last dividend...... | ............. | ............. | $48,014 48 |

Amount loaned on mortgages in other States:—

Massachusetts...................... ...............$65,000 00
Connecticut....................................105,000 00
New York............................. ...........125,470 00
Illinois............................................77,000 00

Total...................... ................$372,470 00

Description of stocks and bonds held by the bank, names of the institutions in which invested, with their several amounts :

671 shares First National Bank, Pawtucket......................................... ...$139,360 00
83 shares Pacific National Bank, Pawtucket................................. ................ 19,460 00
129 shares Slater    "    "    "     ........ ...............................  5,810 00
34 shares National Bank of Redemption, Boston....................................  4,250 00
50 shares Globe National Bank, Providence.................................  ............  2,500 00

$171,380 00

# PROVIDENCE INSTITUTION FOR SAVINGS.

### S. C. BLODGET, *Treasurer.*

| | RESOURCES. | LIABILITIES. | MISCELLANEOUS. |
|---|---|---|---|
| Amount invested in mortgages on real estate.............. | $4,487,206 21 | ............ | |
| Amount invested in stocks... | 342,900 00 | ............ | |
| Amount invested in bonds..... | 2,318,000 00 | ............ | |
| Amount loaned on personal security................... | 941,874 99 | ............ | |
| Amount loaned on collaterals of personal property.......... | 400,900 00 | ............ | |
| Amount of real estate ......... | 30,000 00 | ............ | |
| Amount of cash on hand...... | 143,672 79 | ............ | |
| Amount of deposits............. | ............ | $8,402,887 33 | |
| Amount of profit on hand...... | ............ | 261,666 66 | |
| | $8,664,553 99 | $8,664,553 99 | |
| Number of depositors.......... | ............ | ............ | 19959 |
| of $500 and under $1000... | ............ | ............ | 3458 |
| of $1000 and upwards...... | ............ | ............ | 2707 |
| Largest amount due to any one depositor. ................ | ............ | ............ | $9,228 33 |
| Amount, date and rate per cent. of last dividend............ | $238,306 89 | July 17, 1876. | 3 pr. ct. 6 mo. |
| Average rate of dividend for the last three years............ | ............ | ............ | 6$\frac{41}{100}$prct.pr.an |
| Amount of reserved profits at time of last dividend...... | ............ | ............ | 159,260 55 |

Amount loaned on mortgages in other States:—

Illinois.........................................$125,000 00

Description of Stocks and Bonds held by the Bank, names of the Institutions in which invested, with their several amounts :

| | |
|---|---|
| American National Bank,.................................... ..................... | $8,800 00 |
| National Eagle Bank,........ ........................................ ... . ..| 13,400 00 |
| Blackstone Canal National Bank,................................ ..................... | 27,450 00 |
| National Bank of Commerce,................................ ..................... | 20,000 00 |
| National Exchange Bank,................................ ..................... | 40,000 00 |
| Manufacturers National Bank,................................ ..................... | 30,000 00 |
| Mechanics National Bank,................................ ..................... | 12,100 00 |
| Merchants National Bank,.......... ......... ......... ..................... | 48,000 00 |
| Phenix National Bank,........ ................. ..................... | 3,650 00 |
| Providence National Bank,................................ ..................... | 15,200 00 |
| Roger Williams National Bank,.... ......................... ..................... | 10,650 00 |
| Pawtuxet Bank,................................ ..... . ... | 11,550 00 |
| American Exchange National Bank, New York...... .... ............... ................ | 25,000 00 |
| Metropolitan National Bank New York,. ................................ ........ | 25,000 00 |
| National Bank State of New York,.... ......................... ............ | 10,000 00 |
| Rhode Island Hospital Trust Company,........ ................. ..................... | 50,000 00 |
| | $342,900 00 |

## BONDS.

United States bonds,..................................................................$500,000 00
Rhode Island State bonds,.................................................55,000 00
Maine State bonds,...........................................................25,000 00
Iowa State bonds,.............................................................50,000 00
Illinois State and County bonds,..................................87,000 00
Ohio State bonds,.............................................................56,000 00
New York State and County bonds,............................50,000 00
City of Providence bonds,.............................................150,000 00
City of New York bonds,.................................................49,000 00
City of Brooklyn bonds,..................................................50,000 00
City of Newport bonds,...................................................50,000 00
City of Boston bonds,.......................................................30,000 00
City of Chicago bonds,....................................................25,000 00
City of St. Louis bonds,..................................................150,000 00
City of New Bedford bonds,...........................................50,000 00
City of Springfield bonds,...............................................35,000 00
City of Newark bonds,.....................................................40,000 00
City of Cincinnati bonds,...............................................100,000 00
City of Indianapolis bonds,............................................50,000 00
Town of North Providence bonds,................................22,000 00
Town of Westerly bonds,.................................................40,000 00
Town of Meriden bonds,..................................................60,000 00
American Dock and Improvement Company bonds,.....25,000 00
New York Central Railroad bonds,...............................100,000 00
Providence and Worcester Railroad bonds,...............100,000 00
Providence and Springfield Railroad bonds,..............175,000 00
Pawtuxet Valley Railroad bonds,.................................20,000 00
Carthage and Burlington Railroad bonds,..................10,000 00
Dixon, Peoria and Hannibal Railroad bonds,............10,000 00
Chicago and Alton Railroad bonds,.............................14,000 00
Chicago, Burlington and Quincy Railroad bonds,.....80,000 00
Chicago, Wilmington and Vermillion Coal Company bonds,..............80,000 00
Narragansett Hotel Company bonds,..........................40,000 00

$2,818,000 00

## RHODE ISLAND INSTITUTION FOR SAVINGS, PROVIDENCE.

### *STEPHEN H. TABOR, Treasurer.*

| | RESOURCES. | LIABILITIES. | MISCELLANEOUS. |
|---|---|---|---|
| Amount invested in mortgages on real estate............... | $673,760 00 | ............ | |
| Amount invested in stocks..... | 31,440 00 | ............ | |
| Amount invested in bonds..... | 60,535 00 | ............ | |
| Amount loaned on personal security................... | 220,585 64 | ............ | |
| Amount loaned on collaterals of personal property........... | 25,000 00 | ............ | |
| Amount of cash on hand....... | 14,933 62 | ............ | |
| Amount of deposits............ | ............ | $968,351 27 | |
| Amount of profit on hand...... | ............ | 57,902 99 | |
| | $1,026,254 26 | $1,026,254 26 | |
| Number of depositors.......... | ............ | ............ | 1,645 |
| of $500 and under $1,000.. | ............ | ............ | 247 |
| of $1,000 and upwards..... | ............ | ............ | 257 |
| Largest amount due to any one depositor................... | ............ | ............ | $16,383 00 |
| Amount date and rate per cent. of last dividend........... | 27,513 24 | June 16,1876. | 6 per.ct.pr.an. |
| Average rate of dividend for the last three years......... | ............ | ............ | 7 pr ct. pr.an. |
| Amount of reserved profits at time of last dividend...... | ............ | ............ | $35,407 14 |

Amount loaned on mortgages in other States..................None.

Description of stocks and bonds held by the Bank, names of the Institutions in which invested, with their several amounts:

Social Manufacturing Company, First Mortgage 7 per cent. bonds...................... ...$50,000 00
Manhattan Bleaching and Dying Company First Mortgage 7 per cent. $10,000 cost..... ....9,500 00
Chicago 7 per cent Sewerage bond......... ...................... ....................1,025 00
400 shares stock National Bank of Commerce, Providence,...............................$1,200 00
200 " " Rhode Island National Bank, Providence,...................................5,000 00
80 " " Commercial National Bank, Providence,.................,......... ............4,240 00
10 " " Manufacturers National Bank, Providence,.................................1,000 00
$91,975 00

## SAVINGS BANK OF NEWPORT.

*W. H. SHERMAN, Treasurer.*

| | RESOURCES. | LIABILITIES. | MISCELLANEOUS. |
|---|---|---|---|
| Amount invested in mortgages on real estate.............. | $1,182,730 94 | ..... . .... | |
| Amount invested in stocks...... | 228,740 00 | .............. | |
| Amount invested in bonds...... | 2,620,000 00 | .............. | |
| Amount loaned on personal security...................... | .............. | ... ......... | |
| Amount loaned on collaterals of personal property.......... | 46,000 00 | ............ | |
| Banking house................. | 30,000 00 | ......... .. | |
| Amount of cash on hand....... | 197,006 13 | $4,211,880 80 | |
| Amount of deposits............ | .............. | 92,596 27 | |
| Amount of profit on hand...... | .............. | ....... ..... | |
| | $4,304,477 07 | $4,304,477 07 | |
| Number of depositors.......... | .............. | .............. | 5238 |
| of $500 and under 1,000.... | .............. | .......... .. | 734 |
| of $1,000 and upwards..... | .............. | .......... .. | 1149 |
| Largest amount due to any one depositor ... .......... | .............. | 31,768 22 | |
| Amount. date and rate per cent. of last dividend........... | 121,596 45 | July 15, 1876. | 3 pr. ct. 6 m. |
| Average rate of dividend for the last three years.... .. .. | .............. | ..... ........ | 6⅜ pr.ct.pr.an. |
| Amount of reserved profits at time of last dividend...... | ..... .. .... | .............. | 31,841 89 |

Amount loaned on mortgages in other States.................None.

Description of stocks and bonds held by the bank, names of the institutions in which invested, with their several amount:

### STOCKS.

Blackstone National Bank, Boston................................................... .. .........$50,000 00
Exchange National Bank,     "     .............. ...................................................14,000 00
Second National Bank,     "     ............. ................................................16,000 00
Commerce National Bank,   "     .................. ...........................................13,300 00
North America National Bank, "  ............. ................................................12,000 00
Shawmut National Bank,    "     .................. ....................................... .. ...10,000 00
Metropolitan National Bank,     New York................ .................... .....12,000 00
Commerce National Bank,     "     .............. .................................. .......13,700 00
Gallatin National Bank.     "     .............. .............................. .... 5,000 00
American Exchange National Bank, "  ............. .................... ......... 5,000 00
Continental National Bank,     "     .... ................................ ..........2,000 00
Hanover National Bank,     ..     .................................. ............... 2,500 00
North American National Bank,   "     ............. ...................................... 5,000 00

| | | |
|---|---|---|
| Mechanics National Bank, New Bedford | .......................................... | 3,500 00 |
| First National Bank, " | .......................................... | 14,800 00 |
| Commerce National Bank, " | .......................................... | 1,800 00 |
| Merchants National Bank, " | .......................................... | 2,800 00 |
| Rhode Island National Bank, Newport | .......................................... | 1,000 00 |
| First National Bank, " | .......................................... | 2,000 00 |
| Newport National Bank, " | .......................................... | 5,940 00 |
| New England Commercial Bank, " | .......................................... | 2,300 00 |
| Mechanics National Bank, Providence | .......................................... | 9,200 00 |
| Eagle National Bank, " | .......................................... | 2,300 00 |
| Roger Williams National Bank, " | .......................................... | 800 00 |
| Weybosset National Bank, " | .......................................... | 3,000 00 |
| American National Bank, " | .......................................... | 5,000 00 |
| Pacific National Bank, North " | .......................................... | 1,100 00 |
| Fall River National Bank, Fall River | .......................................... | 6,900 00 |
| | | $228,748 00 |

## BONDS.

| | | |
|---|---|---|
| United States five-twenty bonds, 1867 | .......................................... | $490,500 00 |
| United States 5's, 1881 " | .......................................... | 75,000 00 |
| United States currency " | .......................................... | 120,000 00 |
| New York City " | .......................................... | 445,000 00 |
| Providence City " | .......................................... | 200,000 00 |
| Newport City " | .......................................... | 83,500 00 |
| Boston City " | .......................................... | 30,000 00 |
| Charlestown, Mass., " | .......................................... | 50,000 00 |
| Chelsea, " | .......................................... | 50,000 00 |
| Salem, " | .......................................... | 50,000 00 |
| Malden, " | .......................................... | 50,000 00 |
| Lynn, " | .......................................... | 50,000 00 |
| Fitchburg, " | .......................................... | 50,000 00 |
| Medford, " | .......................................... | 50,000 00 |
| Lowell, " | .......................................... | 50,000 00 |
| Arlington, " | .......................................... | 50,000 00 |
| Woburn, " | .......................................... | 50,000 00 |
| Lawrence, " | .......................................... | 50,000 00 |
| Fall River, " | .......................................... | 50,000 00 |
| Somerville, " | .......................................... | 25,000 00 |
| Springfield, " | .......................................... | 25,000 00 |
| Waterbury, Conn., " | .......................................... | 50,000 00 |
| Middletown, " | .......................................... | 35,000 00 |
| Meriden, " | .......................................... | 50,000 00 |
| New Britain, " | .......................................... | 25,000 00 |
| Jamestown, R. I., " | .......................................... | 18,900 00 |
| Portsmouth, " | .......................................... | 4,000 00 |
| Chicago, Ill., " | .......................................... | 80,000 00 |
| Brooklyn, " | .......................................... | 50,000 00 |
| Newark, " | .......................................... | 50,000 00 |
| Jersey, " | .......................................... | 25,000 00 |
| Elizabeth, " | .......................................... | 25,000 00 |
| Rhode Island, " | .......................................... | 54,000 00 |
| Connecticut, " | .......................................... | 5,000 00 |
| Maine, " | .......................................... | 20,000 00 |
| Missouri, " | .......................................... | 20,000 00 |
| Tennessee, " $18,000 for | .......................................... | 10,000 00 |
| Delaware and Hudson Canal Company, | .......................................... | 35,000 00 |
| Old Colony Railway Company, | .......................................... | 2,000 00 |
| | | $2,620,000 00 |

## SMITHFIELD SAVINGS BANK, GREENVILLE, R. I.

*WILLIAM WINSOR, Treasurer.*

| | RESOURCES. | LIABILITIES. | MISCELLANEOUS. |
|---|---|---|---|
| Amount invested in mortgages on real estate.............. | $273,454 00 | ............. | |
| Amount invested in stocks..... | 16,677 50 | ............. | |
| Amount invested in bonds...... | ............. | ............. | |
| Amount loaned on personal security.................... | 2,000 00 | ............. | |
| Amount loaned on collaterals of personal property.......... | ............. | ............. | |
| Amount of cash on hand....... | 2,301 04 | ............. | |
| Amount of deposits............. | ............. | $288,641 77 | |
| Amount of profit on hand...... | ............. | 5,790 77 | |
| | $294,432 54 | $294,432 54 | |
| Number of depositors.......... | ............. | ............. | 570 |
| of $500 and under $1,000... | ............. | ............. | 74 |
| of $1,000 and upwards...... | ............. | ............. | 73 |
| Largest amount due to any one depositor.................. | ............. | ............. | $15,707 50 |
| Amount, date and rate per cent. of last dividend........... | $8,012 88 | Nov. 15, 1876. | 6 pr.ct. pr.an. |
| Average rate of dividend for the last three years........ | ............. | ............. | 7 1-6 per cent. |
| Amount of reserved profits at time of last dividend...... | ............. | ............. | $5,675 27 |

Amount loaned on mortgages in other States...................None.

Description of stocks held by the Bank, names of the Institutions in which invested, with their several amounts:

297 shares of the Rhode Island National Bank, Providence, R. I............................$7,175 00
263 shares of the National Exchange Bank, Greenville, R. I................................ 9,502 50

$16,677 50

## UNION SAVINGS BANK, PROVIDENCE.

*JOSEPH C. JOHNSON, Treasurer.*

|  | RESOURCES. | LIABILITIES. | MISCELLANEOUS. |
|---|---|---|---|
| Amount invested in mortgages on real estate............. | $665,970 00 | ............. | |
| Amount invested in stocks..... | 231,250 00 | ............. | |
| Amount invested in bonds...... | 106,000 00 | ............. | |
| Amount loaned on personal security.................... | 368,028 89 | ............. | |
| Amount loaned on collaterals of personal property.......... | 140,388 00 | ............. | |
| Amount of cash on hand....... | 28,870 48 | ............. | |
| Amount of deposits............. | ............. | $1,514,263 06 | |
| Amount of profit on hand...... | ............. | 26,244 31 | |
|  | $1,540,507 37 | $1,540,507 37 | |
| Number of depositors.......... | ............. | ............. | 2,748 |
| of $500 and under $1,000... | ............. | ............. | 462 |
| of $1,000 and upwards...... | ............. | ............. | 439 |
| Largest amount due to any one depositor.... ........... | ............. | ............. | $20,245 43 |
| Amount, date and rate per cent. of last dividend........... | $44,976 67 | July 16, 1876. | 3 pr. ct. 6 m. |
| Average rate of dividend for the last three years............. | ............. | ............. | 6 1-2 pr. ct. |
| Amount of reserved profits at time of last dividend....... | ............. | ............. | $3,215 19 |

Amount loaned on mortgages in other States.................None.

Description of stocks and bonds held by the Bank, names of the Institutions in which invested, with their several amounts.

| | |
|---|---|
| Union Bank Providence,................................. ...............$221,250 00 |
| New York, Providence and Boston Railroad bonds.......................35,000 00 |
| New Haven, New London and Stonington Railroad bonds.................10,000 00 |
| Pawtuxet Valley Railroad bonds,................,............ .............5,000 00 |
| City of Elizabeth, New Jersey bonds,......... .................................56,000 00 |
| $337,250 00 |

# WAKEFIELD INSTITUTION FOR SAVINGS.

*DANIEL M. C. STEDMAN, Treasurer.*

| | RESOURCES. | LIABILITIES. | MISCELLANEOUS. |
|---|---|---|---|
| Amount invested in mortgages on real estate.............. | $166,069 07 | ............. | |
| Amount invested in stocks..... | 64,300 00 | ............. | |
| Amount invested in bonds..... | 22,000 00 | ............. | |
| Amount loaned on personal security.................... | 118,125 94 | ........ .... | |
| Amount loaned on collaterals of personal property......... | ............. | ............. | |
| Amount of cash on hand....... | ............. | ............. | |
| Amount of deposits............ | ......... .... | $360,776 62 | |
| Due Wakefield National Bank, | ............. | 7,040 73 | |
| Amount of profit on hand...... | ............. | 2,677 66 | |
| | $370,495 01 | $370,495 01 | |
| Number of depositors........... | ..... .... | ... ....... | 864 |
| of $500 and under $1,000... | ............. | ............. | 122 |
| of $1,000 and upwards..... | ............. | ............. | 90 |
| Largest amount due to any one depositor................ | ............. | ............. | $6,612 62 |
| Amount, date and rate per cent. of last dividend,.......... | $20,269 38 | Oct. 4, 1876. | 6 pr.ct. 1 year. |
| Average rate of dividend for the last three years........... | ............. | ............. | 6½ pr.ct.pr.an. |
| Amount of reserved profits at time of last dividend....... | ............. | ............. | $3,593 92 |

Amount loaned on mortgages in other States:—

| | |
|---|---|
| Connecticut,........................................ | $20,000 00 |
| Minnesota,.............................................. | .700 00 |
| Iowa,.............. ..... ................... | 1,500 00 |
| Kansas, ...........................................  | 1,400 00 |
| Nebraska,........................... .............  | 1,400 00 |
| | $25,000 00 |

Description of stocks and bonds held by the Bank, names of the Institutions in which invested, with their several amounts:

| | | |
|---|---|---|
| National Niantic Bank, Westerly......... .  | ........................................ | $6,000 00 |
| Wakefield National Bank.... | ........................ | 5,000 00 |
| National Bank of Commerce, Providence, including premium,.......................... | | 10,000 00 |
| Commercial National Bank, " | ............... ................. | 3,150 00 |
| American National Bank, " | ..................................... | 5,500 00 |
| Weybosset National Bank, " | ....... ....................... | 3,880 00 |
| City National Bank, " | ....... .................................. | 6,000 00 |
| National Bank of North America, " | ................. .. ....................... | 12,000 00 |
| Merchants National Bank, " | ......... ... ........................ | 12,000 00 |
| | | $64,300 00 |
| United States five twenty Bonds,.................................................. ......... | | $12,000 00 |
| Narragansett Pier Railroad Bonds,.... ................................................. | | 10,000 00 |
| | | $22,000 00 |

## WARREN INSTITUTION FOR SAVINGS.

*W. P. FREEBORN, Treasurer.*

| | RESOURCES. | LIABILITIES. | MISCELLANEOUS. |
|---|---|---|---|
| Amount invested in mortgages on real estate.............. | $345,824 00 | ............. | |
| Amount invested in stocks ..... | 23,500 00 | ............. | |
| Amount invested in bonds. .... | 73,000 00 | ............. | |
| Amount loaned on personal security.................... | 207,677 26 | ............. | |
| Amount loaned on collaterals of personal property.. ....... | 50,205 00 | ............. | |
| Amount of cash on hand........ | 5,393 51 | ............. | |
| Amount of deposits............ | ............. | $694,190 85 | |
| Amount of profit on hand...... | ............. | 11,408 92 | |
| | $705,599 77 | $705,599 77 | |
| Number of depositors.......... | ............. | ............. | 1348 |
| $500 and under $1,000..... | ............. | ............. | 188 |
| of $1,000 and upwards..... | ............. | ............. | 214 |
| Largest amount due to any one depositor................. | ............. | ............. | 5,961 60 |
| Amount, date and rate per cent. of last dividend........... | $19,918 05 | Nov. 6, 1876. | 3 pr. ct. 6 mo. |
| Average rate of dividend for the last three years........... | ............. | ............. | 6⅞ pr.ct.pr.an. |
| Amount of reserved profits at time of last dividend....... | ............. | ............. | $7,500 00 |

Amount loaned on Mortgages in other States:—

     Massachusetts,.................................$32 750 00

Description of stocks and bonds held by the Bank, names of the Institutions in which invested, with their several amounts:

| | |
|---|---|
| First mortgage bonds Morris Run Coal Company............................................. | $4,000 00 |
| First mortgage bonds New York, Providence and Boston Railroad,........................ | 10,000 00 |
| First mortgage bonds Smithfield Manufacturers Company,.... ............................. | 5,000 00 |
| United States 6 per cent. Registered Bonds,........................ ...................... | 54,000 00 |
| Old National Bank, Providence......................................... ........ ........... | 3,000 00 |
| National Bank of North America, Providence............................................... | 1,000 00 |
| Fourth National Bank,     " | 5,000 00 |
| Commercial National Bank,     " | 1,000 00 |
| Weybosset National Bank,     " | 1,000 00 |
| Merchants National Bank,     " | 1,000 00 |
| National Bank of Commerce,     " | 2,000 00 |
| American National Bank,     " | 600 00 |
| National Eagle Bank,     " | 1,500 00 |
| First National Bank, Warren...... | 1,000 00 |
| | $96,600 00 |

## WARWICK INSTITUTION FOR SAVINGS.

### *M. FIFIELD, Treasurer.*

| | RESOURCES. | LIABILITIES. | MISCELLANEOUS. |
|---|---|---|---|
| Amount invested in mortgages on real estate.............. | $844,153 55 | ............. | |
| Amount invested in stocks..... | 132,575 00 | ............. | |
| Amount invested in bonds..... | ............. | ............. | |
| Amount loaned on personal security...................... | 196,179 64 | ............. | |
| Amount loaned on collaterals of personal property.......... | 50,000 00 | ............. | |
| Real estate..................... | 49,000 00 | ............. | |
| Amount of cash on hand........ | 6,223 10 | ............. | |
| Amount of deposits............. | ............. | $1,239,185 62 | |
| Amount of profit on hand...... | ............. | 25,945 67 | |
| Bills Payable.................. | ............. | 15,000 00 | |
| | $1,280,131 29 | $1,280,131 29 | |
| Number of depositors.......... | ............. | ............. | 2105 |
| of $500 and under $1,000 .. | ............. | ............. | 234 |
| of $1,000 and upwards,.... | ............. | ............. | 229 |
| Largest amount due to any one depositor.................. | ............. | ............. | $22,780 65 |
| Amount, date and rate per cent. of last dividend.......... | 36,578 08 | Nov. 25, 1876. | 3 pr. ct. 6 mos. |
| Average rate of dividend for the last three years.......... | ............. | ............. | 6¼ pr.ct.pr.an. |
| Amount of reserved profits at time of last dividend....... | ............. | ............. | $25,945 67 |

Amount loaned on mortgages in other States..................None.

Description of stocks held by the Bank, names of the Institutions in which invested, with their several amounts:

Stock—Merchants National Bank, Providence......,...................................... ...$5,400 00
National Bank of North America, Providence..........................................35,000 00
Northern Bank,       "     ..........................................10,000 00
Rhode Island National Bank.    "     .................................. ...........4,525 00
American National Bank,      ..    .... ................... ................25,000 00
National Bank of Commerce,    "     .... .......................... ........26,100 00
Merchants National Bank,      ..    ......... .....................1,450 00
Globe National Bank,      "     .......................... ........10,500 00
Centreville National Bank, of Warwick....... ............................14,600 00

$132,575 00

## WESTERLY SAVINGS BANK, WESTERLY.

*SIMEON F. PERRY, Treasurer.*

| | RESOURCES. | LIABILITIES. | MISCELLANEOUS. |
|---|---|---|---|
| Amount invested in mortgages on real estate............... | $560,608 59 | ............. | |
| Amount invested in stocks..... | 71,400 00 | ............. | |
| Amount invested in bonds..... | 242,500 00 | ............. | |
| Amount loaned on personal security..................... | 89,585 00 | ............. | |
| Amount loaned on collaterals of personal property.......... | 8,475 00 | ............. | |
| Amount of cash on hand....... | 13,325 59 | ............. | |
| Amount of deposits............. | ............. | $925,464 45 | |
| Amount of profit on hand...... | ............. | 60,429 73 | |
| | $985,894 18 | $985,894 18 | |
| Number of depositors.......... | ............. | ............. | 1,961 |
| of $500 and under $1,000.. | ............. | ............. | 269 |
| of $1,000 and upwards...... | ............. | ............. | 267 |
| Largest amount due to any one depositor.................. | ............. | ............. | $10,000 00 |
| Amount date and rate per cent. of last dividend........... | $27,053 94 | June 1, 1876. | 3 per.ct.6 mos |
| Average rate of dividend for the last three years............ | ............. | ............. | 6¼ pr.ct.pr.an. |
| Amount of reserved profits at time of last dividend...... | ............. | ............. | $33,250 68 |

Amount loaned on mortgages in other States:—

Connecticut............$149,503 00  Indiana............. ............$10,000 00
Massachusetts............1,460 00  Michigan...................6,000 00
Illinois..................09,500 00  West Virginia.............5,000 00

Description of stocks and bonds held by the bank, names of the institutions in which invested, with their several amounts :

American National Bank, Providence...5,000 00
Blackstone Canal Nat. "    "    2,000 00
City National    "    3,000 00
Commercial National Bank,    "    3,000 00
Eagle National Bank,    "    3,000 00
First National Bank,    "    2,000 00
Merchants National Bank,    "    5 000 00
National Bank of Commerce,    "    10,000 00
National Bank of North America,    "    2,050 00
Rhode Island National Bank,    "    3,750 00
Third National Bank,    "    3,000 00
Weybosset National Bank,    "    3,000 00
Amer. Ex,    "    "    N. Y.    5,000 00
Continental    "    "    "    3,000 00
Merchants    "    "    "    2,000 00
Metropolitan    "    "    "    2,000 00
National Bank of Commerce,    "    5,000 00
National Bank of the Republic,    "    5,000 00
Nat. Mechanics Bank'g Ass'n.    "    2,000 00
" Shoe and Leather Bank,    "    2,500 00
Albany & Susquehanna R. R. bds.    10,000 00
Boston & Maine    "    10,000 00

Burlington C. R. and Mln.    bds.    12,000 00
Chesapeake & Ohio R. R.    "    2,000 00
Cleveland & Pittsburg R. R.    "    9,500 00
Lake Erie, Wab. & St. Louis    "    14,000 00
Milwaukee & St. Paul R. R.    "    4,700 00
Morris & Essex    "    5,000 00
New Jersey Midland    "    3,000 00
N. Y. Central & H. River R. R.    "    20,000 00
New London Northern    "    8,000 00
N, Y, Prov. & Boston    "    5,000 00
St. Louis, Alton & Terre Haute "    3,400 00
St Louis & Iron Mountain    "    9,790 00
Toledo & Wabash    "    3,000 00
Union Pacific    "    4,800 00
School District No. 1, Westerly,    27,500 00
Delaware & Hudson Canal,    8,000 00
City of Portsmouth, Ohio,    9,700 00
"    "    Toledo,    "    3,500 00
United States 5.30 bonds.    70,000 00

Total ......................$313,900 00

## WICKFORD SAVINGS BANK.

### *S. B. REYNOLDS, Treasurer.*

| | RESOURCES. | LIABILITIES. | MISCELLANEOUS. |
|---|---|---|---|
| Amount invested in mortgages on real estate............... | $303,679 12 | ............. | |
| Amount invested in stocks..... | 63,047 35 | ............. | |
| Amount invested in bonds..... | 54,061 84 | ............. | |
| Amount loaned on personal security .................. | 61,131 54 | ............. | |
| Amount loaned on collaterals of personal property ......... | 11,300 00 | ............. | |
| Deposit at R. I. H. Trust Co. | 8,152 73 | ............. | |
| City of Providence notes...... | 20,000 00 | ............. | |
| School Dis. Nos. 3 and 4, N. K. | 15,000 00 | ............. | |
| Amount of cash on hand...... | 2,500 00 | ............. | |
| Amount of deposits........,... | ............. | $522,011 52 | |
| Amount of profit on hand...... | ............. | 16,861 06 | |
| | $538,872 58 | $538,872 58 | |
| Number of depositors........... | ............. | ............. | 1088 |
| of $500 and under $1,000,... | ............. | ............. | 166 |
| of $1,000 and upwards..... | ............. | ............. | 50 |
| Largest amount due to any one depositor................. | ............. | ............. | $5,788 20 |
| Amount, date and rate per cent. of last dividend........ .. | 15,317 20 | July 1, 1876. | 3 pr ct. 6 mos. |
| Average rate of dividend for the last three years........... | ............. | ............. | 6¼pr ct. pr.an. |
| Amount of reserved profits at time of last dividend .... | ............. | ............. | $4,542 65 |

Amount loaned on mortgages in other States :—

Brooklyn, N. Y...............................$5,000 00

Description of stocks and bonds held by the bank, names of the institutions in which invested, with their several amount:—

Stock—Wickford National Bank.............. ..........$800 00
     Fourth   "   " Providence.............................2,400 00
     National Bank of Commerce Providence.............5,109 60
     American National Bank   " ......4,000 00
     Butchers and Drovers Bank,   " ......3,000 00
     Westminster   " ......500 00
     Lime Rock National   " ......2,500 00
     Globe   "   " ......1,600 00
     Merchants   "   " ......3,000 00
     Rhode Island   "   " ......750 00
     National Bank of North America," ......5,000 00
     Manufacturers National Bank   " ......1,700 00
     Commercial   "   "   " ......5,187 75
     National Bank of Commerce,   New York.............10,000 00
     American Exchange National Bank,   " ......5,000 00
     Merchants   "   " ......2,500 00
     Fourth   "   " ......10,000 00

        Total............................................$63,047 35
Bonds—New Haven, New London & Stonington first mortgage 6 per cent. ......6,561 84
     United States bonds,6's of 1881............................3,000 00
     "   "   " 5. 20's............................36,500 00
     "   "   " 10-40's............................8,000 00

        Total............................................$54,061 84

## WOONSOCKET INSTITUTION FOR SAVINGS.

### HENRY L. BALLOU, *Acting Treasurer.*

| | RESOURCES. | LIABILITIES. | MISCELLANEOUS. |
|---|---|---|---|
| Amount invested in mortgages on real estate............. | $1,875,208 11 | ............. | |
| Amount invested in stocks..... | 104,100 00 | ............. | |
| Amount invested in bonds..... | 684,000 00 | ............. | |
| Amount loaned on personal security.................... | 469,305 68 | ............. | |
| Amount loaned on collaterals of personal property......... | 64,914 00 | ............. | |
| Amount loaned to School Dist.. | 18,000 00 | ............. | |
| Amount of cash on hand....... | 8,760 21 | | |
| Amount of deposits.......... | ............. | $3,137,619 41 | |
| Amount of profit on hand.... | ............. | 86,668 59 | |
| | $3,224,288 00 | $3,224,288 00 | |
| Number of depositors......... | | | 6460 |
| of $500 and under $1,000.. | | | 1017 |
| of 1,000 and upwards...... | | | 1051 |
| Largest amount due to any one depositor.................. | | | $14,919 00 |
| Amount, date and rate per cent. of last dividend........... | 92,188 49 | Nov. 1, 1876. | 6 pr ct. 6 mos. |
| Average rate of dividend for the last three years......... .. | | | 6$\frac{1}{4}$ pr ct. pr an |
| Amount of reserved profits at time of last dividend...... | | | 77,176 13 |

Amount loaned on mortgages in other States................None.

Description of stocks and bonds held by the Bank, names of the institutions in which invested, with their several amounts :

**STOCKS.**

| | | |
|---|---|---|
| Old National Bank, Providence,.................................................. | 10,000 00 |
| Fourth " " .................................................. | 20,000 00 |
| National Bank of North America, Providence,.................................... | 11,000 00 |
| Weybosset National Bank, " ...................................... | 1,000 00 |
| Roger Williams National Bank, " ...................................... | 3,700 00 |
| Manufacturers " " ...................................... | 16,000 00 |
| National Bank of Commerce, " ...................................... | 10,000 00 |
| American National Bank, " ...................................... | 13,000 00 |
| Globe " " ...................................... | 3,300 00 |
| National Eagle, " ...................................... | 2,800 00 |
| " Globe, " Woonsocket,...................................... | 7,500 00 |
| First National " ...................................... | 5,000 00 |
| Woonsocket National Bank, " ...................................... | 3,100 00 |

Total.......... ..............................................$104,100 00

| | |
|---|---|
| United States 20 year 6 per cent. 1881 bonds........................ | 50,000 00 |
| City of Chicago 7 per cent. bonds................................. | 50,000 00 |
| City of Newport 7 3-10 per cent. bonds............................ | 100,000 00 |
| City of Covington 7 3-10 per cent. bonds.......................... | 65,000 00 |
| " " 8 per cent. bonds.......................... | 17,000 00 |
| City of Newark 7 per cent. bonds................................. | 100,000 00 |
| City of Minneapolis 8 per cent. bonds............................ | 120,000 00 |
| Town of Woonsocket 7 per cent. bonds............................ | 92,000 00 |
| Bernon Manufacturing Company 7 per cent. mort. bonds........... | 30,000 00 |
| Social " " 7 per cent. mort. bonds........... | 30,000 00 |
| Woonsocket " " 7 per cent. mort. bonds........... | 30,000 00 |

Total.................................................$684,000 00

## RHODE ISLAND HOSPITAL TRUST COMPANY.

*WM. BINNEY, President.*

---

### ASSETS.

| | |
|---|---|
| Cash | $105,146 97 |
| Due from Banks and Bankers | 114,049 73 |
| Iowa land account | 42,704 15 |
| Bills Receivable | 2,313,016 57 |
| Mortgages | 989,200 00 |
| United States Bonds | 600,000 00 |
| Rhode Island Bonds | 125,000 00 |
| State, Municipal and R. R. Bonds | 2,436,816 00 |
| Stock of R. I. H. Trust Co. | 17,000 00 |
| Real Estate, South Main street, Providence | 75,000 00 |
| Expense account | 700 00 |
| U. S. Treasurer, redemption account | 16,000 00 |
| Call Loans and on Collateral | 51,650 00 |
| Premium account | 133,346 56 |
| General Treasurer, State of Rhode Island, over draft | 3,291 87 |
| Interest, (earned but not yet paid) | 17,885 13 |
| | $7,040,806 98 |

### LIABILITIES.

| | |
|---|---|
| Capital | $500,000 00 |
| Reserve | 125,000 00 |
| Commissions | 15,598 93 |
| Profit and Loss | 77,179 16 |
| Guarantee account | 30,100 00 |
| Internal Revenue | 5,380 67 |
| Deposits | 2,239,843 44 |
| Due Banks and Bankers | 113,996 97 |
| Moneys in trust | 3,905,683 05 |
| Balances of trust accounts | 24,329 76 |
| Coupon account | 2,400 00 |
| Dividends unpaid | 1,295 00 |
| | $7,040,806 98 |

## AGGREGATE OF THIRTY-NINE INSTITUTIONS FOR SAVINGS,

*Showing Amount of Deposits and Number of Depositors in the Savings Institutions of Rhode Island, on Tuesday, November 28, 1876.*

| NAMES. | AMOUNT OF DEPOSITS. | NUMBER OF DEPOSITORS. |
|---|---|---|
| Ashaway Savings Bank, Ashaway.............. | $75,889 67 | 393 |
| Bristol County Savings Bank, Bristol......... | 6,025 89 | 108 |
| Bristol Institution for Savings, Bristol.......... | 349,361 20 | 1,223 |
| Citizens Savings Bank, Providence............ | 565,838 11 | 756 |
| Citizens Savings Institution, Woonsocket...... | 308,640 84 | 556 |
| City Savings Bank, Providence................ | 1,981,282 20 | 2,818 |
| Coddington Savings Bank, Newport............ | 557,155 98 | 1,525 |
| Coventry Savings Bank, Anthony.............. | 244,124 30 | 574 |
| *Cranston Savings Bank, Providence.......... | 715,646 51 | 4,400 |
| East Greenwich Ins. for Savings, E. Greenwich | 199,025 15 | 528 |
| Franklin Savings Bank, Pawtucket............ | 1,588,981 70 | 2,521 |
| *Franklin Institution for Savings, Providence | 819,764 38 | 5,818 |
| Hopkinton Savings Bank, Wyoming........... | 222,745 08 | 777 |
| Island Savings Bank, Newport................ | 205,716 12 | 408 |
| Jackson Institution for Savings, Providence.... | 437,727 60 | 788 |
| Kingston Savings Bank, Kingston............. | 247,445 21 | 542 |
| Mechanics Savings Bank, Providence.......... | 6,774,698 38 | 10,335 |
| Mechanics Savings Bank, Westerly............ | 315,743 85 | 704 |
| Mechanics Savings Bank, Woonsocket......... | 52,512 84 | 279 |
| Merchants Savings Bank, Providence.......... | 309,478 73 | 460 |
| Niantic Savings Bank, Westerly.............. | 400,968 96 | 910 |
| Pascoag Savings Bank, Pascoag.............. | 554,348 37 | 1,110 |
| Pawtucket Institution for Savings, Pawtucket.. | 2,347,512 24 | 3,973 |
| Peoples Savings Bank, Providence............ | 4,311,764 20 | 6,229 |
| Peoples Savings Bank, Woonsocket........... | 536,471 32 | 1,055 |
| Phenix Savings Bank, Phenix................ | 351,575 32 | 745 |
| Producers Saving Bank, Woonsocket.......... | 270,412 66 | 503 |
| Providence Institution for Savings, Providence | 8,402,887 33 | 19,959 |
| Providence County Savings Bank, Pawtucket. | 3,495,849 86 | 5,841 |
| Rhode Island Institution for Savings, Providence | 968,351 27 | 1,645 |
| Savings Bank of Newport, Newport ........... | 4,211,880 80 | 5,238 |
| Smithfield Savings Bank, Greenville.......... | 208,641 77 | 570 |
| Union Savings Bank, Providence............. | 1,514,263 06 | 2,748 |
| Wakefield Institution for Savings, Wakefield... | 360,776 62 | 864 |
| Warren Institution for Savings, Warren........ | 694,190 85 | 1,348 |
| Warwick Institution for Savings, Centreville.... | 1,239,185 62 | 2,105 |
| Westerly Savings Bank, Westerly.............. | 925,464 45 | 1,961 |
| Wickford Savings Bank, Wickford............ | 522,011 52 | 1,088 |
| Woonsocket Institution for Savings, Woonsocket | 3,137,619 41 | 6,460 |
| | $50,511,979 41 | 99,865 |

*In liquidation.

## INSTITUTIONS FOR SAVINGS.

A Summary of the Condition of the Savings Institutions in Rhode Island, on Tuesday, November 28, 1876.

#### RESOURCES.

| | |
|---|---|
| Loans on Mortgages of Real Estate | $29,416,757 08 |
| Bank and other Stocks | 2,485,342 65 |
| National, State, City and Town Bonds | 6,934,710 87 |
| Railroad and other Bonds | 2,291,680 76 |
| City, Town and District Notes | 191,000 00 |
| Loans on Personal Security | 7,878,837 88 |
| Loans on Collaterals | 1,714,334 07 |
| Cash on hand | 774,959 86 |
| Real Estate | 524,149 02 |
| Miscellaneous | 76,517 95 |
| | $52,287,389 64 |

#### LIABILITIES.

| | |
|---|---|
| Amount due Depositors | $50,511,979 41 |
| Amount due National Banks | 25,235 71 |
| Amount due on Certificates | 5,057 00 |
| Amount of other Liabilities | 23,173 71 |
| Profits or Excess of Assets over Liabilities | 1,721,943 81 |
| | $52,287,389 64 |

#### MISCELLANEOUS.

| | |
|---|---|
| Number of Savings Institutions in the State | 39 |
| Whole Number of Depositors | 99,865 |
| Number of Depositors of $500, and under $1000 | 13,586 |
| Number of Depositors of $1000 and upwards | 14,716 |
| Average to each Depositor | $505 80 |
| Largest amount due any one Depositor | 48,092 87 |
| Decrease of deposits from previous year | 799,351 21 |

Average rate per cent. of last dividend, a small fraction over 6 per cent. per annum.

| | |
|---|---|
| Decrease in number of depositors from previous year of those depositing less than $500 each | 1,490 |
| Amount loaned on Mortgages of Real Estate in other States | $2,567,230 23 |

TABLE SHOWING THE LARGEST AMOUNT DUE TO ANY ONE DEPOSITOR
FROM EACH SAVINGS INSTITUTION IN THE STATE, WITH THE
EXCEPTION OF THE CRANSTON AND FRANKLIN, OF
PROVIDENCE, ON TUESDAY, NOV. 28, 1876.

| | |
|---|---|
| Ashaway Savings Bank, Ashaway | $3,442 84 |
| Bristol County Savings Bank, Bristol | 1,948 21 |
| Bristol Institution for Savings, Bristol | 3,135 60 |
| Citizens Savings Bank, Providence | 31,563 88 |
| Citizens Savings Institution, Woonsocket | 8,259 52 |
| City Savings Bank, Providence | 25,806 02 |
| Coddington Savings Bank, Newport | 12,815 62 |
| Coventry Savings Bank, Anthony | 12,262 03 |
| East Greenwich Institution for Savings, East Greenwich | 6,295 75 |
| Franklin Savings Bank, Pawtucket | 20,000 00 |
| Hopkinton Savings Bank, Wyoming | 6,066 87 |
| Island Savings Bank, Newport | 12,161 63 |
| Jackson Institution for Savings, Providence | 10,000 00 |
| Kingston Savings Bank, Kingston | 16,096 89 |
| Mechanics Savings Bank, Providence | 27,300 00 |
| Mechanics Savings Bank, Westerly | 6,380 78 |
| Mechanics Savings Bank, Woonsocket | 2,435 81 |
| Merchants Savings Bank, Providence | 10,552 95 |
| Niantic Savings Bank, Westerly | 12,087 92 |
| Pascoag Savings Bank, Pascoag | 8,811 23 |
| Pawtucket Institution for Savings, Pawtucket | 30,000 00 |
| Peoples Savings Bank, Providence | 24,656 38 |
| Peoples Savings Bank, Woonsocket | 4,734 68 |
| Phenix Savings Bank, Phenix | 6,755 50 |
| Producers Savings Bank, Woonsocket | 2,793 86 |
| Providence Institution for Savings, Providence | 9,228 33 |
| Providence County Savings Bank, Pawtucket | 48,092 87 |
| Rhode Island Institution for Savings, Providence | 16,383 00 |
| Savings Bank of Newport, Newport | 31,768 22 |
| Smithfield Savings Bank, Greenville | 15,707 50 |
| Union Savings Bank, Providence | 20,245 43 |
| Wakefield Institution for Savings, Wakefield | 6,612 62 |
| Warren Institution for Savings, Warren | 5,961 60 |
| Warwick Institution for Savings, Centreville | 22,780 65 |
| Westerly Savings Bank, Westerly | 10,000 00 |
| Wickford Savings Bank, Wickford | 5,788 20 |
| Woonsocket Institution for Savings, Woonsocket | 14,919 00 |

☛ SEE TABLE ON NEXT PAGE.

## Savings Bank Returns.

A TABLE SHOWING THE AMOUNT OF DEPOSITS IN THE SAVINGS INSTITUTION
TO THIS DEPARTMENT, GIVING ALSO THE WHOLE NUMBER OF DEPOSITO

| NAMES AND LOCATION. | Amount of Deposits, Nov. 30, 1867. | No. of Depositors. | Amount of Deposits, Dec. 1, 1868. | No. of Depositors. | Amount of Deposits, Dec. 8, 1869. | No. of Depositors. | Amount of Depositor |
|---|---|---|---|---|---|---|---|
| Ashaway Savings Bank, Ashaway........ | ........ | ........ | ........ | ........ | ........ | ........ | |
| Bristol County Savings Bank, Bristol..... | ........ | ........ | ........ | ........ | ........ | ........ | |
| Bristol Institution for Savings Bristol.... | $173,873 76 | 885 | $174,289 34 | 901 | $175,312 79 | 904 | |
| Citizens Savings Bank. Providence........ | ........ | ........ | ........ | ........ | ........ | ........ | |
| Citizens Savings Institution, Woonsocket. | 173.714 79 | 508 | 214,666 53 | 561 | 261,815 23 | 614 | |
| City Savings Bank, Providence .......... | 1,295.535 43 | 2,338 | 1,465,469 74 | 2,606 | 1,515,631 78 | 2,174 | |
| Coddington Savings Bank, Newport...... | 174,812 14 | 1,193 | 234,482 61 | 1,279 | 270,564 73 | 1,348 | |
| Coventry Savings Bank, Anthony........ | ........ | ........ | ........ | ........ | ........ | ........ | |
| Cranston Savings Bank, Providence ...... | ........ | ........ | ........ | ........ | ........ | ........ | |
| East Greenwich Institution for Savings... | 65,965 14 | 323 | 87,980 58 | 352 | 96,780 26 | 400 | |
| Franklin Savings Bank, Pawtucket....... | 374,227 78 | 1,011 | 560,126 90 | 1,245 | 565,314 84 | 1,296 | |
| Franklin Institution for Savings, Prov.... | 1,318,989 77 | 4,386 | 1,621,802 01 | 4,935 | 1,912,603 22 | 5,617 | |
| Hopkinton Savings Bank, Wyoming...... | ........ | ........ | ........ | ........ | ........ | ........ | |
| Island Savings Bank, Newport ........ | ........ | ........ | ........ | ........ | ........ | ........ | |
| Jackson Institution for Savings, Prov .... | ........ | ........ | ........ | ........ | ........ | ........ | |
| Kingston Savings Bank, Kingston...... | 80,425 61 | 314 | 87,362 91 | 328 | 113,182 86 | 361 | |
| Mechanics Savings Bank, Providence..... | 2,333,011 04 | 5,455 | 2,635,072 28 | 5,899 | 3,005,090 21 | 6,218 | |
| Mechanics Savings Bank, Westerly...... | ........ | ........ | ........ | ........ | ........ | ........ | |
| Mechanics Savings Bank, Woonsocket.... | ........ | ........ | ........ | ........ | ........ | ........ | |
| Merchants Savings Bank Providence...... | ........ | ........ | ........ | ........ | ........ | ........ | |
| Niantic Savings Bank. Westerly.......... | ........ | ........ | ........ | ........ | ........ | ........ | |
| Pascoag Savings Bank, Pascoag......... | 141,113 96 | 356 | 198,303 27 | 472 | 259,774 36 | 621 | |
| Pawtucket Institution for Savings........ | 1,036,920 72 | 2,807 | 1,003,860 01 | 2,840 | 1,196,601 79 | 2,908 | |
| Peoples Savings Bank, Providence ...... | 2,619,361 20 | 5,626 | 2,905,040 27 | 5,924 | 3,103,106 09 | 6,671 | |
| Peoples Savings Bank, Woonsocket...... | 214,106 37 | 577 | 231,814 62 | 627 | 393,532 33 | 765 | |
| Phenix Savings Bank, Phenix............ | 176,933 04 | 553 | 206,050 52 | 603 | 337,629 42 | 651 | |
| Producers Savings Bank, Woonsocket..... | ........ | ........ | ........ | ........ | ........ | ........ | |
| Providence Institution for Savings....... | 4,601,421 05 | 16,074 | 4,918,188 85 | 16,484 | 5,017,120 88 | 16,553 | |
| Prov. County Savings Bank, Pawtucket.. | 1,445,191 45 | 3,042 | 1,666,496 70 | 3,374 | 1,896,787 96 | 3,637 | |
| R. I. Institution for Savings, Providence.. | 199,034 73 | 311 | 306,794 22 | 548 | 410,995 35 | 711 | |
| Savings Bank of Newport, Newport...... | 1,742,048 96 | 3,487 | 1,940,027 04 | 3,688 | 2,175,504 99 | 3,895 | |
| Smithfield Savings Bank. Greenville...... | ........ | ........ | ........ | ........ | ........ | ........ | |
| Union Savings Bank, Providence......... | 194,012 15 | 263 | 391,976 96 | 546 | 547,434 00 | 781 | |
| Wakefield Institution for Savings. Wak'ld. | 133,743 96 | 463 | 152.477 11 | 494 | 168,047 46 | 527 | |
| Warwick Institution for Savings, Cen. | 788,788 92 | 1,956 | 876.761 62 | 2,086 | 963,314 90 | 2,118 | |
| Woonsocket Institution for Savings...... | 1,377,006 23 | 4,213 | 1,580,573 07 | 4,510 | 1,818,532 63 | 4,963 | |
| Warren Institution for Savings.......... | 164,193 71 | 640 | 183,687 27 | 704 | 223,343 71 | 812 | |
| Westerly Savings Bank................. | 375,566 55 | 1,453 | 426,730 49 | 1,486 | 522,736 74 | 1,736 | |
| Wickford Savings Bank............ ... | 270,716 67 | 830 | 306,712 73 | 909 | 343,029 29 | 887 | |
| | 21,413,647 14 | 59,071 | 24,404,635 95 | 63,501 | 27,067,072 18 | 67,838 | |

ISLAND, FROM 1867 TO 1876, INCLUSIVE, COMPILED FROM STATEMENTS MADE

| Amount of Deposits, Dec. 6, 1871. | No. of Depositors. | Amount of Deposits, Dec. 6, 1872. | No. of Depositors. | Amount of Deposits, Dec. 4, 1873. | No. of Depositors. | Amount of Deposits, Dec. 3, 1874. | No. of Depositors. | Amount of Deposits, Nov. 27, 1875. | No. of Depositors. | Amount of Deposits, Nov. 28, 1876. | No. of Depositors. |
|---|---|---|---|---|---|---|---|---|---|---|---|
| $1,906 71 | 94 | $25,897 01 | 217 | $54,646 69 | 337 | $64,504 13 | 368 | $71,996 60 | 382 | $75,889 67 | 393 |
| | | | | | | | | | | 6,025 89 | 108 |
| 1,811 72 | 877 | 229,893 82 | 978 | 261,127 84 | 1,033 | 291,774 84 | 1,087 | 342,803 22 | 1,207 | 349,361 20 | 1,223 |
| 696 25 | 117 | 100,149 27 | 358 | 155,702 63 | 308 | 234,194 57 | 447 | 396,071 97 | 604 | 555,438 11 | 756 |
| 530 22 | 709 | 357,980 13 | 743 | 359,128 93 | 703 | 353,496 94 | 670 | 337,017 05 | 623 | 306,640 84 | 556 |
| 320 10 | 3,076 | 2,231,054 24 | 3,258 | 2,270,054 52 | 3,144 | 2,199,457 22 | 3,109 | 2,317,096 48 | 3,155 | 1,981,282 20 | 2,818 |
| 755 68 | 1,532 | 496,553 95 | 1,637 | 533,307 92 | 1,673 | 530,140 25 | 1,591 | 567,431 26 | 1,597 | 557,155 98 | 1,595 |
| | | 67,926 00 | 191 | 193,318 09 | 477 | 218,746 44 | 518 | 240,119 94 | 555 | 244,124 30 | 574 |
| 760 96 | 798 | 1,027,962 78 | 2,379 | 2,180,810 74 | 5,115 | 1,103,669 99 | 4,400 | 882,456 07 | 4,400 | 715,646 51 | 4,400 |
| 904 51 | 434 | 153,977 71 | 479 | 155,021 80 | 461 | 173,653 43 | 508 | 191,159 79 | 527 | 199,025 15 | 528 |
| 475 17 | 1,585 | 1,160,833 33 | 2,157 | 1,326,040 96 | 2,205 | 1,461,476 23 | 3,047 | 1,584,189 80 | 2,897 | 1,588,961 70 | 2,521 |
| 311 76 | 6,558 | 2,784,573 28 | 6,894 | 2,677,607 51 | 6,558 | 2,158,270 60 | 6,552 | 972,003 73 | 5,915 | 819,764 38 | 5,818 |
| 254 48 | 399 | 155,198 37 | 597 | 207,340 20 | 715 | 224,146 94 | 770 | 239,909 59 | 799 | 222,745 08 | 777 |
| | | | | 36,237 41 | 83 | 91,556 62 | 240 | 178,286 24 | 376 | 205,716 12 | 406 |
| 900 00 | 125 | 164,018 41 | 388 | 252,712 53 | 513 | 318,484 66 | 625 | 411,899 10 | 758 | 437,727 60 | 788 |
| 297 94 | 477 | 209,777 45 | 493 | 231,722 88 | 511 | 248,393 53 | 525 | 251,189 21 | 529 | 247,445 21 | 542 |
| 237 13 | 7,418 | 4,715,586 67 | 8,300 | 5,112,623 10 | 8,604 | 5,755,275 51 | 9,573 | 6,616,542 76 | 10,344 | 6,774,696 38 | 10,335 |
| | | 129,033 90 | 470 | 171,945 14 | 593 | 232,068 40 | 556 | 260,097 09 | 650 | 315,748 85 | 704 |
| 14,638 00 | 52 | 87,132 56 | 182 | 175,998 26 | 279 | 233,873 27 | 368 | 313,779 61 | 199 | 52,512 84 | 279 |
| 374 54 | 520 | 228,398 54 | 705 | 312,980 82 | 799 | 374,626 55 | 892 | 391,600 68 | 461 | 309,478 73 | 460 |
| 500 29 | 787 | 530,045 41 | 925 | 551,760 23 | 1,013 | 583,682 49 | 1,073 | 633,339 69 | 921 | 400,968 96 | 910 |
| 454 18 | 3,765 | 1,983,535 73 | 3,748 | 2,063,972 57 | 3,866 | 2,253,461 87 | 4,042 | 2,378,601 88 | 1,195 | 554,348 37 | 1,110 |
| 957 04 | 6,388 | 3,871,326 52 | 6,367 | 3,867,992 61 | 6,010 | 4,019,836 09 | 6,065 | 4,341,768 49 | 4,122 | 2,347,512 28 | 3,973 |
| 480 16 | 938 | 470,089 22 | 1,049 | 479,851 19 | 1,029 | 517,506 42 | 1,055 | 570,396 91 | 6,307 | 4,311,764 20 | 6,299 |
| 069 54 | 635 | 285,636 36 | 670 | 310,471 94 | 674 | 339,980 53 | 721 | 350,626 98 | 1,118 | 536,471 32 | 1,055 |
| 019 32 | 384 | 234,864 36 | 457 | 254,413 16 | 467 | 360,742 40 | 471 | 286,722 03 | 747 | 351,573 32 | 745 |
| 083 61 | 16,978 | 6,473,671 52 | 17,744 | 6,739,579 06 | 17,415 | 7,075,773 18 | 19,364 | 8,118,008 88 | 509 | 270,412 66 | 503 |
| 504 04 | 4,749 | 3,327,156 85 | 5,154 | 3,562,286 04 | 5,694 | 3,831,071 10 | 5,896 | 3,870,860 82 | 19,936 | 8,402,887 33 | 19,959 |
| 707 77 | 1,232 | 597,146 58 | 1,093 | 620,497 58 | 1,192 | 749,393 32 | 1,534 | 964,355 10 | 5,841 | 3,495,849 86 | 5,841 |
| 591 39 | 4,385 | 3,201,674 44 | 4,685 | 3,510,758 76 | 4,879 | 3,763,799 27 | 5,020 | 4,058,092 83 | 1,744 | 968,351 27 | 1,645 |
| | | 40,041 45 | 138 | 122,678 51 | 342 | 131,608 11 | 420 | 239,690 54 | 5,203 | 4,211,680 80 | 5,238 |
| 749 27 | 1,470 | 1,337,255 68 | 2,123 | 1,341,162 97 | 2,250 | 1,356,676 42 | 2,463 | 1,619,661 69 | 540 | 288,641 77 | 570 |
| 408 35 | 500 | 266,855 00 | 714 | 293,742 21 | 786 | 328,533 84 | 536 | 364,334 58 | 2,863 | 1,514,268 06 | 2,748 |
| 218 50 | 2,428 | 1,343,648 93 | 2,495 | 1,360,373 19 | 2,523 | 1,341,618 59 | 2,337 | 1,395,431 60 | 822 | 360,776 62 | 864 |
| 625 29 | 5,948 | 2,677,294 83 | 6,512 | 2,871,058 36 | 6,615 | 3,238,325 44 | 6,850 | 3,390,124 36 | 2,376 | 1,239,185 62 | 2,105 |
| 650 73 | 1,061 | 480,943 06 | 1,194 | 547,016 53 | 1,247 | 619,489 53 | 1,269 | 678,068 19 | 6,910 | 3,137,619 41 | 6,460 |
| 192 19 | 1,987 | 809,603 80 | 2,025 | 891,436 57 | 2,033 | 944,561 02 | 1,997 | 928,677 65 | 1,383 | 694,190 85 | 1,348 |
| | 1,000 | 487,936 50 | 1,044 | 459,901 78 | 1,065 | 488,835 12 | 1,066 | 515,893 06 | 2,029 | 925,464 45 | 1,961 |
| | | | | | | | | | 1,090 | 522,011 52 | 1,088 |
| 96,289,703 | 179,676 | 42,583,538 66 | 88,664 | 46,617,183 03 | 93,124 | 48,771,501 86 | 96,359 | 51,311,330 62 | 101685 | 50,511,979 41 | 99,865 |

# FIRST ANNUAL REPORT

OF THE

# 𝕳arbor Commissioners,

MADE TO THE

# GENERAL ASSEMBLY

AT ITS

## JANUARY SESSION, 1877.

PROVIDENCE:
ANGELL, BURLINGAME & CO., PRINTERS TO THE STATE.
1877.

# REPORT.

To the Honorable the General Assembly of the State of Rhode Island, etc. :—

The Board of Harbor Commissioners, established by Chapter 556 of the Public Laws, passed at the January Session of 1876, respectfully submit their first annual report.

The members of the Board were appointed on the 14th day of June, and organized on the 28th of the same month.

The Commissioners are aware that the duties which have been assigned to them are of a very important nature, and it will be their constant endeavor to aid and foster all the facilities for navigation now possessed and all improvements therein which may be projected by the citizens of the State and to avoid interference with any private enterprise looking to such improvements, except in cases where, in their judgment, public injury would otherwise result.

The admirable location of Narragansett Bay, reaching well inland at the northern limit of that portion of our Atlantic Coast, which can be reached by vessels from the middle and southern States, without passing the dangerous outer shore of Cape Cod, renders its improvement for navigable purposes of unusual importance. Within its shores there is sufficient room for the present commerce of the world to ride in safety. At its head lies a city of over one hundred thousand inhabitants, situated upon territory which gives a rare combination of suitable high ground for dwellings, and level ground for business, within easy reach of three streams furnishing large water-power for manufacturing purposes, and to which, at a comparatively moderate expenditure, twenty feet navigation at low water can be brought. Two broad and deep entrances from the sea, one or the other of which can be made in a storm blowing from any direction, furnish easy access and make this bay an attractive haven to seafaring men.

An Advisory Board, consisting of Commodore Daniel Ammen, Chief of Bureau of Navigation ; Major Gouverneur K. Warren, United States Engineer ; Captain Carlisle P. Patterson, Sup't. U. S. Coast Survey, has been appointed by the President of the United States, to aid this Board in the consideration of such subjects as are of national interest, and their advice, which is rendered gratuitously, will be of the highest value.

Maps and plans in relation to our harbors and channels, obtained from the Coast Survey and from the Engineer Department of the United States, as well as others in possession of the city of Providence, and some from the office of the Secretary of State, with a few from other sources, have been or are being copied and collated so as to give us valuable information in regard to the changes which have occurred or may be going on within our public waters.

Believing that the ship channels have been injuriously shoaled by the dumping of ashes from steamers, the Commissioners requested the agents of the various lines to prohibit the throwing out of ashes above Sand Point, east of Prudence Island, above North Point east of Conanicut Island and above Sand Point in the western passage.

A dumping ground for the deposit of dredged material has been designated at the " deep hole " northwest of Rumstick Point, where all such material is now required to be carried. This ground is about nine miles from Providence harbor, but no suitable place above this is known to the Commissioners, and to go farther down the bay would not only cause increased expense but would subject the scows, at times, to a rougher sea than they could be expected to live in. A considerable portion, and perhaps the whole, of the dredged material can be taken care of in the construction of wharves within Providence harbor, if plans now under consideration are perfected, and it will be the aim of the Commissioners to aid in this result so far as they can.

The Commissioners, having studied the needs of Providence harbor, advised with the Harbor Committee of the City Council, as to the most desirable points for expending the money appropriated by the City Council for dredging, from which good accommodations for the heavy coastwise steamers at this port will probably result.

Consultations have been had with the Commissioners of Shell Fisheries in regard to the respective duties of the two boards.

The attention of the officers of the Providence and Worcester Railroad has been called to the injury likely to result to the harbor from the cutting off of an estimated volume of more than three million cubic feet from the tidal flow by the construction of a railroad embankment, without an opening, across a portion of Seekonk river, near Walker's Point. This volume should be restored to the tidal flow, without delay, by the construction of an adequate passage-way through the embankment.

Complaint having been made to the Commissioners of injury to the Pawtucket harbor, from the washing in of earth by storm waters from the highways of the town, and by the deposit of material above the dam, which washes into the harbor below, notice has been given to various parties responsible for such injury, to the end that a remedy may be provided.

Meetings have been held in Bristol, East Greenwich and Pawtucket, to give opportunity to the inhabitants to offer any suggestions in regard to the public waters. It is intended to hold similar meetings in other towns.

Many other subjects of interest in the development or preservation of the trusts committed to the Commissioners have been acted upon or are under consideration.

The Commissioners offer the following suggestions :

An office should be provided for the use of the Commissioners and the keeping of plans and records.

The harbor line of East Providence is unsuitable, in the opinion of the Commissioners, and they would suggest the repeal of the act establishing it. A new line will soon be proposed.

It is desirable that the duties of the commission in reference to improvements within harbor lines, be more fully defined. The experience of the Massachusetts Harbor Commissioners will probably be useful in this regard.

The commission would have greater apparent authority and probably greater weight in its appeals to Congress for aid in improving the harbor, if a clause directly conferring authority to act for the State, in such appeals, were added to the act.

Additional legislation may be needed to insure suitable wharf accommodations for transient shipping. on account of the practice of permanently occupying wharves for private business.

The desirability of requiring compensation, in kind or in money, for tidal space occupied by permanent structures, as is done in some States, should be considered. If such compensation is required in money, the funds resulting therefrom should be devoted exclusively to dredging ship channels near, or valuable to, the wharves or other structures, on account of which the money has been paid. While it is desirable to encourage, or at least to offer no obstacle to, the development of wharf property, such development should, in our opinion, only follow the legitimate demand, including a fair amount of accommodation in excess of immediate needs, for the purpose of inviting an increase of trade, and a moderate tax in compensation for public property resigned to private control and use ought not to be objected to, especially when it is made for the purpose of obtaining a fund to expend in repairing the injury caused by such private occupation and in increasing the value of the property so taxed. The reason for imposing such a tax consists chiefly in the fact that the main channels are preserved by the scour of the tides, and the efficiency of this force depends upon the volume of water which passes into and out of a basin at each tide. Any lessening of this volume will have a tendency to cause the channels to fill up, and to preserve them dredging must be resorted to. The question arises then as to the source from which funds for this dredging should be obtained, and although a part of it may fairly be raised by a general tax upon the community benefited by the increased facilities for trade, it seems most proper that the structures causing the injury should bear an additional part of the cost of the remedy. By this plan, also, the State which surrenders public property to private use, receives indirect compensation therefor. There are rare cases in which the occupation of a moderate amount of tidal space, between high and low water, does not injure the channels, but it has been laid down as a law by high authority that " *Where the high water level of the surface of the river, estuary, or basin is the same as, or higher than, the level seaward of the point of abstraction, a diminution of tide-covered area will reduce the effective backwater.*" Backwater being the term by which the volume of water between high and low tide levels is designated.

Where the inner waters rise higher than the outer it may be concluded that the space for receiving the tidal flow is already smaller than is required for the fullest effect of tidal scour. This is the case with the waters of Narragansett Bay and Providence harbor; the waters pile up as they flow inland and it is safe to say that any lessening of the space between high and low water, to receive the tide is an injury and that artificial means must be resorted to to preserve the channels.

In view of all the facts of the case we recommend that a compensation fund be established from a tax to be levied on parties who displace tide waters by structures or otherwise, and that the fund thus obtained be used by the Board of Harbor Commissioners at their discretion in improving the channels most affected by the displacement.

It is supposed to be the duty of the commission to foster and develop the rights and interests of the State in the public waters as well as to prevent direct injury. In this view it is desirable that an amendment be made to the act, empowering the Commissioners to make such examinations and observations as they may deem necessary.

It is made the duty of the Harbor Commissioners to recommend such further legislation as they may deem proper, and they therefore submit herewith a new draft of the act, under which they were appointed, embodying such changes as seem to them desirable.

J. HERBERT SHEDD,
N. F. POTTER, } *Harbor Commissioners.*
JEDEDIAH WILLIAMS,

## REPORT OF THE WOMEN'S BOARD OF VISITORS TO THE PENAL AND CORRECTIONAL INSTITUTIONS OF THE STATE.

*To the Senate and House of Representatives of the General Asembly of the State of Rhode Island, January Session,* 1877 :

The Women's Board of Visitors to the Penal and Correctional Institutions of the State, respectfully presents to the Legislature this, its Annual Report:

We have, during the past year, endeavored faithfully to perform the duties required of us, namely to visit frequently, the Institutions subject to our inspection, and to make to the proper authorities such suggestions as we have deemed necessary.

The State Prison and County Jail present the same aspect as formerly, of order, cleanliness and discipline, tempered by as much kindness as is compatible with their crowded condition, and the degree of enlightenment at present entering into our penal system. We hope that, with the new building, will come greater privileges and advantages, such as will render this institution a place for a wise and healthy physical, mental and moral culture. More room without and within, a broader sunshine, purer air and additional comforts, will aid much in the reformation of character, and in the preparation of the inmates to return safely to life in the outside world.

The institutions at the State Farm, we believe to be in a more encouraging condition than ever before. Evening schools in the work-house, both for the men and the women, are regularly organized, the women are permitted more exercise in the open air, and we think much credit is due to the officers for their efforts in the way of reform. We cannot hope, however, for any great progress in this direction, while the present large dormitories remain in use. Any advance during the day, must, in most cases, be materially arrested at night, by the crowding together in the same apartment, of all classes of the inmates.

We also look for greater improvement, when the women can be employed in gardening, or in any suitable out-door work.

There is one subject to which we wish to call your attention, that has always been a matter of concern to some members of our board; and has been the occasion of much conversation and remonstrance with individual members of the Board of State Charities. And that is the practice of supplying the inmates with tobacco. We believe it has a tendency unnaturally to stimulate the appetite and so prevents the eradication of the desire for strong drink; and also, that it excites and irritates the nervous system, rendering its victims more unmanageable. The women are not officially provided with it; but knowing that the men have it, there is a continual endeavor, on their part, to procure it from them; and, on the part of the men, to convey it to the women. This is a constant source of excitement, irritation and disregard of the rules of non-intercourse between the two; and, so entirely are the barriers overcome that the weekly or monthly supply to the men, is always followed by a corresponding supply to the women. The matrons have assured us, that this one thing gives them more trouble with the women than all other causes combined. They say, also, that in a number of cases young girls, who had never used tobacco before, have learned to use it in the State work-house. The cost of the tobacco for the last year, was nine hundred and thirty-two dollars. This, which seems to us worse than thrown away, would go far toward defraying the expense of much needed improvements. In our judgment, some stringent legislation in this matter is required. And we should beg for the substitution of greater variety in food.

In regard to the state of the Alms-house, we need add nothing to the appeal of the Board of State Charities for better accomodations. We believe the best is done for the inmates, that the circumstances allow.

The insane appear to be well cared for.

It is with great pleasure, that we are able to report our satisfaction with the condition of the Reform School. The new superintendent and matron, Mr. and Mrs. Eldredge, seem to us well fitded for their work. Although they have not yet had time to show all the results of their experiment, still the effect of their firm but gentle treatment, the kindness they are constantly bestowing, and the refining influences they are introducing, is already obvious, in the improved appearance of the inmates, particularly the girls. The expression on their faces is more hopeful and happy, and we feel more encouraged in their behalf.

But, our experience in all these institutions. confirms and deepens our conviction, that it is the duty of the State to provide, as speedily as possible, an educational institution for the prevention of pauperism and crime. To this school, children now consigned to the Alms-house, and other children deprived of the guardianship of parents, should be sent, not as offenders, but as wards, to be trained into habits of honest, self-supporting industry, at the same time that they are instructed in all that is necessary to make them intelligent, useful citizens. Into this school should enter no influence, which shall, in the slightest manner, cast a shadow of disgrace or shame over the after-life of the inmates. For this reason, we urge, that it shall be wholly under the management of a board of trustees having no connection with any penal institution, which shall be composed of men and women, who shall be appointed guardians of the children to be sent there. In closing we are compelled to express the hope, that the recommendation of the Governor, that women be placed on the Boards of Direction of all the Penal and Correctional institutions of the State, will be carried out. Our experience on this Board, has made us positively certain that the aid of women is absolutely necessary to the good ordering of these places, at the same time, that our helplessness has painfully oppressed and hampered us. If the service of women is needed and appreciated, it deserves an equal place in authority and power.

ELIZABETH B. CHACE,
ELIZA C. WEEDEN,
SARAH E. H. DOYLE,
ANNA E. ALDRICH,
HARRIET A. COOK,

(Who endorses all but the remonstrance against tobacco.)
PROVIDENCE, February 7, 1877.

## THE INDUSTRIAL ARTS IN THE PUBLIC SCHOOLS.

---

# REPORT

OF THE

# Committee on Education,

*MADE TO THE HOUSE OF REPRESENTATIVES, AT ITS*
*JANUARY SESSION, 1877.*

PROVIDENCE:
ANGELL, BURLINGAME & CO., PRINTERS TO THE STATE.
1877.

# REPORT.

*To the Honorable the House of Representatives, at the January Session, 1877 :—*

At the January session of 1876, the following resolution was adopted by the House of Representatives :—

" RESOLVED, That the Committee on Education be and hereby is instructed to inquire and report to this House, whether or not the public money now expended on schools above the grade of Grammar schools, could not be expended more. to the public advantage in instructing the pupils attending the public schools in the Industrial Arts."

The state of Rhode Island appropriates annually to public education, in addition to the Government Land Grant fund given some years ago to Brown University, the income of which is made available in the education of from thirty to forty students, the sum of ninety thousand dollars. Of the money thus appropriated, $63,000 is distributed to the towns according to the number of children under fifteen years of age; and $27,000 in proportion to the number of school districts in each.

As children ordinarily do not complete the Grammar school course, until they are over fourteen, it can hardly be assumed that any "public money" is expended upon schools above that grade, if we interpret the expression "public money" to mean the amount mentioned as such in the statute relating to its appropriation, and the only amount over whose disbursement this General Assembly has any direct control.

We are satisfied, however, that such a strict construction of the resolution was not intended, and that the subject referred to us, embraced expenditures for, and instruction in all the public schools, whether under state or municipal patronage. This view of the general scope of the resolution offers us four special topics for consideration, which, taken in their order, appear to be,

1st. The proper limit of free education.

2d. The importance of the High School in the system.

3d. The variety and kind of instruction in the schools.

4th. Industrial Art education.

### THE PROPER LIMIT OF FREE EDUCATION.

The fundamental principle underlying our public school system is, that the safety of the state depends upon the education of all its people ; and although this principle is universally recognized, there exist differences of opinion as to the precise amount of education the state should furnish.

There are those who maintain that when a child is fourteen or fifteen years of age, and has mastered the rudiments of an English education, this modicum of knowledge will suffice to meet all the necessities of the case, and a boy without further scholastic advantages can enter upon some mechanical pursuit, employment in commerce, or general business of life, and in due time fulfil all the requirements demanded by good citizenship. Others carry the idea still farther, in pronouncing more extended advantages of an educational nature a positive detriment to the body politic, because they have a tendency to diminish the number of good artisans, by fostering in the minds of the young an aversion to mechanical trades or manual labor in any form. They attribute the increase in the number of non-producers to a superabundance in the education of the masses, and aver that it is unwarranted in justice to tax property in order to afford greater opportunities for education than are now presented in the elementary schools.

These objections to an extension of the system beyond the Grammar schools are but a sample of the various opinions upon the subject, and they are perhaps among the most familiar to those who have carefully noted the history of public schools during the last few years. Emanating as these sentiments do, not merely from the ignorant and thoughtless, but also, in many instances, from those whose mental ability and liberal intellectual culture give weight to their opinions, and enable them to appreciate the advantages of a good education, we have given them careful and respectful consideration, but. nevertheless, feel constrained to withhold our concurrence

A recent report of our State Commissioner of Schools shows that Reading, Spelling, Penmanship, Arithmetic, and Geography, are taught in all our schools of an intermediate and grammar grade. History of the United

States, and English Grammar, are taught in most of the grammar schools, and Vocal Music and Drawing in some of them. These branches are undoubtedly taught with varying degrees of thoroughness in the different schools, but allowing for an adequate instruction in all of them, we believe that such a curriculum embraces only the *minimum* which the state absolutely requires for its *safety*, and that more is essential to its *welfare* and *prosperity*.

Under our democratic institutions, the possibilities open to every child are far greater than under monarchical rule; the requirements, more exacting. We have no hereditary class, born to rule and hence educated for it from infancy, but, on the contrary, our future magistrates and legislators, national, state, and municipal, must come from the people generally, without regard to class distinctions. Already in our history, more than once, the chief position in our national government, has been filled by those who were born in the humblest sphere of life, and from Congress to Town Councils we have seen the various offices filled, not only by those who have previously enjoyed, but also by those who have been deprived of, good educational advantages.

The jury-box, too, that important feature in our institutions, draws its complement from no class, but from the whole people, and the welfare of all is dependent upon the degree of intelligence possessed by those placed in that responsible position. Ignorance in the voters is dangerous to the state, and a lack of suitable educational preparation in those who are to perform the multifarious duties attendant upon the workings of democratic institutions in all their ramifications, is highly detrimental, to say the least.

Our state is largely dependent for its prosperity upon its manufacturing and mechanical industries, and these require a cultivated intelligence in order to keep pace with similar works in other states and countries in making constant progress in skill and improvements, in methods and machinery. With all these great interests in view, we cannot safely trust to the chance that natural ability will develop itself, or that those who could be really benefited by a higher education, will, in some way, manage to secure it. The example of other countries teaches us that supremacy can only be secured and maintained by advancing the general education of the masses.

The statement, that any advance beyond the rudiments of an English education tends to unfit its recipients for the practical duties of life, does not seem justifiable, unless it be granted that such advance is made under the tuition and supervision of persons deficient in the qualifications for the exalted position of teacher.

True education looks to the fostering and perfecting of all that is ennobling in character; cultivates correct thinking and reasoning powers; enlarges the mind to a better realization of the duties and responsibilities of every-day life; helps to perceive the dignity of labor in every form, whether mental or manual, and prevents from narrow-minded or one-sided views of social questions. There may be a shallow imitation, giving a superficial knowledge of a few facts, dates or figures, which might engender self-conceit,

and puff up the mind of the scholar to such a degree as to
cause him to depreciate honest labor, but if such a sham is
disseminated in any of our schools, the sooner it is exposed
and eradicated, the better for the community.   An ideal education has not yet been obtained, and ideal educators are
not yet found in every school, but to do them justice, our
teachers, as a class, are striving earnestly to implant in the
minds of their scholars correct views as to the proper conduct of life.

It cannot be denied, however, that false notions of life in
all its details, do exist prevalently, permeating all classes of
society, producing social drones, conducing to extravagance
and caste in an odious form, setting at defiance all true principles of democracy, and tending to subvert the best elements not only of social life, but almost, it may be said, of
true Christianity.   While we deplore the existence of social
influences so baleful in their nature, so repugnant to the
spirit of our institutions, and as palpably absurd as they
are widely diffused, it is not our province, even if it were
in our power, to do more than give them a passing recognition as facts or problems requiring solution at the hands of
experts in philosophy, religion and sociology.

We are compelled, however, as the result of our observation, to deny the propriety of ascribing them to our public
school system, and venture the assertion that the closest
analysis cannot locate their origin inside of our school doors,
and connect it inherently with our school training.

We learn from reliable statistics, that not more than three
per cent. of the pupils in our public schools ever enter a

High School, and probably less than two per cent. complete the course ; hence, admitting all the alleged evil effects of a surplus of education, it can, in no case, contaminate more than a very small proportion of the rising generation. We hope the time is not far distant when all of the children in our state may be thoroughly instructed in the branches now taught in the Grammar schools, but we cannot agree with these objectors in fixing upon that as the limit of free public education.

What may be the exact place, if any, in our system of public education, where it should cease to be entirely free of expense to the scholar ; whether admission in all cases to the higher grades, should be made dependent upon the degree of capacity and merit shown in the lower ones, upon the development of adaptability for further advantages, or upon competitive examinations for free scholarships, and other suggestions that are frequently made upon this subject, are not strictly within the scope of this report, and have not received consideration in this connection.

### IMPORTANCE OF THE HIGH SCHOOL IN THE SYSTEM.

Higher education is the fountain of popular education, and we see that in all countries where great success has attended the efforts to instruct the masses, it has been due to the influences emanating from the higher seminaries of learning. Whatever influences operate detrimentally to the High schools, in the same degree, militate against the real efficiency of the elementary schools. The prospect of advancement to the upper grade, serves as a valuable

2

stimulus to the mind of the scholar just laboring to grasp the rudiments, and the high school furnishes a goal for the laudable ambition of many a child, who, without it would be listless in his efforts and indifferent as to their results. The facilities afforded to any child possessed of superior mental ability, however poor, to attain the highest round of the ladder of education, render our system of public education truly substantial and democratic.

It is undoubtedly true that some who have received the advantages of the higher training, fail to develop in their subsequent career, proportionately beneficial results, but it is equally true, that many others who contribute largely to all that makes up the prosperity of the State, would have been unable to do so, but for the opportunities afforded them by the High school.

Aside from its relation to the lower grades as a goal of ambition to be eagerly sought for, it occupies an intermediate position in furnishing suitable preparation to those boys for whom the State has provided free scholarships in Brown University.

From an economical and practical point of view the High school is not an extravagant and useless appendage to the system, only to be criticised on account of its expense, for it serves admirably as a fountain, from which are drawn needed supplies of teachers for the elementary schools, which could be obtained in sufficient numbers from no other source. In this way the community is directly compensated for the increased expenditure for higher education. The Normal School is indispensable, but unless enlarged far beyond any present anticipations, would prove inadequate to the full supply of teachers for all the schools of the State, for many years to come. At the present time, more than eighty-five per cent. of the teachers in the schools of Providence have come from the High school, and this ratio would undoubtedly be maintained in Newport, and other places in the State, where good High schools exist.

The question of the importance of High schools and the necessity for their existence has received such thorough agitation and discussion during the period when they were first established in our State, that we deem it supererogatory to give it at this time, more than a merely general consideration and leave it with the expression of our conviction, that it is *inexpedient*, in view of the interests of the public, that High schools should be dispensed with as a part of our system of public instruction. They may be *modified*, *altered* or *improved* as the exigencies of the various localities require, but *never abolished*.

THE VARIETY AND KIND OF INSTRUCTION IN THE SCHOOLS.

The branches now taught in the elementary schools, all seem well adapted to the purpose, and none in our judgment could well be omitted. If more can be included, so much the better.

The great desideratum, however, is that they should be *taught thoroughly*, so that scholars who have finished their course, shall really *know* what they have spent so much time in learning. The urgent need of this is instanced in an item in a recent report of the Board of Visitors at West Point, which states, that during the preceding five years, thirty-five per cent. of the applicants for admission to the military academy, from Rhode Island, as well as from other New England States where there are good educational facilities, had failed to pass the preliminary examination in these elementary branches.

There has been in the past, undoubtedly, a tendency in many schools to follow blindly the topics as arranged in the text books, leading to unnecessary minuteness of detail in Geography and Grammar, but we believe it is now the practice with all judicious committees and teachers to consult common sense in making omissions which save much time and incur no loss to the scholar. As time advances, the qualifications of teachers will attain a higher standard, and the quality of their instruction become correspondingly improved ; meanwhile the friends of good education will continue to insist upon *accuracy*.

Criticisms upon the curriculum of the High Schools are very common, and differences of opinion are to be expected, when we consider the varying aims of the pupils who enter them. Some propose to take a College course, others commercial pursuits, others, girls, of course, hope to become teachers, while still others anticipate only a year or two in the High School and then some business or mechanical pursuit. Under such circumstances it would seem evident that whatever may be the regular course of study prescribed, it should not be inelastic, but on the contrary, should offer to the necessities of each scholar that which is best

adapted to them, and include optional branches.  We know
of some High Schools in this State, where great latitude
in this respect is allowed, and arrangements are made with
marked success, to meet the exigencies of all classes of
pupils; this should be the case in all of them.  Undoubtedly, in every place, those who direct the schools, are influenced not only by their own belief as to what is best for
them but also by the opinions of the community in which
they live.  This has led to changes and modifications from
time to time, reflecting the average controlling sentiment of
each community, and will continue to do so in future.
The conditions of the problem of public education are
constantly changing.  Continued immigration has in this
state added an important element to its difficulties.  The
people have changed in modes of thought, habits of life
and methods in business ; the variety of employments has
increased and mechanical arts have made such progress,
that the schools and methods of culture which served the
purpose formerly, would not answer the requirements of
the present time.  Once the public school house and the
meeting-house were built near together, and education and
religion went hand in hand ; the schoolmaster and the parson
labored, if not always together, at least in the same sphere of
duty and were bound by a common sympathy.  Now, however, education is remanded to the teacher in the public school,
while religion is banished from the school, and relegated to
the home, the church and the Sabbath School.  Again, in
the earlier history of public schools, manual labor was far
more common than now, from necessity, and hard work de-

veloped the physical energies of the people to such a
degree, that the need of greater intellectual culture was
seen and led to earnest efforts in that direction.   Hence the
schools have endeavored to carry out the idea, by giving
greatest attention to the cultivation of the brain, educators
believing that even strictly disciplinary studies were important as a part of the preparation for the practical duties
of life.   Now, however, we find quite prevalent among the
people, indications of desire for some modification of the
system of instruction,  that shall look to a more direct and
specific training  for such of the scholars as may become
artisans, or rather, such a training as may tend to induce
them to become artisans.

These are but instances of many changed conditions in
school matters, which have called for the exercise of the
most careful discretion by the managers of the schools, who
have probably given in each locality, such a curriculum for
the High school, as in their judgment the true interests of
the whole people required.   That, in any case, perfection
has been attained in the course of study designated, in the
methods of teaching, or in any of the details of the system
no sensible person will claim, while all friends of public
education will unite in demanding that the schools shall
advance harmoniously with the spirit of the age.

INDUSTRIAL ART EDUCATION.

Recognizing the fact that our public school system is not
perfected beyond criticism or improvement,  and that it is
progressive in its nature, as  well as  elastic in  its adap-

tation to the wants of the people, we must take cognizance of the sentiment quite prevalent in the community, that the results are not fully commensurate with the expenditure of money, and that the element of "practicality" is not as large a factor as it should be, in the great educational problem of the period. The importance of this opinion is acknowledged by the warmest friends of public education, and the popular demand has become so urgent, that at last, it has found expression in that part of the resolution before us, requiring a consideration of the question of industrial art education in the public schools.

The subject of industrial education is by no means new, and were it only the *general* subject, referred to us, the task would be easier than now, since we are confined to the specific consideration of its aspect as an integral part of our present established system, or at least a supplement of it. We find that we are not the only inquirers upon this subject, as our investigations have developed the fact that, in all parts of our country, the subject has recently risen to prominence, and school-boards, educators, and legislators, are seeking for information. The National Board of Trade of the United States has interested itself in this matter, and in January last, sent a memorial to this General Assembly, as to each of the legislatures of the other states, reading as follows :—

"Your memorialists, representing merchants and manufacturers of the United States, beg leave respectfully to represent unto your Honorable body, that the interference and dictation of Trades Union, and similar organizations with the system of apprenticeship, in earlier times prevailing in this and other countries, the active competition of foreign manufacturers with American industries in both home and foreign markets, and the increased attention being given by governments abroad, to the development and improvement of skilled labor, by instruction in science and art, as applied to mechanics and manufacturing, renders it in the opinion of this Board of great importance to our material progress, that suitable provision be made for the establishment of Art and Science schools in each of the several states, where workmen and their children may receive such technical instruction as will improve and create skilled labor, to the end that the poorer classes of society may become better fitted for a higher development of industry, and our mechanical and manufacturing interests be enabled more successfully to compete with those of other countries ; therefore, your petitioners would respectfully pray that your Honorable body will adopt measures for the establishment of such a school, or schools, as is herein indicated, within the state of Rhode Island.

Respectfully submitted, by order of National Board of Trade,

FREDERICK FRALEY,

*President."*

JANUARY, 1877.

NEGLECT OF INDUSTRIAL EDUCATION, A NATION'S WEAKNESS.

The Universal Exhibiton in 1851 at London, bringing together, for the first time, so extensive a collection of the industrial products of all nations, enabled each one to obtain a correct view of its own condition, compared with that of others. The succeeding exhibitions in 1856, 1861, and 1867 furnished valuable lessons to all of the European countries, but especially to England, whose utter discomfiture at the Paris exhibition in 1867, led to systematic inquiries, as to the reasons for the more rapid progress made in other nations in many of those industries in which, every thing else being equal, the English ought to excel.

Government commissioners composed of representatives of the educated professions, applied sciences, engineering, education and manufacturers, were sent to the Paris exhibition, and a deputation of over fifty skilled artisans, also, whose reports all concurred in the statement, that the superiority of other nations in industrial products, was due entirely to the greater interest given to the industrial edu cation of their people.

These statements, admitting inferiority on their own part, noting the rapid advancement of other countries since previous exhibitions, and attributing it solely to the one cause, were most startling, and thoroughly alarmed all Englishmen who had patriotic pride in maintaining for their country, precedence in manufacturing and mechanical industries.

They examined continental systems of industrial education, published elaborate reports, and, at once, adopted such educational measures as were deemed useful to them. During the last ten years, since the Paris exhibition, England has made wondrous efforts in this direction, and her advancement in the industrial arts was made manifest by the many exhibits of her productions at the Centennial Exhibition, last year. Meanwhile, other European countries, taught by experience, had also improved upon the industrial schools, which had given them the advantage of at least one generation of workmen, and were determined to continue in the lead.

The French manufacturers did not fail to note the extraordinary exertions England was making to contend for

8

precedence in industrial arts, They called the attention of the Government to the matter, and demanded increased educational advantages, in addition to those already in existence. A government commission, upon full investigation, learned that their system was very defective in comparison with that of Germany, and the result was, an energetic movement on the part of the state and of parties interested, which has, long ago, worked a great improvement in every branch of industry.

Switzerland, Germany, Austria, Russia and other countries were alike stimulated by the necessity of the case, to renewed interest in all that pertains to the advancement of the arts of industry, and their schools which had been good, were made better, while those which had been best of all, were advanced to a still higher standard. The process of improvement is still going on, and will continue to receive the utmost attention in each country that hopes to compete in the markets of the world, with the products of her industry.

However satisfactory may be the present development of Rhode Island mechanical and manufacturing industries; whatever there may have been of inventive genius, artistic skill or business enterprise to arouse feelings of pride in our achievements in the past, we must not lapse into a spirit of self-complacency, but rather take to ourselves the lesson from the experience of other countries, that no State can secure and maintain pre-eminence in mechanics and manufactures. except by the systematic and thorough training of the young in the industrial arts; that the palm of superiority, by an unfailing law, will surely go to that country, where the *hand of the laborer is guided by a cultivated taste and a scientifically trained intellect.*

From the last census of this State we learn, that in every 1,000 of our population, 560 are engaged in manufacturing or mechanical industries, and this fact in itself is sufficient to give us an interest in the great question of industrial education, and should lead us to the adoption of any measures that furnish a prospect of success in solving this great problem.

It will be interesting to briefly note what has been done in European countries, where, as we have stated, the interest in this subject has become synonymous with their self-interest, and where the competition of different countries has compelled attention to it, under penalty of banishment from the best markets of the world.

### INDUSTRIAL EDUCATION IN GERMANY.

The system of general education in Germany is well known as being most comprehensive, and as having been successful in reducing illiteracy toward its minimum, but in its arrangements for industrial education it is equally broad and systematic. The proportion of the population engaged in mechanics and manufactures is less than in Rhode Island, but there is no place of any considerable size, wanting in some sort of instruction having in view the various industries.

"Improvement" schools, "Real" schools, "Trade" schools, "Weaver's" schools, and special schools of many kinds, are found thickly, scattered over the entire country, affording facilities not only for general but for special technical instruction that are unsurpassed. In the lower order of these institutions, 'there is a similarity to our elementary schools, with the distinction that, *invariably*, the strictest attention is given to instruction in *drawing*. Of the secondary schools, we give the curriculum of one of the best, styled the "City-trade School of Berlin." It was founded " to give a more appropriate education for the mechanic arts and higher trades, than can be had through the courses of the other schools," and has the city of Berlin as its patron. The subjects of instruction are Religion, German, French, English. Arithmetic, Algebra, Geometry, Geography, History, Natural History, Physics, Chemistry, Technology, Writing, Drawing and Vocal Music.

The school is provided amply with laboratories, apparatus, and all the paraphernalia of instruction, and technology is taught by describing and illustrating the different arts and trades by models and visits to workshops of which there are none connected with the institution. Pupils enter after they are twelve years of age, and remain five years to complete the course. Higher than this in order and forming the summit in the grade of industrial schools, is the Royal Trade Academy at Berlin, which embraces in its course, far more advanced mathematical studies, and has extensive workshops connected with it, where various branches of practical mechanics are taught. The pupil begins with the making of a screw, and proceeds in regular order to the most difficult mechanical operations.

An Industrial Drawing School in Berlin, also, trains designers of patterns for printing silk, woolen and cotton tissues, and paper hangings, together with all the theoretical and practical branches of weaving.

Among the large number whose organization we have noted, the Royal School of Machinery at Augsburg, in Bavaria, is interesting, devoting, as it does, more time to the practical side of mechanics. The requisites for admission are a thorough knowledge of Algebra and Geometry and a certain amount of practice in linear drawing. The pupils who must be fifteen years old pursue a theoretical course in higher Mathematics, Mechanics, Physics, Drawing, etc., but devote an average of three hours daily to the work shops.

The scholar is placed at a vise, and a coarse file and a piece of iron are given him. He practises first in filing planes at right angles, and then parallel to one another, then he does the same with a finer file. Nothing can be done superficially and no one can go on to other work until he has been thoroughly successful. Next, he is practised in boring, cutting screws, and in making faucets. Then comes the turning of round surfaces and of screws, smoothing off, etc., all of which is done with simple pieces of iron, out of which paper-weights, etc., are made. Other simple operations follow until the end of the course, when scholars are generally able to support themselves by work in any factory.

Enough examples have been furnished to show the general scope and variety of industrial schools in Germany,

and while from the hundreds of them in operation, covering very many special trades and occupations, we might
select some of unusual interest, we have not space for the
details in this report.

In Austria, the agencies for the education of skilled
labor are of various kinds and increasing in number. They
have as in Germany, the " improvement " and the ordina-
· ry technical schools, but the great impulse which the art-
industrial movement has received during the last twenty-
five years, has called into existence new establishments of
a similar nature, but largely devoted to special trades and
industries.

These comprise theoretical schools and school shops, in
which the practical and theoretical teachings are combined.
The number of these schools has increased, in the last five
years, from *ten* to *one hundred and thirty.* In the highest
of the industrial schools, nearly one-third of the time is
devoted to free-hand and geometrical drawing.

### FRANCE.

France is equally aroused with her continental neighbors
to exertions for increased facilities for industrial-art education, and has rapidly augmented the number of schools for
the elementary training of the young in this respect.
While perhaps, failing to equal Germany in the universal-
ity of the system, she compares quite favorably in certain
localities, and in the higher class of technical schools.

In 1802, when Napoleon was First Consul, he visited one
of the government institutions and was extremely dissatis

fied with the answers of the pupils about to graduate, as
to their intentions for the future. These, he said, unless
they entered the army, would become " a burden rather
than an aid to their families. " He had observed workmen in the manufacturing establishments, who were experts in the manual labor of their trades but deficient in
the theoretical part, and hence he determined to change
the course at this institution, so that it should be devoted
to " the study of trades, with so much theory as is necessary to their progress. " This was done by an order soon
after published, and the result has been one of the most
successful institutions in the world for this purpose, at
Chalons.

The plan has been modified during the last few years, so
that instead of teaching a number of trades, it is devoted
to general mechanical industries for which theoretical
knowledge is indispensable. The shops connected with it,
are the Pattern shop, Smithy, Foundry and Fitting shop.
The pupils, who must be fifteen years of age, devote five
hours or more daily, to the work shops, in which the
general plan of instruction and practice is very similar to
that previously described, at Augsburg.

The general principles are, to make only one piece of the
same kind, and to do all work, as far as practicable, by
hand, and with the simplest tools. The school curriculum embraces Mathematics, Drawing and the elementary
branches.

Paris has numerous industrial schools of every grade,
and throughout the country are found local institutions,

often under the patronage of industrial societies, or established by individuals from philanthropic motives.

Notwithstanding all that had been done previously, a government report after the exhibition of 1867, states that " additional efforts must be put forth to maintain French industry at the level which it has reached, and enable it to meet the rivalry of other countries in fields, once by universal confession, exclusively their own. "

The result has been, as in other countries, a period of remarkable activity in this direction during the last ten years, the beneficial results of which were seen in the display of industrial products at our Centennial, and will be far more evident at the next exhibition in 1878, on their own soil.

It would be a pleasing labor, if our time and space allowed, to note in detail the progress of other countries of Europe and to give comparative views of their advance in industrial art education.

England, Holland, Italy, Sweden, Russia and the other countries have been actively working, and in each of them we find much to interest and instruct, but enough has been written to demonstrate the fact that in all of them, the problem of industrial education is considered of vital importance, and that in its solution they are many years in advance of our own country.

### OUR OWN COUNTRY.

We have had in this country a few technical schools of a high order, whose pupils were instructed in the theory

but not in practice, unless we except the chemical labo-
ratory work. A prominent educator, connected with one
of the best of them, remarked not long since; "Our
graduates go out into the world with their brains well-
stocked with theories, but *with their hands tied behind
them.*"

In occasional instances, institutions have been established where theory and practice were conjoined, as in
the Worcester school, and the "Illinois Industrial Col
lege," with good results. The latter institution was established by the State of Illinois, in carrying out the intention of the act of Congress in 1862, giving grants of
the public lands and prescribing, in return, the promotion
of the "liberal and practical education of the industrial
classes in the several pursuits and professions in life,"
as conditions, accompanying acceptance. The State of
Illinois has added liberally to the original fund, and the
university now has property valued at nearly a million
dollars, including a system of mechanical workshops and
other paraphernalia for a complete industrial training.

In the State of Massachusetts much attention has been
given to the subject, and throughout the State drawing
has been taught in the public schools, being correctly
deemed the true foundation of industrial art.

In Philadelphia, an association of private gentlemen
organized the Pennsylvania Museum of Art, early in
1876, and took advantage of opportunities offered at
the Centennial Exhibition to secure a large collection of

4

industrial masterpieces. to form the foundation of the museum, which like its prototype, the South Kensington Museum, in England, which within twenty years has revolutionized many branches of industry and created new ones, is expected to become an important aid to industrial education and culture. The State of Pennsylvania is moving in this matter, and recently at the Governor's request, Prof. Smith of Boston, made an address to the legislature of that State, which made such a favorable impression upon the members, as to leave little doubt of a speedy legislative enactment making Drawing an obligatory branch in the public schools of that State.

In New York city, the schools of industrial-art, organized through the munificence of private individuals and associations, have for some years past been doing a noble work, especially for young women, hundreds of whom, have been enabled by the instruction there obtained, to secure remunerative and congenial employment, adapted to their sex. There are various institutions in other states as well as individual organizations prompted by philanthropic motives, which have accomplished a good work, but, for the people as a whole, it must be admitted, we have done very little. Probably, our wonderful progress in inventions, and our ability to draw from Europe, by the popularity of our democratic institutions, and a higher rate of wages, constant supplies of skilled workmen, have induced our past apathy, but the vital importance of immediate action is now generally recognized.

In his paper, read before the Boston Society of Arts, on the " Social and Political Economy of Universal Industrial Education," Dr. Bartol says : " Industrial education of the whole people would make the whole people honest. It would detect the mechanical or artistic genius, which now is left to be discovered by an accident, or to be buried in a studiously neglected nature, as in a living grave. Often in the circle of my acquaintance, some gift for artistic hand-work has struggled forth ; had it been searched for and tempted forth by the expert educator at an early stage, it would have won the prize it now lags behind. Industrial education can do more to ameliorate woman's lot and man's than the ballot, an external implement which wielded intelligently, is a blessing, ignorantly, a curse to the land."

Sentiments like these, emanating from a man of such marked culture and mental ability, fitted by his training and long experience in matters affecting the public welfare to give a sound opinion, are a sure indication that the subject of the education of the hand is worthy of general consideration, both as a question of morals and of political economy. While many persons of the highest intellectual resources, are endeavoring by thought, study and speech to aid in obtaining a satisfactory solution of the question, others, in a quiet way, are striving to work it out by experiment. One instance of this has come to our knowledge and in reply to a request for specific information, we have received the following letter, which is extremely interesting in furnishing the details of a simple experiment, which has so far, proved to be so practical and successful as to deserve imitation. We quote the letter as follows :—

BOSTON, FEB. 1877.

DEAR SIR :

Our "*whittling school*" has opened its jack-knife every winter for five years. Thirty or forty boys from twelve to sixteen years of age have belonged to it, and with the aid of jig-saws, a turning lathe and a few simple tools, they have made brackets, match-boxes, small chests checker boards, and such trifling things. We have accommodated the school in our chapel, and found no difficulty in accomplishing the little thus described, with portable work-benches, etc. The value of such a school, is not in the amount of skill the boys attain to, but in the bent it gives their taste, and in the innocent enjoyment it gives to their leisure hours. The boys say they do six times as much work at home as they do at the school.

This year, our school is on a different basis. The city has given us the use of one of its ward-rooms on Church street, and we have put up excellent work-benches, with a vise to each, a box or drawer, and three chisels to each boy. We have planned a course of twenty four lessons in wood carving, and begun with thirty-two boys. The lessons are graded and pursue a natural and progressive course, just as writing is taught in our public schools, beginning with straight lines and going on to curves. I wish you would go down to the Church, Street ward-room any Tuesday or Friday evening, from 7 to 9 o'clock, and see the school. To my eye, it is the finest sight in Boston. It shows what can be done for hand-culture, and how easily it can be done. Mr. Frank Rowell of Allen & Rowell, Photographers, is at the head of the school. He has been the superintendent of our whittling school from the first. He has two practical wood carvers under him, at $7.50 an evening. We who care for the work, have formed a society called the "Industrial Educational Association" and we meet every other Tuesday evening, in Hollis street Chapel.

We devote ourselves, for the present, to this one school, hoping to make it a demonstration to the School Board, that Hand-Schools can be systematized and conducted by them, if they will do it. Please accept this as an answer to your inquiry, and use it as you like."

Sincerely yours,

GEO. L. CHENEY.

Other individual enterprises in various parts of the country have come to our knowledge, interesting in their details and successful as to results, but enough has been given to show that, the people of this country are aroused to the importance of this branch of a complete education, and are eagerly looking for something that may offer to the rising generation, in connection with the culture of the intellect, a coresponding training for the hands.

The teaching of specific trades has often been urged, but the objections are so numerous, and the experience of the past so decidedly in opposition to such a plan, that aside from the difficulties arising from the option as to the particular trades to be taught, the expense of any general system would condemn it.

What is desired, is some system that will teach *the arts which underlie many industrial occupations*; something that will educate the hands and eyes; something that will furnish such a course of manual training, as will enable our children, when they complete their course in the public schools, to secure some kind of employment, and not feel that they are incompetent to live, except " *by their wits.*"

If we can secure this, without limiting or abridging the usefulness of the system of education  · · now have in operation with such great success, we shall succeed in achieving for our day and generation and posterity, a blessing comparable in value with that which the founders of free public schools handed down to us.

In a careful study of very many systems of industrial instruction in Europe, we have found that all agree in one respect, namely, that *Drawing is an indispensable basis.* From the primary grades to the highest institutions of technology, Drawing is invariably a prominent feature of the curriculum. In all of these schools, the same general principles are followed in uniting manual and mental instruction and in familiarizing scholars with the use of tools. The details of instruction, in the scores of schools we have studied, have differed more or less, but in nearly all of them the plan of manual instruction, involved the methods of the apprentice system. In the school at Chalons, and also in that at Augsburg, there is an advance upon the old methods, but in Russia, at the Imperial Technical School, at Moscow, they have taken an entirely "new departure" in manual education, by conforming it strictly to the system and well established principles which have proved successful in developing skill in other arts and sciences. By this system, they *analyze the processes requiring manual skill, and teach each process by itself to a class.*

The first principles are taught and exercises in practice accompany them, leading the pupil on from the simplest to the most difficult manipulations. Just as in teaching one to play upon the piano, the "scales" and simple exercises come first and receive entire attention, rather than set tunes, which are tried only after months of preliminary practice; or, as in Drawing, the pupil first practises upon straight lines and their various combinations, and then after long exercise, attempts anything requiring skill; or, as in penmanship, the first efforts are upon lines, curves and parts of letters, before writing words; so, in manual instruction at this institution, the systematic progress of the pupil, is the paramount consideration.

The collection of implements and pieces of machinery contributed by the Russian government to illustrate the work done at that school, formed an interesting exhibit in Machinery Hall, at our Centennial Exhibition, and furnished to interested observers, a definite idea of the plan, system and results obtainable from it.

Among those whose attention was specially attracted by it was President Runkle, of the Massachusetts Institute of Technology, whose skill as an educator and penetration as a man of science, enabled him at once to discern the novelty and special merits of the system and its adaptability for use, as an adjunct to his own institution, the need of which, he had keenly felt for a long time. He mastered the details of the plan and upon returning to Boston, so favorably impressed the Mass. Charitable Mechanics Association and private individuals interested in industrial education, that in a short time they placed enough money at his disposal to enter upon the experiment. Inexpensive shops were built and fully equipped, in the different rooms, with all the appliances for vise-work, forging, planing, turning, drilling and iron-founding.

In response to the polite invitation of President Runkle,

who had been informed of the inquiry of this Assembly
in regard to industrial education, we spent a day with him,
for the purpose of receiving a full explanation of the plan,
and of having ocular demonstration of the results thus
far achieved. The pupils, since the commencement of the
lessons, had completed the course in "filing," and we saw,
in the results of only *eighty hours* of practice and instruction, such exquisite workmanship as could not be surpassed
by an apprentice of two years experience in an ordinary
shop. We found a class of thirty-two boys, at work on a
"chipping" exercise, with hammer and chisel, under the
instruction and constant supervision of an expert mechanic, employed as teacher of practical mechanics, and
it was easy to perceive that the class instruction in
this branch of education, was as systematic and simple as
the teaching of a class in Arithmetic or Grammar in one
of our best public schools. Our attention was directed to
the fact, that these shops are for *in*struction and not
for *con*struction. The object of the labor performed is not
to produce salable articles, but to impart mechanical skill,
and hence, the student can here receive systematic instruction, proceeding from first principles to difficult manipulations, while in ordinary construction shops, an apprentice
is taught only those things which accord with the convenience and profit of his employer. The fact, that the
instruction is given to so many pupils at a time, in class,
is a marked economical feature, carrying out, as in so many
other respects, the analogy with our general system of
mental training.

Our space forbids a full description of the many interesting details which came under our observation, as well as any account of the testimony already given by practical and expert mechanics, as well as by thoughtful and skilled educators, as to the wonderful results already secured in this experiment of an altogether novel method of industrial training, but we are fully satisfied, that enough has been shown, in the few months of trial, to warrant us in the opinion, that in this well-tried system, at once so simple and so economical, we can find a way to the solution of the great question of the *adaptation of industrial education to our existing system of mental training in the public schools*.

From the data and figures furnished us by President Runkle, based upon actual expenditures, we find that any school committee or city council can add an industrial department to their High School, erecting the necessary shops and completely furnishing them, at an outlay of from $6,000 to $8,000, according to the extent of appliances, capable of giving instruction and practice to four hundred pupils per annum, at a cost not exceeding $18.00 per scholar, and probably even less than that.

Everything necessary for the equipment of such shops, is made in our own state, and there is no doubt, that when our manufacturers are informed that it is proposed to teach *practical mechanics* in connection with our schools, they would vie with each other in furnishing the proper appliances, rejoicing in the prospect of relief from stupid and clumsy apprentices, and of securing, in their place, from the graduates of our public schools, boys with *cultured minds and*

5

*skilled hands.* From the large number of expert mechanics, now engaged in our shops, a suitable instructor could
easily be found, as was the case in Boston, whose mental
and mechanical qualifications would enable him, after a few
days observation and study of the plan of instruction, to
take charge of the classes.

As it is unlikely, that at first there would be enough
boys in the High School to take all the time and room in
the industrial annex, arrangements could be made to secure
these great advantages to older boys in the Grammar
Schools, to whom it would serve as an incentive to study.
With such practical training in prospect, many a boy now
withdrawn from the schools in order to find employment,
would be continued in them, in order to secure such ad
vantages as would better enable him to obtain more remunerative employment.

The High School would be popularized, and the benefits
it now bestows so lavishly upon three per cent. of the
school population, would soon be distributed to a larger
proportion especially of boys, and that too, without any
proportionate increase in the expense of their mental training. Those, who now fail to comprehend the advantage
or necessity of the High School in our system, would
soon be able to recognize it, as the crowning glory of our
series of schools, dispensing to rich and poor alike, the
blessings arising from such a harmonious blending of
mental and manual culture, and rendering back to the
community, in skilled hands and intelligent minds an ample
return for all its expenditures.

The importance of some suggestion in this report, having special reference to the industrial training of girls is not forgotten, and has been the subject of careful consideration, but we have not reached any definite conclusion in the matter, excepting that in respect to *Drawing* in the schools, which of course, would apply to, and equally benefit both sexes. Individual efforts, notably in connection with the Cooper Institute of New York, have resulted in great benefit to young women, in preparing them in the Schools of Design, for a more extended sphere of labor, than has heretofore been open to them, and there is now pending in this House, an application for an Act of Incorporation of a School of Design in this State, which is an auspicious indication of the deep interest, our own people are beginning to take in these important matters. Hence, with the knowledge, that so many of the best minds are now searching for whatever plan may seem practicable for the industrial education of girls, we must, in omitting further consideration of this part of our subject, content ourselves with the consciousness, that all of the great advantages now offered in our schools, are common to both sexes, and will be in future, so far as may be consistent with the physical constitution of each.

In response to the resolution of inquiry referred to us, and in the light of the considerations heretofore submitted in this report, we beg to present the following specific suggestions as a plan for the " instruction of the pupils attending the public schools in the industrial arts," viz:—

1st *Instruction in Drawing in all of the schools.*

2d *Instruction in the Mechanic arts, in work-shops, as a co-ordinate branch with the mental training in the higher grades.*

In harmony with these suggestions, the practicability of which, we have endeavored to demonstrate, we submit herewith, the form of an act to accomplish the first, and a resolution in regard to the second, recommending the passage of both by this House, if in the wisdom of its members it should seem expedient.

The act is as follows :—

An Act to supply a foundation for Industrial Education in the Public Schools.

*Be it enacted by the General Assembly as follows:*

Section 1.　In all towns of the state having a population of more than 5000 persons, provision shall be made for instruction in Drawing in the Public Schools.

Section 2.　This act shall take effect on and after Sept. 1st, 1877.

The Resolution is as follows :—

Whereas, the experience of nations has proved that superiority in the mechanical and manufacturing industries can only be maintained by the most assiduous care in the industrial training of the young and,

Whereas, we believe that there is a deficiency in such training, in the State of Rhode Island, which must, sooner or later, unless remedied, result disastrously to the most important interests of the State, therefore,

Resolved, That this General Assembly (the Senate concurring) recommends to the attention of the people of the towns of the State, the importance of as speedy action as may be practicable, to promote the introduction of the best methods to insure a thorough *manual* education, as a supplement to the instruction now given in the Public Schools.

In a state so absolutely dependent upon its mechanical and manufacturing industries, as Rhode Island unquestion-ably is, it certainly is the most important and practical question of the day, how the permanent prosperity of those industries can best be promoted, for upon them depend very largely, the comfort and happiness of a large propor-tion of our people.

Experience teaches us that this can only be accomplish-ed, by such an education of the masses as may develop manual skill and good taste in connection with their men-tal training. Common sense tells us, this should be effect-ed by means of our public schools.

The increasing facilities for transportation and commu-nication, are rapidly opening the markets of the whole world to the competition of nations, and in this great con-test, if our country is to rank among the successful ones we must prepare at once by training our young to become masters of the arts of industry.

Our chief competitors are, in this respect, far in advance of us, and already have educated hosts of artisans, to take their part in this industrial contest.

In one great exigency in our nation's history, we pro-duced an immense army of soldiers, almost extemporane ously; in a still more recent one, during the perilous period of a closely contested and disputed presidential election, an extemporaneous outpouring of a spirit of peace and submission to law, saved us from threatened anarchy ; but in the industrial struggle of nations, no *extemporaneous efforts* will avail to help us, for, those who achieve the victory, must be artisans and mechanics, trained to the service by long experience, based upon the solid foundation of an adequate industrial training in early manhood.

Respectfully submitted for the Committee on Education.

HENRY H. FAY,
*Chairman.*

Providence, March 11th, 1877.

# REPORT ON LIQUOR LICENSES.

STATE OF RHODE ISLAND,
AUDITOR'S OFFICE, Providence, March 6, 1877. }

To THE HONORABLE GENERAL ASSEMBLY :—

In response to a resolution of inquiry adopted by your honorable body at its present session, as to the payment to the State, by towns, of moneys due for liquor licenses, I respectfully present the following report :

I find that subsequent to the enactment of the law now in force to regulate the sale of intoxicating liquors, enacted June 25, 1875, fourteen of the cities and towns have granted licenses under said act, viz.: Charlestown, Cranston, East Greenwich, East Providence, Johnston, Newport, North Providence, Providence, Richmond, Smithfield, Warren, Warwick, West Greenwich, and Woonsocket. I have been officially advised by the Town Clerks of twenty-two towns, that such licenses have not been granted by their respective Town Councils at any time since the enactment of the present law.

The sum total of moneys paid to the General Treasurer by the City and Town Treasurers is $133,916 43, as follows :—

| | | |
|---|---|---:|
| Charlestown, | January 1, 1876..... ............ | $75 00 |
| Cranston, | January 1, 1876.................. | 1,050 00 |
| " | January 1, 1877.............. .... | 450 00 |
| East Greenwich, | January 1, 1876.................. | 250 00 |
| " " | June 2, 1876.................. | 75 00 |
| " " | January 2, 1877.................. | 375 00 |
| East Providence, | January 1, 1877.................. | 1,340 83 |

| | | |
|---|---|---:|
| Johnston, | January 1, 1876.................. | 1,400 00 |
| " | January 1, 1877.................. | 450 00 |
| Newport, | January 1, 1876.................. | 6,475 00 |
| " | July   10, 1876.................. | 300 00 |
| " | January 1, 1877.................. | 5,850 00 |
| North Providence, | January 1, 1876.................. | 250 00 |
| "     " | January 1, 1877.................. | 275 00 |
| Providence, | January 1, 1876.............. .. | 54,363 79 |
| " | June   30, 1876.................. | 2,746 58 |
| " | January 1, 1877.................. | 48,919 48 |
| Richmond, | January 1, 1877.................. | 300 00 |
| Smithfield, | January 1, 1877.................. | 150 00 |
| Warren, | July   15, 1876.................. | 300 00 |
| Warwick, | January 1, 1876.................. | 3,000 00 |
| " | February 15, 1877.................. | 383 75 |
| West Greenwich, | January 1, 1876............  .... | 300 00 |
| "     " | January 9, 1877........  ........ | 150 00 |
| Woonsocket, | January 1, 1876.................. | 4,687 50 |

In the town of Charlestown no licenses were granted in the year 1876. The town of East Providence granted no licenses previous to May 25, 1876, and none have been granted since the 9th of November 1876. The Town Council of Richmond granted four licenses on the 6th day of July, 1875, and on May 29, 1876, granted licenses to the same persons, being all the licenses issued during the said time. The town of Smithfield granted licenses, three in number, from September 6th, 1875, to March 6th, 1876, amounting to the sum of $500. No licenses have been granted by the Town Council of Warren subsequent to January 31, 1876 ; none by the Town Council of Woonsocket since July 30, 1875. I would respectfully call the attention of your honorable body to certain facts in reference to moneys due from the city of Providence and the town of East Providence.

Contrary to the practice heretofore invariably adopted by the Treasurers of the several cities and towns, of paying into the State Treasury one-half of the sum or amount exacted for each license, the Treasurer of the city of Providence deducted from the gross amount due the State, one-half of the expenses for Printing, contracted by the License Commissioners and one-half of the sum paid for office rents of said commission. The Treasurer of the town of East Providence also deducted one-half of certain expenses incurred for printing by the commissioners of said town. In the performance of my duties under the provisions of the law requiring the Auditor to examine and settle all accounts between the State and Treasurers of the several cities and towns, I examined the returns of these officers and notified the General Treasurer that I could not certify to him that the sums or amounts so returned by the city Treasurer of Providence and the town Treasurer of East Providence, were the actual balances due from these persons into the State Treasury. It is due to the City Treasurer of Providence, that I make note of the fact, that this departure from a long established usage was in conformity to an opinion given by the City Solicitor, based upon the fact that the present law regulating the sale of intoxicating liquors makes it the duty of the Board of Aldermen to elect three commissioners, who shall have and exercise all the powers and duties conferred upon Boards of Aldermen and Town Councils by the provisions of the act, and that consequently the State should pay one-half of the current expenses of the commission, the actual compensation of the commissioners being paid by the city of Providence. I would therefore respectfully ask that some legislation may be had in reference to this matter, especially as to the right or legality of cities and towns, where licenses are granted through commissioners, withholding moneys due and payable to the State, and simply suggest that the city of Newport, granting licenses through its Board of Aldermen, and certain towns granting licenses through their several Town Councils, incur sundry expenses, without doubt, for instance, printing, and should have the same allowance and consideration with reference to sums or proportions of moneys actually received, that they may be required to pay into the State Treasury, as the city and town to which your attention has thus been respectfully called.

Respectfully submitted,

JOEL M. SPENCER,

*State Auditor.*

# REPORT

OF THE

## Special Committee

ON

# WOMAN SUFFRAGE,

MADE TO THE

### HOUSE OF REPRESENTATIVES, JANUARY SESSION, 1877.

PROVIDENCE:
ANGELL, BURLINGAME & CO., PRINTERS TO THE STATE.
1877.

# REPORT.

Your special Committee, to which was referred the numerous petitions and memorials, upon the subject of Woman Suffrage, asking for a change in our fundamental law to effectuate that object, respectfully report as follows :—

Your committee gave the petitioners two hearings, and were at each time addressed by some of their ablest speakers. It was of course an *ex parte* hearing, no one appearing in opposition, and we feel it incumbent upon us to set forth briefly the arguments of the advocates, that the members of the House may have the benefit of knowing what may have influenced your committee in their report. The "right to petition" implies the right to be heard, and that further implies the right to have their cause fairly stated to this body, before which they cannot appear, and in which they can now have no voice, except through this committee, or such as may voluntarily espouse their cause. Your committee feel that whatever their individual opinions may have been, they now have a duty to perform ; a duty both to the petitioners and to the members of this body. All the petitioners ask of us is that their cause may be submitted to the people, the fountain of all political power, and by the consent of whom we now occupy these seats. We could go no further if we would.

The argument upon which the petitioners lay greatest stress is that of taxation without representation. If this was not, as some scholars claim, the immediate cause of our Revolution, it is one upon which the American mind has ever been extremely sensitive.

The simple question presented to us is, does this principle apply to
men and not to women, and if it does not so apply, upon what
ground may the principle be said to change.    Where is the distinction ?    The petitioners say to us, we hold our property by the
same title that you hold yours; in the use of our property we are
governed by the same laws; we purchase and sell by the same kind
of conveyance; our property is levied upon under the same tax law,
by one and the same board of assessors, collected by the same collector and paid into the same general fund to be used and expended
for the same purposes, and they ask why they should not have a
voice in the expenditure of their own money, as well as we in ours.

The question is very difficult of answer in the negative.  We
should blush to say, in the face of your petitioners, that they did
not possess the requisite amount of intelligence.

Your committee are of the opinion that many men who have the
highest, the most chivalric regard for women, oppose this measure with the greatest fervency.  They are afraid of it, not
because of any disadvantage to themselves, but of its effect upon
their wives, their sisters, and their friends.  Men know too well
that contact with the world, especially the political world, has a
tendency to destroy those qualities of mind which give to womanhood its greatest charm.  This feeling, call it prejudice if you will,
these petitioners will find more difficulty in allaying than in con-
vincing the judgment.  Even if we admit that, logically, nothing
can be said against woman suffrage that cannot with equal truth be
said of man suffrage, still this sentiment remains, and men having
the power will be slow to relinquish it.  But your petitioners address themselves to the removal of this objection also, and attempt
to dislodge from our minds what they call an illusion.  They assure
us that their presence at the ballot box will exert the same good
and potent influence that it has wherever else they have been
admitted.  In early times, the Germans would not admit women to
their banqueting halls, because of the scenes of revelry and drunkenness, but when at last they were admitted, the license and the
debauchery disappeared, and into the hundred places where women
have but recently been admitted, they challenge us to show they
are the worse for it, while we admit that we are the better for their

presence. Civilization is a growth, and this question is one of development. Under the first forms of society, women had no rights, and the average man but few. One of the first forms of marriage was simply one of capture upon the part of the husband. He took her forcibly away from her friends, and from that time she was his slave. They inform us also that under the Roman law woman was but little better than a slave, and from the civil law we derived much of our own. But recently, under our common law, upon marriage, woman not only lost her legal existence, but all rights of property. The husband was sole owner, and the laws that to-day we pride ourselves upon, in our own State, were as strongly opposed but recently as this movement is to-day. Besides these arguments, they bring positive evidence of the good effects of woman suffrage wherever tried. They introduce the testimony of Judge Kingman, of the Supreme Court of Wyoming, and call our attention to the fact that in England to-day unmarried women and widows vote upon the same basis as men, except in the election of members to parliament.

It is only within a hundred years that women have taken an influential position in literature, and to-day, because of prejudice against woman's work, the two ablest romancists of the century use for *noms de plume* the names of men. A note in Howell's State Trials quotes from an ancient work, "Probation by Witnesses," by Sir George Mackenzie, in which he says, "the reason why women are excluded from witnessing, must be either that they are subject to too much compassion, and so ought not to be more received in criminal cases than in civil cases; or else the law was unwilling to trouble them, and thought it might learn them too much confidence, and make them subject to too much familiarity with men and strangers, if they were necessitated to vague up and down at all courts upon all occasions." Hume says, "this was held as late as the beginning of the eighteenth century."

About the year 1790, women were first recognized as school teachers in Massachusetts. These facts of history, compared with the facts of our own time, show us how great the change has been, and yet the present condition neither alarms us, nor appears strange. As a matter of fact, we boast of the privileges accorded to women in our day, and call it a test or measure of our civilization. The question before us now is, how far shall we go in the proposed innovation? That there should be vehement protests, your petitioners will expect, when they remember that, "when Sir Samuel Romilly proposed to abolish the death penalty for stealing a handkerchief, the law officers of the crown said it would endanger the whole criminal law of England," and "when the bill abolishing the slave trade, passed the House of Lords, Lord St. Vincent rose and stalked out, declaring that he washed his hands of the ruin of the British empire."

In view of all the progress of women from the position of slave, to a position of honor, trust, confidence, and as a companion of man, they ask us by what authority we now say, you can go no further, cannot have this particular privilege asked for. If we reply, it will injure woman herself, they ask, who made us their judges? There is no standard, no absolute measure, of womanhood, and our ideal woman of to-day may be as false as was the Roman's, while he regarded her as his property. Your committee find this question also difficult of answering. To the statement that neither all women, nor a considerable number, desire the ballot, it might be sufficient to reply, that if it be a right, (a right in the same sense as man claims it,) numbers neither add to nor diminish the force of the argument.

It is, perhaps, too late, after so much has been accomplished by woman in every position in which she has been allowed to labor, to say much upon the question of woman's intelligence in the use of the ballot, if it should be allowed to her. Since the Reformation in England, three queens have come to the throne by inheritance, Queen Elizabeth, Queen Ann and Queen Victoria, the worst of whom has been fully equal to any king, that, in the same time, has come to it by inheritance, and the other two were immeasurably superior. In the list of European sovereigns, there are few brighter than those of Isabella of Spain, Maria Theresa, and Queen Victoria. In the schools and colleges to which she has been admitted, she has won some of the greenest laurels. It is claimed also by your petitioners, that " the ignorant and depraved women bear no greater proportion to the whole of their sex, than the ignorant and depraved men do to theirs;" and if, in the one matter of government they are not generally so well informed, they ask us, whether one of the reasons urged for the extension of suffrage to the freedman, viz.: that "the ballot itself is an educator," would not apply equally to them. If, however, the ballot were to-day given to women upon the same terms as to men, it is doubtful if the fears of the one would be realized, or the hopes of the other fulfilled.

They also call to our attention the names of those who have espoused their cause, and in this country, notably those of George William Curtis, Col. T. W. Higginson, and the Hon. George F. Hoar; the latter of whom, in a speech before the joint special committee of the Massachusetts Legislature, in 1869, said : " Now, in turning in my own mind, what I ought to say to you here to-day, I have failed to think of a single reason which I can give, why you or I should have the right of suffrage which does not include woman ; and I think I may safely challenge any human being to come forward and state why it is that I am permitted to cast my vote—to give any general rule which shall define·the qualities or capabilities, or interests, which should entitle a person to have a share in the administration of the government from which women are excluded." Perhaps the foremost of English thinkers and writers who have given the weight of their names to this movement, is the late John Stuart Mill.

In conclusion, while some of your committee, if for no other purpose than that of bringing the matter squarely before the people, would report favorably upon all that the petitioners ask, others, more conservative, prefer a different course, as, in any event, the recommendation of a committee gives the matter a *quasi* endorsement. The other view of the office of the committee being, that unless the matter of a petition appear almost wholly frivolous, the committee should recommend the granting the prayer thereof, as the only way of properly bringing the subject under consideration.

Your committee, however, join in recommending that upon any proposition to impose a tax, unmarried women and widows shall have the privilege of voting, subject to the same regulations and limitations as men, and submit the following resolution :

*Resolved,* A majority of all the members elected to each house of the General Assembly concurring herein, that the following article be proposed as an amendment to the Constitution of the State, and that the Secretary of State cause the same to be published, and printed copies thereof to be distributed in the manner provided in Article XII of the Constitution.

### ARTICLE.

Upon any proposition to impose a tax, unmarried women and widows shall have the privilege of voting, subject to the same regulations and limitations as men.

All of which is respectfully submitted.

DEXTER B. POTTER,
SAMUEL P. COLT,
ALVORD O. MILES,
AMOS SHERMAN,
ALMON K. GOODWIN.

# REPORT OF THE COMMITTEE ON EDUCATION,

## ON THE PROPOSITION TO REDUCE THE NUMBER OF THE SCHOOL COMMITTEE IN PROVIDENCE, AND CHANGE THE MODE OF ELECTION.

*To the Honorable the House of Representatives, January Session,* 1877 :

The Committee on Education beg to report, that in the matter of the reduction of the numbers of the School Committee of the city of Providence, and a change in the manner of electing some of its members, which was referred to us, we have given patient and careful investigation, and have had the benefit of the views of many gentlemen interested, pro and con, at five public hearings. At these hearings, His Honor Mayor Doyle and Arthur F. Dexter, Esq., chairman of the committee which reported the proposition to the City Council, presented views in advocacy of the changes mentioned, while Prof. Clarke, Ex. Gov. Padelford, Prof. Greene and many others ably represented the remonstrants.   The prominent position and high character of the gentlemen representing both sides of the question, the cogency of the arguments advanced by each, and the importance of the subject itself, have combined to impress the committee with a lively sense of the responsibility resting upon them and they have not united in any recommendation, without attempting to examine the case in every aspect.

The proposition to deprive the people of the power to elect the school committee, is not, in this case, supported by reasons sufficiently valid, to compensate for such a limitation of a prerogative now

exercised, and we believe there are some positive advantages gained
by annually calling the attention of the people to the fact, that they
have a direct duty to perform in relation to their schools, and a
great interest in providing for them a suitable management.

In regard to the number of the committee, we are satisfied that
sixty is too large, and the evidence presented to that effect was con-
vincing. It was stated upon unquestionable authority that the
meetings of the committee are ordinarily attended by from thirty-
three to forty members only, and that there is generally delay and
sometimes great difficulty in securing a legal quorum for the transaction of business. It is evident that twenty or thirty members are
generally absent from the regular meetings which are but *quarterly*,
and this in our judgment is a dereliction of duty that must tend to
impair the efficiency of the committee. Such absence indicates a
lack of interest in the proceedings or a disgust with the manner of
transacting business or an unlimited confidence in the ability of a
few to fulfil the duties of the entire body. We believe the last to
be the true cause, but either case furnishes a good reason for reducing the number.

It is claimed that some who do not attend the quarterly meetings,
are capable in other respects, and especially that they are diligent
in visiting the schools. This is no extenuation ; for, such visitation
without due report and opportunity for questioning and exchange
of views, does not benefit the other members, and the result is, a
sort of "guerilla" work, which can accomplish very little good and
may do harm. It appears evident to us, that if the schools are to
depend upon the members of the Committee for the only examinations and inspection they receive outside of the Superintendent's
work, and the whole committee only meet regularly four times a
year, that it must be difficult, if not impossible, for all the members
to secure a proper knowledge of the actual condition of the schools.
The testimony of a prominent member of the School Committee,
distinctly states that at present, the reports from the schools " are
neither valuable nor reliable, and that the members, for the most
part, have only a general knowledge of the workings of the schools,
in those things upon which educational efficiency depends."

We are aware that at present the system of examination includes the services of Grammar School principals as examiners, and this unquestionably meets the exigencies of the case partly, but there should be in addition, thorough examinations by qualified persons outside of the corps of teachers and superior to them in authority. The ability to examine a school and furnish a correct and valuable report as to the efficiency of the teacher and the progress of the scholars is possessed by few who are not, from previous experience in educational matters, *experts*, and it would be surprising if out of any sixty men elected by the people, more than a small proportion should be competent for that work. The present committee has many in its number who are well qualified and devote much time to the work, but it cannot be expected that with other occupations they should give all of their time. Hence, it seems to us, in view of the magnitude of the moral, political and pecuniary interests that Providence has in her 212 schools, that it would be in the line of true economy to give the Superintendent of Schools at least two competent assistants, and that upon the three should devolve the systematic examination and inspection of schools under the direction of the School Committee.

It is unnecessary to detail fully the reasons leading us to recommend a reduction in the number, but prominent among them are the following :—

1. That individual responsibility will be increased.

2. The proportion of well-qualified members will be augmented.

3. Business at the meetings could be transacted with greater facility and dispatch.

4. A larger number of regular meetings could be held.

5. The entire School Committee would be better acquainted with the entire school work.

6. The experience of other cities of equal and greater size, is entirely on the side of smaller numbers.

We recommend the accompanying substitute for the bill proposed, by which provision is made for the reduction of the committee to thirty-three members, including those ex-officio, or three from each ward. As the term of office is three years, this will enable each ward to elect one member every year, instead of two as at present.

His Honor Mayor Doyle has urged upon the committee, public ly and privately, that the Mayor should not be named in the bill as one of the ex-officio members, for the reason that the chief magistrate of the city has enough of other public business to engage all his time; but knowing the eminent ability and high qualifications which have characterized the selections for that office in the past, we do not feel justified in making a recommendation that will deprive the school committee of such wise councils, without previously receiving the suggestions from some other source.

The advantages obtained by the substitute are obvious. The changes made in the present law are very few, and they are effected gradually, without turning out of office any member previously elected by the people. The time required to accomplish the reduction is two years, which will prevent any sudden disadjustment of the machinery of organization, and the mode adopted will avoid all friction.

This reduction will meet the views of many of the remonstrants, who objected more to the manner of the reduction than to the thing itself, while the continued election of the committee by the people is not objected to by the representatives of the City Council who presented the original bill. It may not please extremists on either side, but seems to be the most unobjectionable mode of accomplishing what we believe to be a necessary change.

For the Committee on Education,

HENRY H. FAY, *Chairman.*

# REPORT

OF THE

## Joint Special Committee

ON THE SUBJECT OF ESTABLISHING A

# State Industrial School,

MADE TO THE

GENERAL ASSEMBLY OF THE STATE OF RHODE ISLAND,
AT ITS JANUARY SESSION, A. D. 1877.

PROVIDENCE:
ANGELL, BURLINGAME & CO., PRINTERS TO THE STATE.
1877.

# REPORT.

*To the General Assembly, at its January Session, 1877 :—*

The Joint Special Committee, to whom was referred a resolution in relation to an Industrial School, recommended in the Governor's message, respectfully submit the following report :—

In a report of this character, it is impossible to give as full and as extended a statement of the reasons why some action should be adopted looking to the establishment of such an institution as the nature of the subject seems to demand.

That there are grave public reasons why the State should interpose its authority in this behalf, is, in the minds of your committee, a self-evident fact. In the consideration of this subject, your committee were highly favored by listening to thoughts and suggestions from Rev. H. W. Rugg, Prof. Geo. I. Chace, Hon. Thomas B. Stockwell, and members of the Board of Lady Visitors to our Penal and Correctional Institutions. There was some diversity of opinion expressed as to the location and nature of the institution, but as to the main facts, great unanimity seemed to prevail. Economical considerations, as well as considerations of duty, urge to this course. In the words of His Excellency Gov. Lippitt, " it is much cheaper to educate and train a child and to fit him by habits of industry, economy and self-government, to become a useful citizen, than to allow him to grow up in ignorance and vice and afterwards provide for him in reformatories and prisons." Therefore, we believe it is the duty of the State to take care of the various classes

of children, which are now living without that proper assistance so
desirable to prevent their growing up in idleness and sin.   Most of
the States are acting on this principle, they are removing the children from their parents and gathering them into primary schools
and orphan asylums  where they may receive a kindly nurture
and training.   When they have reached the proper age, they are
either transferred to Industrial Schools, or what is better, placed in
families, where they may grow up under healthy influences and
become respectable and respected citizens.   The question naturally
suggests itself, how much will the State devote to this object, and
what class or classes of children will it provide with this home?
Those at the almshouses, the offspring of vicious and criminal parents, those in mills and work shops, who do not attend public
schools at all—and the truants and vagrants.   It is quite an alarming fact at this time in our history, that so many children of school
age do not attend our Public Schools, and it would seem that some
action should be taken by the Legislature to remedy this evil.  The
right of the State to take the children of paupers and vicious parents
and educate and train them to habits of industry and virtue
is beyond question.   Nor is it merely a right, it is a duty which it
owes alike to them and society—a duty which cannot be evaded or
disregarded without the entailment of the gravest evils.  It appears
to your committee, if it is a benefit to one class, it must necessarily
be a benefit to all, and we would therefore recommend that the
action taken be so broad in its scope as to include all either now or
in some future legislation.  It must be obvious to every one, that it
is very necessary that children now growing up in idleness and
ignorance should be taught at least the fundamental principles of
an English education, and some practical knowledge of the business
of life.   The State is now required to support the children at the
Alms House; but the place and the surroundings are not what they
ought to be for children.   Your committee advise that the institution to be established should not be of a penal nature, but simply
educational and reformatory; and any child enjoying its benefits
should be as free from taint or crime as if brought up in the home.
Your committee would also recommend that the trustees, directors
or supervisors of the institution have authority conferred upon them.

to place any such children in their discretion in any good and suitable home where they may be supported and educated—the Board always retaining the right to take them away for any good and sufficient reasons, and placing them elsewhere, or taking them again to the State School. Your committee are of the opinion that no further legislation is required to enable the Board of State Charities and Corrections, and the Overseers of the Poor in the different towns to transfer to a State Industrial School, when it shall be established, the children under their charge, provided the Legislature do not deem it advisable to include truants, vagrants and absentees from our Public Schools. The building for such a School they think should be large enough to accommodate not less than one hundred children. Already more than twice that number have been inmates of the State Alms House, a very considerable portion of whom should have been retained and educated as wards of the State. How large a number of children would come from the poor houses of the several towns in the State, they have not the means of judging. Your committee recommend that a majority, at least, of the directors, trustees or supervisors of the institution, be ladies, for the reasons that a better and gentler influence would be exerted over the children, and from the nature of woman and her mission would aid more in making it humane and Christian in its character. The Children's Home on Tobey street, in Providence, is and always has been under the management of a Board composed solely of ladies. No institution of the kind was ever more ably conducted. More than a thousand children have been rescued by these ladies from the haunts of wretchedness and vice and trained up to become virtuous men and women and useful and respected citizens. Lastly, as to where it shall be located. On this point we found a variety of opinions. The first location we will allude to, is the "Duncan Homestead Estate," on Smith's Hill, in the city of Providence. Accompanying this report is a letter from Albert W. Smith, to His Excellency Gov. Lippitt, marked "A," to which we would call your attention. The second named to your committee, is "Hope Island," in Narragansett Bay, accompanying which is a letter from Hiram B. Aylsworth, and a printed circular, descriptive of the Island, marked "B" to which your attention is also called. It was also brought to the attention of your committee, that there was an estate in the town of Smithfield, that could be purchased for a reasonable compensation, having on it a good water power. "Lapham Institute," in North Scituate, was also named as a suitable site for such a school. And lastly, lands owned by the State, in the town of Cranston, were recommended as a suitable location—objections, however, were offered to the latter place, that it would be in the vicinity, and that it might be unfavorably connected with the criminal institutions there. It was shown to the committee, however, that these objections could be obviated by placing it on some portion of the extended tract of land quite remote from the other buildings. The advantages of this location are, 1st. There will be no outlay for the site—the State already owns it. 2d. A plenty of good building materials on the ground. 3d. The command of any amount of labor from the State Work House. 4th. A plentiful supply of good water. 5th. Milk, vegetables and fruit from the Farm. 6th. Economy of administration in connection with the other State Institutions located in Cranston. Looking at this subject simply with a view to what would be best for the children in question, and believing that more depends upon the conduct and general management of the School than its location, we therefore recommend the adoption of the accompanying act and resolution.

                                        N. T. VERRY, *Chairman.*

## A.

His Excellency Gov. LIPPITT, Providenc e :

SIR: I desire to call attention to the Duncan Homestead Estate, Smith's Hill, as a suitable place for the Industrial School. The estate contains about three acres, substantially enclosed by a stone wall, on three streets, and the buildings are such as I should suppose well adapted for the purpose proposed.

I would be glad to dispose of the property for such a purpose at a reasonable price.

If you deem the matter worthy your conside ration, I should be very happy to have you visit the property.

　　　　I am, very respectfully, your obedient servant,

　　　　　　　　　ALBERT W. SMITH.

## B.

PROVIDENCE, Jan. 17, 1877.

*To the Chairman of the Joint Special Committee on Industrial Schools :*

Permit me to call your attention to Hope Island as a location for the proposed school. The within circular furnishes information concerning location, &c. I will sell it to the State at an appraised value, by three disinterested men, to be chosen as such appraisers usually are.

　　　　Yours respectfully,

　　　　　　　　　HIRAM B. AYLSWORTH.

[CIRCULAR.]

A group of Islands in Narragansett Bay, embracing Hope, Despair and Gooseberry, also Seal, Ball, Scup and Gull Rocks. Hope Island contains about seventy acres of as good land as we have in the state. The Island proper will measure, at water mark, about one hundred acres. It is beautifully located in the centre of the Bay, about eighteen miles below Providence, eight above Newport, four from Wickford, eight from East Greenwich, four from Rocky Point and Oakland Beach, and two from Conanicut Park. Newport, Gould's Island, Conanicut Park, Patience, Prudence, Fall River, Bristol, Warren, Rocky Point, Oakland Beach, Buttonwoods, East Greenwich, Wickford, and nearly all points of interest in Narragansett Bay can be seen from this Island. The American Steamboat Co., and Providence and Newport steamers, pass within a few hundred of the Island, ten or twelve times each day, (Sundays excepted), six months in the year.

The Wickford and Newport steamers pass within a short distance, six times each day, making the Island accessible nearly every hour in the day, through that portion of the year when a residence would be desirable, and this can be accomplished at a small expense. The water is very bold at all points, as shown by the United States Coast Surveyors' Map, published recently.

The boldness of the water, and the location of the Island, make it the centre of fishing-grounds on the Bay, no place surpassing it in this respect.

Fall and Spring water-fowl shooting from the Island is equal to any place on the coast.

Gooseberry Island, located at the west of Hope, presents a natural Breakwater, making a fine harbor and anchorage for yachts and vessels such as would be desirable for the residents. The size of the Island, its location and general surroundings make it particularly desirable for an association of friends, acquaintances and neighbors residing in an inland city, who desire to keep up their home associations at their summer residence by the sea; to such, this Island presents a rare opportunity; its nearness to New port, (the most desirable summer resort in America), makes it a desirable location for head-quarters for a yacht or fishing-club. A portion of the Island being some two hundred feet above the level of the sea, affords a good location for a first-class Hotel, every room of which would command a perfect view of Narragansett Bay. It is a very desirable place for a gentleman with means, who wishes to lavish a portion of his wealth where he would receive in return, the benefit of a sea-breeze unsurpassed, excellent bathing-grounds, beauty of location unequaled, and all the requisites desirable to a summer residence of this nature.

# REPORT

OF THE

# State Board of Pharmacy,

MADE TO THE

# GENERAL ASSEMBLY.

## 1877.

———•———

PROVIDENCE:
ANGELL, BURLINGAME & CO., PRINTERS TO THE STATE.
1877.

# REPORT.

To the Honorable the General Assembly, of the State of Rhode Island,
at its January Session, A. D. 1877 :—

The State Board of Pharmacy, in compliance with the provisions
of "Chapter 119 of the General Statutes, of Medicines and
Poisons," respectfully present this their seventh annual report
"On the Condition of Pharmacy; together with a list of all persons
registered as Pharmacists and Assistant Pharmacists."

The term of office of the Board, appointed July 1st, A. D. 1873,
for the three years then ensuing, having expired by limitation,
His Excellency the Governor appointed the following persons to
constitute the Board for three years from July 1st, A. D. 1876,
viz.: Albert L. Calder, William B. Blanding, Norman N. Mason
and William E. Clarke, of Providence ; James H. Taylor, of Newport ; Albert J. Congdon, of East Greenwich, and Walter E. Colwell, of Pawtucket. The first four being of the former Board and
the latter two to take the places of Dr. Ossian Sumner and Bela P.
Clapp, both of whom declined a re-appointment.

The new Board met for organization July 6th, 1876, in Providence, and elected Albert L. Calder for President, and Norman N.
Mason, Secretary and Registrar, both for the full term of their
appointment.

The Centennial year just closed was to the Pharmacists of the
country a season of rare pleasure and improvement, marking as it
did a notable gathering of the members of the profession from all

parts of the country, together with many distinguished Pharmacists from abroad, in the annual meeting of the American Pharmaceutical Association, held in Philadelphia during the month of September. This meeting, backed as it was by the unprecedented display of Pharmaceutical and Chemical products and apparatus at the Exposition, enabled those who attended it to gather much valuable information, the fruits of which will enure to the benefit of the great public who are so largely dependent upon the skill and intelligence of the dispensing pharmacist for their safety and welfare in their hours of illness.

The increasing intelligence and desire for knowledge in the profession has led to the formation of an association of the Pharmacists of the State, whose meetings have tended greatly to the advantage and mutual improvement of the members. This association has also established during the winter a course of lectures on practical Pharmacy by Professor Markoe, of Boston. These lectures have been well attended by an interested and attentive audience, and give encouraging proof of the awakened interest felt in the improvement and advancement of our profession, and it is not too much to say that this increased intelligence and desire for knowledge may be traced almost directly to the passage of the eminently judicious and practical law regulating the sale of medicines and poisons.

The provisions of the so-called Liquor Law, granting to the Registered Pharmacists of the State the long desired privilege of selling the officinal and other wines and liquors in small quantities as wanted for strictly medicinal purposes, still continues to give great satisfaction, not only to the Pharmacists, but to the many persons who using such medicines only occasionally desire to procure them where they find their other medicinal supplies. The Board is informed by the License Commissioners of Providence that they hear no complaints of infractions of the law, and none have been made known from other parts of the State.

The Board desire especially to thank the executive and prosecuting authorities of Providence for their zeal in prosecuting offenders against the law in that city. In some other parts of the state, the law has not been so well executed, and although the notice of the proper officers has been called to repeated and continued violations of the law, the delinquents have remained unmolested. It is to be hoped that this state of things will improve in the future, now that it has been so fully demonstrated that a judicious enforcement of the law is of such wide benefit to the community.

The Board has held monthly meetings at their rooms in Elizabeth Building, with the exception of the July meeting, which was held at Newport for the benefit and convenience of persons residing in that part of the state. At these meetings the Board examined the qualifications of eighteen persons who presented themselves for registration as Registered Pharmacists. Ten of this number were granted registration on the first examination; two, on a second examination, and two on a third examination, and the remainder were refused. They also examined seven applicants for registration as Assistant Pharmacists, all of whom were registered on the first examination. Three persons were granted certificates to sell the usual domestic medicines as provided in section fifth of the law.

Annexed is a list of the Pharmacists and Assistant Pharmacists.

All of which is respectfully submitted.

ALBERT L. CALDER, *President.*
WM. B. BLANDING,·
W. E. CLARKE,
JAMES H. TAYLOR,
WALTER E. COLWELL,
NORMAN M. MASON, *Secretary.*

## NAMES OF REGISTERED PHARMACISTS.

Henry J. Alfreds..........................Providence.
A. O. Austin...............................      "
B. D. Bailey...............................      "
Alfred Barth...............................
August J. Berg.............................
William B. Blanding........................
C. B. Burrington...........................
Albert L. Calder...........................
E. A. Calder...............................
George B. Calder...........................      "
G. S. Calder.. ............................
J. H. Carpenter............................      "
James H. Chace. ...........................      "
Robert B. Chambers... .....................      "
Charles F. Clarke..........................
Charles H. Clark...........................
William E. Clarke..........................
George W. Davis............................
Thomas E. Eddy.............................      "
George E. B. Fairbanks.....................
Albert Fenner..............................      "
Peter M. Forsyth...........................      "
Charles A. Gladding.....  .................      "
A. J. Greene...............................      "
Willard H. Greene..........................
William H. Greene. Jr......................
Thomas J. Griffin..........................
William H. Hinds...........................      "
W. W. Handy................................
Harvey I. Leith............................      "

William E. MaCartney..................... Providence.
Norman N. Mason........................ "
E. F. Mattison............................ ::
Charles H. Newell........................
John F..Oates............................
John E. Potter..........................
F. J. Phillips............................
James A. Packard........................ -
William K. Reynolds..................·.... ..
C. A. Ross............................... ..
William Francis Ryan.................... ..
Thomas E. Simmons......................
Andrew J. Smith.........................
Byron Smith.............................
Ferdinand Smith..........................
W. G. Stewart........................... ..
George C. Sumner........................ ..
Ossian Sumner..........................
E. P. Sumner............................
Cyrus T. Thurber........... ............
Walter A. Walling.......................
Horatio J. Watson.......................
Wayland A. Wheaton..................... "
William H. Abbott...................... Pawtucket.
Mowry P. Arnold........................ Foster Centre.
Thomas A. Barber....................... Ashaway.
Nathan C. Bedell......................... Bristol.
William H. Buffington.................... "
George H. Brown......................... Warren.
Otis Bullock............................. "
E. C. Capwell........................... Phenix.
Albert P. Carpenter...................... Central Falls.
Bela P. Clapp........................... Pawtucket.
Albert B. Collins........................ Westerly.
Walter E. Colwell....................... Pawtucket.
A. J. Congdon........................... East Greenwich,
C. H. Congdon........................... "
Richard E. Congdon.....................

William H. Cotton........................Newport.
Charles E. Davis...........................Pawtucket.
George T. Dana............................. "
Stephen H. Farnham.....................Wickford.
George E. Greene.............·...........Wyoming.
Lucius C. Greene.,,,.....................Centreville.
William Ray Greene.....................East Greenwich.
R. N. Hazard............................Newport.
Simeon Hunt...........................East Providence.
Frank A. Jackson.......................Woonsocket.
John L. Jones...........................Central Falls.
E. H. Knowles...........................Westerly.
Clarence W. Locke.....................Woonsocket.
E. J. Luther...........................Watchemoket.
E. T. Luther...........................Olneyville.
William J. McCaw......................Warren.
J. Mott, Jr.............................Olneyville.
William N. Orcutt.......................Woonsocket.
Edward Saunders........................Warren.
William D. Smith........................Valley Falls.
W. F. Teston...........................Woonsocket.
James H. Taylor.........................Newport.
Enoch W. Vars..........................Niantic.
Nathan G. West.....................  .....Bristol.

———

Licensed to sell Medicines in conformity with the **Pharmacy and Poison Act** of the State of Rhode Island :

Charles Noyes................  ...........Hopkinton.
H. W. Parkis...................... .......Slatersville.
I. H. Parkis...........................Forestville.

# REGISTERED ASSISTANT PHARMACISTS.

| | Employed by | In |
|---|---|---|
| Charles G. Abbe | Wm. B. Blanding | Providence. |
| E. P. Anthony | " | " |
| John L. Ashton | R. I. Hospital | :: |
| W. F. Bowen | Wm. B. Blanding | .. |
| A. F. Bosworth | F. J. Phillips | " |
| William E. Boutelle | Wm. E. Clarke | " |
| A. F. Burns | | " |
| William J. Burton | Wm. E. Clarke | . |
| John W. Cone | Wm. B. Blanding | .. |
| Francis X. Dion | | " |
| James M. Fenner, Jr., | Albert Fenner | " |
| Henry K. Gardner | Wm. B. Blanding | " |
| Edward B. Hanes | Ferdinand Smith | |
| Willis F. Hobbs | Norman N. Mason | .. |
| Clarence J. Luce | | .. |
| John W. Miller | G. S. Calder | .. |
| Andrew J. Myers | Wm. E. Clarke | .. |
| William Russell | Wm. H. Hinds | .. |
| Arthur P. Sanborn | Albert L. Calder | .. |
| Peter B. Schurman | Byron Smith | |
| Samuel A. Slack | Mason, Chapin & Co. | . |
| William O. Stanton | Thomas E. Eddy | |
| Charles S. Thomas | F. A. Hatch | |
| Walter D. Watson | George L. Claflin & Co. | " |
| M. A. A. Whitney | | .. |
| F. E. Willis | Wm. B. Blanding | " |
| C. I. Collins | A. B. Collins | Westerly. |
| John Howland | J. Mott, Jr., | Olneyville. |

W. T. Parker..........James H. Taylor......Newport.
A. W. Wellington......Wm. H. Cotton........    "
H. A. Whitney........F. A. Jackson.........Woonsocket.
Herbert C. Whitney....Caswell, Hazard & Co...Newport.
James T. Wright.......          "
J. H. Young....,,.....N. C. Bedell.,,......Bristol.

# ANNUAL REPORT

OF THE

# Commissioners on Inland Fisheries

MADE TO THE

## GENERAL ASSEMBLY

OF THE

## STATE OF RHODE ISLAND,

AT ITS

### January Session, A. D. 1877.

PROVIDENCE:

ANGELL, BURLINGAME & CO., PRINTERS TO THE STATE.

1877.

# REPORT.

*To the Honorable General Assembly of the State of Rhode Island, at its January Session,* 1877 :

The Commissioners of Inland Fisheries beg leave to submit their seventh annual report :

The State hatching house and its appurtenances are in excellent condition. We received the past year from Mr. C. S. Atkins 20,-000 land-locked or Schoodic salmon ova. These were hatched and distributed as follows, with a loss of only about 2 per cent.:

Wallum Pond............................. in Burrillville.
Moswansicut Pond........................... in Scituate.
Steers Pond........................ ............ in Scituate.
Searles Pond.............................. in Foster.
Lilly Pond................................ in Foster.
Gorton's Pond................... .. .......... in Warwick.
Warwick Pond............................ in Warwick.
Beach Pond................................ in Richmond.

The following ponds have been stocked with black bass by the present commissioners, which we append in this order for convenience of reference :

### JUNE AND JULY, 1870.

Wauchog Pond........................... in Charlestown.
Moswansicut Pond........................ in Scituate.
Sneach Pond.............................. in Cumberland.
Herring Pond............................ in Burrillville.

### JUNE AND JULY, 1871.

| | |
|---|---|
| Steere's Pond | in Scituate. |
| Hope Pond | in Scituate. |
| Ponegansett Pond | in Scituate. |
| Searle's Pond | in Foster. |
| Spear's Pond | in Foster. |
| Scott's Pond | in Lincoln. |
| New Reservoir | in Lonsdale. |
| Warwick Pond | in Warwick. |
| Gorton Pond | in Warwick. |

### JUNE AND JULY, 1872.

| | |
|---|---|
| Stafford Pond | in Tiverton. |
| Easton's Pond | in Newport and Middletown. |

### JUNE AND JULY, 1873.

| | |
|---|---|
| Yawgoo Pond | in South Kingstown. |
| Worden's Pond | in South Kingstown. |
| Bellville Pond | in North Kingstown. |
| Johnson's Pond | in Coventry. |
| Wickaboxet Pond | in West Greenwich. |
| Deep Pond | in Exeter. |
| Yawgook Pond | in Hopkinton. |
| Eaton's Pond | in Newport. |
| Two Ponds | on Block Island. |

### JUNE AND JULY, 1874.

| | |
|---|---|
| Blue Pond | in Hopkinton |

We also received 120,000 salmon ova which were hatched with about a like success, and placed in the following-named streams: 20,000 in Wood and Pawcatuck rivers, 15,000 in the Slatersville Branch of the Blackstone, and 80,000 in the Pawtuxet and its branches.

In October last, we received a letter from Prof. Baird, the United States Commissioner, asking us how many California eggs we would take; but the extreme drought of the past summer made us unable to avail ourselves of his kindness. Under the present circumstances, we believe we have in the past five years, done all that is necessary to demonstrate if our streams are capable of supporting salmon. Of course the very numerous dams will forever bar the retnrn of these fish to the upper parts of the streams, where they pass the first year, and some authorities say, two of their lives. Once over the dams, there is no return for them. Their instinct at a certain age prompting them to seek the sea. Now all we can demonstrate is, will our streams support these fish in their young state till that age is reached. That they once did is certain, but the quality and temperature of the water has undergone such a change, that he would be a bold fish commissioner, who would make a positive statement. We are encouraged to hope they will, for very many of these young salmon have been taken, by various modes of capture, in different stages of growth. But it is difficult to study what is going on under the water, and so we at present are more or less in the dark. Five years ago a great hue and cry was raised for fishways over the dams in all the New England States; many thousands of dollars have been spent on them, and with our present light we cannot but congratulate the people of Rhode Island on holding aloof up to date.

### BLACK BASS.

We are happy to be able to reiterate all we have said in our past reports as to our success in making this capital fish a native of our waters. The bass have become very popular and are destined to become more so, as our people learn better how to take them.

The past season we have only placed them in one locality namely, the Stillwater Reservoir in Smithfield. Private parties have however stocked numerous ponds with fish taken from the waters previously stocked by the State. A good many have been taken from the Blackstone River the past year which no doubt found their way there from Whitinsville. The reservoir at that place having given away some five years ago. To show the rapidity of the increase of these fish ; five years since in October, 8 bass were put into Steer's pond in Rockland, of about 8 acres in area, and

about 18 feet in average depth. Last year the pond was drawn
down to repair the dam, and a number of bass were taken, from 3
to 4 pounds in weight, and small ones innumerble. Quite a number we hear have been taken through the ice the past winter, by
parties fishing for pickerel, some of upwards of 4 pounds in weight.

Bass make a round nest in the gravel near the shore in from 3
to 5 feet of water, and deposit their eggs about June 1st, or a little
later ; as near as can be ascertained about two weeks are required
to hatch the eggs, and as soon as the sack is absorbed the little
ones retire to the grass and weeds along the shore for safety. The
old fish during the time the eggs and young are in the nest, are
watching near by, and driving off all intruders, The young seem
to grow very rapidly.

## SHAD.

Owing to the extreme heat of the past season we were unable to
get our usual supply of young shad. The source of supply is the
Connecticut river, where the United States Commissioner now has
charge of the works. The labor there was rendered almost naught
the past summer by the over heating of the water, and we. as
well as the other New England States suffered in consequence.
We hope the coming season to do better, for our past success with
shad has been very great, and these fish have been more abundant
and cheaper in our State for the past two years than for a great
length of time, and a good portion of our supply was taken in our
own immediate waters. All the expense necessary to obtain the
young fish, is for transportation, they being furnished free.

## TROUT.

We have done nothing with trout for the past two years owing
to the extreme droughts we are occasionally subjected to, our supply of water sometimes gives out, and then in a very short time
our labors and outlay are vain. We do not recommend any one
attempting to raise these fish on a large scale unless sure of an unfailing supply of water.

## IN CONCLUSION.

We would say as our report briefly shows that the past year has not been an active one in our department for the reason that we having accomplished what was needful in the few previous years in stocking the waters of the State, must now lay upon our oars and watch the success of our labors. We think we do not claim too much in saying that with black bass it has been entire and fully equal to our most sanguine expectations (and fish commissioners are always sanguine.) Shad have increased in our waters vastly within the past three years, and as for salmon, we hope, and can ray no more, and we would only add that our sincere wish is that the same unanimity of wise and generous action would prevail in our councils and community, in regard to our Bay fisheries, as have been granted to us in our efforts to improve those of our inland waters.

Aware that we are now upon dangerous grounds and that the pursuance of the topic will doubtless bring us a strong hint to stick to our legitimate business, we close our report with a statement of our cash account, and would say that no appropriation is needed for the coming year.

The following is a list of the commissioners of the various states.

## COMMISSIONERS OF FISHERIES.

### UNITED STATES.

Prof. Spencer F. Baird.................... Washington, D. C.

### ARKANSAS.

N. H. Fish................. ............... Pine Buffs
J. R. Steelman...................... ...... Little Rock
N. B. Pearce.......................... Fayetville

### CALIFORNIA.

B. B. Redding.......................... Sacramento
S. R. Throckmorton.......... ... ........... San Francisco
J. F. Farwell.......................... San Francisco

### CONNECTICUT.

William M. Hudson...................... Hartford
Robert G. Pike..................... ...... Middletown
James A. Bill..................,......... Lyme

### GEORGIA.

Thomas P. James.........................
(Duties embracing the work of the fish interest assigned to Commissioner of Agriculture).

### IOWA.

Samuel B. Evans.......................... Ottumwa
B. F. Shaw............................... Anamora
Charles A. Haynes........................ Waterloo

### KENTUCKY.

Pack Thomas.............................. Louisville.

### MAINE.

E. M. Stillwell.......................... Bangor.
Henry O. Stanfield....................... Dixfield.

### MARYLAND.

T. B. Ferguson........................... Baltimore.
T. W. Downes............................. Denton.

### MASSACHUSETTS.

Theodore Lyman.......... ................. Brookline.
Asa French............................... South Braintree.
E. A. Brackett........................... Winchester

### MICHIGAN.

George Clark..... ....................... Ecorse.
A. J. Kellogg............................ Allegan.
E. R. Miller............................. Richland.

### MINNESOTA.

R. O. Sweeney............................ St. Paul.
Robert Owesly............................ .....
William Golcher.......................... ....

### NEW HAMPSHIRE.

Colonel Samuel Webber.................... Manchester.
Albina H. Powers......................... Grantham.
Luther H. Hayes.........................., Milton.

## NEW YORK.

| | |
|---|---|
| Horatio Seymour | Utica. |
| Robert R. Roosevelt | New York City. |
| Edward M. Smitts | Rochester. |

## NEW JERSEY.

| | |
|---|---|
| B. P. Howell | Woodbury. |
| J. R. Shortwell | Rahway. |
| G. A. Anderson | Trenton. |
| George Ricardo | Hackensack. |

## OHIO.

| | |
|---|---|
| John C. Fisher | Coshocton. |
| John H. Klipput | Columbus. |
| Robert Cummings | Toledo. |

## PENNSYLVANIA.

| | |
|---|---|
| J. H. Reeder | Easton. |
| B. L. Hewett | Hollidaysburg. |
| James Duffy | Marietta. |

## RHODE ISLAND.

| | |
|---|---|
| Newton Dexter | Providence. |
| Alfred A. Reed, Jr | Providence. |
| John H. Barden | Scituate. |

## UTAH TERRITORY.

| | |
|---|---|
| A. P. Rockwood | Salt Lake City. |

(Superintendent of Fisheries, Zion's Co-operative Society.)

## VERMONT.

| | |
|---|---|
| M. C. Edmunds | Weston. |
| M. Goldsmith | Rutland. |

## VIRGINIA.

| | |
|---|---|
| A. Moseley | Richmond. |
| W. B. Robertson | Lynchburg. |
| M. G. Ellyzer | Blacksburg. |

## WISCONSIN.

William Welch......................... Madison.
A. Palmer............................. Bescobel.
P. R. Hoy............................. Racine

### DOMINION OF CANADA.

W. F. Whitcher........................ Ottawa.
W. H. Vining.......................... St. John, N. B.
  (Inspector of fisheries for New Brunswick and Nova Scotia.)

ALFRED. A. REED, JR.,
NEWTON DEXTER,
JOHN H. BARDEN.

*State of Rhode Island in* ̇ *count with Commissioner's on Inland Fisheries.*

---

## Dr.

1877.

Jan. 1st. To amount paid for labor.......................... $235 7¢

"      "      watching Moswansicut Pond, Paw-

tuxet Cove and River ............ 55 00

"      expenses to Holyoke for shad..... 14 10

"      105 black bass..... .............. 3 00

"      express on salmon eggs............ 34 63

"      expenses of J. H. Barden, Commis-

"      sioner to Centennial Fish Meeting 45 18

"      rent of land...................... . 13 00

"      stationery, etc............. ......... 5 50

"      traveling expenses........ ........ 14 15

"      placing land-locked salmon in fol-

lowing ponds, viz.: Moswansicut,

Johnson, Beach, Wickaboxet, Mill-

ville, Rockville, Spring Grove,

Tucker, Wells, Jackson, Harrisville

Natick, Pontiac, Warwick, Hope,

Arctic,     Washington,     Quidnick,

Crompton, River Point, Mashapaug

and Lilly and Centreville; Slaters-

ville River, Pawcatuck River, and

six different places on Hood's River 61 50

         $471 31

Balance carried forward ........... ..... ............... 488 30

         ——$960 11

## Cr.

1877.

Feb. 29th. By balance on hand.. ............ ... ............ $460 11

By amount of appropriation for the year 1876......... . 500 00

         —— $960 11

1877.

Jan. 1st. By balance cash on hand brought forward........... $488 30

PROVIDENCE *January* 1st, 1877.

# REPORT OF THE INSPECTOR

OF THE

# 𝕳artford, 𝕻rovidence and 𝕱ishkill 𝕽. 𝕽. 𝕮ompany.

— • —

*To the Honorable General Assembly of the State of Rhode Island, at its January Session at Providence, A. D. 1877:*

The Inspector of the Hartford, Providence and Fishkill Rail-Road respectfully presents herewith his report for the year ending September 30th, 1876:

On the 10th day of February, A. D. 1877, at the office of the Trustees of the Hartford, Providence and Fishkill Rail Road Company, in Hartford, Conn., I examined the books and accounts of the said Trustees, and therefrom make the following report of the condition and the receipts and expenditures for the year ending September 30th, 1876:

| | |
|---|---:|
| Funded Debt in State of Connecticut, - - - | $1,574,500 00 |
| Funded Debt in State of Rhode Island, - - - | 481,000 00 |
| | |
| Annual interest on said Funded Debt. - - - | 143,885 00 |
| Hartford Sinking Fund.        Not ascertained. | |
| Providence Sinking Fund,        " | |

Whole amount of receipts for one year, ending September 30th, 1876 :

| | |
|---|---|
| Transportation of Passengers, - - | $470,982 14 |
| Freight, - - - - - | 417,059 81 |
| Mails, - - - - - | 10,300 00 |
| Express, - - - - - | 15,596 40 |
| Rents, - - - - - - | 36,806 13 |

Operating expenses for the year ending September 30th, 1876 :

| | |
|---|---|
| Maintenance of Way, New Iron, &c., - | $182,323 19 |
| Repairs of Engines, - - - - | 36,544 94 |
| Repairs of Passenger Cars, - - - | 27,796 74 |
| Repairs of Freight Cars, - - - | 41,771 72 |
| Salaries and Labor, - - - - | £41,807 66 |
| Bridge Repairs, - - - - | 17,508 20 |
| Repairs of Fences, &c., - - - | 7,945 67 |
| Repairs of Stations, - - - - | 25,919 6) |
| Wood, - - - - - - | 8,677 11 |
| Coal, - - - - - - | 94,513 62 |
| Oil, - - - - - - | 11,201 75 |
| Cotton Waste for Cleaning, - - - | 1,705 51 |
| Printing and Stationery, - - - | 6,473 68 |
| Station Rents, - - - - - | 39,397 39 |
| Damage of Cars, Freight, &c., - - | 3,986 14 |
| Insurance, - - - - - | 8,536 63 |
| Taxes, - - - - - | 19,401 68 |
| Interest, - - - - - | 25,893 62 |
| Incidental, - - - - - | 8,638 73 |

| | |
|---|---|
| Net Earnings for the Year, - - - - | $140,700 81 |

Respectfully submitted,

GEORGE A. SPINK,

Inspector H. P. and F. R. Road.

Lightning Source UK Ltd.
Milton Keynes UK
UKHW012135180219
337529UK00012B/1373/P